*The National Association of
Base Ball Players, 1857–1870*

ALSO BY MARSHALL D. WRIGHT

The International League: Year-by-Year Statistics, 1884–1953
(McFarland, 1998)

The American Association: Year-by-Year Statistics for the Baseball Minor League, 1902–1952
(McFarland, 1997)

Nineteenth Century Baseball: Year-by-Year Statistics for the Major League Teams, 1871 through 1900
(McFarland, 1996)

The National Association of Base Ball Players, 1857–1870

by
MARSHALL D. WRIGHT

McFarland & Company, Inc., Publishers
Jefferson, North Carolina, and London

ISBN 0-7864-0779-4 (softcover : 50# alkaline paper) ∞

Library of Congress Cataloguing-in-Publication data are available

British Library Cataloguing-in-Publication data are available

©2000 Marshall D. Wright. All rights reserved

Cover image © 2000 Wood River Gallery

No part of this book may be reproduced or transmitted in any form or by any means, electronic or mechanical, including photocopying or recording, or by any information storage and retrieval system, without permission in writing from the publisher.

Manufactured in the United States of America

McFarland & Company, Inc., Publishers
  Box 611, Jefferson, North Carolina 28640
    www.mcfarlandpub.com

To Denny,
who, like his cousin Henry Dennison from long ago,
enjoys playing the game.

TABLE OF CONTENTS

Acknowledgments		ix
Introduction		xi
Prelude	The Knickerbocker Club	1
1857	The Association Begins	7
1858	New York vs. Brooklyn	15
1859	Baseball Clubs	28
1860	Spreading the Gospel	41
1861	Home and Home	54
1862	Throwing and Pitching	64
1863	Battlefields and Ballfields	73
1864	The Fly Game	82
1865	The Atlantics of Brooklyn	94
1866	Country Clubs	110
1867	National Tour	139
1868	Bases on Hits	186
1869	The Reds of Sixty-Nine	238
1870	End Game	284
Postlude	Breaking Away	328
Selected Bibliography		330
Index		334

ACKNOWLEDGMENTS

As I meandered through the long journey that culminated in this volume, I had a lot of help along the way—help essential to the completion of the task at hand.

First, I would to acknowledge the institutions that provided fundamental services. The National Baseball Library at Cooperstown and the New York Historical Society provided key pieces to the puzzle. The New York Public Library with its Spalding Collection was a focal research location. The librarians and staff at the Thomas Crane Library in Quincy, Massachusetts, were quite tolerant as I spent many hours copying microfilm. And finally, a special thanks to the Harvard Theatre Collection for their patience while I copied page after page of the *New York Clipper.*

On a more personal level, I would like to thank the many friends who provided research help, encouragement and general nurturing during the writing process. First and foremost in this group is my friend Gary Austin who provided key information concerning early Michigan baseball. Next, Karen Wright who helped with the fine photography. Finally, a special thanks to my colleagues at Howe Sportsdata, especially the intrepid members of the night crew.

Most importantly, I would like to thank my family for their patience and support. My sister, Karen, provided much needed assistance during my New York research sojourns. My father, Robert, once more offered helpful suggestions with the text portion of the book. My beloved wife Jane spent many hours poring over the text making sure the prose flowed smoothly. And finally many thanks to my son Denny, who provided me with cheerful companionship during the whole journey. This book is dedicated to you.

INTRODUCTION

Several years ago when compiling a book on the major league teams and players of the 19th century, I chanced upon an untapped lode of unchronicled baseball activity. Before the onset of the first professional leagues in 1871, there had existed a myriad of teams and players going back to the 1840s. Fascinated, I made a note to myself to do further research on the subject when time permitted. The volume that follows is the result.

In digging into baseball's early roots, I found that the early years centered around an organization known as the National Association of Base Ball Players. This group, whose antecedents date to 1857, governed the world of baseball for the next 14 years right until the formation of the first all-professional league in 1871. The story of this organization—from its humble beginnings through its explosive growth after the Civil War, culminating with its coast-to-coast size of several hundred amateur and professional clubs—was a natural centerpiece for a book on early baseball. Thus, the National Association is the focal point of this tome.

In May 1857, delegates from 16 New York and Brooklyn baseball clubs met to set guidelines for the game of baseball. This led to a subsequent convention in March 1858, where the delegates voted to form an organization which they named the National Association of Base Ball Players. This association wrote a constitution and by-laws which governed all aspects of the game from the rules on the field to the behavior and conduct of clubs and players off the field. The convention also agreed to hold annual meetings (every March) at which most of the new business was transacted.

Most sources date the beginning of the National Association to the March 1858 convention where the original constitution was written. But I have decided to include 1857 as well. The original nucleus of the Association held formal meetings before the 1857 season in which business was transacted much the same as in 1858 and subsequent years. The lack of a formal title until 1858 doesn't lessen the legitimacy of the activity in 1857. Thus it is included here.

In 1858, the National Association included 25 teams. Recorded in this total was a team from New Jersey, the first team from outside the New York metropolitan area. By the March 1859 convention, the Association's roster of teams had doubled, including several teams from upstate New York. At the March 1860 convention, over 80 teams sent delegates, including one from far-off Detroit, Michigan. The Association also voted to henceforth have their annual convention in December starting with a meeting in December 1860.

In 1861, attendance at the National Association's conference was sharply curtailed, primarily due to the Civil War engulfing the nation. During the course of the war, the Association maintained its annual meetings although attendance dwindled. At the 1864 meeting, only 30 teams sent delegates—less than half of the pre-war total.

After the Civil War ended in April 1865, the country's interest in baseball exploded. Ninety-one teams sent delegates to the 1865 convention followed by an astonishing 202 at the meeting in 1866. This huge upturn caused a necessary change in the Association's constitution concerning the admittance of members. Up until 1866, a team had to be present at the convention to be considered for membership. Beginning in 1867 two new rules governed membership. The first stated that clubs could now be represented by state representatives at the convention (to cut back on the sheer numbers) and secondly that clubs could apply for probationary membership any time of the year—not just at convention time.

These new rule changes pushed the membership past the 400 level in 1867, continuing to nearly 1,000 in 1869. The numbers were getting too unwieldy to be managed by one organization. Something had to be done to divide the group. In 1869 a solution was found.

All during the 1860s, several of the good teams paid some of their players although the constitution of the National Association specifically forbade the practice. The "payment" usually consisted of a share of the gate receipts or a well paying "job" for which the participant did little work. However in 1869, this subterfuge was shunted aside. A team in Cincinnati, Ohio, known as the Red

Stockings, openly paid an entire team of players. Later that same year, nearly another dozen teams followed suit. By 1870, nearly 20 teams advertised themselves as all-professional outfits. The National Association was now clearly divided into two camps—the amateurs and the professionals. It was becoming clear that the two could not exist under the same umbrella.

Just before the 1871 season, several of the professional clubs formed a new group which they called the National Association of Professional Base Ball Players. This group, which consisted of most of the old Association's top teams, then commenced to play a schedule of games mostly among themselves. Unfazed, the remaining teams formed a new group which they proudly billed the National Association of Amateur Base Ball Players. But without the glamour clubs to bolster them, taking most of the country's interest with them, the amateur Association faded away without fanfare within two years. This brought an end to the first chapter of baseball's story—also to the story contained within these pages.

To accurately tell the story of the National Association, one needs to divide the work into three general categories: (1) the clubs, (2) the games they played, and (3) the players on their rosters.

The first stage was a need to determine the individual clubs which graced the roster of the National Association during its 14 years of existence. In a modern baseball league, its members are easily determined in a perusal of the local newspaper. For the National Association it was not this easy, for its members consisted of clubs who attended the annual convention or later belonged to a state association. The primary sources for this information were the booklet published each year by the National Association which chronicled the proceedings of the meeting as well as listing the attending clubs. A second source, beginning in 1860, was the "Beadle Guide" (a baseball annual) which contained a roster of member clubs in addition to team statistics. Thirdly, the sporting weekly entitled The "New York Clipper" quite often carried coverage of the convention including a list of participants. Unfortunately, these three sources often disagreed.

To complicate matters, beginning in 1867, clubs could be admitted as probationary members during the course of the season. Shortly thereafter, state associations of teams were granted membership in the National Association, sometimes on a probationary status as well. Lists of members of these groups were nonexistent in many cases and sketchy in others, so the list of Association teams, especially in 1869 and 1870, requires much guess work and remains incomplete.

I have combed the available sources in an attempt to determine which clubs actually belonged to the National Association in a given year. This is an important distinction. Since this book is about the National Association only teams that are members are covered in these pages.

In published sources, the number of teams present at the conventions would be considered the amount of member teams for that year (i.e., 91 teams at the 1865 convention—91 members for 1865). I have chosen a different interpretation. Since many new teams were present at each December meeting, it doesn't make sense to backdate their inclusion in the just completed season. I have let the roster at the conventions govern inclusion in the subsequent season (i.e., 91 attendees in 1865—91 teams for the 1866 season). For the years 1857–1860 when the convention was held in March before the season, I've let those totals remain the same as published sources.

During the years of the National Association, teams were known by their club name, secondarily by the city they played in. For instance, the team in Philadelphia was known as the Keystone club rather than the Philadelphia Keystones. Keeping true to this style, all the teams are listed by club name followed by the city and state.

The second stage in telling the story of the National Association is the record of the games they played. To understand the kind of schedules the clubs played it is necessary to understand the nature of the clubs themselves. During the early years of the National Association, baseball clubs were just that—private clubs formed by a group of gentlemen to serve as a recreational outlet. These groups were originally very self-serving and much of their activity centered around their own members' needs. The clubs' members mostly practiced and played among themselves—occasionally responding to a challenge from a rival organization—usually no more than 10 per year. As professionalism crept into the Association during the post–Civil War years, challenges from other clubs became more frequent and schedules subsequently lengthened.

Originally, any game a team played with another organization counted as a game played in the club's record—even though their opponent was not an Association member. Also games that a team played with a "picked nine" (an all-star group) counted in some instances. In 1865, the rules changed to state that only contests with other Association clubs would count on a club's tally sheet. By 1867, with several hundred teams belonging to the Association, this rule was relaxed somewhat as it was difficult to determine which nines actually belonged to the group.

To locate game scores, I had to rely on a variety of sources. The *New York Clipper* kept a good account of quite a few games. For pre-1867 game scores I relied heavily on *American Pastimes* by Charles Peverelly. This fascinating work, written in 1867, chronicled America at play, including a substantial section on baseball. Here, Peverelly listed over 30 teams with their game dates and scores from the 1840s all the way through the 1866 season. Lastly, the *Beadle's Guides* contained much information regarding each team's opponents.

In looking at the game scores, one will notice a couple of salient points. First, these early teams plated runs in bunches—scores in the thirties and forties were the norm. Second, each year several tie games were played. The rules stated it was up to the participating teams whether or not to play extra innings to determine the outcome.

The third stage of the National Association's story concerns the individual player and his statistical legacy. From the beginning of recorded baseball history, statistics have held a central role. However, to a modern baseball fan they look not the least bit familiar.

Before the formation of the National Association, recorded baseball games usually kept track of only one statistic for each player—runs scored. Occasionally, the recording source would list the times each player was called out (called hands lost). By the late 1850s, most of the games were keeping track of both.

The reason these two statistics were chronicled above all others was because they were already present in another bat and ball game at the time—the game of cricket. Baseball simply borrowed them until its own uniqueness led to other statistical categories.

After the Civil War, baseball scribes were searching for new ways to evaluate a player's batting ability. To this end, late in the 1867 season, two new statistics were added to the mix. In some of the important matches, the scorer began tallying hits and total bases for the combatants, noting correctly that these were the true measure of a batter's worth. In 1868 and after, these new stats were kept by most teams. Also, in 1869 and 1870, for one or two teams, rudimentary pitching statistics began to be noted.

Yearly totals for the players were also compiled in a different way. Scribes kept track of the total games, hands lost and runs a given player achieved during the year. To gauge accurately how many hands lost and runs each player had per game the "average and over" system was used, borrowed from the game of cricket. Simply stated, this is how it worked: let us say a player named Smith played in 10 games during the season where he was put out 27 times and scored 33 runs. His "average and over" for hands lost would be 2 and 7 and for runs 3 and 3. In other words, he averaged 2 outs per game with 7 left over and 3 runs per game with 3 left over. (Note: in the body of the text these averages and over are listed 2,7 or 3,3.) When hits and total bases were introduced in 1868, their yearly totals were summarized in a similar way.

Beginning in 1868, teams started using a decimal system to convey the same information. Thus our Mr. Smith would be given 2.7 outs and 3.3 runs per game. When most teams began using the decimal method in 1870, the tables for that year reflect the trend. Also in 1870, one or two teams began to list the number of times a player came to the plate, dividing this total by the number of hits obtained. These new "batting averages" are also included for the couple of instances present.

The only statistical categories present in the book are the principal ones listed above. Some teams kept track of other statistics such as home runs, but most did not. In other cases, for the later years, it would have been possible to "modernize" the numbers by extrapolating at bats, batting averages and slugging averages from the available data. To remain true to the times, this was not done. For the players and fans of the era, the four categories mentioned previously—hands lost, runs, hits, and total bases—were immediately recognizable as a player's batting average. Only at the very end of the National Association era did what we know as a "batting average" creep into consciousness. Occasionally a mention of other categories (mostly home runs) occurs in the text when the information is pertinent to the story.

To reliably interpret the four categories above one must understand what constituted good averages. The hands lost category was a negative measurement of times a batter was put out. Since there were usually 27 outs in each game for each team, all things being equal, the nine players should have three outs each or an average of three per game. The stronger players naturally wouldn't be called out as often so their hands lost average would be in the two range. Occasionally, a weak hitter would have an average over four.

In the high scoring games of the 1850s and 1860s, an average player would score about two runs a game, good players would score three or more with poor players averaging one or less. The same numbers hold true for hits per game: good players three, average two and poor one. For total bases, five, four and three were the benchmarks of excellence, tolerability and mediocrity.

The players' statistics were again found in a variety of sources. The most reliable was the yearly *Beadle's Guides*. In addition the *New York Clipper* contained some season-ending stats. Beginning in 1867, several sporting publications featuring baseball emerged. The *Baseball Players Chronicle* (1867), *American Chronicle of Sports and Pastimes* (1868), *New England Base Ballist* (1868) and *National Chronicle* (1869-70) all featured detailed player records.

To compile the yearly averages, the above sources relied on the individual clubs to send in their season ending totals. Not all clubs complied, especially those with less than stellar records. On the other hand, teams that wanted to tout their prowess were more than happy to let the world know of their exploits. Occasionally in the records of the better teams, an embarrassing loss against a weaker foe is mysteriously missing from the total account. In most, but not all cases, the forgotten game can be added into the mix.

To fill the gaps in players' statistical information I turned to the source—the boxscores located in the newspapers of the era. The best sources were the various sports weeklies like the *Clipper*. However, several daily papers like the *Boston Herald* and the *New York Times* were consulted as well. Information gleaned included (1) player positions, (2) teams not included in the guides and (3) all teams in 1857 and 1858 before any guides were published.

With this information now at hand on the three phases of the National Association (teams, games, and players) I decided to arrange it in the following fashion. Each chapter consists of one year starting with an explanatory essay featuring one aspect of that season, usually a team, player or trend in the game. Following the essay, teams are listed in the order of most wins. Each team heading contains the following information: club name, wins, losses, ties, and city/state. Next follows a list of games played including date, opponent, score, and decision.

After the games comes the list of individual players. They are listed with the nine starters followed by the substitutes. If no starters are indicated, a team's players are listed in order of most games played. For each player the following categories are noted: position, games played, hands lost (outs) with average and over, runs with average and over. Beginning in 1868, hits and total bases are added to the mix. In 1869 and 1870, where available, pitching totals are mentioned which include innings pitched, hits or runs allowed and average hits or runs per inning. Season leader totals are indicated by bold face.

For 1869 and 1870, with the advent of professional teams, variations of this format were used. First the professional teams are listed, then the amateur clubs. For each of the professional teams, wins, losses and ties with other professionals are placed in parentheses alongside the wins, losses and ties for all games. In addition, at the end of the professional section, a table is included showing a set of standings for the pro teams. Finally, in 1870 the professional players' stats are divided by pro games and amateur contests.

After the list of teams comes a list of the team totals where each club is given a line which chronicles: name, city/state, games played, wins, losses, ties, winning percentage, runs scored, and runs scored against. Finally is a list of Association teams where nothing is known but name and location.

In compiling this information, it became evident how frustratingly incomplete it was. For some Association clubs complete information was available—for others only tantalizing fragments from spotty press coverage. For the games, sometimes the playing date remains unknown, sometimes a score as well. For the players, in several cases, box scores were not extant thus making their record incomplete. In other instances, players were given stats in more games than their team played because of their participation in "picked nine" (all-star) games.

In order to include a complete record as possible, compromises had to be made. In the teams category, only two types of teams were given complete coverage: a team with a complete schedule, or a team with batting information for at least five games. Other clubs with win or loss totals for at least four games are listed in the team totals at the end of the section. Incomplete team records are noted in italics.

For the players, most sources of the period only contain records of participants in five or more games. In the team listings I have done the same although some team stats include the record of all the players, especially in the early years, if they are available. In the cases were fewer than nine players qualify for inclusion, they are in order of most games. In summary, I have endeavored to include as many partial details as possible yet still give an accurate assessment of the total.

Sprinkled throughout the text of the book, the reader will notice baseball terminology not widely used today. Words such as "muffin" (used to describe the most awkward and inexperienced players) and "first nine" (used to describe the first string team of a club) are totally unknown in baseball circles today. Whenever an unusual term crops up in the body of the text, a full explanation follows. Also, to spice up the text, I have liberally quoted from the sources of the era to give it a unique flavor.

In delving into the world of Civil War–era baseball, I found a game that would be recognizable to us on the playing field, but certainly not in the box score. I found teams that were named in seemingly peculiar fashion after famous people and patriotic concepts, yet a few of their names survive to this day. I found players who could rival any modern day athlete in greed and avarice, yet nominally were not paid for their services. In short, virtually every facet of the game we know today had its start in the days of the National Association of Base Ball Players. Please read on and find out how.

PRELUDE
THE KNICKERBOCKER CLUB

Of all the ball games played by groups of young men in the first half of the nineteenth century, only one developed into the game we call baseball. This was entirely due to the efforts of one entity.

In the early years of the nineteenth century, there were several outdoor games that were enjoyed by those seeking recreation. Of these, the ones that involved striking a thrown ball with a wooden bat seemed the most popular. For instance, the game of cricket, imported from England, drew much attention. Also, a game called town ball was played widely.

Town ball was a game played with one team in the field with another at bat. The team at bat did their best to strike the ball, pitched to them by a member of the fielding group. Once struck, the batter would then endeavor to make a circuit of four bases placed in a square in order to score a run. The fielding team would do their best to stop them by catching a hit ball before it hit the ground, or by throwing and striking a baserunner in between the bases. When all the players on one team had received a chance to hit, they switched sides and the other team took their turn at bat.

Dissatisfied with town ball, a group of New Yorkers decided to tinker with the rules. First, they laid out the playing area in the shape of a diamond instead of town ball's square. Second, they eliminated the practice of hitting a runner with a thrown ball to retire him. Instead, they offered the option of tagging him with the ball. Third, they stopped the practice of letting the entire team bat at once. As an alternative, this group suggested that the teams switch places after three men had been put out. Last, the number of runs necessary for victory was set at 21. This group of men called themselves the Knickerbocker Club.

Formed in September 1845, the Knickerbocker Club was one of the earliest ball playing clubs to be formed but certainly not the first. That honor fell to the Olympic Club of Philadelphia which dated to the early 1830s and the New York and Eagle clubs which started around 1840. However, the Knickerbocker outfit was the first to codify and play under the new rules.

Two men were the driving force behind the Knicks—Alexander Cartwright and Daniel Adams. Cartwright's contribution included organizing the club in 1845 and setting down the basic rule changes mentioned above in a club constitution. Daniel Adams' role came later in refining the rules such as (1) setting the number of players at nine, (2) putting in a new fielding position "shortstop" to play midway between third and second and (3) determining the distances between the bases and the distance between the pitcher and batter.

Anxious to test their new game, the Knickerbockers staged several games in the fall of 1845, playing what we would call intersquad games. Several accounts found their way into the New York papers. By the spring of the following year, the Knickerbockers were ready to test their mettle against a real opponent.

On June 19, 1846, the Knickerbocker club met the New York club on the field. Played at Elysian Field in Hoboken, New Jersey, the Knicks were soundly thrashed 21–1. This match, chronicled in the press, was also immortalized by a Currier and Ives print which depicted the momentous occasion for all to see.

For the next several years the Knickerbockers honed their game through practices and intersquad games. This was a necessity as there were no other teams to play. Their 1846 opponents, the New York club, dwindled to nothing as most of their members joined the Knickerbocker outfit. It wasn't until the next decade that another opponent appeared.

Sometime in 1850, another baseball club was formed in New York. Dubbed the Washington club, the team faced the Knickerbocker nine in a pair of 1851 matches losing them both 21–11 and 22–20. In the spring of 1852, the Washington team renamed themselves the Gotham club and were joined by a third New York team—the Eagle club. In 1854, two new teams joined the mix including the first from Brooklyn—the Excelsior—while another seven joined the group in 1855, with an additional four in 1856.

On the field, the Knickerbocker nine ruled their opponents, winning 13 of 21 matches, including eight in a row, from 1851 to 1854.

Other teams of note included Brooklyn's Atlantic which won six without a defeat in 1855 and 1856, and the Eagle club of New York who also bested six opponents from 1854 to 1856. (Note: For a complete list of game scores, please see end of chapter.)

Off the field, the Knickerbocker club continued to show the way by further refining the rules of the game. In 1848, the distances between the bases were set at 42 paces between home and second, first and third which translates to about 90 feet apart. In 1854, the pitcher was placed 15 paces (approx. 45 ft.) from the batter. Also, a new rule stated that a runner could be put out by a fielder touching the base to which he was forced to advance.

When it came time for baseball's next logical organizational step, the Knickerbocker club was once more at the forefront. At a team meeting in December 1856, the club's president Daniel Adams suggested holding a convention of ballplayers with the thought of organizing a national association. This would have the benefit of putting down on paper one set of rules for all teams. In addition, a national convention would be an ideal way for players and clubs to socialize and schedule matches.

All agreed. The call went out to all teams to send delegates to a meeting scheduled for January 1857. Baseball was about to take a giant step forward.

GAME SCORES 1846-1856

KNICKERBOCKER
New York, NY

DATE	OPPONENT	SCORE			W	L	T
06/19/46	New York (New York)	1	21			L	
06/03/51	Washington (New York)	21	11		W		
06/17/51	Washington (New York)	22	20	(10)	W		
---/---/52	Gotham (New York)	--	--		W		
---/---/52	Gotham (New York)	--	--		W		
07/05/53	Gotham (New York)	21	12		W		
10/14/53	Gotham (New York)	21	14		W		
06/30/54	Gotham (New York)	21	16	(16)	W		
09/20/54	Gotham (New York)	24	13		W		
---/---/54	Gotham (New York)	12	12	(12)			T
11/10/54	Eagle (New York)	4	21			L	
11/17/54	Eagle (New York)	21	22			L	
06/01/55	Gotham (New York)	12	21	(11)		L	
06/05/55	Eagle (New York)	27	14		W		
09/13/55	Gotham (New York)	22	7		W		
09/20/55	Eagle (New York)	21	10		W		
08/30/56	Empire (New York)	21	21				T
09/05/56	Gotham (New York)	7	21			L	
09/19/56	Eagle (New York)	24	17		W		
09/25/56	Empire (New York)	21	12		W		
10/09/56	Eagle (New York)	10	21			L	

GOTHAM
New York, NY

DATE	OPPONENT	SCORE			W	L	T
---/---/52	Knickerbocker (New York)	--	--			L	
---/---/52	Knickerbocker (New York)	--	--			L	
07/05/53	Knickerbocker (New York)	12	21			L	
10/14/53	Knickerbocker (New York)	14	21			L	
06/30/54	Knickerbocker (New York)	16	21	(16)		L	
09/20/54	Knickerbocker (New York)	13	24			L	
---/---/54	Knickerbocker (New York)	12	12	(12)			T
06/01/55	Knickerbocker (New York)	21	12	(11)	W		
06/22/55	Eagle (New York)	21	3		W		
09/05/55	Empire (New York)	25	4		W		
09/13/55	Knickerbocker (New York)	7	22			L	
10/01/55	Eagle (New York)	22	11		W		
09/05/56	Knickerbocker (New York)	21	7		W		
09/26/56	Eagle (New York)	18	18				T
10/17/56	Eagle (New York)	2	6			L	
10/28/56	Eagle (New York)	23	4		W		

PRELUDE

EAGLE
New York, NY

DATE	OPPONENT	SCORE		W	L	T
11/10/54	Knickerbocker (New York)	21	4	W		
11/17/54	Knickerbocker (New York)	22	21	W		
06/05/55	Knickerbocker (New York)	14	27		L	
06/22/55	Gotham (New York)	3	21		L	
09/20/55	Knickerbocker (New York)	10	21		L	
10/01/55	Gotham (New York)	11	22		L	
10/15/55	Empire (New York)	21	15	W		
09/10/56	Empire (New York)	10	21		L	
09/19/56	Knickerbocker (New York)	24	17	W		
09/26/56	Gotham (New York)	18	18			T
10/09/56	Knickerbocker (New York)	21	10	W		
10/17/56	Gotham (New York)	6	2	W		
10/28/56	Gotham (New York)	4	23		L	

EMPIRE
New York, NY

DATE	OPPONENT	SCORE		W	L	T
09/05/55	Gotham (New York)	4	25		L	
10/15/55	Eagle (New York)	15	21		L	
08/30/56	Knickerbocker (New York)	21	21			T
09/10/56	Eagle (New York)	21	10	W		
09/25/56	Knickerbocker (New York)	21	12		L	

UNION
Morrisania, NY

DATE	OPPONENT	SCORE		W	L	T
10/25/55	Young America (New York)	25	8	W		
07/31/56	Baltic (New York)	23	17	W		
08/27/56	Baltic (New York)	15	12	W		
09/17/56	Eckford (Brooklyn)	8	22		L	
09/25/56	Baltic (New York)	25	11	W		
10/15/56	Eckford (Brooklyn)	6	22		L	

EXCELSIOR
Brooklyn, NY

DATE	OPPONENT	SCORE		W	L	T
10/08/56	Putnam (Brooklyn)	16	15	W		
10/25/56	Putnam (Brooklyn)	15	21		L	

ATLANTIC
Brooklyn, NY

DATE	OPPONENT	SCORE		W	L	T
10/21/55	Harmony (Brooklyn)	24	22	W		
11/05/55	Harmony (Brooklyn)	27	10	W		
09/18/56	Baltic (New York)	21	19	W		

ATLANTIC (cont.)
Brooklyn, NY

DATE	OPPONENT	SCORE		W	L	T
09/27/56	Columbia (Brooklyn)	34	7	W		
10/04/56	Columbia (Brooklyn)	23	4	W		
10/07/56	Baltic (New York)	27	7	W		

HARMONY
Brooklyn, NY

DATE	OPPONENT	SCORE		W	L	T
10/21/55	Atlantic (Brooklyn)	22	24		L	
11/05/55	Atlantic (Brooklyn)	10	27		L	

ECKFORD
Brooklyn, NY

DATE	OPPONENT	SCORE		W	L	T
09/17/56	Union (Morrisania, NY)	22	8	W		
10/15/56	Union (Morrisania, NY)	22	6	W		

BALTIC
New York, NY

DATE	OPPONENT	SCORE		W	L	T
07/31/56	Union (Morrisania, NY)	17	23		L	
08/27/56	Union (Morrisania, NY)	12	15		L	
09/18/56	Atlantic (Brooklyn)	19	21		L	
09/25/56	Union (Morrisania, NY)	11	25		L	
10/07/56	Atlantic (Brooklyn)	7	27		L	

PUTNAM
Brooklyn, NY

DATE	OPPONENT	SCORE		W	L	T
10/08/56	Excelsior (Brooklyn)	15	16		L	
10/25/56	Excelsior (Brooklyn)	21	15	W		

1857
THE ASSOCIATION BEGINS

On January 22, 1857, a group of men belonging to the prominent baseball clubs of New York and Brooklyn met to discuss the formation of a national baseball fraternity. This informal gathering agreed to meet at a later date in a more formal setting to iron out the details.

In May 1857, 16 clubs from New York and Brooklyn sent three delegates to the first meeting of its kind. The clubs represented were the Knickerbocker, Gotham, Eagle, Empire, Baltic, Harlem and Union from New York as well as the Putnam, Excelsior, Atlantic, Harmony, Continental, Eckford, Bedford, Nassau and Olympic from Brooklyn. No formal set of guidelines issued from this gathering, but a few rule changes were discussed and implemented.

The most important of these rule changes was the elimination of the 21 run dictum. Up until 1857, once a team scored 21 runs, the game was over. It could take four innings or it could take twelve—21 runs was the top score in virtually all cases.

However in 1857, the duration of a game was set at the familiar length of nine innings with any amount of runs possible—from zero to well over one hundred.

At season's end, one club stood head and shoulders above their competition in the winning column. Brooklyn's Atlantic nine played nine matches during the season winning seven of them. The only blemishes on their stellar record was a tie with the Continentals on October 1, and a late season, loss to the Gothams. In this match, the New York club jumped out to a 20–6 lead after six innings only to witness the Brooklynites chop eleven runs off the lead in the seventh and eighth. The Gotham club put away the match with four more in the ninth to win 24–19. The *New York Clipper* was effusive in its praise of the teams—especially the fielding:

> Wadsworth, on the part of Gotham, made a most brilliant catch; Commerford did the same, it being in its execution hardly second to Wadworth's...Of Tooker [Gotham] we have nothing to say, his nimbleness in putting two men out at once, knocking our descriptive powers into a 'cocked hat'. The gentlemen from Long Island [Atlantic] excelled even themselves in this department, Price at first base, O'Brien as pitcher, with Bergen as catcher, backed by Phelps at second base, and Pierce as short, with the assistance of a brilliant field, brought out the very best qualities of the Gothamites at batting, and towards the close of the game gave the spectators the unequalled treat of witnessing this beautiful game played in its brilliancy and perfection;...

Other teams that won as many as they lost included the Eagle and Empire who each won five and lost five, the Gotham who had four up with two down, and the Unions who vanquished three of five. The Knickerbockers also finished at the .500 mark although they only played in four matches. Only an 18-17 squeaker over the Eagle in their final 1857 game allowed them to square their accounts for the season.

Individually, the season's best batters graced the rosters of the winningest teams. Mr. Gelston, starting catcher of the Eagle club, scored the most runs (33) followed by the Atlantic's John Price and Dicky Pearce with 30 and 28. The best average and over of runs per game was posted by Price (3,6), Gelston (3,6) and Mattie and Peter O'Brien of the Atlantics (3,5).

At the end of 1857, the state of baseball was pronounced healthy by its chief chronicler—the *Clipper*. In its issue of December 26, 1857, the editors stated:

> This game is over for the present, but appearances indicate an increased and more wide-spread interest in the sport next season. It is a beautiful exercise, and equally fascinating to player and spectator. As we stated a few weeks since, the game is confined chiefly to this vicinity, but we hope to see it 'caught up' in other localities on the opening of the season of 1858.

By the time of this summation in the *Clipper*, plans were already underway to make its stirring prose a reality. In a request sent by the presidents of the four most senior clubs—Knickerbocker, Gotham, Eagle and Empire—delegates were invited to the next convention of ballplayers scheduled for March 1858. Here, the true keel of the National Association was laid.

ATLANTIC   7 - 1 - 1
Brooklyn, NY

DATE	OPPONENT	SCORE		W	L	T
08/21	Continental (Brooklyn)	37	21	W		
09/03	Gotham (New York)	41	11	W		
09/15	Eckford (Brooklyn)	26	17	W		
09/24	Putnam (Brooklyn)	19	3	W		
10/01	Continental (Brooklyn)	34	34			T
10/06	Continental (Brooklyn)	26	13	W		
10/20	Putnam (Brooklyn)	37	15	W		
10/22	Eckford (Brooklyn)	29	11	W		
---/---	Gotham (New York)	19	24		L	

BATTER	POS	GP	HL	A	O	R	A	O
John Price	1B	8	24	3	0	30	3	6
John Holder	2B	6	17	2	5	22	3	4
Dicky Pearce	SS	8	22	2	6	28	3	4
Polkert Boerum	3B,C	8	19	2	3	22	2	4
Archie McMahon	OF	7	22	3	1	22	3	1
Tice Hamilton	OF	8	25	3	1	21	2	5
Peter O'Brien	OF	8	21	2	5	29	3	5
L. M. Bergen	C	5	12	2	2	19	3	4
Mattie O'Brien	P	6	17	2	5	23	3	5
A. J. Dayton	2B	2	6	3	0	6	3	0
William Babcock	3B,P	2	5	2	1	7	3	1
S.V. Millard	3B	2	6	3	0	8	4	0
Steven Mann	OF	1	2	2	0	1	1	0

EAGLE   5 - 5
New York, NY

DATE	OPPONENT	SCORE		W	L	T
06/08	Knickerbocker (New York)	25	16	W		
06/16	Eckford (Brooklyn)	34	20	W		
07/10	Gotham (New York)	20	43		L	
07/21	Empire (New York)	39	17	W		
08/20	Empire (New York)*	15	39		L	
09/08	Gotham (New York)	15	9	W		
09/15	Knickerbocker (New York)	17	18		L	
09/22	Eckford (Brooklyn)	23	22	W		
09/30	Empire (New York)	21	23		L	
10/09	Gotham (New York)	19	25		L	

* Box score not available

BATTER	POS	GP	HL	A	O	R	A	O
Winslow	1B,P	5	15	3	0	8	1	3
Houseman	2B	*6	10	2	2	20	3	2
Smith	SS	7	23	3	2	14	2	0
Place	3B	*9	17	2	3	23	2	5
Williams	OF	*9	19	2	5	26	2	8
Wandell	OF	5	15	3	0	12	2	2
Sam Yates	OF,1B	*7	11	2	1	23	3	2
Gelston	C	*9	19	2	5	33	3	6
Bixby	P,1B	*9	27	3	6	19	2	1
Norman Welling	OF,SS	*4	4	2	0	10	2	2
Brinckerhoff	OF	*1	11	3	2	8	2	0
Gilman	2B	3	10	3	1	7	2	1
Armfield	OF	*2	5	5	0	7	3	1

EAGLE (cont.)
New York, NY

BATTER	POS	GP	HL	A	O	R	A	O
Van Nice	OF	*1	-	-	-	2	2	0
Baker		*1	-	-	-	1	1	0

* Hands lost not counted in all games

EMPIRE   5 - 5
New York, NY

DATE	OPPONENT	SCORE		W	L	T
06/24	Knickerbocker (New York)	23	37		L	
06/30	Eckford (Brooklyn)	28	20	W		
07/21	Eagle (New York)	17	39		L	
07/29	Eckford (Brooklyn)*	33	35		L	
08/20	Eagle (New York)*	39	15	W		
09/07	Baltic (New York)	23	13	W		
09/10	Knickerbocker (New York)	28	17	W		
09/16	Gotham (New York)	17	19		L	
09/30	Eagle (New York)	23	21	W		
10/09	Eckford (Brooklyn)	13	23		L	

* box score not available

BATTER	POS	GP	HL	A	O	R	A	O
Leavy	1B	*8	21	3	3	12	1	4
Miller	2B,OF	*8	15	2	3	24	3	0
H. Smith	SS	5	16	3	1	12	2	2
Moore	3B,2B,OF	5	12	2	2	15	3	0
Hoyt	OF	*7	11	2	1	21	3	0
Benson	OF	5	16	3	1	8	1	3
Ed Ward	OF,3B	3	9	3	0	4	1	1
Gorff	C	*8	11	1	5	24	3	0
Dick Thorn	P	*8	18	3	0	21	2	5
Scott		*3	5	5	0	6	2	0
Wandell		*3	3	3	0	6	2	0
Tice		*3	5	5	0	6	2	0
Newkirk	OF	2	8	4	0	2	1	0
Fays	3B	*2	2	1	0	7	3	1
Myers	C	1	1	2	0	2	2	0
Belden		*1	-	-	-	2	2	0

* Hands lost not counted in all games

GOTHAM   4 - 2
New York, NY

DATE	OPPONENT	SCORE		W	L	T
07/10	Eagle (New York)	43	20	W		
09/03	Atlantic (Brooklyn)	11	41		L	
09/08	Eagle (New York)	9	15		L	
09/16	Empire (New York)	19	17	W		
10/19	Eagle (New York)	25	19	W		
---/---	Atlantic (Brooklyn)	24	19	W		

BATTER	POS	GP	HL	A	O	R	A	O
Wadsworth	1B,OF	6	17	2	5	13	2	1
Johnson	2B,C	6	18	3	0	13	2	1
Commerford	SS,2B	6	21	3	3	11	1	5
McCosker	3B,1B	5	13	2	3	13	2	3

GOTHAM (cont.)
New York, NY

BATTER	POS	GP	HL	A	O	R	A	O
Sheridan	OF	5	16	3	1	14	2	4
Cudlipp	OF	4	9	2	1	12	3	0
Griswold	OF	3	8	2	2	8	2	2
Vail	C	3	9	3	0	8	2	3
T.G. Van Cott	P	6	11	1	5	19	3	1
Turner	3B,1B,OF	5	18	3	3	9	1	4
Tooker	SS	2	5	2	1	6	3	0
Winslow	OF	1	4	4	0	4	4	0
Andrew Dupignac	2B	1	4	4	0	1	1	0
Seaman	OF	1	4	4	0	0	0	0

UNION 3 - 2
Morrisania, NY

DATE	OPPONENT	SCORE		W	L	T
08/03	Harlem (New York)	22	21	W		
09/08	Harlem (New York)*	14	25		L	
09/16	Excelsior (Brooklyn)	30	8	W		
09/25	Adriatic (Newark)	28	11	W		
09/28	Excelsior (Brooklyn)	21	43		L	

* Box score not available

BATTER	POS	GP	HL	A	O	R	A	O
Booth	1B	3	8	2	2	10	3	1
Balcolm	2B	3	7	2	1	9	3	0
Ferdon	SS	3	8	2	2	11	3	2
Todd	3B,C	4	9	2	1	13	3	1
E. Durell	OF,2B	3	9	3	0	5	1	2
Rodman	OF	3	7	2	1	10	3	1
Dickerson	OF	3	11	3	2	7	2	1
Gifford	C	3	5	1	2	14	4	2
Pinckney	P	4	12	3	0	12	3	0
Roosa	3B	1	1	1	0	5	5	0
Henry	OF	1	3	3	0	3	3	0
Mann		1	3	3	0	2	2	0
Brandon	1B	1	4	4	0	2	2	0
Tremper	OF	1	6	6	0	0	0	0
Frisbee		1	6	6	0	0	0	0

KNICKERBOCKER 2 - 2
New York, NY

DATE	OPPONENT	SCORE		W	L	T
06/08	Eagle (New York)	16	25		L	
06/24	Empire (New York)	37	23	W		
09/10	Empire (New York)	17	28		L	
09/15	Eagle (New York)	18	17	W		

BATTER	POS	GP	HL	A	O	R	A	O
Stephens	1B	*3	5	2	1	6	2	0
Mott	2B,3B	2	6	3	0	4	2	0
Alfred Vredenburgh	SS	*2	2	2	0	5	2	1
Fraley Neibuhr	3B	*2	3	3	0	7	3	1
James Davis	OF	*4	6	3	0	9	2	1
Daniel Adams	OF,SS	*4	4	2	0	12	3	0
Tucker	OF	*2	6	6	0	2	1	0

KNICKERBOCKER (cont.)
New York, NY

BATTER	POS	GP	HL	A	O	R	A	O
Charles DeBost	C	*3	9	4	1	8	2	2
Norman Welling	P,OF	*4	5	2	1	12	3	1
Nap McLaughlin	P	*3	1	1	0	8	2	2
Samuel Kissam		*2	0	0	0	5	2	1
Edgar Lasak		*1	-	-	-	3	3	0
Richard Stevens	2B	1	4	4	0	2	2	0
Richard Conover	OF	1	3	3	0	2	2	0
Dan Stansbury		*1	-	-	-	2	2	0
William Grenelle		*1	-	-	-	1	1	0

* Hands lost not counted in all games

PUTNAM   2 - 2
Brooklyn, NY

DATE	OPPONENT	SCORE		W	L	T
07/14	Excelsior (Brooklyn)*	37	20	W		
09/24	Atlantic (Brooklyn)	3	19		L	
09/25	Continental (Brooklyn)	46	17	W		
10/20	Atlantic (Brooklyn)*	15	37		L	

* Box score not available

BATTER	POS	GP	HL	A	O	R	A	O
Gesner		2	4	2	0	7	3	1
Burr		2	5	2	1	2	3	0
Dakin		2	3	1	1	6	2	0
Dan Ketchum		2	5	2	1	4	2	0
Hoyt		1	3	3	0	5	5	0
Smith		1	4	4	0	5	5	0
Gibbs		1	3	3	0	5	5	0
Davidson		1	3	3	0	5	5	0
Gillespie		1	2	2	0	5	5	0
McKinstry		1	1	1	0	1	1	0
J. Smith		1	1	1	0	0	0	0
Morrell		1	2	2	0	0	0	0
F. Smith		1	2	2	0	0	0	0
Griswold		1	2	2	0	0	0	0

ECKFORD   2 - 5
Brooklyn, NY

DATE	OPPONENT	SCORE		W	L	T
06/16	Eagle (New York)	20	34		L	
06/30	Empire (New York)	20	28		L	
07/29	Empire (New York)*	35	33	W		
09/15	Atlantic (Brooklyn)	17	26		L	
09/22	Eagle (New York)	22	23		L	
10/09	Empire (New York)	23	13	W		
10/22	Atlantic (Brooklyn)*	11	29		L	

* Box score not available

BATTER	POS	GP	HL	A	O	R	A	O
Tostivan	1B,C	*5	6	3	0	15	3	0
Welling	2B,1B	*3	3	3	0	7	2	1
George Grum	SS	*5	3	1	0	19	3	4
Logan	3B	*5	12	4	0	6	1	1
Harry Manolt	OF	*3	9	3	0	7	2	1

ECKFORD (cont.)
Brooklyn, NY

BATTER	POS	GP	HL	A	O	R	A	O
Gray	OF	*4	7	3	1	8	2	0
Curtis	OF	*3	7	3	1	5	1	2
Frank Pidgeon	C,P	*5	6	2	0	16	3	1
McVoy	P	*4	12	4	0	10	2	2
Caulkins	2B	*2	4	4	0	2	1	0
Webster	2B	*2	2	2	0	5	2	1
Brown	OF	1	2	2	0	2	2	0
A. Mills	OF	1	4	4	0	0	0	0
Vanderbilt		*1	-	-	-	0	0	0
Smith	OF	*1	-	-	-	1	1	0

* Hands lost not counted in all games

EXCELSIOR   1 - 2
Brooklyn, NY

DATE	OPPONENT	SCORE		W	L	T
07/14	Putnam (Brooklyn)*	20	37		L	
09/16	Union (Morrisania, NY)	8	30		L	
09/28	Union (Morrisania, NY)	41	23	W		

* box score not extant

BATTER	POS	GP	HL	A	O	R	A	O
William Young	1B	1	3	3	0	5	5	0
Wells	2B	2	7	3	1	5	2	1
R. Fleet	SS	1	3	3	0	0	0	0
James Rogers	3B,SS	2	5	2	1	7	3	1
A. Markham	OF	1	1	1	0	1	1	0
John Zuill	OF	1	2	2	0	1	1	0
George Cole	OF	1	3	3	0	5	5	0
Joe Leggett	C	1	1	1	0	8	8	0
C. Etheridge	P,OF	2	4	2	0	8	4	0
A. Dayton	P	1	4	4	0	4	4	0
Sunderling	3B	1	4	4	0	3	3	0
Pomeroy	1B	1	3	3	0	1	1	0
T. Morris	C	1	2	2	0	1	1	0
P. Chadwick	OF	1	3	3	0	0	0	0

CONTINENTAL   1 - 3 - 1
Brooklyn, NY

DATE	OPPONENT	SCORE		W	L	T
08/21	Atlantic (Brooklyn)*	21	37		L	
09/25	Putnam (Brooklyn)	17	46		L	
09/30	Nassau (Brooklyn)	36	26	W		
10/01	Atlantic (Brooklyn)	34	34			T
10/06	Atlantic (Brooklyn)	13	26		L	

* Box score not available

BATTER	POS	GP	HL	A	O	R	A	O
Brown	1B,3B	2	7	3	1	4	2	0
Knapp	2B	3	9	3	0	7	2	3
Ryno	SS,1B	4	8	2	0	11	3	2
J.F. Law	3B	2	5	2	1	7	3	1
John Oliver	OF	3	11	3	2	6	2	0
N.B. Law	OF	3	8	2	2	8	2	2

CONTINENTAL (cont.)
Brooklyn, NY

BATTER	POS	GP	HL	A	O	R	A	O
Berry	OF	2	5	2	1	7	3	1
Masten	C	3	10	3	1	10	3	1
Kelly	P	3	6	2	0	14	4	2
Durkee	P,OF	3	5	1	2	9	3	0
Briggs	2B	2	4	2	0	6	3	0
Walton	3B,1B	2	5	2	1	4	2	0
J. Law, Jr.	OF	2	7	3	1	4	2	0

TEAM TOTALS

TEAM	CITY/STATE	GP	W	L	T	PCT	R	OR
Atlantic	Brooklyn, NY	9	7	1	1	.833	268	149
Eagle	New York, NY	10	5	5	0	.500	228	232
Empire	New York, NY	10	5	5	0	.500	244	239
Gotham	New York, NY	6	4	2	0	.667	131	131
Union	Morrisania, NY	5	3	2	0	.600	115	108
Knickerbocker	New York, NY	4	2	2	0	.500	88	93
Putnam	Brooklyn, NY	4	2	2	0	.500	101	93
Eckford	Brooklyn, NY	7	2	5	0	.286	148	186
Baltic	New York, NY	2	1	1	0	.500	69	33
Harlem	New York, NY	2	1	1	0	.500	46	36
Excelsior	Brooklyn, NY	3	1	2	0	.333	69	90
Continental	Brooklyn, NY	5	1	3	1	.300	121	169
Nassau	Brooklyn, NY	3	0	3	0	.000	51	109

OTHER TEAMS

TEAM	CITY/STATE
Olympic	Brooklyn, NY
Bedford	Brooklyn, NY
Harmony	Brooklyn, NY

1858
NEW YORK VS. BROOKLYN

In the 1850s, New York and Brooklyn were not lumped into the broader category of New York City as they are today. They were separate entities—each blessed with their own uniqueness. Separated by one mile of water, the cities were two of the leading centers of commerce on America's 19th century seaboard. In matters of shipping, manufacturing, and industry the two were natural rivals. Their rivalry naturally extended to social and sports arenas such as baseball. This baseball rivalry reached a fever pitch in 1858.

New York, what we now consider the island of Manhattan, was the larger of the two. First settled by Dutch immigrants in the 17th century, the population grew northward from its original nucleus on the southern tip of the island. The populace also grew in number, reaching the 750,000 mark by the mid–19th century. Despite this growth the northern boundary of New York had only reached streets numbered in the mid-forties by 1850. Anything north of there was called "God's country"—populated by scattered farms and squatters.

Brooklyn developed differently. Instead of one population center growing outward, Brooklyn originally consisted of several villages scattered throughout the region. By 1840, the population had reached 30,000. In 1854, the villages of Brooklyn, Williamsburg, and Bushwick all joined under the common banner of Brooklyn. However, several of the outlying communities such as Greenpoint and Bedford were considered part of the several districts of greater Brooklyn.

Although New York developed the first several baseball clubs, Brooklyn quickly followed suit. By the time of the first organized baseball meetings in May 1857, the Brooklynites had fully the same amount of clubs present. When the call went out for the next meeting in March 1858, a total of nine Brooklyn clubs answered the summons.

The March 1858 convention was a landmark event in at least two areas: (1) For the first time, a non–New York area team attended. The Liberty Club of New Brunswick would be the first link in a long history of expansion. And (2) the convention produced a written set of by-laws, rules, and a constitution while giving themselves a name. Henceforth the organization governing the game of baseball would be called the National Association of Base Ball Players. This latter act of permanence causes many to use 1858 as the starting date for the National Association.

In late June, the *New York Clipper* reported plans for a series of matches. These were to be no ordinary games. Instead, they would pit an "All New York Nine" against an "All Brooklyn Nine." In other words, the nine best players from the New York clubs would square off against their Brooklyn counterparts. The New York group consisted of players from the Gotham, Knickerbocker, Eagle, Empire, and Union clubs, while the Brooklyn contingent was made up of members of the Atlantic, Excelsior, Putnam, and Eckford nines.

On July 20, 1858, at the Fashion Race Course in Brooklyn, the first match came off. The *Clipper's* issue of July 24 described the scene:

> The stands at the Fashion on Tuesday [7/20] were crowded, the ladies seeming to preponderate; on different parts of the course were gathered immense numbers of spectators, while hundreds of vehicles were arranged at various places around the track. There could not have been less than 10,000 persons present.

The game itself proved to be close and exciting. In the end, New York bested their Brooklyn brethren 22–18. Very complete statistics were kept on the game—even to the level of measuring the pitch count which saw an astounding 547 pitches tossed by all hurlers.

In the return match played on August 17 at the same location, the Brooklyn contingent soundly thrashed New York by the count of 29–8. The *Clipper* described the inability of the Gothamites to score as follows: "Of the nine innings played on each side, New York included 5 round 0's, their highest score being 4; while the Brooklynites had but 1 round 0, and the good score of 6 in their first and fourth innings."

With the series knotted at one each, the tie-breaking match was eagerly anticipated. On September 10, once again at the Fashion Race Course, the "All New York Nine" took on the "All Brooklyn Nine." With New York at bat first, the *Clipper* described the action: "Gelston began by making a homerun. Benson was out first by being caught on the fly by Pidgeon; Tooker by Boerum on a foul ball, and Gelston on the 1st base by Price. Gelston, Wadsworth, Pinckney, Thorne, DeBost, Burns and McCosker each made a run." Trailing by seven after the first one-half inning, the demoralized Brooklyn squad never recovered and lost decisively, 29–18.

These three matches were the pinnacle of baseball interest up to this point. Never before had so much interest been placed in the game—both in the sheer volume of spectators and in the press coverage that followed. Each contributed to the expansion of the sport.

In the regular season, New York wrested the laurels of best club away from their Brooklyn neighbors. The Mutual club won their first eleven matches of the season, only to fall to the Empires 37–22 in their final game. Their 11–1 record stood as the season's best although several other clubs like the Empire (8–1–1) and Atlantic (7–0) finished with gaudy records as well.

Individually, Brooklyn's Eckford and Atlantic clubs boasted the top batting stars. Atlantic first baseman John Price led all with 32 runs, while Eckford third baseman William Young posted the highest average (4,1). Other top scorers included Price's teammates Peter O'Brien (28) and Young's clubmate A. Dayton (27). Price finished with the second best average (4,0) while Dayton ended third (3,6).

Through the rest of the Association years, all-star groups from New York and Brooklyn continued to tilt on the playing field. Once formal league play commenced in the 1870s, teams from the two cities still valued a win against one another, more than all others.

As early as the 1830s, efforts were made to incorporate Brooklyn into New York. The Brooklynites thought little of the idea and it was quashed. In the 1870s, the mile of water separating the two was spanned by the Brooklyn Bridge, forging a permanent link. In 1898, incorporation was accomplished as Brooklyn (along with Queens, the Bronx and Staten Island) was made part of greater New York. For Brooklyn it was time. The borough had grown up and now contained nearly a million citizens of its own.

However even as a part of a whole, baseball rivalries between the two continued well into the 20th century. If a typical Brooklyn Dodgers fan of the 1940s or 1950s were asked if his team was in the same city—on equal footing with the New York Yankees or Giants— his response, if printable, would not have been a surprise.

MUTUAL 11 - 1
New York, NY

DATE	OPPONENT	SCORE		W	L	T
07/29	Monument (New York)	70	13	W		
08/10	St. Nicholas (New York)*	31	24	W		
08/13	Monument (New York)	67	17	W		
08/23	Baltic (New York)	48	21	W		
08/26	Independent (New York)*	56	12	W		
08/30	Hoboken (Hoboken, NJ)*	29	25	W		
09/10	Baltic (New York)*	47	26	W		
09/22	St. Nicholas (New York)	51	21	W		
09/26	Hoboken (Hoboken,NJ)*	31	19	W		
09/30	Empire (New York)*	18	17	W		
10/06	Independent (New York)*	54	13	W		
10/18	Empire (New York)*	22	37		L	

* Box score not available

BATTER	POS	GP	HL	A	O	R	A	O
L. Clancy	1B,P	4	10	2	2	30	7	2
P. Gavagan	2B,3B,C	4	9	2	1	30	7	2
P. Kivelin	SS	4	12	3	0	26	6	2
J. Curtis	3B,2B,1B	3	11	3	2	15	5	0
Green	OF	3	10	3	1	19	6	1
W. Anderson	OF	3	7	2	1	18	6	0
H.B. Taylor	OF	2	6	3	0	12	6	0
J. Beard	C,3B	4	12	3	0	30	7	2
S. Burns	P,1B	3	8	2	2	22·	7	1
W. Powell	OF,P	4	10	2	2	30	7	2
A.B. Taylor	2B,OF,3B	3	9	3	0	18	6	0

EMPIRE 8 - 1 - 1
New York, NY

DATE	OPPONENT	SCORE		W	L	T
07/17	St. Nicholas (New York)*	30	13	W		
07/21	Empire (Newark)*	27	7	W		
08/20	Eagle (New York)*	39	13	W		
09/03	Gotham (New York)*	22	11	W		
09/15	St. Nicholas (New York)	24	3	W		
09/22	Knickerbocker (New York)	21	21			T
09/27	Baltic (New York)*	40	27	W		
09/30	Mutual (New York)*	17	18		L	
10/18	Mutual (New York)*	37	22	W		
10/27	Gotham (New York)*	23	17	W		

* Box score not available

BATTER	POS	GP	HL	A	O	R	A	O
Ed Ward	1B	2	4	2	0	8	4	0
Miller	2B	2	5	2	1	4	2	0
H. Smith	SS	1	3	3	0	3	3	0
Goff	3B,OF	2	6	3	0	4	2	0
Culyer	OF	2	5	2	1	5	2	1
Moore	OF	2	8	4	0	4	2	0
Russell	OF	1	4	4	0	2	2	0
Benson	C	2	7	3	1	4	2	0
Dick Thorn	P	2	4	2	0	6	3	0
Hoyt	SS	1	3	3	0	2	2	0
Fays	3B	1	2	2	0	3	3	0

EXCELSIOR   8 - 5
Brooklyn, NY

DATE	OPPONENT	SCORE		W	L	T
06/10	Putnam (Brooklyn)*	18	31		L	
06/24	Eagle (New York)	32	13	W		
07/08	Knickerbocker (New York)	31	13	W		
07/22	Union (Morrisiana)	30	18	W		
08/05	Harlem (New York)	16	17		L	
08/20	Knickerbocker (New York)*	15	14	W		
09/14	Gotham (New York)	24	13	W		
09/23	Pastime (Brooklyn)	43	14	W		
09/28	Eagle (New York)	36	25	W		
10/08	Pastime (Brooklyn)*	27	11	W		
10/16	Putnam (Brooklyn)*	15	19		L	
11/09	Atlantic (Brooklyn)*	10	22		L	
11/16	Atlantic (Brooklyn)*	6	27		L	

* Box score not available

BATTER	POS	GP	HL	A	O	R	A	O
Ed Russell	1B	3	13	4	1	6	2	0
Thomas Reynolds	2B	5	14	3	4	17	3	2
George Cole	SS	7	28	4	0	16	2	2
William Young	3B,1B	7	18	2	4	29	4	1
A. Markham	OF,1B	7	19	2	5	24	3	3
Samuel Kissam	OF	7	22	3	1	20	2	6
John Holder	OF,2B,3B	7	19	2	5	26	3	5
Joe Leggett	C	7	19	2	5	23	3	2
A. Dayton	P	7	18	2	4	27	3	6
Bergen	OF	3	8	2	2	12	4	0
Wells	3B	1	3	3	0	4	4	0
C. Etheridge	3B	1	2	2	0	6	6	0
H. Polhemus	3B	1	3	3	0	2	2	0

ATLANTIC   7 - 0
Brooklyn, NY

DATE	OPPONENT	SCORE		W	L	T
06/17	Putnam (Brooklyn)	17	13	W		
09/12	Liberty (New Brunswick, NJ)	24	8	W		
10/11	Liberty (New Brunswick, NJ)*	61	14	W		
10/18	Putnam (Brooklyn)*	18	7	W		
10/25	Gotham (New York)*	31	17	W		
11/09	Excelsior (Brooklyn)*	22	10	W		
11/16	Excelsior (Brooklyn)*	27	6	W		

BATTER	POS	GP	HL	A	O	R	A	O
John Price	1B	8	18	2	2	32	4	0
John Oliver	2B	7	22	3	1	20	2	6
Dickey Pearce	SS	8	26	3	2	21	2	5
Charles Smith	3B	5	14	2	4	15	3	0
Peter O'Brien	OF	8	22	2	6	28	3	2
Tice Hamilton	OF	7	15	2	1	18	2	4
Archie McMahon	OF	7	20	2	6	23	3	2
Polkert Boerum	C	8	19	2	3	26	3	2
Mattie O'Brien	P,3B	7	19	2	5	22	3	1
Steven Mann	OF	2	8	4	0	7	3	1
John Ireland	3B	1	3	3	0	3	3	0
L.M. Bergen	C	1	2	2	0	2	2	0
John Holder	2B	1	4	4	0	2	2	0
George Phelps	P	1	5	5	0	1	1	0
Edwin Connor	3B	1	3	3	0	1	1	0

ECKFORD
Brooklyn, NY   5 - 1

DATE	OPPONENT	SCORE		W	L	T
08/31	Gotham (New York)	23	17	W		
09/04	Putnam (Brooklyn)*	29	10	W		
09/08	Harlem (New York)	40	22	W		
09/14	Continental (Brooklyn)	33	18	W		
10/12	Continental (Brooklyn)*	13	9	W		
10/19	Gotham (New York)*	6	23		L	

* Box score not available

BATTER	POS	GP	HL	A	O	R	A	O
A. Mills	1B	2	6	3	0	5	2	1
Welling	2B,1B	3	10	3	1	8	2	3
George Grum	SS	3	6	2	0	16	5	1
Tostivan	3B	3	12	4	0	10	3	1
Webster	OF	3	10	3	1	7	2	1
Brown	OF	3	11	3	2	9	3	0
Harry Manolt	OF	3	6	2	0	12	4	0
Vanderbilt	C	3	9	3	0	9	3	0
Frank Pidgeon	P	3	6	2	0	14	4	2
Smith	2B	1	2	2	0	5	5	0

PUTNAM
Brooklyn, NY   4 - 3

DATE	OPPONENT	SCORE		W	L	T
06/10	Excelsior (Brooklyn)*	31	18	W		
06/17	Atlantic (Brooklyn)	13	17		L	
07/07	St. Nicholas (New York)	45	19	W		
09/04	Eckford (Brooklyn)*	10	29		L	
09/27	Gotham (New York)	30	28	W		
10/16	Excelsior (Brooklyn)*	19	15	W		
10/18	Atlantic (Brooklyn)*	7	18		L	

* Box score not available

BATTER	POS	GP	HL	A	O	R	A	O
Kelly	1B	1	5	5	0	0	0	0
Gesner	2B,OF	3	8	2	2	10	3	1
McKinstry	SS	3	8	2	2	11	3	2
Pierce	3B,1B	2	6	3	0	7	3	1
Jackson	OF	2	7	3	1	6	3	0
Burr	OF,1B	3	9	3	0	10	3	1
Gillespie	OF,3B	3	10	3	1	8	2	2
Masten	C	3	7	2	1	11	3	2
Dakin	P	3	7	2	1	11	3	2
Dan Ketchum	2B	2	4	2	0	9	4	1
Messerole	OF	1	4	4	0	2	2	0
Headford	OF	1	3	3	0	3	3	0

HARLEM
New York, NY   3 - 1

DATE	OPPONENT	SCORE		W	L	T
07/21	Baltic (New York)	46	24	W		
08/05	Excelsior (Brooklyn)	17	16	W		
09/08	Eckford (Brooklyn)	22	40		L	
10/04	Baltic (New York)*	21	20	W		

* Box score not available

HARLEM (cont.)
New York, NY

BATTER	POS	GP	HL	A	O	R	A	O
Marsh	1B	3	10	3	1	10	3	1
Robinson	2B	2	5	2	1	4	2	0
Hughes	SS	3	9	3	0	8	2	2
John Wood	3B	2	4	2	0	11	5	1
Liscomb	OF	3	12	4	0	8	2	2
Dyer	OF	3	8	2	2	10	3	1
Kanski	OF	3	10	3	1	9	3	0
James Wood	C	3	8	2	2	10	3	1
G. Thompson	P	3	10	3	1	8	2	2
Robertson	2B	1	2	2	0	5	5	0
B. Thompson	3B	1	3	3	0	2	2	0

METROPOLITAN   3 - 2
New York, NY

DATE	OPPONENT	SCORE		W	L	T
07/08	Continental (Brooklyn)	25	32		L	
07/21	Manhattan (New York)	46	19	W		
08/13	Manhattan (New York)	39	13	W		
10/04	Continental (Brooklyn)*	15	16		L	
10/07	Hamilton (Brooklyn)*	15	14	W		

* Box score not available

BATTER	POS	GP	HL	A	O	R	A	O
Robbins	1B	2	3	1	1	11	5	1
Kirk	2B,OF	3	10	3	1	9	3	0
Lacour	SS	3	12	4	0	8	2	2
Overheiser	3B	2	5	2	1	8	4	0
Postley	OF	3	6	2	0	14	4	2
Wilson	OF,1B	2	8	4	0	7	3	1
McGregor	OF	1	3	3	0	5	5	0
Hudson	C	3	2	0	2	20	6	2
Jackson	P	3	11	3	2	12	4	0
Brown	3B	2	5	2	1	6	3	0
Dave Birdsall	2B	1	4	4	0	5	5	0
Folsom	OF	1	3	3	0	4	4	0
Decker		1	3	3	0	1	1	0

OSCEOLA   3 - 2
Brooklyn, NY

DATE	OPPONENT	SCORE		W	L	T
07/15	Nassau (Brooklyn)	41	29	W		
07/31	Hiawatha (Brooklyn)	18	27		L	
08/12	Nassau (Brooklyn)	21	25		L	
08/17	Hiawatha (Brooklyn)	45	30	W		
10/01	Nassau (Brooklyn)*	28	12	W		

* Box score not available

BATTER	POS	GP	HL	A	O	R	A	O
Beebe	1B,SS,2B	3	8	2	2	11	3	2
Bynner	2B	3	7	3	1	9	3	0
Simonson	SS,3B	3	3	1	1	11	3	2
Hall	3B	2	8	4	0	3	1	1
Phillips	OF	3	7	2	1	8	2	2
Solomon	OF	2	6	2	0	4	2	0

OSCEOLA (cont.)
Brooklyn, NY

BATTER	POS	GP	HL	A	O	R	A	O
Morrison	OF	2	3	1	1	8	4	0
Perrin	C,OF	3	6	2	0	13	4	1
Wheeler	P,SS	3	2	0	2	14	4	2
A.F. Tomes	P,C	2	4	2	0	10	5	0
John Smith	OF	2	2	1	0	10	5	0
F.H. Tomes	C,1B	2	7	3	1	8	4	0
Mumford	3B,1B	2	4	2	0	8	4	0
James Smith	OF	2	6	3	0	5	2	1
F.W. Massey	1B,P	2	10	5	0	3	1	1

CONTINENTAL   3 - 3
Brooklyn, NY

DATE	OPPONENT	SCORE		W	L	T
07/08	Metropolitan (New York)	32	25	W		
07/28	Baltic (New York)	21	15	W		
09/14	Eckford (Brooklyn)	18	33		L	
09/25	Oriental (Brooklyn)*	17	19		L	
10/04	Metropolitan (New York)*	16	15	W		
10/12	Eckford (Brooklyn)*	9	13		L	

* Box score not available

BATTER	POS	GP	HL	A	O	R	A	O
Durkee	1B	2	5	2	1	6	3	0
Walton	2B	3	8	2	2	9	3	0
Henry	SS,3B	2	6	3	0	3	1	1
Yates	3B	1	3	3	0	2	2	0
Briggs	OF	3	8	2	2	8	2	2
Knapp	OF	2	5	2	1	6	3	0
Voorhees	OF	1	4	4	0	2	2	0
Winants	C	2	5	2	1	6	3	0
Barto	P	3	5	1	2	10	3	1
A.B. Law		1	3	3	0	4	4	0
Coles		1	3	3	0	4	4	0
Ryno		1	3	3	0	3	3	0
Wadlington	SS	1	1	1	0	3	3	0
J.F. Law	OF	1	2	2	0	2	2	0
Parmalee	C	1	4	4	0	1	1	0
J. Law, Jr.	P	1	4	4	0	1	1	0
Beardsley	OF	1	3	3	0	1	1	0

ORIENTAL   2 - 2
Brooklyn, NY

DATE	OPPONENT	SCORE		W	L	T
08/24	Pastime (Brooklyn)	10	32		L	
08/27	Phoenix (Brooklyn)	39	24	W		
09/25	Continental (Brooklyn)*	19	17	W		
10/28	Phoenix (Brooklyn)*	8	20		L	

* Boxscore not available

BATTER	POS	GP	HL	A	O	R	A	O
W. Urell	1B	1	3	3	0	3	3	0
W. Cornell	2B	1	5	5	0	2	2	0
S. Wright	SS	1	1	1	0	6	6	0
W. Vanderbilt	3B	1	2	2	0	6	6	0

ORIENTAL (cont.)
Brooklyn, NY

BATTER	POS	GP	HL	A	O	R	A	O
H. Moore	OF	1	3	3	0	4	4	0
J. Mallison	OF	1	3	3	0	4	4	0
W. B. Overton	OF	1	3	3	0	4	4	0
F. Reed	C	1	3	3	0	4	4	0
G.H. Davis	P	1	0	0	0	6	6	0
Robbins	3B	1	3	3	0	2	2	0
Ryno	SS	1	1	1	0	2	2	0
Tuttle	OF	1	2	2	0	2	2	0
Burr	P	1	4	4	0	1	1	0
Gesner	C	1	5	5	0	1	1	0
Bartlett	1B	1	1	1	0	1	1	0
Witt	2B	1	4	4	0	1	1	0
Gregory	OF	1	5	5	0	0	0	0
Denton	OF	1	2	2	0	0	0	0

EAGLE 2 - 3
New York, NY

DATE	OPPONENT	SCORE		W	L	T
06/24	Excelsior (Brooklyn)	13	32		L	
07/29	Knickerbocker (New York)	45	18	W		
08/20	Empire (New York)	15	39		L	
08/29	St. Nicholas (New York)	33	18	W		
09/28	Excelsior (Brooklyn)*	25	36		L	

* Box score not available

BATTER	POS	GP	HL	A	O	R	A	O
Sam Yates	1B,3B,OF	4	13	3	1	12	3	0
Hazzard	2B	3	9	3	0	10	3	1
Gelston	SS,C	3	7	2	1	11	3	2
Place	3B,2B	3	8	2	2	10	3	1
Williams	OF	4	15	3	3	15	3	3
Brinckerhoff	OF,C	4	10	2	2	16	4	0
Van Nice	OF	2	5	2	1	9	4	1
Wandell	C	1	3	3	0	3	3	0
Bixby	P,1B,SS	4	9	2	1	13	3	1
Smith	SS,OF	3	6	2	0	10	3	1
Winslow	1B,P	3	15	5	0	4	1	1
Houseman	2B	1	4	4	0	2	2	0
Radeau	OF	1	3	3	0	1	1	0

PASTIME 2 - 3
Brooklyn, NY

DATE	OPPONENT	SCORE		W	L	T
08/24	Oriental (Brooklyn)	32	10	W		
09/23	Excelsior (Brooklyn)*	14	43		L	
10/08	Excelsior (Brooklyn)	8	27		L	
10/28	Adriatic (Newark)*	13	45		L	
---/---	Reserve Nine (Newark)	33	23	W		

* Box score not available

BATTER	POS	GP	HL	A	O	R	A	O
McKenzie	1B,OF	2	7	3	1	4	2	0
Carroll	2B,1B	2	8	4	0	6	3	0
E. Holt	SS	2	3	1	1	11	5	1

PASTIME (cont.)
Brooklyn, NY

BATTER	POS	GP	HL	A	O	R	A	O
Barry	3B,SS,OF	3	8	3	2	9	3	0
McNamee	OF	2	2	1	0	9	4	1
Cornish	OF	2	8	4	0	2	1	0
Bennett	OF	1	4	4	0	2	2	0
G. Holt	C,OF	2	4	2	0	7	3	1
Biggs	P	3	10	3	1	6	2	0
Story	C,2B,3B	3	5	1	2	11	3	2
Labon	2B	1	3	3	0	4	4	0
Saxton	3B	1	5	5	0	1	1	0
James Rogers	OF	1	7	7	0	1	1	0
Van Wagner	1B	1	4	4	0	0	0	0

UNION 1 - 1
Morrisania, NY

DATE	OPPONENT	SCORE		W	L	T
07/22	Excelsior (Brooklyn)	18	30		L	
08/05	Adriatic (Newark)	33	16	W		

BATTER	POS	GP	HL	A	O	R	A	O
Ferdon	1B,SS	2	5	2	1	5	2	1
Pinckney	2B	2	6	3	0	7	3	1
Brandow	SS	1	4	4	0	3	3	0
Todd	3B	2	8	4	0	3	1	1
Dickinson	OF	2	5	2	1	7	3	1
Parker	OF	2	7	3	1	6	3	0
Balcolm	OF	2	7	3	1	4	2	0
Booth	C	2	6	3	0	6	3	0
Gifford	P	2	4	2	0	6	3	0
E. Durell	1B	1	2	2	0	4	4	0

LIBERTY 1 - 2
New Brunswick, NJ

DATE	OPPONENT	SCORE		W	L	T
09/12	Atlantic (Brooklyn)	8	24		L	
10/11	Atlantic (Brooklyn)*	14	61		L	
---/---	Independent (Somerville, NJ)	59	10	W		

* Box score not available

BATTER	POS	GP	HL	A	O	R	A	O
J. Hutchings	1B	2	5	2	1	7	3	1
Baker	2B	1	3	3	0	0	0	0
C. Thompson	SS	2	7	3	1	6	3	0
M. Van Nuyse	3B	2	6	3	0	8	4	0
W. H. Cortelew	OF	2	8	4	0	6	3	0
H.S. Cortelew	OF	2	4	2	0	10	5	0
Sturges	OF	1	3	3	0	2	2	0
M. Hilderbrant	C	2	6	3	0	9	4	1
Strong	P	1	1	1	0	1	1	0
J. Conover		1	2	2	0	8	8	0
G. Story		1	4	4	0	6	6	0
L. Gerard		1	5	5	0	4	4	0

GOTHAM 1 - 6
New York, NY

DATE	OPPONENT	SCORE		W	L	T
08/31	Eckford (Brooklyn)	17	23		L	
09/03	Empire (New York)*	11	22		L	
09/14	Excelsior (Brooklyn)	13	24		L	
09/27	Putnam (Brooklyn)	28	30		L	
10/19	Eckford (Brooklyn)*	23	6	W		
10/25	Atlantic (Brooklyn)*	17	31		L	
10/27	Empire (New York)*	14	23		L	

* Box score not available

BATTER	POS	GP	HL	A	O	R	A	O
Turner	1B,OF	3	12	4	0	4	1	1
Salsman	2B,3B	3	8	2	2	6	2	0
Tooker	SS,OF	3	12	4	0	5	1	2
Hackett	3B	1	3	3	0	2	2	0
Sheridan	OF	2	9	4	1	3	1	1
Cudlipp	OF	2	5	2	1	6	3	0
Bertis	OF	2	4	2	0	7	3	1
McCosker	C	3	5	1	2	10	3	1
T.G. Van Cott	P	3	8	2	2	3	1	0
Wadsworth	1B	2	5	2	1	7	3	1
Commerford	SS	1	1	1	0	2	2	0
Forsyth	OF	1	2	2	0	2	2	0
Vail	2B	1	4	4	0	1	1	0

BALTIC 1 - 7
New York, NY

DATE	OPPONENT	SCORE		W	L	T
07/21	Harlem (New York)	24	46		L	
07/28	Continental (Brooklyn)	15	21		L	
08/18	Newark (Newark)	34	16	W		
08/23	Mutual (New York)	21	48		L	
09/10	Mutual (New York)*	26	47		L	
09/27	Empire (New York)*	27	40		L	
10/04	Harlem (New York)*	20	21		L	
11/09	Mohawk (Brooklyn)*	11	27		L	

* Box score not available

BATTER	POS	GP	HL	A	O	R	A	O
C. Cooper	1B	4	15	3	3	7	1	3
R. Brown	2B,C,OF	4	12	3	0	10	2	2
H. Holden	SS,P	4	13	3	1	9	2	1
J. Kettleman	3B	3	8	2	2	9	3	0
W. Fisher	OF	4	11	2	3	10	2	2
B. Foster	OF	4	14	3	2	8	2	0
P. Weeks	OF	2	5	2	1	5	2	1
Sears	C,P	3	7	2	1	12	4	0
C. Lewis	P,2B	3	6	2	0	10	3	1
Van Horn	2B	1	2	2	0	5	5	0
Salters	SS	1	3	3	0	3	3	0
W. Lippincott	2B	1	3	3	0	3	3	0
C. Hawkins	2B	1	1	1	0	3	3	0
Walker	P	1	2	2	0	2	2	0
M. Hawkins	C	1	2	2	0	2	?	0
Auten	1B	1	2	2	0	2	2	0
Smith	3B	1	2	2	0	2	2	0
Brower	3B	1	5	5	0	1	1	0
Pinckney	OF	1	4	4	0	1	1	0

BALTIC (cont.)
New York, NY

BATTER	POS	GP	HL	A	O	R	A	O
Finn	OF	1	3	3	0	0	0	0
Anderson	OF	1	3	3	0	0	0	0

KNICKERBOCKER 0 - 3 - 1
New York, NY

DATE	OPPONENT	SCORE		W	L	T
07/08	Excelsior (Brooklyn)	13	31		L	
07/29	Eagle (New York)	18	45		L	
08/20	Excelsior (Brooklyn)*	14	15		L	
09/22	Empire (New York)	21	21			T

* Box score not available

BATTER	POS	GP	HL	A	O	R	A	O
Stephens	1B	3	8	2	2	5	1	2
Norman Welling	2B,P	3	7	2	1	6	2	0
Daniel Adams	SS,2B	3	7	2	1	8	2	2
Clarke	3B	1	3	3	0	2	2	0
James Davis	OF	3	11	3	2	6	2	0
Morrow	OF	2	6	3	0	2	1	0
Alfred Vredenburgh	OF,SS	3	10	3	1	6	2	0
Charles DeBost	C	2	7	3	1	4	2	0
Harry Wright	P,C	2	5	2	1	6	3	0
William Grenelle	OF	1	3	3	0	2	2	0
Fraley Neibuhr	3B	1	2	2	0	2	2	0
Nap McLaughlin	P	1	3	3	0	1	1	0
Mott	3B	1	4	4	0	0	0	0
Samuel Kissam	OF	1	2	2	0	0	0	0

ST. NICHOLAS 0 - 6
New York, NY

DATE	OPPONENT	SCORE		W	L	T
07/07	Putnam (Brooklyn)	19	45		L	
07/17	Empire (New York)*	13	30		L	
08/10	Mutual (New York)*	24	31		L	
08/29	Eagle (New York)	18	33		L	
09/15	Empire (New York)	3	24		L	
09/22	Mutual (New York)	21	51		L	

* Box score not available

BATTER	POS	GP	HL	A	O	R	A	O
Schaeffer	1B	2	9	4	1	0	0	0
Wood	2B,P,C	2	4	2	0	6	3	0
Connor	SS	3	5	1	2	7	2	1
J.A. Bogart	3B	3	14	4	2	1	0	1
Crawford	OF	4	13	3	1	6	1	2
Weaver	OF,SS	4	15	3	3	4	1	0
Brooks	OF,2B	4	12	3	0	5	1	1
Clarke	C,1B	4	9	2	1	9	2	1
P. Bogart	P,C	4	12	3	0	8	2	0
Benson	C,OF	2	4	2	0	7	3	1
H. Bogart	OF,3B	2	5	2	1	6	3	0
Merritt	OF	1	3	3	0	2	2	0
Barry	2B	1	3	3	0	0	0	0

TEAM TOTALS

TEAM	CITY/STATE	GP	W	L	T	PCT	R	OR
Mutual	New York, NY	12	11	1	0	.917	524	245
Empire	New York, NY	10	8	1	1	.850	280	152
Excelsior	Brooklyn, NY	13	8	5	0	.615	303	237
Atlantic	Brooklyn, NY	7	7	0	0	1.000	200	75
Eckford	Brooklyn, NY	6	5	1	0	.833	144	99
Putnam	Brooklyn, NY	7	4	3	0	.571	155	144
Harlem	New York, NY	4	3	1	0	.750	106	100
Metropolitan	New York, NY	5	3	2	0	.600	140	94
Osceola	Brooklyn, NY	5	3	2	0	.600	153	123
Continental	Brooklyn, NY	6	3	3	0	.500	113	120
Oriental	Brooklyn, NY	4	2	2	0	.500	76	93
Eagle	New York, NY	5	2	3	0	.400	131	143
Pastime	Brooklyn, NY	5	2	3	0	.400	100	148
Union	Morrisania, NY	2	1	1	0	.500	51	46
Liberty	New Brunswick, NJ	3	1	2	0	.333	81	95
Nassau	Brooklyn, NY	3	1	2	0	.333	66	90
Gotham	New York, NY	7	1	6	0	.143	123	159
Baltic	New York, NY	8	1	7	0	.125	178	266
Knickerbocker	New York, NY	4	0	3	1	.125	66	112
Columbian	New York, NY	1	0	1	0	.000	21	39
Hamilton	Brooklyn, NY	1	0	1	0	.000	14	15
Monument	New York, NY	2	0	2	0	.000	30	137
Amity	Brooklyn, NY	2	0	2	0	.000	20	50
St. Nicholas	New York, NY	6	0	6	0	.000	98	214

OTHER TEAMS

TEAM	CITY/STATE
Stuyvesant	New York, NY

1859
BASEBALL CLUBS

Mid-19th century baseball teams were very different than the teams we know today. Virtually all aspects of their makeup, from personnel to uniforms, nicknames to customs, seem quaint and old fashioned to modern tastes.

To start with, a baseball club of the 1850s was in every sense a club. Ball clubs were formed by groups of men thrown together in social or working conditions who also shared an interest in the game. For instance, the Knickerbocker club originally contained several bank clerks among its membership, while Brooklyn's Eckford club was composed of shipyard workers. A member of the latter group, Frank Pidgeon, describes in his reminiscences the formation of the club:

> A year ago last August [1856], a small number of young men of that part of the city known as the Island [Brooklyn], formed themselves into a club, for the purpose of enjoying this noble and manly game. Being shipwrights and mechanics, we could not make it convenient to practice more than once a week... Still, we had some merry times among ourselves; we would forget business and everything else on Tuesday afternoons, go out in the green fields, don our ball suits, and go at it with a perfect rush. At such times we were boys again. Such sport as this brightens a man up, and improves him, both in mind and body.

Once organized, a name for the group was chosen. Many of the names featured some patriotic concept (Liberty, Columbia or E Pluribus Unum), or work ethic (Exercise, Enterprise, or Athletic). Convoluted and strange to our way of thinking, these type of names reflected the mind-set of the American people less than 100 years after the Revolutionary War. As a matter of fact, one of these names is still used today. The Athletic club of Philadelphia, formed nearly

140 years ago, is a direct ancestor to the Philadelphia Athletics, now the Oakland Athletics of the American League.

These clubs played their games wherever open space permitted. Due to a lack of space, most New York clubs played and practiced at Elysian Fields, just a short ferry ride away in Hoboken, New Jersey. Brooklyn clubs played in a variety of locations in their outlying districts. Most of these ball fields were just that—a field with no enclosed boundaries whatsoever. Seating was also nonexistent. Any spectators would have to bring their own chairs or stand.

The uniforms worn by the clubs varied greatly. Originally modeled after firemen's uniforms of the era, most of the costumes were quite elaborate. Here is a description of a Brooklyn Excelsior uniform as found in the pages of Peverelly's *American Pastimes*:

> Uniform - Blue pants with white cord; white shirts trimmed with blue, and the letter "E" in German text over the chest; white cap, trimmed with blue cord at the bottom and blue braid at the top, white vizor; belt, white enameled leather with the word Excelsior in old English.

Once formed, named, located, and outfitted, many clubs wanted a chance to test their mettle against others. A formal invitation, written from one club secretary to another, arranged and set up the match. The two would then agree on a time and a place for the contest, with the inviting team acting as host.

When one club held a tilt with another, the game on the field was just part of the story. After the contest, the host team was expected to provide viands and entertainment. The farther the visitors traveled, the more elaborate the show. The *New York Clipper* described the après-game activities when the Excelsior club of Brooklyn visited their counterparts in Baltimore:

> At the close of the game, the guests and hosts returned to the Monument House, where at 8 p.m., the company, to the number of fifty and more, sat down to a most sumptuous entertainment,... After full justice had been done the good things there spread before them, and the appetites created by the exercise in the field had made things rapidly disappear, Dr. Hawks, President of the Baltimore club, in a few appropriate remarks welcomed the Excelsiors, and closed by toasting them as the Champion club of the United States...And so the time passed, until the 'wee small hours...' gave evidence of the dawn's appearance.

In March 1859, 50 of these convivial baseball clubs sent delegates to the convention of the National Association, doubling its size. The circle of expansion also spread from the New York/Brooklyn hub. Teams from New Jersey (Trenton, Jersey City and Hoboken) and outlying areas of New York state (Buffalo) joined several new New York and Brooklyn nines in the Association's register.

Brooklyn clubs proved to be dominant during the 1859 season. The Association's top four clubs hailed from that area and included the Excelsior (12-3), Atlantic (11-1), Eckford (11-3) and Star (8-1) clubs. So strong was this quartet that out of their eight losses, only two were to non-Brooklyn clubs.

Perhaps the most interesting match of the season occurred in the season's opening days. The powerful Excelsior club of Brooklyn visited the grounds of the Charter Oak, a neophyte club, on May 12. Overconfident, several of the Excelsior's first nine decided not to make the trip. Struggling throughout the match, the Excelsior nine managed to plate two in the top of the ninth to knot the score at 17. Their hosts then proceeded to squeeze home a run in the bottom of the frame to win 18-17, posting the biggest upset of the year. A month later, the Excelsiors were better prepared, as they thumped the Charter Oaks, 62-13.

The most runs scored by an Association club member was accomplished by Joe Leggett of the Excelsiors and John Grum of the Eckfords, both with 49, followed by Excelsior A. Pearsall (46). Mr. T. Morris of the Stars finished with the highest run average (4,2), besting Grum (4,1) and his teammate Harry Manolt (3,10).

Beginning in the 1860s, the club system and its trappings began to change. No longer did a team have to feed their opponents after the game. Club names became less patriotic. Uniforms gradually became less elaborate. However, the most important change concerned the personnel of the clubs themselves.

Starting in the 1860s, clubs began to search the ranks outside their social circles for good ball players to bolster their chances. Not content to present a socially pleasant group, clubs would actively recruit talented ball playing members of other outfits if they thought it would improve their chances on the field. This practice marked the first significant step away from a club that played baseball and towards a baseball team that could club the ball.

EXCELSIOR 12 - 3
Brooklyn, NY

DATE	OPPONENT	SCORE		W	L	T
05/12	Charter Oak (Brooklyn)	17	18		L	
06/09	Charter Oak (Brooklyn)	62	13	W		
06/18	Neosho (New Utrecht, NY)	46	11	W		
06/30	Knickerbocker (New York)	26	22	W		
07/28	Baltic (New York)	30	19	W		
08/02	Knickerbocker (New York)	20	5	W		
08/11	Baltic (New York)	41	16	W		
08/18	Pastime (Brooklyn)	20	12	W		
09/03	Star (Brooklyn)	12	17		L	
09/08	Eagle (New York)	24	20	W		
09/14	Empire (New York)	25	20	W		
09/29	Gotham (New York)	37	12	W		
10/05	Union (Morrisania, NY)	15	19		L	
10/22	Putnam (Brooklyn)	19	17	W		
10/25	Union (Morrisania, NY)	13	3	W		

BATTER	POS	GP	HL	A	O	R	A	O
A. Pearsall	1B	15	32	2	2	46	3	1
H. Brainard	2B	9	15	1	6	16	1	7
Thomas Reynolds	SS	13	30	2	4	42	3	3
John Whiting	3B	11	32	2	10	19	1	8
A. Markham	OF	11	31	2	9	25	2	3
H. Polhemus	OF	14	38	2	10	31	2	3
Charles Whiting	OF	15	41	2	11	43	2	13
Joe Leggett	C	15	30	2	0	49	3	4
Ed Russell	P	11	22	2	0	36	3	3
William Young		7	26	3	5	23	3	2
John Holder		5	10	2	0	12	2	2
George Cole		3	8	2	2	14	4	2
R. Fleet		3	12	4	0	4	1	1
C. Etheridge		2	6	3	0	5	1	2
William Kendall		2	2	1	0	3	1	1
Biggs		1	4	4	0	2	2	0
James Rogers		1	3	3	0	2	2	0

ATLANTIC 11 - 1
Brooklyn, NY

DATE	OPPONENT	SCORE		W	L	T
06/23	Pastime (Brooklyn)	29	15	W		
07/08	Eckford (Brooklyn)	25	15	W		
08/15	Pastime (Brooklyn)	22	13	W		
08/20	Baltic (New York)	48	10	W		
09/08	Eckford (Brooklyn)	16	22		L	
09/15	Baltic (New York)	55	11	W		
09/19	Mutual (New York)	39	20	W		
09/27	Union (Morrisania, NY)	39	5	W		
10/05	Harlem (New York)	24	11	W		
10/12	Eckford (Brooklyn)	22	12	W		
10/14	Mutual (New York)	15	5	W		
10/19	Star (Brooklyn)	15	12	W		

BATTER	POS	GP	HL	A	O	R	A	O
John Price	1B,C,P	12	33	2	9	36	3	0
John Oliver	2B	11	27	2	5	41	3	8
Dickey Pearce	SS	12	23	1	11	44	3	8
Charles Smith	3B,2B	6	9	1	1	22	3	4
Peter O'Brien	OF	12	27	2	3	39	3	3
Tice Hamilton	OF	12	33	2	9	38	3	2
Archie McMahon	OF	10	34	3	4	20	2	0

ATLANTIC (cont.)
Brooklyn, NY

BATTER	POS	GP	HL	A	O	R	A	O
Polkert Boerum	C	11	42	3	9	20	1	9
Mattie O'Brien	P,1B	10	30	3	0	26	2	6
E. Webber	3B	6	20	3	2	16	2	4
George Phelps	P,OF	3	11	3	2	8	2	2
R. Seinsoth	1B	2	8	4	0	7	3	1
T. Seinsoth	OF	1	2	2	0	7	7	0
W. Hawkhurst	OF	1	4	4	0	5	5	0
Edwin Connor	3B	1	4	3	1	2	2	0

ECKFORD   11 - 3
Brooklyn, NY

DATE	OPPONENT	SCORE		W	L	T
07/01	Putnam (Brooklyn)	23	17	W		
07/08	Atlantic (Brooklyn)	15	25		L	
08/02	Continental (Brooklyn)	79	19	W		
08/09	Empire (New York)	21	8	W		
08/12	Gotham (New York)	17	10	W		
08/17	Hoboken (Hoboken, NJ)	40	16	W		
08/20	Harlem (New York)	15	13	W		
09/08	Atlantic (Brooklyn)	22	16	W		
09/28	Eckford (Brooklyn)	28	5	W		
10/07	Hoboken (Hoboken, NJ)	51	13	W		
11/12	Atlantic (Brooklyn)	12	22		L	
11/24	Newburgh (Newburgh, NY)	58	19	W		
---/---	Gotham (New York)	23	6	W		
---/---	Gotham (New York)	27	38		L	

BATTER	POS	GP	HL	A	O	R	A	O
A. Mills	1B,2B	6	19	3	1	12	2	0
Lamphier	2B	4	13	3	1	9	2	1
John Grum	SS	12	31	2	7	49	4	1
George Grum	3B	3	11	2	3	7	2	1
Harry Manolt	OF	11	25	2	8	43	3	10
John Snyder	OF	3	7	2	1	7	2	1
Waddy Beach	OF,3B	4	15	3	3	7	1	3
Brown	C	6	17	2	5	19	3	1
Frank Pidgeon	P	12	32	2	8	40	3	4

STAR   8 - 1
Brooklyn, NY

DATE	OPPONENT	SCORE		W	L	T
05/26	Charter Oak (Brooklyn)	26	22	W		
07/08	Hamilton (Jersey City)	26	12	W		
07/19	Niagara (Brooklyn)	14	8	W		
09/03	Excelsior (Brooklyn)	17	12	W		
09/26	Knickerbocker (New York)	33	11	W		
10/19	Atlantic (Brooklyn)	12	15		L	
---/---	Charter Oak (Brooklyn)	19	12	W		
---/---	Hamilton (Jersey City)	--	--	W		
---/---	Hoboken (Hoboken, NJ)	--	--	W		

BATTER	POS	GP	HL	A	O	R	A	O
F. Whiting	1B,3B	8	27	3	3	20	2	4
Gus Ticknor	2B	5	14	2	4	15	3	0

STAR (cont.)
Brooklyn, NY

BATTER	POS	GP	HL	A	O	R	A	O
S. Patchen	SS,2B	9	26	2	8	24	2	6
Fuller	3B	4	15	3	3	9	2	1
George Flanly	OF,SS	6	19	3	1	14	2	2
T. Morris	OF,C	5	8	1	3	22	4	2
J. Patchen	OF	8	27	3	3	13	1	5
Tracy	C,OF	8	28	2	7	19	2	3
James Creighton	P	6	19	3	1	15	2	3
E. Patchen	OF,3B	5	11	2	1	16	3	1
Henry Fairbanks	OF,P	4	11	2	3	11	2	3
H. Brainard	2B	3	7	2	1	9	3	0
John Whiting	OF,1B	3	9	3	0	7	2	1
Bob Manly	3B,1B	3	7	2	1	4	1	1
Belknap	OF	2	9	4	1	2	1	0
Forker	OF	2	9	4	1	2	1	0

EAGLE   6 - 3
New York, NY

DATE	OPPONENT	SCORE		W	L	T
06/24	Putnam (Brooklyn)	8	28		L	
07/29	Gotham (New York)	22	36		L	
08/09	St. Nicholas (New York)*	37	30	W		
08/19	Gotham (New York)	12	11	W		
08/26	Hoboken (Hoboken, NJ)	26	25	W		
09/02	Pastime (Brooklyn)	24	19	W		
09/08	Excelsior (Brooklyn)	20	24		L	
09/23	Empire (New York)	23	8	W		
10/04	Gotham (New York)	25	21	W		

* Box score not available

BATTER	POS	GP	HL	A	O	R	A	O
Sam Yates	1B	6	16	2	4	17	2	5
Houseman	2B	1	4	4	0	0	0	0
Van Nice	3B	4	8	2	0	15	3	3
Greglietta	SS,C	6	14	2	2	15	2	3
Bensell	OF	3	10	3	1	4	1	1
Williams	OF	6	20	3	2	12	2	0
Howe	OF	3	12	4	0	2	0	2
Brinckerhoff	C	5	12	2	2	15	3	0
Bixby	P,SS	6	17	2	5	12	2	0
Gelston		3	6	2	0	11	3	2
Winslow	P	3	12	4	0	7	2	1
Schwab	3B	2	6	3	0	4	2	0
Place		1	1	1	0	5	5	0
Commerford		1	2	2	0	3	3	0
Smith	OF	1	3	3	0	2	2	0
Chipcase	2B	1	3	3	0	1	1	0
Thornell		1	4	4	0	1	1	0

EMPIRE   4 - 4
New York, NY

DATE	OPPONENT	SCORE		W	L	T
08/11	Knickerbocker (New York)	33	59		L	
08/18	Mutual (New York)	17	13	W		
08/26	Eckford (Brooklyn)	8	21		L	
08/29	Mutual (New York)	27	23	W		

EMPIRE (cont.)
New York, NY

DATE	OPPONENT	SCORE		W	L	T
09/14	Excelsior (Brooklyn)	20	25		L	
09/23	Eagle (New York)	8	23		L	
10/06	Pastime (Brooklyn)	20	13	W		
10/14	Union (Morrisania, NY)	26	8	W		

BATTER	POS	GP	HL	A	O	R	A	O
Ed Ward	1B	6	15	2	3	13	2	1
Miller	2B,OF	7	11	1	4	26	3	5
Hoyt	SS	6	16	2	4	16	2	4
Moore	3B,OF	5	9	1	4	15	3	0
Russell	OF	7	23	3	2	15	2	1
Gough	OF,2B,C	6	15	2	3	16	2	4
Culyer	OF	3	13	4	1	1	0	1
Benson	C,3B	6	19	3	1	12	2	0
Dick Thorn	P	7	18	2	4	18	2	4
Levy		3	11	3	2	6	2	0
H. Smith	OF	2	9	4	1	1	0	1
Haydock		1	3	3	0	2	2	0
Gaunt		1	2	2	0	1	1	0
Fays	3B	1	4	4	0	0	0	0
Grady	OF	1	4	4	0	0	0	0
Leaning		1	4	4	0	0	0	0

GOTHAM   4-5
New York, NY

DATE	OPPONENT	SCORE		W	L	T
07/29	Eagle (New York)	36	22	W		
08/12	Eckford (Brooklyn)	10	17		L	
08/19	Eagle (New York)	11	12		L	
09/07	Newark (Newark)	21	13	W		
09/15	Mutual (New York)	37	25	W		
09/29	Excelsior (Brooklyn)	12	37		L	
10/04	Eagle (New York)	21	25		L	
---/---	Eckford (Brooklyn)	23	6	W		
---/---	Eckford (Brooklyn)	27	38		L	

* Box score not available

BATTER	POS	GP	HL	A	O	R	A	O
Curtis	1B	5	12	2	2	14	2	4
Turner	2B	4	13	3	1	10	2	2
Tooker	SS	1	2	2	0	2	2	0
McKeever	3B	5	16	3	1	10	2	0
Cohen	OF	4	11	2	3	11	2	3
Burtis	OF	4	11	2	3	6	1	2
Commerford	OF	2	7	3	1	2	1	0
McCosker	C	3	10	3	1	7	2	1
T.G. Van Cott	P	4	11	2	3	7	1	3
Anderson		3	7	2	1	10	3	1
Forsyth		3	11	3	2	8	2	2
Andrew Dupignac		3	12	4	0	5	1	2
Hackett		2	5	2	1	5	2	1
Minne		1	4	4	0	2	2	0
Griswold		1	2	2	0	1	1	0

PUTNAM   3 - 3
Brooklyn, NY

DATE	OPPONENT	SCORE		W	L	T
06/24	Eagle (New York)	28	8	W		
07/01	Eckford (Brooklyn)	17	23		L	
07/30	Oriental (Brooklyn)	47	7	W		
08/31	Hoboken (Hoboken, NJ)	38	8	W		
10/07	Union (Morrisania, NY)	22	23		L	
10/22	Excelsior (Brooklyn)	17	19		L	

BATTER	POS	GP	HL	A	O	R	A	O
Pierce	1B	5	12	2	2	14	2	4
Gesner	2B	4	9	2	1	7	1	3
McKinstry	SS,C	5	15	3	0	17	3	2
Sandford	3B,2B	5	12	2	2	18	3	3
Gillespie	OF	5	10	2	0	15	3	0
Burr	OF	6	9	1	3	26	4	2
Dan Ketchum	OF,3B	4	13	3	1	12	3	0
Masten	C	5	9	1	4	16	3	1
Dakin	P	4	9	2	1	12	3	0
Parmalee	1B,SS	4	13	3	1	10	2	2
Van Valkenberg	OF,2B	3	5	1	2	13	3	1
Kelly	P	2	7	3	1	6	3	0
Jackson	OF	1	4	3	1	3	3	0
Tappan		1	5	5	0	0	0	0

MUTUAL   3 - 5
New York, NY

DATE	OPPONENT	SCORE			W	L	T
08/04	Hoboken (Hoboken, NJ)	19	15	(10)	W		
08/06	Jefferson (New York)	33	17		W		
08/18	Empire (New York)	13	17			L	
08/29	Empire (New York)	23	27			L	
09/15	Gotham (New York)	25	37			L	
09/19	Atlantic (Brooklyn)	20	39			L	
09/26	Hoboken (Hoboken, NJ)	31	19		W		
10/14	Atlantic (Brooklyn)	5	15			L	

* Box score not available

BATTER	POS	GP	HL	A	O	R	A	O
L. Clancy	1B	3	11	3	2	8	2	2
A.B. Taylor	2B	5	12	2	2	16	3	1
S. Burns	SS	3	9	3	0	10	3	1
Wismer	3B	1	2	2	0	4	4	0
H.B. Taylor	OF	4	9	2	1	14	3	2
McMahon	OF	4	17	4	1	6	1	2
Harris	OF	1	4	4	0	3	3	0
J. Beard	C	5	12	2	2	19	3	4
W. Powell	P	5	12	2	2	16	3	1
P. Gavagan		4	10	2	2	12	3	0
Spence		3	11	3	2	3	1	0
Bogart		2	6	3	0	5	2	1
Green		1	2	2	0	4	4	0
Mott		1	4	4	0	3	3	0
Bradford		1	3	3	0	2	2	0
Kelso		1	5	5	0	2	2	0
P. Kivelin		1	5	5	0	1	1	0

UNION 2 - 3
Morrisania, NY

DATE	OPPONENT	SCORE		W	L	T
09/27	Atlantic (Brooklyn)	5	39		L	
10/05	Excelsior (Brooklyn)	19	15	W		
10/07	Putnam (Brooklyn)	23	22	W		
10/14	Empire (New York)*	8	26		L	
10/25	Excelsior (Brooklyn)	3	13		L	

* Box score not available

BATTER	POS	GP	HL	A	O	R	A	O
Parker	1B	3	7	2	1	4	1	1
William Abrams	2B	4	7	1	3	6	1	2
Bogle	SS	4	14	3	2	3	0	3
Bennett	3B	4	9	2	1	7	1	3
Bernard Hannegan	OF	4	11	2	3	7	1	3
Booth	OF	4	13	3	1	6	1	2
Balcolm	OF	3	10	3	1	4	1	1
Gifford	C	4	12	3	0	5	1	1
Pinckney	P	4	9	2	1	7	1	3
Ferdon		1	3	3	0	1	1	0

PASTIME 2 - 6
Brooklyn, NY

DATE	OPPONENT	SCORE		W	L	T
05/26	Neosho (New Utrecht, NY)	22	26		L	
06/23	Atlantic (Brooklyn)	15	29		L	
07/08	Atlantic (Jamaica, NY)	25	13	W		
07/18	Charter Oak (Brooklyn)	29	23	W		
08/15	Atlantic (Brooklyn)	13	22		L	
08/18	Excelsior (Brooklyn)	12	20		L	
09/02	Eagle (New York)	19	24		L	
10/06	Empire (New York)	13	20		L	

BATTER	POS	GP	HL	A	O	R	A	O
Carroll	1B	7	17	2	3	18	2	4
Boyd	2B,OF	5	14	2	4	10	2	0
Beers	SS	4	13	3	1	5	1	1
G. Holt	3B,OF	5	9	1	4	10	2	0
Barre	OF,SS,3B	7	21	3	0	12	1	5
McNamee	OF	7	19	2	5	16	2	2
Biggs	OF,P	6	18	3	0	6	1	0
Story	C,OF	7	22	3	1	10	1	3
A. Dayton	P	5	18	3	3	2	0	2
Labon	2B	2	5	2	1	6	3	0
Reynolds	OF	2	6	3	0	2	1	0
Furey	3B	1	3	3	0	2	2	0
Williams	OF	1	4	4	0	2	2	0
G. Dayton		1	2	2	0	1	1	0
J. Dayton		1	4	4	0	1	1	0
E. Holt	SS	1	4	4	0	1	1	0
McKenzie	P	1	5	5	0	0	0	0

CHARTER OAK 1 - 3
Brooklyn, NY

DATE	OPPONENT	SCORE		W	L	T
05/12	Excelsior (Brooklyn)	18	17	W		
06/09	Excelsior (Brooklyn)	13	62		L	

CHARTER OAK (cont.)
Brooklyn, NY

DATE	OPPONENT	SCORE	W	L	T
10/10	Star (Brooklyn)	12 19		L	
05/26	Star (Brooklyn)	22 26		L	

BATTER	POS	GP	HL	A	O	R	A	O
Jerry Fruin	1B,2B	4	11	2	3	9	2	1
Piper	2B,C,OF	4	11	2	3	9	2	1
McBain	SS,3B	3	10	3	1	4	1	1
Randolph	3B,OF,SS	3	9	3	0	2	0	2
Crowell	OF	3	7	2	1	6	2	0
Fish	OF,1B	3	9	3	0	5	1	2
Thomas	OF,3B	2	5	2	1	5	2	1
Parks	C,2B	3	12	4	0	5	1	2
Vanderhoef	P,OF	4	10	2	2	9	2	1
Shurman	SS	1	2	2	0	3	3	0
Murphy	C	1	2	2	0	2	2	0
Showman	3B	1	3	3	0	2	2	0
Jerome	OF	1	2	2	0	2	2	0
Falkenbergh	OF	1	4	4	0	1	1	0
Boyle	P	1	3	3	0	1	1	0
Phillips	OF	1	5	5	0	0	0	0

KNICKERBOCKER   1 - 3
New York, NY

DATE	OPPONENT	SCORE	W	L	T
06/30	Excelsior (Brooklyn)	22 26		L	
08/02	Excelsior (Brooklyn)	5 20		L	
08/11	Empire (New York)	59 33	W		
09/26	Star (Brooklyn)	11 33		L	

BATTER	POS	GP	HL	A	O	R	A	O
Stephens	1B	4	13	3	1	11	2	3
Norman Welling	2B	4	10	2	2	11	2	3
Harry Wright	SS,C	4	8	2	0	14	3	2
Daniel Adams	3B,OF	4	10	2	2	11	2	3
James Davis	OF	4	12	3	0	12	3	0
Samuel Kissam	OF	3	13	4	1	6	2	0
Morrow	OF	3	7	2	1	5	1	2
Charles DeBost	C,SS	4	12	3	0	12	3	0
Nap McLaughlin	P	4	17	4	1	6	1	2
Wood	3B	2	4	2	0	10	5	0

HARLEM   0 - 3
New York, NY

DATE	OPPONENT	SCORE	W	L	T
08/20	Eckford (Brooklyn)	13 15		L	
09/28	Eckford (Brooklyn)	5 28		L	
10/05	Atlantic (Brooklyn)	11 24		L	

HARLEM (cont.)
New York, NY

BATTER	POS	GP	HL	A	O	R	A	O
Dyer		3	8	2	2	5	1	2
Hughes		3	7	2	1	3	1	0
Liscomb		3	8	2	2	5	1	2
Marsh		3	9	3	0	3	1	0
McKellar		3	6	2	0	4	1	1
Robertson		3	9	3	0	2	0	2
Thompson		3	11	3	2	1	0	1
James Wood		3	9	3	0	4	1	1
Eels		1	1	1	0	1	1	0
Ferdon		1	3	3	0	1	1	0
John Wood		1	4	4	0	0	0	0

BALTIC   0 - 4
New York, NY

DATE	OPPONENT	SCORE		W	L	T
07/28	Excelsior (Brooklyn)	19	30		L	
08/11	Excelsior (Brooklyn)	16	41		L	
08/20	Atlantic (Brooklyn)	10	48		L	
09/15	Atlantic (Brooklyn)	11	55		L	

BATTER	POS	GP	HL	A	O	R	A	O
Andreas	1B,OF	6	17	2	5	12	2	0
Martin	2B	2	7	2	1	0	0	0
C. Cooper	SS	5	16	3	1	13	2	3
H. Holden	3B	4	13	3	1	6	1	2
E. Durell	OF,2B	5	12	2	2	17	3	2
W. Fisher	OF	5	10	2	0	14	2	4
C. Lewis	OF	3	7	2	1	7	2	1
J. Kettleman	C	6	17	2	5	15	2	3
Brown	P	3	12	4	0	5	1	2
Brower	1B	5	14	2	4	11	2	1
Van Horn	3B	3	9	3	0	9	3	0
W. Lippincott		2	9	4	1	2	1	1
Estes		1	2	2	0	5	5	0

HOBOKEN   0 - 6
Hoboken, NJ

DATE	OPPONENT	SCORE			W	L	T
08/04	Mutual (New York)	15	19	(10)		L	
08/17	Eckford (Brooklyn)	16	40			L	
08/26	Eagle (New York)	25	26			L	
08/31	Putnam (Brooklyn)	8	38			L	
09/26	Mutual (New York)	19	31			L	
10/07	Eckford (Brooklyn)	13	51			L	

BATTER	POS	GP	HL	A	O	R	A	O
Mott	1B,OF	4	11	2	3	4	1	0
Dewey	2B	6	14	2	2	11	1	5
Scott	SS,OF	2	1	0	1	7	3	1
J. Idell	3B	6	12	2	0	9	1	3
Newkirk	OF	5	16	3	1	4	0	4
Benson	OF	4	11	2	3	9	2	1
Morse	OF	2	6	3	0	0	0	0
Vanderwerken	C	6	14	2	2	11	1	5
Salisbury	P	6	16	2	4	9	1	3

HOBOKEN (cont.)
Hoboken, NJ

BATTER	POS	GP	HL	A	O	R	A	O
Chamberlin		2	9	3	1	2	2	0
Parisen		2	3	1	1	4	2	0
Currier		2	7	3	1	3	1	1
Norton		1	0	0	0	4	4	0
Olmstead		1	4	4	0	2	2	0
Norman Welling	SS	1	3	3	0	2	2	0
T. Idell		1	4	4	0	2	2	0
Beck		1	4	4	0	1	1	0
Sheldon	1B	1	3	3	0	1	1	0
Tryon	OF	1	3	3	0	0	0	0

TEAM TOTALS

TEAM	CITY/STATE	GP	W	L	T	PCT	R	OR
Excelsior	Brooklyn, NY	15	12	3	0	.800	407	224
Atlantic	Brooklyn, NY	12	11	1	0	.917	349	151
Eckford	Brooklyn, NY	14	11	3	0	.786	431	227
Star	Brooklyn, NY	9	8	1	0	.889	201	92
Eagle	New York, NY	9	6	3	0	.667	197	202
Liberty	New Brunswick, NJ	6	5	1	0	.833	161	120
Empire	New York, NY	8	4	4	0	.500	159	185
Gotham	New York, NY	9	4	5	0	.444	198	195
Putnam	Brooklyn, NY	6	3	3	0	.500	169	88
Mutual	New York, NY	8	3	5	0	.375	169	186
Niagara	Buffalo, NY	2	2	0	0	1.000	52	25
Oriental	Brooklyn, NY	3	2	1	0	.667	74	87
Hamilton	Brooklyn, NY	3	2	1	0	.667	71	69
Union	Morrisania, NY	5	2	3	0	.400	58	115
Atlantic	Jamaica, NY	6	2	4	0	.333	108	119
Pastime	Brooklyn, NY	8	2	6	0	.250	148	177
Charter Oak	Brooklyn, NY	4	1	3	0	.250	65	124
Knickerbocker	New York, NY	4	1	3	0	.250	97	112
Continental	Brooklyn, NY	1	0	1	0	.000	19	79
Harlem	New York, NY	3	0	3	0	.000	29	67
Baltic	New York, NY	4	0	4	0	.000	56	174
Hoboken	Hoboken, NJ	6	0	6	0	.000	96	205

OTHER TEAMS

TEAM	CITY/STATE
Amity	Brooklyn, NY
Ashland	New York, NY
Astoria	Astoria, NY
Chelsea	New York, NY
Columbian	New York, NY
E Pluribus Unum	New York, NY
Esculapian	New York, NY
Exercise	Brooklyn, NY
Good Intent	New Utrecht, NY
Hamilton	Jersey City, NJ
Hiawatha	Brooklyn, NY
Independent	New York, NY
Ivanhoe	Brooklyn, NY
Katydid	New York, NY
Lexington	New York, NY
Manhattan	New York, NY
Metropolitan	New York, NY
Monument	New York, NY

OTHER TEAMS

TEAM	CITY/STATE
Nassau	Brooklyn, NY
Neosho	New Utrecht, NY
Olympic	Brooklyn, NY
Olympic	S. Brooklyn, NY
Osceola	Brooklyn, NY
St. Nicholas	New York, NY
Stuyvesant	New York, NY
Tiger	New York, NY
United	Trenton, NJ
Washington	Hempstead, NY

1860
SPREADING THE GOSPEL

As the game of baseball expanded beyond its New York origins, two methods were used to spread the gospel. The first involved the growing coverage of the sport in the press. The writer behind this coverage was Henry Chadwick. His role in promoting baseball greatly exceeded the boundaries of an average sportswriter.

Born in England, Chadwick and his family moved to Brooklyn in the late 1830s. In October 1856, he chanced upon a baseball game between the Gotham and Eagle clubs. Chadwick described (as reported by Frederick Ivor-Campbell, in his article "Henry Chadwick" in *Baseball's First Stars*) what happened next:

> The game was being sharply played on both sides and I watched it with deeper interest than any previous match of the kind I had seen. It was not long before I was struck with the idea that base ball was just the game for a national sport for Americans,...

By 1857, Chadwick had become the baseball writer for the *New York Clipper*, the nation's chief sporting weekly, while also contributing to at least six New York and Brooklyn papers on the subject. Not content just to write about the sport, Chadwick also sought a way to measure the value of a player through statistics. He also was searching for a way to help new clubs organize in a logical manner. He soon found a way to accomplish both.

Following the 1859 season, Chadwick wrote team summaries on several of the New York and Brooklyn clubs in the Clipper. Included in the summaries was a statistical table on the club's leading players. Following up on this idea in the spring of 1860, Chadwick began writing a series of baseball guides. Published under the banner Beadle's dime guides, which printed guidebooks on a variety of topics, the *Beadle's Dime Base Ball Player* or *Guides* included the following items: (1) team and individual statistics, (2) a summary of the Association's annual convention and most importantly (3) guidelines in forming new teams.

In these *Beadle's Guides*, Chadwick laid the groundwork for new teams. The guides contained everything a new club needed, including suggestions for a constitution and detailed rules for scoring so that accurate statistics could be maintained.

Chadwick also pushed out the boundaries of statistics further than just the runs and outs that were generally tabulated. He devised a complex system of fielding statistics far more detailed than anything used today. Later, he was the first to see the importance of counting a batter's hits and total bases. Chadwick summed up the role he saw for statistics in the game of baseball. Speaking in the *Beadle's Guides* he stated:

> These averages will not only be found interesting at the close of the year, but they must be regarded as the only fair criterion of a player's skill, ... Many a dashing general player, who carries off a great deal of *eclat* in prominent matches, has all "the gilt taken off the gingerbread" as the saying is, by these matter-of-fact figures, given at the close of the season; and we are frequently surprised to find that the modest but efficient worker, who has played earnestly and steadily through the season, apparently unnoticed, has come in, at the close of the race, the real victor.

The National Association's convention in March 1860 saw the addition of several new teams which pushed the roster close to 80. The tentacles of membership spread further from New York to encompass clubs in Maryland, Massachusetts, and even Michigan.

During the season, interest in baseball was spread via a second route. Not only could interested parties read Chadwick's missives on the exploits of the game, they could witness the game themselves. This was accomplished by the first baseball tour.

On the morning of July 1st, Brooklyn's Excelsior nine left their stomping grounds en route to upper-state New York. There, beginning on July 2, they played six different teams over the space of the next nine days. The Excelsior's opponents included: the Champion club of Albany, the Victory of Troy, the Niagara of Buffalo, the Flour City and Live Oak of Rochester and the Hudson River of Newburgh.

The Excelsior's tour was wildly successful. A whole new segment of the populace witnessed an elite ball club. The Brooklynites thoroughly enjoyed the trip as well, as they were feted at every stop.

Ten days after their trip north, the Excelsiors turned south. This trip was much shorter and involved only two stops—one in Baltimore to play the Excelsiors (named after their Brooklyn guests) and one in Philadelphia to play an all-star contingent.

The Excelsior club was also involved in the most memorable game of the season—memorable for the wrong reasons. On August 23, the Excelsior nine took the field against the Atlantic club in their third meeting of the season. With the Excelsiors leading 8–6 and batting in the top of the sixth, several Atlantic errors put runners in scoring position. The *Clipper* described what happened next:

> These successive errors in fielding did not improve the temper either of the Atlantics or their very questionable friends [gamblers], and the rowdy spirit of the crowd again began to display itself still more forcibly,... and so insulting were the epithets bestowed on the Excelsiors, that Leggett [Excelsior captain] decided to withdraw his forces from the field, and we certainly think he acted wisely in so doing, and we only regret that he was not supported in his course by the Atlantic nine.

The umpire then declared the game a draw. As a result of this bad feeling, the two teams did not play one another for many years.

At season's close, the Excelsiors finished with the best record. The only blemishes in their 21 game season were one-run losses to the Charter Oak (for the second straight year) and Atlantic, and the aforementioned draw. The Eckford team did nearly as well, winning their first 14 before finishing with a 15–2 record.

The Excelsior team also featured the top run getters as Joe Leggett scored 70 followed by John Whiting with 58 and John Grum of the Eckfords with 57. Fellow Excelsior Charles Whiting finished with the top average (4,1), while Leggett (3,10) and Grum (3,9) finished second and third.

In spreading the gospel of baseball, the accomplishments of Henry Chadwick were legion. In short, baseball had no greater advocate in the mid–19th century. However, one should not overlook the tours undertaken by the Excelsiors and others. It is one thing to read about baseball in the papers and guides; it was quite another to witness the games themselves as the Excelsiors traveled the countryside. As a matter of fact, no fewer than five of the Excelsiors' opponents in the summer of 1860 joined the Association at its next meeting—first hand witnesses of baseball's popularity.

EXCELSIOR
Brooklyn, NY 18 - 2 - 1

DATE	OPPONENT	SCORE		W	L	T
05/17	Charter Oak (Brooklyn)	11	12		L	
06/21	Charter Oak (Brooklyn)	36	9	W		
06/28	Star (Brooklyn)	16	5	W		
07/02	Champion (Albany)	24	6	W		
07/03	Victory (Troy)	13	7	W		
07/05	Niagara (Buffalo)	50	19	W		
07/07	Flour City (Rochester)	21	1	W		
07/09	Live Oak (Rochester)	27	9	W		
07/11	Hudson River (Newburgh, NY)	59	14	W		
07/19	Atlantic (Brooklyn)	23	4	W		
07/22	Excelsior (Baltimore)	51	6	W		
07/24	Picked Nine (Philadelphia)	15	4	W		
08/04	Putnam (Brooklyn)	23	7	W		
08/09	Atlantic (Brooklyn)	14	15		L	
08/23	Atlantic (Brooklyn)	#8	6			T
08/25	Knickerbocker (New York)	32	9	W		
09/01	Empire (New York)	23	7	W		
09/07	Union (Morrisania, NY)	7	4	W		
09/15	Independent (Brooklyn)	46	14	W		
09/29	Empire (New York)	23	7	W		
11/05	St. George Cricket Club (New York)	25	0	W		

After rowdy behavior disrupted play in the sixth inning, the umpire declared the game a draw.

BATTER	POS	GP	HL	A	O	R	A	O
A. Pearsall	1B	18	57	3	3	54	3	0
John Holder	2B,OF	10	25	2	5	26	2	6
Thomas Reynolds	SS	9	33	3	6	12	1	3
John Whiting	3B,SS,2B	20	59	2	19	58	2	18
Asa Brainard	OF,2B	19	58	3	1	48	2	10
H. Polhemus	OF	14	38	2	10	41	2	13
Ed Russell	OF,SS,1B	13	43	3	4	35	2	9
Joe Leggett	C	20	46	2	6	70	3	10
James Creighton	P,OF	20	56	2	16	47	2	7
George Flanly	OF	12	40	3	4	29	2	5
William Young	OF,3B	11	31	2	9	33	3	0
Charles Whiting	OF,3B,2B	5	13	2	3	21	4	1
F. Whiting	3B	5	14	2	4	13	2	3
Charles Gulick	OF	1	4	4	0	3	3	0
H.P. Bostwick		1	3	3	0	2	2	0
Henry Fairbanks	OF	1	3	3	0	2	2	0
B. Kimberly		1	4	4	0	2	2	0

ECKFORD
Brooklyn, NY 15 - 2 - 0

DATE	OPPONENT	SCORE		W	L	T
05/23	Union (Morrisania, NY)	22	19	W		
06/13	Putnam (Brooklyn)	36	29	W		
06/25	Continental (Brooklyn)	30	15	W		
07/11	Star (Brooklyn)	19	6	W		
07/24	Enterprise (Brooklyn)	20	10	W		
08/01	Union (Elizabeth, NJ)	35	19	W		
08/08	Empire (New York)	21	13	W		
08/29	Newburgh (Newburgh, NY)	36	22	W		
09/05	Star (Brooklyn)	16	8	W		
09/10	Union (Elizabeth, NJ)	47	6	W		
09/19	Union (Morrisania, NY)	41	5	W		
09/26	Enterprise (Brooklyn)	31	18	W		
10/04	Empire (New York)	26	10	W		
10/08	Metropolitan (New York)*	28	10	W		
10/15	Atlantic (Brooklyn)	15	17		L	

ECKFORD (cont.)
Brooklyn, NY

DATE	OPPONENT	SCORE		W	L	T
10/22	Atlantic (Brooklyn)	20	15	W		
10/29	Atlantic (Brooklyn)	11	20		L	

* Box score not available

BATTER	POS	GP	HL	A	O	R	A	O
Campbell	1B,2B,OF	15	41	2	11	37	2	7
A. Mills	2B,3B,1B	13	35	2	9	43	3	4
Josh Snyder	SS	14	38	2	10	43	3	1
George Grum	3B,SS	10	31	3	1	26	2	6
Harry Manolt	OF	16	46	2	14	51	3	3
John Snyder	OF	15	47	3	2	40	2	10
Brown	OF	8	24	3	0	20	2	4
Waddy Beach	C,OF	16	43	2	11	50	3	2
John Grum	P,OF	16	45	2	13	57	3	9
Frank Pidgeon	2B,P	9	27	3	0	32	3	5
James Wood	OF,2B	4	8	2	0	10	2	2
Lamphier	2B	3	6	2	0	11	3	2
McCutcheon	3B	3	8	2	2	9	3	0

ATLANTIC   12 - 2 - 2
Brooklyn, NY

DATE	OPPONENT	SCORE		W	L	T
05/25	Star (Brooklyn)	30	11	W		
06/08	Union (Morrisania, NY)	15	4	W		
06/29	Putnam (Brooklyn)	14	11	W		
07/16	Enterprise (Brooklyn)	38	20	W		
07/19	Excelsior (Brooklyn)	4	23		L	
07/30	Mutual (New York)	34	15	W		
08/09	Excelsior (Brooklyn)	15	14	W		
08/16	Enterprise (Brooklyn)	16	14	W		
08/20	Mutual (New York)	26	14	W		
08/23	Excelsior (Brooklyn	#6	8			T
09/03	Harlem (New York)	28	8	W		
09/27	Liberty (New Brunswick, NJ)	16	16			T
10/08	Liberty (New Brunswick, NJ)	15	10	W		
10/15	Eckford (Brooklyn)	17	15	W		
10/22	Eckford (Brooklyn)	15	20		L	
10/29	Eckford (Brooklyn)	20	11	W		

\# After rowdy behavior disrupted play in the sixth inning, the umpire declared the game a draw.

BATTER	POS	GP	HL	A	O	R	A	O
John Price	1B,P	15	37	2	7	38	2	8
John Oliver	2B	12	29	2	5	24	2	0
Dickey Pearce	SS,C	16	46	2	14	37	2	5
Charles Smith	3B,C	16	36	2	4	40	2	8
Joe Oliver	OF	16	39	2	7	29	1	7
Peter O'Brien	OF,2B,SS,3B	13	39	2	13	25	1	12
Tice Hamilton	OF	8	22	2	6	13	1	5
Polkert Boerum	C	4	19	4	3	2	0	2
Mattie O'Brien	P,3B	14	16	3	4	25	1	11
F. Seinsoth	OF,1B,3B	8	23	2	7	17	2	1
Archie McMahon	OF,SS	5	13	2	3	16	3	1
G. Seinsoth	OF	3	6	2	0	11	3	2
Gus Ticknor	2B,SS	3	8	2	2	10	3	1
W. Hawkhurst	OF	3	10	3	1	4	1	1
E. Webber	OF,3B	2	6	3	0	5	2	1
William Bliss	1B	1	5	5	0	2	2	0
T. Swalton	OF	1	3	3	0	2	2	0

ATLANTIC (cont.)
Brooklyn, NY

BATTER	POS	GP	HL	A	O	R	A	O
Alec Babcock		1	3	3	0	1	1	0
R. Seinsoth		1	3	8	2	1	1	0

GOTHAM   8 - 1 - 4
New York, NY

DATE	OPPONENT	SCORE		W	L	T
06/26	Newark (Newark)	26	15	W		
07/10	Eagle (New York)	18	18			T
07/17	Mutual (New York)	25	25			T
07/23	Baltic (New York)	35	16	W		
07/24	Jefferson (New York)	13	13			T
08/22	Independent (Brooklyn)	12	18		L	
08/24	Enterprise (Brooklyn)	56	15	W		
08/29	Enterprise (Brooklyn)	21	15	W		
09/04	Mutual (New York)	18	18			T
09/11	Eagle (New York)	25	11	W		
09/17	Independent (Brooklyn)	19	13	W		
09/27	Mutual (New York)	19	12	W		
10/08	Jefferson (New York)	22	3	W		

BATTER	POS	GP	HL	A	O	R	A	O
Wadsworth	1B	6	19	3	1	9	1	3
Turner	2B	6	20	2	2	10	1	4
McKeever	SS,P	8	26	3	2	16	2	0
T.S.Van Cott	3B	6	16	2	4	16	2	4
Connell	OF,1B	7	20	2	6	17	2	3
Cohen	OF,C	7	21	3	0	15	2	1
Mimnie	OF,SS	6	19	3	1	13	2	1
Burtis	C,2B,OF	9	18	2	0	29	3	2
Purtell	P	2	8	4	0	2	1	0
Vanderwerken	C,OF	6	15	2	3	15	2	3
Milton Sweet	OF	6	16	2	4	10	1	4
McCosker		3	9	3	0	6	2	0
Griswold		3	10	3	1	5	1	2
Forsyth		2	3	1	1	4	2	0
Hopkins		1	3	3	0	1	1	0
T.G. Van Cott		1	3	3	0	1	1	0
Hackett	2B	1	4	4	0	0	0	0

CHARTER OAK   5 - 2
Brooklyn, NY

DATE	OPPONENT	SCORE		W	L	T
05/17	Excelsior (Brooklyn)	12	11	W		
05/30	Independent (Brooklyn)	12	4	W		
06/12	Star (Brooklyn)	27	3	W		
06/21	Excelsior (Brooklyn)	9	36		L	
07/09	Putnam (Brooklyn)	8	26		L	
07/24	Eagle (New York)	25	16	W		
09/06	Adriatic (Newark)	13	11	W		

BATTER	POS	GP	HL	A	O	R	A	O
S. Patchen		7	17	2	3	17	2	3
Murphy		7	25	3	4	10	1	3
Vanderhoef		6	18	3	0	10	1	4

CHARTER OAK (cont.)
Brooklyn, NY

BATTER	POS	GP	HL	A	O	R	A	O
Carroll		6	19	3	1	9	1	3
J. Patchen		6	19	3	1	6	1	0
Piper		5	15	3	0	10	2	0
Shields		5	17	3	2	10	2	0
Randolph		5	14	2	4	5	1	1

EAGLE 4 - 4 - 1
New York, NY

DATE	OPPONENT	SCORE		W	L	T
06/12	Union (Morrisania, NY)	26	15	W		
07/02	Adriatic (Newark)	18	15	W		
07/06	Mutual (New York)	24	10	W		
07/10	Gotham (New York)	18	18			T
07/14	Empire (New York)	14	33		L	
07/24	Charter Oak (Brooklyn)	16	25		L	
09/07	Harlem (New York)	9	17		L	
09/11	Gotham (New York)	11	25		L	
---/---	Hamilton (Brooklyn)	37	25	W		

BATTER	POS	GP	HL	A	O	R	A	O
Brinckerhoff	1B	8	28	3	4	18	2	2
Bixby	2B,P	9	29	3	2	16	1	7
R. Sloat	SS,C	9	27	3	0	21	2	3
Howe	3B	6	21	3	3	7	1	1
Sam Yates	OF	9	21	2	3	28	3	1
Schaub	OF	5	12	2	2	14	2	4
Van Nice	OF	4	10	2	2	8	2	0
Commerford	C	7	16	2	2	20	2	6
Williams	P	8	22	2	6	17	2	1
Sanger		6	16	2	4	14	2	2
Thornell	SS	3	11	3	2	4	1	1
Salisbury		2	5	2	1	1	0	1
Hazzard		1	2	2	0	2	2	0
Norman Welling		1	3	3	0	2	2	0
Hussey	OF	1	4	4	0	1	1	0
Powers	OF	1	4	4	0	1	1	0
Bensell		1	6	5	0	1	1	0
Ed Duffy	2B	1	3	3	0	1	1	0

EUREKA 4 - 5 - 1
Newark, NJ

DATE	OPPONENT	SCORE		W	L	T
06/07	Hamilton (Jersey City)	18	35		L	
06/29	Harlem (New York)	15	21		L	
08/03	Harlem (New York)	34	18	W		
08/10	Enterprise (Brooklyn)	21	25		L	
08/22	Adriatic (Newark)	34	6	W		
08/27	Enterprise (Brooklyn)	21	13	W		
09/14	Harlem (New York)	10	23		L	
09/19	Adriatic (Newark)	12	12			T
09/26	Newark (Newark)	28	14	W		
10/26	Baltic (Belleville, NJ)	20	24		L	

BATTER	POS	GP	HL	A	O	R	A	O
Harry Northrup	1B	6	15	2	3	15	2	3
Albert Pennington	2B	10	29	2	9	30	3	0

EUREKA (cont.)
Newark, NJ

BATTER	POS	GP	HL	A	O	R	A	O
C. Van Houton	SS	7	27	3	6	14	2	0
Charles Thomas	3B	8	26	3	2	14	1	6
R. Davison	OF	9	24	2	6	25	2	7
T. Oliver	OF	8	25	3	1	16	2	0
J. Collins	OF	10	27	2	7	24	2	4
G. Rogers	C	8	27	3	3	17	2	1
J. Linen	P	10	31	3	1	22	2	2
H. Brientnall		5	18	3	3	7	1	2
A. Littlewood		3	6	2	0	9	3	0
E. Benedict		2	6	3	0	4	2	0
P. Baldwin		1	2	2	0	3	3	0
E. Thomas		1	3	3	0	2	2	0
T. Price		1	6	6	0	1	1	0
R. Elsden		1	4	4	0	0	0	0

DETROIT   3 - 2
Detroit, MI

DATE	OPPONENT	SCORE		W	L	T
07/17	Early Riser (Detroit)	25	22	W		
08/06	Early Riser (Detroit)	32	39		L	
09/05	Franklin (Detroit)*	--	--		L	
09/---	Franklin (Detroit)	28	15	W		
10/19	Ypsilanti (Ypsilanti, MI)	42	16	W		

* Box score not available

BATTER	POS	GP	HL	A	O	R	A	O
James Craig	1B	3	10	3	1	10	3	1
F. Folsom	2B	4	8	2	0	18	4	2
S. Newberry	SS,OF	4	13	3	1	8	2	0
Parcher	3B,P	3	9	3	0	12	4	0
Sines	OF,1B	3	9	3	0	12	4	0
G. Niles	OF	3	7	2	1	11	3	2
J. Seaman	OF	2	9	4	1	6	3	0
J.J. Dumon	C	4	15	3	3	13	3	1
R.H. Anderson	P,SS	4	11	2	3	16	4	0
S. Pittman		2	6	3	0	8	4	0
Robinson	OF	2	6	3	0	6	3	0
J. Newberry		1	2	2	0	3	3	0

PUTNAM   3 - 3
Brooklyn, NY

DATE	OPPONENT	SCORE		W	L	T
06/13	Eckford (Brooklyn)	29	36		L	
06/29	Atlantic (Brooklyn)	11	14		L	
07/09	Charter Oak (Brooklyn)	26	8	W		
07/17	Union (Morrisania, NY)	18	12	W		
08/04	Excelsior (Brooklyn)	7	23		L	
09/15	Union (Morrisania, NY)	12	6	W		

BATTER	POS	GP	HL	A	O	R	A	O
Stimson	1B,P	4	10	2	2	9	2	1
Burr	2B,OF	6	16	2	4	16	2	4
McKinstry	SS	5	11	2	1	12	2	2

PUTNAM (cont.)
Brooklyn, NY

BATTER	POS	GP	HL	A	O	R	A	O
Masten	3B,2B,C	6	18	3	0	12	2	0
Gillespie	OF,3B	4	16	4	0	8	2	0
Van Valkenberg	OF	4	15	3	3	2	0	2
McDonald	OF,3B	3	8	2	2	4	1	1
Wanzier	C,1B,OF	6	13	2	1	15	2	3
Dakin	P,1B	6	21	3	3	9	1	3
E. Brown	SS,2B,1B	6	16	2	4	14	2	2
Chapman	OF	2	7	3	1	1	0	1
Gibson	OF	1	4	4	0	1	1	0
Smith	OF	1	4	4	0	0	0	0

EMPIRE 3 - 4
New York, NY

DATE	OPPONENT	SCORE		W	L	T
07/14	Eagle (New York)	33	14	W		
08/08	Eckford (Brooklyn)	13	21		L	
08/13	Mutual (New York)	17	7	W		
08/14	Henry Eckford (New York)	28	11	W		
09/01	Excelsior (Brooklyn)	7	23		L	
09/29	Excelsior (Brooklyn)	7	23		L	
10/04	Eckford (Brooklyn)	10	26		L	

BATTER	POS	GP	HL	A	O	R	A	O
Miller	1B,2B,SS	7	16	2	2	12	1	5
Ed Ward	2B,1B	5	12	2	2	11	2	1
Dewey	SS,2B	6	15	2	3	10	1	4
Benson	3B,C	7	21	3	0	9	1	2
Moore	OF,1B	7	21	3	0	10	1	5
Culyer	OF	6	18	3	0	11	1	5
Leavy	OF,3B	6	20	3	2	3	0	3
Russell	C,OF	7	18	2	4	15	2	1
Dick Thorn	P	7	19	2	5	15	2	1
Loper	OF	3	12	4	0	2	0	2
Haydock		1	3	3	0	3	3	0
Gaunt	2B	1	3	3	0	1	1	0
Wandell	3B	1	3	3	0	1	1	0

UNION 3 - 7
Morrisania, NY

DATE	OPPONENT	SCORE		W	L	T
05/23	Eckford (Brooklyn)	19	22		L	
06/08	Atlantic (Brooklyn)	4	15		L	
06/26	Eagle (New York)	15	26		L	
07/17	Putnam (Brooklyn)	12	18		L	
08/---	Adriatic (Newark)	17	8	W		
09/07	Excelsior (Brooklyn)	4	7		L	
09/15	Putnam (Brooklyn)	6	12		L	
09/19	Eckford (Brooklyn)	5	41		L	
10/12	Independent (Brooklyn)	20	9	W		
10/27	Constellation (Brooklyn)	36	4	W		

BATTER	POS	GP	HL	A	O	R	A	O
Gifford	1B	8	19	2	3	14	1	6
William Abrams	2B,C,3B	8	21	2	5	15	3	0

UNION (cont.)
Morrisania, NY

BATTER	POS	GP	HL	A	O	R	A	O
Bogle	SS	9	30	3	3	17	1	8
Bennett	3B	3	8	2	2	3	1	0
Balcolm	OF	10	32	3	2	13	1	3
Bernard Hannegan	OF,P	9	23	2	5	15	1	7
E. Durell	OF,2B	5	15	3	0	5	1	2
Parker	C	9	19	2	1	15	1	6
Pinckney	P,2B	9	21	2	3	22	2	4
Todd	OF	3	4	1	1	4	1	1
Kinloch	OF,3B	3	9	3	0	0	0	0
Borland	3B	2	9	4	1	6	3	0
Albro		2	5	2	1	1	0	1
Jackson		1	3	3	0	2	2	0
Frisbee		1	1	1	0	1	1	0
Milliken		1	2	2	0	0	0	0
Mallory		1	5	5	0	0	0	0
Stearns		1	2	2	0	0	0	0
Valentine		1	4	1	1	0	0	0

ENTERPRISE 2 - 7
Brooklyn, NY

DATE	OPPONENT	SCORE		W	L	T
07/16	Atlantic (Brooklyn)	20	38		L	
07/24	Eckford (Brooklyn)	10	20		L	
08/01	Hamilton (Brooklyn)	26	10	W		
08/10	Eureka (Newark)*	25	21	W		
08/17	Atlantic (Brooklyn)	14	16		L	
08/24	Gotham (New York)*	15	56		L	
08/27	Eureka (Newark)	13	20		L	
08/29	Gotham (New York)	15	21		L	
09/26	Eckford (Brooklyn)	18	31			L

* Box score not available

BATTER	POS	GP	HL	A	O	R	A	O
John Chapman	1B,C,SS	7	21	3	0	13	1	6
Boyd	2B	6	18	3	0	9	1	3
R. Cornwell	SS,OF	7	15	2	1	16	2	2
Joe Start	3B,1B	6	15	2	3	13	2	1
Leland	OF,1B	5	14	2	4	10	2	0
Meigs	OF	4	13	3	1	5	1	1
E. Smith	OF	4	10	2	2	6	1	2
O'Neil	C	6	22	3	4	12	2	0
Oddie	P,OF	7	18	2	4	16	2	2

ATLANTIC 1 - 0
Jamaica, NY

DATE	OPPONENT	SCORE		W	L	T
08/31	Exercise (Brooklyn)	15	13	W		

BATTER	POS	GP	HL	A	O	R	A	O
Bennett	1B	1	2	2	0	2	2	0
Crawford	2B	1	0	0	0	4	4	0
Young	SS	1	2	2	0	2	2	0
Manwaring	3B	1	3	3	0	1	1	0
Conklin	OF	1	2	2	0	2	2	0
Brush	OF	1	3	3	0	0	0	0

ATLANTIC (cont.)
Jamaica, NY

BATTER	POS	GP	HL	A	O	R	A	O
Powell	OF	1	2	2	0	1	1	0
Ashmead	C	1	2	2	0	2	2	0
Emmons	P	1	2	2	0	1	1	0

MUTUAL 1-8-2
New York, NY

DATE	OPPONENT	SCORE		W	L	T
07/06	Eagle (New York)	10	18		L	
07/17	Gotham (New York)	25	25			T
07/30	Atlantic (Brooklyn)	15	34		L	
08/03	Henry Eckford (New York)*	15	11	W		
08/13	Empire (New York)	7	17		L	
08/20	Atlantic (Brooklyn)	14	26		L	
09/04	Gotham (New York)	18	18			T
09/13	Henry Eckford (New York)	12	16		L	
09/24	Jefferson (New York)	17	18		L	
09/27	Gotham (New York)	12	19		L	
10/15	Henry Eckford (New York)	19	24		L	

* Box score not available

BATTER	POS	GP	HL	A	O	R	A	O
A.B. Taylor	1B,2B	10	35	3	5	17	1	7
Harris	2B, P,C	10	33	3	3	16	1	6
Bogart	SS,OF	7	17	2	3	11	1	4
W. Powell	3B	5	13	2	3	9	1	4
Mott	OF,P	8	27	3	4	12	1	4
H.B. Taylor	OF	5	13	2	3	11	2	1
Spence	OF,3B,P	4	13	3	1	6	1	2
Billy McMahon	C,SS,2B	9	27	3	0	15	1	6
S. Burns	P	6	18	3	0	10	1	4
J. Beard	SS,C	7	24	3	3	11	1	4
P. Gavagan	3B	4	12	3	0	4	1	0
Dalton		2	4	2	0	6	3	0
McConnell	OF	1	1	1	0	3	3	0
Kelso	1B	1	2	2	0	2	2	0
Freeland	OF	2	7	3	1	2	1	0
L. Clancy		1	5	5	0	1	1	0
Wildey	OF	1	3	3	0	1	1	0

STAR 0-5-1
Brooklyn, NY

DATE	OPPONENT	SCORE		W	L	T
05/25	Atlantic (Brooklyn)	11	30		L	
06/12	Charter Oak (Brooklyn)	3	27		L	
06/28	Excelsior (Brooklyn)	5	16		L	
07/11	Eckford (Brooklyn)*	6	19		L	
09/05	Eckford (Brooklyn)	8	16		L	
10/06	Brooklyn (Brooklyn)	12	12			T

* Box score not available

BATTER	POS	GP	HL	A	O	R	A	O
Forker	1B,OF	3	8	2	2	2	0	2
C. Morris	2B,OF	5	14	2	4	3	0	3
Bob Manly	SS,3B,1B	4	15	3	4	1	0	1
Mitchell	3B,2B,SS	3	8	2	2	3	1	0

STAR (cont.)
Brooklyn, NY

BATTER	POS	GP	HL	A	O	R	A	O
Tracy	OF,P,1B	5	15	3	0	6	1	1
Fuller	OF,P,1B	3	10	3	1	1	0	1
Boyd	OF,SS	4	9	2	1	7	1	3
T. Morris	C	3	8	2	2	5	1	2
S. Holt	P,OF	3	10	3	1	0	0	0
Weeks	SS,C	3	10	3	1	3	1	0

KNICKERBOCKER 0 - 1
New York, NY

DATE	OPPONENT	SCORE		W	L	T
08/25	Excelsior (Brooklyn)	9	32		L	

BATTER	POS	GP	HL	A	O	R	A	O
Keeler	1B	1	3	3	0	1	1	0
Hayward	2B	1	4	4	0	0	0	0
Charles DeBost	SS	1	2	2	0	1	1	0
Norman Welling	3B	1	2	2	0	2	2	0
James Davis	OF	1	4	4	0	1	1	0
Botsford	OF	1	3	3	0	1	1	0
Walker	OF	1	3	3	0	1	1	0
Harry Wright	C	1	3	3	0	1	1	0
Morrow	P	1	3	3	0	1	1	0

TEAM TOTALS

TEAM	CITY/STATE	GP	W	L	T	PCT	R	OR
Excelsior	Brooklyn, NY	21	18	2	1	.881	547	165
Eckford	Brooklyn, NY	17	15	2	0	.882	454	242
Atlantic	Brooklyn, NY	16	12	2	2	.813	309	214
Gotham	New York, NY	13	8	1	4	.769	309	192
Harlem	New York, NY	7	5	2	0	.714	135	120
Charter Oak	Brooklyn, NY	7	5	2	0	.714	106	107
Eagle	New York, NY	9	4	4	1	.500	173	183
Eureka	Newark, NJ	10	4	5	1	.450	213	191
Jefferson	New York, NY	6	3	2	1	.583	106	98
Detroit	Detroit, MI	5	3	2	0	.600	127	92
Putnam	Brooklyn, NY	6	3	3	0	.500	103	99
Empire	New York, NY	7	3	4	0	.429	115	125
Union	Morrisania, NY	10	3	7	0	.300	138	162
Potomac	Washington, DC	5	2	3	0	.400	136	153
Enterprise	Brooklyn, NY	9	2	7	0	.222	156	233
Atlantic	Jamaica, NY	1	1	0	0	1.000	15	13
Independent	Brooklyn, NY	3	1	3	0	.250	44	63
Excelsior	Baltimore, MD	4	1	3	0	.250	80	131
Mutual	New York, NY	11	1	8	2	.182	164	226
Star	Brooklyn, NY	6	0	5	1	.083	45	120
Knickerbocker	New York, NY	1	0	1	0	.000	9	32

OTHER TEAMS

TEAM	CITY/STATE
Ashland	New York, NY
Astoria	Astoria, NY

OTHER TEAMS (cont.)

TEAM	CITY/STATE
Baltic	New York, NY
Bowdoin	Boston, MA
Brooklyn	Brooklyn, NY
Champion	Albany, NY
Champion	New York, NY
Chelsea	New York, NY
Continental	Brooklyn, NY
E Pluribus Unum	New York, NY
Esculapian	New York, NY
Exercise	Brooklyn, NY
Good Intent	New Utrecht, NY
Hamilton	Brooklyn, NY
Hamilton	Jersey City, NJ
Hiawatha	Brooklyn, NY
Hoboken	Hoboken, NJ
Hudson River	Newburgh, NY
Katydid	New York, NY
Lexington	New York, NY
Liberty	New Brunswick, NJ
Manhattan	New York, NY
Metropolitan	New York, NY
Monument	New York, NY
Morphy	Brooklyn, NY
Neosho	New Utrecht, NY
Newark	Newark, NJ
Niagara	Buffalo, NY
Olympic	S. Brooklyn, NY
Pastime	Brooklyn, NY
Poughkeepsie	Poughkeepsie, NY
Quinnipiack	New Haven, CT
St. Nicholas	New York, NY
Stuyvesant	New York, NY
Union	Elizabeth, NJ
Victory	Troy, NY
Vigilant	Brooklyn, NY
Washington	Hempstead, NY

1861
HOME AND HOME

In determining a champion, most modern baseball leagues use a tried and true method. Whichever team wins the most games concurrently with the highest winning percentage is declared the winner. In the days of the National Association, this wasn't so. Their method of determining the top-ranked club was quite different.

During the first couple of years of the Association, the organization wasn't particularly concerned about naming a champion. Each club kept track of how many wins and losses they obtained, informally comparing itself to other outfits. Soon this all changed.

In 1859, Henry Chadwick credited the Atlantic team of Brooklyn as the best in the country. They retained the honor the following year not by winning 11 of 12 games, but by not being defeated in a home and home series.

When scheduling games with opponents, most baseball clubs scheduled what they called a home and home series. Basically, the series consisted of a game with your opponent at home, followed by a game at the opponent's site. If each won one of the games, a third game would be played ostensibly at a neutral site, although it could be hosted by one of the participants. These games did not have to be consecutive. They could be spaced over several months or even years with many other games taking place in the interim. Logically then, the only way to unseat a champion would be to prevail in a home and home series.

In 1860, the closest the Atlantic nine came to losing its laurels was in the match with the Excelsior club. In the first game, they got stepped on, 23-4. Three weeks later, the Atlantic club slipped by the Excelsiors, 15-14. After a two week interval, the teams met in the famous drawn game, where the Excelsiors pulled their team off the field. This act prevented the Excelsiors from unseating them and preserved the Atlantic's championship status.

In March 1860, the delegates of the National Association voted henceforth to hold their meetings after the season in December. The first of these December meetings was held in December 1860. Here, 55 clubs sent delegates, electing by their presence to be members for the 1861 season.

The 1861 season started earlier than most, featuring a most unusual game. On February 4, fully 12,000 people came to Litchfield's pond in South Brooklyn to witness the Charter Oak and Atlantic clubs try a whole new game—a baseball game on ice. Some of the rules had to be modified to accommodate the slippery conditions. For instance, each team was allowed an extra player in the field to snare wayward passed balls and each team was allowed to overslide the bases without penalty. When play started, the Atlantics jumped to a 18–2 lead, eventually finishing with a 36–27 decision. The *New York Clipper* summed up the game thusly:

> [I]t will be readily understood that the game, when played upon the ice with skates, is altogether a different sort of an affair from that the Clubs are familiar with. The best player finds himself out of his reckoning when he has got to depend on his skates, and the best skater is apt to prove, for the nonce, the best player.

This unusual brand of baseball proved popular as it was played by various clubs over the next few years.

Of the teams playing matches through the spring, summer and fall of 1861, the Mutual team from New York turned the most heads. Following an abysmal 1860 campaign which saw the team win only one game, the 1861 group reversed course. Featuring virtually the same nine as the year before, the Mutuals nearly ran the table in 1861. After an inaugural defeat by the Eckford club (18–10), the Mutuals posted eight wins in a row including a 23–18 win over the powerful Brooklyn Atlantics before tasting defeat in the season finale. It turned out to be a fine 8–2 season for the Mutuals.

Another contending club was the Eckford of Brooklyn. The team had a record similar to the Mutuals until the end of September. Then, the Ecks lost a close pair to the Enterprise outfit 20–19 and 26–23 falling out of the elite class, and finishing with an 8–4 record.

However, history shows that neither of these teams held the championship in 1861. That honor, according to *Richter's History and Records of Base Ball*, still fell to the Atlantics. On paper, this did not appear to be a logical choice. The Atlantic nine played only seven games during the season, winning five. The only team of note they contested was the aforementioned Mutual club, who whipped them 23–18 on October 3. The second game of the home and home between the Atlantic and Mutual on October 16, however, told a far different tale. The *Clipper* described the scene as follows:

> The Atlantics turned out the finest team they have ever presented in a match, and the result proved that one and all did their duty...the feature of their play was their unusually fine batting. Indeed we question whether the annals of the game can parallel their play. In this respect, in their 3rd innings, in which they scored no less than 26 runs, every member of their nine, save one, getting three runs each...

The demoralized Mutual team gave up the ghost after only six innings on the short end of a 52–27 score. This singular win kept the championship with the Atlantics, because they never scheduled the Mutes in a deciding game of the home and home series.

Individually, in 1861, honors fell to the following players. The most runs were scored by the Atlantic's Dickey Pearce who plated 37, Billy McMahon of the Mutuals who scored 35 and Charles Smith (Atlantics) who came home 33 times. The highest run average was shared by two. A pair of first basemen, the Eckford's Campbell and the Enterprise's Joe Start, each averaged 4,1 followed by Pearce (3,7).

Through the rest of the decade, the championship of the National Association was decided by a home and home series. In reflecting back, one can see at least two major flaws in this championship system. In the scheduling system of the time, a championship team had no compulsion to face a strong opponent and risk losing its crown. More importantly a weak team could conceivably beat any strong team in a best of three series leaving pointless the strong team's superior record. When the first professional leagues were formed, these weaknesses were scrapped, and a championship system using set schedules was put into place.

Although no longer used to determine a regular season champion, the home and home series survives in some form to this day. Now called the World Series, this expanded 20th century version is still used to determine the best team in the land. And like the home and home series of yore, the best team doesn't always win.

1861

MUTUAL   8 - 2
New York, NY

DATE	OPPONENT	SCORE		W	L	T
06/08	Eckford (Brooklyn)	10	18		L	
07/12	Alpine (New York)	36	12	W		
07/22	Alpine (New York)	37	15	W		
08/07	Gotham (New York)	25	22	W		
08/22	Empire (New York)	22	16	W		
08/27	Jefferson (New York)	32	12	W		
09/03	Eagle (New York)	18	7	W		
09/25	Enterprise (Brooklyn)	33	21	W		
10/03	Atlantic (Brooklyn)	23	18	W		
10/16	Atlantic (Brooklyn)	27	52		L	

BATTER	POS	GP	HL	A	O	R	A	O
S. Burns	1B,OF	7	17	2	5	20	2	6
Ed Brown	2B,C	8	20	2	4	26	3	2
Charles Hunt	SS	9	34	3	7	23	2	5
Bogart	3B	9	25	2	7	25	2	7
A.B. Taylor	OF,2B	9	27	3	0	27	3	0
H.B. Taylor	OF	7	19	2	5	23	3	2
Mott	OF	6	13	2	1	20	3	2
Billy McMahon	C,OF	11	25	2	3	35	3	2
Harris	P	11	27	2	5	30	2	8
Stephens	1B	4	20	5	0	13	3	1
Lloyd	OF	2	6	3	0	6	3	0
Greer		1	3	3	0	4	4	0
Spence	OF	1	4	4	0	3	3	0
W. Powell	SS	1	4	4	0	2	2	0
L. Clancy	1B	1	4	4	0	0	0	0

ECKFORD   8 - 4
Brooklyn, NY

DATE	OPPONENT	SCORE		W	L	T
06/05	Enterprise (Brooklyn)	52	19	W		
06/08	Mutual (New York)	18	10	W		
07/23	Eagle (New York)	23	32		L	
08/15	Harlem (New York)	26	16	W		
08/28	Newark (Newark)	18	12	W		
09/05	Exercise (Brooklyn)	27	20	W		
09/13	Eureka (Newark)	11	9	W		
09/16	Newark (Newark)	24	25		L	
10/01	Exercise (Brooklyn)	27	12	W		
10/04	Enterprise (Brooklyn)	19	20		L	
10/17	Enterprise (Brooklyn)	23	26		L	
11/12	Newburgh (Newburgh, NY)	38	17	W		

BATTER	POS	GP	HL	A	O	R	A	O
Campbell	1B,P	6	13	2	1	25	4	1
James Wood	2B	10	29	2	9	32	3	2
Josh Snyder	SS	9	23	2	5	25	2	7
Al Reach	3B,1B,SS	9	25	2	7	20	2	2
Brown	OF	9	28	3	1	20	2	2
Harry Manolt	OF,3B	8	18	2	2	27	3	3
John Snyder	OF	8	24	3	0	21	2	5
Waddy Beach	C	11	38	3	5	31	2	9
John Grum	P	8	20	2	4	23	2	7
George Grum	2B,3B,1B	4	11	2	3	6	1	2
Moss	P,OF,3B	3	10	3	1	8	2	2
A. Mills	1B	2	6	3	0	4	2	0
West	OF	2	6	3	0	4	2	0

ECKFORD (cont.)
Brooklyn, NY

BATTER	POS	GP	HL	A	O	R	A	O		
Lamphier	3B	1	3	3	0	2	2	0	1	
Orr	OF	1	4	4	0	2	2	0	0	

ATLANTIC 5 - 2
Brooklyn, NY

DATE	OPPONENT	SCORE	W	L	T
08/05	Newark (Newark)	21 11	W		
08/16	Exercise (Brooklyn)	32 17	W		
08/25	Newark (Newark)	36 18	W		
09/14	Exercise (Brooklyn)	36 14	W		
10/03	Mutual (New York)	18 23		L	
10/16	Mutual (New York)	52 27	W		
10/28	Liberty (New Brunswick, NJ)	11 31		L	

BATTER	POS	GP	HL	A	O	R	A	O
R. Seinsoth	1B,OF	6	18	3	0	23	3	5
F. Seinsoth	2B,1B,OF,3B	7	18	2	4	22	3	1
Peter O'Brien	SS,OF,P	7	21	3	0	19	2	5
Charles Smith	3B,2B	9	22	2	4	33	3	6
Joe Oliver	OF	8	25	3	1	24	3	0
W. Hawkhurst	OF	3	8	2	2	9	3	0
G. Seinsoth	OF	3	8	2	2	8	2	2
Dickey Pearce	C,SS	10	27	2	7	37	3	7
Mattie O'Brien	P	3	10	3	1	9	3	0
John Oliver	2B,P	3	10	3	1	6	2	0
T. Thwaite	OF	2	5	2	1	7	3	1
John Price	1B	2	6	3	0	7	3	1
Archie McMahon	OF,SS	2	5	2	1	5	2	1
Polkert Boerum	C	1	1	1	0	6	6	0
Colyer	2B	1	2	2	0	5	5	0
Ross	SS	1	3	3	0	4	4	0
A. Smith	1B	1	2	2	0	2	2	0
Alec Babcock	OF	1	2	2	0	1	1	0
Boughton	OF	1	7	7	0	0	0	0
Seibert	OF	1	5	5	0	0	0	0

ENTERPRISE 5 - 4
Brooklyn, NY

DATE	OPPONENT	SCORE	W	L	T
06/05	Eckford (Brooklyn)	19 52		L	
06/26	Hamilton (Brooklyn)	38 27	W		
07/10	Eureka (Newark)	5 27		L	
08/20	Gotham (New York)	13 14		L	
09/10	Hamilton (Brooklyn)	41 23	W		
09/25	Mutual (New York)	21 33		L	
10/04	Eckford (Brooklyn)	20 19	W		
10/17	Eckford (Brooklyn)	26 23	W		

(Only scores extant)

BATTER	POS	GP	HL	A	O	R	A	O
Joe Start	1B,3B	7	12	1	5	29	4	1
Fred Crane	2B,3B,SS,OF	10	24	2	4	30	3	0
R. Cornwell	SS	7	21	3	0	18	2	4
W. H. Murtha	3B,OF	5	13	2	3	18	3	3
Leland	OF	5	15	3	0	9	1	4
Dick	OF	5	12	2	5	16	3	1

ENTERPRISE (cont.)
Brooklyn, NY

BATTER	POS	GP	HL	A	O	R	A	O
Meigs	OF,3B	4	11	2	3	5	1	1
John Chapman	C,2B,SS,1B	10	26	2	6	30	3	0
Earl	P	4	12	3	0	9	2	1
O'Neil	C	5	14	2	4	18	3	3
Weddie	P	4	11	2	3	10	2	2
Ibbottson	OF,1B	3	11	3	2	2	2	2
Vanderhoef	OF,1B	3	11	3	2	8	2	2
Oddie	P,2B,OF	3	12	4	0	5	1	2
E. Smith	OF,SS	3	14	4	2	0	0	0
Henry	OF	2	4	2	0	8	4	0
Boyd	2B	2	9	4	1	1	0	1
Stump	2B	1	3	3	0	5	5	0
Orr	OF	1	6	6	0	1	1	0

STAR 4 - 2
Brooklyn, NY

DATE	OPPONENT	SCORE		W	L	T
05/21	Powhatan (Brooklyn)	46	11	W		
---/---	Powhatan (Brooklyn)	--	--	W		
---/---	Hamilton (Brooklyn)	--	--	W		
---/---	Brooklyn (Brooklyn)	--	--	W		
---/---	Olympic (S. Brooklyn)	--	--		L	
---/---	Hamilton (Brooklyn)	--	--		L	

BATTER	POS	GP	HL	A	O	R	A	O
Hope Waddell		6	15	2	3	16	2	4
Kelly		6	18	3	0	10	1	4
Mitchell		6	17	2	5	9	1	3
Skaats		5	16	3	1	6	1	1
Boyd		4	8	2	0	11	2	3
Forker		4	10	2	2	8	2	0
Hunter		4	11	2	3	8	2	0
Bradish		3	9	3	0	2	0	2
Holt		2	6	3	0	5	2	1
Gignoux		2	4	2	0	2	2	0
Weeks		2	6	3	0	4	2	0
W. Forker		1	1	1	0	3	3	0
Galpin		1	2	2	0	2	2	0
Henry		1	1	1	0	2	2	0
Conduit		1	3	3	0	1	1	0
C. Morris		1	3	3	0	1	1	0
Barnett		1	4	4	0	0	0	0
Jerome		1	3	3	0	0	0	0

EXERCISE 4 - 4
Brooklyn, NY

DATE	OPPONENT	SCORE		W	L	T
08/16	Atlantic (Brooklyn)	17	32		L	
09/05	Eckford (Brooklyn)	20	27		L	
09/14	Atlantic (Brooklyn)	14	36		L	
10/01	Eckford (Brooklyn)	12	27		L	
10/09	Woodlawn (Bronx)	23	8	W		
10/22	Hamilton (Brooklyn)	12	8	W		
---/---	Hamilton (Brooklyn)	--	--	W		

(Only scores extant)

EXERCISE (cont.)
Brooklyn, NY

BATTER	POS	GP	HL	A	O	R	A	O
John Galvin	1B,OF	8	20	2	4	19	2	1
Simonson	2B	9	19	2	1	26	2	8
Hough	SS,C	8	19	2	3	16	2	0
Dean	3B,OF	6	20	3	2	12	2	0
Bergen	OF,3B	5	11	2	1	9	1	4
Myers	OF,SS	4	14	3	2	6	1	2
Demarest	OF,3B	4	10	2	2	7	1	3
F.W. Massey	C,SS,1B	9	26	2	8	17	1	8
Joe Sprague	P,OF	7	23	3	2	12	1	5
A.F. Tomes	OF	4	11	2	3	5	1	1
Pike	OF	3	7	2	1	6	2	0
Smith	SS,P	2	6	3	0	4	2	0
F.H. Tomes	OF	2	6	3	0	4	2	0
Granger	OF	1	2	2	0	3	3	0
Harvey		1	4	4	0	1	1	0
Povee		1	3	3	0	2	2	0
George Cole	OF	1	4	4	0	1	1	0
C. Tomes	OF	1	3	3	0	1	1	0

JEFFERSON   3 - 2
New York, NY

DATE	OPPONENT	SCORE		W	L	T
08/27	Mutual (New York)	12	32		L	
09/02	Henry Eckford (New York)	27	31		L	
09/16	Henry Eckford (New York)	--	--	W		
09/20	Empire (New York)	25	15	W		
09/24	Eagle (New York)	22	18	W		

BATTER	POS	GP	HL	A	O	R	A	O
Zeller	1B	5	20	4	0	6	1	1
John Goldie	2B	4	7	1	3	13	3	1
Vincelette	SS	4	8	2	0	9	2	1
Callahan	3B	3	7	2	1	5	1	2
J. Raymond	OF	4	10	2	2	6	1	2
Calvert	OF	4	13	3	1	4	1	0
Tipson	OF	4	11	2	3	8	2	0
Conner	C	4	8	2	0	13	3	1
Rowland	P	1	5	2	1	5	2	1
H. Springsteen	3B	3	10	3	1	3	1	0
Love	OF	2	7	3	1	3	1	1
Jackson	P	1	3	3	0	3	3	0
Reed		1	1	1	0	2	2	0
Davis		1	3	3	0	1	1	0
Greer		1	3	3	0	1	1	0
Totten		1	5	5	0	0	0	0

NEWARK   2 - 3
Newark, NJ

DATE	OPPONENT	SCORE		W	L	T
08/05	Atlantic (Brooklyn)	11	21		L	
08/22	Atlantic (Brooklyn)	18	36		L	
08/28	Eckford (Brooklyn)	12	18		L	
09/05	Adriatic (Newark)	17	14	W		
09/16	Eckford (Brooklyn)	25	24	W		

NEWARK (cont.)
Newark, NJ

BATTER	POS	GP	HL	A	O	R	A	O
Dusenberry	1B	5	16	3	1	10	2	0
Terrell	2B	5	14	2	4	7	1	2
Coleman	OF	5	13	2	3	9	1	4
Osborne	C	5	9	1	4	12	2	2
R. Stout	P	5	17	3	2	7	1	2

EAGLE   2-3
New York, NY

DATE	OPPONENT	SCORE		W	L	T
07/23	Eckford (Brooklyn)	32	23	W		
09/03	Mutual (New York)	7	18		L	
09/24	Jefferson (New York)	18	22		L	
10/15	Gotham (New York)	30	15	W		
10/29	Union (Morrisania, NY)	18	33		L	

BATTER	POS	GP	HL	A	O	R	A	O
Sam Yates	1B	5	13	2	3	16	3	1
Howe	2B	5	16	3	1	11	2	1
Thornell	SS,OF	4	15	3	3	7	1	3
Bixby	3B	2	6	3	0	3	1	1
Brinckerhoff	OF	4	7	1	3	12	3	0
Van Nice	OF	3	9	3	0	5	1	2
Williams	OF	3	7	2	1	6	2	0
R. Sloat	C	4	8	2	0	13	3	1
Salisbury	P	4	10	2	2	13	3	1
Smith	OF	2	7	3	1	3	1	1
J. Sloat	OF	1	5	5	0	2	2	0
Commerford	SS	1	4	4	0	1	1	0
Curry	OF	1	5	5	0	0	0	0
Hussey	OF	1	4	4	0	0	0	0

EMPIRE   2-3
New York, NY

DATE	OPPONENT	SCORE		W	L	T
08/14	Henry Eckford (New York)	28	11	W		
08/22	Mutual (New York)	16	22		L	
09/02	Jefferson (New York)	15	25		L	
09/22	Hamilton (Jersey City)	15	14	W		
09/26	Henry Eckford (New York)	9	18		L	

BATTER	POS	GP	HL	A	O	R	A	O
Ed Ward	1B,SS	5	18	3	3	9	1	4
Miller	2B	5	11	2	1	14	2	4
Dewey	SS,C	5	14	2	4	7	1	2
Loper	3B	5	20	4	0	7	1	2
Culyer	OF	5	17	3	2	9	1	4
Moore	OF,1B	4	13	3	1	4	1	0
Sebring	OF	3	11	3	2	4	1	1
Russell	C	4	7	1	3	13	3	1
Dick Thorn	P	5	14	2	4	13	2	3
Benson	OF	2	4	2	0	4	2	0
Burd	OF	1	5	5	0	0	0	0
Haydock	OF	1	4	4	0	0	0	0

GOTHAM 1 - 2
New York, NY

DATE	OPPONENT	SCORE		W	L	T
08/07	Mutual (New York)	22	25		L	
08/20	Enterprise (Brooklyn)	14	13	W		
10/15	Eagle (New York)	15	30		L	

BATTER	POS	GP	HL	A	O	R	A	O
A. Saunders	1B,OF	3	10	3	1	5	1	2
Turner	2B,SS	3	8	2	2	7	2	1
Forsyth	SS,OF	3	10	3	1	5	1	2
T.S. Van Cott	3B	4	14	3	2	7	1	3
Griswold	OF	2	3	1	1	6	3	0
Vanderwerken	OF,2B	2	7	3	1	4	2	0
Milton Sweet	OF	2	7	3	1	2	1	0
Cohen	C	5	14	2	4	6	1	1
McKeever	P	5	9	1	4	14	2	4
Hopkins	1B	1	4	4	0	1	1	0
Wadsworth	1B	1	5	5	0	1	1	0
Smith	OF	1	2	2	0	0	0	0

HAMILTON 1 - 5
Brooklyn, NY

DATE	OPPONENT	SCORE		W	L	T
06/26	Enterprise (Brooklyn)	27	38		L	
09/10	Enterprise (Brooklyn)	23	41		L	
10/22	Exercise (Brooklyn)	8	12		L	
---/---	Star (Brooklyn)	--	--	W		
---/---	Star (Brooklyn)	--	--		L	
---/---	Exercise (Brooklyn)	--	--		L	

BATTER	POS	GP	HL	A	O	R	A	O
Rogers	1B,2B	3	12	4	0	2	0	2
Kipp	2B,OF	4	8	2	0	11	2	3
Coe	SS	4	14	3	2	5	1	1
Bergen	3B,P	5	12	2	2	14	2	4
Hall	OF,2B	5	12	2	2	6	1	1
Maxfield	OF,SS	4	13	3	1	9	2	1
Halsey	OF	4	8	2	0	6	1	2
Davenport	C	6	21	3	3	9	1	3
Payne	P	2	7	3	1	4	2	0
S. Mundell		3	9	3	0	5	1	2
Maxon	OF	3	10	3	1	5	1	2
Albert	OF	2	6	3	0	6	3	0
Johnson	1B	2	7	3	1	4	2	0
Evans	OF	1	3	3	0	3	3	0
C.U. Mundell		1	3	3	0	3	3	0
Doneldson		1	5	5	0	1	1	0
Elmendorf	3B	1	3	3	0	1	1	0
Whiting	1B	1	4	4	0	1	1	0

TEAM TOTALS

TEAM	CITY/STATE	GP	W	L	T	PCT	R	OR
Mutual	New York, NY	10	8	2	0	.800	263	193
Eckford	Brooklyn, NY	12	8	4	0	.667	306	218
Atlantic	Brooklyn, NY	7	5	2	0	.714	206	141

TEAM TOTALS (cont.)

TEAM	CITY/STATE	GP	W	L	T	PCT	R	OR
Enterprise	Brooklyn, NY	9	5	4	0	.556	228	**230**
Star	Brooklyn, NY	6	4	2	0	.667	104	69
Exercise	Brooklyn, NY	8	4	4	0	.500	143	159
Olympic	Philadelphia, PA	3	3	0	0	1.000	84	55
Union	Morrisania, NY	4	3	1	0	.750	98	67
Jefferson	New York, NY	5	3	2	0	.600	86	*102*
Henry Eckford	New York, NY	*6*	*3*	*3*	*0*	*.500*	*102*	*108*
Athletic	Philadelphia, PA	4	2	2	0	.500	97	89
Newark	Newark, NJ	*5*	*2*	*3*	*0*	*.400*	*83*	*113*
Eagle	New York, NY	5	2	3	0	.400	105	111
Empire	New York, NY	5	2	3	0	.400	83	90
Liberty	New Brunswick, NJ	1	1	0	0	1.000	31	11
National	Washington, DC	2	1	1	0	.500	51	30
Gotham	New York, NY	3	1	2	0	.333	51	68
Hamilton	Brooklyn, NY	6	1	**5**	0	.167	96	149

OTHER TEAMS

TEAM	CITY/STATE
Adriatic	Newark, NJ
Alpine	New York, NY
Baltic	Belvidere, NJ
Baltic	New York, NY
Benedict	Philadelphia, PA
Bowdoin	Boston, MA
Brooklyn	Brooklyn, NY
Charter Oak	Brooklyn, NY
Chelsea	New York, NY
Continental	Brooklyn, NY
Continental	Jersey City, NJ
Englewood	Englewood, NJ
Equity	Philadelphia, PA
Eureka	Newark, NJ
Excelsior	Baltimore, MD
Excelsior	Brooklyn, NY
Flour City	Rochester, NY
Good Intent	New Utrecht, NY
Harlem	New York, NY
Hudson River	Newburgh, NY
Independent	New York, NY
Knickerbocker	New York, NY
Lexington	New York, NY
Malta	New York, NY
Manhattan	New York, NY
Metropolitan	New York, NY
New Rochelle	New Rochelle, NY
New York	New York, NY
Pastime	Brooklyn, NY
Powhatan	Brooklyn, NY
Putnam	Brooklyn, NY
Quickstep	Bergen, NJ
St. Nicholas	New York, NY
Union	Elizabeth, NJ
United	Philadelphia, PA
Victory	Troy, NY
Winona	Philadelphia, PA

1862
THROWING AND PITCHING

The role of the pitcher in the early National Association was quite different than the role of the pitcher today. In the 1850s and 1860s, the rulemakers of the game meant the pitcher to be a ball-server to the batters, allowing the hitters to put the spheroid in play.

Strict rules governed how the pitcher was to deliver the goods. The ball was to be thrown with the arm below the waist—essentially underhand. The wrist had to be stiff—no snapping off a throw was allowed. To govern this, section six of the Association's playing rules stated, "The ball must be pitched, not jerked or thrown to the bat."

This can be clarified by a definition of pitching and throwing found in an issue of the *New York Clipper* from the 1870s. In looking back at the previous decade, the article states:

> The difference between a pitched ball and an underhand throw, as far as the style of delivery is concerned, is that a pitched ball is sent in with a straight arm, swinging perpendicularly to the side of the body, while an underhand throw is made by the same swinging motion, but with the addition of bending the arm and wrist with a motion similar to that made when snapping a whip.

During the first few years of the National Association, the straight arm tenet was strictly obeyed. However, beginning in 1859, this rule was bent by a young new talent gracing the roster of the Niagara nine from Brooklyn. Not yet 20, this player threw, not pitched, like none before.

James Creighton was born in April 1841. Originally from New York, he and his family crossed the river to live in Brooklyn when he was a boy. At the age of 16, he helped found the Young America

Baseball Club. The next year, in 1858, Creighton was in on the ground floor with a new Brooklyn club, the Niagara.

In 1859, Creighton found himself playing the infield. However, changes were in store. Blessed with a strong throwing arm which garnered praise, Creighton found himself utilizing his talents in another direction. In the game of July 19 against the Star club, Creighton was inserted as a relief pitcher. What the Star club witnessed was a blistering delivery—a virtually unhittable pitch. An 1860s account of this event, as quoted by Mark Rucker in *Nineteenth Century Stars*, ran like this:

> On the final inning of the game when the Stars were a number of runs ahead, the Niagaras changed pitchers, and Jimmy [Creighton] took that position...[W]hen Creighton got to work something new was seen in base ball - the low swift delivery, the ball rising from the ground past the shoulder to the catcher. The Stars soon saw they could not cope with such pitching.

What the Stars saw of Creighton they coveted. After one more game in a Niagara uniform, he was enticed to the Star outfit. There, Creighton pitched in the club's remaining six games, winning five.

Creighton technically obeyed the pitching rules of the time, but it was his ability to conceal his wrist movement which led to his success. His subterfuge was investigated but allowed to continue.

Before the 1860 season, Creighton joined the Excelsior nine, making a previously strong squad almost unbeatable. With Creighton pitching nearly every game, the team won 18 of 21 games, holding their opponents to only 7.6 runs a game, the lowest total of the era. Included in this total was the first recorded shutout in National Association annals—a 25-0 whitewashing of the St. George Cricket club on November 11.

During the 1861 season, the Excelsor nine did not play any matches with other clubs, although Creighton pitched a Brooklyn all-star team to an 18-6 victory over a New York contingent in October. In 1862, Creighton and the Excelsiors won four of six games. These contests not only featured Creighton's pitching, but his hitting as well. In the six games, he was put out only four times (0,4), easily the best average of the National Association era.

In October 1862, Creighton fell ill after a game with the Unions of Morrisania (in what now is the Bronx). A few days later he died. He was 21 years old. Originally, contemporary accounts stated that he was injured in this game with the Unions and died as a result. But since there is no account of this injury in the report of the game, it has been dismissed as apocryphal.

Nevertheless, the outpouring of grief was immense. One of the tributes ran in the *Clipper*:

> As a base ball player, Creighton had no equal. As a pitcher he stood alone, and in his skill in batting and fielding he never had a superior... His funeral on Sunday was attended by a large concourse of the fraternity, among whom his sudden decease was painfully felt.

He was buried in Brooklyn's Greenwood Cemetery. A granite obelisk, adorned with a marble baseball, marks the spot.

During the 1862 season, the Eckford nine wrested the bunting from their Brooklyn rivals, the Atlantics. In an exciting home and home series begun in August, the Eckfords bested the Atlantics in the first game 20–14. One week later, the Atlantics thrashed their neighbors, 39–5. In the deciding game in September, the Eckfords won an 8–3 decision, in a remarkably well fielded game. The Eckfords now had the right to claim the championship as theirs. Overall, the team finished with a 14–2 record—easily the best among Association teams.

The Eckford team also boasted the three top run producers of the year: A. Mills (39), James Wood (37) and Harry Manolt (33). These three, in the same order, also posted the top averages (4,7, 4,5 and 4,4). (Note: The statistics for 1862 are particularly scanty due to a plethora of missing box scores. Because of this paucity, all located records are included.)

Larger in death than in life, Creighton's legacy lived on. Ball players across the land strove to emulate him. Soon, every pitcher was attempting to imitate Creighton's speed and ball movement. One outfit in Virginia took matters a step further. The Creighton team of Norfolk even named themselves after the great ballplayer.

Creighton's legacy to baseball was primarily in his role as pitcher. Before he unleashed his talent, a baseball pitch was merely a throw—an adjunct—a necessity to put the ball in play. Afterward, it would be seen that pitching could be used as a way to shut down the opposition—a strategy used to this day.

1862

ECKFORD 14 - 2
Brooklyn, NY

DATE	OPPONENT	SCORE		W	L	T
05/20	Enterprise (Brooklyn)*	19	20		L	
07/04	Hudson River (Newburgh, NY)	74	29	W		
07/29	Eagle (New York)*	18	5	W		
08/11	Atlantic (Brooklyn)*	20	14	W		
08/13	Harlem (New York)*	42	25	W		
08/18	Atlantic (Brooklyn)*	5	39		L	
08/19	Newark (Newark)*	35	19	W		
08/24	Mutual (New York)*	28	24	W		
08/29	Union (Morrisania, NY)	27	11	W		
09/18	Atlantic (Brooklyn)*	8	3	W		
09/24	Mutual (New York)	28	14	W		
10/07	Union (Morrisania, NY)	13	10	W		
10/21	Picked Nine (Philadelphia)	39	8	W		
10/22	Olympic (Philadelphia)	39	13	W		
10/23	Athletic (Philadelphia)	32	25	W		
10/24	Keystone (Philadelphia)	26	2	W		

* Box score not extant

BATTER	POS	GP	HL	A	O	R	A	O
Al Reach	1B,OF,3B,SS	*7	15	2	3	25	4	1
James Wood	2B	*8	15	2	1	36	4	4
Tom Devyr	SS,3B	*8	27	4	6	22	2	6
A. Mills	3B,P	*8	14	2	0	39	4	7
Harry Manolt	OF,C	*8	19	2	5	37	4	5
John Snyder	OF	3	9	3	0	9	3	0
Dan Ketchum	OF	*4	12	4	0	14	3	2
Waddy Beach	C,OF	*8	17	2	3	34	4	2
Joe Sprague	P	5	14	2	4	15	3	0
Campbell	1B	*4	10	3	1	18	4	2
Frank Pidgeon	OF,P	*3	8	2	2	10	3	1
Spence	OF	3	11	3	2	4	1	1
McAuslan	OF	1	-	-	-	7	7	0
Brown	OF	1	2	2	0	5	5	0
Burr	OF	1	3	3	0	3	3	0

* Hands lost not counted in all games

MUTUAL 8 - 5
New York, NY

DATE	OPPONENT	SCORE			W	L	T
07/19	Gotham (New York)*	52	14		W		
07/27	Gotham (New York)*	9	14			L	
07/28	Jefferson (New York)*	58	25		W		
08/04	Eckford (Brooklyn)*	24	28			L	
08/14	Gotham (New York)*	14	15			L	
08/21	Eureka (Newark)*	14	13	(10)	W		
08/26	Adriatic (Philadelphia)	33	5		W		
08/27	Olympic (Philadelphia)	10	7		W		
08/28	Athletic (Philadelphia)	10	17			L	
09/08	Harlem (New York)*	47	16		W		
09/22	Atlantic (Brooklyn)	15	10		W		
09/24	Eckford (Brooklyn)	14	28			L	
10/07	Harlem (New York)*	24	13		W		

* Box score not available

BATTER	POS	GP	HL	A	O	R	A	O
Ed Ward	1B	3	9	3	0	5	1	2
Ed Brown	2B	5	15	3	0	11	2	1
Dewey	SS	3	11	3	2	4	1	1

MUTUAL (cont.)
New York, NY

BATTER	POS	GP	HL	A	O	R	A	O
Bogart	3B	4	12	3	0	8	2	0
Harris	OF	5	12	2	2	11	2	1
Billy McMahon	OF,SS,3B	4	13	3	1	5	1	1
John Zeller	OF	2	5	2	1	3	1	1
Bill Wansley	C	5	11	2	1	12	2	2
S. Burns	P	5	15	3	0	9	1	4
Charles Hunt	SS	2	4	2	0	4	2	0
John Goldie	1B	2	7	3	1	3	1	1
Mott	OF	2	9	4	1	2	1	0
H.B. Taylor	OF	2	6	3	0	2	1	0

GOTHAM 6 - 3
New York, NY

DATE	OPPONENT	SCORE		W	L	T
07/09	Mutual (New York)*	14	52		L	
07/29	Mutual (New York)*	14	9	W		
08/07	Charter Oak (Brooklyn)*	17	13	W		
08/14	Mutual (New York)*	15	14	W		
08/---	Eureka (Newark)*	13	18		L	
09/04	Harlem (New York)*	15	29		L	
09/09	Eagle (New York)*	17	16	W		
10/14	Harlem (New York)	19	10	W		
10/20	Harlem (New York)	24	17	W		

* Box score not available

BATTER	POS	GP	HL	A	O	R	A	O
McGrath	1B	2	5	2	1	6	3	0
T.S. Van Cott	2B,3B	2	4	2	0	6	3	0
Squires	SS	2	4	2	0	6	3	0
McKeever	3B	1	4	4	0	1	1	0
Burtis	OF	2	8	4	0	4	2	0
Turner	OF	1	2	2	0	1	1	0
Roe	OF	1	3	3	0	1	1	0
Vincellette	C	2	7	3	1	3	1	1
Dick Thorn	P	2	5	2	1	6	3	0
Milton Sweet	OF	1	2	2	0	3	3	0
Cohen	2B	1	4	4	0	2	2	0
Forsyth	OF	1	3	3	0	3	3	0

UNION 5 - 5
Morrisania, NY

DATE	OPPONENT	SCORE		W	L	T
07/03	Jefferson (New York)*	15	42		L	
07/10	Henry Eckford (New York)*	26	10	W		
07/18	Harlem (New York)*	23	13	W		
07/26	Excelsior (Brooklyn)*	12	4	W		
08/02	Newark (Newark)*	12	11	W		
08/27	Newark (Newark)	13	14		L	
08/29	Eckford (Brooklyn)	11	27		L	
09/27	Star (Brooklyn)	14	10	W		
10/07	Eckford (Brooklyn)	10	13		L	
10/14	Excelsior (Brooklyn)	9	13		L	

* Box score not available

UNION (cont.)
Morrisania, NY

BATTER	POS	GP	HL	A	O	R	A	O
E. Durell	1B	5	17	3	2	6	1	1
Pinckney	2B	2	5	2	1	3	1	1
Bassford	SS,OF	3	7	2	1	6	2	0
Hyatt	3B,SS,OF	5	13	2	3	6	1	1
Nicholson	OF,2B	5	13	2	3	7	1	2
Sammy Collins	OF	4	12	3	0	3	0	3
Albro	OF,3B	3	8	2	2	1	0	1
Williams Abrams	C,SS	5	15	3	0	9	1	4
Bernard Hannegan	P	5	11	2	1	11	2	1
Bogle	2B	2	7	3	1	2	1	0
Gaynor	C	2	8	4	0	1	0	1
Van Horn	OF	2	6	3	0	0	0	0
F. Durrell	OF	1	1	1	0	1	1	0
Parker	SS	1	3	3	0	1	1	0

EXCELSIOR 4 - 1 - 1
Brooklyn, NY

DATE	OPPONENT	SCORE		W	L	T
06/26	Charter Oak (Brooklyn)*	20	19	W		
07/10	Bowdoin (Boston)*	41	15	W		
07/11	Lowell/Tri Mountain (Boston)*	39	13	W		
07/26	Union (Morrisania, NY)*	4	12		L	
10/04	Star (Brooklyn)	5	5			T
10/14	Union (Morrisania, NY)	13	9	W		

* Box score not available

BATTER	POS	GP	HL	A	O	R	A	O
Ed Russell	1B	1	2	2	0	1	1	0
H. Brainard	2B,3B	2	4	2	0	2	1	0
George Flanly	SS,P	2	5	2	1	3	1	1
H. Polhemus	3B	1	3	3	0	0	0	0
George Cook	OF	2	5	2	1	0	0	0
Asa Brainard	OF,P	2	3	1	1	3	1	1
William Young	OF	1	1	1	0	2	2	0
Masten	C	2	5	2	1	1	0	1
James Creighton	P,2B	6	4	0	4	22	3	4
McKenzie	OF	1	2	2	0	1	1	0
Jerold	SS	1	2	2	0	1	1	0
H.P. Bostwick	OF	1	3	3	0	0	0	0
Joe Leggett	1B	1	1	1	0	0	0	0

STAR 4 - 2 - 1
Brooklyn, NY

DATE	OPPONENT	SCORE		W	L	T
05/21	Powhatan (Brooklyn)	45	11	W		
06/11	Charter Oak (Brooklyn)	12	17		L	
06/28	Resolute (Brooklyn)	35	12	W		
09/13	Olympic (S. Brooklyn)	18	11	W		
09/27	Union (Morrisania, NY)	10	14		L	
10/04	Excelsior (Brooklyn)	5	5			T
---/---	Olympic (S. Brooklyn)*	47	24	W		

* Box score not available

STAR (cont.)
Brooklyn, NY

BATTER	POS	GP	HL	A	O	R	A	O
Hope Waddell	1B,OF	6	20	3	2	14	2	2
Galpin	2B	5	11	2	1	14	2	4
McCullough	SS,OF	3	10	3	1	3	1	0
B. Chilton	3B,2B	5	18	3	3	11	2	1
Chappell	OF	4	9	2	1	15	3	2
Henry	OF	3	8	2	2	10	3	1
Thompson	OF	2	5	2	1	5	2	1
Mitchell	C	6	19	3	1	11	1	5
Kelly	P,OF	4	10	2	2	7	1	3
Jerome	1B,SS	3	7	2	1	13	4	1
Thomas	OF,1B	2	4	2	0	7	3	1
Bob Manly	3B	2	9	4	1	3	1	1
Povee	3B	2	2	1	0	3	1	1
T. Morris	SS	1	2	2	0	5	5	0
C. Morris	2B	1	2	2	0	2	2	0
Anderson	SS	1	2	2	0	2	2	0
Mudge	OF	1	4	4	0	1	1	0
Field	OF	1	2	2	0	0	0	0
Skaats	OF	1	4	4	0	0	0	0

ATLANTIC   2 - 3
Brooklyn, NY

DATE	OPPONENT	SCORE		W	L	T
08/11	Eckford (Brooklyn)	14	20		L	
08/18	Eckford (Brooklyn)	39	5	W		
09/16	Harlem (New York)	27	12	W		
09/18	Eckford (Brooklyn)	3	8		L	
09/22	Mutual (New York)	10	15		L	

BATTER	POS	GP	HL	A	O	R	A	O
Joe Start	1B	4	11	2	3	6	1	2
John Oliver	2B	3	10	3	1	5	1	2
Peter O'Brien	SS	5	15	3	0	11	2	1
Charles Smith	3B	4	10	2	2	11	2	3
Fred Crane	OF	5	16	3	1	10	2	0
Joe Oliver	OF	4	13	3	1	10	2	2
John Chapman	OF	4	12	3	0	9	2	1
Dickey Pearce	C	5	13	2	3	13	2	3
Mattie O'Brien	P	3	7	2	1	7	2	1
F.W. Massey	P	3	10	3	1	3	1	0
Simonson	3B	2	7	3	1	3	1	1
Seibert	OF	1	4	4	0	3	3	0
Sid Smith	P	1	4	4	0	1	1	0
F. Seinsoth	1B	1	3	3	0	1	1	0

HARLEM   2 - 7
New York, NY

DATE	OPPONENT	SCORE		W	L	T
07/18	Union (Morrisania, NY)*	13	23		L	
08/13	Eckford (Brooklyn)*	25	42		L	
09/04	Gotham (New York)*	29	15	W		
09/08	Mutual (New York)*	16	47		L	
09/16	Atlantic (Brooklyn)*	12	27		L	
09/20	Resolute (Brooklyn)	25	21	W		
10/07	Mutual (New York)*	13	24		L	

HARLEM (cont.)
New York, NY

DATE	OPPONENT	SCORE		W	L	T
10/14	Gotham (New York)	10	19		L	
10/20	Gotham (New York)	17	24		L	

* Box score not available

BATTER	POS	GP	HL	A	O	R	A	O
Seaver Page	1B,OF	2	6	3	0	2	1	0
W.F. Hudson	2B,C	3	5	1	2	10	3	1
Graff	SS	2	5	2	1	4	2	0
Rooney	3B	2	6	3	0	3	1	1
Stephens	OF	2	4	2	0	5	2	1
Estes	OF,2B,1B	3	4	1	1	9	3	0
Armour	OF	2	5	2	1	4	2	0
Dave Birdsall	C,P	2	7	3	1	3	1	1
G. Thompson	P	2	7	3	1	1	0	1
Dan Ketchum	2B	1	0	0	0	4	4	0
Kingsland	OF	1	2	2	0	2	2	0
J. Kettleman	OF	1	2	2	0	2	2	0
Mott	SS	1	3	3	0	2	2	0
Price	OF	1	3	3	0	1	1	0
Colgate	3B	1	3	3	0	0	0	0
Marsh	1B	1	4	4	0	0	0	0

POWHATAN 0 - 1
Brooklyn, NY

DATE	OPPONENT	SCORE		W	L	T
05/21	Star (Brooklyn)	11	45		L	

BATTER	POS	GP	HL	A	O	R	A	O
McCarty	1B	1	3	3	0	1	1	0
Brown	2B	1	2	2	0	1	1	0
Snediker	SS	1	2	2	0	2	2	0
Bennett	3B	1	3	3	0	1	1	0
Irwin	OF	1	3	3	0	1	1	0
Vanderveer	OF	1	1	1	0	2	2	0
Lyons	OF	1	2	2	0	1	1	0
Thompson	C	1	2	2	0	1	1	0
Earl	P	1	3	3	0	1	1	0

TEAM TOTALS

TEAM	CITY/STATE	GP	W	L	T	PCT	R	OR
Eckford	Brooklyn, NY	16	14	2	0	.875	453	261
Mutual	New York, NY	13	8	5	0	.615	324	205
Gotham	New York, NY	9	6	3	0	.667	148	178
Union	Morrisania, NY	10	5	5	0	.500	145	157
Excelsior	Brooklyn, NY	6	4	1	1	.750	122	73
Star	Brooklyn, NY	7	4	2	1	.643	172	94
Jefferson	New York, NY	3	2	1	0	.667	112	83
Atlantic	Brooklyn, NY	5	2	3	0	.400	93	60
Harlem	New York, NY	9	2	7	0	.222	160	242
Empire	New York, NY	1	1	0	0	1.000	39	21
Victory	Troy, NY	4	1	3	0	.250	110	191
Eagle	New York, NY	4	1	3	0	.250	86	92
Powhatan	Brooklyn, NY	1	0	1	0	.000	11	45

OTHER TEAMS

TEAM	CITY/STATE
Adriatic	Newark, NJ
Alpine	New York, NY
Brooklyn	Brooklyn, NY
Charter Oak	Brooklyn, NY
Continental	Brooklyn, NY
Enterprise	Brooklyn, NY
Eureka	Newark, NJ
Exercise	Brooklyn, NY
Favorita	Brooklyn, NY
Good Intent	New Utrecht, NY
Hamilton	Brooklyn, NY
Henry Eckford	New York, NY
Independent	New York, NY
Knickerbocker	New York, NY
Metropolitan	New York, NY
New York	New York, NY
Newark	Newark, NJ
Olympic	S. Brooklyn, NY
Putnam	Brooklyn, NY
Union	Elizabeth, NJ

1863
BATTLEFIELDS AND BALLFIELDS

Baseball had no real effect on the Civil War, but the war certainly had a profound influence on the game. As a matter of fact, the conflict helped cement baseball's claim as the national pastime.

The Civil War may have become inevitable in 1860 when long-simmering tensions between the northern and southern regions of the United States boiled over. In December, South Carolina voted to secede from the United States. Several other southern states followed suit. By February 1861, this group of southern entities decided to form a new country—the Confederate States of America. After several skirmishes, war between the North and South broke out in earnest in July at the Battle of Bull Run. America's bloodiest war—the Civil War—had begun.

The war's effect was felt immediately. During the summer of 1861, one of baseball's strongest clubs, the Excelsior of Brooklyn, played no inter-club games because of a war-depleted roster. After the season, at the December 1861 convention of the National Association only 34 clubs sent delegates—half of the previous year's total. Of these 34, none were from further south than New Jersey.

Although many clubs suspended competition or disbanded during the Civil War, interest in baseball did not wither—it merely moved from a team to an individual setting. Members of various clubs, not wanting to be deprived of the game they loved, took the game with them when they went to war. However, for enthusiasts of America's other favorite bat and ball game—cricket—this was not possible.

Before the Civil War, cricket and baseball shared a place in the hearts of ball-playing enthusiasts. The English game of cricket had been in America for years, but when it came time for the game to be brought to the front—to the men who needed it for recreation—cricket fell short. This was due simply to the rules and trappings of the game.

The game of cricket needed an immaculate sward of perfectly level ground to be played properly. Such plots were scarce in the wartime staging areas. Also, cricket needed several accoutrements such as wickets and pads to accompany it. In addition, a cricket match needed an inordinate amount of time to complete—sometimes more than one day.

On the other hand, soldiers on both sides of the conflict found they could take baseball anywhere. Needing only a bat, a ball, two hours and a rudimentary field, many ball players brought the game to the wartime theatre.

Baseball games between soldiers usually consisted of a contest pitting one regiment against another, although many informal contests occurred. There is also evidence detailing games played by Union detainees in Confederate prisoner of war camps, and even by opposing troops in the lull of battle.

The turmoil wracking the country also affected the membership of individual clubs. As reported in the *New York Clipper*, Brooklyn's Excelsior club dealt with A. Pearsall in the following fashion:

> Some time he [Pearsall] was heard from in Richmond [the Confederate capital], as a Brigade Surgeon, on the rebel General Morgan's staff. He had charge of some Union prisoners, taking them along the streets of Richmond, when he recognized a gentleman of Brooklyn, formerly a member of the Excelsior club, and entered into conversation. He asked particularly about Leggett, Flanley, Creighton and Brainard, whom as members of the Club, he wished particularly to be remembered to. These facts came to the knowledge of the Club, and they expelled him by a unanimous vote.

This was largely a symbolic gesture, but it reflected the strong emotional influence the conflict held on the populace in general.

As the Civil War moved forward, further shrinkage occurred in the National Association. At the 1862 convention only 32 clubs sent representatives, although two Philadelphia clubs (Keystone and Athletic) were present in the group.

During the summer of 1863, while the Civil War raged in places like Gettysburg, Pennsylvania, and Vicksburg, Mississippi, National Association baseball continued. Several strong teams emerged in the New York area. The best of the group was once again the Eckfords of Brooklyn.

The Eckfords started the season with a trio of narrow victories over the Athletic (10–5), Mutual (10–9) and Union (8–4) clubs. As the summer progressed, they posted two strong wins (31–10 and 21–10) over the Atlantics. Finally, they rounded out the year with an 18–10 decision over the Mutual nine. In all, the Eckford club played 10 games during the season and won them all, the first time an Association club had gone undefeated in that many contests. By losing nary a game, the Eckfords guaranteed the retention of their championship.

Other strong clubs included the Mutual who won 10-of-14, the Atlantic who vanquished 8-of-11 and the Athletic of Philadelphia who bested 7-of-12. Interestingly, half of the Athletic's 12 contests came in the space of six days in June as they embarked on a trip to play the major clubs in New York and New Jersey. Although they won only two of the six, all parties thoroughly enjoyed the competition. In the years to come, excursions between Philadelphia and New York became a staple of the schedule for most leading clubs.

Not surprisingly, the leading batsmen came from the best clubs. The most runs were scored by Ed Brown (39) of the Mutuals followed by his clubmate Bill Wansley (36), and James Wood (35) of the Eckfords. The highest scoring average was obtained by Wood (3,5) while his teammate Joe Sprague finished second (3,1). Five other Association players tied with an average of 3,0.

After 1863, the Civil War still had two more years to run before hostilities ended at Appomattox Courthouse. All during that time, baseball continued to flourish both in the National Association and by the people that needed it the most—the soldiers in the field. The *Clipper* reported: "Our soldier boys will have their 'hand in' at base ball, it seems, and we commend them therefore, as it must be a very agreeable change from dodging leaden balls."

After the war, the game of baseball continued to gain support, while the game of cricket languished. It seemed that the factors that made cricket unsuitable for the soldiers at the front made it unpopular for the population in general. In a choice between the two, baseball won the battle, pushed to victory by the War between the States.

ECKFORD 10 - 0
Brooklyn, NY

DATE	OPPONENT	SCORE		W	L	T
06/17	Athletic (Philadelphia)	10	5	W		
07/22	Mutual (New York)	10	9	W		
07/30	Union (Morrisania, NY)	8	4	W		
08/04	Hudson River (Newburgh, NY)	50	13	W		
08/14	Resolute (Brooklyn)	16	5	W		
09/02	Atlantic (Brooklyn)	31	10	W		
09/08	Atlantic (Brooklyn)	21	10	W		
09/16	Resolute (Brooklyn)	24	8	W		
09/24	Union (Morrisania, NY)	29	5	W		
10/06	Mutual (New York)	18	10	W		

BATTER	POS	GP	HL	A	O	R	A	O
Al Reach	1B	8	27	3	3	16	2	0
James Wood	2B	10	22	2	2	35	3	5
Tom Devyr	SS	6	19	3	1	5	0	5
Ed Duffy	3B	10	27	2	7	24	2	4
Harry Manolt	OF	9	23	2	5	27	3	0
Josh Snyder	OF	9	27	3	0	18	2	0
Marty Swandell	OF	8	32	4	0	11	1	3
Waddy Beach	C	10	27	2	7	30	3	0
Joe Sprague	P	9	19	2	1	28	3	1

MUTUAL 10 - 4
New York, NY

DATE	OPPONENT	SCORE		W	L	T
06/16	Athletic (Philadelphia)	17	11	W		
07/13	Gotham (New York)	21	15	W		
07/20	Empire (New York)	24	12	W		
07/22	Eckford (Brooklyn)	9	10		L	
07/28	Gotham (New York)	19	5	W		
08/03	Atlantic (Brooklyn)	27	26	W		
08/06	Empire (New York)	21	16	W		
08/11	Eureka (Newark)	13	7	W		
08/24	Eagle (New York)	25	12	W		
09/04	Star (Brooklyn)	32	19	W		
09/10	Atlantic (Brooklyn)	11	15		L	
09/17	Star (Brooklyn)	23	12	W		
09/24	Atlantic (Brooklyn)	18	42		L	
10/06	Eckford (Brooklyn)	10	18		L	

BATTER	POS	GP	HL	A	O	R	A	O
John Goldie	1B,OF	13	38	2	12	34	2	8
Ed Brown	2B	13	32	2	6	39	3	0
Billy McMahon	SS,3B	13	33	2	7	33	2	7
Charles Hunt	3B,SS	2	5	2	1	5	2	1
John Zeller	OF	13	39	3	0	17	1	4
Harris	OF	10	37	3	7	17	1	7
Mott	OF	9	28	3	1	13	1	4
McKever	P	9	31	3	4	12	1	3
Bill Wansley	C	14	30	2	2	36	2	8
J. Beard		7	26	3	5	13	1	6
Campbell	1B,P	6	19	3	1	13	2	1

ATLANTIC 8 - 3
Brooklyn, NY

DATE	OPPONENT	SCORE		W	L	T
06/18	Athletic (Philadelphia)	21	13	W		
08/03	Mutual (New York)	26	27		L	
08/06	Henry Eckford (New York)	14	10	W		
08/13	Henry Eckford (New York)	30	13	W		
08/31	Eureka (Newark)	16	15	W		
09/02	Eckford (Brooklyn)	10	31		L	
09/08	Eckford (Brooklyn)	10	21		L	
09/10	Mutual (New York)	15	11	W		
09/24	Mutual (New York)	42	18	W		
10/22	Nassau (Princeton, NJ)	18	13	W		
10/26	New York Cricket Club (New York)	23	8	W		

BATTER	POS	GP	HL	A O		R	A O	
Joe Start	1B,OF,SS	9	26	2	8	23	2	5
Peter O'Brien	SS	7	20	2	6	16	2	2
John Galvin	2B	5	9	2	1	13	2	3
Charles Smith	3B	11	28	2	6	33	3	0
John Chapman	OF,P	11	35	3	2	19	1	8
Joe Oliver	OF	9	26	2	8	20	2	2
Fred Crane	OF,2B	10	28	2	8	23	2	3
Dickey Pearce	C	11	32	2	10	30	2	8
Tom Pratt	P,SS	7	20	2	6	17	2	3
John Price	1B	4	10	2	2	9	2	1
Sid Smith	P	4	17	4	1	4	1	0
John Oliver	2B	3	10	3	1	3	1	0
Gus Ticknor	OF	2	4	2	0	5	2	1
Galpin	OF	2	8	4	0	5	2	1
James Smith	OF	1	3	3	0	3	3	0
Davenport	2B	1	2	2	0	2	2	0
F. Seinsoth	OF	1	2	2	0	2	2	0
Earl	OF	1	5	5	0	1	1	0
Joe Sprague	P	1	5	5	0	0	0	0

ATHLETIC 7 - 5
Philadelphia, PA

DATE	OPPONENT	SCORE			W	L	T
03/22	Nassau (Princeton, NJ)	29	18		W		
06/15	Excelsior (Brooklyn)	18	17	(10)	W		
06/16	Mutual (New York)	11	17			L	
06/17	Eckford (Brooklyn)	5	10			L	
06/18	Atlantic (Brooklyn)	13	21			L	
06/19	Star (Brooklyn)	37	17		W		
06/20	Eureka (Newark)	6	8			L	
09/04	Keystone (Philadelphia)	25	5		W		
09/11	Mountain (Altoona, PA)	73	22		W		
09/29	Keystone (Philadelphia)	14	13		W		
10/26	Nassau (Princeton, NJ)	13	29			L	
---/---	Bridgeton (Bridgeton, NJ)	--	--		W		

BATTER	POS	GP	HL	A O		R	A O	
Nate Berkenstock	1B,OF	9	25	2	7	19	2	1
Paul	2B,1B	9	22	2	4	24	2	6
Dick McBride	SS,P	10	27	2	7	25	2	5
Mike Smith	3B,OF,1B	10	33	3	3	22	2	2
Isaac Wilkins	OF,3B,SS	9	30	3	3	11	1	2
Charles Gaskill	OF	8	28	3	4	17	?	1
Colonel Moore	OF,1B	8	22	2	6	15	1	7
Dan Kleinfelder	C	11	28	2	6	33	3	0
Tom Pratt	P,2B	7	20	2	6	16	2	2

EXCELSIOR   5 - 4
Brooklyn, NY

DATE	OPPONENT	SCORE			W	L	T
06/15	Athletic (Philadelphia)	17	18	(10)		L	
08/03	Hudson River (Newburgh, NY)	16	13		W		
08/15	Union (Morrisania, NY)	9	20			L	
09/10	Newark (Newark)	17	10		W		
09/16	Henry Eckford (New York)	25	21		W		
09/23	Newark (Newark)	19	17		W		
09/30	Henry Eckford (New York)	15	8		W		
10/17	Eagle (New York)	5	6			L	
10/20	Nassau (Princeton, NJ)	11	12			L	

BATTER	POS	GP	HL	A	O	R	A	O
Whiting	1B	9	26	2	8	18	2	0
John Clyne	2B,OF	5	16	1	3	5	1	0
H. Brainard	SS	10	32	3	2	24	2	4
George Cook	3B	5	13	2	3	13	2	3
George Flanly	OF,2B	10	22	2	2	28	2	8
Langley	OF	7	25	3	4	12	1	5
McKenzie	OF	7	22	3	1	12	1	5
Joe Leggett	C	5	18	3	3	6	1	1
Asa Brainard	P	10	22	2	2	28	2	8

STAR   5 - 5
Brooklyn, NY

DATE	OPPONENT	SCORE		W	L	T
06/10	Gotham (New York)	41	16	W		
06/19	Athletic (Philadelphia)	17	37		L	
08/18	Empire (New York)	28	9	W		
09/04	Mutual (New York)	19	32		L	
09/11	Gotham (New York)	23	19	W		
09/17	Mutual (New York)	12	23		L	
---/---	Hudson River (Newburgh, NY)	--	--	W		
---/---	Resolute (Brooklyn)	--	--	W		
---/---	Resolute (Brooklyn)	--	--		L	
---/---	Nassau (Princeton, NJ)	--	--		L	

BATTER	POS	GP	HL	A	O	R	A	O
Hope Waddell	1B	9	25	2	7	24	2	6
Pete Flanders	2B,SS,3B	9	28	3	1	20	2	2
Worth	SS	9	24	2	6	20	2	2
Mitchell	3B,C	10	33	3	3	21	2	1
Lennon	OF	9	27	3	0	19	2	1
Frank Norton	OF	8	29	3	5	14	1	6
T. Smith	OF	2	8	4	0	5	2	1
Thompson	C	7	21	3	0	12	1	5
Kelly	P	9	29	3	2	13	1	4
Bob Manly		5	12	2	2	11	2	1

HENRY ECKFORD   4 - 8
New York, NY

DATE	OPPONENT	SCORE		W	L	T
06/24	Empire (New York)	--	--	W		
07/29	Empire (New York)	16	21		L	
08/06	Atlantic (Brooklyn)	10	14		L	
08/13	Atlantic (Brooklyn)	13	30		L	
09/16	Excelsior (Brooklyn)	21	25		L	

HENRY ECKFORD (cont.)
New York, NY

DATE	OPPONENT	SCORE		W	L	T
09/30	Excelsior (Brooklyn)	8	15		L	
---/---	Union (Morrisania, NY)	--	--	W		
---/---	Mystic (New York)	--	--	W		
---/---	Baltic (New York)	--	--	W		
---/---	Union (Morrisania, NY)	--	--		L	
---/---	Union (Morrisania, NY)	--	--		L	
---/---	Empire (New York)	--	--		L	

BATTER	POS	GP	HL	A	O	R	A	O
H. Dalton	1B	12	36	3	0	18	1	6
W.F. Hudson	2B	11	23	2	1	31	2	9
T. Dalton	SS	13	33	2	7	26	2	0
McCarthy	3B	8	24	3	0	17	2	1
A. Saunders	OF	10	31	3	1	15	1	5
Nat Jewett	OF	8	26	3	2	13	1	5
Wright	OF	7	22	3	1	11	1	4
Dan Patterson	C	10	26	2	6	24	2	4
William Bell	P	13	31	2	5	30	2	4
Snow		6	17	2	5	13	2	1

UNION 3 - 3
Morrisania, NY

DATE	OPPONENT	SCORE		W	L	T
07/30	Eckford (Brooklyn)	4	8		L	
08/15	Excelsior (Brooklyn)	20	9	W		
09/24	Eckford (Brooklyn)	5	29		L	
---/---	Henry Eckford (New York)	--	--	W		
---/---	Henry Eckford (New York)	--	--		L	
---/---	Henry Eckford (New York)	--	--	W		

BATTER	POS	GP	HL	A	O	R	A	O
William Abrams		7	19	2	5	16	2	2
Bernard Hannegan		7	19	2	5	14	2	0
Nicholson		7	19	2	5	12	1	5
Dave Birdsall		7	19	2	5	10	1	3
Hyatt		6	13	2	1	14	2	2
Sammy Collins		5	11	2	1	8	1	3

GOTHAM 3 - 4
New York, NY

DATE	OPPONENT	SCORE		W	L	T
06/10	Star (Brooklyn)	16	41		L	
06/23	Eagle (New York)	19	15	W		
07/01	Empire (New York)	16	14	W		
07/13	Mutual (New York)	15	21		L	
07/28	Mutual (New York)	5	19		L	
09/11	Star (Brooklyn)	19	23		L	
---/---	Empire (New York)	--	--	W		

BATTER	POS	GP	HL	A	O	R	A	O
Stokem		8	23	2	7	14	1	6
Dick Thorn		8	28	3	4	12	1	4
Harry Wright		7	16	2	2	14	2	0
Norman Welling		7	23	3	2	12	1	5

GOTHAM (cont.)
New York, NY

BATTER	POS	GP	HL	A	O	R	A	O
Squires		5	12	2	2	9	1	4
Vincelette		5	16	3	1	9	1	4
Forsyth		5	19	3	4	5	1	0

RESOLUTE   3 - 6
Brooklyn, NY

DATE	OPPONENT	SCORE		W	L	T
07/01	Eagle (New York)	27	5	W		
08/14	Eckford (Brooklyn)	5	16		L	
09/16	Eckford (Brooklyn)	8	24		L	
---/---	Star (Brooklyn)	--	--	W		
---/---	Hudson River (Newburgh, NY)	--	--	W		
---/---	Star (Brooklyn)	--	--		L	
---/---	Hudson River (Newburgh, NY)	--	--		L	
---/---	Nassau (Princeton, NJ)	--	--		L	
---/---	Union (Brooklyn)	--	--		L	

BATTER	POS	GP	HL	A	O	R	A	O
Morrison		8	21	2	5	13	1	5
Weeden		8	22	2	4	11	1	4
Wilson		8	24	3	0	10	1	2
Stanton		8	28	3	4	6	0	6
M. Rogers		7	21	3	0	14	2	0
W. Warnock		7	16	2	2	11	1	4
T. Allen		7	22	3	1	11	1	4
Bliss		7	17	2	3	10	1	3
Taylor		6	17	2	5	5	0	5

EMPIRE   2 - 6
New York, NY

DATE	OPPONENT	SCORE		W	L	T
06/24	Henry Eckford (New York)	--	--		L	
07/01	Gotham (New York)	14	16		L	
07/20	Mutual (New York)	12	24		L	
07/21	Eagle (New York)	19	10	W		
07/29	Henry Eckford (New York)	21	16	W		
08/06	Mutual (New York)	16	21		L	
08/18	Star (Brooklyn)	9	28		L	
---/---	Gotham (New York)	--	--		L	

BATTER	POS	GP	HL	A	O	R	A	O
Westervelt		6	15	2	3	18	3	0
Russell		6	14	2	2	15	2	3
Miller		6	17	2	5	13	2	1
Wilson		6	15	2	3	11	1	5
James Ryder		6	20	3	2	10	1	4
Sebring		5	17	3	2	7	1	2

TEAM TOTALS

TEAM	CITY/STATE	GP	W	L	T	PCT	R	OR
Eckford	Brooklyn, NY	10	10	0	0	1.000	217	79
Mutual	New York, NY	14	10	4	0	.714	270	220
Atlantic	Brooklyn, NY	11	8	3	0	.727	225	180
Athletic	Philadelphia, PA	12	7	5	0	.583	244	177
Excelsior	Brooklyn, NY	9	5	4	0	.556	134	125
Star	Brooklyn, NY	10	5	5	0	.500	183	187
Henry Eckford	New York, NY	12	4	8	0	.333	204	244
Union	Morrisania, NY	6	3	3	0	.500	88	83
Knickerbocker	Albany, NY	6	3	3	0	.500	164	136
Gotham	New York, NY	7	3	4	0	.429	116	155
Resolute	Brooklyn, NY	9	3	6	0	.333	116	126
Empire	New York, NY	8	2	6	0	.250	91	115
Eagle	New York, NY	5	1	4	0	.200	48	95
Hudson River	Newburgh, NY	5	1	4	0	.200	26	66
Keystone	Philadelphia, PA	4	0	4	0	.000	46	76

OTHER TEAMS

TEAM	CITY/STATE
Baltic	New York, NY
Charter Oak	Brooklyn, NY
Constellation	Brooklyn, NY
Continental	Brooklyn, NY
Eureka	Newark, NJ
Favorita	Brooklyn, NY
Hamilton	Brooklyn, NY
Harlem	New York, NY
Independent	New York, NY
Jefferson	New York, NY
Knickerbocker	New York, NY
Metropolitan	New York, NY
New York	New York, NY
Newark	Newark, NJ
Olympic	S. Brooklyn, NY
Union	Brooklyn, NY
Victory	Troy, NY

1864
THE FLY GAME

At the crack of the bat, the outfielder races in to attempt to catch the short fly ball. Unable to reach the landing point, he pulls up and gracefully fields the ball on one hop. Seeing the spheroid held triumphantly aloft by the outfielder, the umpire declares the batter out. This action describes not an arcane interpretation of the game of baseball used in some far-flung district, but any typical National Association game of the early 1860s. For at that time, any fly ball caught on a bounce was considered an out.

The game of baseball played in the early days of the Association used some rules that would be unrecognizable to us today. For instance, a batter could wait for a perfect pitch before swinging. He would be in no danger of striking out because no strikes would be called against him. As a result, an at-bat could take 10 minutes or longer. Another rule stated that a ball was fair if it first hit the ground anywhere in fair territory. This would still hold true if the ball then skittered into foul territory well short of first or third base.

However, the rule governing the out on one bounce seems the strangest to modern sensibilities, although it had been an integral part of the game since the beginning. In the playing rules set down by Alexander Cartwright and the Knickerbocker club in 1845, rule 12 stated: "If a ball be struck, or tipped, and caught, either flying or on the first bound, it is a hand out." When the rules were modified in 1857, the rule remained on the books "Section 13: [the striker is out]... if a fair ball is struck, and the ball is caught either without having touched the ground or upon the first bound."

The exact reasoning for this rule is lost in the mists of antiquity. No doubt it had something to do with making the game easier. In the first place, it was simpler to retire a batter when you could catch the ball on one bounce or bound. Secondly, it would be easier on the gloveless hands of baseball's early competitors to have most of the sting of impact absorbed by the ground.

Despite its being an original part of the game, no rule was more hotly contested than the bound out rule. Beginning as early as 1858, several teams led by the Knickerbocker contingent tried to get the delegates to vote the rule out. These players were in favor of the fly game, which stated the ball had to be caught in the air to put the batter out. The reasoning behind the desire for the rule change was summarized in the report of the 1859 convention of the National Association in the *New York Clipper*:

> The committee on rules and by-laws ... were equally divided on the question of catching the ball on the fly. An alteration in that respect would seem necessary to make the game more manly, as all the little boys are now able to play the game on equal terms with the older clubs, whilst they may put a hand out while catching the ball on the bound.

These reformers, led by sportswriter Henry Chadwick and others, were continually frustrated by the National Association's delegates reluctance to abandon the bound catch. In 1860 the delegates voted 55 to 37 against the fly rule. For the next several years, the votes were similar. The 1863 result was particularly galling to the fly catch enthusiasts. Henry Chadwick expressed his frustration in the pages of the 1864 *Beadle's Guide*:

> When the question of the fly game came up for action, it elicited considerable discussion. On putting the question to vote, it was decided in the negative by a vote of 25 to 22. It was a noteworthy fact that all, or nearly all, of those opposed to it belong to the muffin fraternity, whose fun the fly game would put a stop to altogether.

(Note: "Muffin" was a term used to describe the less-skilled player.)

Despite not being on the books, many teams played fly games anyway, eschewing the easier bound game. The Knickerbockers played a series of exhibitions with the Excelsiors in 1859 which drew strong praise from the sporting press.

Defeated at the 1863 convention, the fly game was put on hold for the 1864 season. Despite this, baseball remained hugely popular, regularly drawing thousands for the important matches.

Most of the important games of 1864 involved the Atlantic club of

Brooklyn. The team won its first two encounters, tied their third against the Empire, then won the rest—eighteen more in all. The team finished with 20 wins and one tie—the Association's best record to date.

Finishing not far behind were the Mutuals, who also won 20. But included in their record were three losses, two at the hand of the Atlantics 26–16 and 21–16. Other teams of note included the up and coming Athletics of Philadelphia and the Excelsior outfit with eight wins each.

The defending champion Eckfords of Brooklyn had a particularly disappointing season. Starting later than usual, the team lost their first game in almost two years 24–18 to an all-star contingent in June. After a win against the Newark club in July, the team played only three more games the rest of the way, losing all of them. Two of these losses were to the strong Mutual club, who in turn lost a pair to the Atlantics. As a result, the Atlantics were given the championship mantle in 1864.

Individually, all of the best marks were attained by the Atlantic nine. Charles Smith scored an even 100 runs, followed by Dickey Pearce (94) and John Chapman (88). Smith also held the highest average (5,5), followed by teammates John Galvin (5,0) and Pearce (4,14).

After the season, at the December Association convention, baseball's reformers finally got their way. By a vote of 33 to 19, the bound game was relegated to the shelf. The fly game now governed the National Association.

Baseball's other seemingly odd rules also changed over the years. Beginning in 1863, the umpire was entitled to call balls on the pitcher thus speeding up every at-bat. However, the fair-foul rule had to wait until the formation of the National League before being changed to its present configuration. These rule changes, especially the fly catch out, were helpful in developing the game of baseball. They elevated the skill level needed to play the game properly—thus changing a boy's pastime into a man's profession.

ATLANTIC
Brooklyn, NY   20 - 0 - 1

DATE	OPPONENT	SCORE		W	L	T
05/30	Field Nine (Brooklyn)	45	11	W		
06/27	Mutual (New York)	26	16	W		
06/30	Empire (New York)	13	13			T
07/06	Nassau (Princeton, NJ)	42	7	W		
07/08	Empire (New York)	33	8	W		
07/18	Resolute (Brooklyn)	18	1	W		
07/20	Eagle (New York)	45	12	W		
07/26	Eureka (Newark)	25	13	W		
07/30	Star (Brooklyn)	35	16	W		
08/04	Star (Brooklyn)	35	17	W		
08/08	Camden (Camden, NJ)	64	10	W		
08/09	Keystone (Philadelphia)	65	10	W		
08/10	Olympic (Philadelphia)	58	11	W		
08/11	Athletic (Philadelphia)	43	16	W		
08/23	Gotham (New York)	14	9	W		
09/01	Resolute (Brooklyn)	53	6	W		
09/12	Mutual (New York)	21	16	W		
09/19	Gotham (New York)	38	12	W		
09/22	Young Canadian (Woodstock, ON)	75	11	W		
09/23	Ontario (Rochester)	54	5	W		
10/19	Empire (New York)	15	7	W		

BATTER	POS	GP	HL	A	O	R	A	O
Joe Start	1B,3B	18	47	2	11	82	4	10
Fred Crane	2B,OF	18	51	2	15	85	4	13
John Galvin	SS,2B,3B	16	38	2	6	82	5	0
Charles Smith	3B,SS,2B	19	50	2	12	100	5	5
Peter O'Brien	OF	19	57	3	0	80	4	4
Sid Smith	OF	14	46	3	4	56	3	14
John Chapman	OF,P,C,SS,3B	22	68	3	2	88	4	0
Dickey Pearce	C,SS,OF	20	62	3	2	94	4	14
Tom Pratt	P,SS	21	67	3	4	84	4	0
Joe Sprague	SS,1B	6	20	3	2	29	4	5
Joe Oliver	OF,SS	6	18	3	0	15	2	3

MUTUAL
New York, NY   20 - 3

DATE	OPPONENT	SCORE		W	L	T
06/20	Newark (Newark)	19	18	W		
06/27	Atlantic (Brooklyn)	16	26		L	
07/04	Nassau (Princeton, NJ)	10	19		L	
07/14	Eagle (New York)	39	8	W		
07/20	Empire (New York)	24	12	W		
07/27	Empire (New York)	20	16	W		
08/02	Eureka (Newark)	16	10	W		
08/04	Knickerbocker (Albany)	24	16	W		
08/12	Gotham (New York)	23	7	W		
08/17	Excelsior (Brooklyn)	21	10	W		
08/22	Eckford (Brooklyn)	29	17	W		
08/26	Active (New York)	22	3	W		
08/30	Utica (Utica, NY)	26	8	W		
08/31	Knickerbocker (Albany)	36	29	W		
09/01	Victory (Troy)	34	13	W		
09/02	Hudson River (Newburgh, NY)	18	11	W		
09/12	Atlantic (Brooklyn)	16	21		L	
09/14	Newark (Newark)	24	10	W		
09/24	Active (New York)	14	8	W		
09/26	Excelsior (Brooklyn)	33	22	W		
09/28	Empire (New York)	13	8	W		
10/03	Gotham (New York)	12	10	W		
10/10	Eckford (Brooklyn)	23	19	W		

MUTUAL (cont.)
New York, NY

BATTER	POS	GP	HL	A	O	R	A	O
John Goldie	1B	20	48	2	8	57	2	17
Ed Brown	2B,OF,C	20	60	3	0	55	2	15
Tom Devyr	SS	15	55	3	10	34	2	4
Ed Duffy	3B,SS	12	39	3	3	32	2	8
John Zeller	OF,2B,P	21	58	2	16	58	2	16
Dan Patterson	OF,2B	15	40	2	10	39	2	9
Billy McMahon	OF,SS,C,3B,2B	20	59	2	19	54	2	14
Bill Wansley	C,1B	17	51	3	0	50	2	16
Harris	P,OF	16	48	3	0	33	2	1
McCullough	3B,OF	8	23	2	7	17	2	1
Charles Hunt	OF,C,SS	7	20	2	6	20	2	6
Mott	P,OF	5	14	2	4	10	2	0

ATHLETIC   8 - 1
Philadelphia, PA

DATE	OPPONENT	SCORE		W	L	T
06/09	Camden (Camden, NJ)	21	10	W		
06/20	Keystone (Philadelphia)	13	8	W		
06/27	Mercantile (Philadelphia)	68	25	W		
06/30	Nassau (Princeton, NJ)	14	9	W		
07/28	Resolute (Brooklyn)	29	12	W		
08/11	Atlantic (Brooklyn)	16	43		L	
08/25	Camden (Camden, NJ)	42	12	W		
09/27	Mountain (Altoona, PA)	63	2	W		
11/24	Keystone (Philadelphia)	23	15	W		

BATTER	POS	GP	HL	A	O	R	A	O
Nate Berkenstock	1B	8	20	2	4	28	3	4
Luengene	2B,OF	6	21	3	0	18	2	2
Fergy Malone	SS,1B,2B	7	19	2	5	17	2	3
Gratz	3B	5	14	2	4	18	3	3
Charles Gaskill	OF,1B	10	32	3	2	33	3	3
Mike Smith	OF,3B	9	23	2	5	27	3	0
Isaac Wilkins	OF,3B,SS	8	27	3	3	24	3	0
Dan Kleinfelder	C,P	11	30	2	8	40	3	7
Dick McBride	P,C	8	21	3	0	18	2	2
Hicks Hayhurst	OF,P	7	23	3	2	27	3	6

EXCELSIOR   8 - 3
Brooklyn, NY

DATE	OPPONENT	SCORE		W	L	T
07/16	Enterprise (Brooklyn)	25	19	W		
08/10	Newark (Newark)	24	20	W		
08/13	Enterprise (Brooklyn)	33	6	W		
08/17	Mutual (New York)	10	21		L	
09/10	Newark (Newark)	19	35		L	
09/23	St. George Cricket Club (New York)	28	15	W		
09/26	Mutual (New York)	22	33		L	
10/01	Union (Morrisania, NY)	8	6	W		
10/08	Union (Morrisania, NY)	33	26	W		
10/11	Eagle (New York)	32	22	W		
10/19	Newark (Newark)	27	5	W		

EXCELSIOR (cont.)
Brooklyn, NY

BATTER	POS	GP	HL	A	O	R	A	O
George Fletcher	1B,SS,3B,OF	9	24	2	6	25	2	7
George Flanly	2B,1B	9	22	2	4	28	3	1
J. Patchen	SS,OF	10	29	2	9	20	2	0
John Clyne	3B,1B	11	36	3	3	25	2	3
Moore	OF	8	27	3	3	19	2	3
Langley	OF,3B	7	17	2	4	17	2	4
Dakin	OF,P	6	14	2	2	20	3	2
H. Brainard	C,2B	10	25	2	5	36	3	6
Asa Brainard	P,2B	10	31	3	1	24	2	4

KNICKERBOCKER   8 - 6
Albany, NY

DATE	OPPONENT	SCORE		W	L	T
06/16	Eckford (Albany)	26	18	W		
07/12	Eckford (Albany)	27	8	W		
07/16	Union College (Albany)	37	8	W		
08/04	Mutual (New York)	16	24		L	
08/25	Empire (New York)	18	32		L	
08/24	Hudson River (Newburgh, NY)	51	11	W		
08/31	Mutual (New York)	29	36		L	
09/22	Union (Green Island, NY)	35	15	W		
10/04	Union (Green Island, NY)	24	14	W		
10/08	Utica (Utica)	32	28	W		
10/26	Utica (Utica)	22	31		L	
11/22	Resolute (Brooklyn)	11	16		L	
---/---	Enterprise (Troy)	48	11	W		
---/---	Star (Brooklyn)	--	--		L	

BATTER	POS	GP	HL	A	O	R	A	O
Winne	1B	8	25	3	1	19	2	3
Umpleby	2B	8	18	2	2	23	2	7
Turner	SS,OF	5	14	2	4	11	2	1
Delavarge	3B,C	5	12	2	2	15	3	0
Corey	OF,1B	8	21	2	5	22	2	6
Lathrop	OF	7	18	2	4	21	3	0
McDonald	OF,SS	5	10	2	0	19	3	4
Gardner	C,3B	7	18	2	4	27	3	6
Ford	P	8	29	3	5	15	1	7

EMPIRE   7 - 13 - 2
New York, NY

DATE	OPPONENT	SCORE		W	L	T
06/11	Active (New York)	29	16	W		
06/21	Eagle (New York)	19	10	W		
06/30	Atlantic (Brooklyn)	13	13			T
07/08	Atlantic (Brooklyn)	8	33		L	
07/13	Active (New York)	16	37		L	
07/20	Mutual (New York)	12	24		L	
07/26	Gotham (New York)	13	22		L	
07/27	Mutual (New York)	16	20		L	
08/---	Union (Morrisania, NY)	16	23		L	
08/02	Enterprise (Brooklyn)	18	13	W		
08/25	Knickerbocker (Albany)	32	18	W		
08/26	Eckford (Albany)	45	10	W		
08/31	Union (Morrisania, NY)	16	23		L	
09/---	Hudson River (Newburgh, NY)	25	28		L	
09/21	Enterprise (Brooklyn)	23	11	W		

EMPIRE (cont.)
New York, NY

DATE	OPPONENT	SCORE		W	L	T
09/28	Mutual (New York)	8	13		L	
10/05	Active (New York)	3	9		L	
10/11	Gotham (New York)	12	12			T
10/19	Atlantic (Brooklyn)	7	15		L	
---/---	Eureka (Newark)	--	--		L	
---/---	New York Cricket Club (New York)	--	--	W		
---/---	Eureka (Newark)	--	--		L	

BATTER	POS	GP	HL	A	O	R	A	O
Miller	1B	19	52	2	14	41	2	3
Ryder	2B,3B,C	22	59	2	15	51	2	7
Russell	SS,OF,2B	16	47	2	15	22	1	6
Westervelt	3B,OF,2B	21	56	2	14	54	2	12
Wilson	OF,3B,2B	21	55	2	13	48	2	6
Ed Ward	OF,P	11	36	3	3	20	1	9
Sebring	OF,P,1B	8	23	2	7	12	1	4
Nat Jewett	C,SS	17	55	3	4	24	1	7
William Bell	P,OF	21	70	3	7	41	1	20
Simms	1B,OF,3B	8	22	2	6	19	2	3
Al Martin	2B,OF,P	7	23	3	2	12	1	5
Reeves	3B,OF	5	10	2	0	13	2	3
Benson	SS,OF,C	5	15	3	0	7	1	2
Snow	OF	5	18	3	3	6	1	1

HUDSON RIVER   6 - 4
Newburgh, NY

DATE	OPPONENT	SCORE		W	L	T
08/24	Knickerbocker (Albany)	11	51		L	
09/02	Mutual (New York)	11	18		L	
09/17	Star (Brooklyn)	26	27		L	
09/---	Empire (New York)	28	25	W		
10/---	Resolute (Brooklyn)	23	12	W		
---/---	Goshen (Goshen, NY)	--	--	W		
---/---	Poughkeepsie (Poughkeepsie, NY)	--	--	W		
---/---	Enterprise (Troy, NY)	--	--	W		
---/---	Orange County (Orange County, NY)	--	--	W		
---/---	Picked Nine (Orange County, NY)	--	--		L	

BATTER	POS	GP	HL	A	O	R	A	O
Kelly	1B,2B,P	10	28	2	8	27	2	7
Halsey	2B,SS	7	18	2	4	28	4	0
Fisher	SS	7	26	3	5	19	2	5
S.W. Miller	3B,2B	11	28	2	6	41	3	8
Millspaugh	OF,1B	11	26	2	4	44	4	0
Adams	OF	8	23	2	7	33	4	1
Andy Leonard	OF,2B,1B	5	17	3	2	8	1	3
Boyd	C	10	31	3	1	28	2	8
Mapes	P,OF	11	33	3	0	39	3	6

ACTIVE   5 - 4
New York, NY

DATE	OPPONENT	SCORE		W	L	T
06/11	Empire (New York)	16	29		L	
07/04	Eureka (Newark)	29	27	W		
07/13	Empire (New York)	37	16	W		

ACTIVE (cont.)
New York, NY

DATE	OPPONENT	SCORE		W	L	T
07/27	Eagle (New York)	20	18	W		
08/26	Mutual (New York)	3	22		L	
09/14	Eureka (Newark)	10	11		L	
09/21	Mutual (New York)	8	14		L	
10/05	Empire (New York)	9	3	W		
10/27	Rose Hill (Fordham, NY)	32	16	W		

BATTER	POS	GP	HL	A	O	R	A	O
Rogers	1B,OF	8	26	3	2	17	2	1
Seaver Page	2B	7	18	2	4	16	2	2
Stoutenberg	SS	5	17	3	2	8	1	3
William Rooney	3B,SS,C,OF,1B	8	25	3	1	15	1	7
Hibbard	OF	8	24	3	0	17	2	1
Simonson	OF,3B	6	20	3	2	14	2	2
Vanderwerken	OF,C	6	18	3	0	9	1	3
William Kelley	C	5	13	2	3	6	1	1
Charley Walker	P	8	22	2	6	11	1	3

UNION 4 - 3
Morrisania, NY

DATE	OPPONENT	SCORE		W	L	T
08/---	Empire (New York)	23	16	W		
08/17	Newark (Newark)	8	10		L	
08/31	Empire (New York)	23	16	W		
09/20	Resolute (Brooklyn)	26	19	W		
10/01	Excelsior (Brooklyn)	6	8		L	
10/08	Excelsior (Brooklyn)	26	33		L	
---/---	Resolute (Brooklyn)	--	--	W		

BATTER	POS	GP	HL	A	O	R	A	O
Dave Birdsall		7	19	2	5	19	2	5
Bernard Hannegan		7	17	2	3	18	2	4
E. Durell		7	19	2	5	15	2	1
W.F. Hudson		6	15	2	3	15	2	3
Sammy Collins		6	19	3	1	11	1	5
William Abrams		5	15	3	0	10	2	0
Bogle		5	12	2	2	6	1	1

EUREKA 4 - 4
Newark, NJ

DATE	OPPONENT	SCORE		W	L	T
07/04	Active (New York)	27	29		L	
07/06	Atlantic (Brooklyn)	13	25		L	
07/07	Nassau (Princeton, NJ)	24	12	W		
08/02	Mutual (New York)	10	16		L	
09/14	Active (New York)	11	10	W		
---/---	Empire (New York)	--	--	W		
---/---	Empire (New York)	--	--	W		
---/---	Mutual (New York)	--	--		L	

BATTER	POS	GP	HL	A	O	R	A	O
Harry Northrup	1B	7	18	2	4	19	2	5
Charles Thomas	SS,P	7	17	2	3	20	2	6
H. Brientnall	C,OF	7	19	2	5	16	2	2
Fred Calloway	OF,3B	7	23	3	2	14	2	0

EUREKA (cont.)
Newark, NJ

BATTER	POS	GP	HL	A	O	R	A	O
A. Littlewood	OF	7	22	3	1	13	1	6
Ev Mills	3B,1B	7	19	2	5	9	1	2
Burroughs	P,SS	7	23	3	2	9	1	2
Ted Bomeisler	OF,2B,C	6	20	3	2	8	1	2

STAR 3 - 4
Brooklyn, NY

DATE	OPPONENT	SCORE		W	L	T
05/21	Field Nine (Brooklyn)	19	21		L	
07/05	Nassau (Princeton, NJ)	22	26		L	
07/30	Atlantic (Brooklyn)	16	35		L	
08/04	Atlantic (Brooklyn)	17	35		L	
09/17	Hudson River (Newburgh, NY)	27	26	W		
09/26	Resolute (Brooklyn)	16	12	W		
---/---	Knickerbocker (Albany, NY)	--	--	W		

BATTER	POS	GP	HL	A	O	R	A	O
Lennon	1B,OF	5	19	3	4	5	1	0
Worth	2B,OF	5	13	2	3	13	2	3
Pete Flanders	SS	7	21	3	0	16	2	2
Mitchell	3B,OF	7	14	2	0	23	3	2
Tom McDiarmid	OF,2B,3B	9	26	2	8	21	2	3
Thompson	OF,C	6	18	3	0	11	1	5
C. Morris	OF	5	16	3	1	14	2	4
Frank Norton	C,OF	7	17	2	3	17	2	3
Kelly	P	8	18	2	2	18	2	2

EAGLE 3 - 6
New York, NY

DATE	OPPONENT	SCORE		W	L	T
06/21	Empire (New York)	10	19		L	
07/01	Gotham (New York)	16	22		L	
07/14	Mutual (New York)	8	39		L	
07/20	Atlantic (Brooklyn)	12	45		L	
07/27	Active (New York)	18	30		L	
08/30	Eckford (Brooklyn)	16	14	W		
09/12	Resolute (Brooklyn)	34	23	W		
10/11	Excelsior (Brooklyn)	22	32		L	
---/---	New York Cricket Club (New York)	--	--	W		

BATTER	POS	GP	HL	A	O	R	A	O
Clarke		10	25	2	5	23	2	3
Collins		7	20	2	6	16	2	2
R. Sloat		6	15	2	3	15	2	3
Salisbury		6	15	2	3	13	2	1
N.B. Shaffer		6	20	3	2	10	1	4
Bogart		6	19	3	1	10	1	4
Sam Yates		5	15	3	0	13	2	3
Chapin		5	17	3	2	6	1	1

1864

NEWARK 3 - 6
Newark, NJ

DATE	OPPONENT	SCORE		W	L	T
06/20	Mutual (New York)	18	19		L	
07/08	Gotham (New York)	12	25		L	
07/21	Eckford (Brooklyn)	22	37		L	
08/10	Excelsior (Brooklyn)	20	24		L	
08/17	Union (Morrisania, NY)	10	8	W		
08/30	Gotham (New York)	18	14	W		
09/10	Excelsior (Brooklyn)	35	19	W		
09/14	Mutual (New York)	10	24		L	
10/19	Excelsior (Brooklyn)	5	27		L	

BATTER	POS	GP	HL	A	O	R	A	O
Thorne	1B,OF	9	25	2	7	20	2	2
Joe Tyrell	2B	9	22	2	4	17	1	8
Mahlon Stockman	SS,C,2B	8	30	3	6	13	1	5
Eaton	3B,SS	6	16	2	4	14	2	2
Lewis	OF	10	23	2	3	25	2	5
R. Stout	OF,1B	4	13	3	1	5	1	1
McFarland	OF,SS	4	11	2	3	7	1	3
Osborne	C	7	15	2	1	17	2	3
T. Buckley	P,2B	9	26	2	8	17	1	8

GOTHAM 3 - 7 - 1
New York, NY

DATE	OPPONENT	SCORE		W	L	T
07/01	Eagle (New York)	22	16	W		
07/08	Newark (Newark)	25	12	W		
07/26	Empire (New York)	22	13	W		
07/---	Newark (Newark)	10	44		L	
08/12	Mutual (New York)	7	23		L	
08/23	Atlantic (Brooklyn)	9	14		L	
08/30	Newark (Newark)	14	18		L	
09/09	Enterprise (Brooklyn)	11	17		L	
09/19	Atlantic (Brooklyn)	12	38		L	
10/02	Mutual (New York)	10	12		L	
10/11	Empire (New York)	12	12			T

BATTER	POS	GP	HL	A	O	R	A	O
Harry Wright	1B,SS,3B	7	8	2	4	14	2	0
Andrew Gibney	2B	9	24	2	6	19	2	1
Squires	SS	6	19	3	1	8	1	2
Cohen	3B,2B,OF	6	20	3	2	18	1	2
Stokem	OF	6	18	3	0	13	2	1
Patsy Dockney	OF,C	6	17	2	5	12	2	0
Ed Beadle	OF,1B	6	18	3	0	9	1	3
George Wright	C	8	19	2	3	19	2	3
Dick Thorn	P	9	25	2	7	13	1	4

RESOLUTE 3 - 11
Brooklyn, NY

DATE	OPPONENT	SCORE		W	L	T
07/18	Atlantic (Brooklyn)	1	18		L	
07/28	Athletic (Philadelphia)	12	29		L	
07/29	Camden (Camden, NJ)	13	14		L	
07/29	Keystone (Philadelphia)	32	20	W		
07/30	Olympic (Philadelphia)	23	24		L	
09/01	Atlantic (Brooklyn)	6	53		L	

RESOLUTE (cont.)
Brooklyn, NY

DATE	OPPONENT	SCORE		W	L	T
09/12	Eagle (New York)	23	34		L	
09/20	Union (Morrisania, NY)	19	26		L	
09/26	Star (Brooklyn)	12	16		L	
10/---	Hudson River (Newburgh, NY)	12	23		L	
10/---	Monitor (Goshen, NY)	22	36		L	
11/22	Knickerbocker (Albany)	16	11	W		
---/---	Field Nine (Brooklyn)	--	--	W		
---/---	Union (Morrisania, NY)	--	--		L	

BATTER	POS	GP	HL	A	O	R	A	O
Carhart	1B,3B,SS	7	19	2	5	16	2	2
J. Weeden	2B	10	37	3	7	13	1	3
J. Wilson	SS,OF	9	28	3	1	12	1	3
T. Allen	3B	8	20	2	4	19	2	3
G. Wilson	OF,3B	13	37	2	11	25	1	12
Stearns	OF,2B,3B	10	31	3	1	18	1	8
Creagh	OF	6	13	2	1	10	1	4
J.S. Lockwood	C,OF	11	32	2	10	19	1	8
Mort Rogers	P	16	40	2	8	39	2	7
Bush	1B,OF	7	20	2	6	10	1	3
Bowie	1B	6	21	3	3	11	1	5
W. Warnock	SS	6	15	2	3	8	1	2

ECKFORD   1 - 4
Brooklyn, NY

DATE	OPPONENT	SCORE		W	L	T
06/07	Field Nine (Brooklyn)	18	24		L	
07/21	Newark (Newark)	37	22	W		
08/22	Mutual (New York)	17	29		L	
08/30	Eagle (New York)	14	16		L	
10/10	Mutual (New York)	19	23		L	

BATTER	POS	GP	HL	A	O	R	A	O
Harry Manolt		5	10	2	0	14	2	4
Brown		5	13	2	3	14	2	4
C.C. Smith		5	12	2	2	13	2	3
Marty Swandell		5	19	3	4	8	1	3
James Wood		4	9	2	1	16	4	0
A. Mills		4	11	2	3	11	2	3
Al Reach		4	9	2	1	11	2	3
Josh Snyder		4	10	2	2	9	2	1

ENTERPRISE   1 - 4
Brooklyn, NY

DATE	OPPONENT	SCORE		W	L	T
07/16	Excelsior (Brooklyn)	19	25		L	
08/02	Empire (New York)	13	18		L	
08/13	Excelsior (Brooklyn)	6	33		L	
09/09	Gotham (New York)	17	11	W		
09/21	Empire (New York)	11	23		L	

BATTER	POS	GP	HL	A	O	R	A	O
W. Cornwell		6	18	3	0	14	2	2
W. H. Murtha		5	14	2	4	6	1	1

ENTERPRISE (cont.)
Brooklyn, NY

BATTER	POS	GP	HL	A	O	R	A	O
Leland		4	7	1	3	9	2	1
Flynn		4	13	3	1	8	2	0
O'Neil		4	9	2	1	6	1	2
R. Cornwell		4	15	3	3	5	1	1

TEAM TOTALS

TEAM	CITY/STATE	GP	W	L	T	PCT	R	OR
Atlantic	Brooklyn, NY	21	20	0	1	.976	817	227
Mutual	New York, NY	23	20	3	0	.870	512	321
Athletic	Philadelphia, PA	9	8	1	0	.889	289	136
Excelsior	Brooklyn, NY	11	8	3	0	.727	261	208
Knickerbocker	Albany, NY	14	8	6	0	.571	376	252
Empire	New York, NY	22	7	13	2	.364	391	398
Hudson River	Newburgh, NY	10	6	4	0	.600	332	242
Active	New York, NY	9	5	4	0	.556	164	156
Union	Morrisania, NY	7	4	3	0	.571	136	113
Eureka	Newark, NJ	8	4	4	0	.500	120	114
Star	Brooklyn, NY	7	3	4	0	.429	147	162
Eagle	New York, NY	9	3	6	0	.333	173	218
Newark	Newark, NJ	9	3	6	0	.333	150	197
Gotham	New York, NY	11	3	7	1	.318	154	219
Resolute	Brooklyn, NY	14	3	11	0	.214	213	309
National	Washington, DC	3	2	1	0	.667	83	66
Eckford	Brooklyn, NY	5	1	4	0	.200	105	114
Enterprise	Brooklyn, NY	5	1	4	0	.200	66	110
Keystone	Philadelphia, PA	7	1	6	0	.143	102	212

OTHER TEAMS

TEAM	CITY/STATE
Constellation	Brooklyn, NY
Hamilton	Brooklyn, NY
Henry Eckford	New York, NY
Jefferson	New York, NY
Metropolitan	New York, NY
Monitor	Goshen, NY
Mystic	New York, NY
New York	New York, NY
Olympic	S. Brooklyn, NY

1865
THE ATLANTICS OF BROOKLYN

Since the game of baseball developed in the New York/Brooklyn area, it was no great surprise that many of the country's top clubs emerged from that locale. In the 1840s and 1850s, New York's Knickerbocker club bested most opponents. As the 1850s gave way to the 1860s the Excelsior and Eckford nines from Brooklyn dominated play with the Eckford club enjoying an undefeated season in 1863. With the decade of the 1860s reaching its middle portions, another Brooklyn squad reached the peak of excellence. This team, resplendent in light blue pants with white flannel shirts emblazoned with an Old English "A," was known as the Atlantic club.

The Atlantic club was created in the summer of 1855 in the Bedford section of Brooklyn. Its membership was formed, according to club historian F. Prescott Rivers, "...by a number of good natured youths, who liking something more lively than cricket, chose this then youthful game." In the fall of the same year, the new team played their first matches against the Harmony club, winning both 24–22 and 27–10. The next summer they doubled their output, besting all four of their opponents.

In 1857, the Atlantic club was one of the 16 New York area teams which sent delegates to the first meeting organizing the teams. The following year, they were a charter member of the National Association.

On the field, the Atlantic nine continued to dominate the opposition. From 1857 through 1863 they beat 52 of 65 opponents—a winning percentage of .800. During these years, they were recognized as the Association's champion from 1859–1861.

During the 1864 season, the Atlantics reached full powerhouse status. Playing its longest schedule to date, the team snatched the pennant back from their cross-town rivals, the Eckfords. In 21 games, the Atlantic nine tasted defeat nary once as they won 20 with one tie. This mark was the Association's best up to this time. Good as this was, the club would surpass even this lofty total the very next year.

The Atlantics' success on the diamond was a direct result of their superior personnel. Batters like their shortstop Dickey Pearce and third baseman Charles Smith were near the top of the statistical charts virtually every year. When big first baseman Joe Start joined the club in 1862, the team had its first legitimate power-hitter. Start would hold down the firstbase position for many years, earning him the sobriquet "Old Reliable."

Joining the Atlantics for the 1865 National Association season were 29 other clubs—all attendees at the December 1864 annual meeting. At this meeting, it was determined that only matches against other Association clubs would count for both statistical and championship purposes.

The Brooklyn champions came flying out of the gate in 1865 winning their first five Association matches with ease. Their first real test came on August 3rd when they tilted with New York's Mutual club. Rain notwithstanding, several thousand spectators were on hand to witness the event. Leading 12–8 after four, the Brooklyn nine plated a run in the top of the fifth only to see the Mutuals score four of their own in the bottom. While playing the sixth inning, the rain turned into a downpour, thus washing out any possibility of a complete game. The score then reverted back to the fifth inning making the Atlantics the grateful beneficiary of a 13–12 win.

Nine days later, the champions had another narrow escape. Playing the Eurekas of Newark, the Atlantic club watched the New Jerseyites nearly overcome a six-run last inning lead before hanging on to a 21–20 decision. It was with some trepidation then that the Atlantic club awaited their rematch with the Eurekas.

In late August, the rematch occurred. The *New York Clipper* described the action:

> On Thursday the 31st ult., the champions had another very narrow escape from defeat. They had just returned from Washington and were entirely jaded out. So little sleep had they enjoyed for several days that one of them fell asleep while waiting his turn at the bat. Of course, under such circumstances, good play could scarcely be expected from them. Nevertheless, by perseverance, they succeeded in winning the game, though only by *one* run.

This time, like a true champion, the Atlantic club scored four in the bottom of the ninth to win 38–37.

The club cruised through the rest of the campaign, finishing with an 18–0 record against Association teams with another six wins versus non-Association foes. This was the best record shown in baseball to this date. More importantly, it marked the second year in a row the Atlantic club had finished the season unscathed.

One jarring note marked the end of the Association season which illustrated a disturbing part of the game. On the 28th of September, the heavily favored Mutuals lost to the Eckfords 23–11 in a game marked by loose New York fielding, including 10 miscues by Mutual catcher Bill Wansley. Many of the attendees smelled a rat, suspecting that all was not square. When pressed, Wansley admitted that he, shortstop Tom Devyr and third baseman Ed Duffy had accepted a substantial bribe from gamblers to throw the game.

In the early days of baseball, gambling was an unfortunate adjunct to the game. While attending games, seasoned wagerers would bark out the odds for all to hear. Substantial money would then change hands as a result of a batter's performance or the contest's outcome. Quite often, the players themselves would be involved, which tainted the purity of competition as well as altering the final score.

After a hearing, Wansley, Devyr and Duffy were booted out of the Association. To the chagrin of many, Devyr was reinstated two years later as Association resolve wilted under pressure from the powerful Mutual club.

The 1865 Atlantics were led by Joe Start and Charles Smith who both scored more than four runs per game. As a matter of fact, the entire starting nine averaged over three runs per game. This was not surprising considering the Atlantics outscored their opponents 32–15 per game.

The Atlantics' main competitor in 1865 was the Athletics of Philadelphia whom they played twice. The first tilt came in October when the Atlantics prevailed 21–15. The rematch one week later, played before thousands in Philadelphia, saw another close Atlantic win, 27–24. The Athletic squad only lost one other game the rest of the season, finishing 15–3.

Most of the Association's top batters graced the Atlantic roster. The top three run getters Joe Start (82), Fred Crane (71), and Charles Smith (70) all held positions in the team's infield. Two of the three best averages were also posted by Atlantics: Start (4,10) and Smith (4,6) who finished second and third. The top average belonged to Mitchell (5,1) who played for the Star club.

In the years to come, the Atlantics continued to be one of the Association's top clubs, winning two more titles in the 1860s, before sliding from the top perch. However, never again would they finish the season undefeated.

The Atlantic club's legacy was twofold. Firstly, their run of success in the mid–1860s was unprecedented. From September 8, 1863, to June 14, 1866, the club never lost—a span of 49 games (including non–Association games). Secondly, their overall winning percentage of .862 easily put them in the top five of all Association teams.

Peverelly's account in *The National Game* summed up the success of the Atlantic nine:

> Unlike many of its kindred associations, who place a strong nine in the field for one summer, and perhaps a weak body of players for the ensuing season, the Atlantics have always and at all times had a nine from whom any rival club might almost despair of winning any lasting laurels. It is this extraordinary and unvarying success which has gained for them the title of 'Champion'.

ATLANTIC
Brooklyn, NY   18 - 0

DATE	OPPONENT	SCORE		W	L	T
06/21	Empire (New York)	21	10	W		
07/14	Gotham (New York)	38	21	W		
07/24	Union (Morrisania, NY)	15	5	W		
07/27	Empire (New York)	65	3	W		
07/29	Keystone (Philadelphia)	33	13	W		
08/03	Mutual (New York)	13	12	W		
08/10	Star (Brooklyn)	26	13	W		
08/14	Mutual (New York)	40	28	W		
08/18	Eureka (Newark)	21	20	W		
08/23	Active (New York)	24	19	W		
08/28	Eagle (New York)	48	10	W		
08/29	National (Washington)	33	19	W		
08/31	Eureka (Newark)	38	37	W		
09/21	Eckford (Brooklyn)	28	23	W		
10/05	Union (Morrisania, NY)	58	30	W		
10/13	Eckford (Brooklyn)	35	8	W		
10/30	Athletic (Philadelphia)	21	15	W		
11/06	Athletic (Philadelphia)	27	24	W		

BATTER	POS	GP	HL	A	O	R	A	O
Joe Start	1B	18	39	2	3	82	4	10
Fred Crane	2B,3B	18	42	2	6	71	3	17
John Galvin	SS,OF,2B,3B	14	39	2	11	45	3	3
Charles Smith	3B	16	40	2	8	70	4	6
Peter O'Brien	OF	15	48	3	3	46	3	1
Sid Smith	OF	16	50	3	2	51	3	3
John Chapman	OF,P,3B	18	54	3	0	67	3	13
Dickey Pearce	C,SS,2B	17	55	3	4	64	3	13
Tom Pratt	P	13	37	2	11	44	3	5

ATHLETIC
Philadelphia, PA   15 - 3

DATE	OPPONENT	SCORE		W	L	T
06/08	Keystone (Philadelphia)	21	12	W		
06/12	Eureka (Newark)	12	9	W		
06/13	Eagle (New York)	24	14	W		
06/14	Union (Morrisania, NY)	31	21	W		
06/15	Resolute (Brooklyn)	39	14	W		
06/16	Gotham (New York)	28	20	W		
07/01	Resolute (Brooklyn)	46	12	W		
07/04	Star (Brooklyn)	25	14	W		
08/03	Union (Morrisania, NY)	26	13	W		
08/08	Eureka (Newark)	38	28	W		
08/10	Active (New York)	13	28		L	
08/23	Empire (New York)	40	28	W		
08/28	National (Washington)	87	12	W		
09/20	Mountain (Altoona)*	41	16	W		
10/11	Excelsior (Brooklyn)	45	11	W		
10/30	Atlantic (Brooklyn)	15	21		L	
11/06	Atlantic (Brooklyn)	24	27		L	
11/11	Keystone (Philadelphia)	49	5	W		

* Box score not available

BATTER	POS	GP	HL	A	O	R	A	O
Nate Berkenstock	1B	15	38	2	8	59	3	14
Al Reach	2B	15	44	2	14	57	3	12
Isaac Wilkins	SS,P	11	39	3	6	36	3	3
Mike Smith	3B,OF	12	31	2	1	60	4	0
Charles Gaskill	OF	11	37	3	4	39	3	6
Luengene	OF,2B,SS,3B,1B	16	52	3	4	47	2	15

ATHLETIC (cont.)
Philadelphia, PA

BATTER	POS	GP	HL	A O	R	A O
Hicks Hayhurst	OF	10	30	3 0	31	3 7
Dan Kleinfelder	C,3B	15	51	3 6	54	3 9
Dick McBride	P,SS	15	31	2 1	60	4 0

UNION 13 - 10
Morrisania, NY

DATE	OPPONENT	SCORE	W	L	T
06/14	Athletic (Philadelphia)	21 31		L	
06/21	Eckford (Brooklyn)	27 8	W		
06/30	Pioneer (Newark)	18 13	W		
07/04	Active (New York)	25 16	W		
07/08	Eureka (Newark)	5 30		L	
07/15	Excelsior (Brooklyn)	14 43		L	
07/24	Atlantic (Brooklyn)	5 15		L	
07/28	Newark (Newark)	30 8	W		
08/03	Athletic (Philadelphia)	13 26		L	
08/05	Keystone (Philadelphia)	24 7	W		
08/10	Eckford (Brooklyn)	34 22	W		
08/19	Active (New York)	12 22		L	
09/01	Newark (Newark)	18 17	W		
09/07	Eureka (Newark)	10 30		L	
09/13	Mystic (New York)	54 9	W		
09/15	Excelsior (Brooklyn)	34 35		L	
09/23	Active (New York)	10 32		L	
09/25	Star (Brooklyn)	37 12	W		
10/05	Atlantic (Brooklyn)	30 58		L	
10/11	Mystic (New York)	55 19	W		
10/14	Star (Brooklyn)	57 21	W		
11/10	Hudson River (Newburgh, NY)	21 13	W		
---/---	Pioneer (Newark)	31 9	W		

BATTER	POS	GP	HL	A O	R	A O
George Smith	1B	21	53	2 11	65	3 2
Charley Pabor	2B,OF	14	48	3 2	18	1 4
Bernard Hannegan	SS,2B,OF,3B	21	55	2 13	64	3 1
Nicholson	3B,2B	17	46	2 12	39	2 5
E. Durell	OF,2B	18	52	2 16	42	2 6
W.F. Hudson	OF,2B,SS	19	46	2 8	63	3 6
Dan Ketchum	OF,SS	19	47	2 9	50	2 12
Dave Birdsall	C,P	21	62	2 20	48	2 6
Sammy Collins	P	8	22	2 6	16	2 0
William Abrams	OF,3B	8	31	3 7	11	1 3
Henry Austin	2B,OF	7	20	2 6	20	2 6

MUTUAL 12 - 4
New York, NY

DATE	OPPONENT	SCORE	W	L	T
06/28	Empire (New York)	12 5	W		
07/11	Gotham (New York)	27 4	W		
07/20	Empire (New York)	26 15	W		
07/25	Keystone (Philadelphia)	31 12	W		
07/31	Eureka (Newark)	27 12	W		
08/03	Atlantic (Brooklyn)	12 13		L	

MUTUAL (cont.)
New York, NY

DATE	OPPONENT	SCORE			W	L	T
08/10	Hudson River (Newburgh, NY)	34	14		W		
08/14	Atlantic (Brooklyn)	28	40			L	
08/22	Gotham (New York)	18	12		W		
08/25	Eckford (Brooklyn)	19	10		W		
08/30	Active (New York)	22	21	(11)	W		
09/14	Eureka (Newark)	19	20			L	
09/21	Active (New York)	26	20		W		
09/22	Hudson River (Newburgh, NY)	36	23		W		
09/28	Eckford (Brooklyn)	11	23			L	
10/30	Eagle (New York)	18	7		W		

BATTER	POS	GP	HL	A	O	R	A	O
John Goldie	1B	13	34	2	8	38	2	12
Ed Brown	2B	11	29	2	7	34	3	1
Tom Devyr	SS	10	31	3	1	22	2	2
Ed Duffy	3B	11	32	2	10	29	2	7
John Zeller	OF	14	37	2	9	37	2	9
Dan Patterson	OF,2B	13	42	3	3	32	2	6
Charles Hunt	OF,SS,1B	6	16	2	4	14	2	2
Bill Wansley	C,2B	11	36	3	3	27	2	5
Dick Thorn	P	9	28	3	1	16	1	7
Harris	P,OF	8	28	3	4	12	1	4

ACTIVE 10 - 7
New York, NY

DATE	OPPONENT	SCORE			W	L	T
06/13	Newark (Newark)	12	11		W		
06/24	Resolute (Brooklyn)	37	26		W		
07/04	Union (Morrisania, NY)	16	35			L	
07/08	Empire (New York)	15	21			L	
07/29	Enterprise (Brooklyn)	27	12		W		
08/10	Athletic (Philadelphia)	28	13		W		
08/19	Union (Morrisania, NY)	22	12		W		
08/23	Atlantic (Brooklyn)	19	24			L	
08/30	Mutual (New York)	21	22	(11)		L	
09/02	Enterprise (Brooklyn)	28	18		W		
09/15	Eagle (New York)	54	9		W		
09/21	Mutual (New York)	20	26			L	
09/23	Union (Morrisania, NY)	32	10		W		
09/29	Gotham (New York)	23	9		W		
10/07	Empire (New York)	24	15		W		
10/20	Eureka (Newark)	3	6			L	
11/24	Gotham (New York)	24	30			L	

BATTER	POS	GP	HL	A	O	R	A	O
William Rooney	1B	16	41	2	9	46	2	14
Seaver Page	2B	15	36	2	6	58	3	13
Mahlon Stockman	SS	12	44	3	8	27	3	3
G. Rooney	3B,SS	14	41	2	9	46	2	14
George Ebbetts	OF,C	13	31	2	5	41	3	2
Rogers	OF,3B,1B	14	53	3	11	30	2	2
Vanderwerken	OF	8	30	3	6	19	2	3
William Kelley	C	16	42	2	10	44	2	12
Charley Walker	P	14	41	2	13	30	2	2
Crawford		6	15	2	3	19	3	1
Hibbard	OF,SS	6	13	2	1	17	2	5
John Hatfield	OF	5	15	3	0	12	2	2

EUREKA 9 - 5
Newark, NJ

DATE	OPPONENT	SCORE		W	L	T
06/12	Athletic (Philadelphia)	9	12		L	
07/08	Union (Morrisania, NY)	30	5	W		
07/24	Keystone (Philadelphia)	50	11	W		
07/31	Mutual (New York)	12	27		L	
08/08	Athletic (Philadelphia)	28	38		L	
08/18	Atlantic (Brooklyn)	20	21		L	
08/24	Pioneer (Newark)	12	5	W		
08/31	Atlantic (Brooklyn)	37	38		L	
09/07	Union (Morrisania, NY)	30	10	W		
09/14	Mutual (New York)	20	19	W		
10/05	Americus (Newark)	85	12	W		
10/20	Active (New York)	6	3	W		
---/---	Pioneer (Newark)	--	--	W		
---/---	Newark (Newark)	--	--	W		

BATTER	POS	GP	H	L	A	O	R	A	O
Ev Mills	1B	14	38		2	10	45	3	3
Ted Bomeisler	2B,C,3B	14	42		3	0	42	3	0
Charles Thomas	SS	10	27		2	7	33	3	3
Harry Northrup	3B,OF	10	30		3	0	32	3	2
Fred Calloway	OF	14	42		3	0	52	3	10
Collins	OF,3B	11	40		3	7	35	3	2
A. Littlewood	OF	11	34		3	1	30	2	8
H. Brientnall	C	13	35		2	9	43	3	4
Faitoute	P	14	37		2	9	39	2	11
Albert Pennington	2B	6	16		2	4	15	2	3
Fryatt	OF	5	15		3	0	21	4	1

ECKFORD 8 - 6
Brooklyn, NY

DATE	OPPONENT	SCORE		W	L	T
06/21	Union (Morrisania, NY)	18	27		L	
06/30	Newark (Newark)	22	5	W		
07/14	Eagle (New York)	38	7	W		
07/26	Keystone (Philadelphia)	16	18		L	
08/02	Empire (New York)	48	35	W		
08/09	Union (Morrisania, NY)	22	34		L	
08/25	Mutual (New York)	10	19		L	
08/28	Enterprise (Brooklyn)	21	20	W		
09/05	Gotham (New York)	18	9	W		
09/13	Enterprise (Brooklyn)	26	25	W		
09/21	Atlantic (Brooklyn)	23	28		L	
09/28	Mutual (New York)	23	11	W		
10/10	Empire (New York)	32	8	W		
10/13	Atlantic (Brooklyn)	8	35		L	

BATTER	POS	GP	H	L	A	O	R	A	O
Klein	1B,3B	13	35		2	9	35	2	9
George Fox	2B,3B	9	25		2	2	23	2	5
George Grum	SS,P,2B	9	24		2	6	28	3	1
A. Mills	3B,1B	11	23		2	1	35	3	2
Marty Swandell	OF	13	45		3	6	27	2	1
Butler	OF	8	21		2	5	23	2	7
Harry Manolt	OF	7	20		2	6	21	3	0
Charley Mills	C	14	40		2	12	33	2	5
George Zettlein	P	8	31		3	7	13	1	5
Farrell	P,SS	7	16		2	2	24	3	3
John Snyder	3B,OF	6	17		2	5	16	2	4
Ed Pinkham	2B,OF	5	18		3	3	9	1	4

EMPIRE 7 - 9
New York, NY

DATE	OPPONENT	SCORE		W	L	T
06/17	Mystic (New York)	42	5	W		
06/21	Atlantic (Brooklyn)	10	21		L	
06/28	Mutual (New York)	5	12		L	
07/08	Active (New York)	21	15	W		
07/12	Resolute (Brooklyn)	29	26	W		
07/20	Mutual (New York)	15	26		L	
07/27	Atlantic (Brooklyn)	3	65		L	
08/02	Eckford (Brooklyn)	35	48		L	
08/08	Gotham (New York)	29	6	W		
08/16	Enterprise (Brooklyn)	37	33	W		
08/23	Athletic (Philadelphia)	28	40		L	
08/26	Keystone (Philadelphia)	15	45		L	
09/13	Eagle (New York)	37	6	W		
09/27	Mystic (New York)	50	6	W		
10/10	Eckford (Brooklyn)	8	32		L	
10/11	Active (New York)	15	24		L	

BATTER	POS	GP	HL	A	O	R	A	O
Miller	1B,OF	12	39	3	3	27	2	3
Kelly	2B,C	14	35	2	7	45	3	3
James Ryder	SS,2B	12	40	3	4	24	2	0
Fred Waterman	3B,OF	14	29	2	1	45	3	3
Wilson	OF	16	43	2	11	46	2	14
Ed Ward	OF,SS	13	45	3	6	28	2	2
Duncan	OF,1B,3B	12	32	2	8	32	2	8
Nat Jewett	C,SS	12	35	2	11	33	2	9
Al Martin	P	15	40	2	10	37	2	7
Westervelt	3B,OF	7	16	2	2	20	2	6
Russell	OF,2B	5	13	2	3	18	3	3

HUDSON RIVER 6 - 6
Newburgh, NY

DATE	OPPONENT	SCORE		W	L	T
08/01	Gotham (New York)	5	34		L	
08/07	Enterprise (Brooklyn)	28	38		L	
08/09	Mystic (New York)	34	13	W		
08/10	Mutual (New York)	14	34		L	
08/11	Gotham (New York)	26	29		L	
09/22	Mutual (New York)	23	36		L	
10/07	Eagle (New York)	45	10	W		
11/10	Union (Morrisania, NY)	13	21		L	
11/15	Knickerbocker (Albany)	24	18	W		
---/---	Monitor (Goshen)	--	--	W		
---/---	Mystic (New York)	--	--	W		
---/---	Enterprise (?)	--	--	W		

BATTER	POS	GP	HL	A	O	R	A	O
Andy Leonard	1B	7	28	4	0	19	2	5
Adams	2B,OF,3B	11	25	2	3	45	4	1
Halsey	SS	11	30	2	8	37	3	4
S.W. Miller	3B,OF	12	40	3	4	31	2	7
Fisher	OF,2B	12	44	3	8	36	3	0
Lindley	OF,2B,1B	11	26	2	4	38	3	5
Mapes	OF	12	32	2	8	43	3	7
Boyd	C	10	30	3	0	22	2	2
Kelly	P	12	39	3	3	39	3	3
Millspaugh	OF,1B	8	22	2	6	30	3	6

KNICKERBOCKER 5 - 2
Albany, NY

DATE	OPPONENT	SCORE			W	L	T
06/15	National (Albany)	53	15		W		
07/15	Utica (Utica)	27	15		W		
09/21	Resolute (Brooklyn)	13	12		W		
10/05	Utica (Utica)	13	8		W		
10/26	National (Albany)	21	24			L	
11/02	National (Albany)	20	6		W		
11/15	Hudson River (Newburgh, NY)	18	24			L	

BATTER	POS	GP	HL	A	O	R	A	O
Bliss		6	18	3	0	19	3	1
Corey		6	17	2	5	17	2	5
Archie Bush		6	21	3	3	13	2	1
Lamoure		5	12	2	2	16	3	1
Ford		5	18	3	3	14	2	4

GOTHAM 5 - 7
New York, NY

DATE	OPPONENT	SCORE			W	L	T
06/06	Enterprise (Brooklyn)	19	18	(13)	W		
06/16	Athletic (Philadelphia)	20	28			L	
07/11	Mutual (New York)	4	27			L	
07/14	Atlantic (Brooklyn)	21	38			L	
07/18	Eagle (New York)	38	16		W		
08/01	Hudson River (Newburgh, NY)	34	5		W		
08/08	Empire (New York)	6	29			L	
08/11	Hudson River (Newburgh, NY)	29	26		W		
08/22	Mutual (New York)	12	18			L	
09/05	Eckford (Brooklyn)	9	18			L	
09/29	Active (New York)	9	25			L	
11/24	Active (New York)	30	24		W		

BATTER	POS	GP	HL	A	O	R	A	O
Ed Beadle	1B,OF	10	33	3	3	23	2	3
Joe Simmons	2B,OF,3B	7	21	3	0	13	1	6
Cohen	SS,3B,2B,C	9	23	2	5	18	2	0
Courtney	3B,OF,2B	5	13	2	3	10	2	0
John Hatfield	OF	7	20	2	6	16	2	3
Harry Wright	OF,SS,P	7	16	2	2	22	3	1
William Wright	OF,3B	5	15	3	0	9	1	4
Patsy Dockney	C	9	25	2	7	26	2	8
Stevens	P,2B	8	25	3	1	11	1	3
Andrew Gibney	2B	5	12	2	2	11	2	1

EXCELSIOR 4 - 3
Brooklyn, NY

DATE	OPPONENT	SCORE		W	L	T
05/20	Pioneer (Newark)	14	32		L	
07/15	Union (Morrisania, NY)	43	14	W		
09/15	Union (Morrisania, NY)	35	34	W		
09/26	Enterprise (Brooklyn)	46	21	W		
10/09	National (Washington)	30	36		L	
10/11	Athletic (Philadelphia	11	45		L	
11/11	Enterprise (Brooklyn)	43	16	W		

EXCELSIOR (cont.)
Brooklyn, NY

BATTER	POS	GP	HL	A	O	R	A	O
John Clyne		7	22	3	1	26	3	5
Asa Brainard		7	20	2	6	25	3	4
George Fletcher		7	15	2	1	24	3	3
Herbert Jewell		6	19	3	1	22	3	4
J. Patchen		6	17	2	5	21	3	3
James Mitchell		6	16	2	4	20	3	2
George Flanly		5	11	2	1	22	4	2
McCullough		5	11	2	1	16	3	1

STAR 4 - 5
Brooklyn, NY

DATE	OPPONENT	SCORE		W	L	T
05/30	Eagle (New York)	31	40		L	
06/24	Enterprise (Brooklyn)	44	36	W		
07/04	Athletic (Philadelphia)	14	25		L	
07/05	Keystone (Philadelphia)	32	31	W		
07/28	Keystone (Philadelphia)	37	34	W		
08/05	Enterprise (Brooklyn)	47	38	W		
08/10	Atlantic (Brooklyn)	13	26		L	
09/25	Union (Morrisania, NY)	12	37		L	
10/14	Union (Morrisania, NY)	21	57		L	

BATTER	POS	GP	HL	A	O	R	A	O
Hope Waddell	1B	8	27	3	3	24	3	0
Tom McDiarmid	2B,OF,C	5	12	2	2	21	4	1
Pete Flanders	SS	9	27	3	0	26	2	8
Bob Manly	3B,1B	8	14	1	6	28	3	4
Herb Worth	OF,2B	9	26	2	8	26	2	8
Mitchell	OF,3B	5	8	1	3	26	5	1
Frank Thompson	OF	6	15	2	3	33	3	5
Norton	C,OF	6	19	3	1	19	3	1
Sullivan	P	9	28	3	1	24	2	6
T. Smith	OF	5	16	3	1	14	2	4

KEYSTONE 4 - 8
Philadelphia, PA

DATE	OPPONENT	SCORE		W	L	T
06/08	Athletic (Philadelphia)	12	21		L	
06/29	Resolute (Brooklyn)	46	16	W		
07/05	Star (Brooklyn)	31	32		L	
07/24	Eureka (Newark)	11	50		L	
07/25	Mutual (New York)	12	31		L	
07/26	Eckford (Brooklyn)	18	16	W		
07/27	Resolute (Brooklyn)	30	15	W		
07/28	Star (Brooklyn)	34	37		L	
07/29	Atlantic (Brooklyn)	13	33		L	
08/05	Union (Morrisania, NY)	7	24		L	
08/26	Empire (New York)	45	15	W		
11/11	Athletic (Philadelphia)	5	49		L	

BATTER	POS	GP	HL	A	O	R	A	O
Mulholland	1B,3B	8	32	4	0	13	1	5
William Wallace	2B,SS	11	33	3	0	20	1	9

KEYSTONE (cont.)
Philadelphia, PA

BATTER	POS	GP	HL	A	O	R	A	O
Eddie Woods	SS,3B,OF	12	30	2	6	33	2	9
Billy Dick	3B,C	12	33	2	9	29	2	5
Brown	OF,P,1B	9	21	2	3	21	2	3
Ned Cuthbert	OF,2B	12	23	1	11	33	2	9
W.M. Deal	OF	8	22	2	6	17	2	1
Fergy Malone	C,3B,P	10	31	3	1	25	2	5
Elias Cope	P,OF,SS	11	23	2	1	34	3	1
F.A. Frazier	OF,1B,2B	7	17	2	3	22	3	1

MYSTIC   4 - 8
New York, NY

DATE	OPPONENT	SCORE		W	L	T
06/17	Empire (New York)	5	42		L	
07/13	Pioneer (Newark)	24	60		L	
08/09	Hudson River (Newburgh, NY)	13	34		L	
08/23	Americus (Newark)	48	30	W		
09/06	Americus (Newark)	39	5	W		
09/13	Union (Morrisania, NY)	9	54		L	
09/27	Empire (New York)	16	50		L	
10/04	Eclectic (New York)	25	23	W		
10/11	Union (Morrisania, NY)	11	55		L	
10/17	Eclectic (New York)	21	35		L	
---/---	Pioneer (Newark)	--	--	W		
---/---	Hudson River (Newburgh, NY)	--	--		L	

BATTER	POS	GP	HL	A	O	R	A	O
T. Dalton	1B,OF,2B	10	25	2	5	25	2	5
W. Glover	2B,OF	9	31	3	4	16	1	7
Tom Haines	SS,P	11	32	2	10	26	2	4
A. Saunders	3B	7	21	3	0	18	2	4
C. Glover	OF,1B	11	30	2	8	30	2	8
Graham	OF,C,SS	7	29	4	1	13	1	6
Manson	OF,C	10	31	3	1	22	2	2
Kelley	C	5	14	2	4	14	2	4
J. Reynolds	P,C,OF	12	26	2	2	37	3	1
R. Clark	3B	5	14	2	4	13	2	3

ECLECTIC   3 - 1 - 1
New York, NY

DATE	OPPONENT	SCORE		W	L	T
09/20	Americus (Newark)	45	6	W		
10/04	Mystic (New York)	23	25		L	
10/12	Americus (Newark)	18	11	W		
10/17	Mystic (New York)	35	21	W		
10/20	Knickerbocker (New York)	31	31			T

BATTER	POS	GP	HL	A	O	R	A	O
Clarke		5	9	1	4	23	4	3
William Bell		5	8	1	3	23	4	3
M. Humphrey		5	13	2	3	17	3	2
Coon		4	12	3	0	11	2	3
G. Humphrey		4	13	3	1	11	2	3
Wardwell		4	14	3	2	11	2	3

NATIONAL   3 - 2
Washington, DC

DATE	OPPONENT	SCORE		W	L	T
08/22	Jefferson (Washington)#	34	13	W		
08/28	Athletic (Philadelphia)	12	87		L	
08/29	Atlantic (Brooklyn)	19	34		L	
09/---	Jefferson (Washington)#	22	10	W		
10/08	Excelsior (Brooklyn)	36	30	W		

non-Association game statistics included in totals

BATTER	POS	GP	HL	A	O	R	A	O
Prouty		5	12	2	2	18	3	3
Ed Parker		5	13	2	3	16	3	1
Arthur Gorman		5	16	3	1	15	3	0
Sam Yeatman		5	14	2	4	13	2	3
Harry Berthrong		5	12	2	2	13	2	3
Will Williams		5	14	2	4	13	2	3

PIONEER   2 - 5
Newark, NJ

DATE	OPPONENT	SCORE		W	L	T
05/20	Excelsior (Brooklyn)	32	14	W		
06/30	Union (Morrisania, NY)	13	18		L	
07/13	Mystic (New York)	60	24	W		
08/24	Eureka (Newark)	5	12		L	
---/---	Union (Morrisania, NY)	9	31		L	
---/---	Eureka (Newark)	--	--		L	
---/---	Mystic (New York)	--	--		L	

BATTER	POS	GP	HL	A	O	R	A	O
Walters		6	17	2	5	18	3	0
Duval		6	18	3	0	15	2	3
Ford		6	19	3	1	14	2	2
Nagle		6	20	3	2	13	2	1
Dunlap		5	13	2	3	16	3	1
Hoagland		5	14	2	4	13	2	3
Currier		5	12	2	2	7	1	2

KNICKERBOCKER   1 - 4 - 1
New York, NY

DATE	OPPONENT	SCORE		W	L	T
07/06	Excelsior (Brooklyn)#	20	27		L	
07/25	Excelsior (Brooklyn) #	45	60		L	
08/17	New York (New York)	13	58		L	
09/21	Excelsior (Brooklyn) #	22	17	W		
10/05	New York (New York)	11	28		L	
10/20	Eclectic (New York)	31	31			T

"Friendly" game statistics included in totals

BATTER	POS	GP	HL	A	O	R	A	O
Hinsdale	1B	5	8	1	3	19	3	4
Taylor	2B	5	15	3	0	16	3	1
Thomas	SS	3	8	2	2	12	4	0
Churchill	3B,OF	3	10	3	1	6	2	0
Bensel	OF	3	11	3	2	7	2	1
Homans	OF	3	8	2	2	8	2	2
Samuel Kissam	OF	5	9	1	4	16	3	1
De Mott	C	5	11	2	1	17	3	2
Davis	P	5	18	3	3	15	3	0

NEWARK 1 - 5
Newark, NJ

DATE	OPPONENT	SCORE		W	L	T
06/13	Active (New York)	11	12		L	
06/20	Eagle (New York)	43	32	W		
06/30	Eckford (Brooklyn)	5	22		L	
07/28	Union (Morrisania, NY)	8	30		L	
09/01	Union (Morrisania, NY)	17	18		L	
---/---	Eureka (Newark)	--	--		L	

BATTER	POS	GP	HL	A	O	R	A	O
Terrell		5	11	2	1	12	2	2
Thorne		5	16	3	1	12	2	2
A. Bailey		5	16	3	1	8	1	3
Hugh Campbell		5	15	3	0	7	1	2
T. Buckley		5	20	4	0	6	1	1

EAGLE 1 - 9
New York, NY

DATE	OPPONENT	SCORE		W	L	T
05/30	Star (Brooklyn)	40	31	W		
06/13	Athletic (Philadelphia)	14	24		L	
06/20	Newark (Newark)	32	43		L	
07/14	Eckford (Brooklyn)	7	38		L	
07/18	Gotham (New York)	16	38		L	
08/28	Atlantic (Brooklyn)	10	48		L	
09/13	Empire (New York)	6	37		L	
09/15	Active (New York)	9	54		L	
10/07	Hudson River (Newburgh, NY)	10	45		L	
10/30	Mutual (New York)	7	13		L	

BATTER	POS	GP	HL	A	O	R	A	O
N.B. Shaffer		10	27	2	7	20	2	0
R. Sloat		8	18	2	2	19	2	3
Collins		8	16	2	0	19	2	3
Sam Yates		8	32	4	0	11	1	3
Reed		8	22	2	6	9	1	1
Doremus		6	16	2	4	14	2	2
Chapin		5	15	3	0	11	2	1

ENTERPRISE 1 - 10
Brooklyn, NY

DATE	OPPONENT	SCORE			W	L	T
06/06	Gotham (New York)	18	19	(13)		L	
06/24	Star (Brooklyn)	36	44			L	
07/29	Active (New York)	12	27			L	
08/05	Star (Brooklyn)	38	47			L	
08/07	Hudson River (Newburgh, NY)	38	28		W		
08/16	Empire (New York)	33	37			L	
08/28	Eckford (Brooklyn)	20	21			L	
09/02	Active (New York)	18	28			L	
09/13	Eckford (Brooklyn)	25	26			L	
09/26	Excelsior (Brooklyn)	21	46			L	
11/11	Excelsior (Brooklyn)	16	43			L	

BATTER	POS	GP	HL	A	O	R	A	O
W.H. Murtha	1B,OF	12	38	3	2	35	2	11
E. Smith	2B	11	23	2	1	45	4	1

ENTERPRISE (cont.)
Brooklyn, NY

BATTER	POS	GP	HL	A	O	R	A	O
Edwards	SS	10	32	3	2	31	3	1
Bob Ferguson	3B,SS	5	14	2	4	16	3	1
George Cook	OF,3B	12	38	3	2	34	2	10
Herbert Jewell	OF	8	20	2	4	31	2	7
W. Cornwell	OF,C	7	21	3	0	25	3	4
O'Neil	C	7	22	3	1	18	2	4
Leland	P	7	19	2	5	21	3	0
Connorton	P	6	21	3	3	11	1	5
R. Cornwell		5	15	3	0	17	3	2

RESOLUTE   0 - 7
Brooklyn, NY

DATE	OPPONENT	SCORE		W	L	T
06/15	Athletic (Philadelphia)	14	39		L	
06/24	Active (New York)	26	37		L	
06/29	Keystone (Philadelphia)	16	46		L	
07/01	Athletic (Philadelphia)	12	46		L	
07/12	Empire (New York)	26	29		L	
07/27	Keystone (Philadelphia)	15	30		L	
09/21	Knickerbocker (Albany)*	12	13		L	

BATTER	POS	GP	HL	A	O	R	A	O
J.S. Lockwood		7	19	2	5	16	2	2
Kelly		7	27	3	6	10	1	3
Mort Rogers		5	13	2	3	18	3	3
J. Wilson		5	16	3	1	12	2	2
Fraley Rogers		5	15	3	0	9	1	4

TEAM TOTALS

TEAM	CITY/STATE	GP	W	L	T	PCT	R	OR
Atlantic	Brooklyn, NY	18	18	0	0	1.000	584	310
Athletic	Philadelphia, PA	18	15	3	0	.833	604	305
Union	Morrisania, NY	23	13	10	0	.565	585	496
Mutual	New York, NY	16	12	4	0	.750	366	251
Active	New York, NY	17	10	7	0	.588	405	299
Eureka	Newark, NJ	14	9	5	0	.643	339	201
Eckford	Brooklyn, NY	14	8	6	0	.571	325	281
Empire	New York, NY	16	7	9	0	.438	379	410
Hudson River	Newburgh, NY	12	6	6	0	.500	212	233
Knickerbocker	Albany, NY	7	5	2	0	.714	165	104
Gotham	New York, NY	12	5	7	0	.417	231	272
Excelsior	Brooklyn, NY	7	4	3	0	.571	222	198
Star	Brooklyn, NY	9	4	5	0	.444	251	324
Keystone	Philadelphia, PA	12	4	8	0	.333	264	339
Mystic	New York, NY	12	4	8	0	.333	259	432
Eclectic	New York, NY	5	3	1	1	.700	152	94
National	Washington, DC	5	3	2	0	.600	123	174
Pioneer	Newark, NJ	7	2	5	0	.400	129	121
National	Albany, NY	4	1	3	0	.250		
Knickerbocker	New York, NY	6	1	4	1	.250	142	221
Newark	Newark, NJ	6	1	5	0	.167	84	114
Eagle	New York, NY	10	1	9	0	.100	151	371
Enterprise	Brooklyn, NY	11	1	10	0	.091	275	366
Eckford	Albany, NY	4	0	4	0	.000	62	115

TEAM TOTALS (cont.)

TEAM	CITY/STATE	GP	W	L	T	PCT	R	OR
Americus	Newark, NJ	5	0	5	0	.000	64	235
Resolute	Brooklyn, NY	7	0	7	0	.000	121	240

OTHER TEAMS

TEAM	CITY/STATE
Monitor	Goshen, NY
Mountain	Altoona, PA
New York	New York, NY
Utica	Utica, NY

1866
COUNTRY CLUBS

From the beginning, National Association activity never strayed far from a New York epicenter. Although a few teams wandered in from places such as Detroit or Washington, D.C., most of the Association teams were based in New York, Brooklyn, or their near environs. In addition, because of the Civil War, the Association was limited numerically as well. By mid-decade, both of these trends were in the midst of change.

During the 1865 season, baseball experienced a spurt of rapid growth with new teams forming in all quadrants. The reason behind this was simple. In the spring of 1865, the War between the States had ended. War weary players, ready for baseball's pleasures, revived many clubs. Their enthusiasm also spread, leading to the formation of many new clubs. Many of these organizations, since they didn't hail from the metropolis of New York, were called "country clubs," a reference to their rustic nature and lack of sophistication.

Many of these clubs, country and otherwise, sent delegates to the Association's annual meeting in December 1865, more than tripling the previous year's total. During the Civil War years, the convention had been sparsely attended with rarely more than 30 clubs represented. With an attendance history such as this, Association officers were not prepared for the crush. The *New York Clipper* described the scene: "The locale of the convention was room 24 of the Cooper Institute, and it proved entirely inadequate for the purpose as one-third of the delegates were unable to obtain seats." In all, 91 teams sent representatives, the highest total in nine conventions.

Of all the delegates sent to Association conventions from 1858 to 1864, over 80 percent had come from New York, Brooklyn or nearby areas. Of the 91 teams represented at the 1865 festivities, only 55 percent came from the greater New York area. The rest were distributed mostly on the eastern seaboard, but a handful of clubs like the Frontier, Empire, Lookout and Louisville hailed from far-flung areas such as Kansas, Missouri, Tennessee and Kentucky.

To honor the explosion of non–Gotham clubs, two movements made themselves heard at the convention. The first was a suggestion to move the next convention to a non–New York site. The second was a serious bid for the Association presidency by Colonel Moore of Philadelphia, the first aspirant to the title outside of New York. Although losing by seven votes, Moore's attempt would be mimicked at future conventions with more success. In addition, the convention would be held in Philadelphia, Washington and Boston before the end of the decade.

Once the 1866 season began, three teams rose to the top of the Association ladder. Two of the three were familiar dwellers in the upper echelons, while the third was a newcomer to the heights.

The defending champion Atlantic club cruised into the season not having lost since October 1863. After easily beating the Harvard club 37–15 in their season opener, they were about to be rudely surprised by what most considered a country club.

The Irvington club was a new Association entrant in 1866. Located in Irvington, New Jersey (20 miles west of New York), the club issued an invitation to the Atlantic club. The *Clipper* described the scene:

> ...on one of the practice days of the Atlantics, a committee of the Irvington club visited the grounds of the club,... "We are a mere country club, Mr. Babcock" [the Atlantic club president] said one of the committee, "and we would like the champions come out to our place and teach us a few points; we will treat them well and do the best we can to beat them, but if they beat us one hundred to ten we shan't cry about it."

Heartened at the thought of an easy romp in the country, the Atlantic club accepted the offer and scheduled a game for June 14th.

The *Clipper* next described the Atlantic's "preparations" for the Irvington junket:

> Babcock, [the Atlantic club president] thinking that the Irvingtons were a mere country club, did not take pains to have the full nine out. On asking the players, one said he couldn't go, as he had to go on a picnic. Another declined on the ground that his not going would give some of the second nines a chance, etc. Finally, a nine was made up for the game, and the party went "over to New Jersey," in gay spirits, to have a practice game with a country club,...

The Atlantics' spirits were not so happy several hours later after they blew a 15-9 lead and lost their first game in three years, 23-17.

What the Atlantics didn't realize was that just because the Irvingtons were a country club didn't mean that they weren't a good club. Three of the Irvington nine that day were top-notch players. Charlie Sweasy and Andy Leonard went on to star with the famed Cincinnati club, while pitcher Rynie Wolters became a mainstay of the Mutual club.

Embarrassed by their misfortune, the Atlantic squad finished the season strong, winning 16 of their last 18 games. Included in the totals was a 10 inning victory over the Irvingtons in October. Of their three losses, no two of them came from the same team ensuring the Atlantics their championship banner for another year.

The second of the three elite teams hailed from Philadelphia. The Athletic nine, fresh on the heels of two strong campaigns in 1864 and 1865, increased their win total dramatically in 1866. This offensive powerhouse only lost two games of 25 while scoring better than 50 runs a game. Included in the total was a triple-digit slaughter of the Alert club of Philadelphia on August 11, during which they pounded out 29 home runs.

One of the two losses handed the Athletics came at the hands of the Atlantic club. The other came courtesy of the third first-tier squad, the Union contingent from Morrisania, NY. The Unions, charter members of the National Association, had toiled for years in mediocrity before breaking through in 1866. Hailing from the village of Morrisania, located in what is now the Bronx, the Unions won 25 games while losing only three. Two of the losses came in one June week to the Mutuals and Athletics, while the third was a one-run heartbreaker to the Excelsior team in October. The Union and Atlantic clubs never faced off during the season thus giving the Morrisania crew no shot at the flag. This would be remedied the following year.

All of the year's top batters came from one team- the Athletics. In amongst seven 100 run scorers, the three best were Dick McBride with 160, Kleinfelder with 141 and Al Reach with 134. The entire Athletic first nine and three of the second scored at least five runs per game, spearheaded by McBride (6,10), Hicks Hayhurst (6,4) and Lip Pike (6,4). All six of these totals and averages set new Association records.

The influx of new blood into the Association stable led to larger schedules of games for member clubs. It also led to frequent mismatches. Most of the new clubs were not like the Irvingtons, but instead were more enthusiastic than talented which led to continual waxings by more experienced foes. Thus it was no great shock that the Athletic nine set a multitude of scoring records in 1866. Like today, most offensive records in National Association years were set in expansion years.

As the 1860s progressed, the expansion of 1866 proved to be no fluke. Each successive convention brought more and more clubs into the fold. Many of the newcomers came from locales far from the bustling cities of the east. Though many of the established teams would still call these organizations country clubs, soon they would be calling them something else. They would be calling them champions.

UNION 25 - 3
Morrisania, NY

DATE	OPPONENT	SCORE		W	L	T
05/19	Una (Mt Vernon, NY)	25	11	W		
05/24	Surprise (W. Farms, NY)	52	4	W		
06/06	Eckford (Brooklyn)	15	11	W		
06/09	Active (New York)	56	13	W		
06/12	Eureka (Newark)	28	26	W		
06/16	Enterprise (Brooklyn)	42	16	W		
06/20	Mutual (New York)	23	25		L	
06/26	Athletic (Philadelphia)	20	33		L	
07/04	National (Washington)	22	8	W		
07/17	Gotham (New York)	52	25	W		
07/19	Excelsior (Brooklyn)	20	15	W		
07/24	Uncas (Norwich, CT)	51	1	W		
07/25	Chester (Norwich, CT)	45	25	W		
07/26	Charter Oak (Hartford)	32	20	W		
07/27	Waterbury (Waterbury, CT)	71	11	W		
08/16	National (Albany)	53	18	W		
08/22	Surprise (W. Farms, NY)	46	9	W		
09/18	Eureka (Newark)	25	23	W		
10/02	Excelsior (Brooklyn)	29	30		L	
10/06	Enterprise (Brooklyn)	43	16	W		
10/18	Eckford (Brooklyn)	20	9	W		
10/20	Hudson River (Newburgh, NY)	43	4	W		
10/22	Oriental (Greenpoint, NY)	24	5	W		
10/27	Athletic (Philadelphia)	42	29	W		
11/03	Excelsior (Brooklyn)	43	14	W		
11/17	Waterbury (Waterbury, CT)	53	27	W		
---/---	Una (Mt Vernon, NY)	--	--	W		
---/---	Oriental (Greenpoint, NY)	--	--	W		

BATTER	POS	GP	HL	A O	R	A O
George Smith	1B,OF	28	66	2 10	138	4 26
Al Martin	2B,OF	28	83	2 27	118	4 6
Bernard Hannegan	SS,OF	25	58	2 8	109	4 9
William Abrams	3B	13	32	2 6	63	4 11
Dan Ketchum	OF,2B,3B	28	78	2 22	113	4 1
Henry Austin	OF	21	67	3 4	75	3 12
Albro Aiken	OF,C,SS	20	55	2 15	80	4 0
Dave Birdsall	C	25	73	2 23	95	3 20
Charley Pabor	P	28	110	3 26	86	3 2
W.F. Hudson	OF,3B	15	32	2 2	66	4 6
George Wright	SS,C	9	12	1 3	42	4 6
John Goldie	1B	5	15	3 0	17	3 2

ATHLETIC 23 - 2
Philadelphia, PA

DATE	OPPONENT	SCORE		W	L	T
06/14	Alert (Danville, PA)	92	2	W		
06/15	Susquehanna (Wilkesbarre, PA)	66	11	W		
06/26	Union (Morrisania, NY)	33	20	W		
06/27	Star (Brooklyn)	37	19	W		
06/28	Empire (New York)	64	10	W		
07/02	National (Washington)	22	6	W		
07/16	Alert (Philadelphia)	67	25	W		
07/17	Irvington (Irvington, NJ)	77	9	W		
07/30	Philadelphia (Philadelphia)	68	10	W		
08/11	Alert (Philadelphia)	100	5	W		
08/24	Columbia (Bordentown, NJ)	65	6	W		
08/27	Eureka (Newark)	48	8	W		
08/28	Irvington (Irvington, NJ)	18	11	W		
09/07	Liberty (New Brunswick, NJ)	53	9	W		

ATHLETIC (cont.)
Philadelphia, PA

DATE	OPPONENT	SCORE		W	L	T
09/12	Camden (Camden, NJ)	49	11	W		
09/13	Olympic (Philadelphia)	57	16	W		
09/19	Camden (Camden, NJ)	33	4	W		
10/15	Atlantic (Brooklyn)	17	27		L	
10/22	Atlantic (Brooklyn)	31	12	W		
10/27	Union (Morrisania, NY)	29	42		L	
10/30	Keystone (Philadelphia)	40	16	W		
11/05	Keystone (Philadelphia)	27	23	W		
11/09	Columbia (Bordentown, NJ)	63	26	W		
11/17	Philadelphia (Philadelphia)	58	15	W		
11/29	Burlington (Burlington, NJ)	73	7	W		

BATTER	POS	GP	HL	A	O	R	A	O
Wes Fisler	1B,OF,3B,2B	16	45	2	13	85	5	5
Al Reach	2B	23	61	2	15	134	5	19
Isaac Wilkins	SS,OF	23	50	2	4	125	5	10
Lip Pike	3B,OF,2B	16	49	2	11	100	6	4
Dan Kleinfelder	OF,C	24	69	2	21	141	5	21
Charles Gaskill	OF	18	52	2	16	100	5	10
Hicks Hayhurst	OF,3B,P	13	39	3	0	82	6	4
Patsy Dockney	C,OF	20	60	3	0	118	5	18
Dick McBride	P,3B,SS	25	58	2	8	**160**	6	10
Nate Berkenstock	1B	13	48	3	9	66	4	1
John Sensenderfer	OF,2B	12	29	2	5	65	5	5
McCleary	OF	5	16	3	1	28	5	3

ATLANTIC   17 - 3
Brooklyn, NY

DATE	OPPONENT	SCORE			W	L	T
05/30	Harvard (Cambridge)	37	15		W		
06/14	Irvington (Irvington, NJ)	17	23			L	
06/18	Peconic (Brooklyn)	43	19		W		
07/19	Peconic (Brooklyn)	64	7		W		
07/21	Atlantic (Jamaica, NY)	38	4		W		
08/08	Union (Lansingburgh, NY)	46	11		W		
08/18	Eureka (Newark)	10	36			L	
09/13	Mutual (New York)	17	15		W		
09/19	Eckford (Brooklyn)	28	12		W		
09/24	Irvington (Irvington, NJ)	28	11		W		
09/27	Eureka (Newark,)	30	20		W		
10/02	Keystone (Philadelphia)	28	18		W		
10/03	Camden (Camden, NJ)	35	7		W		
10/11	Star (Brooklyn)	46	18		W		
10/15	Athletic (Philadelphia)	27	17		W		
10/18	Mutual (New York)	34	24		W		
10/22	Athletic (Philadelphia)	12	31			L	
10/25	Eureka (Newark)	38	13		W		
10/29	Irvington (Irvington, NJ)	12	6	(10)	W		
---/---	Atlantic (Jamaica, NY)	--	--		W		

BATTER	POS	GP	HL	A	O	R	A	O
Joe Start	1B	16	37	2	5	69	4	5
Fred Crane	2B	12	28	2	4	42	3	6
Dickey Pearce	SS,OF	12	39	3	3	41	3	5
Bob Ferguson	3B,OF	18	64	3	10	44	2	8
John Chapman	OF,2B,1B	18	46	2	10	69	3	15
Dan McDonald	OF	10	28	2	8	41	4	1
Sid Smith	OF,3B,SS	12	27	2	3	50	4	2
Charley Mills	C	15	48	3	3	44	2	14

ATLANTIC (cont.)
Brooklyn, NY

BATTER	POS	GP	HL	A	O	R	A	O
George Zettlein	P	8	38	4	2	18	2	2
John Galvin	SS,OF	12	29	2	5	36	3	0
Tom Pratt	P	7	20	2	6	16	2	2

EXCELSIOR 13 - 6 - 1
Brooklyn, NY

DATE	OPPONENT	SCORE		W	L	T
06/01	Harvard (Cambridge, MA)	46	28	W		
06/19	Star (Brooklyn)	27	20	W		
07/05	National (Washington)	46	33	W		
07/19	Union (Morrisania, NY)	15	20		L	
07/24	Contest (Brooklyn)	34	5	W		
07/28	Active (New York)	7	9		L	
08/07	Peconic (Brooklyn)	32	4	W		
08/14	Mutual (New York)	13	32		L	
08/17	National (Albany)	48	29	W		
08/24	Independent (Brooklyn)	30	11	W		
08/28	Eureka (Newark)	24	12	W		
09/04	Star (Brooklyn)	32	9	W		
09/14	Enterprise (Brooklyn)	16	18		L	
09/18	National (Washington)	33	28	W		
09/19	Union (Washington)	40	23	W		
09/21	Keystone (Philadelphia)	18	18			T
09/22	Olympic (Philadelphia)	41	16	W		
10/02	Union (Morrisania, NY)	30	29	W		
10/22	Mutual (New York)	6	23		L	
11/03	Union (Morrisania, NY)	14	43		L	

BATTER	POS	GP	HL	A	O	R	A	O
George Fletcher	1B,3B,P	19	53	2	5	62	3	5
Fred Crane	2B	6	14	2	2	25	4	1
George Flanly	SS,1B,2B	16	36	2	4	59	3	11
Frank Norton	3B,SS,OF,C	20	60	3	0	70	3	10
John Clyne	OF,SS	18	54	3	0	60	3	6
James Mitchell	OF,3B	17	53	3	2	50	2	16
Anthony Elmendorf	OF	15	45	3	0	39	2	9
Joe Leggett	C,SS	14	40	2	12	45	3	3
Asa Brainard	P	14	46	3	4	35	2	7
Whitney	1B	11	24	2	2	35	3	2
Herbert Jewell	OF	6	21	3	3	20	3	2
Candy Cummings	P,SS	6	19	3	1	13	2	1
Dickey Pearce	SS,3B	5	10	2	2	19	3	4

MUTUAL 10 - 2
New York, NY

DATE	OPPONENT	SCORE		W	L	T
06/20	Union (Morrisania, NY)	25	23	W		
06/28	Eureka (Newark)	24	13	W		
07/12	Active (New York)	23	16	W		
08/14	Excelsior (Brooklyn)	32	13	W		
08/21	Star (Brooklyn)	45	16	W		
08/25	Harlem (New York)#	34	20	W		
09/06	Harlem (New York)#	40	1	W		
09/13	Atlantic (Brooklyn)	15	17		L	
10/11	Eckford (Brooklyn)	18	10	W		

MUTUAL (cont.)
New York, NY

DATE	OPPONENT	SCORE		W	L	T
10/18	Atlantic (Brooklyn)	24	34			T
10/22	Excelsior (Brooklyn)	23	6	W		
10/29	Star (Brooklyn)	16	13	W		

non-Association game statistics included in totals

BATTER	POS	GP	HL	A	O	R	A	O
John Goldie	1B	6	17	2	5	26	4	2
Billy McMahon	2B,OF	9	23	2	5	25	2	7
Dan Patterson	SS,2B,OF	9	20	2	2	33	3	6
Fred Waterman	3B	12	30	2	6	41	3	5
Richard Hunt	OF,SS	12	23	1	11	51	4	3
John Zeller	OF,1B	12	30	2	6	43	3	7
John Hatfield	OF	6	16	2	4	21	3	3
Nat Jewett	C	12	49	4	1	21	1	9
Al Martin	P,OF	12	52	4	4	24	2	0
James Reed	SS,OF	7	27	3	6	16	2	2
Charles Hunt	OF	6	18	3	0	16	2	4

NATIONAL   10 - 5
Washington, DC

DATE	OPPONENT	SCORE		W	L	T
05/10	Union (Washington)	37	7	W		
06/26	Union (Washington)	66	16	W		
07/02	Athletic (Philadelphia)	6	22		L	
07/03	Keystone (Philadelphia)	26	9	W		
07/04	Union (Morrisania, NY)	8	22		L	
07/05	Excelsior (Brooklyn)	33	46		L	
07/06	Gotham (New York)	22	34		L	
07/07	Liberty (New Brunswick, NJ)	29	9	W		
09/18	Excelsior (Brooklyn)	28	33		L	
09/27	Potomac (Washington)	67	19	W		
10/16	Keystone (Philadelphia)	41	26	W		
---/---	Jefferson (Washington)	--	--	W		
---/---	Jefferson (Washington)	--	--	W		
---/---	Jefferson (Washington)	--	--	W		
---/---	Jefferson (Washington)	--	--	W		

BATTER	POS	GP	HL	A	O	R	A	O
Hodges	1B	14	41	2	13	58	4	2
Ed Parker	2B	15	39	2	9	71	4	11
Eb Smith	SS,3B	13	28	2	2	60	4	8
George Fox	3B,C	10	21	2	1	51	5	1
Sy Studley	OF	15	38	2	8	68	4	8
Harry McLean	OF,3B,C	12	35	2	11	51	4	3
Sam Yeatman	OF	5	16	3	1	19	3	4
Harry Berthrong	C,SS,OF	14	30	2	2	72	5	2
Will Williams	P	12	33	2	9	47	3	11
M.E. Urell	OF	5	16	3	1	9	1	4

ACTIVE   10 - 6
New York, NY

DATE	OPPONENT	SCORE		W	L	T
06/02	Harvard (Cambridge, MA)	24	15	W		
06/09	Union (Morrisania, NY)	13	56		L	

1866

ACTIVE (cont.)
New York, NY

DATE	OPPONENT	SCORE			W	L	T
06/16	Una (Mt Vernon, NY)	23	17		W		
06/30	Enterprise (Brooklyn)	31	26		W		
07/04	Enterprise (Brooklyn)	29	26	(10)	W		
07/12	Mutual (New York)	16	23			L	
07/21	Star (Brooklyn)	32	33			L	
07/28	Excelsior (Brooklyn)	9	7		W		
08/15	Empire (New York)	28	9		W		
08/18	Una (Mt Vernon, NY)	43	22		W		
08/22	Eckford (Brooklyn)	19	16		W		
09/08	Eagle (New York)	29	10		W		
09/12	Eureka (Newark)	9	24			L	
10/03	Irvington (Irvington, NJ)	19	10		W		
10/06	Star (Brooklyn)	17	20			L	
10/17	Eureka (Newark)	12	44			L	

BATTER	POS	GP	HL	A	O	R	A	O
George Eaton	1B	9	22	2	4	22	2	4
Collins	2B,C,1B,SS,3B	14	33	2	5	40	2	12
Mahlon Stockman	SS,2B,OF	14	41	2	13	35	2	7
Moran	3B,OF	15	41	2	11	37	2	7
George Ebbetts	OF,1B	12	33	2	9	33	2	9
Tom Haines	OF,3B,SS	9	22	2	4	28	3	1
Hibbard	OF	8	23	2	7	19	2	3
William Kelley	C	13	36	2	10	25	1	12
Charley Walker	P	16	37	2	5	36	2	4
John Hatfield	OF,2B,C	6	20	3	2	18	3	0
T.F. Kelley	2B	6	18	3	0	8	1	2
Rogers	OF	5	17	3	2	9	1	4

MOHAWK   9 - 3
Brooklyn, NY

DATE	OPPONENT	SCORE		W	L	T
06/21	Surprise (W. Farms, NY)	40	10	W		
09/07	Greenwood (Brooklyn)	31	13	W		
10/11	Eclectic (New York)	27	25	W		
11/02	Eclectic (New York)	22	24		L	
11/13	Eclectic (New York)	56	24	W		
11/29	Surprise (W. Farms, NY)	28	15	W		
---/---	Powhatan (Brooklyn)	--	--	W		
---/---	Powhatan (Brooklyn)	--	--	W		
---/---	Independent (Brooklyn)	--	--	W		
---/---	Peconic (Brooklyn)	--	--	W		
---/---	Independent (Brooklyn)	--	--		L	
---/---	Surprise (W. Farms, NY)	--	--		L	

BATTER	POS	GP	HL	A	O	R	A	O
Silleck	1B	5	8	1	3	20	4	0
Forker	2B	7	16	2	2	27	3	6
Delisser	SS	10	23	2	3	33	3	3
O'Connor	3B	8	13	1	5	40	5	0
A. Steiner	OF	10	29	2	9	35	3	5
J. Steiner	OF	10	36	3	6	28	2	8
Hoagland	OF,3B	8	24	3	0	25	3	1
Weeks	C	2	4	2	0	12	6	0
Ryder	P	5	13	2	3	18	3	3
Behr	OF	6	9	1	3	23	3	5

ENTERPRISE 9 - 6
Brooklyn, NY

DATE	OPPONENT	SCORE			W	L	T
06/16	Union (Morrisania, NY)	16	42			L	
06/20	Eckford (Brooklyn)	21	39			L	
06/30	Active (New York)	26	31			L	
07/04	Active (New York)	20	26	(10)		L	
07/21	Pacific (New Utrecht, NY)	30	15		W		
08/25	Peconic (Brooklyn)	46	38		W		
09/04	Eclectic (New York)	24	14		W		
09/10	Eckford (Brooklyn)	22	17		W		
09/14	Excelsior (Brooklyn)	18	16		W		
09/18	Waterbury (Waterbury, CT)	37	21		W		
09/29	Peconic (Brooklyn)	33	14		W		
10/06	Union (Morrisania, NY)	16	43			L	
10/24	Pacific (New Utrecht, NY)	52	19		W		
---/---	Empire (New York)	--	--			L	
---/---	Eclectic (New York)	--	--		W		

BATTER	POS	GP	HL	A	O	R	A	O
George Hall	1B,OF	12	29	2	5	39	3	5
Herbert Jewell	2B,C,P,OF	15	36	2	6	54	3	9
Edwards	SS,C	15	45	3	0	44	2	14
W. Cornwell	3B,2B	9	22	2	4	25	2	7
George Cook	OF	15	48	3	3	47	3	2
W. H. Murtha	OF	12	35	2	11	37	3	1
Tom Patterson	OF,2B	10	25	2	5	40	4	0
Richards	C,SS,3B	4	11	2	3	12	3	0
Ed Pinkham	P,2B	14	34	2	6	46	3	4
R. Cornwell		9	24	2	6	24	2	6
George Cornwell	3B,SS	6	16	2	4	14	2	2
Leland	OF,1B	5	16	3	1	11	2	1

EUREKA 9 - 6
Newark, NJ

DATE	OPPONENT	SCORE		W	L	T
05/31	Harvard (Cambridge, MA)	42	39	W		
06/12	Union (Morrisania, NY)	26	28		L	
06/22	Americus (Newark)	67	7	W		
06/28	Mutual (New York)	13	24		L	
07/10	Kearney (Rahway, NJ)	45	6	W		
08/14	Atlantic (Brooklyn)	36	10	W		
08/20	Empire (New York)	15	11	W		
08/27	Athletic (Philadelphia)	8	48		L	
09/12	Active (New York)	24	9	W		
09/18	Union (Morrisania, NY)	23	25		L	
09/27	Atlantic (Brooklyn)	20	30		L	
10/17	Active (New York)	44	12	W		
10/25	Atlantic (Brooklyn)	13	38		L	
---/---	Kearney (Rahway, NJ)	--	--	W		
---/---	Empire (New York)	--	--	W		

BATTER	POS	GP	HL	A	O	R	A	O
Ev Mills	1B	15	40	2	10	53	4	8
Albert Pennington	2B	8	26	3	2	26	3	2
Charles Thomas	SS	7	20	2	6	17	2	3
Ted Bomeisler	3B,SS,OF	5	18	3	3	12	2	2
Joe Tyrell	OF,2B,3B	15	44	2	14	48	3	3
Ford	OF	14	40	2	12	50	4	8
Fred Calloway	OF	9	29	3	2	37	4	1
H. Brientnall	C	13	23	1	10	49	3	10
Faitoute	P,OF	6	18	3	0	17	2	5

EUREKA (cont.)
Newark, NJ

BATTER	POS	GP	HL	A	O	R	A	O
Osborne	C	13	28	2	2	48	3	9
Shugard	SS,OF	6	15	2	3	21	3	3
Harry Lex	P	6	16	2	4	15	2	3
Burroughs	SS	5	16	3	1	12	2	2
A. Littlewood	OF	5	13	2	3	11	2	1

ECKFORD   9 - 8
Brooklyn, NY

DATE	OPPONENT	SCORE		W	L	T
06/06	Union (Morrisania, NY)	11	15		L	
06/20	Enterprise (Brooklyn)	39	21	W		
06/24	Eagle (New York)	38	33	W		
07/02	Irvington (Irvington, NJ)	22	37		L	
07/04	M.M. Van Dyke (New York)	60	5	W		
08/01	Empire (New York)	53	23	W		
08/22	Active (New York)	16	19		L	
08/24	Oriental (Greenpoint, NY)	33	12	W		
08/28	Unionville (Unionville, NY)	56	20	W		
09/04	Empire (New York)	32	19	W		
09/10	Enterprise (Brooklyn)	17	22		L	
09/12	Irvington (Irvington, NJ)	13	20		L	
09/19	Atlantic (Brooklyn)	12	28		L	
10/11	Mutual (New York)	10	18		L	
10/18	Union (Morrisania, NY)	9	20		L	
10/19	M.M. Van Dyke (New York)	57	12	W		
10/24	Oriental (Greenpoint, NY)	27	9	W		

BATTER	POS	GP	HL	A	O	R	A	O
Klein	1B	18	56	3	2	60	3	6
Ed Brown	2B,OF	9	24	2	6	25	2	7
Butler	SS,OF	7	24	3	3	25	3	4
Josh Snyder	3B,SS	8	26	3	2	26	3	2
Marty Swandell	OF,2B,P	18	58	3	4	53	2	17
Harry Manolt	OF,C	14	36	2	8	52	3	10
Ryan	OF,SS	11	24	2	2	43	3	10
Waddy Beach	C,OF	18	47	2	11	67	3	13
Southworth	P,OF	12	40	3	4	42	3	16
George Grum	3B	10	26	2	6	37	3	7
John Grum	OF,2B	6	17	2	5	25	4	1
A. Mills	3B	5	16	3	1	16	3	1
Wilson	SS	5	9	1	4	12	2	2

AMERICUS   8 - 5
Newark, NJ

DATE	OPPONENT	SCORE		W	L	T
06/08	Eclectic (New York)	11	40		L	
06/22	Eureka (Newark)	7	67		L	
06/26	National (Jersey City, NJ)	54	42	W		
07/11	Star (New Brunswick, NJ)	48	38	W		
07/28	Social (New York)	28	21	W		
08/07	National (Jersey City, NJ)	47	33	W		
08/15	Star (New Brunswick, NJ)	19	24		L	
09/05	Social (New York)	28	20	W		
09/19	Eclectic (New York)	28	20	W		
09/---	Star (New Brunswick, NJ)	18	56		L	

AMERICUS (cont.)
Newark, NJ

DATE	OPPONENT	SCORE		W	L	T
10/02	National (Jersey City)	30	21	W		
10/19	Newark (Newark)	32	12	W		
11/17	Eclectic (New York)	17	25		L	

BATTER	POS	GP	HL	A	O	R	A	O
H. Ward	1B	6	15	2	3	23	3	5
Collins	2B	5	18	3	3	19	3	4
Ayres	SS	5	12	2	2	16	3	1
Jeralemon	3B	7	19	2	5	23	3	2
Bunting	OF	6	17	2	5	27	4	3
Mayhew	OF	7	21	3	0	25	3	4
W. Ward	OF	6	15	2	3	24	4	0
Joyce	C	7	17	2	3	29	4	1
Pilch	P	5	20	4	0	14	2	4

IRVINGTON   8 - 6
Irvington, NJ

DATE	OPPONENT	SCORE			W	L	T
06/14	Atlantic (Brooklyn)	23	17		W		
07/02	Eckford (Brooklyn)	37	22		W		
07/17	Athletic (Philadelphia)	9	77			L	
08/10	Contest (Brooklyn)	22	14		W		
08/28	Athletic (Philadelphia)	11	18			L	
08/30	Contest (Brooklyn)	29	14		W		
09/05	Olympic (Paterson, NJ)	16	20			L	
09/12	Eckford (Brooklyn)	20	13		W		
09/24	Atlantic (Brooklyn)	11	28			L	
10/03	Active (New York)	10	19			L	
10/29	Atlantic (Brooklyn)	6	12	(10)		L	
---/---	Kearney (Rahway, NJ)	--	--		W		
---/---	Kearney (Rahway, NJ)	--	--		W		
---/---	Olympic (Paterson, NJ)	--	--		W		

BATTER	POS	GP	HL	A	O	R	A	O
Mike Campbell	1B	13	45	3	6	43	3	4
Charlie Sweasy	2B	15	53	3	8	50	3	5
Harry Crawford	SS	14	39	2	11	42	3	0
T. Buckley	3B,C	17	65	3	14	39	2	5
A. Bailey	OF	16	49	3	1	66	4	2
Hugh Campbell	OF,1B	17	41	2	7	56	3	5
Billy Lewis	OF,1B	14	42	3	0	50	3	8
Andy Leonard	C,3B	16	40	2	8	59	3	11
Rynie Wolters	P	16	35	2	3	69	4	5
J. Campbell	OF	7	20	2	6	14	2	0

STAR   8 - 6
Brooklyn, NY

DATE	OPPONENT	SCORE		W	L	T
06/02	Independent (Brooklyn)	46	24	W		
06/19	Excelsior (Brooklyn)	20	27		L	
06/27	Athletic (Philadelphia)	19	37		L	
07/04	Monitor (Goshen, NY)	25	22	W		
07/21	Active (New York)	33	32	W		
08/11	Unionville (Unionville, NY)	74	14	W		

STAR (cont.)
Brooklyn, NY

DATE	OPPONENT	SCORE		W	L	T
08/21	Mutual (New York)	16	45		L	
08/25	Eagle (New York)	82	19	W		
09/04	Excelsior (Brooklyn)	9	32		L	
10/06	Active (New York)	20	17	W		
10/11	Atlantic (Brooklyn)	18	46		L	
10/29	Mutual (New York)	13	16		L	
11/03	Unionville (Unionville, NY)	23	17	W		
11/29	Independent (Brooklyn)	15	14	W		

BATTER	POS	GP	HL	A	O	R	A	O
Hope Waddell	1B	14	39	2	11	46	3	4
Tom McDiarmid	2B	14	38	2	10	52	3	10
Pete Flanders	SS	9	22	2	4	26	2	8
Bob Manly	3B	13	29	2	3	44	3	5
Lewis	OF	13	38	2	12	39	3	0
Herb Worth	OF	10	15	1	5	38	3	8
Fraley Rogers	OF,SS	9	27	3	0	32	3	5
Thompson	C	11	33	3	0	38	3	5
Sullivan	P	12	40	3	4	35	2	11
T. Smith	OF,1B	7	18	2	4	28	4	0

FULTON MARKET   6 - 2
New York, NY

DATE	OPPONENT	SCORE			W	L	T
07/20	Kearney (Rahway, NJ)	14	45			L	
08/21	Kearney (Rahway, NJ)	16	39		W		
08/29	M.M. Van Dyke (New York)	37	35	(10)	W		
10/29	Kearney (Rahway, NJ)	71	14		W		
11/07	Constellation (Brooklyn)	24	30			L	
---/---	M.M. Van Dyke (New York)	--	--		W		
---/---	Constellation (Brooklyn)	--	--		W		
---/---	Williamsburgh (Brooklyn)	--	--		W		

BATTER	POS	GP	HL	A	O	R	A	O
Storer		6	13	2	1	32	5	2
Campbell		6	15	2	3	28	4	4
Brower		6	25	4	1	23	3	5
Owens		5	10	2	0	30	6	0
Hubbs		5	8	1	3	29	5	4
Dunham		5	13	2	3	24	4	4
Sullivan		5	18	3	3	19	3	4
Betts		5	12	2	2	16	3	1

CHARTER OAK   6 - 3
Hartford, CT

DATE	OPPONENT	SCORE		W	L	T
05/26	Yale (New Haven, CT)	18	15	W		
06/13	Yale (New Haven, CT)	22	10	W		
06/23	Chester (Norwich, CT)	57	15	W		
07/04	Harvard (Cambridge, MA)	14	16		L	
07/05	Waterbury (Waterbury, CT)	25	5	W		
07/20	Chester (Norwich, CT)	32	51		L	
07/26	Union (Morrisania, NY)	20	32		L	
07/28	Waterbury (Waterbury, CT)	25	21	W		
09/29	Chester (Norwich, CT)	39	22	W		

CHARTER OAK (cont.)
Hartford, CT

BATTER	POS	GP	HL	A O	R	A O
Edward Jewell	1B	10	23	2 3	34	3 4
H.L. Bunce	2B	10	28	2 8	29	2 9
C.L. Perry	SS	7	18	2 4	21	3 0
F.L. Bunce	3B	10	35	3 5	33	3 3
V.D. Perry	OF	9	21	2 3	31	3 4
Tate	OF	9	35	3 8	21	3 2
Lane	OF	6	17	2 5	14	2 2
Hubbell	C	10	29	2 9	34	3 4
Blackwell	P	8	19	2 3	25	3 1
Hills	OF	5	12	2 2	22	4 2

OLYMPIC   6 - 3
Paterson, NJ

DATE	OPPONENT	SCORE	W	L	T
07/19	Eagle (New York)	28 24	W		
07/31	Gotham (New York)	10 21		L	
08/20	Eclectic (New York)	21 9	W		
09/05	Irvington (Irvington, NJ)	20 16	W		
09/19	Star (New Brunswick, NJ)	27 20	W		
09/24	M.M. Van Dyke (New York)	58 33	W		
09/28	Eagle (New York)	18 23		L	
11/21	Eclectic (New York)	17 15	W		
---/---	Irvington (Irvington, NJ)	-- --		L	

BATTER	POS	GP	HL	A O	R	A O
Tynan	1B,3B	7	18	2 4	27	3 6
Fitzgerald	2B	8	27	3 3	22	2 6
Lamb	SS	6	15	2 3	24	4 0
Cocker	3B,OF,1B	7	16	2 2	15	2 1
Sears	OF,1B	7	20	2 6	18	2 4
Kilt	OF	6	22	3 4	13	2 1
Mullen	OF	6	17	2 5	11	1 5
McKiernan	C	8	23	2 7	27	3 3
Tuomey	P	8	21	2 5	22	2 6

INDEPENDENT   6 - 5
Brooklyn, NY

DATE	OPPONENT	SCORE	W	L	T
06/02	Star (Brooklyn)	24 46		L	
07/14	Greenwood (Brooklyn)	46 15	W		
08/24	Excelsior (Brooklyn)	11 30		L	
09/01	Resolute (Elizabeth, NJ)#	24 22	W		
09/08	Powhatan (Brooklyn)	19 36		L	
10/31	Resolute (Brooklyn)	34 20	W		
11/29	Star (Brooklyn)	14 15		L	
---/---	Greenwood (Brooklyn)	-- --	W		
---/---	Resolute (Brooklyn)	-- --	W		
---/---	Mohawk (Brooklyn)	-- --	W		
---/---	Mohawk (Brooklyn)	-- --		L	

non-Association game statistics included in totals

BATTER	POS	GP	HL	A O	R	A O
R. Edwards	1B	11	36	3 3	26	2 4
H.S. Peck	2B,C	11	25	2 3	38	3 5

INDEPENDENT (cont.)
Brooklyn, NY

BATTER	POS	GP	HL	A	O	R	A	O
Browne	SS	7	18	2	4	22	3	1
Moore	3B,OF	10	28	2	8	33	3	3
W.S. Colvin	OF,SS	9	20	2	2	32	3	5
C.H. Edwards	OF,P	9	34	3	7	28	3	1
G. Noyes	OF,SS,3B	7	22	3	1	24	3	3
George Bailey	C,OF	7	18	2	4	16	2	2
W.S. Taylor	P	9	20	2	2	29	3	2
R. McCoskry	2B	6	20	3	2	18	3	0

ECLECTIC   6 - 13
New York, NY

DATE	OPPONENT	SCORE		W	L	T
06/05	Americus (Newark)	40	11	W		
06/20	Irvington (Irvington, NJ)	18	57		L	
07/04	Hudson River (Newburgh, NY)	14	26		L	
07/10	Gotham (New York)	12	20		L	
07/25	Una (Mt. Vernon, NY)	25	23	W		
08/15	Harlem (New York)	19	21		L	
08/20	Olympic (Paterson, NJ)	9	21		L	
08/24	Social (New York)	23	27		L	
09/04	Enterprise (Brooklyn)	14	24		L	
09/19	Americus (Newark)	20	28		L	
10/03	Una (Mt. Vernon, NY)	8	37		L	
10/11	Mohawk (Brooklyn)	25	27		L	
10/20	Enterprise (Brooklyn)	18	31		L	
10/24	Social (New York)	16	14	W		
10/26	Una (Mt. Vernon, NY)	29	21	W		
11/02	Mohawk (Brooklyn)	24	22	W		
11/13	Mohawk (Brooklyn)	24	56		L	
11/17	Americus (Newark)	25	17	W		
---/---	Olympic (Paterson, NJ)	--	--		L	

BATTER	POS	GP	HL	A	O	R	A	O
Dalton	1B	12	35	2	11	18	1	6
Taylor	2B,3B	7	19	2	5	9	1	2
Stilwaggon	SS	5	13	2	3	10	2	0
M. Humphrey	3B	8	24	3	0	11	1	3
William Bell	OF,P	19	52	2	14	45	2	7
Brown	OF	16	38	2	6	40	2	8
Glover	OF,3B,1B	11	35	3	2	19	1	8
Bunting	C,2B	16	33	2	1	47	2	15
McGee	P,OF	8	24	3	0	11	1	3
Ryder		13	24	1	11	37	2	11
G. Ackerson	OF	9	18	2	0	21	2	3
G. Humphrey		7	16	2	2	14	2	0
A.H. Wright	2B,SS	5	12	2	2	15	3	0
James	SS,C	5	13	2	3	9	1	4

POWHATAN   5 - 4
Brooklyn, NY

DATE	OPPONENT	SCORE		W	L	T
07/28	Greenwood (Brooklyn)	23	5	W		
08/17	Mohawk (Brooklyn)	17	42		L	
08/28	Atlantic (Jamaica, NY)	51	26	W		

POWHATAN (cont.)
Brooklyn, NY

DATE	OPPONENT	SCORE	W	L	T
09/04	Atlantic (Jamaica, NY)	9 14		L	
09/08	Independent (Brooklyn)	36 19	W		
09/22	Unionville (Unionville, NY)	41 15	W		
10/04	Peconic (Brooklyn)	17 25		L	
10/31	Unionville (Unionville, NY)	16 9	W		
---/---	Mohawk (Brooklyn)	-- --		L	

BATTER	POS	GP	HL	A O	R	A O
Clark	1B,3B	5	8	1 3	17	3 2
A.V. Bergen	2B	6	17	2 5	14	2 2
Snediker	SS	6	12	2 0	24	4 0
Shields	3B,OF	5	9	1 4	18	3 3
Irwin	OF	6	21	3 3	17	2 5
McCarty	OF,1B	6	19	3 1	15	2 3
Bennett	OF	5	15	3 0	14	2 4
Brown	C	6	17	2 5	17	2 5
Earle	P	6	17	2 5	16	2 4

KEYSTONE 5-5-1
Philadelphia, PA

DATE	OPPONENT	SCORE	W	L	T
06/09	Camden (Camden, NJ)	45 17	W		
07/03	National (Washington)	9 26		L	
08/09	Camden (Philadelphia)	32 31	W		
09/21	Excelsior (Brooklyn)	18 18			T
10/02	Atlantic (Brooklyn)	18 25		L	
10/16	National (Washington)	26 41		L	
10/17	Union (Washington)	27 20	W		
10/18	Jefferson (Washington)	22 13	W		
10/30	Athletic (Philadelphia)	16 40		L	
11/05	Athletic (Philadelphia)	23 27		L	
---/---	Alert (Philadelphia)	-- --	W		

BATTER	POS	GP	HL	A O	R	A O
Mulholland	1B	5	19	3 4	9	1 4
Eddie Woods	2B,SS	9	21	2 3	22	2 4
W.M. Deal	SS,OF	8	28	3 4	18	2 2
Mike Smith	3B	6	15	2 3	15	2 3
Ned Cuthbert	OF,1B,C	9	14	1 5	30	3 3
Brown	OF,3B	8	18	2 2	22	2 6
W. Shane	OF,1B	6	19	3 1	14	2 2
Billy Dick	C,2B,SS	9	25	2 7	28	3 1
Elias Cope	P	9	25	2 7	26	2 8
Charley Weaver	OF	6	15	2 3	18	3 0
William Wallace	C	5	15	3 0	15	3 0
Bratton	OF	5	20	4 0	13	2 3

JEFFERSON 5-7-1
Washington, DC

DATE	OPPONENT	SCORE	W	L	T
05/25	Union (Washington)	40 30 (10)	W		
06/29	Union (Washington)	36 45		L	
10/18	Keystone (Philadelphia)	13 22		L	
11/22	Union (Washington)	19 27		L	

JEFFERSON (cont.)
Washington, DC

DATE	OPPONENT	SCORE	W	L	T
---/---	Union (Washington)	-- --	W		
---/---	Union (Washington)	-- --	W		
---/---	Potomac (Washington)	-- --	W		
---/---	Potomac (Washington)	-- --	W		
---/---	National (Washington)	-- --		L	
---/---	National (Washington)	-- --		L	
---/---	National (Washington)	-- --		L	
---/---	National (Washington)	-- --		L	
---/---	Union (Washington)	-- --			T

BATTER	POS	GP	HL	A O	R	A O
Daniels	1B	8	27	3 3	23	2 5
McClelland	2B,C	11	31	2 9	41	3 8
Seaver Page	SS	10	31	3 1	28	2 8
Sam Yeatman	3B	5	13	2 3	17	3 2
George Joyce	OF,1B,3B	12	31	2 7	34	2 10
A.V. Robinson	OF	12	35	2 11	38	3 2
Stone	OF,2B	12	29	2 5	35	2 11
McCauley	C,SS	13	36	2 10	42	3 3
Anderson	P	11	38	3 5	23	2 1
A. Finney	OF	7	23	3 2	19	2 5

HUDSON RIVER   4 - 1
Newburgh, NY

DATE	OPPONENT	SCORE	W	L	T
07/04	Eclectic (New York)	26 14	W		
07/20	Undercliff (Cold Spring, NY)	23 21	W		
10/20	Union (Morrisania, NY)	4 43		L	
---/---	Undercliff (Cold Spring, NY)	-- --	W		
---/---	Pacific (New Utrecht, NY)	-- --	W		

BATTER	POS	GP	HL	A O	R	A O
Andy Leonard	1B	5	17	3 2	6	1 1
Lindley	2B,SS	5	15	3 0	15	3 0
Halsey	SS	5	11	2 1	14	2 4
J.W. Miller	3B	5	13	2 3	11	2 1
Millspaugh	OF	5	10	2 0	13	2 3
Wilson	OF	5	16	3 1	6	1 1
Garrison	OF,1B,2B	5	10	2 0	9	1 4
Boyd	C	5	10	2 0	13	2 3
Kelly	P	5	18	3 3	8	1 3

LIBERTY   4 - 2
New Brunswick, NJ

DATE	OPPONENT	SCORE	W	L	T
06/15	Star (New Brunswick, NJ)	40 35	W		
06/29	Star (New Brunswick, NJ)	39 15	W		
07/07	National (Washington)	9 29		L	
08/17	Gotham (New York)	41 29	W		
08/31	Gotham (New York)	24 23	W		
09/07	Athletic (Philadelphia)	9 53		L	

LIBERTY (cont.)
New Brunswick, NJ

BATTER	POS	GP	HL	A	O	R	A	O
Bergen		6	12	2	0	23	3	5
M. Van Nuyse		6	15	2	3	23	3	5
Hyde		6	19	3	1	18	3	0
A. Solomon		6	14	2	2	17	2	5
W.H. Cortelyew		6	17	2	5	17	2	5
H.S. Cortelyew		6	17	2	5	17	2	5
Wanser		6	20	3	2	9	1	3
Towle		5	17	3	2	6	1	1

GOTHAM   4 - 4
New York, NY

DATE	OPPONENT	SCORE			W	L	T
06/26	Eagle (New York)	29	12		W		
07/06	National (Washington)	34	22		W		
07/10	Eclectic (New York)	20	12		W		
07/17	Union (Morrisania, NY)	25	52			L	
07/31	Olympic (Paterson, NJ)	21	10		W		
08/17	Liberty (New Brunswick, NJ)	29	41			L	
08/31	Liberty (New Brunswick, NJ)	23	24			L	
09/25	Jefferson (New York)	20	21			L	

BATTER	POS	GP	HL	A	O	R	A	O
Ed Beadle	1B	8	22	2	7	25	3	1
William Goodspeed	2B	5	14	2	4	15	3	0
Pete Shreves	SS	5	10	2	0	17	3	2
Connell	3B	6	13	2	1	25	4	1
Andrew Dupignac	OF	8	29	3	5	22	2	6
Milton Sweet	OF,P	7	18	2	4	22	3	1
Mehl	OF	5	19	3	4	12	2	2
George Wright	C	5	9	1	4	21	4	1
Stevens	P	5	20	4	0	8	1	3

M.M. VAN DYKE   4 - 4
New York, NY

DATE	OPPONENT	SCORE			W	L	T
08/01	Fulton Market (New York)	30	43			L	
08/15	Constellation (Brooklyn)	71	23		W		
08/29	Fulton Market (New York)	35	37	(10)		L	
09/05	Oriental (Greenpoint, NY)	36	27		W		
09/18	Oriental (Greenpoint, NY)	28	23		W		
09/24	Olympic (Paterson, NJ)	43	58			L	
10/17	Constellation (Brooklyn)	43	38		W		
10/19	Eckford (Brooklyn)	12	57			L	

BATTER	POS	GP	HL	A	O	R	A	O
Bennett	1B	5	18	3	3	21	4	0
Wade	2B	6	18	3	0	22	3	4
Hogan	SS,P	5	14	2	4	15	3	0
Briggs	3B,SS,OF	5	12	2	2	21	4	1
Butler	OF,P,3B	5	7	1	2	23	4	3
Baldwin	OF,C	5	13	2	3	15	3	0
Quinn	OF,SS	5	13	2	3	19	3	4
William Hobby	C	5	17	3	2	19	3	4
Samuel Galbraith	P,OF,1B	6	13	2	1	28	4	4

NATIONAL   4 - 4
Albany, NY

DATE	OPPONENT	SCORE		W	L	T
07/19	Victory (Troy)	42	27	W		
08/02	Knickerbocker (Albany)	17	22		L	
08/14	Lorillard (Rhinebeck, NY)	38	11	W		
08/15	Undercliff (Cold Spring, NY)	81	20	W		
08/16	Union (Morrisania, NY)	18	53		L	
08/17	Excelsior (Brooklyn)	29	48		L	
09/05	Knickerbocker (Albany)	8	24		L	
---/---	Rivermont (?)#	--	--	W		

non-Association game statistics included in totals

BATTER	POS	GP	HL	A	O	R	A	O
Lansing	1B	7	16	2	2	34	4	6
McClure	2B,OF	6	18	3	0	29	4	3
Woolverton	SS	7	23	3	2	32	4	4
Sprague	3B	6	17	2	5	38	6	2
Ross	OF	7	19	2	5	41	5	6
Ertsberger	OF	5	13	3	3	27	5	2
Johnson	OF	5	13	2	3	25	5	0
Archie Bush	C	6	14	2	2	37	6	1
Waddell	P	7	24	3	3	35	5	0

PACIFIC   4 - 5
New Utrecht, NY

DATE	OPPONENT	SCORE		W	L	T
07/14	Unionville (Unionville, NY)	27	43		L	
07/21	Enterprise (Brooklyn)	15	30		L	
10/24	Enterprise (Brooklyn)	19	52		L	
11/10	Unionville (Unionville, NY)	47	26	W		
11/17	Contest (Brooklyn)	14	15		L	
---/---	Unionville (Unionville, NY)	--	--	W		
---/---	Contest (Brooklyn)	--	--	W		
---/---	Greenwood (Brooklyn)	--	--	W		
---/---	Hudson River (Newburgh, NY)	--	--		L	

BATTER	POS	GP	HL	A	O	R	A	O
Berry	1B	5	15	3	0	15	3	0
Ran	2B	6	16	2	4	26	4	2
Brown	SS	7	10	1	3	36	5	1
Slater	3B,OF	7	24	3	3	21	3	0
Moore	OF	7	21	3	0	23	3	2
G. Wardwell	OF,P	6	17	2	5	17	2	5
Weir	OF	5	15	3	0	13	2	3
Ryder	C	6	13	2	1	21	3	3
Lake	P	6	12	2	0	25	4	1
Van Pelt	C	5	12	2	2	25	5	0
W. Wardwell	OF	5	8	1	3	23	4	3

CONTEST   3 - 4
Brooklyn, NY

DATE	OPPONENT	SCORE		W	L	T
07/07	Greenwood (Brooklyn)	57	13	W		
07/24	Excelsior (Brooklyn)	5	34		L	
08/10	Irvington (Irvington, NJ)	14	22		L	
08/30	Irvington (Irvington, NJ)	14	29		L	

CONTEST (cont.)
Brooklyn, NY

DATE	OPPONENT	SCORE		W	L	T
11/17	Pacific (New Utrecht, NY)	15	14	W		
---/---	Greenwood (Brooklyn)	--	--	W		
---/---	Pacific (New Utrecht, NY)	--	--		L	

BATTER	POS	GP	HL	A	O	R	A	O
Boone	1B	5	16	3	1	13	2	3
Hough	2B,C	5	10	2	0	18	3	3
Tompkins	SS,2B	5	13	2	3	17	3	1
Shannon	3B,1B	6	9	1	3	24	4	1
Gibson	OF	5	23	4	3	8	1	3
Van Pelt	OF	5	15	3	0	12	2	2
Garvey	OF,P	5	14	2	4	12	2	2
Janes	C	5	14	2	4	14	2	4
Davenport	P	6	20	3	2	14	2	2

OLYMPIC 3 - 4
Philadelphia, PA

DATE	OPPONENT	SCORE		W	L	T
06/20	Camden (Camden, NJ)	26	47		L	
07/12	Minerva (Philadelphia)	50	11	W		
08/02	Camden (Camden, NJ)	24	28		L	
08/22	Equity (Philadelphia)	38	15	W		
09/13	Athletic (Philadelphia)	16	47		L	
09/22	Excelsior (Brooklyn)	16	41		L	
---/---	Equity (Philadelphia)	--	--	W		

BATTER	POS	GP	HL	A	O	R	A	O
Hurn		6	13	2	1	26	4	2
Dodson		6	18	3	0	19	3	1
Kuen		6	19	3	1	17	2	5
Anspach		5	11	2	1	19	3	4
Croasdale		5	13	2	3	19	3	4
Tiers		5	10	2	0	18	3	3
Richards		5	16	3	1	17	3	2
Waldie		5	17	3	2	13	2	3

WATERBURY 3 - 5
Waterbury, CT

DATE	OPPONENT	SCORE		W	L	T
07/05	Charter Oak (Hartford)	5	25		L	
07/25	Charter Oak (Hartford)	21	25		L	
07/27	Union (Morrisania, NY)	11	71		L	
09/17	Eagle (New York)	31	20	W		
09/18	Enterprise (Brooklyn)	21	37		L	
09/19	Empire (New York)	26	21	W		
11/17	Union (Morrisania, NY)	27	53		L	
---/---	Yale (New Haven)	--	--	W		

BATTER	POS	GP	HL	A	O	R	A	O
Terry	1B,SS	5	15	3	0	11	2	1
Adams	2B,OF	5	13	2	3	13	2	3
Commerford	SS	5	14	2	4	12	2	2
White	3B,OF	5	12	2	2	11	2	1
J. W. Blakeslee	OF,2B	6	14	2	2	16	2	4

WATERBURY (cont.)
Waterbury, CT

BATTER	POS	GP	HL	A	O	R	A	O
Cate	OF	5	16	3	1	8	1	3
McCarty	OF	5	14	2	4	11	2	1
Greenman	C	6	15	2	3	19	3	1
V. Blakeslee	P	6	15	2	2	15	2	3

UNA 3 - 6
Mt Vernon, NY

DATE	OPPONENT	SCORE		W	L	T
05/19	Union (Morrisania, NY)	11	25		L	
06/16	Active (New York)	17	23		L	
06/27	Constellation (Brooklyn)	42	9	W		
07/25	Eclectic (New York)	23	25		L	
08/03	Union (Morrisania, NY)	18	27		L	
08/18	Active (New York)	22	43		L	
09/03	Constellation (Brooklyn)	39	23	W		
10/02	Eclectic (New York)	37	8	W		
10/26	Eclectic (New York)	21	29		L	

BATTER	POS	GP	HL	A	O	R	A	O
C. Sageman	1B	5	17	3	2	6	1	1
Lawrence	2B,OF	5	11	2	1	13	2	3
Selchow	SS	6	15	2	3	9	1	3
Hathaway	3B	7	18	2	4	19	2	4
Downs	OF,C	7	13	1	6	19	2	4
D. Van Cott	OF,C,1B	7	17	2	3	16	2	2
W. H. Van Cott	OF	5	9	1	4	11	2	1
Manson	C	5	12	2	2	12	2	2
Stevens	P	7	15	2	1	17	2	3
T. S. Van Cott	2B	5	10	2	0	15	3	0
Dusenbury	OF,SS	2	5	2	1	6	3	0

EMPIRE 3 - 7
New York, NY

DATE	OPPONENT	SCORE		W	L	T
06/28	Athletic (Philadelphia)	10	64		L	
08/01	Eckford (Brooklyn)	23	53		L	
08/08	Eagle (New York)	45	19	W		
08/15	Active (New York)	9	28		L	
08/20	Eureka (Newark)	11	15		L	
09/04	Eckford (Brooklyn)	19	32		L	
09/10	Jefferson (New York)	31	21	W		
09/19	Waterbury (Waterbury, CT)	21	26		L	
---/---	Enterprise (Brooklyn)	--	--	W		
---/---	Eureka (Newark)	--	--		L	

BATTER	POS	GP	HL	A	O	R	A	O
Wilson		9	22	2	4	28	3	1
Duncan		9	22	2	4	27	3	0
Miller		9	29	3	2	22	2	4
Samuel Hosford		9	31	3	4	21	2	3
Ed Ward		8	26	3	2	20	2	4
Sebring		7	21	3	0	19	2	5
Coulter		7	21	3	0	10	1	3
Amor Williamson		6	16	2	4	15	2	3

NATIONAL 2 - 4 - 1
Jersey City, NJ

DATE	OPPONENT	SCORE		W	L	T
06/26	Americus (Newark)	42	54		L	
08/07	Americus (Newark)	33	47		L	
09/07	Social (New York)	30	13	W		
09/19	Eagle (New York)	30	15	W		
10/26	Eagle (New York)	13	29		L	
---/---	Star (New Brunswick, NJ)	--	--			T
---/---	Star (New Brunswick, NJ)	--	--		L	

BATTER	POS	GP	HL	A	O	R	A	O
Denmead		6	12	2	0	24	4	0
Willis		6	9	1	3	23	3	5
Dingler		5	11	2	1	16	3	1
Bacot		5	11	2	1	12	2	2
Gough		5	11	2	1	12	2	2
Clark		5	12	2	2	11	2	1
Ransom		5	15	3	0	11	2	1
Edwards		5	12	2	2	8	1	3

STAR 2 - 4 - 1
New Brunswick, NJ

DATE	OPPONENT	SCORE		W	L	T
06/15	Liberty (New Brunswick, NJ)	35	40		L	
06/29	Liberty (New Brunswick, NJ)	15	39		L	
07/11	Americus (Newark)	38	48		L	
09/---	Americus (Newark)	56	18	W		
09/19	Olympic (Paterson, NJ)	20	27		L	
---/---	National (Jersey City)	--	--	W		
---/---	National (Jersey City)	--	--			T

BATTER	POS	GP	HL	A	O	R	A	O
Dayton		5	14	2	4	15	3	0
R. Stout		5	12	2	2	12	2	2
J.B. Kirkpatrick		5	12	2	2	15	3	0
Wiley		5	11	2	1	15	3	0

CAMDEN 2 - 5
Camden, NJ

DATE	OPPONENT	SCORE		W	L	T
06/09	Keystone (Philadelphia)	17	45		L	
06/20	Olympic (Philadelphia)	47	26	W		
08/02	Olympic (Philadelphia)	28	24	W		
08/09	Keystone (Philadelphia)	31	32		L	
09/12	Athletic (Philadelphia)	11	49		L	
09/19	Athletic (Philadelphia)	4	33		L	
10/03	Atlantic (Brooklyn)	7	35		L	

BATTER	POS	GP	HL	A	O	R	A	O
George Albertson		8	24	3	0	16	2	0
Birdsall		7	16	2	2	13	1	6
C. Evans		7	21	3	0	13	1	6
Barber		7	27	3	6	11	1	4
Bergen		6	13	2	1	14	2	2
Mulliner		6	20	3	2	13	2	1
Stinson		6	12	2	0	10	1	4
John Radcliff		6	19	3	1	10	1	4

SURPRISE 2 - 5
W. Farms, NY

DATE	OPPONENT	SCORE			W	L	T
05/24	Union (Morrisania, NY)	4	52			L	
06/21	Mohawk (Brooklyn)	10	40			L	
07/20	Union (Morrisania, NY)	9	46			L	
09/21	Harlem (New York)#	6	13			L	
11/29	Mohawk (Brooklyn)	15	28			L	
---/---	Harlem (New York)#	--	--		W		
---/---	Mohawk (Brooklyn)	--	--		W		

non-Association game statistics included in totals

BATTER	POS	GP	HL	A	O	R	A	O
Cuthill		5	13	2	3	9	1	4
Magill		5	14	2	4	7	1	2
A. Sloane		5	12	2	2	7	1	2
Valentine		5	16	3	1	5	1	0

UNION 2 - 8 - 1
Washington, DC

DATE	OPPONENT	SCORE			W	L	T
05/10	National (Washington)	7	37			L	
05/25	Jefferson (Washington)	30	40	(10)		L	
06/26	National (Washington)	16	66			L	
06/29	Jefferson (Washington)	45	36		W		
08/04	Potomac (Washington)	14	40			L	
09/19	Excelsior (Brooklyn)	23	40			L	
10/17	Keystone (Philadelphia)	20	27			L	
11/22	Jefferson (Washington)	27	19		W		
---/---	Jefferson (Washington)	--	--				T
---/---	Jefferson (Washington)	--	--			L	
---/---	Jefferson (Washington)	--	--			L	

BATTER	POS	GP	HL	A	O	R	A	O
Quantrell		9	28	3	1	26	2	8
Cassiday		8	11	1	3	29	3	5
Babcock		8	28	3	4	17	2	1
Wood		6	15	2	3	18	3	0
M.E. Urell		6	21	3	3	17	2	5
Harmon		6	17	2	5	13	2	1
Pearson		5	11	2	1	17	3	2
Alden		5	13	2	3	12	2	2

EAGLE 2 - 9
New York, NY

DATE	OPPONENT	SCORE		W	L	T
06/26	Gotham (New York)	12	29		L	
07/19	Olympic (Paterson, NJ)	24	28		L	
07/24	Eckford (Brooklyn)	33	38		L	
08/08	Empire (New York)	19	45		L	
08/25	Star (Brooklyn)	19	82		L	
09/08	Active (New York)	10	29		L	
09/17	Waterbury (Waterbury, CT)	20	31		L	
09/19	National (Jersey City)	15	30		L	
09/28	Olympic (Paterson, NJ)	23	18	W		
10/19	Empire (New York)	20	25		L	
10/26	National (Jersey City)	29	13	W		

EAGLE (cont.)
New York, NY

BATTER	POS	GP	HL	A	O	R	A	O
N.B. Shaffer		9	21	2	3	27	3	0
W.B. Shaffer		9	22	2	4	23	2	5
Reed		8	22	2	6	20	2	4
Norton		6	15	2	3	17	2	5
Demarest		6	19	3	1	13	2	1
Doremus		6	21	3	3	13	2	1
Nat Hicks		5	11	2	1	14	2	4
Kane		5	15	3	0	11	2	1

CONSTELLATION 1 - 5
Brooklyn, NY

DATE	OPPONENT	SCORE		W	L	T
06/27	Una (Mt Vernon, NY)	9	42		L	
08/15	M.M. Van Dyke (New York)	23	71		L	
09/03	Una (Mt Vernon, NY)	23	39		L	
10/17	M.M. Van Dyke (New York)	38	43		L	
11/07	Fulton Market (New York)	30	24	W		
---/---	Fulton Market (New York)	--	--		L	

BATTER	POS	GP	HL	A	O	R	A	O
H. Thomas		5	9	1	4	15	3	0
J. Smith		5	8	1	3	14	2	4
Moore		5	12	2	2	14	2	4
G. Thomas		5	13	2	3	10	2	0

HARVARD 1 - 5
Cambridge, MA

DATE	OPPONENT	SCORE		W	L	T
05/30	Atlantic (Brooklyn)	15	37		L	
05/31	Eureka (Newark)	39	42		L	
06/01	Excelsior (Brooklyn)	28	46		L	
06/02	Active (New York)	15	24		L	
07/04	Charter Oak (Hartford)	16	14	W		
07/14	Lowell (Boston)	27	37		L	

BATTER	POS	GP	HL	A	O	R	A	O
Frank Wright	1B,P,OF	6	20	3	2	18	3	0
Nelson	2B,OF	5	13	2	3	12	2	2
G.A. Flagg	SS,C	6	16	2	4	17	2	5
Parker	3B	5	20	4	0	7	1	2
Abercrombie	OF	6	20	3	2	13	2	1
Hunnewell	OF,SS,P	6	16	2	4	20	3	2
Nathaniel Smith	OF,3B	6	17	2	5	15	2	3
Ames	C,2B	6	20	3	2	13	2	1
Miller	P,1B,SS	5	8	1	3	17	3	2

KEARNEY 1 - 6
Rahway, NJ

DATE	OPPONENT	SCORE		W	L	T
07/10	Eureka (Newark)	6	45		L	
07/20	Fulton Market (New York)	45	14	W		

KEARNEY (cont.)
Rahway, NJ

DATE	OPPONENT	SCORE		W	L	T
07/27	Eureka (Newark)	6	36		L	
08/21	Fulton Market (New York)	16	39		L	
10/29	Fulton Market (New York)	14	71		L	
---/---	Irvington (Irvington, NJ)	--	--		L	
---/---	Irvington (Irvington, NJ)	--	--		L	

BATTER	POS	GP	HL	A	O	R	A	O
Tufts		5	11	2	1	17	3	2
Baldwin		5	12	2	2	11	2	1
Martin		5	11	2	1	11	2	1
Lang		5	12	2	2	8	1	3
G. Bramhall		5	15	3	0	5	1	0
McDonald		5	17	3	2	3	0	2

ORIENTAL 1 - 6
Greenpoint, NY

DATE	OPPONENT	SCORE		W	L	T
08/24	Eckford (Brooklyn)	12	33		L	
09/05	M.M. Van Dyke (New York)	27	36		L	
09/18	M.M. Van Dyke (New York)	23	28		L	
10/20	Eckford (Brooklyn)	9	27		L	
10/22	Union (Morrisania, NY)	5	24		L	
---/---	Social (New York)	--	--	W		
---/---	Union (Morrisania, NY)	--	--		L	

BATTER	POS	GP	HL	A	O	R	A	O
Elijah Holmes		6	14	2	2	13	2	1
George Russell		6	13	2	1	10	1	4
A. Oppenheimer		6	13	2	1	9	1	3
Ed Holmes		6	19	3	1	6	1	0
Percy Butler		5	10	2	0	9	1	4
G.H. Davis		5	14	2	4	6	1	1
English		5	16	3	1	6	1	1

PECONIC 1 - 6
Brooklyn, NY

DATE	OPPONENT	SCORE		W	L	T
06/18	Atlantic (Brooklyn)	19	43		L	
07/19	Atlantic (Brooklyn)	7	64		L	
08/07	Excelsior (Brooklyn)	4	32		L	
08/25	Enterprise (Brooklyn)	38	46		L	
09/29	Enterprise (Brooklyn)	14	33		L	
10/04	Powhatan (Brooklyn)	25	17	W		
---/---	Mohawk (Brooklyn)	--	--		L	

BATTER	POS	GP	HL	A	O	R	A	O
Wright	1B	7	14	2	0	21	3	0
Hall	2B	6	19	3	1	13	1	6
Hartman	SS	7	22	3	1	13	1	6
Thorp	3B	5	13	2	3	12	2	2
Chapman	OF,P	7	22	3	1	13	1	6
Davis	OF	7	17	2	3	14	2	0
Wilcox	OF,3B	7	7	1	0	15	2	1
Kiers	C	6	21	3	3	10	1	4
Stark	P	5	13	2	3	13	2	3

SOCIAL
New York, NY   1 - 7

DATE	OPPONENT	SCORE		W	L	T
07/28	Americus (Newark)	21	28		L	
08/16	Jefferson (New York)	27	44		L	
08/24	Eclectic (New York)	27	23	W		
08/30	Jefferson (New York)	29	31		L	
09/05	Americus (Newark)	20	28		L	
09/07	National (Jersey City)	13	30		L	
10/24	Eclectic (New York)	14	16		L	
---/---	Oriental (Greenpoint, NY)	--	--		L	

BATTER	POS	GP	HL	A	O	R	A	O
Byrnes		6	12	2	0	12	2	0
Chase		5	7	1	2	12	2	2
Fields		6	14	2	2	12	2	0
Foster		5	10	2	0	10	2	0
Layman		5	14	2	4	10	2	0
Trayo		5	6	1	1	12	2	2
Vogel		5	12	2	2	11	2	1

UNIONVILLE
Unionville, NY   1 - 7

DATE	OPPONENT	SCORE		W	L	T
08/11	Star (New Brunswick, NJ)	14	74		L	
08/28	Eckford (Brooklyn)	20	56		L	
09/22	Powhatan (Brooklyn)	15	41		L	
10/31	Powhatan (Brooklyn)	9	16		L	
11/03	Star (New Brunswick, NJ)	17	23		L	
11/10	Pacific (New Utrecht, NY)	26	47		L	
---/---	Pacific (New Utrecht, NY)	--	--	W		
---/---	Pacific (New Utrecht, NY)	--	--		L	

BATTER	POS	GP	HL	A	O	R	A	O
J. Williams		5	10	2	0	15	3	0
Morris		5	11	2	1	11	2	1
C. Bennett		5	14	2	4	10	2	0
Maxwell		5	14	2	4	7	1	2

ALERT
Danville, PA   0 - 1

DATE	OPPONENT	SCORE		W	L	T
06/14	Athletic (Philadelphia)	2	92		L	

BATTER	POS	GP	HL	A	O	R	A	O
Pinneo	1B	1	1	2	2	0	0	0
Magill	2B	1	2	2	0	0	0	0
Clark	SS	1	3	3	0	0	0	0
Forrister	3B	1	2	2	0	0	0	0
Boyd	OF	1	2	2	0	0	0	0
Gerhart	OF	1	2	2	0	0	0	0
Byorly	OF	1	1	1	0	2	2	0
Biddle	C	1	2	2	0	0	0	0
Adams	P	1	2	2	0	0	0	0

EON
Portland, ME

0 - 1

DATE	OPPONENT	SCORE	W	L	T
07/04	Lowell (Boston)	23 33		L	

BATTER	POS	GP	HL	A	O	R	A	O
Means	1B	1	2	2	0	5	5	0
Hackes	2B	1	5	5	0	2	2	0
Armstrong	SS	1	3	3	0	3	3	0
Randall	3B	1	3	3	0	2	2	0
McAllister	OF	1	1	1	0	2	2	0
Foster	OF	1	4	4	0	2	2	0
Dennis	OF	1	3	3	0	2	2	0
Evans	C	1	2	2	0	3	3	0
Braughton	P	1	4	4	0	2	2	0

UNCAS
Norwich, CT

0 - 1

DATE	OPPONENT	SCORE	W	L	T
07/24	Union (Morrisania, NY)	1 51		L	

BATTER	POS	GP	HL	A	O	R	A	O
Abbott	1B	1	3	3	0	0	0	0
Meech	2B	1	2	2	0	0	0	0
Pierce	SS	1	3	3	0	0	0	0
Muzzey	3B	1	2	2	0	1	1	0
Case	OF	1	4	4	0	0	0	0
Palmer	OF	1	3	3	0	0	0	0
Whitaker	OF	1	3	3	0	0	0	0
Hilliard	C	1	4	4	0	0	0	0
Toll	P	1	3	3	0	0	0	0

GREENWOOD
Brooklyn, NY

0 - 7

DATE	OPPONENT	SCORE	W	L	T
07/07	Contest (Brooklyn)	13 57		L	
07/14	Independent (Brooklyn)	15 46		L	
07/28	Powhatan (Brooklyn)	5 23		L	
09/07	Mohawk (Brooklyn)	13 31		L	
---/---	Pacific (New Utrecht, NY)	-- --		L	
---/---	Independent (Brooklyn)	-- --		L	
---/---	Contest (Brooklyn)	-- --		L	

BATTER	POS	GP	HL	A	O	R	A	O
J. Scrimgeour		6	12	2	0	12	2	0
Sloane		6	13	2	1	11	1	5
F. Scrimgeour		6	14	2	2	11	1	5
Ross		6	13	2	3	10	1	4
J. Blair		5	9	1	4	8	1	3
Youngs		5	13	2	3	8	1	3
Byrd		5	11	2	1	6	1	1
W. Blair		5	13	2	3	6	1	1

TEAM TOTALS

TEAM	CITY/STATE	GP	W	L	T	PCT	R	OR
Union	Morrisania, NY	**28**	**25**	**3**	**0**	.893	1022	454
Athletic	Philadelphia, PA	25	23	2	0	**.920**	**1287**	350
Atlantic	Brooklyn, NY	20	17	3	0	.850	634	314
Excelsior	Brooklyn, NY	20	13	6	1	.675	552	410
Mutual	New York, NY	12	10	2	0	.833	319	182
National	Washington, DC	15	10	5	0	.667	593	325
Active	New York, NY	16	10	6	0	.625	353	358
Mohawk	Brooklyn, NY	12	9	3	0	.750	363	244
Eureka	Newark, NJ	15	9	6	0	.600	446	311
Enterprise	Brooklyn, NY	15	9	6	0	.600	361	335
Eckford	Brooklyn, NY	17	9	8	0	.529	505	333
Americus	Newark, NJ	13	8	5	0	.638	367	419
Irvington	Irvington, NJ	14	8	6	0	.571	377	297
Star	Brooklyn, NY	14	8	6	0	.571	413	362
Fulton Market	New York, NY	8	6	2	0	.750	295	146
Charter Oak	Hartford, CT	9	6	3	0	.667	252	187
Olympic	Paterson, NJ	9	6	3	0	.667	205	161
Independent	Brooklyn, NY	11	6	5	0	.545	304	279
Eclectic	New York, NY	19	6	13	0	.316	376	**497**
Powhatan	Brooklyn, NY	9	5	4	0	.556	210	155
Keystone	Philadelphia, PA	11	5	5	1	.500	236	238
Jefferson	Washington, DC	13	5	7	1	.423	347	429
Hudson River	Newburgh, NY	5	4	1	0	.800	129	110
Liberty	New Brunswick, NJ	6	4	2	0	.667	162	184
Gotham	New York, NY	8	4	4	0	.500	201	194
M.M. Van Dyke	New York, NY	8	4	4	0	.500	298	306
National	Albany, NY	8	4	4	0	.500	233	205
Pacific	New Utrecht, NY	9	4	5	0	.444	280	248
Alert	Cumberland, MD	3	3	0	0	1.000	40	16
Jefferson	New York, NY	4	3	1	0	.750	132	103
Contest	Brooklyn, NY	7	3	4	0	.429	162	150
Olympic	Philadelphia, PA	7	3	4	0	.429	226	243
Waterbury	Waterbury, CT	8	3	5	0	.375	142	252
Una	Mt. Vernon, NY	9	3	6	0	.333	230	212
Empire	New York, NY	10	3	7	0	.300	215	315
Knickerbocker	Albany, NY	2	2	0	0	1.000	46	25
Lowell	Boston, MA	2	2	0	0	1.000	70	50
National	Jersey City, NJ	7	2	4	1	.357	155	175
Star	New Brunswick, NJ	7	2	4	1	.357	164	172
Camden	Camden, NJ	7	2	5	0	.286	145	244
Surprise	W. Farms, NY	7	2	5	0	.286	44	179
Union	Washington, DC	11	2	8	1	.227	182	305
Eagle	New York, NY	11	2	9	0	.182	224	368
Undercliff	Cold Spring, NY	4	1	3	0	.250	140	127
Atlantic	Jamaica, NY	4	1	3	0	.250	44	98
Chester	Norwich, CT	4	1	3	0	.250	113	173
Harvard	Cambridge, MA	6	1	5	0	.167	140	200
Constellation	Brooklyn, NY	6	1	5	0	.167	123	219
Kearney	Rahway, NJ	7	1	6	0	.143	87	205
Oriental	Greenpoint, NY	7	1	6	0	.143	122	179
Peconic	Brooklyn, NY	7	1	6	0	.143	130	264
Social	New York, NY	8	1	7	0	.125	151	200
Unionville	Unionville, NY	8	1	7	0	.125	101	257
Alert	Danville, PA	1	0	1	0	.000	2	92
Eon	Portland, ME	1	0	1	0	.000	23	33
Uncas	Norwich, CT	1	0	1	0	.000	1	51
Allegheny	Allegheny, PA	3	0	3	0	.000	16	40
Greenwood	Brooklyn, NY	7	0	7	0	.000	85	285

OTHER TEAMS

TEAM	CITY/STATE
Alert	Philadelphia, PA
Burlington	Burlington, NJ
Cedar Grove	Fishkill, NY
Central City	Syracuse, NY
Clinton	Brooklyn, NY
Columbia	Bordentown, NJ
Eckford	Albany, NY
Empire	St. Louis, MO
Enterprise	Clifton, NY
Equity	Philadelphia, PA
Fallkill	Poughkeepsie, NY
Frontier	Ft. Leavenworth, KS
Knickerbocker	New York, NY
Lookout	Chattanooga, TN
Lorillard	Rhinebeck, NY
Louisville	Louisville, KY
Minerva	Philadelphia, PA
Monitor	Goshen, NY
Mount Airy	Philadelphia, PA
Mountain	Altoona, PA
Mystic	New York, NY
New Jersey	Burlington, NJ
New York	New York, NY
Newark	Newark, NJ
Philadelphia	Philadelphia, PA
Pioneer	Newark, NJ
Potomac	Washington, DC
Resolute	Brooklyn, NY
Susquehanna	Wilkesbarre, PA
Swiftfoot	Philadelphia, PA
Utica	Utica, NY
Victory	Troy, NY
Wayne	Brooklyn, NY
Williamsburgh	Brooklyn, NY
Yale	New Haven, CT

1867
NATIONAL TOUR

During the summer of 1860, baseball experienced its first road trip. Before this time, virtually all teams stayed home playing clubs in their immediate vicinity. However, in the midst of the 1860 season, the Excelsior of Brooklyn club traveled far-afield playing six opponents in upper-state New York. In the ensuing years, teams on the eastern seaboard journeyed to other locales such as Boston or Philadelphia to test their mettle, but none delved into the interior. During the summer of 1867 this all changed as one Association club traveled to the edge of the baseball playing world and back. Surprisingly, this team didn't hail from the baseball meccas of New York or Brooklyn. This club in fact came from the Association's southern border.

At the National Association's convention in December 1866, the attendance more than doubled the previous year's total as an astounding 202 clubs were represented. In addition, other clubs were admitted as probationary members during the season, swelling the ranks even further. Most clubs were still located in the Mid-Atlantic and New England states but some came from more westerly or southerly districts. Several of the southern entities hailed from Washington, D.C., one of which was known as the National club.

The Nationals were first listed on the Association roster in 1861, but soon dropped out because of the Civil War. Reorganized in 1864, the team sported modest records until 1866, when they finished 10-5. In 1867, the National club was poised to make another leap ahead, but not in the usual way. In a small notice published in the *New York Clipper* entitled "The Tour of the Nationals" the following agenda was outlined: "The famous Washington club will start upon their proposed Western trip on the 10th [July], visiting and playing friendly games with the leading clubs of Columbus, Cincinnati, Louisville, Indianapolis, St. Louis and Chicago, reaching the latter place on the 24th,..." The Nationals proposed what no other eastern Association club had attempted—a trans-Allegheny ball playing journey.

There was good reason why no other eastern club had attempted such a trip - it was difficult. Traveling any distance in the 1860s was a tiresome chore. Railroads were still in their adolescence, unreliable at best. As a result, the National party supplemented train travel with a combination of boats and coaches to reach their destinations.

After leaving the capital on July 11th, the National club met their first opponent two days later. On the 13th, they vanquished the Capital club of Columbus, Ohio, 90–10. The Nationals next journeyed to Cincinnati where they bested the Cincinnati (53–10) and Buckeye (88–10) clubs on the 15th and 16th. The very next day, the traveling nine visited Kentucky where they walloped the Louisville team 82–21. Two days later, in Indianapolis, the Nationals reached triple-digits as they torched the Westerns 106–26. The next stop was St. Louis on the 22nd and 23rd where they toyed with the Unions (113–26) and Empires (53–26).

In the last week of July, the Nationals reached Chicago, the final destination of their tour. Here they faced their first real challenge. After mauling seven opponents in four states, the Nationals expected a similar result in their game against the Forest City club of Rockford on July 25th. In his book *America's National Pastime*, baseball magnate Al Spalding, who was the 16 year old pitcher for the Rockford nine that day, described the action:

> Every member of the team cautioned me to take my time and keep cool; but I was not so rattled but that I recognized the fact that every one of them was so scared that none could speak above a whisper. The fact is, we were all frightened nearly to death,...

Spalding overcame his jitters to pitch his team to an unexpected 29–23 victory. Stung by the setback, the Nationals closed out the tour with two convincing wins on the 27th and 29th over the Excelsiors (49–4) and Atlantics (78–17) of Chicago.

While the Nationals played out west, the defending champion Atlantic club of Brooklyn ran aground. On July 31, they were soundly whipped by the Unions of Morrisania 32–19. In their rematch on the

10th of October, the curtain came crashing down. After taking an 11-9 lead in the top of the seventh, the Atlantics watched the Unions plate three in the bottom of the inning. The Brooklynites tied the match in the top of the eighth, but the Unions wrested the advantage back with two of their own. Trailing by two entering the ninth, the Atlantics could score but one and so lost 14–13. The *Clipper* described the aftermath:

> And so the championship, which the Atlantics have held so long, slipped out of their grasp when least expected, and into the hands of a club that has been defeated by the Athletics, Mutuals, Irvingtons, and Unions of Lansingburgh. It seemed hard to realize the fact, so sudden and unexpected.

Though the Unions had lost a total of eight games, the championship was theirs based upon their pair of victories over the Atlantic club.

Enjoying the fruits of their tour, the National club finished with 29 victories in 1867. Good as that total was, it didn't come close to matching the season's best. That honor belonged to the Athletic contingent who won an incredible 44 of 47 games. Other teams with more than 20 victories included the Quaker City (a new entry from Philadelphia) with 28, the Mutuals with 23, the Keystone of Philadelphia with 21 and the aforementioned champion Unions also with 21.

On a sad note, one of Philadelphia's strongest clubs was not included in the official statistics of the National Association. Despite winning a majority of their contests, the Pythian club was banned from Association membership for the simple reason that the club was composed of African-Americans. Founded in 1866 by Octavius Catto, the Pythian club played games against other African-American teams. In 1867, the Pythians dominated, winning eight of nine. In later years, their schedule expanded to include games against white teams. Although they competed on the same ballfield as Association clubs, the Pythians and other African-American clubs never were allowed to join as they were unfortunately looked at as curiosities rather than equals.

The Association's top run scorers all came from the Athletic club as Al Reach (270), Dick McBride (265) and John Sensenderfer (263) each broke the existing record. The three top averages were posted by an obscure trio of players. Eastin and Bettinger of the Active of

Buffalo club each posted the top average (7,8) followed by Sheppard of the Brandywines (W. Chester, PA) at 7,7. (Note: Daly on the Oshkosh [Everett, WI] club averaged 8,0 in five games although no scores are extant.) Among the more established teams, brothers Harry (6,10) and George Wright (6,8) of the Cincinnatis and Nationals as well Harry Wright's teammate Schwartz (6,8) finished with the best averages.

The National's tour of 1867 was considered a smashing success. The Nationals were able to showcase their talents in crushing nine of ten opponents. In being led to the slaughter, many western cities got their first glimpse of first class ball playing thus prodding them into creating first-class nines of their own.

The 1867 tour was soon to be emulated by other teams. During the remaining years of the Association, virtually all of the top clubs took their turns traversing the Alleghenies. With all of the strong teams springing up in the wake of the National's tour in places like Cincinnati and Chicago, no season was considered complete without at least one trip—at least one test against the best of the west.

ATHLETIC   44 - 3
Philadelphia, PA

DATE	OPPONENT	SCORE		W	L	T
04/20	Bachelor (Philadelphia)	41	11	W		
04/27	Commonwealth (Philadelphia)	76	16	W		
---/---	Camden (Camden, NJ)	46	14	W		
05/09	W. Philadelphia (Philadelphia)	64	14	W		
05/13	W. Philadelphia (Philadelphia)	34	13	W		
05/17	Keystone (philadelphia)	19	14	W		
---/---	Hamilton (Philadelphia)	40	7	W		
---/---	Harry Clay (Philadelphia)	80	32	W		
06/11	Eon (Portland, ME)	88	23	W		
06/12	Harvard (Cambridge, MA)	22	10	W		
06/13	Lowell (Boston)	53	8	W		
06/14	Charter Oak (Hartford)	35	19	W		
06/29	Philadelphia (Philadelphia)	72	7	W		
07/03	Harry Clay (Philadelphia)	54	6	W		
07/04	Atlantic (Trenton, NJ)	66	8	W		
07/13	Bristol (Philadelphia)	76	16	W		
07/15	Tyrolean (Harrisburg, PA)	118	11	W		
07/17	Commonwealth (Philadelphia)	75	25	W		
07/20	Arctic (Philadelphia)	55	16	W		
07/25	Union (Camden, NJ)	28	11	W		
08/14	Star (Allentown, PA)	58	4	W		
08/17	Camden (Camden, NJ)	29	3	W		
08/19	Union (Morrisania, NY)	23	10	W		
08/20	Mutual (New York)	18	16	W		
08/21	Eckford (Brooklyn)	23	19	W		
08/26	Hamilton (Philadelphia)	84	9	W		
08/28	Mutual (New York)	21	23		L	
09/06	Union (Lansingburgh, NY)	47	8	W		
09/12	Enterprise (Baltimore)	77	12	W		
09/14	Union (Camden, NJ)	57	27	W		
09/16	Atlantic (Brooklyn)	16	28		L	
09/18	Mutual (New York)	17	18		L	
09/21	Union (Morrisania, NY)	36	32	W		
09/23	Atlantic (Brooklyn)	28	8	W		
09/24	Jefferson (Washington, DC)	50	14	W		
---/---	Monocacy (?)	40	16	W		
10/02	Olympic (Washington, DC)	36	6	W		
10/12	Quaker City (Philadelphia)	57	8	W		
---/---	Union (Washington, DC	65	15	W		
---/---	Bachelor (Philadelphia)	30	14	W		
---/---	Arctic (Philadelphia)	54	13	W		
11/02	W. Philadelphia (Philadelphia)	37	10	W		
---/---	W. Philadelphia (Philadelphia)	37	22	W		
11/09	Quaker City (Philadelphia)	16	10	W		
11/13	National (Washington, DC)	28	12	W		
11/14	Olympic (Washington, DC)	17	5	W		
11/16	Bristol (Philadelphia)	55	14	W		

BATTER	POS	GP	H L	A O	R	A O
Dan Kleinfelder	1B,C,OF	43	117	2 31	229	5 14
Al Reach	2B	45	112	2 22	270	6 0
Isaac Wilkins	SS	44	137	3 5	210	4 34
Wes Fisler	3B,1B	43	117	2 31	229	5 14
John Sensenderfer	OF	47	114	2 20	263	5 28
Tom Berry	OF,2B	35	100	2 30	165	4 25
Ned Cuthbert	OF	25	74	2 24	98	3 23
John Radcliff	C,OF	36	107	2 35	165	4 21
Dick McBride	P,3B	45	109	2 19	265	5 40
Hicks Hayhurst	OF,P	15	55	3 10	88	5 13
Kahmar	3B,OF	14	48	3 6	66	4 10
Pharo	OF,C	10	23	2 3	59	5 9
Woolman	OF	9	31	3 4	57	6 3

NATIONAL   29 - 7
Washington, DC

DATE	OPPONENT	SCORE		W	L	T
06/03	Interior (Washington)	91	8	W		
06/12	Jefferson (Washington)	57	27	W		
06/19	Olympic (Washington)	46	7	W		
07/02	Continental (Washington)	74	26	W		
07/09	Union (Washington)	41	16	W		
07/13	Capital (Columbus, OH)	90	10	W		
07/15	Cincinnati (Cincinnati, OH)	53	10	W		
07/16	Buckeye (Cincinnati, OH)	88	12	W		
07/17	Louisville (Louisville, KY)	82	21	W		
07/19	Western (Indianapolis, IN)*	106	26	W		
07/22	Union (St. Louis, MO)	113	26	W		
07/23	Empire (St. Louis, MO)	53	26	W		
07/25	Forest City (Rockford, IL)*	23	29		L	
07/27	Excelsior (Chicago)*	49	4	W		
07/29	Atlantic (Chicago)*	78	17	W		
08/14	Jefferson (Washington)	52	19	W		
08/19	Capitol (Washington)	48	14	W		
08/24	Capitol (Washington)	43	11	W		
08/26	Mutual (New York)	16	40		L	
08/---	Empire (Washington)	37	17	W		
08/---	Interior (Washington)	80	14	W		
09/04	Union (Lansingburgh, NY)	31	28	W		
09/12	Union (Washington)	24	22	W		
09/13	Empire (Washington)	39	6	W		
09/18	Pastime (Richmond, VA)*	111	9	W		
09/19	Irvington (Irvington, NJ)	33	22	W		
09/20	Maryland (Baltimore, MD)	35	8	W		
09/21	Pastime (Baltimore, MD)	57	17	W		
10/09	Maryland (Baltimore, MD)	53	12	W		
10/16	Olympic (Washington, DC)	33	7	W		
10/21	Union (Lansingburgh, NY)	15	16		L	
10/23	Mutual (New York)	29	37		L	
10/25	Irvington (Irvington, NJ)	23	29		L	
10/26	Excelsior (Brooklyn)	11	26		L	
11/09	Commonwealth (Philadelphia)	30	6	W		
11/13	Athletic (Philadelphia)*	12	35		L	

* statistics not included in totals

BATTER	POS	GP	HL	A	O	R	A	O
Ed Parker	1B,2B	27	82	3	1	143	5	8
George Wright	2B,SS,P	29	64	2	6	182	6	8
Frank Norton	SS,C	17	48	3	14	76	4	8
George Fox	3B	21	40	1	19	126	6	0
George Fletcher	OF,1B,P	30	85	2	25	169	5	19
Sy Studley	OF	22	51	2	7	134	6	2
Eb Smith	OF	19	56	2	18	117	6	3
Harry Berthrong	C,OF	28	70	2	14	161	5	21
Will Williams	P,OF	18	65	3	11	98	5	8
Hodges	OF,3B	17	50	2	16	85	5	0
Harry McLean	OF	7	33	4	5	39	5	4
Asa Brainard	P	6	15	2	3	16	2	4
Andrew Gibney	OF	6	20	3	2	14	2	2

QUAKER CITY   28 - 9
Philadelphia, PA

DATE	OPPONENT	SCORE		W	L	T
05/06	Camden (Camden, NJ)	22	17	W		
05/---	Geary (Philadelphia)	33	15	W		
05/---	Geary (Philadelphia)	39	11	W		
05/23	Alvin (Philadelphia)	48	12	W		

QUAKER CITY (cont.)
Philadelphia, PA

DATE	OPPONENT	SCORE		W	L	T
05/27	W. Philadelphia (Philadelphia)	40	13	W		
06/10	Keystone (Philadelphia)	25	51		L	
06/---	Alvin (Philadelphia)	95	18	W		
06/20	Bachelor (Philadelphia)	29	8	W		
06/24	W. Philadelphia (Philadelphia)	20	11	W		
07/01	Keystone (Philadelphia)	37	42		L	
07/04	Leonore (Philadelphia)	85	11	W		
07/11	Arctic (Philadelphia)	70	26	W		
07/15	Bachelor (Philadelphia)	50	14	W		
07/18	Union (Camden, NJ)	36	14	W		
07/25	Harry Clay (Philadelphia)	49	40	W		
07/27	Eagle (Norristown, PA)	56	5	W		
08/01	Perry (Philadelphia)	45	13	W		
08/12	Columbia (Bordentown, NJ)	48	18	W		
08/19	Columbia (Bordentown, NJ)	30	12	W		
08/24	Harry Clay (Philadelphia)	36	17	W		
08/26	Union (Camden, NJ)	38	28	W		
09/07	Union (Lansingburgh, NY)	10	20		L	
09/13	Pastime (Baltimore)	15	18		L	
09/14	Camden (Camden, NJ)	22	21	W		
09/17	Perry (Philadelphia)	63	3	W		
09/20	Irvington (Irvington, NJ)	27	14	W		
09/24	Atlantic (Brooklyn)	21	24		L	
10/01	Arctic (Philadelphia)	26	16	W		
10/03	Olympic (Washington, DC)	29	11	W		
10/12	Athletic (Philadelphia)	8	57		L	
10/24	Eagle (Norristown, PA)	35	17	W		
11/07	Keystone (Philadelphia)	13	21		L	
11/09	Athletic (Philadelphia)	10	16		L	
11/18	Keystone (Philadelphia)	*9	0	W		
11/28	Wawassett (Wilmington, DE)	65	9	W		
---/---	Bachelor (Philadelphia)	39	9	W		
---/---	Bachelor (Philadelphia)	12	17		L	

* Forfeit

BATTER	POS	GP	HL	A	O	R	A	O
George Heubel	1B,OF	31	101	3	8	110	3	17
William Wallace	2B	10	29	2	9	43	4	3
Dick Flowers	SS,C,	27	60	2	6	112	4	4
Donohue	3B,SS	37	98	2	24	146	3	35
John Chapman	OF,P,2B	28	54	1	26	143	5	3
Deshong	OF,1B	26	66	2	14	107	4	3
Brown	OF,P	16	38	2	6	63	3	15
Fergy Malone	C,1B,SS	34	79	2	11	152	4	16
Tom Pratt	P	24	60	2	12	96	4	0
Potter	3B,2B,OF	22	52	2	8	91	4	3
W. Shane	SS,OF	17	55	3	4	58	3	7
Howell	OF,C,3B	14	45	3	8	89	2	11
Rivers	SS	12	35	2	11	53	4	5

MUTUAL 23 - 6 - 1
New York, NY

DATE	OPPONENT	SCORE		W	L	T
06/12	Jefferson (New York)	58	1	W		
06/19	Eclectic (New York)	32	5	W		
06/28	Irvington (Irvington, NJ)	17	16	W		
06/29	Independent (Brooklyn)	28	26	W		
07/04	Eckford (Brooklyn)	20	20			T
07/12	Eckford (Brooklyn)	28	9	W		
07/22	Hudson River (Newburgh, NY)	27	6	W		

MUTUAL (cont.)
New York, NY

DATE	OPPONENT	SCORE			W	L	T
07/26	Harlem (New York)	45	16		W		
07/30	Harlem (New York)	40	20		W		
08/01	Mohawk (Brooklyn)	17	1		W		
08/05	Champion (Jersey City, NJ)	52	13		W		
08/12	Atlantic (Brooklyn)	15	18			L	
08/14	Union (Morrisania, NY)	8	9	(10)		L	
08/20	Athletic (Philadelphia)	16	18			L	
08/23	Eureka (Newark)	34	21		W		
08/26	National (Washington, DC)	40	16		W		
08/27	Pastime (Baltimore)	31	47			L	
08/28	Athletic (Philadelphia)	23	21		W		
08/30	Keystone (Philadelphia)	20	28			L	
08/31	W. Philadelphia (Philadelphia)	28	23		W		
09/04	Irvington (Irvington, NJ)	19	16		W		
09/14	Independent (Brooklyn)	71	25		W		
09/17	W. Philadelphia (Philadelphia)	32	18		W		
09/18	Athletic (Philadelphia)	18	17		W		
09/23	Union (Morrisania, NY)	28	24		W		
09/25	Union (Lansingburgh, NY)	19	6		W		
09/27	Eckford (Brooklyn)	29	20		W		
10/07	Atlantic (Brooklyn)	17	32			L	
10/22	National (Washington, DC)	37	29		W		
10/28	Jefferson (New York)	52	9		W		

BATTER	POS	GP	HL	A	O	R	A	O
Charley Bearman	1B,P	25	75	3	0	67	2	17
John Hatfield	2B,OF	27	72	2	18	100	3	19
Tom Devyr	SS	29	97	3	9	80	3	3
Fred Waterman	3B	27	59	2	5	106	3	25
Charles Hunt	OF,1B,SS	25	60	2	10	97	3	22
Billy McMahon	OF,3B	24	46	1	22	85	3	13
Lip Pike	OF,3B,2B,1B	21	51	2	9	82	3	19
Nat Jewett	C	27	87	3	6	87	3	6
Al Martin	P,OF	16	50	3	2	54	3	6
Richard Hunt	OF,3B,2B	14	42	3	0	55	3	15
John Zeller	1B,OF	12	38	3	2	37	3	1
Tom Watts	P	10	42	4	2	14	1	4

KEYSTONE   21 - 6 - 1
Philadelphia, PA

DATE	OPPONENT	SCORE		W	L	T
05/17	Athletic (Philadelphia)	14	19		L	
---/---	Union (Camden, NJ)	18	25		L	
05/30	Union (Camden, NJ)	52	25	W		
06/10	Quaker City (Philadelphia)	51	25	W		
---/---	W. Philadelphia (Philadelphia)	31	43		L	
---/---	Arctic (Philadelphia)	27	12	W		
---/---	First Ward (Philadelphia)	40	12	W		
07/01	Quaker City (Philadelphia)	42	37	W		
07/05	Arctic (Philadelphia)	35	55		L	
07/22	Union (Camden, NJ)	45	30	W		
08/05	W. Philadelphia (Philadelphia)	49	39	W		
---/---	Dirigo (Philadelphia)	46	13	W		
08/19	W. Philadelphia (Philadelphia)	36	16	W		
08/23	Ralston (Camden, NJ)	32	22	W		
08/30	Mutual (New York)	28	20	W		
09/10	Eckford (Brooklyn)	6	29		L	
09/14	Pastime (Baltimore)	39	9	W		
09/25	Atlantic (Brooklyn)	12	12			T
---/---	Jefferson (Washington)	68	6	W		

KEYSTONE (cont.)
Philadelphia, PA

DATE	OPPONENT	SCORE		W	L	T
10/02	Excelsior (Brooklyn)	20	15	W		
10/03	Atlantic (Brooklyn)	21	18	W		
10/04	Eckford (Brooklyn)	31	13	W		
---/---	Bachelor (Philadelphia)	21	4	W		
---/---	Union (Washington)	11	7	W		
---/---	Union (Camden, NJ)	29	15	W		
11/07	Quaker City (Philadelphia)	21	13	W		
11/18	Quaker City (Philadelphia)	*0	9		L	
---/---	Bachelor (Philadelphia)	17	14	W		

* Forfeit

BATTER	POS	GP	HL	A	O	R	A	O
Robinson	1B	8	23	2	7	22	2	6
Billy Dick	2B	14	41	2	13	54	3	12
Eddie Woods	SS,OF	13	34	2	8	44	3	5
Mackie	3B	8	22	2	6	19	2	3
Elias Cope	OF,P,SS	13	36	2	10	48	3	3
John McMullin	OF,1B,C	13	31	2	5	47	3	8
Ned Conner	OF,1B,C	12	36	3	0	33	2	9
Ewell	C	9	27	3	0	23	2	5
Joseph Gwynn	P,OF	9	23	2	5	25	2	7
McClarnan	OF,1B,SS	8	23	2	7	29	3	5
Mike Smith	3B,OF,C	7	26	3	5	25	3	4

UNION   21 - 8
Morrisania, NY

DATE	OPPONENT	SCORE		W	L	T
05/18	Atlanta (Tremont, NY)	48	10	W		
05/25	Athlete (Washington Hts, NY)	101	13	W		
06/04	Irvington (Irvington, NJ)	17	26		L	
06/12	Eureka (Newark)	26	12	W		
06/15	Eclectic (New York)	45	10	W		
06/29	Eclectic (New York)	36	32	W		
07/02	Irvington (Irvington, NJ)	22	26		L	
07/08	National (Albany, NY)	41	17	W		
07/09	Union (Lansingburgh, NY)	23	51		L	
07/10	Utica (Utica, NY)	49	26	W		
07/11	Excelsior (Rochester, NY)	34	15	W		
07/12	Niagara (Buffalo, NY)	25	19	W		
07/31	Atlantic (Brooklyn)	32	19	W		
08/06	Atlanta (Tremont, NY)	31	16	W		
08/14	Mutual (New York)	9	8	(10)	W	
08/19	Athletic (Philadelphia)	10	23		L	
08/26	Active (Newark)	22	12	W		
08/27	Eckford (Brooklyn)	25	23	W		
08/31	Pequot (New London, CT)	33	8	W		
08/31	Riverside (?)	66	10	W		
09/10	Eureka (Newark)	33	14	W		
09/12	Excelsior (Rochester, NY)	29	21	W		
09/17	Active (Newark)	22	11	W		
09/19	Oriental (Greenpoint, NY)	19	42		L	
09/21	Athletic (Philadelphia)	32	36		L	
09/23	Mutual (New York)	24	29		L	
09/24	Union (Lansingburgh, NY)	21	26		L	
09/28	Active (New York)	15	11	(10)	W	
10/10	Atlantic (Brooklyn)	14	13	W		

BATTER	POS	GP	HL	A	O	R	A	O
John Goldie	1B	19	54	2	16	76	4	0
Al Martin	2B	28	68	2	12	114	4	3

UNION (cont.)
Morrisania, NY

BATTER	POS	GP	HL	A	O	R	A	O
George Smith	SS,OF,C,1B	29	75	2	17	115	3	28
Dan Ketchum	3B	27	89	3	8	63	2	12
Albro Aiken	OF,SS	28	79	2	23	96	3	12
Henry Austin	OF	28	79	2	23	98	3	14
Tommy Beals	OF	20	56	2	16	67	3	7
Dave Birdsall	C	28	78	2	22	93	3	9
Charley Pabor	P	28	91	3	7	92	3	8
Hudson	OF	8	22	2	6	29	3	5
William Abrams	OF	6	19	3	1	27	4	3
Norton	P	6	20	3	2	21	3	3

TRI MOUNTAIN   19 - 3
Boston, MA

DATE	OPPONENT	SCORE		W	L	T
06/21	King Phillip (Abington, MA)	38	14	W		
07/04	Shields (E. Cambridge, MA)	67	35	W		
08/31	Eureka (E. Cambridge, MA)	55	30	W		
09/04	Lowell (Boston)	18	20		L	
09/23	Lowell (Boston)	40	35	W		
09/24	King Phillip (Abington, MA)	*9	0	W		
09/25	Fraternity (S. Boston)	51	20	W		
09/26	Eagle (Florence, MA)	16	6	W		
09/27	Waban (Newton, MA)	*9	0	W		
09/28	Lowell (Boston)	42	22	W		

(Only scores extant)

* Forfeit

BATTER	POS	GP	HL	A	O	R	A	O
Williams	1B,OF	20	30	1	10	103	5	3
Frank Barrows	2B	21	46	2	4	101	4	17
Freeman	SS	18	35	1	17	81	4	9
Edwards	3B	17	83	1	16	83	4	15
Harris	OF	16	36	2	4	86	5	6
Franklin	OF,3B	14	29	2	1	53	3	11
Kelly	OF	9	18	2	0	35	3	8
Putnam	C	22	49	2	5	97	4	9
O'Brien	P	18	50	2	14	65	3	11
Crosby	1B	10	28	2	8	31	3	1
Stewart	OF	8	26	3	2	38	4	6

ATLANTIC   19 - 5 - 1
Brooklyn, NY

DATE	OPPONENT	SCORE		W	L	T
06/20	Eckford (Brooklyn)	27	14	W		
07/01	Empire (New York)	78	24	W		
07/04	Star (Brooklyn)	39	21	W		
07/05	Eckford (Brooklyn)	11	4	W		
07/31	Union (Morrisania, NY)	19	32		L	
08/05	Irvington (Irvington, NJ)	32	34		L	
08/12	Mutual (New York)	18	15	W		
08/24	Eckford (Brooklyn)	41	9	W		
09/03	Empire (New York)	32	19	W		
09/05	Eureka (Newark)	21	13	W		
09/11	Excelsior (Rochester, NY)	36	13	W		

ATLANTIC (cont.)
Brooklyn, NY

DATE	OPPONENT	SCORE		W	L	T
09/16	Athletic (Philadelphia)	28	16	W		
09/19	W. Philadelphia (Philadelphia)	34	11	W		
09/21	Star (Brooklyn)	34	7	W		
09/23	Athletic (Philadelphia)	8	28		L	
09/24	Quaker City (Philadelphia)	24	21	W		
09/25	Keystone (Philadelphia)	12	12			T
09/26	W. Philadelphia (Philadelphia)	36	31	W		
10/03	Keystone (Philadelphia)	18	21		L	
10/07	Mutual (New York)	32	17	W		
10/10	Union (Morrisania, NY)	13	14		L	
10/12	Princeton (Princeton, NJ)	19	9	W		
10/14	Irvington (Irvington, NJ)	36	12	W		
10/15	Union (Lansingburgh, NY)	41	21	W		
10/24	Oriental (Greenpoint, NY)	35	11	W		

BATTER	POS	GP	HL	A O	R	A O
Joe Start	1B	19	40	2 2	83	4 7
Fred Crane	2B	25	76	3 1	88	3 13
Dickey Pearce	SS,3B,C,OF	23	70	3 1	83	3 14
Bob Ferguson	3B	24	67	2 19	82	3 10
Dan McDonald	OF	26	71	2 19	81	3 3
John Kenney	OF	21	62	2 20	54	2 12
John Galvin	OF	11	32	2 10	35	3 2
Charley Mills	C	24	67	2 19	82	3 10
George Zettlein	P	26	87	3 9	65	2 12
Charles Smith	SS,1B	11	35	3 2	32	2 10
Regan	OF	8	24	3 0	21	2 5
O'Flynn	OF	5	12	2 2	16	3 1

GEARY 19 - 6
Philadelphia, PA

DATE	OPPONENT	SCORE		W	L	T
---/---	Chestnut St. Theatre (Philadelphia)	51	13	W		
---/---	Amateur (Philadelphia)	55	12	W		
05/---	Quaker City (Philadelphia)	15	33		L	
05/---	Quaker City (Philadelphia)	11	39		L	
---/---	Malta (?)	53	7	W		
---/---	South Penn (Philadelphia)	42	13	W		
---/---	Thorn (?)	51	28	W		
---/---	Star (?)	33	59		L	
---/---	Friendship (Beverly, NJ)	43	30	W		
---/---	Chestnut St. Theatre (Philadelphia)	*9	0	W		
---/---	Star (?)	39	18	W		
---/---	Thorn (?)	13	23		L	
---/---	Philadelphia (Philadelphia)	36	17	W		
---/---	Excelsior (Philadelphia?)	60	19	W		
---/---	Thorn (?)	30	12	W		
---/---	Arctic (Philadelphia)	6	16		L	
---/---	Excelsior (Coatesville, PA)	31	12	W		
09/07	Commonwealth (Philadelphia)	26	19	W		
---/---	S.J. Randall (Philadelphia)	50	12	W		
---/---	Ballston (?)	19	18	W		
---/---	Excelsior (Coatesville, PA)	37	26	W		
10/08	Commonwealth (Philadelphia)	26	18	W		
---/---	Arctic (Philadelphia)	20	28		L	
---/---	Harry Clay (Philadelphia)	16	13	W		
---/---	Harry Clay (Philadelphia)	34	31	W		

* Forfeit

GEARY (cont.)
Philadelphia, PA

BATTER	POS	GP	HL	A	O	R	A	O
Levi Meyerle		25	43	1	18	110	4	10
Caton		24	73	3	1	63	2	15
Halbach		20	28	1	8	84	4	4
Hopkins		19	41	2	3	74	3	17
Bradbury		19	49	2	11	57	3	0
Silberman		16	37	2	5	60	3	12
Hamberger		15	30	2	0	61	4	1
Merrell		9	22	2	4	39	4	3
Garvin		9	25	2	7	26	2	8
George Bechtel		8	19	2	3	22	2	6
Bear		7	23	3	2	14	2	0
Matthews		6	19	3	1	22	3	4
Allen		6	16	2	4	16	2	4
Pluck		5	17	3	2	10	2	0

CINCINNATI 16 - 1
Cincinnati, OH

DATE	OPPONENT	SCORE		W	L	T
05/25	Buckeye (Cincinnati)	82	40	W		
05/30	Holt (Newport, KY)	53	33	W		
06/22	Holt (Newport, KY)	93	22	W		
07/04	Louisville (Louisville, KY)	60	24	W		
07/11	Live Oak (Cincinnati)	56	18	W		
07/15	National (Washington, DC)	10	53		L	
07/31	Live Oak (Cincinnati)	51	21	W		
08/29	Western (Indianapolis, IN)	34	27	W		
09/02	Holt (Newport, KY)	109	15	W		
09/06	Louisville (Louisville, KY)	44	22	W		
09/07	Olympic (Louisville, KY)	77	17	W		
09/14	Buckeye (Cincinnati)	28	20	W		
09/26	Hickory (McConnellsville, OH)	28	16	W		
10/05	Buckeye (Cincinnati)	49	23	W		
10/12	Western (Indianapolis, IN)	17	15	W		
10/19	Buckeye (Cincinnati)	37	23	W		
10/25	Active (Indianapolis, IN)	44	24	W		

BATTER	POS	GP	HL	A	O	R	A	O
Arden	1B	11	40	3	7	45	4	1
Storer	2B,OF	9	19	2	1	55	6	1
Con Howe	SS	15	34	2	4	96	6	6
Grant	3B	10	22	2	2	55	5	5
Ellard	OF	13	42	3	3	69	5	4
William Johnson	OF	15	42	2	12	86	5	11
Neff	OF	6	24	4	0	30	5	0
McLean	C	9	22	2	4	51	5	6
Harry Wright	P	17	42	2	9	112	6	10
Schwartz		12	28	2	4	80	6	8
Kemper		8	32	4	0	41	5	1

IRVINGTON 16 - 7
Irvington, NJ

DATE	OPPONENT	SCORE		W	L	T
05/16	Eureka (Newark)	25	17	W		
05/30	Active (Newark)	25	16	W		
06/04	Union (Morrisania, NY)	26	17	W		

IRVINGTON (cont.)
Irvington, NJ

DATE	OPPONENT	SCORE		W	L	T
06/28	Mutual (New York)	16	17		L	
07/02	Union (Morrisania, NY)	26	22	W		
07/04	Neptune (Easton, PA)	36	16	W		
07/16	Eckford (Brooklyn)	44	13	W		
07/21	Neptune (Easton, PA)	38	25	W		
07/27	Star (Brooklyn)	24	10	W		
08/05	Atlantic (Brooklyn)	34	32	W		
08/13	Active (Newark)	52	13	W		
09/04	Mutual (New York)	16	19		L	
09/17	Pastime (Baltimore, MD)	55	17	W		
09/19	National (Washington, DC)	22	33		L	
09/20	Quaker City (Philadelphia)	14	17		L	
09/23	Eckford (Brooklyn)	39	33	W		
09/26	Union (Lansingburgh, NY)	39	7	W		
10/10	Union (Lansingburgh, NY)	9	28		L	
10/14	Atlantic (Brooklyn)	12	36		L	
10/18	Union (Lansingburgh, NY)	27	7	W		
10/22	Eureka (Newark)	22	9	W		
10/25	National (Washington, DC)	29	23	W		
11/02	Star (Brooklyn)	*0	9		L	

BATTER	POS	GP	HL	A	O	R	A	O
Mike Campbell	1B	21	63	3	0	60	2	18
Charlie Sweasy	2B	21	56	2	14	66	3	3
Mahlon Stockman	SS	14	39	2	11	41	2	13
Andy Leonard	3B,OF	21	64	3	2	61	2	19
Billy Lewis	OF,C	19	61	3	4	65	3	8
Hugh Campbell	OF	16	51	3	3	53	3	5
A. Bailey	OF	15	43	2	13	49	3	4
T. Buckley	C	20	62	3	2	61	3	1
Rynie Wolters	P	20	49	2	9	81	4	1
Harry Crawford	OF,SS	15	36	2	6	46	3	1
Lip Pike	3B	6	19	3	1	19	3	1

ORIENTAL   15 - 3
Greenpoint, NY

DATE	OPPONENT	SCORE		W	L	T
05/23	Eclectic (New York)	37	34	W		
06/10	Excelsior (Paterson, NJ)	91	19	W		
06/12	Athlete (Washington Hts, NY)	35	19	W		
---/---	Atlanta (Tremont, NY)	18	9	W		
07/03	Lone Star (Matteawan, NY)	29	31		L	
07/11	Empire (New York)	53	10	W		
07/25	Fulton (New York)	22	27		L	
08/01	Lone Star (Matteawan, NY)	38	33	W		
08/08	Orchard (Brooklyn)	36	11	W		
08/21	Eclectic (New York)	32	22	W		
08/28	Athlete (Washington Hts, NY)	27	25	W		
09/12	Atlanta (Tremont, NY)	26	17	W		
09/19	Union (Morrisania, NY)	42	19	W		
10/03	Lone Star (Mattewan, NY)	27	19	W		
10/04	Hudson River (Newburgh, NY)	29	21	W		
10/10	Knickerbocker (Albany, NY)	22	18	W		
10/22	Fulton (New York)	29	13	W		
10/24	Atlantic (Brooklyn)	11	35		L	

BATTER	POS	GP	HL	A	O	R	A	O
Frank Bliss	1B	11	25	2	3	44	4	0
J. Vanderhoef	2B	8	25	3	1	26	3	2

ORIENTAL (cont.)
Greenpoint, NY

BATTER	POS	GP	HL	A O	R	A O
Percy Butler	SS,3B	18	40	2 4	83	4 11
Samuel Durnham	3B	15	48	3 3	42	2 12
Elijah Holmes	OF,P	17	49	2 15	71	4 3
William Ostrander	OF	12	40	3 4	50	4 2
George Russell	OF	9	29	3 2	33	3 6
Ed Holmes	C	17	43	2 9	62	3 11
Ed Pinkham	P	15	33	2 3	54	3 9
A. Oppenheimer		8	20	2 4	30	3 6
Samuel Galbraith	OF	7	19	2 5	21	3 0
D. Davies	OF,3B	5	15	3 0	25	5 0
William Hobby	2B	5	11	2 1	17	3 2

UNION   14 - 6
Lansingburgh, NY

DATE	OPPONENT	SCORE		W	L	T
05/16	Hudson (Hudson, NY)	53	16	W		
07/09	Union (Morrisania, NY)	51	23	W		
08/06	Eureka (Newark)	42	21	W		
08/14	Eagle (Florence, MA)	17	9	W		
08/---	Hampden (Springfield, MA)	8	6	W		
09/04	National (Washington, DC)	28	31		L	
09/06	Athletic (Philadelphia)	8	47		L	
09/07	Quaker City (Philadelphia)	20	10	W		
09/27	Hudson River (Newburgh, NY)	23	29		L	
09/24	Union (Morrisania, NY)	26	21	W		
09/25	Mutual (New York)	6	19		L	
09/26	Irvington (Irvington, NJ)	7	39		L	
10/10	Irvington (Irvington, NJ)	28	9	W		
10/15	Atlantic (Brooklyn)	21	41		L	
10/21	National (Washington, DC)	16	15	W		
---/---	Eagle (Florence, MA)	--	--	W		
---/---	Hampden (Springfield, MA)	--	--	W		
---/---	Victory (Troy, NY)	--	--	W		
---/---	Hudson River (Newburgh, NY)	--	--	W		
---/---	National (Albany, NY)	--	--	W		

BATTER	POS	GP	HL	A O	R	A O
Sonny Leavenworth	1B	14	38	2 10	45	3 3
John Ward	2B,P	19	56	2 18	68	3 11
Bub McAtee	SS	16	47	2 15	63	3 15
Cal Penfield	3B	19	58	3 1	56	2 18
Mart King	OF,1B,2B	19	56	2 18	65	3 8
Steve King	OF	19	42	2 4	75	3 18
James McKeon	OF	18	57	3 3	57	3 3
Bill Craver	C	19	46	2 8	75	3 18
William Abrams	P,OF	19	56	2 8	69	3 12
Clipper Flynn	2B,OF	9	26	2 8	36	4 0

KNICKERBOCKER   13 - 2
Albany, NY

DATE	OPPONENT	SCORE		W	L	T
07/04	Powhatan (Brooklyn)	48	12	W		
07/11	Chatham (Chatham, NY)	77	23	W		
07/18	Hudson (Hudson, NY)	26	15	W		

KNICKERBOCKER (cont.)
Albany, NY

DATE	OPPONENT	SCORE		W	L	T
08/01	Utica (Utica, NY)	39	38	W		
08/08	National (Albany)	36	28	W		
08/27	Union (Summit, ?)	90	23	W		
08/28	Excelsior (Cobleskill, NY)	100	14	W		
08/29	Hudson (Hudson, NY)	71	16	W		
08/30	Hampden (Springfield, MA)	62	36	W		
09/03	National (Albany)	24	11	W		
09/10	Hampden (Springfield, MA)	51	43	W		
09/16	Union (Cohoes, NY)	39	23	W		
09/26	Victory (Troy, NY)	42	20	W		
10/10	Oriental (Greenpoint, NY)	18	22		L	
10/19	Central City (Syracuse, NY)	17	34		L	

BATTER	POS	GP	HL	A	O	R	A	O
Brumaghim		15	34	2	4	95	6	5
Bliss		15	46	3	1	82	5	7
Mike Powers		14	37	2	9	76	5	6
Lamoure		14	31	2	3	70	5	0
Cliker		14	41	2	13	68	4	12
Crawford		13	32	2	6	64	4	12
Gardner		12	25	2	1	76	6	4
Grace		10	27	2	7	48	4	8
Umpleby		10	31	3	1	43	4	3
O'Brien		8	26	2	8	53	5	8

CENTRAL CITY   13 - 3
Syracuse, NY

DATE	OPPONENT	SCORE		W	L	T
06/15	Plow Boy (Syracuse)	33	6	W		
06/29	Cazenovia (Syracuse)	36	27	W		
07/27	Auburn (Auburn, NY)	32	41		L	
08/10	Auburn (Auburn, NY)	38	55		L	
08/17	Auburn (Auburn, NY)	44	18	W		
08/22	Utica (Utica, NY)	29	35		L	
09/08	Marcellus (?)	47	13	W		
09/30	Binghamton (Binghamton, NY)	30	16	W		
10/01	Amateur (Oswego, NY)	54	24	W		
10/03	Niagara (Buffalo, NY)	39	27	W		
10/04	Excelsior (Rochester, NY)	45	32	W		
10/07	Hamilton College (?)	35	28	W		
10/15	Utica (Utica, NY)	28	19	W		
10/19	Knickerbocker (Albany, NY)	34	17	W		
10/22	Utica (Utica, NY)	30	13	W		
10/25	Binghamton (Binghamton, NY)	51	14	W		

BATTER	POS	GP	HL	A	O	R	A	O
Cruttenden		17	38	3	0	69	4	1
Yale		16	31	1	15	69	4	5
Boswell		16	59	3	11	67	4	3
Dodge		16	50	3	2	67	4	3
Johnson		16	49	3	1	61	3	13
Porter		15	47	3	2	72	4	12
Sanford		14	28	2	0	74	5	4
Telford		10	37	3	7	38	3	8
Adams		8	24	3	0	38	4	6
Loomis		6	21	3	3	20	3	2
Campbell		5	9	1	4	22	4	2

BRANDYWINE 12 - 3
W. Chester, PA

DATE	OPPONENT	SCORE		W	L	T
04/13	Columbia (W. Chester, PA)	91	26	W		
05/11	Columbia (W. Chester, PA)	78	34	W		
05/29	Excelsior (Coatesville, PA)	59	50	W		
06/10	W. Philadelphia (Philadelphia)	19	65		L	
06/11	Camden (Camden, NJ)	4	59		L	
06/27	Excelsior (Coatesville, PA)	22	17	W		
07/11	Oxford (Oxford, PA)	63	44	W		
07/13	Indian Queen (Phoenixville, PA)	98	27	W		
08/07	Penn (Downington, PA)	52	28	W		
08/19	Indian Queen (Phoenixville, PA)	41	16	W		
09/07	Camden (Camden, NJ)	50	37	W		
09/19	Oxford (Oxford, PA)	74	4	W		
10/03	Hamilton (Philadelphia)	32	38		L	
10/24	Hamilton (Philadelphia)	37	29	W		
11/28	Mercantile (Philadelphia)	98	3	W		

BATTER	POS	GP	HL	A	O	R	A	O
Pawling		14	33	2	5	89	6	5
Taylor		14	42	3	0	83	5	13
Hartman		14	49	3	7	68	4	12
Bateman		14	49	3	7	76	4	6
Sheppard		13	27	2	1	98	7	7
Potts		12	27	2	3	75	6	3
Mercer		11	23	2	1	58	5	3
Strickland		10	33	3	3	57	5	7
Allen		8	22	2	6	49	6	1
Hulme		8	19	2	3	51	3	6

HARVARD 11 - 2
Cambridge, MA

DATE	OPPONENT	SCORE		W	L	T
05/11	Granite (Lynn, MA)	67	26	W		
05/15	Lowell (Boston)	28	37		L	
05/24	Lowell (Boston)	32	26	W		
06/01	Lowell (Boston)	39	28	W		
06/12	Athletic (Philadelphia)	10	22		L	
10/07	Excelsior (Brooklyn)	18	6	W		

(Only scores extant)

BATTER	POS	GP	HL	A	O	R	A	O
Shaw	1B	13	30	2	4	70	5	5
Ames	2B	13	37	2	11	64	4	12
Gardner Willard	SS	11	32	2	10	50	4	6
Parker	3B	10	24	2	4	52	5	2
Sprague	OF	13	38	2	12	59	4	7
Nathaniel Smith	OF	12	36	3	0	53	4	5
Mealey	OF	9	19	2	1	41	4	5
G.A. Flagg	C	10	27	2	7	46	4	6
Hunnewell	P	13	40	3	1	63	4	11

CHAMPION 11 - 5
Jersey City, NJ

DATE	OPPONENT	SCORE		W	L	T
---/---	Excelsior (Paterson, NJ)	--	--	W		
---/---	Eagle (New York)	--	--	W		

CHAMPION (cont.)
Jersey City, NJ

DATE	OPPONENT	SCORE		W	L	T
---/---	Active (New York)	--	--	W		
---/---	Olympic (Paterson, NJ)	--	--	W		
---/---	Bergen (Bergen, NJ)	--	--	W		
---/---	Peconic (Brooklyn)	--	--	W		
---/---	Oriental (?)	--	--	W		
---/---	Sparkhill (Piermont, NY)	--	--	W		
---/---	Fulton (New York)	--	--	W		
---/---	World (New York)	--	--	W		
---/---	Athlete (Washington Hts, NY)	--	--	W		
07/23	Empire (New York)	20	23		L	
08/13	Mutual (New York)	13	52		L	
09/14	Empire (New York)	29	35		L	
---/---	Olympic (Paterson, NJ)	--	--		L	
---/---	Athlete (Washington Hts, NY)	--	--		L	

BATTER	POS	GP	HL	A	O	R	A	O
Snowden		16	31	1	15	75	4	11
Delaney		16	40	2	8	62	3	14
Willis		15	30	2	0	76	5	1
McMahon		14	45	3	3	57	4	1
Edwards		14	19	3	7	51	3	9
Bliven		14	43	3	1	50	3	8
Reynolds		11	23	2	1	51	4	7
Johnson		11	34	3	1	42	3	9
Donnelly		6	19	3	1	20	3	2

EXCELSIOR   11 - 5
Brooklyn, NY

DATE	OPPONENT	SCORE		W	L	T
06/15	Independent (Brooklyn)	32	9	W		
06/29	Active (Newark)	6	10		L	
07/26	Active (New York)	14	9	W		
08/01	Eckford (Brooklyn)	21	27		L	
08/16	Charter Oak (Hartford, CT)	52	4	W		
08/23	Eagle (New York)	35	8	W		
09/05	Una (Mt Vernon, NY)	56	13	W		
09/09	Mohawk (Brooklyn)	38	7	W		
09/13	Active (Newark)	39	5	W		
09/20	Eckford (Brooklyn)	26	15	W		
09/23	Eureka (Newark)	41	22	W		
10/02	Keystone (Philadelphia)	15	20		L	
10/04	Lowell (Boston)	21	28		L	
10/07	Harvard (Cambridge)	6	18		L	
10/16	Peconic (Brooklyn)	41	15	W		
10/26	National (Washington, DC)	26	11	W		

BATTER	POS	GP	HL	A	O	R	A	O
E. Thompson	1B	7	25	3	4	14	2	0
George Flanly	2B	14	33	2	5	40	2	12
Bill Lennon	SS,1B	9	28	3	1	28	3	1
Dan Chauncey	3B,OF	11	31	2	9	42	3	9
George Hall	OF,1B	15	42	2	12	48	3	3
John Clyne	OF	15	35	2	5	54	3	9
Fred Treacey	OF	10	29	2	9	39	3	9
Herbert Jewell	C	15	37	2	7	51	3	6
Candy Cummings	P	15	53	3	8	37	2	7
James Mitchell	3B	5	13	2	3	14	2	4
George Cook	OF	5	20	4	0	13	2	3

JEFFERSON 11 - 6 - 1
Washington, DC

DATE	OPPONENT	SCORE		W	L	T
06/12	National (Washington)	27	57		L	
07/04	Maryland (Baltimore, MD)	50	61		L	
07/23	Continental (Washington)	85	16	W		
08/01	Empire (Washington)	36	35	W		
08/08	Capitol (Washington)	41	29	W		
08/14	National (Washington)	19	52		L	
08/27	Capitol (Washington)	37	23	W		
09/24	Athletic (Philadelphia)	14	50		L	
10/14	Olympic (Washington)	10	22		L	
---/---	Empire (Washington)	--	--	W		
---/---	Severn (Annapolis, MD)	--	--	W		
---/---	Pioneer (Alexandria, VA)	--	--	W		
---/---	Severn (Annapolis, MD)	--	--	W		
---/---	Union (Washington)	--	--	W		
---/---	Interior (Washington)	--	--	W		
---/---	Potomac (Washington)	--	--	W		
---/---	Union (Washington)	--	--		L	

(Only scores extant)

BATTER	POS	GP	HL	A O	R	A O
Daniels	1B	14	39	2 11	50	3 8
Seaver Page	2B,OF,SS	14	41	2 13	58	4 2
J. Doyle	SS,3B,2B	13	35	2 9	47	3 8
George Joyce	3B,OF,	16	37	2 5	66	4 2
A. Finney	OF,SS	15	42	2 2	58	3 13
Sam Yeatman	OF	11	29	2 7	39	3 6
Stone	OF	9	23	2 5	24	2 6
Shields	C	15	42	2 12	55	3 10
Anderson	P	15	35	2 5	53	3 8
McCauley	OF	8	19	2 3	34	4 4
McClelland		5	19	3 4	13	2 3

COMMONWEALTH 11 - 11 - 2
Philadelphia, PA

DATE	OPPONENT	SCORE		W	L	T
04/27	Athletic (Philadelphia)	16	76		L	
05/24	Chester (Chester, PA)	33	33			T
05/28	Crescent (?)	50	13	W		
05/31	Alvin (Philadelphia)	83	15	W		
06/14	Minerva (Philadelphia)	43	17	W		
06/20	Olympic (Washington, DC)	16	62		L	
06/21	Knickerbocker (?)	52	31	W		
06/28	Crescent (?)	37	10	W		
07/04	Columbia (Bordentown, NJ)	56	30	W		
07/12	Union (Camden, NJ)	25	27		L	
07/17	Athletic (Philadelphia)	25	75		L	
08/23	Arctic (Philadelphia)	19	36		L	
09/02	Alvin (Philadelphia)	38	36	W		
09/07	Geary (Philadelphia)	19	26		L	
09/13	Malvern (Philadelphia)	34	27	W		
09/27	Woodland (?)	43	28	W		
10/08	Geary (Philadelphia)	18	26		L	
10/12	Union (Washington, DC)	37	25	W		
10/24	W. Philadelphia (Philadelphia)	18	46		L	
10/25	Olympic (Philadelphia)	26	26			T
11/01	W. Philadelphia (Philadelphia)	12	30		L	
11/07	Union (Washington, DC)	32	19	W		
11/08	Olympic (Washington, DC)	6	41		L	
11/09	National (Washington, DC)	6	30		L	

COMMONWEALTH (cont.)
Philadelphia, PA

BATTER	POS	GP	HL	A	O	R	A	O
Oram		24	48	2	0	94	3	22
Kern		18	54	3	0	68	3	14
Furness		17	46	2	12	55	3	4
W. Aitken		15	43	2	13	40	2	10
Fields		13	30	2	4	59	4	7
Borden		13	32	2	6	47	3	8
Adams		13	34	2	8	36	2	10
Hoyt		13	33	2	7	35	2	9
Myers		12	36	3	0	30	2	6
Rorke		11	27	2	5	40	4	4
Schell		9	21	2	3	35	3	8
E.A. Pharo		8	22	2	6	21	2	5
O'Brien		7	20	2	6	24	3	3
R.F. Pharo		7	21	3	0	19	2	5
Pohl		7	24	3	3	19	2	5
Diehl		6	12	2	0	24	4	0
Harrop		5	14	2	4	26	5	1

EXCELSIOR 10 - 1
Chicago, IL

DATE	OPPONENT	SCORE		W	L	T
06/05	Atlantic (Chicago)	48	24	W		
06/07	Garden City (Chicago)	27	10	W		
06/20	Forest City (Rockford, IL)	45	41	W		
07/04	Forest City (Rockford, IL)	28	24	W		
07/27	National (Washington, DC)	4	49		L	
08/21	Rustic (Danby, IL)	124	2	W		
09/19	Egyptian (Centralia, IL)	79	9	W		
09/21	Capitol (Springfield, Il)	38	6	W		
09/27	Bloomington (Bloomington, IL)	25	17	W		
10/05	Detroit (Detroit, MI)	49	20	W		
10/19	Detroit (Detroit, MI)	36	24	W		

BATTER	POS	GP	HL	A	O	R	A	O
Stearns		11	18	1	7	68	6	2
Oberlander		11	24	2	2	59	5	4
Tom Foley		10	16	1	6	64	6	4
McNally		10	29	2	9	36	3	6
Alston		8	19	2	3	45	5	5
Blakeslee		8	18	2	2	41	5	1
Banker		6	13	2	1	25	4	1
Keenan		5	8	1	3	27	5	2
John Zeller		5	7	1	2	24	4	4
Kennedy		5	14	2	4	17	3	2
Budd		5	16	3	1	13	2	3

EMPIRE 10 - 4
New York, NY

DATE	OPPONENT	SCORE		W	L	T
06/17	Powhatan (Brooklyn)	45	31	W		
07/01	Atlantic (Brooklyn)	24	78		L	
07/04	Waterbury (Waterbury, CT)	11	19		L	
07/05	Monitor (Waterbury, CT)	30	22	W		
07/11	Oriental (Greenpoint, NY)	10	53		L	
07/17	Knickerbocker (New York)	41	26	W		

EMPIRE (cont.)
New York, NY

DATE	OPPONENT	SCORE		W	L	T
07/23	Champion (Jersey City, NJ)	23	20	W		
07/31	Jefferson (New York)	41	31	W		
08/21	Exercise (New York)	64	11	W		
08/28	Resolute (Brooklyn)	21	19	W		
09/02	Atlantic (Brooklyn)	19	32		L	
09/14	Champion (Jersey City, NJ)	35	29	W		
09/18	Una (Mt Vernon, NY)	53	31	W		
10/31	Knickerbocker (New York)	51	21	W		

BATTER	POS	GP	HL	A	O	R	A	O
M. Nestler	1B	10	29	2	9	42	4	2
Samuel Hosford	2B,1B	8	24	3	0	30	3	6
Pete Shreves	SS	11	29	2	7	40	3	7
Duncan	3B	11	39	3	6	39	3	6
Wilson	OF,C	13	35	2	9	50	3	11
Joe Simmons	OF,SS,P	11	28	2	6	50	4	6
Hart	OF	10	30	3	0	41	4	1
Quinn	C	6	18	3	0	18	3	0
Sebring	P	10	25	2	5	40	4	0
E. Nestler	OF	10	35	3	5	34	3	4
Way	3B,2B	7	23	3	2	22	3	1

OLYMPIC   10 - 5
Washington, DC

DATE	OPPONENT	SCORE		W	L	T
06/19	National (Washington)	7	46		L	
07/30	Continental (Washington)	98	7	W		
09/13	Interior (Washington)	49	8	W		
09/25	Empire (Washington)	41	10	W		
09/27	Union (Washington)	22	15	W		
10/02	Athletic (Philadelphia)	6	36		L	
10/03	Quaker City (Philadelphia)	11	29		L	
10/12	Capitol (Washington)	18	4	W		
10/14	Jefferson (Washington)	22	10	W		
10/16	National (Washington)	7	33		L	
10/19	Interior (Washington)	31	25	W		
11/08	Commonwealth (Philadelphia)	41	6	W		
11/14	Athletic (Philadelphia)	5	17		L	
11/23	Union (Washington)	25	13	W		
11/28	Maryland (Baltimore, MD)	34	14	W		

BATTER	POS	GP	HL	A	O	R	A	O
Denison	1B	15	39	2	9	48	3	3
Clark	2B	9	24	2	6	28	3	1
Williams	SS	8	20	2	4	27	3	3
Davy Force	3B,SS	14	22	1	8	60	4	4
A.V. Robinson	OF	13	30	2	4	33	2	7
Nick Young	OF	13	34	2	8	31	2	5
W. Burchard	OF	10	25	2	5	37	3	7
Harry McLean	C	12	27	2	3	35	2	11
Ed Leech	P	15	31	2	1	45	3	0
Robbins	OF	9	26	2	8	18	2	0

ACTIVE
Buffalo, NY
10 - 6

DATE	OPPONENT	SCORE		W	L	T
07/13	Niagara (Buffalo)	12	69		L	
07/18	Clifton (Clifton, NY)	42	52		L	
07/25	Clifton (Clifton, NY)	53	94		L	
07/28	Mutual (Buffalo)	31	23	W		
08/02	Star (Batavia, NY)	62	22	W		
08/08	Niagara Falls (Niagara Falls, NY)	124	41	W		
08/---	Mutual (Buffalo)	14	21		L	
08/09	Lock City (Lockport, NY)	54	41	W		
08/10	Alert (Rochester, NY)	44	86		L	
08/12	Churchville (Churchville, NY)	58	32	W		
08/13	Warsaw (Warsaw, NY)	90	43	W		
08/14	Oatka (LeRoy, NY)	47	39	W		
08/15	Star (Batavia, NY)	53	23	W		
08/16	Empire (Dunkirk, NY)	62	41	W		
10/19	Empire (Dunkirk, NY)	13	25		L	
10/30	Empire (Dunkirk, NY)	31	13	W		

BATTER	POS	GP	HL	A	O	R	A	O
Tremaine	1B	7	22	3	1	47	6	5
Dingrus	2B	10	41	4	1	58	5	8
Barnum	SS	14	38	2	10	87	6	3
Walker	3B,1B	5	11	2	1	31	6	1
Eberhardt	OF	15	51	3	6	81	5	6
Eastin	OF	13	22	1	9	99	7	8
Barker	OF	12	37	3	1	74	6	2
Bettinger	C	15	23	1	8	113	7	8
Fox	P	13	47	3	8	71	5	6
Seymour		7	19	2	5	38	5	3
Scobell		6	20	3	2	28	4	4
Burtiss		5	14	2	4	14	2	4
Holloway		5	18	3	3	12	2	2

UNION
St. Louis, MO
9 - 1

DATE	OPPONENT	SCORE		W	L	T
05/09	Pickwick (St. Louis)	36	20	W		
06/20	Hope (St. Louis)	82	29	W		
07/02	Empire (St. Louis)	59	29	W		
07/10	Empire (St. Louis)	34	32	W		
07/22	National (Washington, DC)	26	113		L	
09/05	Magnolia (St. Louis)	59	30	W		
09/14	Hope (St. Louis)	69	27	W		
09/19	Resolute (St. Louis)	60	41	W		
09/28	Resolute (St. Louis)	51	39	W		
10/05	Hope (St. Louis)	44	22	W		

BATTER	POS	GP	HL	A	O	R	A	O
R. Duncan		10	21	2	1	67	6	7
W. Duncan		10	20	2	0	62	6	2
Greenleaf		10	31	3	1	52	5	2
Cabanne		9	20	2	2	60	6	6
Freeman		9	22	2	4	59	6	5
Meacham		9	36	3	0	45	5	0
A.W. Smith		8	24	3	0	40	5	0
Prouty		5	15	3	0	31	6	1

AMERICUS 9 - 5
Newark, NJ

DATE	OPPONENT	SCORE		W	L	T
05/27	Eclectic (New York)	17	32		L	
08/14	Gotham (New York)	32	24	W		
---/---	Sparta (New York)	--	--	W		
---/---	Sparta (New York)	--	--	W		
---/---	Endeavor (New York)	--	--	W		
---/---	Endeavor (New York)	--	--	W		
---/---	Gotham (New York)	--	--	W		
---/---	Eclectic (New York)	--	--	W		
---/---	Kearney (Rahway, NJ)	--	--	W		
---/---	Star (New Brunswick, NJ)	30	13	W		
---/---	Active (Newark)	--	--		L	
---/---	Active (Newark)	--	--		L	
---/---	Eureka (Newark)	--	--		L	
---/---	Star (New Brunswick, NJ)	47	50		L	

BATTER	POS	GP	HL	A	O	R	A	O
McGrath	1B	12	42	3	6	52	4	4
Kelly	2B	12	30	2	6	58	4	10
Helms	SS	8	24	3	0	34	4	2
Mayhew	3B	12	44	3	8	41	3	5
Devine	OF	12	31	2	7	57	4	9
Bunting	OF	11	19	1	8	63	5	8
Charles	OF	10	34	3	4	34	3	4
William Greathead	C	13	39	3	0	56	4	4
Farley	P	14	47	3	5	55	3	13
Joyce	C	8	22	2	6	48	6	0
Leonard	OF	5	15	3	0	22	4	2

TYPOGRAPHICAL 9 - 6
Philadelphia, PA

DATE	OPPONENT	SCORE		W	L	T
---/---	Arctic (Philadelphia)	30	65		L	
---/---	James Page (Philadelphia)	16	49		L	
---/---	Belmont (Philadelphia)	18	34		L	
---/---	Rittenhouse (Philadelphia)	50	32	W		
---/---	Pennsylvania (Philadelphia)	52	22	W		
---/---	Pestaricus (Manayunk, PA)	37	56		L	
---/---	Chestnut St. Theatre (Philadelphia)	46	40	W		
---/---	Pennsylvania (Philadelphia)	56	19	W		
---/---	Hoopla (?)	32	16	W		
---/---	Rittenhouse (Philadelphia)	36	18	W		
---/---	Belmont (Philadelphia)	29	35		L	
---/---	Flomerfelt (?)	41	19	W		
---/---	Arctic (Philadelphia)	16	44		L	
---/---	Hoopla (?)	51	27	W		
---/---	Flomerfelt (?)	*9	0	W		

* Forfeit

BATTER	POS	GP	HL	A	O	R	A	O
Turner		14	40	2	12	56	4	0
Ogborne		13	36	2	10	56	4	4
Heffern		13	22	1	9	54	4	2
Glading		10	23	2	3	43	4	3
Simpson		10	27	2	7	40	4	0
Gelwicks		10	21	2	1	30	3	0
Morrow		6	20	3	2	22	3	4
McCullough		6	14	2	2	19	3	1
Stroman		5	8	1	3	25	5	0
Dunkell		4	11	2	3	16	4	0

TYPOGRAPHICAL (cont.)
Philadelphia, PA

BATTER	POS	GP	HL	A	O	R	A	O
Weldon		4	13	3	1	14	3	2
Patton		4	15	3	3	12	3	0
Allison		3	7	2	1	11	3	2
Stanmire		3	6	2	0	15	3	1
Hooper		3	10	3	1	8	2	2
Eaton		3	8	2	2	6	2	0
Crees		3	9	3	0	6	2	0
McCusker		3	9	3	0	4	1	1

CREIGHTON 8 - 4
Norfolk, VA

DATE	OPPONENT	SCORE		W	L	T
06/01	Old Point (Ft Monroe, VA)	24	39		L	
06/05	Old Point (Ft Monroe, VA)	27	40		L	
07/24	Independent (Petersburg, VA)	38	34	W		
09/16	Independent (Petersburg, VA)	43	9	W		
---/---	Ordinance (Ft Monroe, VA)	47	10	W		
---/---	Old Point (Ft Monroe, VA)	21	5	W		
---/---	Old Point (Ft Monroe, VA)	40	25	W		
---/---	Hope (?)	50	7	W		
---/---	Hope (?)	26	21	W		
---/---	Social (?)	27	18	W		
---/---	Severn (Annapolis, MD)	12	32		L	
---/---	Independent (Petersburg, VA)	17	20		L	

BATTER	POS	GP	HL	A	O	R	A	O
Howell	1B	8	15	1	7	29	3	5
Pearson	2B	13	30	2	4	53	4	1
W. Martin	SS	3	5	1	2	15	3	0
Hayes	3B	4	10	2	2	17	4	1
Gordon	OF	12	28	2	4	48	4	0
Kendall	OF	11	30	2	8	33	3	0
Whitehurst	OF	11	27	2	5	32	2	10
L. Allen	C	8	19	2	3	37	4	5
Calvert	P	13	39	3	0	37	2	11
E.C. Salisbury		8	10	1	2	31	3	7
Donn		5	15	3	0	12	2	2
L. Salisbury		4	14	3	2	7	1	4
Hutchins		3	8	2	2	12	4	0
Spaight		3	13	4	1	8	2	2
Doyle		3	6	2	0	14	2	2

LOWELL 8 - 5
Boston, MA

DATE	OPPONENT	SCORE		W	L	T
05/15	Harvard (Cambridge, MA)	37	28	W		
05/24	Harvard (Cambridge, MA)	26	32		L	
06/01	Harvard (Cambridge, MA)	28	39		L	
06/13	Athletic (Philadelphia)	8	53		L	
06/24	Eon (Portland, ME)	53	29	W		
08/17	Fraternity (S. Boston)	30	14	W		
08/19	Eagle (Natick, MA)	59	21	W		
08/31	Mechanic (Weymouth, MA)	31	15	W		
09/04	Tri Mountain (Boston)	20	18	W		
09/17	Star (Greenfield, MA)	70	21	W		

LOWELL (cont.)
Boston, MA

DATE	OPPONENT	SCORE		W	L	T
09/23	Tri Mountain (Boston)	35	40		L	
09/28	Tri Mountain (Boston)	22	42		L	
10/04	Excelsior (Brooklyn)	28	21	W		

(Only scores extant)

BATTER	POS	GP	HL	A	O	R	A	O
Henry Dennison	1B	8	27	3	3	40	5	0
Sumner	2B	14	37	2	9	57	4	1
Edward Jewell	SS,1B,3B	18	43	2	7	83	4	11
William Joslyn	3B	14	41	2	13	77	5	7
William Alline	OF,3B	17	40	2	6	71	4	3
Lowell	OF	17	48	2	14	76	4	8
A.M. Newton	OF,3B	13	46	3	7	59	4	7
J. Wilder	C	19	55	2	17	80	4	4
James Lovett	P,1B	19	42	2	4	107	5	12
Mort Rogers	OF	6	14	2	2	32	5	2
Thompson	SS	6	18	3	8	16	2	4
Simmons	OF	5	14	2	4	20	4	0

ARCTIC   8 - 6
Philadelphia, PA

DATE	OPPONENT	SCORE		W	L	T
07/05	Keystone (Philadelphia)	55	35	W		
07/08	Bachelor (Philadelphia)	14	18		L	
07/11	Quaker City (Philadelphia)	26	70		L	
07/20	Athletic (Philadelphia)	16	55		L	
07/22	Bachelor (Philadelphia)	28	17	W		
07/26	Maryland (Baltimore, MD)*	24	23	W		
08/23	Commonwealth (Philadelphia)*	36	19	W		
10/01	Quaker City (Philadelphia)	16	26		L	
---/---	Athletic (Philadelphia)*	13	54		L	
---/---	Keystone (Philadelphia)*	12	27		L	
---/---	Geary (Philadelphia)*	16	6	W		
---/---	Geary (Philadelphia)*	28	20	W		
---/---	Typographical (Philadelphia)*	65	30	W		
---/---	Typographical (Philadelphia)*	44	16	W		

* Box score not available

BATTER	POS	GP	HL	A	O	R	A	O
Burleigh		6	13	2	1	21	3	3
Rorke		6	14	2	2	18	3	0
Weaver		6	19	3	1	18	3	0
Hargesheimer		6	12	2	0	15	2	3
Jones		5	15	3	0	14	2	4
Harry Schafer		5	14	2	4	13	2	3
Watt		5	17	3	2	11	2	1

ECLECTIC   8 - 13 - 1
New York, NY

DATE	OPPONENT	SCORE		W	L	T
05/27	Americus (Newark)	32	17	W		
05/23	Oriental (Greenpoint, NY)	34	37		L	
06/15	Union (Morrisania, NY)	10	45		L	
06/19	Mutual (New York)	5	32		L	

ECLECTIC (cont.)
New York, NY

DATE	OPPONENT	SCORE		W	L	T
06/29	Union (Morrisania, NY)	32	36		L	
08/21	Oriental (Greenpoint, NY)	22	32		L	
---/---	Americus (Newark)	--	--		L	

(Only scores extant)

BATTER	POS	GP	HL	A	O	R	A	O
H. Dalton	1B,OF	13	32	2	6	28	2	2
H. Connell	2B,3B	6	18	3	0	13	2	1
Byrnes	SS	12	36	3	0	34	2	10
Brown	3B,OF,SS	5	14	2	4	17	3	2
Stevenson	OF,3B	14	38	2	10	33	2	5
Salts	OF,2B	14	43	3	1	36	2	8
Glover	OF,2B	13	38	2	2	40	3	1
William Bell	P,1B	22	59	2	17	72	3	6
Fisher		17	38	2	4	60	3	9
Gillett		11	25	2	3	29	2	7
T. Dalton		10	19	1	9	25	2	5
Howard		8	23	2	5	28	3	4
Ryder		5	9	1	4	18	3	3
Keteltas		5	12	2	2	12	2	2

PRINCETON 7-3
Princeton, NJ

DATE	OPPONENT	SCORE		W	L	T
05/01	Princeton Class of '69 (Princeton)	29	30		L	
05/03	Princeton Class of '70 (Princeton)	18	10	W		
05/15	Atlantic (Trenton, NJ)	35	22	W		
05/18	Nassau (Princeton)	27	15	W		
05/25	Nassau (Princeton)	26	42		L	
06/07	Star (New Brunswick, NJ)	19	6	W		
06/15	Columbia (Bordentown, NJ)	27	7	W		
09/21	Alvin (Philadelphia)	40	10	W		
10/12	Atlantic (Brooklyn)	9	19		L	
10/19	Nassau (Princeton)	27	24	W		

BATTER	POS	GP	HL	A	O	R	A	O
Rankin		11	30	2	8	39	3	6
Anderson		11	32	2	10	26	2	4
Mellier		10	35	3	5	30	3	0
Hageman		10	32	3	2	21	2	1
Schenck		9	27	3	0	28	3	1
Johnson		8	22	2	6	21	2	5
McIlvaine		8	28	3	4	20	2	4
Olmsted		7	19	2	5	23	3	2
Hope		6	15	2	3	15	2	3
Oliphant		4	13	3	1	12	3	0
Ward		3	3	1	0	13	4	1
Eby		3	10	3	1	8	2	2

LINCOLN 7-4
Pittsburgh, PA

DATE	OPPONENT	SCORE		W	L	T
06/13	Olympic (Allegheny, PA)	27	22	W		
07/09	Hiawatha (Kitanning, PA)	33	32	W		

LINCOLN (cont.)
Pittsburgh, PA

DATE	OPPONENT	SCORE		W	L	T
07/20	Atlantic (Pittsburgh)	33	26	W		
07/24	Hiawatha (Kitanning, PA)	24	19	W		
08/08	Olympic (Allegheny, PA)	53	24	W		
08/15	Ristori (Tarentum, PA)	25	35		L	
08/23	Atlantic (Pittsburgh)	22	29		L	
08/31	Ristori (Tarentum, PA)	50	21	W		
09/03	Enterprise (Allegheny, PA)	22	11	W		
09/09	Enterprise (Allegheny, PA)	31	42		L	
09/27	Enterprise (Allegheny, PA)	24	60		L	

BATTER	POS	GP	HL	A	O	R	A	O
S. Lane		11	25	2	3	49	4	5
W.W. McClelland		11	36	3	3	35	3	2
Lawrence		10	23	2	3	37	3	7
Smith		10	31	3	1	26	2	6
Carpenter		9	22	2	4	31	3	4
C.E. Jones		6	12	2	0	27	4	3
T. McClintock		6	15	2	3	26	4	2
Loughery		6	5	0	5	23	3	5
Orr		6	20	3	2	22	3	4
Telford		5	15	3	0	16	3	1
Worthington		5	15	3	0	13	2	3
Kurtz		3	8	2	2	8	2	2

CAPITOL 7 - 6
Washington, DC

DATE	OPPONENT	SCORE		W	L	T
06/21	Continental (Washington)	33	9	W		
07/20	Gymnastic (Washington)	61	17	W		
08/06	Continental (Washington)	60	13	W		
08/08	Jefferson (Washington)	29	41		L	
08/19	National (Washington)	14	48		L	
08/24	National (Washington)	9	43		L	
08/27	Jefferson (Washington)	23	38		L	
08/30	Interior (Washington)	43	19	W		
09/03	Union (Washington)	14	39		L	
09/12	Pioneer (Alexandria, VA)	52	22	W		
10/02	Interior (Washington)	42	7	W		
10/12	Olympic (Washington)	4	18		L	
11/01	Pioneer (Alexandria, VA)	58	10	W		

BATTER	POS	GP	HL	A	O	R	A	O
Aber	1B	11	26	2	4	34	3	1
Mallory	2B	7	23	3	2	26	3	5
Bayard	SS	9	21	2	3	40	4	4
Clarke	3B	5	8	1	3	19	3	4
Bielaski	OF	11	31	2	9	33	3	0
Yoder	OF	10	20	2	0	37	3	7
Minshall	OF	7	17	2	3	20	2	6
R.L. Clear	C	11	25	2	3	43	3	10
A.W. Clear	P	9	22	2	4	19	2	1
Lawlor		5	11	2	4	16	3	1

BUCKEYE   7 - 8
Cincinnati, OH

DATE	OPPONENT	SCORE		W	L	T
05/11	Holt (Newport, KY)	49	14	W		
05/25	Cincinnati (Cincinnati)	40	82		L	
06/01	Buckeye (Dayton, OH)	43	23	W		
06/11	Live Oak (Cincinnati)	78	38	W		
07/01	Western (Indianapolis, IN)	40	55		L	
07/02	Louisville (Louisville, KY)	37	45		L	
07/03	Olympic (Louisville, KY)	46	33	W		
07/16	National (Washington, DC)	12	88		L	
07/20	Xenia (Xenia, OH)	101	57	W		
08/30	Western (Indianapolis, IN)	62	60	W		
09/14	Cincinnati (Cincinnati)	20	28		L	
09/24	Hickory (McConnellsville,OH)	25	41		L	
10/05	Cincinnati (Cincinnati)	23	49		L	
10/19	Cincinnati (Cincinnati)	23	37		L	
11/02	Live Oak (Cincinnati)	70	39	W		

BATTER	POS	GP	HL	A	O	R	A	O
Charles Gould	1B	13	32	2	6	60	4	8
B.O.M. DeBeck	2B	2	6	3	0	11	5	1
J. Scheidemantle	SS	7	22	3	1	29	4	1
Charles Jones	3B	9	23	2	5	38	4	2
J.L. Boake	OF	13	41	3	2	57	4	5
W. P. Wright	OF	12	34	2	10	50	4	2
W.H. Boake	OF	11	28	2	6	48	4	4
William Skiff	C	7	16	2	2	39	5	4
George Smith	P	5	16	3	1	22	4	2
John Meagher		6	17	2	5	24	4	0
Thomas Tallon		6	16	2	4	22	3	4
J. P. Mack		6	23	3	5	20	3	2
B. Brookshaw		5	10	2	0	26	5	2
G.P. Miller		4	10	2	2	24	6	0
C.S. Foote		3	3	1	0	14	4	2
F. J. Hannon		3	9	3	0	10	3	1
J.E. Sherwood		2	5	2	1	6	3	0

CANACADEA   6 - 2
Hornellsville, NY

DATE	OPPONENT	SCORE		W	L	T
06/13	Challenge (Rogersville, NY)	46	30	W		
07/31	Empire (Dunkirk, NY)	42	29	W		
08/06	Ellicott (Jamestown, NY)	20	35		L	
09/09	Star (Canaseraga, NY)	67	21	W		
09/25	Meteor (Addison, NY)	40	59		L	
10/12	Challenge (Rogersville, NY)	29	25	W		
10/22	University of Alfred (NY)	39	21	W		
10/26	Star (Canaseraga, NY)	38	30	W		

BATTER	POS	GP	HL	A	O	R	A	O
Rose		8	12	1	4	40	5	0
Strawn		8	21	2	5	39	4	7
Carroll		8	28	3	4	33	4	1
E. Morrisey		8	19	2	3	34	4	2
King		8	28	3	4	32	4	0
J. Adsit		6	20	3	2	24	4	0
Simpson		5	7	1	2	28	5	3
Bassett		5	17	3	2	23	4	3
T. Morrisey		4	10	2	2	20	5	0
Badger		4	8	2	0	12	3	0
C. Adsit		2	4	2	0	10	5	0

EUREKA 6 - 2
Chicago, IL

DATE	OPPONENT	SCORE		W	L	T
05/18	Atlantic (Chicago)	39	19	W		
06/01	Resolute (Chicago)	31	11	W		
07/04	Garden City (Chicago)	21	32		L	
08/02	Garden City (Chicago)	56	26	W		
09/07	Atlantic (Chicago)	28	18	W		
09/21	Atlantic (Chicago)	23	29		L	
10/14	Atlantic (Chicago)	42	19	W		
11/09	Garden City (Chicago)	41	30	W		

BATTER	POS	GP	HL	A	O	R	A	O
Gaskins		8	20	2	5	33	4	1
Milton Sweet		7	11	1	4	35	5	0
Whitehead		7	13	1	6	28	4	0
Fred Cone		6	9	1	3	28	4	4
Miles		6	18	3	0	21	3	3
Beach		6	23	3	5	19	3	1
Hough		6	21	3	3	16	2	4
Stearns		5	9	1	4	18	3	3
Jennings		4	12	3	0	16	4	0
Blair		3	7	2	1	15	4	2
Babcock		3	3	1	0	13	4	1
Baker		3	11	3	2	10	3	1
Yost		2	5	2	1	8	4	0
Brown		2	7	3	1	7	3	1
Price		1	2	2	0	6	6	0
Everts		1	4	4	0	4	4	0
Haines		1	5	5	0	3	3	0
Miller		1	4	4	0	2	2	0

MUTUAL 6 - 2 - 1
Meadville, PA

DATE	OPPONENT	SCORE		W	L	T
06/22	Allegheny College (Meadville)	51	41	W		
07/17	Ydrad (W. Greenville, PA)	84	34	W		
07/25	Ydrad (W. Greenville, PA)	19	12	W		
07/31	Ellicott (Jamestown, NY)	17	39		L	
08/09	Venango (Franklin, PA)	49	49			T
08/23	Venango (Franklin, PA)	43	46		L	
08/29	Union (Titusville, PA)	66	44	W		
09/09	Venango (Franklin, PA)	54	32	W		
10/26	Seneca (Oil City, PA)	32	8	W		

BATTER	POS	GP	HL	A	O	R	A	O
McCoy		11	24	2	2	60	5	5
Honeywell		11	28	2	6	56	5	1
Carnahan		10	25	2	5	57	5	7
Comstock		10	30	3	0	43	4	3
McLaren		10	25	2	5	50	5	0
Lord		10	30	3	0	46	4	6
Curry		8	18	2	2	50	6	2
Whitesides		7	13	1	6	33	4	5
Sargeant		6	15	2	3	33	5	3
Hastings		4	9	2	1	20	5	0
Harden		3	7	2	1	12	4	0
Thomas		2	3	1	1	19	9	1

STAR 6-4
Brooklyn, NY

DATE	OPPONENT	SCORE		W	L	T
04/27	Independent (Brooklyn)	24	18	W		
07/04	Atlantic (Brooklyn)	21	39		L	
07/13	Mohawk (Brooklyn)	46	24	W		
07/19	Eckford (Brooklyn)	17	22		L	
07/27	Irvington (Irvington, NJ)	10	24		L	
09/14	Excelsior (Rochester, NY)	37	17	W		
09/21	Atlantic (Brooklyn)	7	34		L	
10/01	Eckford (Brooklyn)	47	23	W		
10/26	Independent (Brooklyn)	31	17	W		
11/02	Irvington (Irvington, NJ)	*9	0	W		

* Forfeit

BATTER	POS	GP	HL	A O	R	A O
Hope Waddell	1B	8	27	3 3	17	2 1
Tom McDiarmid	2B	11	26	2 4	36	3 3
Joseph Johnson	SS,OF	5	16	3 1	8	1 3
McCrea	3B	6	9	1 3	24	4 0
Fraley Rogers	OF	10	27	2 7	27	2 7
Herb Worth	OF,1B	8	18	2 2	27	3 3
Pete Flanders	OF,SS	6	20	3 2	16	2 4
Thompson	C	11	33	3 0	30	2 8
Sullivan	P	7	24	3 3	16	2 2
Greenwood		5	15	3 0	16	3 1
Bob Manly	3B,OF	5	12	2 2	9	1 4

UNA 6-4
Mt. Vernon, NY

DATE	OPPONENT	SCORE		W	L	T
06/12	Surprise (W. Farms, NY)	17	15	W		
06/27	Resolute (Elizabeth, NJ)	25	43		L	
07/04	Independent (Brooklyn)	31	24	W		
07/25	Resolute (Elizabeth, NJ)	43	11	W		
07/30	Atlanta (Tremont, NY)	51	20	W		
08/21	Resolute (Brooklyn, NY)	29	31		L	
09/05	Excelsior (Brooklyn)	13	56		L	
09/11	Surprise (W. Farms, NY)	50	23	W		
09/18	Empire (New York)	31	53		L	
10/03	Resolute (Brooklyn, NY)	45	19	W		

BATTER	POS	GP	HL	A O	R	A O
D. Van Cott		10	26	2 6	46	4 6
Lawrence		10	26	2 6	44	4 4
G. Stevens		9	24	2 6	40	4 4
Minard		8	29	3 5	32	4 0
Downs		9	28	3 1	35	3 8
Hathaway		9	24	2 6	35	3 8
J.O. Stevens		8	32	4 0	28	3 4
C. Sageman		7	18	2 4	28	4 0
W. H Van Cott		4	11	2 3	15	3 3
Jarvis		4	18	4 2	8	2 0
Archer		3	8	2 2	11	3 2

EXCELSIOR 6 - 6
Elmira, NY

DATE	OPPONENT	SCORE		W	L	T
06/04	Union (Elmira)	39	41		L	
06/29	Meteor (Addison, NY)	54	68		L	
07/11	Binghamton (Binghamton, NY)	19	71		L	
07/30	Binghamton (Binghamton, NY)	81	75	W		
08/01	Union (Elmira)	40	39	W		
08/26	Binghamton (Binghamton, NY)	22	61		L	
08/30	Alert (Elmira)	81	26	W		
09/20	Alert (Elmira)	23	27		L	
09/26	Alert (Elmira)	35	41		L	
10/10	Hector (Elmira)	22	13	W		
10/11	Alert (Elmira)	12	10	W		
10/18	Hector (Elmira)	32	20	W		

BATTER	POS	GP	HL	A	O	R	A	O
Charles Roe		11	31	2	9	50	4	6
William H. Davis		10	28	2	8	52	5	2
E. A. Thompson		10	56	2	6	49	4	9
B. Hutchins		10	33	3	3	45	4	5
John Furey		9	23	2	5	49	5	4
S.S. Taylor		9	24	2	6	49	5	4
T. Wormley		9	27	3	0	42	4	6
J. Ellis		9	32	3	5	24	3	7
Charles Sewell		6	18	3	0	27	4	3
E. Grover		5	12	2	2	27	5	2
C. Leavitt		3	15	5	0	7	2	1
John Donahue		2	7	3	1	14	7	0
S. Kingsbury		2	7	3	1	11	5	1
Hosea Billings		2	8	4	0	6	3	0

ECKFORD 6 - 16 - 1
Brooklyn, NY

DATE	OPPONENT	SCORE		W	L	T
06/20	Atlantic (Brooklyn)	14	27		L	
06/26	Powhatan (Brooklyn)	61	23	W		
07/03	Mutual (New York)	20	20			T
07/09	Atlantic (Brooklyn)	4	11		L	
07/12	Mutual (New York)	9	28		L	
07/16	Irvington (Irvington, NJ)	13	44		L	
07/19	Star (Brooklyn)	22	17	W		
07/30	Fulton (New York)	20	28		L	
08/01	Excelsior (Brooklyn)	27	21	W		
08/06	Mohawk (Brooklyn)	42	12	W		
08/21	Athletic (Philadelphia)	19	23		L	
08/24	Atlantic (Brooklyn)	9	41		L	
08/27	Union (Morrisania, NY)	23	25		L	
09/06	Fulton (New York)	23	21	W		
09/10	Keystone (Philadelphia)	29	6	W		
09/11	W. Philadelphia (Philadelphia)	31	45		L	
09/13	Excelsior (Rochester, NY)	12	16		L	
09/20	Excelsior (Brooklyn)	15	26		L	
09/23	Irvington (Irvington, NJ)	33	39		L	
09/27	Mutual (New York)	20	29		L	
09/30	Mohawk (Brooklyn)	18	31		L	
10/01	Star (Brooklyn)	23	47		L	
10/04	Keystone (Philadelphia)	13	31		L	

BATTER	POS	GP	HL	A	O	R	A	O
Andy Allison	1B	10	26	2	6	27	2	7
Tom Patterson	2B	18	53	2	17	34	1	16
Jack Nelson	SS,C,	23	57	2	11	69	3	0

ECKFORD (cont.)
Brooklyn, NY

BATTER	POS	GP	HL	A	O	R	A	O
Klein	3B,1B	21	49	2	7	69	3	6
Fesler	OF	20	48	2	8	53	2	13
Ryan	OF	13	47	3	8	18	1	5
Grim	OF	6	18	3	0	12	2	0
Marty Swandell	C,P	18	59	3	5	51	2	15
Malone	P	14	51	3	9	24	1	10
Josh Snyder	SS,1B,3B	12	35	2	11	30	2	6
George Grum	3B	8	23	2	7	15	1	7
Coleman	3B	6	18	3	0	11	1	5
John Grum	OF,SS	5	8	1	3	19	3	4
Courtney	C	5	17	3	2	6	1	1

NEPTUNE   5 - 2
Easton, PA

DATE	OPPONENT	SCORE		W	L	T
07/04	Irvington (Irvington, NJ)	16	36		L	
07/26	Irvington (Irvington, NJ)	25	38		L	
08/08	Resolute (Elizabeth, NJ)	42	41	W		
08/24	Resolute (Elizabeth, NJ)	27	22	W		
08/27	Harry Clay (Philadelphia)	43	32	W		
09/18	Scranton (Scranton, PA)	41	12	W		
10/01	Scranton (Scranton, PA)	68	25	W		

BATTER	POS	GP	HL	A	O	R	A	O
Brensriger	1B	5	9	1	4	24	4	4
Collins	2B	7	17	2	3	24	3	3
Drinkhouse	SS	3	8	2	2	10	3	1
Stewart	3B	7	20	2	6	23	3	2
Bell	OF	7	29	4	1	25	3	4
Houser	OF	7	22	3	1	22	3	1
Reeder	OF	6	17	2	5	20	3	2
Rinkle	C	7	15	2	1	31	4	3
Smith	P	7	19	2	5	31	4	3
Wikoff		3	9	3	0	13	4	1
Hayden		2	9	4	1	6	3	0

ALERT   5 - 3
Norwalk, CT

DATE	OPPONENT	SCORE		W	L	T
10/08	Liberty (Norwalk)	29	22	W		

(Only scores extant)

BATTER	POS	GP	HL	A	O	R	A	O
J. Hatch		8	17	2	1	29	3	5
Lyon		8	18	2	2	28	3	4
Waterbury		8	19	2	3	28	3	4
Coe		8	20	3	4	28	3	4
C. Hatch		8	23	2	7	24	3	0
Byxbee		7	18	2	4	19	2	5
Woodman		7	26	3	5	16	2	2
Foulks		6	16	2	4	23	3	5
Beard		6	12	2	0	21	3	3
Purdy		2	7	3	1	5	2	1

ECLIPTIC
Middletown, CT
5 - 3

DATE	OPPONENT	SCORE	W	L	T
		(No scores extant)			

BATTER	POS	GP	HL	A	O	R	A	O
Lewis		8	20	2	4	42	5	2
Comstock		7	17	2	3	33	4	5
Murphy		7	22	3	1	33	4	5
Douglass		6	15	2	3	30	5	0
McAllister		6	14	2	2	26	4	2
Ingals		5	13	2	3	21	4	1
Reynolds		4	8	2	0	18	4	2
Welch		3	9	3	0	14	4	2
Camp		2	3	1	1	12	6	0
Eaton		2	5	2	1	10	5	0
Carrigan		2	5	2	1	7	3	1

LONE STAR
Catskill, NY
5 - 3

DATE	OPPONENT	SCORE	W	L	T
		(No scores extant)			

BATTER	POS	GP	HL	A	O	R	A	O
Tolley		8	18	2	2	55	6	7
Smith		8	25	3	1	45	5	5
E. Wilcox		8	31	3	7	35	4	3
H. Wilcox		7	20	2	6	44	6	2
Doane		7	16	2	2	37	5	2
Beach		6	14	2	2	39	6	3
Joesbury		6	22	3	4	27	4	3
Weed		6	20	3	2	23	3	5
Sullivan		4	11	2	3	25	6	1
Day		3	13	4	1	14	4	2
Fiero		3	10	3	1	14	3	2
Mitchell		2	1	0	1	14	7	0
Cornwall		2	9	4	1	8	4	0

ATLANTIC
Chicago, IL
5 - 4

DATE	OPPONENT	SCORE		W	L	T
06/08	Excelsior (Chicago)	24	48		L	
06/29	O.K. (Ottawa, IL)	92	14	W		
07/04	Cream City (Milwaukee, WI)	48	45	W		
07/13	Garden City (Chicago)	41	32	W		
07/26	Cream City (Milwaukee, WI)	71	20	W		
07/29	National (Washington, DC)	17	78		L	
09/07	Eureka (Chicago)	18	28		L	
09/21	Eureka (Chicago)	28	23	W		
10/09	Eureka (Chicago)	19	42		L	

BATTER	POS	GP	HL	A	O	R	A	O
J. O'Neil	1B	7	18	2	4	39	5	4
T. Burton	2B	7	19	2	5	37	5	2
G. Kinzie	SS	9	24	2	6	40	4	4
H. Taylor	3B	8	17	2	1	42	5	2
E. Scates	OF	9	22	2	4	32	3	5

ATLANTIC (cont.)
Chicago, IL

BATTER	POS	GP	H L	A O	R	A O
R. Sheldon	OF	6	13	2 1	24	4 0
J. Holmes	OF	5	16	3 1	18	3 3
F. Drummond	C	5	14	2 4	26	5 1
William Burwell	P	5	17	3 2	24	4 4

PIONEER 5-7-1
Alexandria, VA

DATE	OPPONENT	SCORE		W	L	T
06/25	Old Dominion (Alexandria)	30	21	W		
06/21	Mt. Vernon (Alexandria)	68	25	W		
09/12	Capitol (Washington, DC)	22	52		L	
11/01	Capitol (Washington, DC)	10	58		L	
---/---	Old Dominion (Alexandria)	--	--	W		
---/---	Tuscarora (Leesburg, VA)	--	--	W		
---/---	Awkward (Aldic, VA)	--	--	W		
---/---	Potomac (Washington, DC)	--	--		L	
---/---	Potomac (Washington, DC)	--	--		L	
---/---	Pastime (Washington, DC)	--	--		L	
---/---	Jefferson (Washington, DC)	--	--		L	
---/---	United States (Washington, DC)	--	--		L	
---/---	Monumental (Washington, DC)	--	--			T

BATTER	POS	GP	H L	A O	R	A O
Gordon		13	32	2 6	56	4 4
Strine		13	32	2 6	54	4 2
Brenner		13	46	3 7	43	3 4
Moore		11	29	2 3	37	3 4
Murray		11	23	2 1	39	3 6
Perry		10	21	2 1	42	4 2
Smith		9	28	3 1	33	3 6
Huntington		5	14	2 4	29	5 4
Ryan		5	8	1 3	16	3 1

INDEPENDENT 5-8
Brooklyn, NY

DATE	OPPONENT	SCORE		W	L	T
04/27	Star (Brooklyn)	18	24		L	
05/25	Powhatan (Brooklyn)	39	35	W		
06/15	Excelsior (Brooklyn)	9	32		L	
06/29	Mutual (New York)	26	28		L	
07/04	Una (Mt. Vernon, NY)	24	31		L	
08/17	Resolute (Brooklyn)	44	15	W		
08/19	Mohawk (Brooklyn)	22	13	W		
08/31	Intrepid (Brooklyn)	47	31	W		
09/14	Mutual (New York)	25	71		L	
09/20	Mohawk (Brooklyn)	23	28		L	
09/21	Atlanta (Tremont, NY)	48	12	W		
10/19	Harlem (New York)	10	26		L	
10/26	Star (Brooklyn)	17	31		L	

BATTER	POS	GP	H L	A O	R	A O
R. Edwards	1B	9	29	3 2	30	3 3
T.W. Smith	2B	6	16	2 4	19	3 1
H.B. Browne	SS	10	29	2 9	33	3 3

INDEPENDENT (cont.)
Brooklyn, NY

BATTER	POS	GP	H L	A	O	R	A	O
L.S. Lewis	3B	5	9	1	4	21	4	1
C.H. Edwards	OF	12	31	2	7	39	3	3
R. McCoskry	OF	11	34	3	1	32	2	10
W.S. Colvin	OF	7	18	2	4	20	2	6
H.S. Peck	C	11	33	3	0	28	2	6
W.S. Taylor	P	10	26	2	6	30	3	0

W. PHILADELPHIA   5 - 12
Philadelphia, PA

DATE	OPPONENT	SCORE		W	L	T
05/09	Athletic (Philadelphia)	14	64		L	
05/13	Athletic (Philadelphia)	13	34		L	
05/27	Quaker City (Philadelphia)	13	40		L	
06/10	Brandywine (W. Chester, PA)*	65	19	W		
06/24	Quaker City (Philadelphia)	11	20		L	
08/05	Keystone (Philadelphia)	39	49		L	
08/31	Mutual (New York)	23	28		L	
08/19	Keystone (Philadelphia)*	16	36		L	
09/11	Eckford (Brooklyn)	45	31	W		
09/17	Mutual (New York)	18	32		L	
09/19	Atlantic (Brooklyn)	11	34		L	
09/25	Atlantic (Brooklyn)	31	36		L	
10/24	Commonwealth (Philadelphia)*	46	18	W		
11/01	Commonwealth (Philadelphia)*	30	12	W		
11/02	Athletic (Philadelphia)	10	37		L	
---/---	Athletic (Philadelphia)*	22	37		L	
---/---	Keystone (Philadelphia)*	43	31	W		

* Box score not available

BATTER	POS	GP	H L	A	O	R	A	O
Maguire	1B,OF,3B	8	23	2	7	21	2	5
Helling	2B,1B,SS	4	9	2	1	8	2	0
Ned Cuthbert	SS,C	4	10	2	2	10	2	2
Clinton	3B,2B	7	24	3	3	14	2	0
E. Osterheldt	OF	11	29	2	7	23	2	1
Charley Weaver	OF	10	28	2	8	28	2	8
S. Myers	OF,SS	8	25	3	1	18	2	2
Abel	C	8	21	2	5	18	2	2
Cherokee Fisher	P	10	30	3	0	19	1	9
Dorsey	OF,P,3B	7	19	2	5	19	2	5
George Bechtel	1B,3B	4	8	2	0	12	3	0
J. Weaver	2B	4	12	3	0	5	2	1
William Osterheldt	3B,SS,OF	4	10	2	2	6	1	2

RESOLUTE   4 - 1
Evansville, IN

DATE	OPPONENT	SCORE		W	L	T
---/---	Evansville (Evansville)	--	--	W		
---/---	Evansville (Evansville)	--	--	W		
---/---	Owensboro (Owensboro, KY)	--	--	W		
---/---	Owensboro (Owensboro, KY)	--	--	W		
---/---	Western (Indianapolis, IN)	--	--		L	

RESOLUTE (cont.)
Evansville, IN

BATTER	POS	GP	HL	A O	R	A O
Wentz		5	10	2 0	33	6 3
Ingle		5	11	2 1	32	6 2
Morgan		5	12	2 2	29	5 4
Bennett		5	8	1 3	27	5 2
Edward Babcock		5	13	2 3	24	4 4
Preston		4	11	2 3	14	3 2
Elisha Babcock		4	17	4 1	13	3 1
Rankin		3	10	3 1	18	6 0
Thompson		3	10	3 1	13	4 1
Iglehart		3	13	4 1	12	4 0
Ehrman		2	12	6 0	9	4 1

WALKILL   4 - 2
Middletown, NY

DATE	OPPONENT	SCORE	W	L	T
---/---	Retaliators (Middletown)	-- --	W		
---/---	Resolute (Brooklyn)	-- --	W		
---/---	Wurtsboro (Wurtsboro, NY)	-- --	W		
---/---	Excelsior (Ridgewood, NJ)	-- --	W		
---/---	Delaware (Port Jervis, NY)	-- --		L	
---/---	Delaware (Port Jervis, NY)	-- --		L	

BATTER	POS	GP	HL	A O	R	A O
H.K. Wilcox		6	12	2 0	33	5 3
W. H. Van Sciver		6	15	2 3	28	4 4
W. Van Houghton		6	18	3 0	27	4 3
John Finnegan		5	10	2 0	29	5 4
J. D. Horton		5	13	2 3	24	4 4
W. E. Coulter		5	19	3 4	23	4 3
Daniel Fullerton		5	21	4 1	20	4 0
A.V.N. Powelson		3	10	3 1	15	5 0
C. H. Horton		3	8	2 2	12	4 0

STAR   4 - 7
New Brunswick, NJ

DATE	OPPONENT	SCORE	W	L	T
05/25	Eureka (Newark, NJ)	9 66		L	
06/07	Princeton (Princeton, NJ)	6 19		L	
---/---	Americus (Newark, NJ)	50 47	W		
---/---	Jefferson (New York)	17 7	W		
---/---	Bergen (Bergen, NJ)	58 19	W		
---/---	Jefferson (New York)	44 27	W		
---/---	Liberty (New Brunswick, NJ)	33 40		L	
---/---	Liberty (New Brunswick, NJ)	29 52		L	
---/---	Active (Newark, NJ)	8 36		L	
---/---	Olympic (Paterson, NJ)	23 56		L	
---/---	Americus (Newark, NJ)	13 30		L	

BATTER	POS	GP	HL	A O	R	A O
Meyers	1B	10	30	3 0	24	2 4
O'Neil	2B	5	17	3 2	9	1 4
Dayton	SS	7	20	2 6	18	2 4
R.B. Bonney	3B	5	14	2 4	10	2 0
Joseph Fisher, Jr.	OF	11	32	2 10	37	3 4
Wiley	OF	9	27	3 0	28	3 1

STAR (cont.)
New Brunswick, NJ

BATTER	POS	GP	HL	A	O	R	A	O
R. Stout	OF	7	13	1	6	28	4	0
J.B. Kirkpatrick	C	7	24	3	3	17	2	3
W.G. Bergen	P	5	14	2	4	12	2	2
Helm		4	9	2	1	17	4	1

JEFFERSON 4 - 8
New York, NY

DATE	OPPONENT	SCORE		W	L	T
---/---	Olympic (Paterson, NJ)	49	34	W		
---/---	Social (New York)	36	26	W		
---/---	Gotham (New York)	30	14	W		
---/---	Sparta (new York)	34	10	W		
06/12	Mutual (New York)	1	58		L	
---/---	Star (New Brunswick, NJ)	7	17		L	
---/---	Gotham (New York)	14	44		L	
---/---	Empire (New York)	31	41		L	
---/---	Olympic (Paterson, NJ)	16	20		L	
---/---	Star (New Brunswick, NJ)	27	44		L	
---/---	Olympic (Paterson, NJ)	16	49		L	
10/28	Mutual (New York)	9	52		L	

BATTER	POS	GP	HL	A	O	R	A	O
J. Welsh		12	34	2	10	30	2	6
C. Delany		11	24	2	2	31	2	9
P. Murray		11	27	2	5	22	2	0
J. Raymond		8	19	2	3	27	3	3
S. B. Mettler		8	26	3	2	19	2	3
P. Murphy		8	21	2	5	18	2	2
C. Paul		7	13	1	6	26	3	5
P. D. Braisted		7	19	2	5	15	2	1
H. McGorran		6	16	2	4	15	2	3
H. L. Davis		5	16	3	1	10	2	0
Andrew Gedney		4	9	2	1	10	2	2
E. O. Hedden		4	12	3	0	9	2	1
G. Ackerson		4	13	3	1	9	2	1
J. Chapman		3	8	2	2	7	2	1
H. Springsteen		2	6	3	0	5	2	1
A. Walton		2	6	3	0	4	2	0
G. H. Howe		2	8	4	0	3	1	1

LONE STAR 3 - 3
Springfield, OH

DATE	OPPONENT	SCORE		W	L	T
---/---	Railway Union (Cleveland)	35	45		L	
---/---	Republic (Springfield)	32	29	W		
---/---	Republic (Springfield)	32	24	W		
---/---	Republic (Springfield)	53	56		L	
---/---	Miami (Yellow Springs, OH)	36	46		L	
---/---	Miami (Yellow Springs, OH)	33	20	W		

BATTER	POS	GP	HL	A	O	R	A	O
I.W. Bishop		7	10	1	3	35	5	0
J.C. Davidson		7	17	2	3	40	5	5
Clay Nelson		6	15	2	3	30	5	0

LONE STAR (cont.)
Springfield, OH

BATTER	POS	GP	HL	A	O	R	A	O
John A. Widdecombe		6	20	3	2	22	3	4
L.M. Sprecher		6	27	4	3	20	3	2
C. Frankhouse		5	9	1	4	25	5	0
Lew Selbert		4	8	2	0	21	5	1
C.D. Wallace		4	14	3	2	15	3	3
William Selbert		3	4	1	1	16	5	1
John Harshman		3	10	3	1	12	4	0
E.T. Thomas		3	8	2	2	10	3	1
E.O. McCord		2	6	3	0	9	4	1
George Ford		2	7	3	1	6	3	0
J.B. Kurtz		2	8	4	0	4	2	0

ACTIVE 2 - 3
New York, NY

DATE	OPPONENT	SCORE		W	L	T
07/26	Excelsior (Brooklyn)	9	14		L	
08/27	Fulton (New York)	37	11	W		
09/28	Union (Morrisania, NY)	11	15		L	
---/---	Alert (Elmira, NY)	--	--	W		
---/---	Champion (?)	--	--		L	

BATTER	POS	GP	HL	A	O	R	A	O
H.C. Kelley	1B	5	16	3	1	15	3	0
T.F. Kelley	2B,3B	4	16	4	0	17	4	1
Andrew Dupignac	SS,3B	5	16	3	1	13	2	3
Collins	3B	4	10	2	2	15	3	3
Seaver Page	OF	3	6	2	0	13	4	1
Tom Haines	OF	3	7	2	1	7	2	1
Rogers	OF	2	7	3	1	5	2	1
William Kelley	C	5	12	2	2	17	3	2
Charley Walker	P	4	11	2	3	9	2	1

FULTON 2 - 4
New York, NY

DATE	OPPONENT	SCORE		W	L	T
07/25	Oriental (Greenpoint, NY)	27	22	W		
07/30	Eckford (Brooklyn)	28	20	W		
08/27	Active (New York)	11	37		L	
09/06	Eckford (Brooklyn)	21	23		L	
10/22	Oriental (Greenpoint, NY)	13	29		L	
---/---	Champion (Jersey City, NJ)	--	--		L	

(Only scores extant)

BATTER	POS	GP	HL	A	O	R	A	O
Nape		9	24	2	6	24	2	6
Campbell		8	20	2	4	27	3	3
Harry Manolt		7	23	3	2	14	2	0
Hubbs		6	21	3	3	9	1	3
Devine		5	10	2	0	19	3	4
Betts		5	12	2	2	16	3	1
Storer		5	14	2	4	15	3	0
Carlton		5	13	2	3	14	2	4

MOHAWK   2 - 5
Brooklyn, NY

DATE	OPPONENT	SCORE		W	L	T
07/13	Star (Brooklyn)	24	46		L	
08/01	Mutual (New York)	1	17		L	
08/06	Eckford (Brooklyn)	12	42		L	
08/19	Independent (Brooklyn)	13	22		L	
09/09	Excelsior (Brooklyn)	7	38		L	
09/20	Independent (Brooklyn)	28	23	W		
09/30	Eckford (Brooklyn)	31	18	W		

(Only scores extant)

BATTER	POS	GP	HL	A	O	R	A	O
J. Steiner		10	29	2	9	29	2	9
A. Steiner		10	28	2	8	25	2	5
Davenport		9	26	2	8	23	2	5
Silleck		7	19	2	5	23	3	2
Weeks		6	20	3	2	17	2	5
Miles		6	21	3	3	11	1	5
O'Connor		5	9	1	4	24	4	4

EUREKA   2 - 8
Newark, NJ

DATE	OPPONENT	SCORE		W	L	T
05/16	Irvington (Irvington, NJ)	17	25		L	
05/23	Star (New Brunswick, NJ)	66	9	W		
06/12	Union (Morrisania, NY)	12	26		L	
08/06	Union (Lansingburgh, NY)	21	42		L	
08/23	Mutual (New York)	21	34		L	
08/14	Charter Oak (Hartford, CT)	35	9	W		
09/05	Atlantic (Brooklyn)	13	21		L	
09/10	Union (Morrisania, NY)	14	33		L	
09/23	Excelsior (Brooklyn)	22	41		L	
11/02	Irvington (Irvington, NJ)	9	22		L	

BATTER	POS	GP	HL	A	O	R	A	O
Ev Mills	1B	10	30	3	0	27	2	7
Beans	2B	6	20	3	2	13	2	1
Charles Thomas	SS	9	28	3	1	15	1	6
H. Brientnall	3B,C,2B	7	26	3	5	12	1	5
Fred Calloway	OF	7	15	2	1	21	3	0
A. Littlewood	OF,3B	7	18	2	4	20	2	6
Osborne	OF,C	6	19	3	1	15	2	3
Dockney	C	10	30	3	2	25	2	5
Harry Lex	P	10	28	2	8	23	2	3
Terrell	2B,OF	8	19	2	3	21	2	5

GOTHAM   1 - 3
New York, NY

DATE	OPPONENT	SCORE		W	L	T
08/14	Americus (Newark, NJ)	24	32		L	
---/---	Americus (Newark, NJ)	--	--		L	
---/---	Jefferson (New York)	14	30		L	
---/---	Jefferson (New York)	44	14	W		

(Only scores extant)

GOTHAM (cont.)
New York, NY

BATTER	POS	GP	HL	A	O	R	A	O
William Goodspeed		5	12	2	2	17	3	2
Connell		5	14	2	4	16	3	1
Marks		5	13	2	3	15	3	0
Ed Beadle		5	19	3	4	11	2	1

UNION 1 - 4
Elmira, NY

DATE	OPPONENT	SCORE		W	L	T
06/04	Excelsior (Elmira)	41	39	W		
07/10	Alert (Elmira)	25	34		L	
07/18	Meteor (Addison, NY)	44	83		L	
07/26	Monitor (Corning, NY)	34	65		L	
08/01	Excelsior (Elmira)	39	49		L	

BATTER	POS	GP	HL	A	O	R	A	O
Miller		5	10	2	0	27	5	2
Bachman		5	9	1	4	22	4	2
Porter		5	20	4	0	19	3	5
Millspaugh		5	17	3	2	15	3	0
Haviland		3	11	3	2	12	4	0
Hazard		3	9	3	0	14	4	2
McNeil		3	6	2	0	12	4	0
Graves		3	11	3	2	11	3	2
Callahan		3	14	4	2	10	3	1
Mathews		2	4	2	0	10	5	0
Patrick		2	3	1	1	9	4	1
Hylen		2	6	3	0	6	3	0

EAGLE 0 - 2
New York, NY

DATE	OPPONENT	SCORE		W	L	T
08/23	Excelsior (Brooklyn)	8	35		L	
---/---	Champion (Jersey City, NJ)	--	--		L	

(Only scores extant)

BATTER	POS	GP	HL	A	O	R	A	O
N.B. Shaffer		5	11	2	1	16	3	1
W.B. Shaffer		5	14	2	4	13	2	3
Vitt		5	14	2	4	12	2	2

PECONIC 0 - 2
Brooklyn, NY

DATE	OPPONENT	SCORE		W	L	T
---/---	Champion (Jersey City, NJ)	--	--		L	
10/16	Excelsior (Brooklyn)	15	41		L	

(Only scores extant)

BATTER	POS	GP	HL	A	O	R	A	O
Wilcox		7	16	2	2	45	6	3
Wright		7	19	2	5	42	6	0

PECONIC (cont.)
Brooklyn, NY

BATTER	POS	GP	HL	A	O	R	A	O
Stark		7	19	2	5	39	5	4
E.P. Beavans		6	16	2	4	36	6	0
Hillyer		6	19	3	1	32	5	2
J. Potts		6	14	2	2	32	5	2
Jones		5	8	1	3	33	6	3
Thorpe		5	16	3	1	29	5	4
W. Potts		5	17	3	2	22	4	2

RESOLUTE   0 - 3
Brooklyn, NY

DATE	OPPONENT	SCORE		W	L	T
08/17	Independent (Brooklyn)	15	44		L	
08/28	Empire (New York)	19	21		L	
---/---	Walkill (Middletown, NY)	--	--		L	

(Only scores extant)

BATTER	POS	GP	HL	A	O	R	A	O
Lethbridge		7	17	2	3	22	3	1
J.S. Lockwood		7	25	3	4	18	2	4
Gray		6	14	2	2	24	4	0
A.H. Rogers		6	14	2	2	23	3	5
J. Weeden		5	13	2	3	23	4	3
T. Allen		5	15	3	0	17	3	2
Creagh		5	17	3	2	12	2	2

POWHATAN   0 - 4
Brooklyn, NY

DATE	OPPONENT	SCORE		W	L	T
05/25	Independent (Brooklyn)	35	39		L	
07/04	Knickerbocker (Albany, NY)	12	48		L	
06/17	Empire (New York)	31	45		L	
06/17	Eckford (Brooklyn)	23	61		L	

(Only scores extant)

BATTER	POS	GP	HL	A	O	R	A	O
A.V. Bergen		8	17	2	1	39	4	7
Earl		7	15	2	1	26	3	5
McCarty		6	12	2	0	26	4	2
Clark		6	24	4	0	17	2	5
Brown		5	14	2	4	17	3	2
Cooney		5	14	2	4	17	3	2
Shields		5	16	3	1	16	3	1
Snediker		5	17	3	2	15	3	0
Farr		5	22	4	2	12	2	2

EAGLE   -- --
Flatbush, NY

DATE	OPPONENT	SCORE	W	L	T

(No scores extant)

EAGLE (cont.)
Flatbush, NY

BATTER	POS	GP	HL	A	O	R	A	O
A.J. Vanderveer		7	16	2	2	28	4	0
G. Delano		7	18	2	4	19	2	5
J. Quevedo		6	13	2	1	22	3	4
W. Dallon		6	22	3	4	15	2	3
W. Bergen		5	12	2	2	19	3	4
J. Niefus		5	17	3	2	8	1	3
L. Millard		4	8	2	0	16	4	0
A. Gillen		4	8	2	0	12	3	0
S.H. Spofford		4	12	3	0	10	2	2
A. McCauley		2	6	3	0	6	3	0
J. Edwards		2	6	3	0	5	2	1
A. Bergen		2	6	3	0	4	2	0

EVERETT -- --
Oshkosh, WI

DATE	OPPONENT	SCORE	W	L	T
		(No scores extant)			

BATTER	POS	GP	HL	A	O	R	A	O
Bailey		6	14	2	2	40	6	4
Daly		5	11	2	1	40	8	0
Badger		5	16	3	1	31	6	1
Harmon		5	12	2	2	31	6	1

FAIRMOUNT -- --
Marlboro, MA

DATE	OPPONENT	SCORE	W	L	T
		(No scores extant)			

BATTER	POS	GP	HL	A	O	R	A	O
Felton		13	34	2	8	58	4	6
Hudson		13	34	2	8	58	4	6
Russell		12	34	2	10	60	5	0
John Madden		12	32	2	8	54	4	6
H. Brigham		11	34	3	1	38	3	5
James Madden		11	43	3	10	35	3	2
Putnam		9	27	3	0	29	3	4
Brady		8	20	2	4	29	4	7
Sawin		5	15	3	0	21	4	1
Andrews		5	13	2	3	19	3	4
Dolan		4	11	2	3	18	4	2

LAURENCE -- --
Pittsburgh, PA

DATE	OPPONENT	SCORE	W	L	T
		(No scores extant)			

BATTER	POS	GP	HL	A	O	R	A	O
L. Bloor		4	8	2	0	20	5	0
J.A. Fox		4	9	2	1	20	5	0
J. Brantner		4	11	2	3	19	4	3

LAURENCE (cont.)
Pittsburgh, PA

BATTER	POS	GP	HL	A	O	R	A	O
A. Wells		4	8	2	0	16	4	0
W. Bell		3	6	2	0	18	6	0
D. Maxwell		3	9	3	0	13	4	1
W. Donaldson		3	6	2	0	13	4	1
C. Keally		2	0	0	0	11	5	1
C. Stiehl		2	6	3	0	9	4	1
J.K. Verner		2	4	2	0	8	4	0

WABAN
Newton, MA -- --

DATE	OPPONENT	SCORE	W	L	T

(No scores extant)

BATTER	POS	GP	HL	A	O	R	A	O
Crafts		17	31	1	14	83	4	15
William Bradbury		17	52	3	1	81	4	12
Young		17	39	2	5	75	4	7
G.H. Ellis		17	51	3	0	74	4	6
E.A. Ellis		16	36	2	4	88	5	8
Rice		16	39	2	7	85	5	5
Clarke		15	44	2	14	67	4	7
Dexter		14	47	3	5	60	4	4
Gould		6	20	3	2	21	3	3

TEAM TOTALS

TEAM	CITY/STATE	GP	W	L	T	PCT	R	OR
Athletic	Philadelphia, PA	47	44	3	0	.936	2198	657
National	Washington, DC	36	29	7	0	.806	1856	660
Quaker City	Philadelphia, PA	38	28	9	0	.757	1335	669
Mutual	New York, NY	30	23	6	1	.783	901	530
Keystone	Philadelphia, PA	28	21	6	1	.768	842	557
Union	Morrisania, NY	29	21	8	0	.724	904	586
Trimountain	Boston, MA	22	19	3	0	.902	454	182
Atlantic	Brooklyn, NY	25	19	5	1	.780	724	429
Geary	Philadelphia, PA	25	19	6	0	.760	806	516
Cincinnati	Cincinnati, OH	17	16	1	0	.941	872	413
Irvington	Irvington, NJ	23	16	7	0	.696	630	436
Oriental	Brooklyn, NY	18	15	3	0	.833	604	382
Union	Lansingburgh, NY	20	14	6	0	.700	607	408
Knickerbocker	Albany, NY	15	13	2	0	.867	740	358
Central City	Syracuse, NY	16	13	3	0	.813	605	385
Brandywine	W. Chester, PA	15	12	3	0	.800	818	477
Harvard	Cambridge, MA	13	11	2	0	.846	562	242
Champion	Jersey City, NJ	16	11	5	0	.688	570	110
Excelsior	Brooklyn, NY	16	11	5	0	.688	469	221
Jefferson	Washington, DC	18	11	6	1	.639	434	444
Commonwealth	Philadelphia, PA	24	11	11	2	.500	744	785
Excelsior	Chicago, IL	11	10	1	0	.909	503	226
Empire	New York, NY	14	10	4	0	.714	468	423
Olympic	Washington, DC	15	10	5	0	.667	417	273
Active	Buffalo, NY	16	10	6	0	.625	790	665
Union	St. Louis, MO	10	9	1	0	.900	520	382
Americus	Newark, NJ	14	9	5	0	.643	549	336
Typographical	Philadelphia, PA	15	9	6	0	.600	519	476
Creighton	Norfolk, VA	12	8	4	0	.667	372	260

TEAM TOTALS (cont.)

TEAM	CITY/STATE	GP	W	L	T	PCT	R	OR
Lowell	Boston, MA	13	8	5	0	.615	447	373
Arctic	Philadelphia, PA	14	8	6	0	.571	393	416
Eclectic	New York, NY	22	8	13	1	.386	547	651
Princeton	Princeton, NJ	10	7	3	0	.700	257	185
Lincoln	Pittsburgh, PA	11	7	4	0	.636	344	321
Pastime	Baltimore, MD	11	7	4	0	.636	411	353
Capitol	Washington, DC	13	7	6	0	.538	442	324
Buckeye	Cincinnati, OH	15	7	8	0	.467	669	689
Canacadea	Hornellsville, NY	8	6	2	0	.750	321	250
Eureka	Chicago, IL	8	6	2	0	.750	281	184
Mutual	Meadville, PA	9	6	2	1	.722	415	305
Una	Mt. Vernon, NY	10	6	4	0	.600	335	295
Star	Brooklyn, NY	10	6	4	0	.600	249	218
Excelsior	Elmira, NY	12	6	6	0	.500	460	492
Eckford	Brooklyn, NY	23	6	16	1	.283	500	611
Neptune	Easton, PA	7	5	2	0	.786	262	206
Pequot	New London, CT	7	5	2	0	.786	226	179
Alert	Norwalk, CT	8	5	3	0	.625	225	173
Ecliptic	Middletown, CT	8	5	3	0	.625	322	274
Lone Star	Catskill, NY	8	5	3	0	.625	397	309
Atlantic	Chicago, IL	9	5	4	0	.556	358	330
Pioneer	Arlington, VA	13	5	7	1	.423	454	641
Independent	Brooklyn, NY	13	5	8	0	.385	352	377
W. Philadelphia	Philadelphia, PA	17	5	12	0	.303	450	558
Eon	Portland, ME	5	4	1	0	.800	170	186
Phil. Sheridan	Cohoes, NY	5	4	1	0	.800	272	164
Resolute	Evansville, IN	5	4	1	0	.800	234	184
Walkill	Middletown, NY	6	4	2	0	.667		
Maryland	Baltimore, MD	8	4	4	0	.500	302	244
Western	Indianapolis, IN	8	4	4	0	.500		
Star	New Brunswick, NJ	11	4	7	0	.364	290	399
Jefferson	New York, NY	12	4	8	0	.333	270	409
Lone Star	Springfield, OH	6	3	3	0	.500	221	220
Kickenepawling	Johnstown, PA	4	2	2	0	.500	186	151
Niagara	Buffalo, NY	4	2	2	0	.500	149	118
Auburn	Auburn, NY	4	2	2	0	.500	24	25
Lone Star	Mattewan, NY	4	2	2	0	.500	99	64
Active	New York, NY	5	2	3	0	.400	128	100
Excelsior	Rochester, NY	6	2	4	0	.333	100	161
Fulton	New York, NY	6	2	4	0	.333	100	131
Mohawk	Brooklyn, NY	7	2	5	0	.286	116	206
Camden	Camden, NJ	7	2	5	0	.286	80	73
Eureka	Newark, NJ	10	2	8	0	.200	230	262
Bachelor	Philadelphia, PA	10	2	8	0	.200	68	162
Union	Camden, NJ	10	2	8	0	.200	164	298
Hudson River	Newburgh, NY	4	1	3	0	.250	35	50
Gotham	New York, NY	4	1	3	0	.250	82	76
Union	Elmira, NY	5	1	4	0	.200	183	270
Utica	Utica, NY	5	1	4	0	.200	26	49
Fraternity	S. Boston, MA	6	1	5	0	.167	125	251
Live Oak	Cincinnati, OH	6	1	5	0	.167	75	69
Eagle	New York, NY	2	0	2	0	.000	8	35
Peconic	Brooklyn, NY	2	0	2	0	.000	15	41
Resolute	Brooklyn, NY	3	0	3	0	.000	34	65
Powhatan	Brooklyn, NY	4	0	4	0	.000	101	193
Charter Oak	Hartford, CT	4	0	4	0	.000	62	114
National	Albany, NY	4	0	4	0	.000	17	41
Empire	Washington, DC	5	0	5	0	.000	35	36
Alvin	Philadelphia, PA	5	0	5	0	.000	30	143
Harry Clay	Philadelphia, PA	7	0	7	0	.000	63	139

OTHER TEAMS

TEAM	CITY/STATE
Active	Ballston Spa, NY
Active	Indianapolis, IN
Active	Newark, NJ
Agallian	Middletown, CT
Alert	Cumberland, MD
Alert	Danville, PA
Alert	Elmira, NY
Alert	Hartford, CT
Alert	Philadelphia, PA
Alert	Poultney, VT
Allegheny	Allegheny, PA
Alpha	Springfield, VT
Amateur	Chicago, IL
Amateur	Philadelphia, PA
Amulet	Waterbury, VT
Anchor	Pittsburgh, PA
Antietam	Hagerstown, MD
Armstrong	Philadelphia, PA
Atalanta	Geneva, NY
Athenian	Philadelphia, PA
Athlete	Washington Hts., NY
Athletic	Memphis, TN
Athletic	Portland, ME
Atlanta	Tremont, NY
Atlantic	Jamaica, NY
Atlantic	Memphis, TN
Atlantic	Pittsburgh, PA
Atlantic	Trenton, NJ
Aurora	Plattsburgh, NY
Awkard	Philadelphia, PA
Bergen	Bergen, NJ
Binghamton	Binghamton, NY
Bluff City	Memphis, TN
Bridgeport	Bridgeport, CT
Brookline	Boston, MA
Buffalo	Buffalo, NY
Burlington	Burlington, NJ
Burlington	Burlington, VT
Capital	Columbus, OH
Capital	Madison, WI
Cedar Grove	Fishkill, NY
Champion	Burlington, VT
Champlain	Vergennes, VT
Chester	Norwich, CT
Chestnut St. Th.	Philadelphia, PA
Chittendon	Milton, VT
Clinton	Brooklyn, NY
Clipper	Castleton, VT
Columbia	Bordentown, NJ
Constellation	Brooklyn, NY
Contest	Brooklyn, NY
Continental	Washington, DC
Crescent	New Lisbon, OH
Crescent	St. Albans, VT
Cypress	E. New York, NY
Delaware	Delaware, OH
Diamond State	Wilmington, DE
Dictator	Brooklyn, NY
Dirigo	Philadelphia, PA
Eagle	Flatbush, NY
Eagle	Sparta, WI
Eagle	St. Albans, VT
Eagle	W. Troy, NY
Earnest	Riverhead, NY
Eckford	Albany, NY
Empire	Placedale, RI

OTHER TEAMS (cont.)

TEAM	CITY/STATE
Empire	St. Louis, MO
Endeavor	New York, NY
Enterprise	Allegheny City, PA
Enterprise	Baltimore, MD
Enterprise	Brooklyn, NY
Enterprise	Clifton, NY
Enterprise	Philadelphia, PA
Equity	Philadelphia, PA
Ethan Allen	Winooski, VT
Etruria	E. Liverpool, OH
Eureka	E. Cambridge, MA
Eureka	Pittsburgh, PA
Everett	Oshkosh, WI
Excelsior	Coatesville, PA
Excelsior	Dubuque, IA
Excelsior	Manchester, IA
Excelsior	Paterson, NJ
Excelsior	Philadelphia, PA
Excelsior	St. Louis, MO
Exercise	New York, NY
Fairmount	Marlborough, MA
Fallkill	Poughkeepsie, NY
Fear Naught	Middlebury, VT
First Ward	Philadelphia, PA
Forest City	Middletown, CT
Friendship	Beverly, NJ
Frontier	Ft. Leavenworth, KS
Ft. Clark	Peoria, IL
Ft. Scott	Ft. Scott, KS
Germantown	Philadelphia, PA
Granite	New York, NY
Green Mountain	Bristol, VT
Greenwood	Brooklyn, NY
Gymnast	Philadelphia, PA
Gymnastic	Washington, DC
Harlem	New York, NY
Hector	Elmira, NY
Hiawatha	Kitanning, PA
Hockanum	N. Manchester, CT
Home	Burlington, VT
Hope	Elmira, NY
Hope	Saratoga Springs, NY
Howard	Hartford, CT
Hudson	Hudson, NY
Hunkidori	Wheeling, WV
Idlewild	Cornwall, NY
Independent	Johnstown, PA
Interior	Washington, DC
Intrepid	Brooklyn, NY
Irvington	Columbus, OH
Jamaica	Jamaica Plains, MA
Juniata	Hollidaysburg, PA
Kearney	Rahway, NJ
Kensington	Philadelphia, PA
Kewanee	Kewanee, IL
Keystone	Harrisburg, PA
Knickerbocker	New York, NY
Korndaffer	Philadelphia, PA
Laurence	Pittsburgh, PA
Lawrenceburgh W.M	Lawrenceburgh, IN
Leisure	Philadelphia, PA
Liberty	Jamaica, NY
Liberty	New Brunswick, NJ
Liberty	Norwalk, CT
Lightfoot	Chattanooga, TN
Lone Star	Anderson, IN

OTHER TEAMS (cont.)

TEAM	CITY/STATE
Lookout	Chattanooga, TN
Lorillard	Rhinebeck, NY
Louisville	Louisville, KY
M.M. Van Dyke	New York, NY
Manhattan	New York, NY
Marion	Philadelphia, PA
Marvin	Norwichtown, CT
Mechanic	Memphis, TN
Mechanics	St. Johnsbury, VT
Meteor	Addison, NY
Middlebury	Middlebury, VT
Minerva	Bound Brook, NJ
Minerva	Philadelphia, PA
Mohican	Hightstown, NJ
Momoweta	Greenport, NY
Monitor	Corning, NY
Monitor	Goshen, NY
Monitor	Waterbury, CT
Monitor	Westport, CT
Monmouth	Hoboken, NJ
Monticello	Monticello, NY
Mount Airy	Philadelphia, PA
Mountain	Altoona, PA
Mutual	E. Liberty, PA
Mystic	New York, NY
Nassau	Princeton, NJ
National	Jersey City, NJ
National	Morristown, NJ
National	Philadelphia, PA
New Britain	New Britain, CT
New Jersey	Burlington, NJ
New York	New York, NY
Newark	Newark, NJ
Nonpareil	Burlington, VT
Occidental	Gambrier, OH
Oceanic	Mystic Bridge, CT
Olympic	Louisville, KY
Olympic	Nazareth, PA
Olympic	Norrisville, VT
Olympic	Paterson, NJ
Olympic	Philadelphia, PA
Olympic	Providence, RI
Ontario	Oswego, NY
Orchard	Brooklyn, NY
Orion	Philadelphia, PA
Osceola	Frankford, PA
Pacific	Clinton, IA
Pacific	New Utrecht, NY
Pacific	Rochester, NY
Palisade	Englewood, NJ
Palisade	Yonkers, NY
Penn Treaty	Philadelphia, PA
Philadelphia	Philadelphia, PA
Phoenix	Belvidere, IL
Pine Grove	Fair Haven, CT
Pioneer	Newark, NJ
Pioneer	Portland, OR
Pioneer	Springfield, MA
Potomac	Washington, DC
Queens	Oyster Bay, NY
Quinnipiack	New Haven, CT
Raleigh	Philadelphia, PA
Randolph	Dover, NJ
Resolute	Elizabeth, NJ
Ristori	Farentum, PA
Rittenhouse	Philadelphia, PA

OTHER TEAMS (cont.)

TEAM	CITY/STATE
Rival	Providence, RI
S.J. Randall	Philadelphia, PA
Scranton	Scranton, PA
Sea Side	Long Branch, NJ
S.J. Randall	Philadelphia, PA
Social	Huntington, PA
Social	New York, NY
Sophomore	Cambridge, MA
Sparkhill	Piermont, NY
Sparta	New York, NY
Star	Altoona, PA
Star	Pleasantville, NY
Star	Wakefield, RI
Suffolk	Huntington, NY
Surprise	W. Farms, NY
Susquehanna	Wilkesbarre, PA
Titan	Pournal, VT
Trenton	Trenton, NJ
Tyrolean	Harrisburg, PA
U.V.M.	Burlington, VT
Uncas	Norwich, CT
Undercliff	Cold Spring, NY
Union	Richmond, VA
Union	St. Johnsbury, VT
Union	Titusville, PA
Union	Washington, DC
Unionville	Unionville, NY
Unique	Staten Island, NY
Unity	Port Richmond, PA
Unkidori	Monticello, IA
Vermillion	Danville, IL
Victory	Troy, NY
Viola	Nazareth, PA
W. H. Patterson	Philadelphia, PA
Waban	Newton, MA
Wahkonsa	Ft. Dodge, IA
Wamsutta	New Bedford, MA
Washington	Port Chester, NY
Waterbury	Waterbury, CT
Wayne	Brooklyn, NY
West Point	Highland Falls, NY
Western	Burlington, IA
Western Market	Philadelphia, PA
Wide Awake	Middlebury, VT
Wild Cat	Brookville, PA
Williamsburgh	Brooklyn, NY
Williamsport	Williamsport, PA
Williston	E. Hampton, MA
Winooski	Cabot, VT
Winthrop	Boston, MA
World	New York, NY
Xenia	Xenia, OH
Yale	New Haven, CT

1868
BASES ON HITS

In the report of the September 10, 1867, game between the Eureka and Union clubs, a new wrinkle was added to the box score. As well as the usual hands lost and runs reported, a new category was added. This was explained by a brief addendum in the *New York Clipper*: "In addition to the usual columns of outs and runs we have added ... bases on hits, designated 'B'... We shall pursue this course in all first class games hereafter." With this new statistic, baseball was endeavoring to find a new yardstick to measure a player's worth.

Up until this time, runs were considered the supreme baseball statistic. Without them, a team couldn't win. Naturally, the player who scored the most runs was considered the most valuable. In late 1867, as shown above, run scoring was being analyzed more carefully. Baseball scribes were rightly reasoning that to score runs, a player had to reach base. It followed then that the surest way to reach base was on a safe hit, beyond the reach of any fielder. The new statistic "bases on hits" sought to measure this by tallying all the bases each player earned on safe hits, not bases by means of an error.

For the first time at the National Association's annual convention in December 1867, delegates representing state associations were admitted. Having been overwhelmed by the more than 200 individual delegates present the year before, Association leaders opted for a qualification change. From now on, individual clubs needed to be a part of a state association to be considered for membership. With this new rule, attendance at the 1867 convention was greatly reduced because most clubs didn't attend themselves, but instead were represented by their state delegations. However, the number of Association clubs doubled again. Now, well over 400 clubs claimed membership.

As the 1868 season unfolded, three top teams, the Athletics, Atlantics, and Unions (Morrisania, NY) copied the National's successful tour of the summer before. Expanding on a good idea, each of the three planned to double the stops.

The Athletics were the first of the trio to depart. Heading due west, they met the Olympic club of Pittsburgh, spanking them 30–5. Throughout the month of June the Philadelphia contingent wandered the northern United States beating teams in Detroit, Chicago, St. Louis and points in between. On the trip's penultimate stop, their ambitious schedule caught up with them. The correspondent of the *Philadelphia Post* as reported in the *American Chronicle of Sports and Pastimes* had this to say: "The Athletic club should not have extended its tour into the present week... The result has been seen today,...when they have met defeat at the hands of a second-rate club." The culprit was fatigue. Commonly, the trekking teams spent all their free time in travel, leaving them little time to rest. Consequently, on this day the Excelsiors of Rochester were the better team as they prevailed, 26–20.

Two weeks after the Athletic embarkation, the Atlantic nine left Brooklyn. On the 13th of June, they met and dispatched their first opponent, the Central City squad of Syracuse, 20–14. A few days later, they too met with disaster in upper-state New York as they were bested by the Niagaras of Buffalo, 19–15. Following their win over the Cincinnati club (40–10) on July 6th, the team journeyed home, with only the one blemish on their 17-game trip.

Near the end of July, the Unions of Morrisania started northward playing and winning their first match against the National of Albany 36–19. The Unions fared better against weaker foes than either the Athletic or Atlantic group as they beat them all. However, like their predecessors, they would not finish the trip without a hitch. Playing the powerful Cincinnati club on the journey's last stop, the Unions were edged, 13–12.

Following the end of the tours, a new type of box score was first seen. Breaking down the bases on hits category, the box score of the Atlantic-Athletic matchup on September 7 contained the number of hits garnered by each player in addition to his total bases. As a result of these innovations, these two new categories were included in the season-ending statistics for some teams. Unfortunately, most teams clung to the old ways as they still only kept track of outs and runs.

During the 1868 season, an annoying trend was becoming prevalent. During the course of the season, several players were jumping or "revolving" from club to club in search of greener pastures. This practice was nominally banned by the Association which stated that a player had to be a club member for at least 30 days before participating in a match. Teams skirted the rule by claiming that games played with new members inside the 30 day grace period would be considered "practice" games and would not count towards the season's totals. Neither the practice of revolving nor the status of so-called practice games was seriously monitored by the Association.

Before the end of the season, the Atlantics were able to temporarily snatch the bunting back from the Union nine as the Brooklyn team won a pair of one-sided decisions 31–7 and 24–8 on September 10th and October 5th. Although the Atlantics had twice been soundly waxed by the Athletics, the losses occurred before the Union wins, before the Atlantics had re-taken the flag. For the Brooklyn team, euphoria faded quickly. Shortly after their second triumph over the Unions, the Atlantics lost a pair to the Mutuals 25-22 and 28–17 allowing the New York team to finish 1868 with its first pennant. This convoluted way of determining the champion was inherently flawed. Nevertheless, the system would remain intact for several more years.

The Athletic team certainly had the right to claim the crown as they finished with 47 wins in 50 games losing single games to the Excelsior (Rochester), Mutual and Nassau (Princeton) clubs. The Atlantic club also won 47 but lost seven. The Unions also finished strong, winning 37 of 43 decisions. Other teams winning 30 included the Cincinnati (36) and Mutual (31) clubs.

The leading run gatherers came from the top clubs. The Athletics' John Radcliff (240) finished first while his teammate Wes Fisler (231) finished third. In between, Joe Start of the Atlantics crossed the plate 235 times. The top run averages mostly came from lesser nines. The top mark was achieved by Joe Simmons of the Chicago Excelsiors (6,0) followed by James Lovett of Boston's Lowell club, Whitney of Lowell's Clipper club and Al Reach of the Athletics each at 5,6.

In the new categories of hits and bases, the top performers came from a variety of locales. The most hits were struck by Joe Start (233), John Chapman (218) and Bob Ferguson (194) of the Atlantics. The highest total of bases was garnered by Ferguson (312), Fisler (304) and Chapman (301). The best averages in the hit classification were posted by Start (4,25), John Hatfield of Cincinnati (4,6) and Tom Pratt and Dicky Pearce of the Atlantics tied at 4,5. The best bases per game average was claimed by Fisler (6,21), Lovett (6,9) and Pratt (6,8).

In the judgment of many, hits and bases soon became the best measuring-stick of a player's ability. In the summary of the 1868 season found in the *Beadle's Guide*, Henry Chadwick stated "though...the statistics of outs and runs are better than no data at all, it does not compare with that of bases on hits." Unfortunately, many clubs did not heed this advice as they continued to chart only outs and runs.

By adding these two new categories to baseball's statistical mix, the game as tabulated in the box scores and guides crept closer to our modern equivalent. In a few years, the final evolution would occur, leaving a form that has not changed in over 100 years.

1868

ATHLETIC 47 - 3
Philadelphia, PA

DATE	OPPONENT	SCORE		W	L	T
05/01	Commonwealth (Philadelphia)	61	8	W		
05/09	Bachelor (Philadelphia)	42	5	W		
05/12	Bachelor (Philadelphia)	59	14	W		
05/14	Olympic (Philadelphia)	56	16	W		
05/16	Union (Camden, NJ)	39	15	W		
05/19	Olympic (Philadelphia)	26	9	W		
05/26	Geary (Philadelphia)	36	17	W		
05/28	Keystone (Philadelphia)	34	12	W		
06/01	Olympic (Pittsburgh)	39	5	W		
06/02	Allegheny (Pittsburgh)	27	18	W		
06/04	Xenia (Xenia, OH)	79	8	W		
06/05	Buckeye (Cincinnati)	22	8	W		
06/06	Cincinnati (Cinciinnati)	20	13	W		
06/09	Louisville (Louisville)	51	3	W		
06/10	Active (Indianapolis)	53	21	W		
06/12	Union (St. Louis)	54	12	W		
06/13	Empire (St. Louis)	54	6	W		
06/15	Bloomington (Bloomington, IL)	31	6	W		
06/17	Excelsior (Chicago)	33	13	W		
06/18	Forest City (Rockford, IL)	94	13	W		
06/19	Eureka (Chicago)	37	18	W		
06/22	Detroit (Detroit)	30	17	W		
06/24	Forest City (Cleveland)	85	11	W		
06/26	Erie (Erie, PA)	46	8	W		
06/27	Niagara (Buffalo)	34	14	W		
06/29	Excelsior (Rochester, NY)	20	26		L	
07/01	Central City (Syracuse, NY)	41	12	W		
08/01	Geary (Philadelphia)	42	21	W		
08/03	Union (Camden, NJ)	60	23	W		
08/10	Keystone (Philadelphia)	28	13	W		
08/12	Brandywine (W. Chester, PA)	65	21	W		
08/14	Dirigo (Philadelphia)	52	8	W		
08/17	Olympic (Washington, DC)	35	27	W		
08/22	Olympic (Philadelphia)	32	23	W		
08/26	Columbia (Bordentown, NJ)	60	8	W		
08/29	Keystone (Philadelphia)	47	22	W		
08/31	Atlantic (Brooklyn)	18	9	W		
09/05	Union (Camden, NJ)	47	24	W		
09/07	Atlantic (Brooklyn)	37	13	W		
09/09	National (Albany, NY)	13	6	W		
09/10	Union (Lansingburgh, NY)	36	28	W		
09/15	Eckford (Brooklyn)	26	20	W		
09/18	Brandywine (W. Chester, PA)	37	13	W		
09/21	Mutual (New York)	51	24	W		
09/22	Neptune (Easton, PA)	27	5	W		
09/23	Cincinnati (Cincinnati)	15	12	W		
10/14	Mutual (New York)	15	25		L	
10/17	Olympic (Philadelphia)	36	20	W		
10/24	Olympic (Philadelphia)	21	19	W		
10/31	Nassau (Princeton, NJ)	17	25		L	

BATTERS	POS	GP	HL	A	O	R	A	O	H	A	O	TB	A	O
Wes Fisler	1B	47	111	2	17	231	4	43				304	6	21
Al Reach	2B	42	121	2	37	216	5	6				256	6	4
Isaac Wilkins	SS	41	143	3	20	179	4	15				208	5	3
Tom Berry	3B	49	158	3	11	197	4	1				219	4	23
John Sensenderfer	OF	48	146	3	2	211	4	19				260	5	20
Ned Cuthbert	OF	45	117	2	25	216	4	32				252	5	22
Harry Schafer	OF	31	95	3	2	140	4	16				162	5	7
John Radcliff	C	48	127	2	31	240	5	0				254	5	14
Dick McBride	P	40	121	3	1	172	4	12				212	5	12
Hicks Hayhurst		11	38	3	5	50	4	6						
Kahmar		7	27	3	6	30	4	2						
Dan Kleinfelder	P,OF	6	20	3	2	29	4	5						

ATLANTIC
Brooklyn, NY
47 - 7

DATE	OPPONENT	SCORE		W	L	T
05/11	Mohawk (Brooklyn)	35	10	W		
05/23	Athletic (Brooklyn)	26	3	W		
05/28	Eureka Newark, NJ)	45	8	W		
06/01	Athletic (Brooklyn)	44	13	W		
06/04	Mohawk (Brooklyn)	38	13	W		
06/08	Star (Brooklyn)	13	2	W		
06/13	Central City (Syracuse, NY)	20	14	W		
06/15	Young Canadian (Woodstock, ON)	30	17	W		
06/16	Niagara (Buffalo, NY)	15	19		L	
06/17	Railway Union (Cleveland, OH)	47	12	W		
06/18	Detroit (Detroit, MI)	40	7	W		
06/20	Excelsior (Chicago, IL)	47	7	W		
06/21	Central City (Jackson, MI)	56	8	W		
06/22	Cream City (Milwaukee, WI)	67	13	W		
06/23	Atlantic (Chicago, IL)	51	7	W		
06/24	Forest City (Rockford, IL)	31	29	W		
06/26	Bloomington (Bloomington, IL)	57	19	W		
06/27	Union (St. Louis, MO)	68	9	W		
06/29	Empire (St. Louis, MO)	53	15	W		
07/01	Active (Indianapolis, IN)	103	8	W		
07/02	Louisville (Louisville, KY)	66	11	W		
07/04	Buckeye (Cncinnati, OH)	38	9	W		
07/06	Cincinnati (Cincinnati, OH)	40	19	W		
07/16	Eckford (Brooklyn)	55	11	W		
07/18	Yale (New Haven, CT)	40	16	W		
07/23	Tri Mountain (Boston, MA)	33	5	W		
07/27	Olympic (Paterson, NJ)	28	5	W		
07/30	Olympic (Philadelphia)	35	9	W		
08/03	Oriental (Greenpoint, NY)	36	9	W		
08/06	Active (New York)	25	6	W		
08/10	National (Albany, NY)	19	27		L	
08/13	Olympic (Washington, DC)	55	22	W		
08/19	Active (New York)	37	6	W		
08/17	Mutual (New York)	12	11	W		
08/20	Keystone (Philadelphia)	17	7	W		
08/24	Irvington (Irvington, NJ)	37	6	W		
08/25	Eckford (Brooklyn)	14	2	W		
08/27	Union (Lansingburgh, NY)	40	14	W		
08/31	Athletic (Philadelphia)	9	18		L	
09/05	Star (Brooklyn)	16	7	W		
09/07	Athletic (Philadelphia)	13	37		L	
09/10	Union (Morrisania, NY)	31	7	W		
09/11	Irvington (Irvington, NJ)	13	6	W		
09/22	Eckford (Brooklyn)	48	11	W		
09/29	Union (Lansingburgh, NY)	16	13	W		
10/03	Cincinnati (Cincinnati, OH)	31	12	W		
10/05	Union (Morrisania, NY)	24	8	W		
10/10	Nassau (Princeton, NJ)	27	16	W		
10/12	Mutual (New York)	22	25		L	
10/24	Maryland (Baltimore, MD)	14	11	W		
10/26	Mutual (New York)	17	28		L	
10/29	Eckford (Brooklyn)	14	18		L	

(Only scores extant)

BATTERS	POS	GP	HL	A	O	R	A	O	H	A	O	TB	A	O
Joe Start	1B	52	122	2	18	235	4	27	233	4	25	283	5	23
Charles Smith	2B	38	126	3	12	161	4	9	152	4	0	215	5	25
Dickey Pearce	SS,OF	45	139	3	4	191	4	11	185	4	5	222	4	42
Bob Ferguson	3B	51	158	3	5	212	4	8	194	3	41	312	6	6
John Chapman	OF	54	150	2	42	222	4	2	218	4	2	301	5	31
Fred Crane	OF	47	146	3	5	191	4	3	172	3	31	230	4	42
Dan McDonald	OF,1B	42	100	2	16	163	3	37	152	3	26	228	5	18
Charley Mills	C	50	137	2	37	189	3	39	171	3	21	235	4	35
George Zettlein	P	56	209	3	41	154	2	42	160	2	48	215	3	47

ATLANTIC (cont.)
Brooklyn, NY

BATTERS	POS	GP	HL	A	O	R	A	O	H	A	O	TB	A	O
Tom Pratt	SS,OF	22	64	2	20	97	4	9	93	4	5	140	6	8
John Kenney	2B	13	53	4	1	41	3	2	35	2	9	50	3	11

UNION   37 - 6
Morrisania, NY

DATE	OPPONENT	SCORE			W	L	T
06/01	Olympic (Paterson, NJ)	31	16		W		
06/06	Yale (New Haven, CT)	16	14	(10)	W		
06/20	Star (Brooklyn)	37	16		W		
06/27	Gramercy (New York)	28	7		W		
06/13	Star (Pleasantville, NY)	38	12		W		
06/14	Mohawk (Brooklyn)	34	11		W		
07/10	Endeavor (New York)	53	5		W		
07/17	Yale (New Haven, CT)	19	9		W		
07/18	Star (Pleasantville, NY)	38	4		W		
07/27	National (Albany, NY)	36	19		W		
07/28	Central City (Syracuse)	34	7		W		
07/29	Auburn (Auburn, NY)	67	28		W		
07/31	Forest City (Cleveland)	25	7		W		
08/01	Railway Union (Cleveland)	43	8		W		
08/03	Detroit (Detroit)	33	11		W		
08/04	Central City (Jackson, MI)	65	1		W		
08/06	Atlantic (Chicago)	41	12		W		
08/07	Cream City (Milwaukee)	43	16		W		
08/08	Capital City (Madison, WI)	77	12		W		
08/10	Excelsior (Chicago)	31	21		W		
08/11	Forest City (Rockford, IL)	23	17		W		
08/13	Bloomington (Bloomington, IL)	37	11		W		
08/14	Union (St. Louis)	37	30		W		
08/15	Empire (St. Louis)	37	11		W		
08/17	Active (Indianapolis)	36	8		W		
08/18	Louisville (Louisville)	59	11		W		
08/20	Eagle (Louisville)	59	4		W		
08/22	Buckeye (Cincinnati)	12	7		W		
08/24	Cincinnati (Cincinnati)	12	8		W		
08/25	Cincinnati (Cincinnati)	12	13			L	
09/05	Harlem (New York)	41	11		W		
09/08	Harlem (New York)	69	5		W		
09/10	Atlantic (Brooklyn)	7	31			L	
09/12	Star (Brooklyn)	17	14		W		
09/15	Mutual (New York)	28	12		W		
09/18	Eckford (Brooklyn)	42	26		W		
10/02	Keystone (Philadelphia)	15	24			L	
10/05	Atlantic (Brooklyn)	8	24			L	
10/07	Active (New York)	9	8		W		
10/15	Mutual (New York)	6	14			L	
10/17	Active (New York)	6	8			L	
10/28	Mutual (New York)	27	21		W		
11/06	Eckford (Brooklyn)	29	24		W		

(Only scores extant)

BATTERS	POS	GP	HL	A	O	R	A	O	H	A	O	TB	A	O
John Goldie	1B	44	115	2	27	191	4	15						
Al Martin	2B	30	103	3	13	113	3	23						
George Wright	SS,2B	43	91	2	5	195	4	23						
Ed Shelley	3B,2B	43	132	3	3	144	3	15						
Henry Austin	OF	43	135	3	6	159	3	30						
George Smith	OF,1B	32	88	2	24	128	4	0						
Reynolds	OF	21	59	2	17	65	3	2						
Dave Birdsall	C	43	131	3	2	145	3	16						
Charley Pabor	P	44	141	3	9	159	3	27						

UNION (cont.)
Morrisania, NY

BATTERS	POS	GP	HL	A	O	R	A	O	H	A	O	TB	A	O
Steve Bellan	2B,OF	20	48	2	8	78	3	18						

CINCINNATI   36 - 7
Cincinnati, OH

DATE	OPPONENT	SCORE		W	L	T
05/06	Great Western (Cincinnati)	41	7	W		
05/09	Xenia (Xenia, OH)	51	13	W		
05/21	Copec (Covington, KY)	30	14	W		
05/23	Buckeye (Cincinnati)	28	10	W		
---/---	Live Oak (Cincinnati)	72	5	W		
06/06	Athletic (Philadelphia)	13	20		L	
06/11	Riverside (Portsmouth, OH)	59	17	W		
06/20	Miami (Yellow Springs, OH)	71	12	W		
---/---	Xenia (Xenia, OH)	60	13	W		
07/02	Railway Union (Cleveland)	52	16	W		
07/04	Union (St. Louis)	70	7	W		
07/06	Atlantic (Brooklyn)	19	40		L	
07/24	Riverside (Portsmouth, OH)	34	16	W		
---/---	Live Oak (Cincinnati)	55	11	W		
08/03	Railroad (Columbus, OH)	34	15	W		
08/04	Capital (Columbus, OH)	43	5	W		
08/05	Hickory (McConnellsville, OH)	59	16	W		
08/06	Baltic (Wheeling, WV)	66	8	W		
08/07	Mears (Steubenville, OH)	61	20	W		
08/08	Allegheny (Pittsburgh)	25	15	W		
08/10	Olympic (Pittsburgh)	29	14	W		
08/12	Forest City (Cleveland)	44	22	W		
08/24	Union (Morrisania, NY)	8	12		L	
08/25	Union (Morrisania, NY)	13	12	W		
09/02	Buckeye (Cincinnati)	20	12	W		
09/14	Active (Indianapolis)	54	7	W		
09/19	Great Western (Cincinnati)	30	2	W		
---/---	Excelsior (Chicago)	22	4	W		
09/24	National (Washington)	16	10	W		
09/25	Olympic (Washington)	9	21		L	
09/26	Enterprise (Baltimore)	24	3	W		
09/30	Athletic (Philadelphia)	12	15		L	
10/01	Keystone (Philadelphia)	22	24		L	
10/02	Olympic (Philadelphia)	41	20	W		
10/03	Atlantic (Brooklyn)	19	31		L	
10/04	Mutual (New York)	29	28	W		
10/06	Union (Lansingburgh, NY)	27	8	W		
10/07	National (Albany, NY)	16	1	W		
10/08	Excelsior (Rochester, NY)	21	11	W		
10/09	Niagara (Buffalo, NY)	28	8	W		
10/10	Railway Union (Cleveland)	41	8	W		
---/---	Forest City (Cleveland)	33	14	W		
---/---	Miami (Yellow Springs, OH)	45	10	W		

BATTERS	POS	GP	HL	A	O	R	A	O	H	A	O	TB	A	O
Charles Gould	1B	43	126	2	40	164	3	35	155	3	26			
Asa Brainard	2B,P	38	111	2	35	137	3	23	116	3	2			
Con Howe	SS	38	125	3	11	159	4	7	122	3	8			
Fred Waterman	3B	40	93	2	13	176	4	16	150	3	30			
William Johnson	OF	42	134	3	8	173	4	5	136	3	10			
John Hatfield	OF	42	89	2	5	202	4	34	174	4	6			
Rufus King	OF	39	115	2	37	137	3	20	93	2	15			
Doug Allison	C	27	67	2	13	80	2	26	71	2	17			
Harry Wright	P,2B	40	120	3	0	146	3	26	131	3	11			
Grant	OF	22	64	2	20	106	4	18	82	3	16			

MUTUAL   31 - 10
New York, NY

DATE	OPPONENT	SCORE		W	L	T
05/27	Mohawk (Brooklyn)	29	5	W		
05/30	Star (Brooklyn)	28	6	W		
06/06	Oriental (New York)	26	6	W		
06/10	Oriental (Greenpoint, NY)	58	9	W		
06/13	Star (Brooklyn)	13	5	W		
06/17	Mohawk (Brooklyn)	22	6	W		
06/20	Endeavor (New York)	51	1	W		
06/24	Social (New York)	32	5	W		
07/03	Eckford (Brooklyn)	19	14	W		
07/08	Harlem (New York)	21	9	W		
07/22	Tri Mountain (Boston)	11	7	W		
07/24	Irvington (Irvington, NJ)	41	14	W		
07/27	Champion (Jersey City)	57	15	W		
07/29	Olympic (Philadelphia)	29	5	W		
08/03	National (Albany)	32	20	W		
08/04	Union (Lansingburgh, NY)	12	22		L	
08/08	Irvington (Irvington, NJ)	12	7	W		
08/10	Active (New York)	16	30		L	
08/12	Olympic (Washington, DC)	25	14	W		
08/14	Eckford (Brooklyn)	12	18		L	
08/17	Atlantic (Brooklyn)	11	12		L	
08/22	Keystone (Philadelphia)	26	19	W		
08/26	Union (Lansingburgh, NY)	32	10	W		
09/02	Harlem (New York)	25	13	W		
09/12	Eckford (Brooklyn)	23	16	W		
09/15	Union (Morrisania, NY)	12	28		L	
09/17	Union (Lansingburgh, NY)	11	48		L	
09/21	Athletic (Philadelphia)	24	51		L	
09/22	Olympic (Philadelphia)	9	29		L	
09/30	Active (New York)	37	17	W		
10/04	Cincinnati (Cincinnati)	28	29		L	
10/10	Oriental (New York)	31	5	W		
10/12	Atlantic (Brooklyn)	25	22	W		
10/14	Athletic (Philadelphia) ᵧ	25	15	W		
10/15	Union (Morrisania, NY)	14	6	W		
10/17	Oriental (New York)	33	12	W		
10/24	Maryland (Baltimore)	27	14	W		
10/26	Atlantic (Brooklyn)	28	17	W		
10/28	Union (Morrisania, NY)	21	27		L	
10/31	Active (New York)	33	12	W		
---/---	Oriental (New York)	12	1	W		

BATTERS	POS	GP	HL	A	O	R	A	O	H	A	O	TB	A	O
Charley Bearman	1B	18	58	3	4	50	2	14	49	2	13	57	3	3
George Flanly	2B	42	114	2	30	112	2	28	126	3	0	179	4	11
Mahlon Stockman	SS	17	58	3	7	34	2	0	49	2	15	53	3	2
Tom Devyr	3B,SS	42	106	2	22	127	3	1	141	3	15	174	4	6
Marty Swandell	OF,C,3B	41	107	2	25	122	2	40	142	3	19	183	4	19
Billy McMahon	OF	33	91	2	25	98	2	32	118	3	19	149	4	17
Lip Pike	OF	25	83	3	2	60	2	15	82	3	1	109	4	1
Nat Jewett	C	27	77	2	23	71	2	17						
Rynie Wolters	P	37	109	2	35	101	2	27	116	3	4	133	3	22
Patsy Dockney	C	22	60	2	16	62	2	18	68	3	2	103	4	14
Charles Hunt	OF	18	42	2	6	62	3	8	63	3	9	79	4	7
Pete Shreves	SS,C	11	33	3	0	32	2	10	28	2	6	36	3	3
Ev Mills	1B	10	23	2	3	29	2	9	37	3	7	43	4	3
John Galvin	OF	10	31	3	1	21	2	1	28	2	8	32	3	2
Richard Hunt	1B,OF	7	16	2	2	31	4	3	24	3	3	34	4	6
Kelly	OF,1B	6	21	3	3	18	3	0	17	2	5	20	3	2
Dick Thorn	P,OF	5	18	3	3	10	2	0	7	1	2	10	2	0

ECKFORD
Brooklyn, NY   23 - 12

DATE	OPPONENT	SCORE		W	L	T
06/06	Athletic (Brooklyn)	60	3	W		
06/23	Athletic (Brooklyn)	29	11	W		
06/26	Oriental (New York)	30	16	W		
07/03	Mutual (New York)	14	19		L	
07/16	Atlantic (Brooklyn)	11	35		L	
07/21	Yale (New Haven, CT)	19	11	W		
07/22	Mohawk (Brooklyn)	30	11	W		
07/24	Tri Mountain (Boston)	36	9	W		
07/28	Olympic (Philadelphia)	42	7	W		
07/31	Active (New York)	34	16	W		
08/04	Unique (Staten Island, NY)	37	1	W		
08/07	Irvington (Irvington, NJ)	27	18	W		
08/11	Cypress (E. New York)	41	6	W		
08/14	Mutual (New York)	18	12	W		
08/15	Olympic (Washington, DC)	21	12	W		
08/19	Irvington (Irvington, NJ)	12	14		L	
08/21	Keystone (Philadelphia)	27	24	W		
08/25	Atlantic (Brooklyn)	2	14		L	
08/27	National (Albany)	26	33		L	
09/01	Irvington (Irvington, NJ)	12	6	W		
09/08	Alaska (Brooklyn)	33	5	W		
09/12	Mutual (New York)	16	23		L	
09/15	Athletic (Philadelphia)	20	26		L	
09/16	Cypress (E. New York)	43	15	W		
09/18	Union (Morrisania, NY)	36	42		L	
09/21	Athletic (Brooklyn)	38	10	W		
09/22	Atlantic (Brooklyn)	11	43		L	
09/26	Oriental (New York)	47	17	W		
09/30	Yale (New Haven, CT)	12	15		L	
10/06	Athletic (Brooklyn)	53	14	W		
10/10	Yale (New Haven, CT)	17	19		L	
10/13	Alaska (Brooklyn)	30	1	W		
10/23	Maryland (Baltimore)	14	10	W		
10/29	Atlantic (Brooklyn)	18	14	W		
11/06	Union (Morrisania, NY)	24	29		L	

BATTERS	POS	GP	HL	A	O	R	A	O	H	A	O	TB	A	O
Andy Allison	1B	32	96	3	0	106	3	10	111	3	15	140	4	12
James Wood	2B	18	52	2	16	64	3	10	63	3	9	83	4	11
Jack Nelson	SS	32	86	2	18	111	3	15	101	3	5	134	4	6
Holmes	3B	11	36	3	3	21	1	10	14	1	3	26	2	4
Tom Patterson	OF,2B	32	89	2	23	104	3	8	101	3	5	145	4	17
Dave Eggler	OF	31	93	3	0	96	3	3	102	3	9	137	4	13
Malone	OF,P	25	81	3	6	64	2	14	66	2	16	94	3	19
Charlie Hodes	C	30	82	2	22	78	2	18	96	3	6	128	4	8
Al Martin	P	29	80	2	22	92	3	5	92	3	5	118	4	2
George Grum	3B	11	32	2	10	33	3	0	32	2	10	54	4	10
Courtney	OF,C	9	31	2	4	22	2	4						
Ed Brown	3B	8	26	3	2	17	2	1						
Davenport	P	6	23	3	5	14	2	2						
John Grum	OF,3B	5	12	2	2	23	4	3						
Laing	OF	5	13	2	3	11	2	1						

BUCKEYE
Cincinnati, OH   21 - 5

DATE	OPPONENT	SCORE		W	L	T
05/---	Great Western (Cincinnati)	31	3	W		
05/09	Mutual (Springfield, OH)	53	22	W		
05/21	Great Western (Cincinnati)	45	3	W		
05/23	Cincinnati (Cincinnati)	10	28		L	

BUCKEYE (cont.)
Cincinnati, OH

DATE	OPPONENT	SCORE		W	L	T
06/05	Athletic (Philadelphia)	8	22		L	
06/13	Great Western (Cincinnati)	28	19	W		
06/20	Louisville (Louisville)	28	4	W		
07/03	Railway Union (Cleveland)	49	13	W		
07/04	Atlantic (Brooklyn)	9	38		L	
07/20	Detroit (Detroit)	36	35	W		
07/21	Excelsior (Chicago)	43	22	W		
07/22	Atlantic (Chicago)	27	9	W		
07/23	Forest City (Rockford, IL)	19	11	W		
07/25	Bloomington (Bloomington, IL)	33	17	W		
07/27	Union (St. Louis)	25	8	W		
07/28	Empire (St. Louis)	44	9	W		
07/29	Active (Indianapolis)	64	22	W		
08/05	Mutual (Springfield, OH)	74	11	W		
08/11	Forest City (Cleveland)	13	8	W		
08/22	Union (Morrisania, NY)	7	12		L	
09/02	Cincinnati (Cincinnati)	12	20		L	
09/05	Columbia (Columbia, OH)	55	5	W		
09/15	Forest City (Cleveland)	29	5	W		
09/16	Railway Union (Cleveland)	15	13	W		
09/17	Active (Indianapolis)	44	12	W		
09/29	Live Oak (Cincinnati)*	40	15	W		

* Box score not available

BATTERS	POS	GP	HL	A	O	R	A	O	H	A	O	TB	A	O
Joe Doyle	1B,3B	22	59	2	15	75	3	9						
Charlie Sweasy	2B,3B	25	67	2	17	105	4	5						
B. Brookshaw	SS	22	54	2	10	81	3	15						
Andy Leonard	3B,C	23	57	2	11	106	4	14						
John Meagher	OF	20	72	3	12	57	2	17						
Febiger	OF	12	41	3	5	31	2	7						
J.E. Sherwood	OF	8	21	2	5	39	4	7						
John McMullin	C,1B,OF,2B,P	19	45	2	7	70	3	13						
Cherokee Fisher	P,3B	25	64	2	14	89	3	14						
W.P. Wright	1B,OF,3B	10	36	3	6	24	2	4						
Patsy Dockney	C,SS	6	12	2	0	23	3	5						
Dick Hurley	OF	6	19	3	1	21	3	3						

UNION   15 - 5
Lansingburgh, NY

DATE	OPPONENT	SCORE		W	L	T
05/---	Trojan (Troy, NY)	39	10	W		
06/20	Central City (Syracuse, NY)	48	6	W		
07/03	Hudson River (Newburgh, NY)	44	8	W		
07/08	Excelsior (Rochester, NY)	31	26	W		
07/09	Central City (Syracuse, NY)	35	14	W		
07/---	National (Albany, NY)	29	16	W		
07/27	Tri Mountain (Boston)	63	37	W		
08/04	Mutual (New York)	22	12	W		
08/10	Olympic (Washington, DC)	44	8	W		
08/26	Mutual (New York)	10	32		L	
08/27	Atlantic (Brooklyn)	14	40		L	
08/28	Star (Brooklyn)	23	16	W		
---/---	Excelsior (Rochester, NY)	23	15	W		
09/10	Athletic (Philadelphia)	28	36		L	
09/16	National (Albany, NY)	41	10	W		
09/17	Mutual (New York)	48	11	W		
09/29	Atlantic (Brooklyn)	13	16		L	
10/06	Cincinnati (Cincinnati, OH)	8	27		L	
10/10	Tri Mountain (Boston)	15	10	W		
10/12	Star (Brooklyn)	25	12	W		

UNION (cont.)
Lansingburgh, NY

BATTERS	POS	GP	HL	A	O	R	A	O	H	A	O	TB	A	O
Bub McAtee	1B	18	46	2	10	72	4	0	76	4	4	87	4	15
John Ward	2B	20	63	3	3	76	3	16	81	4	1	93	4	13
J.H. Borker	SS	10	35	3	5	20	2	0	24	2	4	34	3	4
Cal Penfield	3B	11	28	2	6	45	4	1	48	4	4	53	4	9
Clipper Flynn	OF	20	65	3	5	59	2	19	79	3	19	82	4	2
Mart King	OF	20	45	2	5	74	3	14	84	4	4	103	5	3
Steve King	OF	20	51	2	11	63	3	3	80	4	0	96	4	16
Bill Craver	C	20	65	3	5	70	3	10	82	4	2	109	5	9
Rua	P	12	45	3	9	38	3	2	38	3	2	43	3	7
Davis		15	47	2	17	56	3	11	56	3	11	73	4	13
William Abrams		7	23	3	2	15	2	1	25	3	4	29	4	1
Charley Bearman	P	7	24	3	3	15	2	1	21	3	0	26	3	5

CHAMPION   14 - 7
Jersey City, NJ

DATE	OPPONENT	SCORE		W	L	T
06/05	Social (New York)	32	37		L	
06/24	Eureka (Newark)	4	17		L	
06/26	Resolute (Elizabeth, NJ)	24	16	W		
06/30	Athlete (Washington Hts., NY)	16	32		L	
07/14	Olympic (Paterson, NJ)	22	17	W		
07/22	Union (Hudson City, NJ)	59	10	W		
07/27	Mutual (New York)	15	57		L	
07/30	Jefferson (New York)	19	16	W		
08/04	Union (Hudson City, NJ)	63	12	W		
08/05	Social (New York)	50	18	W		
08/19	Resolute (Elizabeth, NJ)	16	24		L	
08/31	Athletic (Brooklyn)	28	5	W		
09/02	Jefferson (New York)	30	8	W		
09/09	Resolute (Elizabeth, NJ)	17	18		L	
09/15	Ivanhoe (Sing Sing, NY)	39	3	W		
09/18	Gotham (New York)	27	20	W		
09/22	Empire (New York)	20	11	W		
10/06	Eagle (New York)	30	21	W		
10/09	Athlete (Washington Hts., NY)	14	25		L	
10/13	Gotham (New York)	22	16	W		
10/26	Ivanhoe (Sing Sing, NY)	15	6	W		

BATTERS	POS	GP	HL	A	O	R	A	O	H	A	O	TB	A	O
Edwards	1B	16	44	2	12	54	3	6						
H. McMahon	2B	11	23	2	2	37	3	4						
C. Tilden	SS,OF	11	33	3	0	28	2	6						
Donnelly	3B,SS,OF	9	26	2	8	38	4	2						
Snowden	OF	17	41	2	7	61	3	10						
Brown	OF,SS,C	11	24	2	2	31	2	9						
J. McMahon	OF,2B,SS	11	31	2	9	28	2	6						
Willis	C,1B,P	17	51	3	0	67	3	16						
Denmead	P,2B	14	40	2	12	48	3	6						
Johnson	OF,2B	10	30	3	0	24	2	4						
Bliven	C	8	26	3	2	25	3	1						
Halpin	OF	6	17	2	5	17	2	5						

HARVARD   13 - 2
Cambridge, MA

DATE	OPPONENT	SCORE		W	L	T
06/13	Athletic (Boston)	67	2	W		
06/20	Eureka (Cambridge)	70	7	W		
06/23	Nassau (Princeton, NJ)	17	16	W		
07/04	Lowell (Boston)	20	23		L	
07/11	Tri Mountain (Boston)	23	11	W		
07/14	Eon (Portland, ME)	42	10	W		
07/21	Lowell (Boston)	28	27	W		
07/25	Yale (New Haven, CT)	25	17	W		
09/19	Eagle (E. Cambridge)	29	7	W		
09/26	Brown (Providence, RI)	37	15	W		
10/03	Lowell (Boston)	27	24	W		
10/09	Lowell (Boston)	30	33		L	
10/19	Lowell (Boston)	28	15	W		
10/24	Brown (Providence, RI)	29	25	W		
10/27	Tri Mountain (Boston)	32	12	W		

BATTERS	POS	GP	HL	A	O	R	A	O	H	A	O	TB	A	O
Peabody	1B	8	23	2	7	32	4	0	26	3	2	35	4	3
Ames	2B	8	25	3	1	31	3	7	29	3	5	33	4	1
Gardner Willard	SS	15	51	3	6	42	2	12	40	2	10	51	3	6
Nathaniel Smith	3B	15	43	2	13	61	4	1	60	4	0	78	5	3
Francis Rawle	OF	15	39	2	9	59	3	14	52	3	7	74	4	14
Shaw	OF,1B	11	30	2	8	52	4	8	45	4	1	53	4	9
Sprague	OF	8	32	4	0	21	3	0	24	3	0	31	3	7
Archie Bush	C	14	32	2	4	59	4	3	51	3	9	75	5	5
Hunnewell	P	8	24	3	0	32	4	0	34	4	2	43	5	3
James Wells	OF	8	20	2	4	27	3	3	23	2	7	30	3	6
Percy Austin	2B	7	16	2	2	25	4	4	15	2	1	21	3	0
Soule	P	7	21	3	0	21	3	0	15	2	1	16	2	2
William Eustis	OF	5	17	3	2	12	2	2	16	3	1	25	5	0
Bowditch	OF	4	13	3	1	18	4	2	16	4	0	19	4	3
Minot		1	4	4	0	2	2	0	1	1	0	1	1	0

NATIONAL   13 - 8
Albany, NY

DATE	OPPONENT	SCORE		W	L	T
06/05	Mohawk (Schnectady, NY)	65	19	W		
06/08	Trojan (Troy, NY)	21	16	W		
07/04	Central City (Syracuse)	24	32		L	
07/21	Union (Cohoes, NY)	43	2	W		
07/27	Union (Morrisania, NY)	19	36		L	
07/28	Tri Mountain (Boston)	44	25	W		
07/---	Union (Lansingburgh, NY)	16	29		L	
08/03	Mutual (New York)	20	33		L	
08/10	Atlantic (Brooklyn)	27	19	W		
08/11	Olympic (Washington)	10	12		L	
08/26	Trojan (Troy, NY)	37	15	W		
08/27	Eckford (Brooklyn)	33	26	W		
09/08	Active (Wappinger Falls, NY)	29	14	W		
09/09	Athletic (Philadelphia)	6	13		L	
09/16	Union (Lansingburgh, NY)	10	41		L	
10/07	Cincinnati (Cincinnati)	1	16		L	
---/---	Union College (?)	--	--	W		
---/---	Union College (?)	--	--	W		
---/---	Live Oak (Albany)	--	--	W		
---/---	Auburn (Auburn, NY)	--	--	W		
---/---	Champion (W. Troy, NY)	--	--	W		

NATIONAL (cont.)
Albany, NY

BATTERS	POS	GP	HL	A	O	R	A	O	H	A	O	TB	A	O
Whitney	1B,OF,SS	13	40	3	1	48	3	9	40	3	1	50	3	11
Spellman	2B	13	37	2	11	41	3	2	34	2	8	41	3	2
Mike Powers	SS	20	28	2	8	72	3	12	66	3	6	90	4	10
Woolverton	3B	19	39	2	1	83	4	7	76	4	0	106	5	11
Stimson	OF	21	65	3	2	63	3	0	60	2	18	79	3	16
Ertsberger	OF	14	39	2	11	36	2	8	29	2	1	35	2	7
Gould	OF,1B	8	24	3	0	30	3	6	30	3	6	37	4	5
Cantwell	C,2B	20	60	3	0	79	3	19	72	3	12	88	4	8
Waddell	P	20	59	2	19	62	3	2	61	3	1	80	4	0
Ross	C,OF	8	33	4	1	29	3	5	26	3	2	30	3	6
Umpleby	1B	7	17	2	3	20	2	6	15	2	1	21	3	0
Archie Bush	2B	5	12	2	2	24	4	4	22	4	2	35	7	0

MARYLAND 12 - 6
Baltimore, MD

DATE	OPPONENT	SCORE		W	L	T
06/02	National (Washington, DC)	28	27	W		
06/15	Olympic (Washington, DC)	19	16	W		
07/04	Olympic (Washington, DC)	29	35		L	
---/---	Pastime (Baltimore)	26	15	W		
---/---	Patapaco (Baltimore)	32	20	W		
---/---	Pastime (Baltimore)	31	28	W		
09/01	Enterprise (Baltimore)	15	36		L	
---/---	Olympic (Washington, DC)	25	13	W		
09/10	Enterprise (Baltimore)	17	15	W		
---/---	Enterprise (Baltimore)	33	21	W		
---/---	Arctic (Baltimore)	53	15	W		
10/02	National (Washington, DC)	13	12	W		
---/---	Arctic (Baltimore)	33	18	W		
10/21	Olympic (Philadelphia)	11	20		L	
10/23	Eckford (Brooklyn)	10	14		L	
10/24	Atlantic (Brooklyn)	11	14		L	
10/24	Mutual (New York)	14	27		L	
---/---	Union (Washington, DC)	38	11	W		

BATTERS	POS	GP	HL	A	O	R	A	O	H	A	O	TB	A	O
Wilson	1B	15	51	3	6	37	2	7						
Hazlehurst	2B,OF	7	17	2	3	23	3	2						
Lucas	SS	13	38	3	12	32	2	6						
G. Lilly	3B,1B	9	28	3	1	20	2	2						
Tully Worthington	OF	16	35	2	3	41	2	9						
Mike Hooper	OF	16	42	2	10	52	3	5						
Sam Armstrong	OF	7	20	2	6	19	2	5						
Keerle	C	16	42	2	10	40	2	8						
Rorke	P	14	39	2	11	32	2	4						
Annan	SS	10	32	3	2	21	2	1						
Doyle	OF	7	10	1	3	19	2	5						
Wally Goldsmith	2B	6	18	3	0	14	2	2						
Ed Mincher	OF	5	10	2	0	10	2	0						

TRI MOUNTAIN 12 - 9
Boston, MA

DATE	OPPONENT	SCORE		W	L	T
06/17	Eagle (Cambridge, MA)	31	13	W		
06/23	Kearsarge (Stoneham, MA)	41	18	W		

TRI MOUNTAIN (cont.)
Boston, MA

DATE	OPPONENT	SCORE		W	L	T
06/27	Eagle (Natick, MA)	31	18	W		
07/04	Gramercy (New York)	42	9	W		
07/11	Harvard (Cambridge, MA)	11	23		L	
07/21	Gramercy (New York)	38	26	W		
07/22	Mutual (New York)	7	11		L	
07/23	Atlantic (Brooklyn)	5	33		L	
07/24	Eckford (Brooklyn)	9	26		L	
07/27	Union (Lansingburgh, NY)	37	63		L	
07/28	National (Albany, NY)	25	44		L	
08/17	Eagle (Natick, MA)	32	12	W		
09/02	Metacomet (Taunton, MA)	31	21	W		
09/05	Hampden (Springfield, MA)	45	11	W		
09/08	Norfolk (Foxboro, MA)	25	13	W		
09/15	Howard (New Bedford, MA)	33	9	W		
09/12	Fairmount (Marlboro, MA)	23	6	W		
09/19	Hampden (Springfield, MA)	19	28		L	
10/07	St. Lawrence (Malone, NY)	29	11	W		
10/10	Union (Lansingburgh, NY)	10	15		L	
10/27	Harvard (Cambridge, MA)	12	32		L	

BATTERS	POS	GP	HL	A	O	R	A	O	H	A	O	TB	A	O
Crosby	1B,OF	14	42	3	0	36	2	8						
Frank Barrows	2B,P,SS,C	20	54	2	14	61	3	1						
Freeman	SS	11	36	3	3	30	2	8						
Sullivan	3B,C,2B,SS	21	55	2	13	76	3	13						
Kelly	OF,SS	21	59	2	17	56	2	14						
Lyons	OF	20	68	3	8	54	2	14						
Franklin	OF	11	35	3	2	22	2	0						
Putnam	C,2B,SS	20	45	2	5	54	2	14						
O'Brien	P	20	63	3	3	54	2	14						
Tom Pratt	2B,SS,P	5	16	3	1	14	2	4						

OLYMPIC 12 - 11 - 1
Washington, DC

DATE	OPPONENT	SCORE			W	L	T
06/15	Maryland (Baltimore)	16	19			L	
06/27	Enterprise (Baltimore)	18	19	(10)		L	
07/04	Maryland (Baltimore)	35	29		W		
07/08	Jefferson (Washington)	33	11		W		
07/11	Union (Washington)	38	13		W		
07/20	Jefferson (Washington)	61	10		W		
08/05	Pastime (Baltimore)	28	10		W		
08/08	Geary (Philadelphia)	25	15		W		
08/10	Union (Lansingburgh, NY)	8	44			L	
08/11	National (Albany, NY)	12	10		W		
08/12	Mutual (New York)	14	25			L	
08/13	Atlantic (Brooklyn)	22	55			L	
08/14	Star (Brooklyn)	13	15			L	
08/15	Eckford (Brooklyn)	12	21			L	
08/17	Athletic (Philadelphia)	27	35			L	
08/18	Olympic (Philadelphia)	37	20		W		
08/19	Keystone (Philadelphia)	*26	26				T
08/20	Harry Clay (Philadelphia)	40	8		W		
08/21	Commonwealth (Philadelphia)	87	22		W		
09/08	Maryland (Baltimore)	13	25			L	
09/21	National (Washington)	15	21			L	
09/25	Cincinnati (Cincinnati)	21	9		W		
10/07	National (Washington)	13	18			L	
11/12	Union (Washington)	40	7		W		

* Disputed, Keystone club claimed a 42-29 victory in 10 innings.

OLYMPIC (cont.)
Washington, DC

BATTERS	POS	GP	HL	A	O	R	A	O	H	A	O	TB	A	O
Denison	1B	19	56	2	18	57	3	0	50	2	12			
Billy Dick	2B	19	40	2	2	73	3	16	61	3	4			
Davy Force	SS	20	56	2	16	65	3	5	63	3	3			
Ed Leech	3B,P	22	71	3	5	52	2	9	47	3	3			
Fergy Malone	OF,C	24	79	3	7	74	3	3	75	3	3			
A.V. Robinson	OF	23	79	3	10	62	2	16	56	2	10			
Eddie Woods	OF	18	34	1	16	56	3	2	52	2	16			
Waddy Beach	C,OF	16	47	2	15	41	2	9	39	2	7			
Elias Cope	P	19	45	2	7	60	3	3	63	3	6			
Harry McLean	3B	15	55	3	10	47	3	2	37	2	7			
Nick Young	OF	9	28	3	1	34	3	7	29	3	2			
Seymour	3B	5	14	2	4	14	2	4	11	2	1			

ATLANTIC   11 - 3
St. Louis, MO

DATE	OPPONENT	SCORE		W	L	T
05/28	Union (St. Louis)	17	52		L	
09/20	Lone Star (Alma, IL)	22	20	W		
09/27	Aetna (St. Louis)	45	16	W		
10/08	Aetna (St. Louis)	25	10	W		
10/09	St. Louis (St. Louis)*	31	19	W		
10/10	Excelsior (Chicago)	7	71		L	
08/01	Dirigo (St. Louis)	38	25	W		
06/21	Baltic (St. Louis)*	34	11	W		
07/12	Aetna (St. Louis)*	53	35	W		
07/19	Hope (St. Louis)*	58	24	W		
07/26	Active (St. Louis)*	57	17	W		
08/17	Resolute (St. Louis)	20	32		L	
09/13	Baltic (St. Louis)	52	14	W		
10/---	Olympic (?)	54	9	W		

* Box score not available

BATTERS	POS	GP	HL	A	O	R	A	O	H	A	O	TB	A	O
Herring		9	17	1	8	36	4	0						
J. Peterson		9	38	4	2	20	2	2						
J. Berry		8	18	2	2	35	4	3						
W.R. Peterson		8	21	2	5	26	3	4						
O'Keefe		6	24	4	0	16	2	4						
E. Chenot		6	19	3	1	15	2	3						
Seaman		5	11	2	1	19	3	4						

FOREST CITY   11 - 4
Rockford, IL

DATE	OPPONENT	SCORE		W	L	T
06/18	Athletic (Philadelphia)	13	94		L	
06/24	Atlantic (Brooklyn)	29	31		L	
07/04	Excelsior (Chicago)	35	27	W		
07/09	Capital City (Madison, WI)	28	9	W		
08/11	Union (Morrisania, NY)	17	23		L	
06/12	Excelsior (Chicago)	20	18	W		
07/22	Buckeye (Cincinnati)	11	19		L	
07/16	Capital City (Madison, WI)	13	12	W		

(Only scores extant)

FOREST CITY (cont.)
Rockford, IL

BATTERS	POS	GP	HL	A	O	R	A	O	H	A	O	TB	A	O
Fred Cone	1B	14	35	2	7	48	3	5						
Bob Addy	2B	15	43	2	3	70	4	10						
Ross Barnes	SS	15	35	2	5	75	5	0						
Ballard Osborne	3B	13	42	4	3	43	3	4						
Al Barker	OF	13	39	3	0	40	3	11						
Gat Stires	OF	10	30	3	10	36	3	6						
Waxham	OF	7	17	1	3	20	2	6						
George King	C	14	49	3	7	43	3	4						
Al Spalding	P	15	28	1	3	67	4	7						
Swasey	3B	5	18	3	3	14	2	4						
Trumbull	OF	6	17	2	5	24	4	0						

LOWELL 11 - 4
Boston, MA

DATE	OPPONENT	SCORE			W	L	T
05/30	Athletic (Boston)	35	31		W		
06/09	Rollstone (Fitchburg, MA)	50	14		W		
06/13	Yale (New Haven, CT)	16	13	(10)	W		
06/15	Charter Oak (Hartford, CT)	61	12		W		
06/17	Brown (Providence, RI)	19	22			L	
07/04	Harvard (Cambridge, MA)	23	20		W		
07/21	Harvard (Cambridge, MA)	27	28			L	
08/01	Kearsarge (Stoneham, MA)	34	13		W		
08/14	Wamsutta (New Bedford, MA)	62	6		W		
08/22	Active (Quincy, MA)	49	19		W		
09/24	Howard (N. Bridgewater, MA)	25	19		W		
09/26	Tufts (Medford, MA)	39	9		W		
10/03	Harvard (Cambridge, MA)	24	27			L	
10/09	Harvard (Cambridge, MA)	33	30		W		
10/19	Harvard (Cambridge, MA)	15	28			L	

BATTERS	POS	GP	HL	A	O	R	A	O	H	A	O	TB	A	O
Hawes	1B,P,3B	8	22	2	6	32	4	0	23	2	7	30	3	6
Sumner	2B,1B	13	37	2	11	46	3	7	43	3	4	64	4	12
Edward Jewell	SS,1B,2B,3B	15	48	3	3	51	3	6	39	2	9	45	3	0
William Joslyn	3B,1B,OF,SS	11	31	2	9	42	3	9	24	2	2	34	3	1
William Alline	OF,3B	13	39	3	0	45	3	6	48	3	9	84	6	6
A.M. Newton	OF	13	42	3	3	46	3	7	29	2	3	35	2	9
Mort Rogers	OF	11	32	2	10	47	4	4	39	3	6	51	4	7
William Bradbury	C	15	43	2	13	53	3	8	57	3	12	81	5	6
James Lovett	P,2B	13	25	1	12	71	5	6	47	3	8	87	6	9
Fred Conant	3B,SS	7	25	3	4	18	2	4	20	2	6	25	3	4
Henry Dennison	OF,1B	6	19	3	3	26	4	2	20	3	2	33	5	3

GREAT WESTERN 11 - 9
Cincinnati, OH

DATE	OPPONENT	SCORE		W	L	T
05/06	Cincinnati (Cncinnati)	7	41		L	
05/---	Buckeye (Cincinnati)	3	31		L	
05/09	Greenwood (California, OH)	58	18	W		
05/21	Buckeye (Cincinnati)	3	45		L	
06/04	Live Oak (Cincinnati)	47	17	W		
06/17	Alert (Plainville, OH)	62	16	W		

GREAT WESTERN (cont.)
Cincinnati, OH

DATE	OPPONENT	SCORE			W	L	T
06/13	Buckeye (Cincinnati)	19	28			L	
06/20	Copec (Covington, KY)	18	44			L	
06/19	Walnut Hill (Cincinnati)*	13	11		W		
07/17	Live Oak (Cincinnati)	11	34			L	
07/21	Copec (Covington, KY)	23	22	(10)	W		
07/29	Avenue (Cincinnati)	65	33		W		
07/31	Greenwood (California, OH)	79	20		W		
08/06	Mutual (Springfield, OH)	55	13		W		
08/14	Riverside (Portsmouth, OH)	15	26			L	
08/26	Live Oak (Cincinnati)*	33	10		W		
09/15	Active (Indianapolis)*	20	18		W		
09/19	Cincinnati (Cincinnati)	2	38			L	
09/24	Columbia (Columbia, OH)	32	18		W		
10/03	Live Oak (Cincinnati)*	15	30			L	

* Box score not available

BATTERS	POS	GP	HL	A	O	R	A	O	H	A	O	TB	A	O
Riemeyer	1B	15	46	3	1	46	3	1						
Beggs	2B	14	32	2	4	55	3	13						
Stiles	SS,OF,P	11	28	2	6	27	2	5						
Thompson	3B	6	15	2	3	23	3	5						
Slebern	OF	14	35	2	7	51	3	9						
Baker	OF,SS,C,3B	12	31	2	7	58	4	10						
Garlick	OF	9	26	2	8	32	3	5						
Kalisch	C,OF	11	31	2	9	31	2	9						
Black	P,OF,3B	16	46	2	14	54	3	6						
Bates	SS,C,1B	7	26	3	5	12	1	5						
Holabird	OF	6	14	2	2	28	4	4						
Mussey	C,OF	5	13	2	3	21	4	1						

FOREST CITY
Cleveland, OH   11 - 11 - 1

DATE	OPPONENT	SCORE		W	L	T
06/04	Railway Union (Cleveland)	14	21		L	
06/16	Detroit (Detroit)	23	45		L	
06/24	Athletic (Philadelphia)	11	85		L	
07/04	Railway Union (Cleveland)	#27	25			T
07/07	Allegheny (Pittsburgh)	12	9	W		
07/17	Detroit (Detroit)	44	7	W		
07/31	Union (Morrisania, NY)	7	25		L	
07/25	Railway Union (Cleveland)	59	25	W		
08/11	Buckeye (Cincinnati)	8	13		L	
08/12	Cincinnati (Cincinnati)	22	44		L	
08/21	Independent (Mansfield, OH)	40	19	W		
08/25	Mutual (Pittsburgh)	32	18	W		
08/29	Railway Union (Cleveland)	32	25	W		
09/15	Buckeye (Cincinnati)	5	29		L	
09/19	Excelsior (Chicago)	5	19		L	
10/03	Railway Union (Cleveland)	28	19	W		

(Only scores extant)

* Box score not available
# With two out in bottom of tenth inning, game declared a draw.

BATTERS	POS	GP	HL	A	O	R	A	O	H	A	O	TB	A	O
Clarke	1B	14	35	2	1	43	3	1						
Hanna	2B	14	38	2	5	38	2	5						
James White	SS,C	23	63	2	17	73	3	4						
H. Brown	3B	20	57	2	19	61	3	1						

FOREST CITY (cont.)
Cleveland, OH

BATTERS	POS	GP	HL	A	O	R	A	O	H	A	O	TB	A	O
Branch	OF	17	56	3	5	46	2	15						
Herse	OF,1B	17	50	2	16	46	2	12						
Burt	OF	14	37	2	9	43	3	1						
Eb Smith	C,SS	21	58	2	16	60	2	19						
C. Brown	P	16	32	2	0	53	3	5						
Johnson	2B	10	30	3	0	27	2	7						
Sheffield	OF	8	22	2	3	18	2	1						
L. White	P,3B	7	24	2	3	18	2	4						
Taylor	OF	6	20	3	2	16	2	2						

OLYMPIC   11 - 11
Philadelphia, PA

DATE	OPPONENT	SCORE		W	L	T
05/14	Athletic (Philadelphia)	16	56		L	
05/19	Athletic (Philadelphia)	9	26		L	
05/27	Harry Clay (Philadelphia)	23	11	W		
06/16	Geary (Philadelphia)	13	11	W		
06/20	Alvin (Philadelphia)	66	15	W		
06/25	Union (Camden, NJ)	44	30	W		
06/29	Keystone (Philadelphia)	49	15	W		
07/01	Alvin (Philadelphia)	55	26	W		
07/08	Geary (Philadelphia)	43	16	W		
07/13	Union (Camden, NJ)	32	23	W		
07/18	Keystone (Philadelphia)	10	25		L	
07/27	Excelsior (Brooklyn)	22	14	W		
07/28	Eckford (Brooklyn)	7	42		L	
07/29	Mutual (New York)	5	29		L	
07/30	Atlantic (Brooklyn)	9	35		L	
08/18	Olympic (Washington)	20	37		L	
08/22	Athletic (Philadelphia)	23	32		L	
09/22	Mutual (New York)	29	9	W		
10/02	Cincinnati (Cincinnati)	20	41		L	
10/17	Athletic (Philadelphia)	20	36		L	
10/21	Maryland (Baltimore)	20	11	W		
10/24	Athletic (Philadelphia)	19	31		L	

BATTERS	POS	GP	HL	A	O	R	A	O	H	A	O	TB	A	O
Oram	1B,2B,OF	22	65	2	21	64	2	20						
Kern	2B,1B	14	43	3	1	28	2	0						
Welsh	SS,2B,OF	17	44	2	10	36	2	2						
Eckendorf	3B,OF	18	56	3	2	47	2	11						
W. Aitken	OF,P	17	55	3	4	44	2	10						
Myers	OF	14	38	2	10	48	3	6						
Bailey	OF,1B	13	35	2	9	40	3	1						
Harrop	C,P	17	49	2	15	55	3	4						
Rorke	P,C,2B	11	29	2	7	39	3	6						
Willing	SS	11	26	2	4	41	3	8						
Miller	C	6	14	2	2	18	3	0						
Harry Schafer	3B,C	6	17	2	5	14	2	2						
Chick Fulmer	SS	5	11	2	1	10	2	0						

EAGLE
New York, NY   10 - 1

DATE	OPPONENT	SCORE		W	L	T
07/01	Social (New York)	36	31	W		
08/03	Empire (New York)	30	20	W		
08/13	Gotham (New York)	25	9	W		
08/25	Knickerbocker (New York)	41	13	W		
09/08	Sparta (New York)	45	15	W		
09/21	Knickerbocker (New York)	25	4	W		
09/25	Sparta (New York)	45	15	W		
09/29	Jefferson (New York)	39	10	W		
10/06	Champion (Jersey City, NJ)	21	30		L	
10/09	Gotham (New York)	20	17	W		
10/13	Bergen (Bergen, NJ)	37	14	W		

(Only scores extant)

BATTERS	POS	GP	HL	A	O	R	A	O	H	A	O	TB	A	O
Norton	1B,OF	12	33	2	9	47	3	11						
T. Gaughan	2B	12	34	2	10	43	3	7						
Kane	SS	10	22	2	2	40	4	0						
Vitt	3B	9	24	2	6	29	3	2						
W.B. Shaffer	OF,P	12	33	2	9	39	3	3						
N.B. Shaffer	OF,3B,SS	10	21	2	1	45	4	5						
W. Gallagher	OF,2B,1B,3B	9	24	2	6	32	3	5						
Nat Hicks	C	11	32	2	10	39	3	6						
Stevens	P	10	22	2	2	35	3	5						
Phillips	OF	6	16	2	4	20	3	2						

NIAGARA
Buffalo, NY   10 - 5

DATE	OPPONENT	SCORE		W	L	T
06/13	Clifton (Clifton, NY)	32	19	W		
06/16	Atlantic (Brooklyn)	19	15	W		
06/25	Clifton (Clifton, NY)	61	32	W		
06/27	Athletic (Philadelphia)	14	34		L	
07/14	Niagara (Lockport, NY)	84	16	W		
07/30	Central City (Syracuse)	21	33		L	
08/07	Niagara (Lockport, NY)	84	2	W		
08/15	Excelsior (Rochester)	19	10	W		
08/22	Alert (Rochester)	13	30		L	
08/26	Alert (Rochester)	23	11	W		
09/03	Alert (Rochester)	34	22	W		
09/08	Detroit (Detroit)	24	14	W		
09/16	Detroit (Detroit)	38	17	W		
09/17	Excelsior (Chicago)	12	31		L	
10/09	Cincinnati (Cincinnati)	11	28		L	

BATTERS	POS	GP	HL	A	O	R	A	O	H	A	O	TB	A	O
Van Velsor	1B	*15	42	2	12	47	3	2	36	3	0	48	4	0
M. Holley	2B	*10	31	3	1	34	3	4	16	2	0	19	2	3
Hawley	SS	*15	36	2	6	71	4	11	55	4	7	59	4	11
Cowing	3B,OF	*15	36	2	6	58	3	13	45	3	9	61	5	1
Emerson	OF	*14	36	2	8	46	3	4	35	3	2	38	3	5
Alfred Holley	OF	*13	47	3	8	39	3	0	35	3	11	45	4	9
Tanner	OF	*9	25	2	7	37	4	1	35	4	3	46	5	6
Bettinger	C,2B	*10	25	2	5	36	3	6	18	2	2	23	2	7
Atwater	P	*15	60	4	0	37	2	7	28	2	4	29	2	5
Burt	C,3B	*5	10	?	0	25	5	0	10	4	2	22	5	2

* Hits and total bases not counted in all games

ATHLETE 9 - 5
Washington Hts., NY

DATE	OPPONENT	SCORE		W	L	T
05/20	Fanwood (New York)	17	5	W		
06/25	Americus (Yorkville, NY)	25	38		L	
06/30	Champion (Jersey City, NJ)	32	16	W		
10/09	Champion (Jersey City, NJ)	25	14	W		

(Only scores extant)

BATTERS	POS	GP	HL	A	O	R	A	O	H	A	O	TB	A	O
Hopkins	1B	12	26	2	2	40	3	4						
Valentine	2B	11	19	1	8	33	3	0						
Guernsey	SS,P	7	19	2	5	40	3	4						
Barry	3B	10	24	2	4	36	3	6						
Sloane	OF	13	27	2	1	38	2	12						
Cregan	OF	8	16	2	0	30	3	6						
Collins	OF	12	35	2	11	34	2	10						
James	C,3B	7	25	3	4	13	1	6						
Truax	P	5	9	1	4	15	3	0						
McManus		5	7	1	2	14	2	4						

STAR 9 - 10
Brooklyn, NY

DATE	OPPONENT	SCORE		W	L	T
05/30	Mutual (New York)	28	6		L	
06/08	Atlantic (Brooklyn)	2	13		L	
06/13	Mutual (New York)	5	13		L	
06/20	Union (Morrisania, NY)	17	36		L	
06/27	Independent (Brooklyn)	24	20	W		
07/04	Yale (New Haven, CT)	14	31		L	
07/11	Independent (Brooklyn)	39	13	W		
07/22	Harlem (New York)	19	34		L	
08/14	Olympic (Washington)	15	13	W		
08/15	Harlem (New York)	57	9	W		
08/28	Union (Lansingburgh, NY)	15	23		L	
08/29	Peconic (Brooklyn)	21	13	W		
09/05	Atlantic (Brooklyn)	7	16		L	
09/12	Union (Morrisania, NY)	14	17		L	
09/23	Active (New York)	37	11	W		
10/01	Harlem (New York)	76	9	W		
10/10	Independent (Brooklyn)	40	3	W		
10/12	Union (Lansingburgh, NY)	13	25		L	
11/14	Active (New York)	25	7	W		

BATTERS	POS	GP	HL	A	O	R	A	O	H	A	O	TB	A	O
John Clyne	1B	*11	34	3	1	29	2	7	36	4	0	47	5	2
Tom McDiarmid	2B	7							17	2	3	26	3	5
Fraley Rogers	SS,OF,2B	*19	64	3	7	57	2	15	56	3	8	67	4	3
Bob Manly	3B,SS	*13	43	3	4	28	2	2	35	3	5	41	4	1
Brown	OF	*12	26	2	2	39	3	3	28	3	1	31	3	4
Joseph Johnson	OF	*11	30	2	8	28	2	6	26	3	2	29	3	5
Worth	OF,SS	*10	35	3	5	22	2	2	40	4	1	48	4	3
Herbert Jewell	C	*11	36	3	3	31	2	9	35	3	8	39	4	3
Candy Cummings	P	*11	33	3	0	35	3	2	33	3	6	44	4	8
Booth	SS	7	25	3	4	22	3	1	26	3	5	29	4	1
George Hall	OF	*7	15	2	1	16	2	2	17	3	2	26	5	1
Thomspon	C	7							15	2	1	19	2	5
Hy Dollard	2B,SS	*6	17	2	5	16	2	4	20	4	0	23	4	3
Sullivan	P	5							10	2	0	14	2	4
Hope Waddell	1B	5							5	1	0	7	1	2

* Hits and total bases not counted in all games.

ORIENTAL   8 - 3
Greenpoint, NY

DATE	OPPONENT	SCORE	W	L	T
06/02	Cypress (E. New York, NY)	24 11	W		
06/10	Mutual (New York)	9 58		L	
06/17	Gramercy (New York)	23 20	W		
07/01	Enterprise (Clifton, NY)	63 10	W		
07/04	Nassau (Princeton, NJ)	54 37	W		
07/09	Eureka (Newark, NJ)	28 22	W		
07/13	Cypress (E. New York, NY)	35 12	W		
07/16	Ivanhoe (Sing Sing, NY)	34 7	W		
08/08	Atlantic (Brooklyn)	9 36		L	
08/26	Gramercy (New York)	20 18	W		
09/09	Oriental (New York)	8 19		L	

BATTERS	POS	GP	HL	A	O	R	A	O	H	A	O	TB	A	O
Percy Butler	1B,2B,OF,3B	11	32	2	10	33	3	0						
William Hobby	2B	6	13	2	1	23	3	5						
Thomas	SS,2B	8	17	2	1	33	4	1						
Stillwaggon	3B,2B	5	14	2	4	17	3	2						
Elijah Holmes	OF,P,1B	11	31	2	9	36	3	3						
William Ostrander	OF	10	29	2	9	29	2	9						
George Cook	OF,2B	9	25	2	7	32	3	5						
Ed Holmes	C	6	21	3	3	18	3	0						
Ed Pinkham	P,SS	10	26	2	6	43	4	3						

CLIPPER   7 - 3
Lowell, MA

DATE	OPPONENT	SCORE	W	L	T
06/17	Webster (Woburn, MA)*	56 5	W		
07/04	Kearsarge (Stoneham, MA)*	32 52		L	
08/22	Kearsarge (Stoneham, MA)	36 38		L	
09/12	Eagle (Natick, MA)	11 7	W		
09/19	Union (Lynnfield Center, MA)	36 14	W		
09/---	Hosford (Lowell)	35 8	W		
---/---	Salmon (Lowell)	-- --	W		
---/---	Sheridan (Lowell)	-- --	W		
---/---	Mishawaum (Woburn, MA)	-- --	W		
---/---	Harvard (Cambridge, MA)	-- --		L	

BATTERS	POS	GP	HL	A	O	R	A	O	H	A	O	TB	A	O
Carter	1B	8	29	3	5	26	3	2						
Temple	2B	9	23	2	5	34	3	7						
White	SS	10	28	2	8	42	4	2						
Parker	3B	4	11	2	3	16	4	0						
Coolidge	OF	8	27	3	3	28	3	4						
Davis	OF	8	20	2	4	26	3	2						
Church	OF	6	18	3	0	15	2	3						
Whitney	C	9	12	1	3	51	5	6						
G. Conway	P	10	25	2	5	42	4	2						
Buttrick		5	11	2	1	25	5	0						
J. Conway		5	14	2	4	23	4	3						
Lowe	3B,OF	5	18	3	3	17	3	2						
Grover	OF	2	6	3	0	9	4	1						
Bailey		1	5	5	0	3	3	0						

NATIONAL 7-3
Washington, DC

DATE	OPPONENT	SCORE		W	L	T
05/23	National, Jr. (Washington)	23	10	W		
06/02	Maryland (Baltimore)	27	28		L	
08/10	Jefferson (Washington)	28	17	W		
08/21	Union (Washington)	43	27	W		
09/21	Olympic (Washington)	21	15	W		
09/24	Cincinnati (Cincinnati)	10	16		L	
10/02	Maryland (Baltimore)	12	13		L	
10/01	Jefferson (Washington)	28	13	W		
10/07	Olympic (Washington)	18	13	W		

(Only scores extant

BATTERS	POS	GP	HL	A	O	R	A	O	H	A	O	TB	A	O
Tom Forker	1B	7	21	3	0	16	2	4	20	2	6	26	3	5
Andrew Gibney	2B,OF	6	17	2	5	17	2	5	14	2	2	21	3	3
Frank Norton	SS,2B	9	28	3	1	31	3	4	25	2	7	42	4	6
George Fox	3B,1B	6	9	1	3	26	4	2	22	3	4	40	4	6
Dennis Coughlin	OF	8	21	2	5	31	3	7	27	3	3	35	4	3
Harry Berthrong	OF,C	7	16	2	2	20	2	6	20	2	6	30	4	2
Sy Studley	OF,1B	7	16	2	2	33	4	5	22	3	1	32	4	4
Ward	C	8	21	2	5	24	3	0	25	3	1	34	4	2
Jones	P	3	10	3	1	6	2	0						
Finney	OF	6	15	2	3	19	3	1	17	2	5	22	3	4
Hodges	OF,3B	5	20	4	0	17	3	2	11	2	1	18	3	3

ENTERPRISE 7-5
Baltimore, MD

DATE	OPPONENT	SCORE			W	L	T
06/27	Olympic (Washington)	19	18	(10)	W		
07/04	Union (Washington)	31	24		W		
07/25	Union (Washington)	14	21			L	
08/01	Union (Washington)*	13	21			L	
08/13	Jefferson (Washington)	33	10		W		
08/18	Union (Washington)	34	16		W		
08/20	Pastime (Baltimore)	35	27		W		
08/28	Jefferson (Washington)*	60	23		W		
09/01	Maryland (Baltimore)	36	15		W		
09/10	Maryland (Baltimore)	15	17			L	
09/15	Maryland (Baltimore)	18	33			L	
09/26	Cincinnati (Cincinnati)	3	24			L	

* Box score not available

BATTERS	POS	GP	HL	A	O	R	A	O	H	A	O	TB	A	O
Wachtel	1B	9	28	3	1	23	2	5						
Wally Goldsmith	2B	9	26	2	8	29	3	2						
Bass	SS	6	12	2	0	25	4	1						
Braden	3B	9	22	2	4	29	3	2						
Chenowith	OF	9	21	2	3	35	3	8						
Ed Mincher	OF	8	27	3	3	19	2	3						
Gorman	OF	6	20	3	2	17	2	5						
Galliker	C	9	34	3	7	27	3	0						
R.J. Fitzsimmons	P	9	31	3	4	17	1	8						

GEARY 7 - 6
Philadelphia, PA

DATE	OPPONENT	SCORE		W	L	T
04/27	Keystone (Philadelphia)	15	18		L	
05/11	Keystone (Philadelphia)	17	15	W		
05/20	Chestnut St. Theatre (Philadelphia)	40	17	W		
05/21	Union (Camden, NJ)	18	10	W		
05/26	Athletic (Philadelphia)	17	36		L	
06/01	Keystone (Philadelphia)	34	18	W		
06/09	Chestnut St. Theatre (Philadelphia)	29	15	W		
06/16	Olympic (Philadelphia)	11	13		L	
06/23	Malvern (Philadelphia)	24	12	W		
07/07	Malvern (Philadelphia)	25	17	W		
07/08	Olympic (Philadelphia)	16	43		L	
08/01	Athletic (Philadelphia)	20	42		L	
08/06	Olympic (Washington)	15	25		L	

(Only scores extant)

BATTERS	POS	GP	HL	A	O	R	A	O	H	A	O	TB	A	O
George Heubel	1B,OF	18	58	3	4	64	3	10						
Opdycke	2B,3B	9	22	2	4	35	3	8						
Halbach	SS	16	48	3	0	61	3	13						
Clinton	3B,2B	18	61	3	7	57	3	3						
Hopkins	OF	11	32	2	10	22	2	0						
Doug Allison	OF,C	10	22	2	2	30	3	0						
Abel	OF,3B	10	23	2	3	31	3	1						
Art Allison	C,1B	15	47	3	2	43	2	13						
Levi Meyerle	P	10	21	2	1	41	4	1						
Donohue	3B	6	22	3	4	24	4	0						
George Bechtel	P	6	17	2	5	19	3	1						
Dorsey	OF,P	6	22	3	4	11	1	5						

UNION 7 - 6
St. Louis, MO

DATE	OPPONENT	SCORE		W	L	T
05/28	Atlantic (St. Louis)	52	17	W		
06/12	Athletic (Philadelphia)	12	54		L	
06/18	Empire (St. Louis)	21	18	W		
06/24	Empire (St. Louis)	39	17	W		
06/27	Atlantic (Brooklyn)	9	68		L	
07/04	Cincinnati (Cincinnati)	7	70		L	
07/27	Buckeye (Cincinnati)	8	25		L	
08/14	Union (Morrisania, NY)	30	37		L	
09/16	Kaw Valley (Lawrence, KS)	32	10	W		
09/23	Mutual (St. Louis)	43	8	W		
09/26	Athlete (St. Louis)	43	14	W		
10/08	Excelsior (Chicago)*	9	27		L	
10/14	Empire (St. Louis)	27	13	W		

* Box score not available

BATTERS	POS	GP	HL	A	O	R	A	O	H	A	O	TB	A	O
H.C. Carr	1B,2B,3B	11	32	2	10	27	2	5						
Turner	2B,P,OF	8	21	2	5	31	3	7						
Cabanne	SS,1B,OF	9	31	3	4	26	2	8						
Easton	3B,2B,OF,1B	9	29	3	2	24	2	6						
Freeman	OF	10	31	3	1	32	3	2						
R. Duncan	OF,SS,3B	10	28	2	8	34	3	4						
Greenleaf	OF,1B,3B,P	8	27	3	3	17	2	1						
Oran	C,SS,OF	11	23	2	1	40	3	7						
Lucas	P,OF,C	9	26	2	8	25	2	7						
A.W. Smith	OF,SS	6	23	3	5	16	2	4						

YALE 7 - 6
New Haven, CT

DATE	OPPONENT	SCORE			W	L	T
06/06	Union (Morrisania, NY)	14	16	(10)		L	
06/13	Lowell (Boston)	13	16			L	
06/24	Liberty (Norwalk, CT)	20	5		W		
06/25	Nassau (Princeton, NJ)	30	23		W		
07/04	Star (Brooklyn)	31	14		W		
07/17	Union (Morrisania, NY)	9	19			L	
07/18	Atlantic (Brooklyn)	16	40			L	
07/21	Eckford (Brooklyn)	11	19			L	
07/25	Harvard (Cambridge, MA)	17	25			L	
---/---	Liberty (Norwalk, CT	40	11		W		
09/30	Eckford (Brooklyn)	15	12		W		
10/10	Eckford (Brooklyn)	19	17		W		
10/31	Bridgeport (Bridgeport, CT)	14	6		W		

BATTERS	POS	GP	HL	A	O	R	A	O	H	A	O	TB	A	O
Shattuck	1B	6	15	2	3	12	2	0						
McClintock	2B,OF,SS	12	35	2	11	32	2	8						
McCutcheon	SS	12	46	3	10	16	1	4						
Cleveland	3B	10	31	3	1	17	1	7						
Selden	OF,2B	12	33	2	9	23	1	11						
Condict	OF,C	11	37	3	4	24	2	2						
Buck	OF,1B	7	25	3	4	16	2	2						
Denning	C,1B,OF	13	29	2	3	36	2	10						
Hooker	P	13	35	2	11	33	2	7						
Lewis	3B,OF	10	23	2	3	28	2	8						

EXCELSIOR 7 - 7 - 1
Chicago, IL

DATE	OPPONENT	SCORE		W	L	T
05/09	Eureka (Chicago)	28	10	W		
06/12	Forest City (Rockford, IL)	18	20		L	
06/17	Athletic (Philadelphia)	13	33		L	
06/20	Atlantic (Brooklyn)	17	47		L	
07/04	Forest City (Rockford, IL)	27	35		L	
07/21	Buckeye (Cincinnati)	22	43		L	
08/10	Union (Morrisania, NY)	21	31		L	
08/29	Enterprise (Chicago)	55	12	W		
09/12	Detroit (Detroit)	12	15		L	
09/17	Niagara (Buffalo)	31	12	W		
09/18	Detroit (Detroit)	31	31			T
09/19	Forest City (Cleveland)	19	5	W		
10/08	Union (St. Louis)*	27	9	W		
10/09	Resolute (St. Louis)*	41	13	W		
10/10	Atlantic (St. Louis)	71	7	W		

* Box score not available

BATTERS	POS	GP	HL	A	O	R	A	O	H	A	O	TB	A	O
George Stearns	1B	11	35	3	2	30	2	8						
McNally	2B	6	23	3	5	9	1	3						
J.W. Stearns	SS	5	13	2	3	20	4	0						
Oberlander	3B,OF	7	22	3	1	25	3	4						
Budd	OF	6	18	3	0	11	1	5						
Kennedy	OF,C	5	12	2	2	16	3	1						
Taylor	OF,SS,3B	5	18	3	3	10	2	0						
Tom Foley	C,3B,2B	12	38	3	2	42	3	6						
Harry Lex	P	11	28	2	6	37	3	4						
Joe Simmons	2B	5	10	2	0	30	6	0						

ACTIVE
Indianapolis, IN
7 - 8

DATE	OPPONENT	SCORE		W	L	T
05/09	Asbury College (Greencastle, IN)	56	22	W		
05/21	Pioneer (Indianapolis)	60	11	W		
05/---	Western Star (Indianapolis)	104	6	W		
06/10	Athletic (Philadelphia)	21	53		L	
06/25	Western (Indianapolis)	35	21	W		
07/01	Atlantic (Brooklyn)	8	103		L	
07/09	Western (Indianapolis)	63	32	W		
07/15	Mutual (Indianapolis)	46	12	W		
07/29	Buckeye (Cincinnati)	22	64		L	
08/08	Live Oak (Cincinnati)	38	19	W		
08/17	Union (Morrisania, NY)	8	36		L	
09/14	Cincinnati (Cincinnati)	7	54		L	
09/15	Great Western (Cincinnati)*	18	20		L	
09/16	Xenia (Xenia, OH)*	29	40		L	
09/17	Buckeye (Cincinnati)	12	44		L	

* Box score not available

BATTERS	POS	GP	HL	A	O	R	A	O	H	A	O	TB	A	O
Spann	1B	8	30	3	6	29	3	5						
McDonald	2B,OF	6	17	2	5	16	2	4						
Norwood	SS,2B	5	13	2	3	6	1	1						
C. Yohn	3B,OF,SS,C,1B	9	20	2	2	31	3	4						
Smithers	OF	8	21	2	5	38	4	6						
Bussell	OF	6	15	2	3	36	6	0						
Brown	OF,3B	5	14	2	4	22	4	2						
Dean	C,SS,1B,2B	11	31	2	9	48	4	4						
Cal McVey	P,2B,3B	13	30	2	4	68	5	3						

HARLEM
New York, NY
7 - 8

DATE	OPPONENT	SCORE		W	L	T
06/06	Fanwood (New York)	49	33	W		
06/13	Fanwood (New York)	33	20	W		
06/24	Active (New York)	8	16		L	
07/01	Americus (Yorkville, NY)	47	39	W		
07/08	Mutual (New York)	9	21		L	
07/15	Gramercy (New York)	12	13		L	
07/22	Star (Brooklyn)*	34	19	W		
08/03	Baltic (New York)	45	11	W		
08/12	Empire (New York)	40	18	W		
08/15	Star (Brooklyn)	9	57		L	
09/02	Mutual (New York)	13	25		L	
09/05	Union (Morrisania, NY)	11	41		L	
09/08	Union (Morrisania, NY)*	5	69		L	
10/01	Star (Brooklyn)	9	76		L	
10/22	Gramercy (New York)	29	25	W		

*Box score not available

BATTERS	POS	GP	HL	A	O	R	A	O	H	A	O	TB	A	O
Asten	1B,OF	8	18	2	2	28	3	4						
Deady	2B,OF	5	10	2	0	20	4	0						
Meyers	SS,OF	11	34	3	1	22	2	0						
Murray	3B,2B	8	18	2	2	22	2	6						
Crooker	OF,3B,C	13	33	2	7	36	2	10						
Helms	OF,SS,C	9	19	2	1	27	3	0						
Smith	OF,3B	6	17	2	5	20	3	2						
Comstock	C	9	31	3	4	17	1	8						
G. Thompson	P,3B	9	27	3	0	29	3	2						
Marsh	3B,1B	7	26	3	5	16	2	2						

OLYMPIC 6 - 2
Providence, RI

DATE	OPPONENT	SCORE		W	L	T
07/22	Hope and Anchor (Pawtucket, RI)	35	41		L	
08/19	Hope and Anchor (Pawtucket, RI)	27	15	W		
09/12	Emmett (Westerly, RI)	36	7	W		
09/22	Emmett (Westerly, RI)	23	21	W		
10/10	Wide Awake (Burrillville, RI)	78	20	W		
10/20	Blackstone (Providence)	28	25	W		
---/---	Hope and Anchor (Pawtucket, RI)	63	27	W		
---/---	Blackstone (Providence)	--	--		L	

BATTERS	POS	GP	HL	A	O	R	A	O	H	A	O	TB	A	O
Wood	1B	5	16	3	1	22	4	2						
Greene	2B	5	16	3	1	23	4	3						
Hart	SS	5	12	2	2	28	5	3						
O'Reilly	3B	5	17	3	2	21	4	1						
Burbanks	OF	6	25	4	1	23	3	5						
Pidge	OF	6	16	2	4	27	4	3						
Ward	OF	5	14	2	4	22	4	2						
Magee	C	5	7	1	2	29	5	4						
Calder	P	4	8	2	0	21	5	1						

OLD POINT 6 - 4
Norfolk, VA

DATE	OPPONENT	SCORE		W	L	T
07/03	Chesapeake (Hampton, VA)	34	26	W		
07/11	Chesapeake (Hampton, VA)	62	15	W		
09/19	Creighton (Norfolk, VA)	9	60		L	

(Only scores extant)

BATTERS	POS	GP	HL	A	O	R	A	O	H	A	O	TB	A	O
Dielman	1B,2B	4	10	2	2	17	4	1						
Baulch	2B	10	28	2	8	25	2	5						
James Ware	SS	8	21	2	5	29	3	5						
Maloney	3B	10	17	1	7	40	4	0						
Moody	OF	6	20	3	2	9	1	3						
Kerr	OF	5	12	2	2	21	4	1						
Hasty	OF	5	12	2	2	22	4	2						
Joseph Ware	C	8	18	2	2	26	3	2						
Bodell	P	10	26	2	6	20	2	0						
Elliott	OF	4	7	1	3	7	1	3						
De Witt	OF	4	13	3	1	7	1	3						

CENTRAL CITY 6 - 5
Syracuse, NY

DATE	OPPONENT	SCORE		W	L	T
05/15	Ontario (Oswego, NY)	22	15	W		
06/13	Atlantic (Brooklyn)	14	20		L	
06/20	Union (Lansingburgh, NY)	6	48		L	
06/27	Fulton (Fulton, NY)	44	15	W		
07/01	Athletic (Philadelphia)	12	41		L	
07/04	National (Albany, NY)	32	24	W		
07/09	Union (Lansingburgh, NY)	14	35		L	
07/10	Ontario (Oswego, NY)	65	10	W		
07/28	Union (Morrisania, NY)	7	34		L	
07/30	Niagara (Buffalo)	33	21	W		
08/29	Fulton (Fulton, NY)	42	12	W		

CENTRAL CITY (cont.)
Syracuse, NY

BATTERS	POS	GP	HL	A	O	R	A	O	H	A	O	TB	A	O
Adams		11	21	1	10	42	3	9						
Cruttendon		11	29	2	7	35	3	2						
Porter		11	35	3	2	33	3	0						
Johnson		11	32	2	10	28	2	6						
Dodge		11	40	3	7	21	1	10						
Yale		7	20	2	6	24	3	4						
Boswell		7	22	3	1	15	2	1						
Telford		7	19	2	5	15	2	1						

UNION   6-6
Camden, NJ

DATE	OPPONENT	SCORE		W	L	T
05/16	Athletic (Philadelphia)	15	39		L	
05/21	Geary (Philadelphia)	10	18		L	
05/23	Bachelor (Philadelphia)	22	18	W		
06/02	Bachelor (Philadelphia)	32	11	W		
06/13	Camden (Camden)	41	20	W		
06/25	Olympic (Philadelphia)	30	44		L	
07/13	Olympic (Philadelphia)	23	32		L	
08/03	Athletic (Philadelphia)	23	60		L	
08/08	Raritan (S. Amboy, NJ)*	15	6	W		
08/13	Camden (Camden)	47	28	W		
08/26	Commonwealth (Philadelphia)*	40	29	W		
09/05	Athletic (Philadelphia)	34	47		L	

* Box score not available

BATTERS	POS	GP	HL	A	O	R	A	O	H	A	O	TB	A	O
L. Horner	1B,2B	10	28	2	8	30	3	0						
Sweeney	2B,OF	7	22	3	1	21	3	0						
Sebley	SS	9	30	3	3	23	2	5						
Donohue	3B	4	12	3	0	6	1	2						
Alcott	OF	10	33	3	3	32	3	2						
Johnson	OF	8	29	3	5	19	2	3						
Doyle	OF,P	6	17	2	5	15	2	3						
Fackler	C,OF,SS,P	9	21	2	3	35	3	8						
Bourquin	P,2B,3B	9	27	3	0	27	3	0						
Bassett	OF,2B	5	15	3	0	16	3	1						

EMPIRE   6-9
St. Louis, MO

DATE	OPPONENT	SCORE		W	L	T
05/21	Commercial (St. Louis)	26	13	W		
06/04	Resolute (St. Louis)	43	35	W		
06/13	Athletic (Philadelphia)	6	54		L	
06/18	Union (St. Louis)	18	21		L	
06/24	Union (St. Louis)	17	39		L	
06/29	Atlantic (Brooklyn)	15	53		L	
07/16	Resolute (St. Louis)	38	12	W		
07/28	Buckeye (Cincinnati)	9	44		L	
08/15	Union (Morrisania, NY)	11	37		L	
08/29	Lone Star (Alma, IL)	65	19	W		
09/03	Aetna (St. Louis)	18	26		L	
09/09	Lone Star (Alma, IL)	53	14	W		
09/15	Kaw Valley (Lawrence, KS)	20	12	W		
10/14	Union (St. Louis)	13	27		L	
10/---	Resolute (St. Louis)	27	32		L	

EMPIRE (cont.)
St. Louis, MO

BATTERS	POS	GP	HL	A	O	R	A	O	H	A	O	TB	A	O
Wirth	1B,2B	15	45	3	0	46	3	1						
Jerry Fruin	2B,P	6	19	3	1	12	2	0						
Barron	SS	15	49	3	4	37	2	7						
O'Connell	3B,OF	8	22	2	6	17	2	1						
Murray	OF,C,2B	12	33	2	9	39	3	3						
Roberts	OF	7	19	2	5	16	2	2						
Hazelton	OF	6	15	2	3	14	2	2						
Shockey	C,OF	14	33	2	5	46	3	4						
Fitzgibbons	P,C	10	30	3	0	25	2	5						
Quinn	P	6	24	4	0	15	2	2						

WAMSUTTA   5 - 2
New Bedford, MA

DATE	OPPONENT	SCORE		W	L	T
07/04	Onward (New Bedford)*	49	13	W		
08/03	Onward (New Bedford)	37	11	W		
08/08	Acushnet (Acushnet, MA)	25	7	W		
08/14	Lowell (Boston)	6	62		L	
09/12	Eagle (Providence)	28	14	W		
10/14	Blackstone (Providence)	38	18	W		
10/16	Independent (Sandwich, MA)	14	34		L	

* Box score not available

BATTERS	POS	GP	HL	A	O	R	A	O	H	A	O	TB	A	O
N.E. Howland		6	17	2	5	18	3	0						
J.H. Tallman		6	14	2	2	17	2	5						
O.N. Pierce		6	17	2	5	17	2	5						
W.C. Gooding		5	11	2	1	15	3	0						

UNIQUE   5 - 5
Staten Island, NY

DATE	OPPONENT	SCORE		W	L	T
05/08	Harmonic (Staten Island)	19	33		L	
05/22	Harmonic (Staten Island)	55	38	W		
06/22	Independent (Brooklyn)	30	23	W		
06/25	Harmonic (Staten Island)	36	26	W		
06/29	Unknown (Elizabeth, NJ)	51	15	W		
07/02	Independent (Brooklyn)	26	55		L	
07/06	Bergen (Bergen, NJ)	40	47		L	
07/09	Knickerbocker (New York)	34	40		L	
07/11	Enterprise (Clifton, NY)	37	20	W		
08/04	Eckford (Brooklyn)	1	37		L	

BATTERS	POS	GP	HL	A	O	R	A	O	H	A	O	TB	A	O
Booraem	1B	9	29	3	2	38	4	2						
Gosman	2B	8	22	2	6	27	3	3						
Harriman	SS,3B	9	24	2	6	41	4	5						
Wilcox	3B,OF	8	18	2	2	24	3	0						
J.B. Staples	OF,C	9	29	3	2	23	2	5						
Brownlee	OF,SS	9	18	2	0	42	4	6						
Simmons	OF	7	20	2	6	31	4	3						
Doubleday	C,P	10	26	2	6	39	3	9						
M. Staples	P,OF	10	34	3	4	36	3	6						

JEFFERSON 5 - 6
Washington, DC

DATE	OPPONENT	SCORE		W	L	T
07/08	Olympic (Washington)	11	33		L	
06/16	Pioneer (Alexandria, VA)	64	13	W		
07/16	Union (Washington)	43	27	W		
07/20	Olympic (Washington)*	10	61		L	
07/30	Union (Washington)	43	17	W		
08/13	Enterprise (Baltimore)	10	33		L	
08/10	National (Washington)	17	28		L	
08/27	Potomac (Washington)*	33	8	W		
08/28	Enterprise (Baltimore)*	23	60		L	
10/01	National (Washington)	13	28		L	
10/22	Union (Washington)	42	20	W		

* Box score not available

BATTERS	POS	GP	HL	A	O	R	A	O	H	A	O	TB	A	O
Daniels	1B	6	10	1	4	28	4	4						
McClelland	2B,OF	5	14	2	4	22	4	2						
J. Doyle	SS	7	23	3	2	19	2	5						
A. Finney	3B	6	17	2	5	21	3	3						
George Joyce	OF	8	23	2	7	27	3	3						
Sam Yeatman	OF	4	9	2	1	22	5	2						
Slater	OF	4	13	3	1	8	2	0						
Shields	C	6	14	2	2	25	4	1						
Anderson	P,OF	7	21	3	0	21	3	0						

ACTIVE 5 - 9
New York, NY

DATE	OPPONENT	SCORE		W	L	T
06/18	Rose Hill (Fordham, NY)	34	36		L	
06/24	Harlem (New York)	16	8	W		
07/02	Gramercy (New York)	28	17	W		
07/25	Empire (New York)	44	6	W		
07/31	Eckford (Brooklyn)	16	34		L	
08/06	Atlantic (Brooklyn)	6	25		L	
08/10	Mutual (New York)	30	16	W		
08/19	Atlantic (Brooklyn)	6	37		L	
09/23	Star (Brooklyn)*	11	37		L	
09/30	Mutual (New York)	17	37		L	
10/07	Union (Morrisania, NY)	8	9		L	
10/17	Union (Morrisania, NY)	8	6	W		
10/31	Mutual (New York)	12	33		L	
11/14	Star (Brooklyn)	7	25		L	

* Box score not available

BATTERS	POS	GP	HL	A	O	R	A	O	H	A	O	TB	A	O
H.C. Kelley	1B	13	43	3	4	25	1	12	29	2	3	35	2	9
T.F. Kelley	2B	11	27	2	5	21	1	10	23	2	1	33	3	0
Tom Haines	SS,OF	13	24	1	11	38	2	12	41	3	2	48	3	9
Collins	3B	11	29	2	7	25	2	3	28	2	6	34	3	1
George Ebbetts	OF,2B	13	24	2	2	27	2	5	34	3	1	39	3	6
Rogers	OF	10	26	2	6	18	1	8	20	2	0	26	?	6
Vanderwerken	OF	7	25	3	4	16	2	2	15	2	1	19	2	4
William Kelley	C	13	41	3	2	23	1	10	31	2	5	37	2	11
Charley Walker	P	12	37	3	1	19	1	7	22	1	10	29	2	5

KEYSTONE
Philadelphia, PA   5- 10 - 1

DATE	OPPONENT	SCORE			W	L	T
04/27	Geary (Philadelphia)	18	15		W		
05/11	Geary (Philadelphia)	15	17			L	
05/28	Athletic (Philadelphia)	12	34			L	
06/01	Geary (Philadelphia)	18	34			L	
06/29	Olympic (Philadelphia)	15	49			L	
07/02	Dirigo (Philadelphia)	24	17		W		
07/09	Harry Clay (Philadelphia)	18	31			L	
07/18	Olympic (Philadelphia)	25	10		W		
08/10	Athletic (Philadelphia)	13	28			L	
08/19	Olympic (Washington)	*42	29	(10)			T
08/20	Atlantic (Brooklyn)	7	17			L	
08/21	Eckford (Brooklyn)	24	27			L	
08/22	Mutual (New York)	19	26			L	
08/28	Athletic (Philadelphia)	23	47			L	
10/01	Cincinnati (Cincinnati)	24	22		W		
10/02	Union (Morrisania, NY)	24	15		W		

* Disputed, Olympic club claimed 26-26 tie after nine innings.

BATTERS	POS	GP	HL	A	O	R	A	O	H	A	O	TB	A	O
George Albertson	1B,3B	15	48	3	3	31	2	1						
Bob Reach	2B	13	44	3	5	41	3	2						
Dick Flowers	SS	17	50	2	16	53	3	2						
Phillip Culp	3B	12	34	2	10	34	2	10						
Ned Conner	OF,1B	14	33	2	5	39	2	11						
Joseph Gwynn	OF,P	14	40	2	12	44	3	2						
McClarnan	OF,3B	11	32	2	10	28	2	6						
Ewell	C,1B	16	51	3	3	29	1	13						
George Bechtel	P	13	38	2	12	38	2	12						
Charley Weaver	OF,P	8	21	2	5	19	2	3						
Burleigh	C	5	12	2	2	13	2	3						

EON
Portland, ME   4 - 2

DATE	OPPONENT	SCORE		W	L	T
06/13	Pioneer (Westbrook, ME)	37	11	W		
06/---	Androscoggin (Lewiston, ME)	*9	0	W		
07/11	Androscoggin (Lewiston, ME)	14	31		L	
07/14	Harvard (Cambridge, MA)	10	42		L	
08/21	Pennessewassee (Norway, ME)	14	10	W		
09/05	Cushnoc (Augusta, ME)	39	8	W		

* Forfeit

BATTERS	POS	GP	HL	A	O	R	A	O	H	A	O	TB	A	O
Evans		5	10	2	0	18	3	3						
Mathews		5	13	2	3	15	3	0						
Moody		5	15	3	0	15	3	0						
Abbott		5	13	2	3	14	2	4						
Dennis		5	10	2	0	13	2	3						

ALPHA
Brooklyn, NY   4 - 3

DATE	OPPONENT	SCORE		W	L	T
05/26	Manhattan (New York)	41	13	W		
06/---	Peconic (Brooklyn)	18	32		L	

ALPHA (cont.)
Brooklyn, NY

DATE	OPPONENT	SCORE		W	L	T
07/01	Alaska (Brooklyn)	31	59		L	
07/14	Athletic (Brooklyn)	16	52		L	
10/30	Excelsior (Brooklyn)	29	11	W		
11/06	Harmonic (Brooklyn)	39	13	W		
11/14	Alaska (Brooklyn)	32	7	W		

BATTERS	POS	GP	HL	A	O	R	A	O	H	A	O	TB	A	O
Howard		7	18	2	4	25	3	4						
Munn		6	13	2	1	24	4	0						
Mesereau		6	19	3	1	20	3	2						
A. Gillen		5	11	2	1	20	4	0						
E. Jackson		5	16	3	1	14	2	4						

SOCIAL   4 - 4
New York, NY

DATE	OPPONENT	SCORE		W	L	T
06/05	Champion (Jersey City, NJ)	37	32	W		
06/24	Mutual (New York)	5	32		L	
07/01	Eagle (New York)	31	36		L	
07/06	Jefferson (New York)	25	36		L	
08/05	Champion (Jersey City, NJ)*	18	50		L	
08/12	Jefferson (New York)	30	25	W		
08/22	Empire (New York)*	20	15	W		
09/09	Empire (New York)	22	19	W		

* Box score not available

BATTERS	POS	GP	HL	A	O	R	A	O	H	A	O	TB	A	O
Layman		6	12	2	0	20	3	2						
J. Clute		6	20	3	2	18	3	0						
Byrnes		5	10	2	0	18	3	3						
Chase		5	15	3	0	9	1	4						

EXCELSIOR   4 - 5 - 1
Brooklyn, NY

DATE	OPPONENT	SCORE		W	L	T
05/---	Alert (S. Orange, NJ)	22	11	W		
06/25	Alert (S. Orange, NJ)	44	17	W		
07/27	Olympic (Philadelphia)	14	22		L	
08/25	Peconic (Brooklyn)*	28	28			T
09/05	Knickerbocker (New York)#	25	51		L	
09/09	Athletic (Brooklyn)	12	33		L	
09/11	Peconic (Brooklyn)	31	18	W		
10/15	Knickerbocker (New York)#	27	36		L	
10/29	Knickerbocker (New York)#	38	25	W		
10/30	Alpha (Brooklyn)	11	29		L	

* Box score not available
# Friendly game

BATTERS	POS	GP	HL	A	O	R	A	O	H	A	O	TB	A	O
Anthony Elmendorf		9	21	2	3	29	3	2	38	4	2	48	5	3
Morrell		9	19	2	1	29	3	2	35	3	8	41	4	5
James Mitchell		9	27	3	0	21	2	3	23	2	5	31	3	4
Milton Sweet		8	18	2	2	25	3	1	32	4	0	29	4	7
George Cornwell		8	23	2	7	19	2	3	20	2	4	28	3	4

EXCELSIOR (cont.)
Brooklyn, NY

BATTERS	POS	GP	HL	A	O	R	A	O	H	A	O	TB	A	O
W.H. Murtha		7	22	3	1	23	3	2	25	3	4	36	5	1
Dan Chauncey		6	17	2	5	16	2	4	17	2	5	25	4	1
Moore		6	12	2	0	19	3	1						

COMMONWEALTH 4 - 6
Philadelphia, PA

DATE	OPPONENT	SCORE		W	L	T
05/01	Athletic (Philadelphia)	8	61		L	
05/22	Malvern (Philadelphia)	11	57		L	
05/---	Harry Clay (Philadelphia)	20	49		L	
07/04	Brandywine (W. Chester, PA)	30	29	W		
07/16	Brandywine (W. Chester, PA)	43	36	W		
08/14	W.H. Patterson (Philadelphia)*	47	11	W		
08/18	Bachelor (Philadelphia)*	28	29		L	
08/21	Olympic (Washington, DC)	21	87		L	
08/26	Union (Camden, NJ)*	29	40		L	
08/28	Columbia (Chester, PA)*	38	21	W		

* Box score not available

BATTERS	POS	GP	HL	A	O	R	A	O	H	A	O	TB	A	O
Cushing		6	17	2	5	16	2	4						
Borden		5	10	2	0	18	3	3						
Fry		5	10	2	0	17	3	2						
Tomlin		5	15	3	0	13	2	3						
Freeman		5	14	2	4	12	2	2						

LIVE OAK 4 - 7
Cincinnati, OH

DATE	OPPONENT	SCORE		W	L	T
06/04	Great Western (Cincinnati)	17	47		L	
07/16	East End (Cincinnati)*	50	20	W		
07/17	Great Western (Cincinnati)	34	11	W		
07/27	Newport (Newport, KY)	37	12	W		
08/08	Active (Indianapolis)	19	38		L	
08/15	Greenwood (California, OH)	72	44	W		
08/26	Great Western (Cincinnati)*	10	33		L	
09/29	Buckeye (Cincinnati)*	15	40		L	
10/03	Great Western (Cincinnati)*	15	30		L	
---/---	Cincinnati (Cincinnati)	5	72		L	
---/---	Cincinnati (Cincinnati)	11	55		L	

* Box score not available

BATTERS	POS	GP	HL	A	O	R	A	O	H	A	O	TB	A	O
M. Bertie	1B	10	21	2	1	42	4	2						
Jones	2B	7	16	2	2	30	4	2						
F. Bertie	SS,OF	8	21	2	5	27	3	4						
Lowe	3B	13	32	2	6	49	3	10						
J.P. Mack	OF	14	36	2	8	53	3	11						
Wunder	OF	12	25	2	1	39	3	3						
Bowman	OF,3B	6	14	2	2	22	3	4						
William Skiff	C	14	47	3	5	46	3	4						
Becklar	P,C	15	46	3	1	42	2	12						
Mortimer	P	5	14	2	4	6	1	1						

LIVE OAK (cont.)
Cincinnati, OH

BATTERS	POS	GP	HL	A	O	R	A	O	H	A	O	TB	A	O
Welsch		4	12	3	0	13	3	1						
DeLille		4	15	3	3	10	2	2						
Piggott	2B	4	11	2	3	8	2	0						
Owen	1B	2	7	3	1	3	1	1						

DETROIT   4 - 10 - 1
Detroit, MI

DATE	OPPONENT	SCORE		W	L	T
05/29	University (Ann Arbor, MI)	24	26 (11)		L	
06/04	University (Ann Arbor, MI)*	18	26		L	
06/10	O.K. (Detroit)*	76	13	W		
06/16	Forest City (Cleveland)	45	23	W		
06/18	Atlantic (Brooklyn)	7	40		L	
06/22	Athletic (Philadelphia)	17	30		L	
07/04	Allegheny (Pittsburgh)	22	4	W		
07/16	Allegheny (Pittsburgh)	18	29		L	
07/17	Forest City (Cleveland)*	7	44		L	
07/20	Buckeye (Cincinnati)	35	36		L	
08/03	Union (Morrisania, NY)	11	33		L	
09/08	Niagara (Buffalo)	14	24		L	
09/12	Excelsior (Chicago)	15	12	W		
09/16	Niagara (Buffalo)	17	38		L	
09/18	Excelsior (Chicago)	31	31			T

* Box score not available

BATTERS	POS	GP	HL	A	O	R	A	O	H	A	O	TB	A	O
Clark	1B	9	27	3	0	28	3	1						
Brown	2B	10	30	3	0	30	3	0						
Joseph Burroughs	SS	10	24	2	4	30	3	0						
Collins	3B,2B	8	18	2	2	18	2	2						
Hinchman	OF	9	22	2	4	19	2	1						
Phelps	OF,3B,C	5	17	3	2	12	2	2						
Irwin	OF	3	9	3	0	8	2	2						
Dawson	C	7	29	4	1	9	1	2						
Lane	P	10	29	2	9	30	3	0						

ALERT   3 - 1
Charleston, SC

DATE	OPPONENT	SCORE		W	L	T
05/16	Carolina (?)	50	5	W		
06/13	Carolina (?)	38	15	W		
07/04	Forest City (Savannah, GA)	16	27		L	
09/07	Forest City (Savannah, GA)	51	16	W		

(Only scores extant)

BATTERS	POS	GP	HL	A	O	R	A	O	H	A	O	TB	A	O
Heslin		9	18	2	0	40	4	4						
Conklin		8	21	2	5	28	3	4						
Easton		7	14	2	0	32	4	4						
Lockwood		6	14	2	2	30	5	0						
Stubbs		6	16	2	4	26	4	2						
Boyce		6	16	2	4	20	3	2						
Cooke		5	10	2	0	22	4	2						

RESOLUTE   3 - 2
St. Louis, MO

DATE	OPPONENT	SCORE		W	L	T
06/04	Empire (St. Louis)	35	43		L	
07/16	Empire (St. Louis)	12	38		L	
08/17	Atlantic (St. Louis)	32	20	W		
08/30	Baltic (St. Louis)	32	23	W		
10/---	Empire (St. Louis)	32	27	W		

BATTERS	POS	GP	HL	A	O	R	A	O	H	A	O	TB	A	O
Chambers		5	14	2	4	18	3	3						
Creamer		5	11	2	1	17	3	2						
Riegel		5	14	2	4	17	3	2						
Carroll		5	18	3	3	15	3	0						
Willard		5	17	3	2	12	2	2						
Grace		5	18	3	3	11	2	1						

AMERICUS   3 - 3
Yorkville, NY

DATE	OPPONENT	SCORE		W	L	T
06/25	Athlete (Washington Hts., NY)	38	25	W		
07/01	Harlem (New York)	39	47		L	
07/09	Baltic (New York)	33	20	W		
07/16	Exercise (New York)	35	36		L	
07/27	Baltic (New York)	70	21	W		
09/01	Oriental (New York)	18	54		L	

BATTERS	POS	GP	HL	A	O	R	A	O	H	A	O	TB	A	O
Smith	P,OF	6	13	2	1	34	5	4						
Roberts	1B,3B	6	19	3	1	22	3	4						
Peffers	C	5	12	2	2	27	5	2						
Truax	2B	5	11	2	1	26	5	1						
McManus	OF	5	17	3	2	22	4	2						
Shelly	OF,3B	5	17	3	2	18	3	3						
McClymont	SS	5	18	3	3	15	3	0						

KNICKERBOCKER   3 - 3
New York, NY

DATE	OPPONENT	SCORE		W	L	T
07/09	Unique (Staten Island)	40	34	W		
08/25	Eagle (New York)	13	41		L	
09/05	Excelsior (Brooklyn)#	51	25	W		
09/21	Eagle (New York)	4	25		L	
10/15	Excelsior (Brooklyn)#	36	27	W		
10/29	Excelsior (Brooklyn)#	25	38		L	

Friendly game

BATTERS	POS	GP	HL	A	O	R	A	O	H	A	O	TB	A	O
Brown	1B	4	12	3	0	10	2	2						
McDonald	2B,SS	3	6	2	0	10	3	1						
Richter	SS,C	4	5	1	1	14	3	2						
Benson	3B	3	9	3	0	11	2	3						
Hinsdale	OF,2B	4	5	1	1	15	3	3						
Samuel Kissam	OF,3B	3	7	2	1	11	3	2						
Slote	OF	3	5	1	2	11	3	2						
Schack	C,SS	5	11	2	1	16	3	1						
James Davis	P	4	11	2	3	9	2	1						

KNICKERBOCKER (cont.)
New York, NY

BATTERS	POS	GP	HL	A	O	R	A	O	H	A	O	TB	A	O
Purdy	1B,C	4	9	2	1	12	3	0						
Stubbs	2B	3	10	3	1	4	1	1						
Brothers	OF	2	7	3	1	7	3	1						
Craven	OF	2	8	4	0	5	2	1						
Vail	SS,3B	2	5	2	1	4	2	0						
Taylor	OF	2	4	2	0	4	2	0						
Cheeseman	OF	2	5	2	1	4	2	0						
Myers	SS	1	3	3	0	5	5	0						
Ball	P	1	2	2	0	5	5	0						
Baldwin	OF	1	2	2	0	5	5	0						
Richard Stevens	OF	1	0	0	0	4	4	0						
Barclay	OF	1	2	2	0	4	4	0						
Dorsett	OF	1	1	1	0	2	2	0						
Kettleton	C	1	5	5	0	0	0	0						

TROJAN 3 - 3
Troy, NY

DATE	OPPONENT	SCORE		W	L	T
05/---	Union (Lansingburgh, NY)	10	39		L	
05/09	McKeon (?)	42	15	W		
05/21	Independent (?)	68	30	W		
06/08	National (Albany, NY)	16	21		L	
07/11	Union (Cohoes, NY)	27	4	W		
08/26	National (Albany, NY)	15	37		L	

BATTERS	POS	GP	HL	A	O	R	A	O	H	A	O	TB	A	O
M. Hayes	1B	6	15	2	3	24	4	0						
Murray	2B	6	20	3	2	18	3	0						
Lillie	SS	6	20	3	2	20	3	2						
P. Hayes	3B	5	17	3	2	14	2	4						
Delaney	OF	6	20	3	2	15	2	3						
Ryan	OF,P	6	13	2	1	23	3	5						
Miller	OF	5	17	3	2	8	1	3						
Purcell	C	6	14	2	2	24	4	0						
Hunt	P	5	18	3	3	12	2	2						

NASSAU 3 - 6
Princeton, NJ

DATE	OPPONENT	SCORE		W	L	T
05/16	Columbia (New York)	59	12	W		
05/---	Princeton (Princeton)	5	30		L	
06/13	Irvington (Irvington, NJ)	18	23		L	
06/23	Harvard (Cambridge, MA)	16	17		L	
06/24	Williams (Williamstown, MA)	24	14	W		
06/25	Yale (New Haven, CT)	23	30		L	
07/04	Oriental (Greenpoint, NY)	37	54		L	
10/10	Atlantic (Brooklyn)*	16	27		L	
10/31	Athletic (Philadelphia)	25	17	W		

* Box score not available

BATTERS	POS	GP	HL	A	O	R	A	O	H	A	O	TB	A	O
Rankin	C	7	20	2	6	23	3	2						
Eby	3B,SS,2B	7	23	3	2	17	?	3						
G. Ward	SS,2B	6	17	2	5	18	3	0						
Mellier	OF,1B	7	24	3	3	16	2	2						

NASSAU (cont.)
Princeton, NJ

BATTERS	POS	GP	HL	A	O	R	A	O	H	A	O	TB	A	O
F.W. Ward	OF	6	20	3	2	17	2	5						
McKibben	P	5	14	2	4	19	3	4						
Buck	OF	5	14	2	4	13	2	3						

ORIENTAL   3 - 6
New York, NY

DATE	OPPONENT	SCORE	W	L	T
06/06	Mutual (New York)	6 26		L	
06/25	Eckford (Brooklyn)	16 30		L	
07/04	Riverside (Norwich, CT)	59 22	W		
07/11	Raritan (S. Amboy, NJ)	12 33		L	
09/01	Americus (Yorkville, NY)	54 18	W		
09/09	Oriental (Greenpoint, NY)	19 8	W		
09/26	Eckford (Brooklyn)	17 47		L	
10/10	Mutual (New York)	5 31		L	
10/17	Mutual (New York)*	12 33		L	

* Box score not available

BATTERS	POS	GP	HL	A	O	R	A	O	H	A	O	TB	A	O
L. Miller		7	18	2	4	27	3	6						
J. Miller		7	19	2	5	23	3	2						
George Bunting		7	19	2	5	21	3	0						
Pennington		6	18	3	0	11	1	5						
C. Smith		5	14	2	4	16	3	1						
Perrine		5	12	2	2	14	2	4						

UNION   3 - 8
Washington, DC

DATE	OPPONENT	SCORE	W	L	T
06/13	National (29th Infantry)	93 31	W		
07/04	Enterprise (Baltimore)	21 34		L	
07/11	Olympic (Washington)	13 38		L	
07/16	Jefferson (Washington)	27 43		L	
07/25	Enterprise (Baltimore)	21 14	W		
07/30	Jefferson (Washington)	17 43		L	
08/01	Enterprise (Baltimore)*	21 13	W		
08/18	Enterprise (Baltimore)	16 34		L	
08/21	National (Washington)	27 43		L	
10/23	Jefferson (Washington)	20 42		L	
11/12	Olympic (Washington)*	7 40		L	

* Box score not available

BATTERS	POS	GP	HL	A	O	R	A	O	H	A	O	TB	A	O
A.W. Clear		9	27	3	0	29	3	2						
Bielaski		8	18	2	2	34	4	2						
Alden		8	21	2	5	26	3	2						
Shepard		7	16	2	2	27	3	6						
Foster		6	20	3	2	17	2	5						
Quantrell		6	14	2	2	15	2	3						
M.E. Urell		5	16	3	1	22	4	2						

ATHLETIC   3 - 9
Brooklyn, NY

DATE	OPPONENT	SCORE		W	L	T
05/23	Atlantic (Brooklyn)	3	26		L	
06/01	Atlantic (Brooklyn)	13	44		L	
06/06	Eckford (Brooklyn)	3	60		L	
06/23	Eckford (Brooklyn)	11	29		L	
07/04	Peconic (Brooklyn)	22	42		L	
07/14	Alpha (Brooklyn)	52	16	W		
07/20	Ivanhoe (Sing Sing, NY)	34	8	W		
08/20	Capitoline (Brooklyn)	17	8	W		
08/31	Champion (Jersey City, NJ)	5	28		L	
09/09	Excelsior (Brooklyn)	12	33		L	
09/21	Eckford (Brooklyn)*	10	38		L	
10/06	Eckford (Brooklyn)*	14	53		L	

* Box score not available

BATTERS	POS	GP	HL	A	O	R	A	O	H	A	O	TB	A	O
Minor		9	26	2	8	23	2	5						
Oliver		7	15	2	1	19	2	5						
Van Buscheten		7	24	3	3	11	1	4						
Barrett		6	19	3	1	15	2	3						
H. Madden		6	17	2	5	18	3	0						
Martin		6	24	4	0	12	2	0						
Woods		6	19	3	1	11	1	5						
Richardson		5	9	1	4	18	3	3						

OLYMPIC   2 - 1
New York, NY

DATE	OPPONENT	SCORE		W	L	T
06/25	Bowery (New York)	55	43	W		
07/29	Post Office (New York)	17	57		L	
10/07	Acme (New York)	27	23	W		

(Only scores extant)

BATTERS	POS	GP	HL	A	O	R	A	O	H	A	O	TB	A	O
Wandell	1B	9	22	2	4	29	3	2						
Neville	2B,OF	16	45	2	13	57	3	9						
Penney	SS	9	20	2	2	35	3	8						
Fanley	3B	5	8	1	3	20	4	0						
Sanders	OF,SS	15	53	3	8	38	2	8						
Conlan	OF	9	24	2	6	28	3	1						
Hardenbrook	OF	5	15	3	0	14	2	4						
White	C,3B	8	23	2	7	28	3	4						
Sutton	P	10	27	2	7	32	3	2						
Jones		8	21	2	5	28	3	4						

FAIRMOUNT   2 - 2
Marlboro, MA

DATE	OPPONENT	SCORE		W	L	T
07/04	Eureka (E. Cambridge, MA)	26	19	W		
08/01	Eureka (E. Cambridge, MA)	21	26		L	
08/15	Eureka (E. Cambridge, MA)	19	15	W		
09/12	Tri Mountain (Boston)	6	25		L	

(Only scores extant)

FAIRMOUNT (cont.)
Marlboro, MA

BATTERS	POS	GP	HL	A	O	R	A	O	H	A	O	TB	A	O
W. Brigham	1B	10	28	2	8	31	3	1						
Russell	2B	8	28	3	4	23	2	7						
Madden	SS	10	22	2	2	40	4	0						
Dolan	3B	7	19	2	5	24	3	3						
H. Brigham	OF	9	25	2	7	33	3	6						
Sawin	OF	6	18	3	0	13	2	1						
Andrews	OF	5	12	2	2	16	3	1						
Hudson	C	10	30	3	0	37	3	7						
Felton	P	10	27	2	7	37	3	7						

BRANDYWINE   2 - 3
W. Chester, PA

DATE	OPPONENT	SCORE		W	L	T
06/25	Hibernia (Phoenixville, PA)	55	12	W		
07/04	Commonwealth (Philadelphia)	29	30		L	
07/16	Commonwealth (Philadelphia)	36	43		L	
08/12	Athletic (Philadelphia)	21	65		L	
08/20	Spartacus (Philadelphia)*	24	13	W		

(Only scores extant)

BATTERS	POS	GP	HL	A	O	R	A	O	H	A	O	TB	A	O
Mercer	1B	12	24	2	0	54	5	4						
Taylor	2B	14	40	2	12	54	3	12						
Sheppard	SS	14	31	2	3	64	4	4						
Hartman	3B	12	38	3	2	42	3	6						
Bateman	OF	12	38	3	2	38	3	2						
McFarland	OF	15	26	1	11	62	4	2						
Darlington	OF,3B	11	28	2	6	47	4	3						
Pawling	C	14	26	1	12	62	4	6						
Jones	P	14	54	3	12	40	2	12						

CREAM CITY   2 - 3
Milwaukee, WI

DATE	OPPONENT	SCORE		W	L	T
06/22	Atlantic (Brooklyn)	13	67		L	
07/04	Garden City (Chicago)	20	52		L	
08/04	Capital City (Madison, WI)	41	15	W		
08/07	Union (Morrisania, NY)	16	43		L	
08/26	Capital City (Madison, WI)	67	23	W		

BATTERS	POS	GP	HL	A	O	R	A	O	H	A	O	TB	A	O
Smith		5	5	1	0	22	4	2						
Wood		5	17	3	2	19	3	4						
McFayden		5	12	2	2	19	3	4						
Norris		5	13	2	3	18	3	3						
Larkin		5	18	3	3	17	3	2						
Wells		5	16	3	1	16	3	1						
Reddington		5	16	3	1	16	3	1						

LOUISVILLE 2 - 4 - 1
Louisville, KY

DATE	OPPONENT	SCORE			W	L	T
06/09	Athletic (Philadelphia)	3	51			L	
06/20	Buckeye (Cincinnati)	4	28			L	
07/02	Atlantic (Brooklyn)	11	66			L	
07/---	Eagle (Louisville)*	35	23		W		
08/10	Eagle (Louisville)*	22	22	(10)			T
08/18	Union (Morrisania, NY)	11	59			L	
08/25	Eagle (Louisville)	14	10		W		

* Box score not available

BATTERS	POS	GP	HL	A	O	R	A	O	H	A	O	TB	A	O
Dickens		5	14	2	4	6	1	1						
Robinson		5	10	2	0	6	1	1						
Booth		5	14	2	4	5	1	0						
Anderson		5	14	2	4	5	1	0						
Tracy		5	17	3	2	4	0	4						

INDEPENDENT 2 - 4
Brooklyn, NY

DATE	OPPONENT	SCORE		W	L	T
06/19	Harmonic (Brooklyn)	91	18	W		
06/22	Unique (Staten Island)	23	30		L	
06/27	Star (Brooklyn)	20	24		L	
07/02	Unique (Staten Island)	55	26	W		
07/11	Star (Brooklyn)	13	39		L	
10/10	Star (Brooklyn)*	3	40		L	

* Box score not available

BATTERS	POS	GP	HL	A	O	R	A	O	H	A	O	TB	A	O
H. Brown		5	12	2	2	26	5	1						
Fenniman		5	10	2	0	26	5	1						
G. Noyes		5	15	3	0	24	4	4						
L.S. Lewis		5	15	3	0	24	4	4						
H. Edwards		5	15	3	0	23	4	3						
R. McCoskry		5	16	3	1	21	4	1						

MUTUAL 2 - 4
E. Liberty, PA

DATE	OPPONENT	SCORE		W	L	T
07/04	Olympic (Allegheny, PA)	17	28		L	
08/20	Dexter (Massillon, OH)	14	28		L	
08/25	Forest City (Cleveland)	18	32		L	
09/18	Independent (Salem, OH)	39	25	W		
09/19	Dexter (Massillon, OH)	15	28		L	
09/21	Star (Ravenna, OH)	34	32	W		

BATTERS	POS	GP	HL	A	O	R	A	O	H	A	O	TB	A	O
Martin		6	14	2	2	21	3	3						
Lylle		6	13	2	1	21	3	3						
S. McKelvy		6	18	3	0	20	3	2						
W.F. McKelvy		6	18	3	0	19	3	1						
Tomer		6	22	3	4	13	2	1						
J. McKelvy		5	13	2	3	10	2	0						

EMPIRE   2 - 6
New York, NY

DATE	OPPONENT	SCORE		W	L	T
07/09	Jefferson (New York)	33	26	W		
07/25	Active (New York)	6	44		L	
08/03	Eagle (New York)	20	30		L	
08/12	Harlem (New York)	18	40		L	
08/22	Social (New York)*	15	20		L	
09/09	Social (New York)	19	22		L	
09/22	Champion (Jersey City, NJ)	11	20		L	
10/01	Gotham (New York)	33	14	W		

* Box score not available

BATTERS	POS	GP	HL	A	O	R	A	O	H	A	O	TB	A	O
Wilson		7	19	2	5	18	2	4						
Miller		6	14	2	2	19	3	1						
E. Nestler		6	17	2	5	12	2	0						
Post		5	16	3	1	11	2	1						
Vosge		5	16	3	1	8	1	3						

IRVINGTON   2 - 6
Irvington, NJ

DATE	OPPONENT	SCORE		W	L	T
06/13	Princeton (Princeton, NJ)	23	18	W		
07/24	Mutual (New York)	14	41		L	
08/07	Eckford (Brooklyn)	18	27		L	
08/08	Mutual (New York)	7	12		L	
08/19	Eckford (Brooklyn)	14	12	W		
08/24	Atlantic (Brooklyn)	6	37		L	
09/01	Eckford (Brooklyn)	6	12		L	
09/11	Atlantic (Brooklyn)	6	13		L	

(Only scores extant)

BATTERS	POS	GP	HL	A	O	R	A	O	H	A	O	TB	A	O
Mike Campbell		10	22	2	2	24	2	4	31	3	1	38	3	8
Hugh Campbell		10	30	3	0	16	1	6	25	2	5	32	3	2
Billy Lewis		10	34	3	4	21	2	1	25	2	5	30	3	0
A. Bailey		10	33	3	3	17	1	7	22	2	2	27	2	7
Ev Mills		9	24	2	6	23	2	5	27	3	0	37	4	1
George Lines		9	29	3	2	16	1	7	21	2	3	26	2	8
George Eaton		9	30	3	3				16	1	7	19	2	1
T. Buckley		6	19	3	1	14	2	2	18	3	0	23	3	5

RIVERSIDE   1 - 2
Portsmouth, OH

DATE	OPPONENT	SCORE		W	L	T
06/11	Cincinnati (Cincinnati)	17	59		L	
07/24	Cincinnati (Cincinnati)	16	34		L	
08/14	Great Western (Cincinnati)	26	15	W		

(Only scores extant)

BATTERS	POS	GP	HL	A	O	R	A	O	H	A	O	TB	A	O
Al Pratt	P	7	17	2	3	27	3	6	24	3	3			
Huddleston	OF,SS	7	21	3	0	20	2	5	19	2	5			
Davis	2B,C	7	20	2	6	20	2	6	16	2	2			
Baden	1B	6	16	2	4	22	3	4	19	3	1			
Lang	OF,3B	6	16	2	4	18	3	0	19	3	1			

RIVERSIDE (cont.)
Portsmouth, OH

BATTERS	POS	GP	HL	A	O	R	A	O	H	A	O	TB	A	O
Lewis	C,2B	6	12	2	0	20	3	2	17	2	5			
B. Pratt	OF	6	21	3	3	16	2	2	10	1	4			

HARMONIC   1 - 6
Brooklyn, NY

DATE	OPPONENT	SCORE		W	L	T
05/08	Unique (Staten Island)	33	19	W		
05/22	Unique (Staten Island)	38	55		L	
06/19	Independent (Brooklyn)	18	91		L	
06/25	Unique (Staten Island)	26	36		L	
07/04	Alert (Norwalk, CT)	16	44		L	
07/09	Enterprise (Clifton, NY)*	41	47		L	
11/06	Alpha (Brooklyn)	13	39		L	

* Box score not available

BATTERS	POS	GP	HL	A	O	R	A	O	H	A	O	TB	A	O
W.J. Bennett		6	15	2	3	19	3	1						
Burns		6	19	3	1	15	2	3						
Murray		5	11	2	1	19	3	4						
Larkin		5	15	3	0	16	3	1						
J.J. Bennett		5	16	3	1	14	2	4						
Byrne		5	12	2	2	13	2	3						
Russell		5	13	2	3	13	2	3						

GRAMERCY   1 - 7
New York, NY

DATE	OPPONENT	SCORE		W	L	T
06/17	Oriental (Greenpoint, NY)	20	23		L	
06/27	Union (Morrisania, NY)	7	28		L	
07/02	Active (New York)	17	28		L	
07/04	Tri Mountain (Boston)	9	42		L	
07/15	Harlem (New York)	13	12	W		
07/21	Tri Mountain (Boston)	26	38		L	
08/26	Oriental (Greenpoint, NY)	18	20		L	
10/22	Harlem (New York)	25	29		L	

BATTERS	POS	GP	HL	A	O	R	A	O	H	A	O	TB	A	O
Jackson	1B,P,OF,3B,SS	6	19	3	1	11	1	5						
Irvine	2B	6	21	3	3	7	1	1						
O'Connor	SS	6	14	2	2	15	2	3						
Sam Wright	3B,C	7	18	2	4	12	1	5						
Bennett	OF,P	7	22	3	1	14	2	0						
L. French	OF,1B	7	17	2	3	13	1	6						
Browne	OF	7	24	3	3	12	1	5						
Bass	C,3B	7	21	3	0	16	2	2						
Lupton	P	6	18	3	0	13	2	1						

RAILWAY UNION   1 - 9 - 1
Cleveland, OH

DATE	OPPONENT	SCORE		W	L	T
06/04	Forest City (Cleveland)	21	14	W		
06/17	Atlantic (Brooklyn)	12	47		L	

RAILWAY UNION (cont.)
Cleveland, OH

DATE	OPPONENT	SCORE		W	L	T
07/02	Cincinnati (Cincinnati)	16	52		L	
07/03	Buckeye (Cincinnati)	13	49		L	
07/04	Forest City (Cleveland)	*25	27			T
07/25	Forest City (Cleveland)	25	59		L	
08/01	Union (Morrisania, NY)	8	43		L	
08/29	Forest City (Cleveland)	25	32		L	
09/16	Buckeye (Cincinnati)	13	15		L	
10/03	Forest City (Cleveland)	19	28		L	
10/10	Cincinnati (Cincinnati)	8	41		L	

* With two out in bottom of tenth inning, game declared a draw.

BATTERS	POS	GP	HL	A	O	R	A	O	H	A	O	TB	A	O
Hardenburg	1B	7	17	2	3	14	2	0						
Crombie	2B	10	39	3	9	16	1	6						
Phelan	SS	9	20	2	2	22	2	4						
Scotton	3B,OF	8	25	3	1	12	1	4						
Melton	OF	11	29	2	7	27	2	5						
Bouse	OF	9	27	3	0	17	1	8						
Bradbury	OF	7	15	2	1	16	2	2						
Doubleday	C	8	19	2	3	16	2	0						
John Riley	P	8	25	3	1	19	2	3						

ATLANTIC   0 - 3
Chicago, IL

DATE	OPPONENT	SCORE		W	L	T
06/23	Atlantic (Brooklyn)	7	51		L	
08/06	Union (Morrisania, NY)	12	41		L	
07/22	Buckeye (Cincinnati)	9	27		L	

(Only scores extant)

BATTERS	POS	GP	HL	A	O	R	A	O	H	A	O	TB	A	O
H. Taylor		12	31	2	7	50	4	2						
Boardman		10	28	2	8	39	3	9						
Ward		9	20	2	4	42	4	6						
Kingon		9	26	2	8	36	4	0						
Graves		9	25	2	7	29	3	3						
Bredberg		7	15	2	1	32	4	4						
Wilson		7	21	3	0	21	4	4						
Standbaugh		6	12	2	0	22	3	4						
Reynolds		6	9	1	3	32	5	2						
Beebe		6	22	3	4	23	3	5						
Dorgan		6	15	2	3	18	3	0						
Mears		6	19	3	1	17	2	5						
Butler		5	9	1	4	18	3	3						

CAPITAL CITY   0 - 5
Madison, WI

DATE	OPPONENT	SCORE		W	L	T
07/09	Forest City (Rockford, IL)	9	28		L	
07/16	Forest City (Rockford, IL)	12	43		L	
08/04	Cream City (Milwaukee)	15	41		L	
08/08	Union (Morrisania, NY)	12	77		L	
08/26	Cream City (Milwaukee)	23	67		L	

CAPITAL CITY (cont.)
Madison, WI

BATTERS	POS	GP	HL	A	O	R	A	O	H	A	O	TB	A	O
Lewis		5	17	3	2	9	1	4						
Bean		5	12	2	2	7	1	2						
Fisher		5	18	3	3	5	1	0						
James Nichols		5	15	3	0	5	1	0						

TEAM TOTALS

TEAM	CITY/STATE	GP	W	L	T	PCT	R	OR
Athletic	Philadelphia, PA	50	47	3	0	.940	1980	737
Atlantic	Brooklyn, NY	54	47	7	0	.870	1845	617
Union	Morrisania, NY	43	37	6	0	.860	1417	578
Cincinnati	Cincinnati, OH	43	36	7	0	.837	1546	577
Mutual	New York, NY	41	31	10	0	.756	1033	621
Eckford	Brooklyn, NY	35	23	12	0	.657	940	561
Buckeye	Cincinnati, OH	26	21	5	0	.808	841	386
Union	Lansingburgh, NY	20	15	5	0	.750	603	362
Champion	Jersey City, NJ	19	14	5	0	.737	562	389
Harvard	Cambridge, MA	15	13	2	0	.867	504	244
National	Albany, NY	21	13	8	0	.619	647	437
Maryland	Baltimore, MD	18	12	6	0	.667	438	357
Tri Mountain	Boston, MA	21	12	9	0	.571	536	442
Olympic	Washington, DC	24	12	11	1	.520	654	487
Atlantic	St. Louis, MO	14	11	3	0	.786	513	355
Forest City	Rockford, IL	15	11	4	0	.733	534	305
Lowell	Boston, MA	15	11	4	0	.636	512	291
Great Western	Cincinnati, OH	20	11	9	0	.550	580	513
Forest City	Cleveland, OH	23	11	11	1	.500	578	428
Olympic	Philadelphia, PA	22	11	11	0	.500	554	571
Eagle	New York, NY	11	10	1	0	.919	364	178
Niagara	Buffalo, NY	15	10	5	0	.667	489	314
Athlete	Washington Hts., NY	14	9	5	0	.643	352	228
Star	Brooklyn, NY	19	9	10	0	.474	468	312
Oriental	Greenpoint, NY	11	8	3	0	.727	307	250
Clipper	Lowell, MA	10	7	3	0	.700	357	205
National	Washington, DC	10	7	3	0	.700	310	162
Enterprise	Baltimore, MD	12	7	5	0	.583	311	249
Geary	Philadelphia, PA	13	7	6	0	.538	281	281
Union	St. Louis, MO	13	7	6	0	.538	332	378
Yale	New Haven, CT	13	7	6	0	.538	249	223
Excelsior	Chicago, IL	15	7	7	1	.500	433	323
Active	Indianapolis, IN	15	7	8	0	.467	527	537
Harlem	New York, NY	15	7	8	0	.467	353	483
Olympic	Providence, RI	8	6	2	0	.750	290	156
Old Point	Norfolk, VA	10	6	4	0	.600	105	101
Central City	Syracuse, NY	11	6	5	0	.545	291	275
Union	Camden, NJ	12	6	6	0	.500	332	352
Empire	St. Louis, MO	15	6	9	0	.400	379	438
Wamsutta	New Bedford, MA	7	5	2	0	.714	197	159
Unique	Staten Island, NY	10	5	5	0	.500	329	334
Jefferson	Washington, DC	11	5	6	0	.455	309	328
Active	New York, NY	14	5	9	0	.357	243	326
Keystone	Philadelphia, PA	16	5	10	1	.344	305	415
Mutual	Janesville, WI	4	4	0	0	1.000	135	103
Montgomery	Montgomery, AL	5	4	1	0	.800	219	169
Eon	Portland, ME	6	4	2	0	.667	123	102
Wide Awake	Alton, IL	6	4	2	0	.667	196	167
Alpha	Brooklyn, NY	7	4	3	0	.571	206	187
Harry Clay	Philadelphia, PA	7	4	3	0	.571	235	202
Social	New York, NY	8	4	4	0	.500	188	245
Excelsior	Brooklyn, NY	10	4	5	1	.450	252	270
Commonwealth	Philadelphia, PA	10	4	6	0	.400	275	420
Live Oak	Cincinnati, OH	16	4	7	0	.364	285	402

TEAM TOTALS (cont.)

TEAM	CITY/STATE	GP	W	L	T	PCT	R	OR
Detroit	Detroit, MI	15	4	10	1	.300	357	409
Active	Quincy, MA	4	3	1	0	.750	86	105
Alert	Charleston, SC	4	3	1	0	.750	155	63
Resolute	St. Louis, MO	5	3	2	0	.600	143	151
Peconic	Brooklyn, NY	6	3	2	1	.583	167	153
Dramatic	Mobile, AL	6	3	3	0	.500	314	275
Americus	Yorkville, NY	6	3	3	0	.500	233	203
Knickerbocker	New York, NY	6	3	3	0	.500	169	190
Trojan	Troy, NY	6	3	3	0	.500	178	146
Nassau	Princeton, NJ	9	3	6	0	.333	223	224
Oriental	New York, NY	9	3	6	0	.333	200	248
Union	Washington, DC	11	3	8	0	.273	283	375
Athletic	Brooklyn, NY	12	3	9	0	.250	196	385
Olympic	New York, NY	3	2	1	0	.667	99	123
Eureka	Newark, NJ	4	2	2	0	.500	77	83
Mobile	Mobile, AL	4	2	2	0	.500	215	195
Fairmount	Marlboro, MA	4	2	2	0	.500	72	85
Union	Hudson City, NJ	4	2	2	0	.500	108	188
Resolute	Elizabeth, NJ	4	2	2	0	.,500	64	87
Bergen	Bergen, NJ	5	2	3	0	.400	156	155
Brandywine	W. Chester, PA	5	2	3	0	.400	165	163
Cream City	Milwaukee, WI	5	2	3	0	.400	157	200
Chestnut St. Th.	Philadelphia, PA	5	2	3	0	.400	117	164
Louisville	Louisville, KY	7	2	4	1	.357	100	259
Independent	Brooklyn, NY	6	2	4	0	.333	205	177
Mutual	E. Liberty, PA	6	2	4	0	.333	137	173
Malvern	Philadelphia, PA	7	2	5	0	.286	195	212
Empire	New York, NY	8	2	6	0	.250	155	216
Irvington	Irvington, NJ	8	2	6	0	.250	94	172
Riverside	Portsmouth, OH	3	1	2	0	.333	59	108
Alaska	Brooklyn, NY	4	1	3	0	.250	72	126
Bachelor	Philadelphia, PA	5	1	4	0	.200	77	183
Excelsior	Rochester, NY	5	1	4	0	.200	86	105
Jefferson	New York, NY	6	1	5	0	.183	121	176
Ivanhoe	Sing Sing, NY	6	1	5	0	.183	52	163
Harmonic	Brooklyn, NY	7	1	6	0	.143	185	331
Gramercy	New York, NY	8	1	7	0	.125	135	220
Railway Union	Cleveland, OH	11	1	9	1	.136	185	407
Atlantic	Chicago, IL	3	0	3	0	.000	28	119
Allegheny	Allegheny, PA	4	0	4	0	.000	44	86
Bloomington	Bloomington, IL	4	0	4	0	.000	53	158
Capital City	Madison, WI	5	0	5	0	.000	71	256
Gotham	New York, NY	6	0	6	0	.000	98	151
Mohawk	Brooklyn, NY	6	0	6	0	.000	78	192

OTHER TEAMS

TEAM	CITY/STATE
Achilles	Morrison, IL
Acme	Waukegan, IL
Active	Ballston Spa, NY
Active	Buffalo, NY
Active	St. Louis, MO
Active	Baltimore, MD
Aetna	Windsor Locks, CT
Alert	Cumberland, MD
Alert	Elmira, NY
Alert	Hartford, CT
Alert	Norwalk, CT
Alert	Paterson, NJ
Alert	Philadelphia, PA
Alert	Poultney, VT

OTHER TEAMS (cont.)

TEAM	CITY/STATE
Alpha	Philadelphia, PA
Alpha	Springfield, VT
Alpha	Chicago, IL
Amateur	Carlisle, PA
Amateur	Philadelphia, PA
Amateur	Princeton, IL
Amateur	Chicago, IL
American	Indianapolis, IN
Americus	Newark, NJ
Amulet	Waterbury, VT
Anchor	Pittsburgh, PA
Arctic	Baltimore, MD
Arctic	Philadelphia, PA
Armstrong	Philadelphia, PA
Associate	Baltimore, MD
Atalanta	Geneva, NY
Athenian	Philadelphia, PA
Athlete	St. Louis, MO
Athlete	Wheaton, IL
Athletic	Chicago, IL
Athletic	Memphis, TN
Athletic	Monmouth, IL
Athletic	Portland, ME
Athletic	Selma, AL
Athletic	Springfield, IL
Atlanta	Tremont, NY
Atlantic	Buffalo, NY
Atlantic	Memphis, TN
Atlantic	Milwaukee, WI
Atlantic	Pittsburgh, PA
Atlantic	Springfield, IL
Atlantic	Trenton, NJ
Auburn	Auburn, NY
Aurora	Chicago, IL
Aurora	Plattsburgh, NY
Avenue	Cincinnati, OH
Badger	Appleton, WI
Badger	Beloit, WI
Badger	Columbus, WI
Bald Eagle	Carlisle, PA
Baltic	St. Louis, MO
Baltic	New York, NY
Belmont	Philadelphia, PA
Binghamton	Binghamton, NY
Black Hawk	Aurora, IL
Blue Wing	New Boston, OH
Bluff City	Memphis, TN
Bower City	Janesville, WI
Bridgeport	Bridgeport, CT
Brookline	Boston, MA
Buckhorn	Indianapolis, IN
Buffalo	Buffalo, NY
Burlington	Burlington, VT
Caledonia	Danville, VT
Camden	Camden, NJ
Canacadea	Hornellsville, NY
Capital	Baton Rouge, LA
Capital	Columbus, OH
Capital City	Montgomery, AL
Capitol	Washington, DC
Catamount	Ridgeway, PA
Central	Centerville, IN
Central City	Selma, AL
Champion	Burlington, VT
Champlain	Vergennes, VT
Charter Oak	Hartford, CT

OTHER TEAMS (cont.)

TEAM	CITY/STATE
Chesterfield	Queen Anne Cty., MD
Chicago	Chicago, IL
Chittendon	Milton, VT
Claybourne	St. Michael's, MD
Clipper	Castleton, VT
Clipper	Monmouth, IL
Cold Spring	Philadelphia, PA
Columbia	Bordentown, NJ
Columbia	Columbia, OH
Columbia	New York, NY
Comet	Beloit, WI
Comet	Chicago, IL
Commercial	St. Louis, MO
Contest	Philadelphia, PA
Continental	Delavan, WI
Creighton	Norfolk, VA
Crescent	Burlington, IA
Crescent	Clinton, WI
Crescent	New Lisbon, OH
Crescent	St. Albans, VT
Crescent	Sycamore, IL
Crescent	Cincinnati, OH
Cypress	E. New York, NY
Delaware	Delaware, OH
Dexter	Baltimore, MD
Diamond	Newton, OH
Dirigo	Philadelphia, PA
Dirigo	St. Louis, MO
Eagle	Beloit, WI
Eagle	Flatbush, NY
Eagle	Sparta, WI
Eagle	St. Albans, VT
Eagle	W. Troy, NY
Earnest	Riverhead, NY
Earthquake	New Harmony, IN
East End	Cincinnati, OH
Eaton	Meriden, CT
Eclectic	New York, NY
Eclipse	Cairo, IL
Ecliptic	Middletown, CT
Eel River	Logansport, IN
Elgin	Elgin, IL
Empire	Champaign, IL
Empire	Placedale, RI
Empire	San Francisco, CA
Empire	Washington, DC
Endeavor	New York, NY
Enterprise	Allegheny City, PA
Enterprise	Alpha, OH
Enterprise	Chicago, IL
Enterprise	Clifton, NY
Enterprise	Renova, PA
Enterprise	Indianapolis, IN
Equity	Philadelphia, PA
Essex	New Brunswick, NJ
Ethan Allen	Winooski, VT
Etruria	E. Liverpool, OH
Eureka	Clinton, IL
Eureka	E. Cambridge, MA
Eureka	Memphis, TN
Eureka	Pittsburgh, OH
Eureka	Baltimore, MD
Eureka	Chicago, IL
Everett	Oshkosh, WI
Excello	Middleton, OH
Excelsior	Coatsville, PA

OTHER TEAMS (cont.)

TEAM	CITY/STATE
Excelsior	Dubuque, IA
Excelsior	Elmira, NY
Excelsior	Manchester, IA
Excelsior	Mt. Joy, PA
Excelsior	Paterson, NJ
Excelsior	St. Louis, MO
Exercise	New York, NY
Expert	Philadelphia, PA
Express	Indianapolis, IN
Fairmount	Fairmount, OH
Fear Naught	Middlebury, VT
First Ward	Philadelphia, PA
Forest City	Middletown, CT
Ft. Clark	Peoria, IL
Fountain City	Fond du Lac, WI
Franklin	Franklin, IN
Fraternity	S. Boston, MA
Fulton	Fulton, IL
Fulton	New York, NY
Garden City	Chicago, IL
Glastenbury	Glastenbury, CT
Govans	Govans, MD
Granite	New York, NY
Green Mountain	Bristol, VT
Greenville	Greenville, AL
Greenwood	California, OH
Gulf City	Mobile, AL
Gulick	New York, NY
Harmony	Cincinnati, OH
Havre	Havre de Grace, MD
Hickory	McConnelsville, OH
Hickory	New Rutland, IL
Hockanum	N. Manchester, CT
Home	Burlington, VT
Hoosier	Lafayette, IN
Hope	Saratoga Springs, NY
Hope	St. Louis, MO
Howard	Hartford, CT
Hudson River	Newburgh, NY
I.X.L.	S. Zanesville, OH
I.X.L.	Cincinnati, OH
Ictoria	Kethsburg, IL
Independent	Cairo, IL
Independent	New London, CT
Interior	Washington, DC
Intrepid	Brooklyn, NY
Intrepid	La Crosse, WI
Invincible	Wetumpka, AL
Ironsides	Cincinnati, OH
Irvington	Columbus, OH
Jamaica	Jamaica Plains, MA
Juneau	Milwaukee, WI
Kekionga	Ft. Wayne, IN
Kendall	Yorkville, IL
Kent	Grand Rapids, MI
Kent Island	Kent Island, MD
Kewanee	Kewanee, IL
Keystone	Harrisburg, PA
Kickenepawling	Johnstown, PA
Knickerbocker	Albany, NY
Korndaffer	Philadelphia, PA
Lake	Baltimore, MD
Lake Shore	Waukegan, IL
Laurel	Cincinnati, OH
Laurence	New York, NY
Liberty	Jamaica, NY

OTHER TEAMS (cont.)

TEAM	CITY/STATE
Liberty	New Brunswick, NJ
Liberty	Norwalk, CT
Liberty	San Francisco, CA
Lightfoot	Madisonville, OH
Lincoln	Pittsburgh, PA
Lively	Toledo, OH
Lively Turtle	Rockford, IL
Logan	Mt. Morris, IL
Logan	Mt. Union, PA
Lone Star	Anderson, IN
Lone Star	Catskill, NY
Lone Star	Chenoa, IL
Lone Star	Mattewan, NY
Lone Star	Springfield, OH
M.M. Van Dyke	New York, NY
Magnolia	St. Louis, MO
Manhattan	New York, NY
Mansion	New York, NY
Marion	Brooklyn, NY
Marion	Philadelphia, PA
Marvin	Norwichtown, CT
Masonic	Manayunk, PA
McLaughlin	Lewisburg, PA
Mechanic	Memphis, TN
Mechanics	Patterson, PA
Mechanics	St. Johnsbury, VT
Meteor	Addison, NY
Middlebury	Middlebury, VT
Milton	Milton, WI
Milton College	Milton, WI
Minerva	Philadelphia, PA
Moline	Moline, IL
Momoweta	Greenport, NY
Monitor	Corning, NY
Monitor	Milwaukee, WI
Monitor	Waterbury, CT
Monitor	Westbury, CT
Monticello	Monticello, NY
Mountain Star	Altoona, PA
Mutual	Columbia, PA
Mutual	Meadville, PA
Mutual	Philadelphia, PA
Mutual	Springfield, OH
Mutual	Baltimore, MD
Napolean	Napolean, OH
National	Philadelphia, PA
National	St. Louis, MO
National	Chicago, IL
Nepperham	Yonkers, NY
Neptune	Easton, PA
New Britain	New Britain, CT
Newark	Newark, NJ
Newtown	Newtown, OH
Niagara	Lockport, NY
Niagara Falls	Niagara Falls, NY
Nonpareil	Burlington, VT
Occidental	Quincy, IL
O.K.	Ottawa, IL
O.K.	Zanesville, OH
Oceanic	Mystic Bridge, CT
Olympian	Blanchester, OH
Olympian	Oxford, OH
Olympic	Detroit, MI
Olympic	Louisville, KY
Olympic	Nazareth, PA
Olympic	Norrisville, VT

OTHER TEAMS (cont.)

TEAM	CITY/STATE
Olympic	Paterson, NJ
Olympic	Sheffield, IL
Omaha	Omaha, NE
Onawa	Williamsburg, OH
Onward	New Bedford, MA
Orchard	Brooklyn, NY
Oriental	Hartford, CT
Orion	New York, NY
Osceola	Frankford, PA
P. Sheridan	Cohoes, NY
Pacific	Clinton, IA
Pacific	Mobile, AL
Pacific	New Utrecht, NY
Pacific	Philadelphia, PA
Pacific	Rochester, NY
Paragon	Danville, IN
Paragon	Baltimore, MD
Pastime	Philadelphia, PA
Pastime	Baltimore, MD
Pastime	Cincinnati, OH
Patapsco	Westminster, MD
Penfield	Oberlin, OH
Penn Treaty	Philadelphia, PA
Pequot	New London, CT
Pestaricus	Manayunk, PA
Philadelphia	Philadelphia, PA
Phoenix	Belvidere, IL
Phoenix	Terre Haute, IN
Pine Grove	Fair Haven, CT
Pioneer	Alexandria, VA
Pioneer	Genesee, IL
Pioneer	Portland, OR
Pioneer	Springfield, MA
Pioneer	Indianapolis, IN
Potomac	Washington, DC
Pottstown	Pottstown, PA
Powhatan	Brooklyn, NY
Prairie	Shannon, IL
Prairie City	Ripon, WI
Prince George	Baltimore, MD
Princeton	Princeton, NJ
Quaker City	Philadelphia, PA
Queens	Oyster Bay, NY
Quickstep	Toledo, OH
Quinniapack	New Haven, CT
Quinnipiack	W. Meriden, CT
Railroad	Columbus, OH
Railroad	Indianapolis, IN
Ralston	Philadelphia, PA
Red Hook	Cincinnati, OH
Red Jacket	Paxton, IL
Red Stick	Baton Rouge, LA
Reno	Philadelphia, PA
Republic	Springfield, OH
Resolute	Baltimore, MD
Resolute	Brooklyn, NY
Resolute	Evansville, IN
Resolute	Terre Haute, IN
Resolute	Chicago, IL
Ristori	Farentum, PA
Rittenhouse	Philadelphia, PA
Rival	Providence, PA
Riverside	Dixon, IL
Riverside	Norwich, CT
Rollstone	Fitchburg, MA
Rural	W. Farrion, PA

OTHER TEAMS (cont.)

TEAM	CITY/STATE
S.J. Randall	Philadelphia, PA
Sans Souci	Connecticut
Sawpitt	Port Chester, NY
Sea Side	Long Branch, NJ
Shabbonna	Ottawa, IL
Social	Elmira, NY
Social	Cincinnati, OH
Sonnissippi	Rockford, IL
Sophomore	Cambridge, MA
Sparta	New York, NY
Spartacus	Philadelphia, PA
Squonnenog	Pequonic, CT
St. Elmo	Mobile, AL
St. Lawrence	Malone, NY
Star	Green Bay, WI
Star	New Brunswick, NJ
Star	Pleasantville, NY
Star	Virden, IL
Star	Wakefield, RI
Star	Wallingford, CT
Stonewall	Wetumpka, AL
Suffolk	Huntington, NY
Surprise	W. Farms, NY
Thomson	Thomson, IL
Tipton	Tipton, IN
Titan	Pournal, VT
Toledo	Toledo, OH
Towson	Towson, MD
Trix	Philadelphia, PA
Tropical	Ocala, FL
Twilight	St. Louis, MO
Typographical	Philadelphia, PA
Tyrolean	Harrisburg, PA
U.V.M.	Burlington, VT
Una	Mt. Vernon, NY
Undercliff	Cold Spring, NY
Union	Cohoes, NY
Union	Elmira, NY
Union	Plainfield, NJ
Union	Richmond, VA
Union	St. Johnsbury, VT
Union	Urbana, OH
Union	Chicago, IL
Unionville	Unionville, NY
Unkidori	Monticello, IA
Unknown	Elizabeth, NJ
Utica	Utica, NY
Valley	Bay City, MI
Vermillion	Danville, IL
Victory	Troy, NY
Viola	Nazareth, PA
W.H. Patterson	Philadelphia, PA
Waban	Newton, MA
Walkill	Middletown, NY
Walnut	Altoona, IL
Walnut Hills	Walnut Hills, OH
Wasello	Rock Island, IL
Waterbury	Waterbury, CT
Wawassett	Wilmington, DE
Wayland	Beaver Dam, WI
Wenona	Wenona, IL
W. Philadelphia	Philadelphia, PA
Western	Indianapolis, IN
Western Star	Janesville, WI
Western Star	Indianapolis, IN
Whitewater	Fond du Lac, WI

OTHER TEAMS (cont.)

TEAM	CITY/STATE
Wide Awake	Middlebury, VT
Wild Cat	Brookville, PA
Winooski	Cabot, VT
Winthrop	Boston, MA
Woolen Mill	Lawrenceburg, IN
Xenia	Xenia, OH

1869
THE REDS OF SIXTY-NINE

In the early 1860s, the Eckford club completed a ten-game campaign without a loss. In the mid 1860s, the Atlantic club enjoyed two seasons without defeat. In 1869, a team from Cincinnati put those records to shame. Nominally called the Cincinnati club, they were more familiarly known as the Red Stockings.

The Cincinnati club was born in 1866. Playing a modest schedule, the team won two and lost two. The next year, the club showed definite signs of improvement as they finished with 16 wins in 17 games. In 1868, the team emerged as a full-fledged power, winning 36 and losing seven. The transformation can be attributed to two men— Aaron Champion and Harry Wright.

Aaron Champion was the principle financial backer of the team. Harry Wright was a veteran ballplayer currently employed as a professional cricket player in Cincinnati. Knowing of Wright's former success as a ballplayer, Champion engaged him to play for the Cincinnati club in 1867. In 1868, Champion made Wright the captain of the club. This position, whose modern equivalent would be manager or general manager, allowed Harry Wright to mold the club into a 36–7 powerhouse. Not content, Wright had ambitious plans for 1869. He wanted to employ an all professional team.

Paying players for their services was not a new concept. As far back as the days of James Creighton, certain ballplayers were compensated for their services. Since the National Association specifically forbade such behavior, the lucre would pass under the table in the form of a share of the gate receipts or in a non-existent job. Quite frequently, the better players would rotate or revolve between clubs several times each season searching for a better deal. To legitimize the professional player, the National Association at its 1868 convention allowed clubs to pay their players aboveboard if they so wished. The era of 19th century free-agency had arrived.

This was the opening Harry Wright was waiting for. Using Champion's checkbook, Wright searched the country recruiting the best ball players. The first place he looked was close to home as he booked his own brother, George, to play shortstop. From the Buckeye nine he plucked outfielder Andy Leonard, second baseman Charlie Sweasy and substitute Dick Hurley.

Another player enticed was Cal McVey from the Actives (Indianapolis). The remainder of the nine, Asa Brainard (pitcher), Doug Allison (catcher) and Charles Gould (first base) were holdovers from the '68 squad. Harry Wright himself would play center field. The entire team's salary, including substitutes, was $9,300. George Wright pulled down the highest compensation as he took home $1,400 for his season's work.

Before the season started, Harry Wright had a new uniform designed for the team. Not content with the standard which included long pants, Wright desired a new look. He decided the team would be outfitted in knickers, with long stockings showing below. The color of the hose was bright red, forever giving the Cincinnati club the more common name "Red Stockings."

After beating up a quartet of soft opponents, the Red Stockings embarked on a lengthy eastern road trip in late May. Scheduled to face over 20 opponents, the team won the first ten with ease. Their first real challenges came as they were set to meet the Association's best clubs in New York and Brooklyn.

On the 15th of June, the Cincinnatis survived their first test as they scored two in the ninth to edge the Mutual club 4–2. On the next two days, they dispatched the Atlantics (32–10) and Eckfords (24–5) with ease.

As the summer progressed, the Red Stockings rolled on to win after win. Their closest call came on August 26 while facing the Union club of Lansingburgh, N.Y. With the score knotted at 17 in the sixth, the *New York Clipper* described what happened next:

> McVey [Cincinnati] struck a foul, which was lifted on the bound by Craver [Union catcher], just as it touched the ground. The umpire called "not out." Craver then called in his nine and stopped the game...The game was given to the Cincinnatis by the umpire, after he had in vain ordered the Haymakers to proceed.

Though the score remained 17-all, Cincinnati's win streak remained intact.

With the team undefeated after 43 games, the Red Stockings undertook an unique venture. Traveling over the recently completed Union Pacific railroad, the team journeyed to far San Francisco. After five one-sided victories over Bay Area teams, the club returned home in mid–October.

To finish the season, the Cincinnati played a pair of big home games against tough foes. On the 18th of October they dispatched the Athletics 17–12 and on November 6th the Red Stockings vanquished the Mutuals.

Though the Red Stockings had finished the season with nary a blemish on their record, they were still not considered the champs. That honor fell in turn to the Eckfords because of their wins over the Mutuals on June 5 and July 3rd. Later the bunting passed to the Atlantics who bested them for the second time on November 8.

In tallying up the season, it was quickly seen that the Red Stockings had enjoyed a season like none other. The team had played 57 opponents and had come away victors each time. They had scored almost 2,400 runs, averaging 42 per contest. In accomplishing this fine record, The Red Stockings were led by several outstanding performances, none better than George Wright. Wright, in perhaps the finest season of any professional player at any time, averaged well over five hits and ten total bases per game. In addition, he swatted 47 homeruns. In compiling approximate batting averages, it can be determined that Wright hit .629 while the team as a whole batted .500. (Note: the Red Stockings were given stats called "Times to Bat" which most likely correspond to our at-bats.) The team also introduced the Association's first pitching statistics

Among the 12 professional teams, the Red Stockings had the finest record as they bested all 19 of their foes. The Athletics, Atlantics and Eckfords also performed well in their matches, winning 15 professional and at least 40 total games each. The top professional batter was easily George Wright as he scored 339 runs (5,54), knocked out 304 hits (5,19) resulting in 614 total bases (10,44). Each of these totals set Association records.

Out of the more than 400 amateur teams in the Association, the best records were posted by the Lone Star (New Orleans) and Forest City (Rockford) clubs. Each of these two won 20, although Brooklyn's Star outfit was generally considered the amateur champion because their 16 wins came against tougher foes. The batting honors were shared by two Forest City players. Scott Hastings scored the most runs (153), had the highest run average (6,9) and cracked out the most hits (125). Bob Addy had the most hits per game (5,9) and most total bases (205) with the accompanying average (8,21).

On the down side, one team deserves mention. The Olympic club of New York engaged 18 foes during the course of the campaign and were beaten by all. They were outscored by an average of 54 to 16 in each game. To compound their woes, the Olympics went on an ill-advised excursion to Boston in August. While there, the club played five contests, giving up more than 80 runs in each of the last three. This sorry campaign ranks as the all-time worst in Association history.

The Cincinnati club would continue their winning ways on into 1870 before finally falling in an epic battle. Sadly, the team itself would not last much past the closing of the next campaign.

The Cincinnati Red Stockings of 1869 rank as the Association's best team. Period. Many years later, as a tribute to the team, Cincinnati scribe Harry Ellard wrote a popular poem singing their praises. Three of the stanzas go like this:

> When I was young and played baseball
> With the Reds of Sixty-nine,
> We then knew how to play the game,
> We were all right in line...
>
> And when our bats would fan the air
> You bet we'd make a hit;
> The ball would fly two hundred yards
> Before it ever lit...
>
> Well, well my boy, those days are gone;
> No club will ever shine...
> Like the one which never knew defeat,
> The Reds of Sixty-Nine.

PROFESSIONAL TEAMS

CINCINNATI 57 - 0 (19 - 0)
Cincinnati, OH

DATE	OPPONENT	SCORE		W	L	T
05/04	Great Western (Cincinnati)	45	9	W		
05/10	Kekionga (Ft. Wayne, IN)	86	8	W		
05/15	Antioch (Yellow Springs, OH)	41	7	W		
05/22	Kekionga (Ft. Wayne, IN)	41	7	W		
06/01	Independent (Mansfield, OH)	48	14	W		
06/02	Forest City (Cleveland)#	25	6	W		
06/03	Niagara (Buffalo)	42	6	W		
06/04	Alert (Rochester, NY)	18	9	W		
06/07	Union (Lansingburgh, NY)#	38	31	W		
06/08	National (Albany, NY)	49	8	W		
06/09	Mutual (Springfield, MA)	80	5	W		
06/10	Lowell (Boston)	29	9	W		
06/11	Tri Mountain (Boston)	40	12	W		
06/12	Harvard (Cambridge, MA)	30	11	W		
06/15	Mutual (New York)#	4	2	W		
06/16	Atlantic (Brooklyn)#	32	10	W		
06/17	Eckford (Brooklyn)#	24	5	W		
06/18	Irvington (Irvington, NJ)#	20	4	W		
06/19	Olympic (Philadelphia)	22	11	W		
06/21	Athletic (Philadelphia)#	27	18	W		
06/22	Keystone (Philadelphia)#	45	30	W		
06/24	Maryland (Baltimore)#	47	7	W		
06/25	National (Washington)#	24	8	W		
06/28	Olympic (Washington)#	16	5	W		
07/03	Olympic (Washington)#	25	14	W		
07/05	Olympic (Washington)#	32	10	W		
07/10	Forest City (Rockford, IL)	34	13	W		
07/13	Olympic (Washington)#	19	7	W		
07/22	Buckeye (Cincinnati)	71	15	W		
07/24	Forest City (Rockford, IL)	15	14	W		
07/30	Cream City (Milwaukee)	85	7	W		
07/31	Forest City (Rockford, IL)	53	32	W		
08/02	Forest City (Rockford, IL)	28	7	W		
08/04	Central City (Syracuse, NY)	37	9	W		
08/05	Central City (Syracuse, NY)	36	22	W		
08/06	Forest City (Cleveland)#	43	27	W		
08/11	Riverside (Portsmouth, OH)	40	0	W		
08/16	Eckford (Brooklyn)#	45	18	W		
08/23	Southern (New Orleans, LA)	35	3	W		
08/26	Union (Lansingburgh, NY)#	*17	17	W		
08/31	Buckeye (Cincinnati)	103	8	W		
09/02	Alert (Rochester, NY)	32	19	W		
09/09	Olympic (Pittsburgh)	54	2	W		
09/15	Union (St. Louis)	70	9	W		
09/16	Empire (St. Louis)	31	14	W		
09/25	Eagle (San Francisco)	35	4	W		
09/27	Eagle (San Francisco)	58	4	W		
09/29	Pacific (San Francisco)	66	4	W		
09/30	Pacific (San Francisco)	54	5	W		
10/01	Atlantic (San Francisco)	76	5	W		
10/11	Omaha (Omaha, NE)	65	1	W		
10/12	Otoes (Omaha, NE)	56	3	W		
10/13	Occidental (Quincy, IL)	51	7	W		
10/15	Marion (Indianapolis)	63	4	W		
10/18	Athletic (Philadelphia)#	17	12	W		
11/03	Kentucky (Louisville)	59	8	W		
11/06	Mutual (New York)#	17	8	W		

Professional games
* Union club withdrew during 6th inning following dispute with umpire, who then declared Cincinnati victors.

CINCINNATI (cont.)
Cincinnati, OH

BATTERS	POS	GP	HL	A	O	R	A	O	H	A	O	TB	A	O
Charles Gould	1B	57	191	3	20	258	4	30	217	3	46	363	6	21
Charlie Sweasy	2B	57	155	2	41	248	4	20	219	3	48	422	7	23
George Wright	SS,P	57	116	2	2	339	5	54	304	5	19	614	10	44
Fred Waterman	3B	57	156	2	42	293	5	8	228	3	55	377	6	35
Harry Wright	OF,P	57	186	3	15	232	4	4	221	3	50	332	5	47
Cal McVey	OF	57	146	2	32	262	4	34	217	3	46	348	6	6
Andy Leonard	OF	54	146	2	38	247	4	31	211	3	49	358	6	34
Doug Allison	C	53	140	2	34	246	4	34	210	3	51	331	6	13
Asa Brainard	P,OF	55	159	2	49	233	4	13	195	3	30	278	5	3

PITCHERS	IP	R	A	O
Asa Brainard	338	405	1	65
Harry Wright	118	145	1	27
George Wright	14	18	1	4

ECKFORD   47 - 8   (15 - 8)
Brooklyn, NY

DATE	OPPONENT	SCORE		W	L	T
05/17	Olympic (New York)	60	5	W		
05/24	Olympic (New York)	35	3	W		
05/27	Alpha (Brooklyn)	30	3	W		
06/03	Rose Hill (Fordham, NY)	10	6	W		
06/05	Mutual (New York)#	6	1	W		
06/12	Mutual (New York)#	8	24		L	
06/17	Cincinnati (Cincinnati)#	5	24		L	
06/19	Union (Lansingburgh, NY)#	22	14	W		
06/24	Athletic (Brooklyn)	32	5	W		
06/26	Harmonic (Brooklyn)	58	6	W		
07/01	Rose Hill (Fordham, NY)	34	14	W		
07/02	Jasper (New York)	50	7	W		
07/03	Mutual (New York)#	31	5	W		
07/07	Harvard (Cambridge, MA)	17	5	W		
07/12	Powhatan (Brooklyn)	52	12	W		
07/19	Oriental (New York)	33	15	W		
07/21	Athletic (Brooklyn)	43	5	W		
07/23	Irvington (Irvington, NJ)#	45	16	W		
07/28	Irvington (Irvington, NJ)#	25	7	W		
07/29	Maryland (Baltimore)#	24	6	W		
08/02	Oriental (New York)	25	12	W		
08/09	Ontario (Oswego, NY)	37	9	W		
08/10	Central City (Syracuse, NY)	41	13	W		
08/11	Alert (Rochester, NY)	38	27	W		
08/12	Forest City (Cleveland)#	41	27	W		
08/13	Independent (Mansfield, OH)	34	19	W		
08/14	Buckeye (Cincinnati)	37	16	W		
08/16	Cincinnati (Cincinnati)#	18	45		L	
08/18	Detroit (Detroit)	42	12	W		
08/19	Niagara (Buffalo)	24	18	W		
08/20	Young Canadian (Woodstock, ON)	29	16	W		
08/21	Union (Lansingburgh, NY)#	20	17	W		
09/01	Mutual (New York)#	25	28		L	
09/02	Resolute (Elizabeth, NJ)	64	17	W		
09/03	Alpha (Brooklyn)	30	17	W		
09/06	Atlantic (Brooklyn)	25	45		L	
09/10	Excelsior (Brooklyn)	14	7	W		
09/11	Active (Wappinger Falls, NY)	31	8	W		
09/16	Athletic (Philadelphia)#	39	16	W		
09/18	Mutual (New York)#	16	8	W		
09/20	Harmonic (Brooklyn)	30	23	W		
09/21	Union (Morrisania, NY)	18	11	W		
10/01	Union (Lansingburgh, NY)#	23	19	W		

ECKFORD (cont.)
Brooklyn, NY

DATE	OPPONENT	SCORE		W	L	T
10/05	Olympic (Washington)#	11	10	W		
10/06	Maryland (Baltimore)#	14	13	W		
10/07	Maryland (Baltimore)#	16	21		L	
10/08	National (Washington)#	2	5		L	
10/09	Atlantic (Brooklyn)#	23	9	W		
10/11	Resolute (Elizabeth, NJ)	17	5	W		
10/18	Powhatan (Brooklyn)	45	4	W		
10/20	Yale (New Haven, CT)	24	8	W		
10/21	Tri Mountain (Boston)	26	17	W		
10/22	Lowell (Boston)	38	33	W		
11/08	Atlantic (Brooklyn)#	12	16		L	
11/18	Mutual (New York)#	11	4	W		

Professional games

BATTERS	POS	GP	HL	A O	R	A O	H	A O	TB	A O
Andy Allison	1B	*53	126	3 3	133	3 10	176	3 20	347	6 29
Tom Patterson	2B	*52	116	2 36	133	3 13	178	3 22	263	5 3
Ed Pinkham	SS,OF	*51	107	2 27	127	3 7	171	3 18	288	5 33
Jack Nelson	3B	*55	130	3 1	128	2 42	171	3 6	251	4 31
Charley Hodes	OF,C	*53	98	2 14	137	3 11	178	3 19	253	4 41
Fred Treacey	OF	*48	90	2 18	125	3 17	153	3 9	230	4 38
John Eggler	OF	*33	77	2 25	74	2 22	81	2 15	125	3 16
Nat Jewett	C	*30	67	3 1	64	2 20	85	2 25	126	4 6
Al Martin	P	*52	116	2 32	132	3 6	164	3 8	204	3 48
James Wood	2B	*23	52	2 12	67	3 7	73	3 4	100	4 21
Tom Devyr	SS	*9	16	2 2	18	2 4	19	2 1	25	2 7
S. Carlton	SS	*7	15	3 2	9	2 1	12	1 5	15	2 1
Courtney	C	6	22	3 4	17	2 5	18	3 0	22	3 4

* Hands lost and runs not counted for all games

ATHLETIC   45 - 8   (15 - 7)
Philadelphia, PA

DATE	OPPONENT	SCORE		W	L	T
04/24	Princeton (Princeton, NJ)	28	27	W		
04/28	Olympic (Philadelphia)	36	23	W		
05/08	Union (Camden, NJ)	36	5	W		
05/15	Intrepid (Philadelphia)	21	8	W		
05/17	Union (Camden, NJ)	37	18	W		
05/26	Olympic (Philadelphia)	45	29	W		
05/29	Intrepid (Philadelphia)	35	21	W		
06/04	Keystone (Philadelphia)#	25	24	W		
06/07	Olympic (Philadelphia)	36	26	W		
06/12	Keystone (Philadelphia)#	38	26	W		
06/16	Young America C.C. (Philadelphia)	76	43	W		
06/21	Cincinnati (Cincinnati)#	18	27		L	
06/28	Olympic (Philadelphia)	30	11	W		
07/03	Expert (Philadelphia)	49	25	W		
07/05	Atlantic (Brooklyn)#	48	51		L	
07/09	Harvard (Cambridge, MA)	21	35		L	
07/12	Atlantic (Brooklyn)#	36	21	W		
07/17	Olympic (Washington)	39	35	W		
07/22	Expert (Philadelphia)	99	19	W		
07/26	Maryland (Baltimore)#	39	27	W		
08/01	Arcadia (Doylestown, PA)	57	6	W		
08/02	Maryland (Baltimore)#	73	23	W		
08/11	National (Philadelphia)	52	19	W		
08/16	Oriental (New York)	49	24	W		
08/18	Schuylkill (Reading, PA)	46	14	W		
08/19	Mountain City (Pottsville, PA)	107	2	W		

ATHLETIC (cont.)
Philadelphia, PA

DATE	OPPONENT	SCORE		W	L	T
08/20	Riverside (Cattawissa, PA)	69	7	W		
08/21	Independent (Bloomsburg, PA)	114	5	W		
08/30	Olympic (Washington)#	30	28	W		
08/31	National (Washington)#	32	20	W		
09/01	Maryland (Baltimore)#	24	28		L	
09/02	Pastime (Baltimore)	33	29	W		
09/06	Union (Lansingburgh, NY)#	18	17	W		
09/08	Mutual (New York)#	45	28	W		
09/13	Schuylkill (Reading, PA)	88	14	W		
09/15	Mutual (New York)#	24	22	W		
09/16	Eckford (Brooklyn)#	16	39		L	
09/18	National (Washington)#	26	16	W		
09/20	Keystone (Philadelphia)#	32	21	W		
09/25	Olympic (Philadelphia)	18	7	W		
09/27	Wissahickon (Germantown, PA)	74	20	W		
09/29	Olive (Philadelphia)	67	7	W		
10/02	Olympic (Philadelphia)	21	17	W		
10/06	Roxborough (Manayunk, PA)	63	19	W		
10/09	Keystone (Philadelphia)#	37	12	W		
10/11	Atlantic (Brooklyn)#	11	20		L	
11/13	Brandywine (W. Chester, PA)	70	20	W		
10/15	Mountaineer (Ebensburgh, PA)	45	12	W		
10/16	Kickenepawling (Johnstown, PA)	49	8	W		
10/18	Cincinnati (Cincinnati)#	12	17		L	
10/25	Atlantic (Brooklyn)#	17	37		L	
10/27	Brandywine (W. Chester, PA)	43	24	W		
11/06	Keystone (Philadelphia)#	44	10	W		

\# Professional games

BATTERS	POS	GP	HL	A	O	R	A	O	H	A	O	TB	A	O
Wes Fisler	1B	39	125	3	8	171	4	15	171	4	15	299	7	26
Al Reach	2B	46	118	2	26	248	5	18	242	5	12	419	9	5
Tom Berry	SS,OF	45	128	2	38	178	3	43	164	3	29	234	5	9
Jim Foran	3B	31	84	2	22	147	4	23	147	4	23	231	7	13
John Sensenderfer	OF	48	128	2	32	240	5	0	219	4	27	356	7	20
Ned Cuthbert	OF	47	137	2	43	241	5	6	205	4	17	362	8	26
Levi Meyerle	OF,C,P	34	98	2	30	135	3	33	128	3	26	205	6	1
John McMullin	C,P	49	134	2	36	238	4	42	222	4	26	352	7	9
Dick McBride	P,2B	34	93	2	25	170	5	0	182	5	12	278	8	6
John Radcliff	C	30	72	2	12	164	5	14	150	5	0	262	8	22
Isaac Wilkins	SS,OF	11	39	3	6	54	4	10	43	3	10	87	7	10
George Heubel	1B	8	30	3	6	28	3	4	28	3	4	40	5	0
Hicks Hayhurst	OF	5	12	2	2	30	6	0	25	5	0	36	7	0

ATLANTIC 40 - 6 - 2 (15 - 6 - 1)
Brooklyn, NY

DATE	OPPONENT	SCORE		W	L	T
04/16	Alpha (Brooklyn)	42	11	W		
05/03	Powhatan (Brooklyn)	17	1	W		
05/06	Alpha (Brooklyn)	32	16	W		
05/07	Keystone (Philadelphia)#	36	23	W		
05/10	Alpha (Brooklyn)	45	14	W		
05/14	Princeton (Princeton, NJ)	24	3	W		
05/17	Champion (Jersey City, NJ)	52	2	W		
05/24	Irvington (Irvington, NJ)#	28	11	W		
05/27	Olympic (New York)	89	7	W		
05/31	Union (Lansingburgh, NY)#	19	19			T
06/03	Eagle (Flatbush, NY)	59	9	W		
06/14	Alpha (Brooklyn)	34	6	W		
06/16	Cincinnati (Cincinnati)#	10	32		L	

ATLANTIC (cont.)
Brooklyn, NY

DATE	OPPONENT	SCORE		W	L	T
06/17	Powhatan (Brooklyn)	55	8	W		
06/19	Picked Nine (Boston)	28	28			T
06/21	Union (Lansingburgh, NY)#	21	4	W		
06/28	Mutual (New York)#	2	1	W		
07/03	Star (Brooklyn)	15	10	W		
07/05	Athletic (Philadelphia)#	51	48	W		
07/12	Athletic (Philadelphia)#	21	36		L	
07/16	Athletic (Brooklyn)	30	22	W		
07/23	Oriental (New York)	81	3	W		
07/30	Maryland (Baltimore)#	24	8	W		
08/02	Union (Lansingburgh, NY)#	10	17		L	
08/05	Union (Morrisania, NY)	34	8	W		
08/09	Union (Lansingburgh, NY)#	25	11	W		
08/12	Athletic (Brooklyn)	29	8	W		
08/14	Eagle (Flatbush, NY)	55	21	W		
08/21	Keystone (Philadelphia)#	34	2	W		
08/25	Union (Brooklyn)	95	12	W		
08/27	Olympic (New York)	89	10	W		
08/28	Star (Brooklyn)	27	22	W		
09/06	Eckford (Brooklyn)#	45	25	W		
09/16	Harmonic (Brooklyn)	38	12	W		
09/23	National (Washington)#	21	10	W		
09/25	Star (Brooklyn)	17	13	W		
09/27	Union (Brooklyn)	64	6	W		
09/29	Union (Lansingburgh, NY)#	13	16		L	
09/30	Harmonic (Brooklyn)	22	9	W		
10/06	Union (Morrisania, NY)	24	14	W		
10/08	Oriental (New York)	32	18	W		
10/09	Eckford (Brooklyn)#	9	23		L	
10/11	Athletic (Philadelphia)#	20	11	W		
10/19	Mutual (New York)#	5	12		L	
10/25	Athletic (Philadelphia)#	37	17	W		
10/26	Keystone (Philadelphia)#	22	13	W		
10/28	Mutual (New York)#	13	10	W		
11/08	Eckford (Brooklyn)#	15	12	W		

Professional games

BATTERS	POS	GP	HL	A	O	R	A	O	H	A	O	TB	A	O
Joe Start	1B	46	119	2	27	202	4	18	203	4	19	341	7	19
Lip Pike	2B	48	112	2	16	193	4	1	175	3	31	325	6	37
Dickey Pearce	SS	47	154	3	13	174	3	33	175	3	34	236	5	1
Charles Smith	3B	33	91	2	25	120	3	21	132	4	0	173	5	8
Curtis Chapman	OF	48	121	2	25	197	4	5	197	4	5	313	6	25
Dan McDonald	OF	42	108	2	24	140	3	14	139	3	13	198	4	30
Fred Crane	OF	41	128	3	5	141	3	18	140	3	17	178	4	14
Bob Ferguson	C	47	138	2	44	174	3	33	167	3	26	274	5	39
George Zettlein	P	33	104	3	5	104	3	5	102	3	3	141	4	9
Oliver Brown	OF	13	50	3	11	36	2	10	40	3	1	62	4	10
Charles Hunt	OF	11	31	2	9	34	3	1	24	2	2	35	3	2
John Kenney	3B	9	34	3	7	43	4	7	40	4	4	61	6	7
Tom Pratt	P	6	22	3	4	12	2	0	19	3	1	22	3	4

MUTUAL 36 - 16 (11 - 15)
New York, NY

DATE	OPPONENT	SCORE		W	L	T
05/04	Olympic (New York)	38	8	W		
05/11	Olympic (New York)	57	9	W		
05/14	Champion (Jersey City, NJ)	39	14	W		
05/20	Irvington (Irvington, NJ)#	28	16	W		
05/24	Tri Mountain (Boston)	69	17	W		

MUTUAL (cont.)
New York, NY

DATE	OPPONENT	SCORE		W	L	T
05/25	Harvard (Cambridge, MA)	43	11	W		
05/26	Lowell (Boston)	26	21	W		
06/01	Irvington (Irvington, NJ)#	23	16	W		
06/04	Oriental (New York)	16	6	W		
06/05	Eckford (Brooklyn)#	1	6		L	
06/08	Gotham (New York)	33	15	W		
06/09	Yale (New Haven, CT)	18	16	W		
06/11	Oriental (New York)	20	15	W		
06/12	Eckford (Brooklyn)#	24	8	W		
06/15	Cincinnati (Cincinnati)#	2	4		L	
06/18	Union (Lansingburgh, NY)#	22	23		L	
06/19	Star (Brooklyn)	12	26		L	
06/23	Yale (New Haven, CT	15	5	W		
06/28	Atlantic (Brooklyn)#	1	2		L	
07/03	Eckford (Brooklyn)#	5	31		L	
07/06	Union (Lansingburgh, NY)#	20	32		L	
07/30	Social (New York)	31	10	W		
07/31	Maryland (Baltimore)#	24	33		L	
08/06	Harmonic (Brooklyn)	46	11	W		
08/10	Irvington (Irvington, NJ)#	32	10	W		
08/14	Star (Brooklyn)	22	18	W		
08/18	Union (Morrisania, NY)	83	8	W		
08/19	Ross (Harlem, NY)	49	5	W		
08/20	Keystone (Philadelphia)#	31	18	W		
08/23	National (Washington)#	16	18		L	
08/24	Olympic (Washington)#	15	32		L	
08/25	Maryland (Baltimore)#	27	18	W		
08/26	Pastime (Baltimore)	21	13	W		
08/27	Keystone (Philadelphia)#	29	19	W		
09/01	Eckford (Brooklyn)#	28	25	W		
09/02	Powhatan (Brooklyn)	49	12	W		
09/03	Irvington (Irvington, NJ)#	34	8	W		
09/08	Athletic (Philadelphia)#	28	45		L	
09/13	Union (Morrisania, NY)	26	10	W		
09/15	Athletic (Philadelphia)#	22	24		L	
09/18	Eckford (Brooklyn)#	8	16		L	
09/21	National (Washington)#	42	16	W		
10/02	Star (Brooklyn)	16	6	W		
10/---	Gramercy (New York)	51	8	W		
10/12	Bergen (Bergen, NJ)	44	10	W		
10/14	Rose Hill (Fordham, NY)	11	10	W		
10/16	Oriental (New York)	22	11	W		
10/19	Atlantic (Brooklyn)#	12	5	W		
10/22	Gramercy (New York)	53	19	W		
10/28	Atlantic (Brooklyn)#	10	13		L	
11/06	Cincinnati (Cincinnati)#	8	17		L	
11/18	Eckford (Brooklyn)#	4	11		L	

Professional games

BATTERS	POS	GP	HL	A	O	R	A	O	H	A	O	TB	A	O
Everett Mills	1B	50	140	2	40	169	3	19	177	3	27	251	5	1
George Flanly	2B	36	91	2	19	129	3	21	130	3	22	174	4	30
James Carlton	SS	24	80	3	8	52	2	4	48	2	0	67	2	19
John Hatfield	3B	48	122	2	26	177	3	33	160	3	16	230	4	38
Martin Swandell	OF	50	149	2	49	131	2	31	136	2	36	189	3	39
Dave Eggler	OF	50	144	2	44	130	2	30	137	2	37	195	3	45
Billy McMahon	OF	26	76	2	24	66	2	14	63	2	11	88	3	10
Charley Mills	C	48	139	2	43	142	2	46	139	2	43	200	4	8
Rynie Wolters	P	43	108	2	22	115	2	29	131	3	2	199	4	27
Charles Hunt	OF	16	46	2	14	42	2	10	40	2	8	57	3	9
Richard Hunt	OF	12	27	2	3	41	3	5	37	3	1	47	3	11
Billy Lewis	OF	11	47	4	3	31	2	9	30	2	8	42	3	9
Tom Devyr	SS	11	39	3	6	29	2	7	27	2	5	39	3	6
Andrew Gedney	OF	10	32	3	2	14	1	4	18	1	8	27	2	7

UNION 24 - 9 - 1 (12 - 8 - 1)
Lansingburgh, NY

DATE	OPPONENT	SCORE		W	L	T
05/31	Atlantic (Brooklyn)#	19	19			T
06/07	Cincinnati (Cincinnati)#	31	37		L	
06/15	Old Elm (Pittsfield, MA)	57	4	W		
06/18	Mutual (New York)#	23	22	W		
06/19	Eckford (Brooklyn)#	14	22		L	
06/21	Atlantic (Brooklyn)#	4	21		L	
07/05	Tri Mountain (Boston)	63	24	W		
07/07	Mutual (New York)#	32	20	W		
07/14	Harvard (Cambridge, MA)	22	10	W		
07/22	National (Albany, NY)	53	14	W		
07/30	Ancient City (Schnectady, NY)	107	2	W		
08/02	Atlantic (Brooklyn)#	17	10	W		
08/07	Alert (Rochester)	53	15	W		
08/09	Atlantic (Brooklyn)#	11	25		L	
08/19	Keystone (Philadelphia)#	31	9	W		
08/21	Eckford (Brooklyn)#	17	20		L	
08/23	Forest City (Cleveland)#	34	21	W		
08/24	Independent (Mansfield, OH)	44	20	W		
08/26	Cincinnati (Cincinnati)#	*17	17		L	
08/28	Kentucky (Louisville)	31	11	W		
08/30	Baltic (Wheeling, WV)	50	16	W		
09/01	National (Washington)#	37	24	W		
09/02	Union (Washington)	73	11	W		
09/03	Pastime (Baltimore)	14	15		L	
09/04	Maryland (Baltimore)#	25	12	W		
09/06	Athletic (Philadelphia)#	17	18		L	
09/07	Keystone (Philadelphia)#	@9	0	W		
09/07	Keystone (Philadelphia)#	29	22	W		
09/09	Niagara (Buffalo)	34	9	W		
09/17	Forest City (Cleveland)#	32	23	W		
09/20	National (Washington)#	24	17	W		
09/29	Atlantic (Brooklyn)#	16	13	W		
10/01	Eckford (Brooklyn)#	19	23		L	
10/07	Buckskin (Gloversville, NY)	33	20	W		

\# Professional games
* Union club withdrew during 6th inning following dispute with umpire, who then declared Cincinnati victors.
@ Forfeit

BATTERS	POS	GP	HL	A	O	R	A	O	H	A	O	TB	A	O
Bub McAtee	1B	30	71	2	11	134	4	14	125	4	5	156	5	6
Charley Bearman	2B,P	31	88	2	26	95	3	2	88	2	26	128	4	4
Mike Powers	SS	32	99	3	3	109	3	13	92	2	28	129	4	1
Steve Bellan	3B	30	87	2	27	99	3	9	91	3	1	142	4	22
Mart King	OF,C,1B	34	71	2	3	137	4	1	146	4	10	234	6	18
Clipper Flynn	OF,2B	34	93	2	15	118	3	16	112	3	13	154	4	18
Steve King	OF	33	85	2	19	127	3	28	112	3	13	158	4	30
Bill Craver	C,OF	32	73	2	9	117	3	21	115	3	13	158	4	30
Cherokee Fisher	P,2B	33	100	3	-1	112	3	13	103	3	4	157	4	25
William Abrams	OF,1B	9	25	2	7	34	3	7	27	3	0	37	4	1

OLYMPIC 22 - 14 (9 - 12)
Washington, DC

DATE	OPPONENT	SCORE		W	L	T
05/18	Jefferson (Washington)	44	10	W		
---/---	Maryland (Baltimore)#	10	14		L	
05/---	Union (Washington)#	60	16	W		
05/20	Maryland (Baltimore)#	26	10	W		
05/25	National (Washington)#	27	33		L	
06/17	Pastime (Baltimore)	22	15	W		
06/18	Maryland (Baltimore)#	41	15	W		

OLYMPIC (cont.)
Washington, DC

DATE	OPPONENT	SCORE		W	L	T
06/22	Maryland (Baltimore)#	13	31		L	
06/28	Cincinnati (Cincinnati)#	5	16		L	
07/03	Cincinnati (Cincinnati)#	14	25		L	
07/05	Cincinnati (Cincinnati)#	10	32		L	
07/06	Kentucky (Louisville, KY)	44	9	W		
07/08	Forest City (Cleveland)#	20	28		L	
07/09	Forest City (Cleveland)#	44	19	W		
07/10	Independent (Mansfield, OH)	49	18	W		
07/12	Buckeye (Cincinnati)	36	11	W		
07/13	Cincinnati (Cincinnati)#	7	19		L	
07/14	Riverside (Portsmouth, OH)	23	15	W		
07/16	Keystone (Philadelphia)#	31	45		L	
07/17	Athletic (Philadelphia)#	35	39		L	
07/19	Star (Brooklyn)	11	49		L	
07/--	National (Washington)#	20	17	W		
08/11	Union (Washington)	29	10	W		
08/17	National (Washington)#	42	18	W		
08/21	National (Washington)#	22	9	W		
08/24	Mutual (New York)#	32	15	W		
08/30	Athletic (Philadelphia)#	28	30		L	
09/09	Jefferson (Washington)	45	5	W		
09/20	Alert (Washington)	56	4	W		
09/27	Excelsior (Brooklyn)	38	13	W		
10/01	Keystone (Philadelphia)#	11	8	W		
10/05	Eckford (Brooklyn)#	10	11		L	
10/09	Union (Washington)	18	6	W		
10/12	Mutual (Washington)	24	15	W		
10/18	National (Washington)#	13	11	W		

(Only scores extant)

Professional games

BATTERS	POS	GP	HL	A	O	R	A	O	H	A	O	TB	A	O
Harry McLean	1B	*22	64	2	20	59	2	15	58	2	14	76	3	10
Bob Reach	2B,SS	*24	76	3	4	74	3	2	62	2	14	86	3	14
Davy Force	SS,3B	*26	66	2	14	99	3	21	80	3	2	121	4	17
M.E. Urell	3B,1B	*16	55	3	7	35	2	3	38	2	6	58	3	10
Nick Young	OF,1B	*26	72	2	20	82	3	4	78	3	0	108	4	4
A.V. Robinson	OF	*25	81	3	6	64	2	14	53	2	3	86	3	11
Eddie Woods	OF	*15	42	2	12	39	2	9	40	2	10	58	3	13
Fergy Malone	C,1B	*25	50	2	0	100	4	0	92	3	17	144	5	19
Ed Leech	P	*26	70	2	18	74	2	22	69	2	17	82	3	4
Dick Hurley	3B	*8	26	3	2	18	2	2	19	2	3	38	4	6
William Miller	1B	*7	24	3	3	18	2	4	21	3	0	29	4	1
Sam Yeatman		*5	10	2	0	7	1	2	10	2	0	11	2	1
Denison	OF,1B	5	16	3	1	17	3	2						
Barrett	3B	5	18	3	3	15	3	0						

* Averages do not include nine "friendly" games.

FOREST CITY 19 - 6 (1 - 6)
Cleveland, OH

DATE	OPPONENT	SCORE		W	L	T
06/02	Cincinnati (Cincinnati)#	6	25		L	
06/24	Boanerges (Hiram College, OH)	20	5	W		
06/29	Independent (Mansfield, OH)	44	7	W		
07/01	Reserve (Hudson, OH)*	75	17	W		
07/05	Detroit (Detroit)	25	10	W		
07/08	Olympic (Washington)#	28	20	W		
07/09	Olympic (Washington)#	19	44		L	
07/23	Detroit (Detroit)	54	9	W		

FOREST CITY (cont.)
Cleveland, OH

DATE	OPPONENT	SCORE		W	L	T
07/30	Central City (Syracuse, NY)	29	23	W		
08/06	Cincinnati (Cincinnati)#*	27	43		L	
08/09	Niagara (Buffalo)	40	36	W		
08/12	Eckford (Brooklyn)#	27	44		L	
08/23	Union (Lansingburgh, NY)#	21	34		L	
09/01	Alert (Rochester, NY)	34	29	W		
09/13	Union (Lansingburgh, NY)#*	23	32		L	
09/14	Central City (Syracuse, NY)	39	11	W		
09/15	Alert (Rochester, NY)	18	8	W		
09/16	Niagara (Buffalo)	32	22	W		
09/24	Star (Painesville, OH)	54	11	W		
10/09	Resolute (Oberlin, OH)	17	2	W		

(Only scores extant)

\# Professional games
* Box score not available

BATTERS	POS	GP	HL	A	O	R	A	O	H	A	O	TB	A	O
Art Allison	1B	15	43	2	13	36	2	6						
Hanna	2B	10	35	3	5	29	2	9						
Eb Smith	SS	16	38	2	6	54	3	6						
A.R. Smith	3B	15	32	2	2	59	3	14						
Burt	OF	15	40	2	10	48	3	3						
John Riley	OF	14	41	2	13	39	2	11						
John Ward	OF,2B,C	13	44	3	5	38	2	12						
James White	C	8	20	2	4	26	3	2						
Al Pratt	P	16	49	3	1	46	2	14						
Sheffield	OF	8	16	2	0	33	4	1						
H. Brown	OF,2B	6	15	2	3	22	3	4						
Bradbeer	OF	5	2	1	8	4	0							

MARYLAND   14 - 13   (7 - 12)
Baltimore, MD

DATE	OPPONENT	SCORE		W	L	T
05/20	Olympic (Washington)#	10	26		L	
06/03	Arctic (Baltimore)	63	19	W		
---/---	Olympic (Washington)#	14	10	W		
06/18	Olympic (Washington)#	15	41		L	
06/22	Olympic (Washington)#	31	13	W		
06/24	Cincinnati (Cincinnati)#	7	47		L	
07/05	Keystone (Philadelphia)#	38	27	W		
07/16	Pastime (Baltimore)	55	19	W		
07/26	Athletic (Philadelphia)#	27	39		L	
07/29	Eckford (Brooklyn)#	6	24		L	
07/30	Atlantic (Brooklyn)#	8	24		L	
07/31	Mutual (New York)#	33	24	W		
08/02	Keystone (Philadelphia)#	24	31		L	
08/03	Athletic (Philadelphia)#	23	73		L	
08/19	Oriental (New York)	28	15	W		
08/25	Mutual (New York)#	18	27		L	
09/01	Athletic (Philadelphia)#	28	24	W		
09/04	Union (Lansingburgh, NY)#	12	25		L	
09/16	National (Washington)#	23	12	W		
09/17	Pastime (Baltimore)	12	31		L	
09/20	Jefferson (Washington)	29	19	W		
09/29	Keystone (Philadelphia)#	11	26		L	
10/01	Pastime (Baltimore)	27	21	W		
10/06	Eckford (Brooklyn)#	13	14		L	
10/07	Eckford (Brooklyn)#	21	16	W		

MARYLAND (cont.)
Baltimore, MD

DATE	OPPONENT	SCORE		W	L	T
10/26	Pastime (Baltimore)	52	16	W		
---/---	Ft. Monroe (Ft. Monroe, VA)	29	3	W		

Professional games

BATTERS	POS	GP	HL	A	O	R	A	O	H	A	O	TB	A	O
Reese	1B	10	31	3	1	24	2	4						
Wally Goldsmith	2B,C	26	75	2	23	76	2	24						
Frank Selman	SS	19	57	3	0	42	2	4						
Buck	3B	17	41	2	7	44	2	19						
Ed Mincher	OF	24	69	2	21	59	2	11						
Sam Armstrong	OF	24	63	2	15	52	2	4						
Mike Hooper	OF	22	52	2	8	77	3	1						
Bill Lennon	C	26	70	2	18	76	2	24						
Elias Cope	P	14	37	2	9	44	3	2						
Tully Worthington	OF	18	48	2	12	44	2	8						
Bobby Mathews	P	15	59	3	14	30	2	0						
Wilson	1B	9	28	3	1	27	3	0						
Lucas	2B,3B,1B	7	24	3	3	9	1	2						
Keerle	SS	6	19	3	1	14	2	2						

NATIONAL   13 - 13   (4 - 12)
Washington, DC

DATE	OPPONENT	SCORE		W	L	T
05/25	Olympic (Washington)#	33	27	W		
06/23	Union (Washington)	34	9	W		
06/25	Cincinnati (Cincinnati)#	8	24		L	
07/04	Jefferson (Washington)	38	15	W		
07/14	Jefferson (Washington)	56	35	W		
07/---	Olympic (Washington)#	17	20		L	
08/17	Olympic (Washington)#	18	42		L	
08/20	Oriental (New York)	48	8	W		
08/21	Olympic (Washington)#	9	22		L	
08/23	Mutual (New York)#	18	16	W		
08/31	Athletic (Philadelphia)#	20	32		L	
09/01	Union (Lansingburgh, NY)#	24	37		L	
09/03	Jefferson (Washington)	15	17		L	
09/13	Jefferson (Washington)	46	15	W		
09/15	Athletic (Philadelphia)#	16	26		L	
09/16	Maryland (Baltimore)#	12	23		L	
09/20	Union (Lansingburgh, NY)#	17	24		L	
09/21	Mutual (New York)#	16	42		L	
09/23	Atlantic (Brooklyn)#	10	21		L	
09/24	Oriental (New York)	36	21	W		
09/25	Excelsior (Brooklyn)	58	11	W		
09/30	Jefferson (Washington)	23	15	W		
10/02	Keystone (Philadelphia)#	13	11	W		
10/08	Eckford (Brooklyn)#	5	2	W		
10/18	Olympic (Washington)#	11	13	W		

(Only scores extant)

Professional games

BATTERS	POS	GP	HL	A	O	R	A	O	H	A	O	TB	A	O
Tom Forker	1B	23	69	3	0	58	2	12	61	2	11	77	3	8
Andrew Gibney	2B,3B	14	29	2	1	53	3	11	53	3	11	81	5	11
Dennis Coughlin	SS,3B	22	55	2	11	68	3	2	69	3	3	95	4	7
Ed Shelley	3B,SS	24	59	2	11	72	3	0	64	2	16	85	3	13
Sy Studley	OF	24	63	2	15	70	2	22	67	2	19	183	3	17
George Joyce	OF	21	64	3	1	55	2	13	44	2	2	55	2	13
George Fox	OF,3B	17	52	3	1	47	2	13	40	2	6	70	4	2

NATIONAL (cont.)
Washington, DC

BATTERS	POS	GP	HL	A	O	R	A	O	H	A	O	TB	A	O
Dave Birdsall	C,P	23	62	2	16	60	2	14	54	2	8	93	4	1
Osborn	P	14	45	3	3	27	1	13	24	1	10	30	2	2
John Hollingshead	OF,2B	16	46	2	14	34	2	2	34	2	2	52	3	4
Brown	OF,C	9	29	3	2	24	2	6						
Lusk	3B,SS	7	20	2	6	19	2	5	16	2	2	52	3	4
Will Williams	P	5	6	1	1	16	3	1	12	2	2	15	3	0

KEYSTONE   12 - 21 - 1   (3 - 17)
Philadelphia, PA

DATE	OPPONENT	SCORE		W	L	T
05/07	Atlantic (Brooklyn)#	23	36		L	
05/14	Olympic (Philadelphia)	10	19		L	
05/11	Chestnut St. Th. (Philadelphia)	32	21	W		
05/18	Chestnut St. Th. (Philadelphia)	52	23	W		
05/22	Olympic (Philadelphia)	15	20		L	
05/25	Expert (Philadelphia)	42	30	W		
05/28	Rescue (Philadelphia)	42	34	W		
06/04	Athletic (Philadelphia)#	24	25		L	
06/08	Expert (Philadelphia)	37	37			T
06/12	Athletic (Philadelphia)#	26	38		L	
06/22	Cincinnati (Cincinnati)#	30	45		L	
07/05	Maryland (Baltimore)#	27	38		L	
07/10	Harvard (Cambridge, MA)	24	18	W		
07/16	Olympic (Washington)#	45	31	W		
07/17	City Item (Philadelphia)	47	14	W		
07/30	City Item (Philadelphia)	80	26	W		
08/02	Maryland (Baltimore)#	31	24	W		
08/17	Oriental (New York)	45	17	W		
08/19	Union (Lansingburgh, NY)#	9	31		L	
08/20	Mutual (New York)#	18	31		L	
08/21	Atlantic (Brooklyn)#	2	34		L	
08/27	Mutual (New York)#	19	29		L	
09/07	Union (Lansingburgh, NY)#	*0	9		L	
09/07	Union (Lansingburgh, NY)#	22	29		L	
09/14	Olympic (Philadelphia)	23	37		L	
09/20	Athletic (Philadelphia)#	21	32		L	
09/28	Olympic (Philadelphia)	7	21		L	
09/29	Maryland (Baltimore)#	26	11	W		
09/30	Pastime (Baltimore)	26	13	W		
10/01	Olympic (Washington)#	8	11		L	
10/02	National (Washington)#	11	13		L	
10/09	Athletic (Philadelphia)#	12	37		L	
10/26	Atlantic (Brooklyn)#	13	22		L	
11/06	Athletic (Philadelphia)#	10	44		L	

\# Professional games
* Forfeit

BATTERS	POS	GP	HL	A	O	R	A	O	H	A	O	TB	A	O
George Albertson	1B,2B,OF	*17	34	2	8	26	2	0	66	2	12	58	3	7
Billy Dick	2B,1B	*35	74	2	16	106	3	19	106	3	1	143	4	3
Dick Flowers	SS,P,C	*35	80	2	24	92	3	8	102	2	32	155	4	15
McClarnan	3B,OF	*15	39	3	0	35	2	9	43	2	13	64	4	4
Charley Weaver	OF,2B	*35	79	2	19	100	3	10	113	3	8	200	5	25
Joseph Gwynn	OF,P	*15	12	2	0	15	2	3	40	2	10	54	3	9
Eddie Woods	OF	*15	30	2	4	18	1	7	34	2	4	43	2	13
Ewell	C,1B	*29	52	2	10	59	2	17	80	2	22	125	4	9
George Bechtel	P,1B	*28	59	2	17	51	2	9	80	2	24	126	4	14
Phillip Culp	SS,2B	*21	50	3	2	38	2	6	59	2	17	93	4	11
Halbach	OF,C,SS	*13	23	1	11	61	5	1	54	4	2	72	5	7

KEYSTONE (cont.)
Philadelphia, PA

BATTERS	POS	GP	HL	A	O	R	A	O	H	A	O	TB	A	O
Dan Kleinfielder	OF,C,P	*12	25	2	5	37	3	7	53	4	5	74	6	2
Chick Fulmer	P	*11	16	2	0	13	1	5	23	2	1	29	2	7
McKenna	1B	*10	19	2	3	15	1	7	13	1	3	18	1	8
Allen	OF,P	5	15	3	0	20	4	0						
John Radcliff	C	5	8	1	3	18	3	3						
Henry	OF,C	5	12	2	2	9	1	4						
Clinton	OF	5	21	4	1	5	1	0						

* Hands lost and runs not available for some games

IRVINGTON 0 - 9 (0 - 8)
Irvington, NJ

DATE	OPPONENT	SCORE		W	L	T
05/20	Mutual (New York)#	16	28		L	
05/24	Atlantic (Brooklyn)#	11	28		L	
06/01	Mutual (New York)#	16	23		L	
06/18	Cincinnati (Cincinnati)#	4	20		L	
06/30	Resolute (Elizabeth, NJ)	15	16		L	
07/23	Eckford (Brooklyn)#	16	45		L	
07/29	Eckford (Brooklyn)#	7	25		L	
08/10	Mutual (New York)#	10	32		L	
09/03	Mutual (New York)#	8	34		L	

Professional games

BATTERS	POS	GP	HL	A	O	R	A	O	H	A	O	TB	A	O
Mike Campbell	1B	8	22	2	6	7	0	7	11	1	3	13	1	5
Mahlon Stockman	2B	4	11	2	3	3	0	3	6	1	2	10	2	2
William Greathead	SS	7	24	3	3	7	1	0	10	1	3	11	1	4
Farrar	3B,C	6	15	2	3	11	1	5	11	1	5	13	2	1
George Eaton	OF	7	18	2	4	11	1	4	16	2	2	21	3	0
George Lines	OF	7	19	2	5	10	1	3	13	1	6	15	2	1
A. Bailey	OF	7	21	3	0	8	1	1	9	1	2	12	1	5
T. Buckley	C	5	18	3	3	7	1	2	9	1	4	10	2	0
Hugh Campbell	P	6	15	2	3	9	1	3	19	3	1	23	3	4

TEAM STANDINGS (Professional Games Only)

CLUB	Cin	Atl	Ath	Eck	Un	Mut	Oly	Mar	Nat	Key	FC	Irv	W	L	T	PCT
Cincinnati	x	1	2	2	2	2	4	1	1	1	2	1	19	0	0	1.000
Atlantic	0	x	3	2	*2	2	0	1	1	3	0	1	15	6	1	.705
Athletic	0	1	x	0	1	2	2	2	2	5	0	0	15	7	0	.682
Eckford	0	1	1	x	3	4	1	2	0	0	1	2	15	8	0	.652
Union	0	*2	0	0	x	2	0	1	2	3	2	0	12	8	1	.595
Mutual	0	1	0	2	0	x	0	1	1	2	0	4	11	15	0	.423
Olympic	0	0	0	0	0	1	x	2	4	1	1	0	9	12	0	.429
Maryland	0	0	1	1	0	1	2	x	1	1	0	0	7	12	0	.368
National	0	0	0	1	0	1	1	0	x	1	0	0	4	12	0	.250
Keystone	0	0	0	0	0	0	1	2	0	x	0	0	3	17	0	.150
Forest City	0	0	0	0	0	0	1	0	0	0	x	0	1	6	0	.143
Irvington	0	0	0	0	0	0	0	0	0	0	0	x	0	8	0	.000

* Union and Atlantic clubs played one tie game

PROFESSIONAL TEAM TOTALS

TEAM	CITY/STATE	GP	W	L	T	PCT	R	OR
Cincinnati	Cincinnati, OH	57	57	0	0	1.000	2395	574
Eckford	Brooklyn, NY	55	47	8	0	.855	1560	758
Athletic	Philadelphia, PA	53	45	8	0	.849	2298	1093
Atlantic	Brooklyn, NY	48	40	6	2	.854	1610	654
Mutual	New York, NY	52	36	16	0	.692	1406	780
Union	Lansingburgh, NY	34	24	9	1	.721	1092	566
Olympic	Washington, DC	36	22	14	0	.611	987	669
Forest City	Cleveland, OH	25	19	6	0	.760	852	510
Maryland	Baltimore, MD	27	14	13	0	.519	657	666
National	Washington, DC	26	13	13	0	.500	640	536
Keystone	Philadelphia, PA	34	12	21	1	.368	1102	925
Irvington	Irvington, NJ	9	0	9	0	.000	103	251

AMATEUR TEAMS

LONE STAR 22 - 3
New Orleans, LA

DATE	OPPONENT	SCORE		W	L	T
01/31	Atlantic (Algiers, LA)	33	25	W		
02/21	Atlantic (Algiers, LA)	20	27		L	
02/28	Atlantic (Algiers, LA)	40	60		L	
03/05	Dramatic (Mobile, AL)	31	17	W		
03/05	Dramatic (Mobile, AL)	22	18	W		
04/04	Pelican (New Orleans)	35	17	W		
04/25	Pelican (New Orleans)	18	5	W		
05/02	Washington (New Orleans)	45	22	W		
05/09	Washington (New Orleans)	44	31	W		
05/16	Pelican (New Orleans)	44	19	W		
05/23	Southern (New Orleans)	36	26	W		
06/06	Comet (New Orleans)	21	16	W		
06/20	Comet (New Orleans)	36	29	W		
07/04	Southern (New Orleans)	26	24	W		
07/11	R.E. Lee (New Orleans)	14	10	W		
07/18	Fearless (New Orleans)	18	3	W		
07/25	Southern (New Orleans)	22	21	W		
08/22	R.E. Lee (New Orleans)	23	25		L	
10/02	Fearless (New Orleans)	26	21	W		
11/14	Surprise (New Orleans)	32	22	W		
11/20	Hancock (New Orleans)	57	16	W		
11/27	Surprise (New Orleans)	25	5	W		
12/05	Hancock (New Orleans)	47	24	W		
12/12	Comet (New Orleans)	54	14	W		
12/19	Pickwick (New Orleans)	37	7	W		

BATTERS	POS	GP	HL	A	O	R	A	O	H	A	O	TB	A	O
James G. Aymer	1B	20	62	3	2	75	3	15						
D.A. Dunn	2B,3B	19	51	2	13	65	3	8						
Ed White	SS	*4	7	3	1	8	2	0						
George Scott	3B	18	48	2	12	71	3	17						
William Tracy	OF	23	66	2	20	80	3	11						
William Carson	OF	15	43	2	13	55	2	10						
Charles Young	OF	14	42	3	0	38	2	10						
R.M. Thebault	C	13	30	2	4	54	4	2						
William Condon	P	23	42	1	19	109	4	17						
L. Keating		6	21	3	3	17	2	5						
McEnery	3B,SS,OF	*5	4	4	0	14	2	4						

* Hands lost not counted in all games

FOREST CITY 20 - 4
Rockford, IL

DATE	OPPONENT	SCORE		W	L	T
05/18	Harvard (Harvard, IL)	110	11	W		
06/09	Beloit (Beloit, WI)	37	9	W		
06/11	Hawkeye (Stillman Valley, IL)	103	6	W		
06/16	Beloit (Beloit, WI)	40	6	W		
06/30	Clipper (Monmouth, IL)	76	1	W		
07/05	Amateur (Chicago)	32	4	W		
07/06	Aetna (Chicago)	25	4	W		
07/10	Cincinnati (Cincinnati)	13	32		L	
07/19	Garden City (Chicago)	31	10	W		
07/20	Garden City (Chicago)	43	9	W		
07/24	Cincinnati (Cincinnati)	14	15		L	
07/26	Buckeye (Cincinnati)	40	1	W		
07/27	Independent (Mansfield, OH)	83	14	W		
07/29	Detroit (Detroit)	32	10	W		
07/31	Cincinnati (Cincinnati)	32	53		L	
08/02	Cincinnati (Cincinnati)	7	28		L	
08/26	Clipper (Monmouth)	47	2	W		
08/27	Occidental (Quincy, IL)	53	7	W		
08/30	Union (St. Louis)	44	11	W		
08/31	Empire (St. Louis)	70	6	W		
09/01	Relic (Jacksonville, IL)	66	3	W		
09/02	Liberty (Springfield, IL)	101	13	W		
09/03	Picked Nine (Chicago)	34	22	W		
10/06	Illinois (Morris, IL)	41	10	W		

BATTERS	POS	GP	HL	A	O	R	A	O	H	A	O	TB	A	O
Fred Cone	1B	23	70	3	1	115	5	0	96	4	4	156	6	18
Scott Hastings	2B	24	59	2	11	153	6	9	125	5	5	202	8	10
Ross Barnes	SS	23	62	2	16	134	5	19	111	4	19	174	7	6
Tom Foley	3B	24	64	2	16	139	5	19	121	5	1	196	8	4
Al Barker	OF	17	57	3	6	96	5	11	78	4	10	90	5	5
Ballard Osborne	OF	13	38	2	12	58	4	6	57	4	5	87	6	9
Chesney	OF	13	43	3	4	53	3	14	61	4	9	93	6	2
Bob Addy	C	23	60	2	14	136	5	21	124	5	9	205	8	21
Al Spalding	P	24	81	3	9	120	5	0	104	4	8	162	6	18
Trumbull		10	28	2	8	38	3	8	42	4	2	52	5	2
Gat Stires	OF	8	23	2	7	50	6	2	37	4	5	77	8	13
Sawyer	OF	8	23	2	7	50	6	2	37	4	5	46	5	6

FAIRMOUNT 17 - 3
Marlboro, MA

DATE	OPPONENT	SCORE			W	L	T
05/08	Lowell (Boston)	23	21	(10)	W		
05/22	Harvard (Cambridge, MA)	16	34			L	
06/07	Somerset (Boston)	38	17		W		
06/12	Somerset (Boston)	20	13		W		
06/17	Excelsior (Boston)	36	13		W		
06/26	Anderson (Lynn, MA)	70	7		W		
06/26	Granite (Lynn, MA)	42	5		W		
07/03	Excelsior (Worcester, MA)	29	27		W		
07/05	Excelsior (Worcester, MA)	52	25		W		
07/17	Upton (Boston)	45	16		W		
07/23	Tri Mountain (Boston)	40	17		W		
08/06	Olympic (New York)	48	17		W		
08/07	Excelsior (Worcester)	34	17		W		
08/13	Lowell (Boston)	28	47			L	
08/30	Dirigo (Augusta, ME)	66	26		W		
08/31	Androscoggin (Lewiston, ME)	26	25		W		
09/01	Union (Lewiston, ME)	63	29		W		
09/03	Field Nine (Portland, ME)	21	10				

FAIRMOUNT (cont.)
Marlboro, MA

DATE	OPPONENT	SCORE		W	L	T
09/09	Lowell (Boston)	36	20	W		
09/18	Harvard (Cambridge, MA)	14	40		L	

BATTERS	POS	GP	HL	A	O	R	A	O	H	A	O	TB	A	O
W. Brigham	1B	20	69	3	9	65	3	5	58	2	18	62	3	2
Hudson	2B	20	57	2	17	84	4	4	74	3	14	92	4	12
Madden	SS	20	50	2	10	92	4	11	85	4	5	126	6	6
Russell	3B	20	67	3	7	85	4	5	72	3	12	82	4	2
H. Brigham	OF	18	59	3	5	66	3	12	57	3	3	81	4	9
Smith	OF	17	39	2	5	76	4	8	57	3	6	70	4	2
A. Brigham	OF	15	41	2	11	53	3	8	49	3	4	64	4	4
Allen	C	20	55	2	15	90	4	10	77	3	17	109	5	9
Felton	P	20	46	2	6	96	4	16	88	4	8	134	6	14

STAR 16 - 6
Brooklyn, NY

DATE	OPPONENT	SCORE		W	L	T
06/12	Eagle (Flatbush, NY)	57	15	W		
06/19	Mutual (New York)	26	12	W		
06/26	Alpha (Brooklyn)	17	15	W		
07/03	Atlantic (Brooklyn)	10	15		L	
07/05	Lowell (Boston)	27	15	W		
07/19	Olympic (Washington)	49	11	W		
07/24	Alpha (Brooklyn)	31	20	W		
07/28	Powhatan (Brooklyn)	26	11	W		
07/31	Harmonic (Brooklyn)	42	25	W		
08/07	Eagle (Flatbush, NY)	37	21	W		
08/14	Mutual (New York)	18	22		L	
08/28	Atlantic (Brooklyn)	22	27		L	
09/04	Athletic (Brooklyn)	57	10	W		
09/15	Champion (Jersey City, NJ)	16	13	W		
09/18	Powhatan (Brooklyn)	42	19	W		
09/25	Atlantic (Brooklyn)	13	17		L	
09/30	Oriental (New York)	18	9	W		
10/02	Mutual (New York)	6	16		L	
10/09	Champion (Jersey City, NJ)	9	24		L	
10/16	Harmonic (Brooklyn)	27	11	W		
10/26	Champion (Jersey City, NJ)	27	8	W		
11/18	Osceola (Brooklyn)	41	2	W		

BATTERS	POS	GP	HL	A	O	R	A	O	H	A	O	TB	A	O
John Clyne	1B	18	52	2	16	51	2	15	52	2	16	80	4	8
Joseph Johnson	2B	14	42	3	0	44	3	2	52	3	10	80	5	10
Hy Dollard	SS	17	48	2	14	60	3	9	57	3	6	76	4	8
Bob Manly	3B	14	40	2	12	38	2	10	40	2	12	46	3	4
Fraley Rogers	OF	22	66	3	0	79	3	13	72	3	6	147	6	15
George Hall	OF	22	56	2	12	76	3	10	71	3	5	113	5	3
Herb Worth	OF	20	54	2	14	69	3	9	66	3	6	100	5	0
Herbert Jewell	C	19	61	3	4	56	2	18	55	2	17	71	3	14
Candy Cummings	P	22	76	3	10	63	2	19	60	2	16	91	4	3
Richard Hunt	2B	8	16	2	0	24	3	0	30	3	6	46	5	6
Tom McDiarmid	OF	6	15	2	3	15	2	3	13	2	1	20	3	2

CLIPPER 14 - 4 - 1
Lowell, MA

DATE	OPPONENT	SCORE		W	L	T
05/19	Sheridan (Lowell)	30	15	W		
06/10	Kearsarge (Stoneham, MA)	19	11	W		
07/04	Picked Nne (Leominster, MA)	20	27		L	
08/10	Olympic (New York)	84	20	W		
08/20	Anderson (Lynn, MA)	36	16	W		
09/01	Eureka (Lowell)	16	13	W		
09/03	Tri Mountain (Boston)	15	22		L	
09/16	Resolute (Nashua, NH)	29	26	W		
09/18	Harvard Sophomore (Cambridge, MA)	13	4	W		
09/22	Lightfoot (Salem, MA)	24	9	W		
09/29	Tri Mountain (Boston)	15	33		L	
10/02	Harvard (Cambridge, MA)	17	17			T
10/05	Salmon (Lowell)	25	10	W		
10/06	Eureka (Lowell)	41	12	W		
10/07	Atalanta (Stoneham, MA)	39	20	W		
10/08	Eureka (Lowell)	26	11	W		
10/09	Mutual (Springfield, MA)	7	17		L	
10/09	Excelsior (Worcester, MA)	19	7	W		
10/30	Clipper (Nashua, MA)	35	6	W		

BATTERS	POS	GP	HL	A	O	R	A	O	H	A	O	TB	A	O
Carter	1B	18	50	2	14	54	3	0						
Temple	2B,SS	16	45	2	13	45	2	13						
White	SS,C	17	35	2	1	60	3	9						
Coolidge	3B	18	47	2	11	46	2	10						
Davis	OF	14	29	2	1	41	2	13						
Church	OF	11	28	2	6	33	3	0						
Parker	OF	10	22	2	2	25	2	5						
Whitney	C,2B	18	49	2	13	59	3	5						
G. Conway	P	18	49	2	13	65	3	9						
Boynton		9	27	3	0	17	1	8						

HARVARD 14 - 5 - 1
Cambridge, MA

DATE	OPPONENT	SCORE		W	L	T
04/27	Lowell (Boston)	41	22	W		
05/22	Fairmount (Marlboro, MA)	34	16	W		
05/25	Mutual (New York)	11	43		L	
06/05	Dartmouth (Hanover, NH)	38	0	W		
06/12	Cincinnati (Cincinnati)	11	30		L	
06/24	Lowell (Boston)	35	19	W		
06/26	Williams College (Williamstown, MA)	45	8	W		
07/03	Lowell (Boston)	21	4	W		
07/05	Yale (New Haven, CT)	41	24	W		
07/07	Eckford (Brooklyn)	5	17		L	
07/09	Athletic (Philadelphia)	35	21	W		
07/10	Keystone (Philadelphia)	18	24		L	
07/13	National (Albany)	58	17	W		
07/14	Union (Lansingburgh, NY)	10	22		L	
09/19	Fairmount (Marlboro, MA)	40	14	W		
09/25	Lowell (Boston)	39	16	W		
10/02	Clipper (Lowell, MA)	17	17			T
10/09	Lowell (Boston)	32	14	W		
10/19	Mutual (Springfield, MA)	26	1	W		
10/26	Lowell (Boston)	36	24	W		

BATTERS	POS	GP	HL	A	O	R	A	O	H	A	O	TB	A	O
Perrin	1B,OF	16	56	3	8	46	2	14	40	2	8	51	3	3
Percy Austin	2B	19	54	2	16	69	3	12	54	2	16	68	3	11

HARVARD (cont.)
Cambridge, MA

BATTERS	POS	GP	HL	A	O	R	A	O	H	A	O	TB	A	O
Gardner Willard	SS	14	45	3	3	39	2	11	30	2	2	37	2	9
John Reynolds	3B	15	50	3	5	42	2	12	37	2	7	45	3	0
William Eustis	OF	20	46	2	6	71	3	11	73	3	13	108	5	8
James Wells	OF	20	61	3	1	68	3	8	55	2	15	84	4	4
Francis Rawle	OF	12	36	3	0	45	3	9	40	3	4	58	4	10
Archie Bush	C	20	52	2	12	74	3	14	69	3	9	120	6	0
Nathaniel Smith	P,3B	14	37	2	9	52	3	10	46	3	4	68	4	12
Goodwin		6	11	1	5	25	4	1	29	4	5	37	6	1
Minot		6	15	2	3	20	3	2	20	3	2	24	4	0
White		6	18	3	0	19	3	1	13	2	1	20	3	3
Peabody	1B	5	14	2	4	15	3	0	16	3	1	19	3	4

LOWELL   14 - 13
Boston, MA

DATE	OPPONENT	SCORE			W	L	T
04/27	Harvard (Cambridge, MA)	22	41			L	
05/08	Fairmount (Marlboro, MA)	21	23	(10)		L	
05/21	Atalanta (Stoneham, MA)	42	5		W		
05/26	Mutual (New York)	21	26			L	
06/05	Granite (Lynn, MA)	42	9		W		
06/09	Cincinnati (Cincinnati)	9	29			L	
06/17	Brown (Providence, RI)	40	13		W		
06/19	King Phillip (E. Abington, MA)	21	17		W		
06/24	Harvard (Cambridge, MA)	19	35			L	
07/01	Eon (Portland, ME)	35	12		W		
07/03	Harvard (Cambridge, MA)	4	21			L	
07/05	Star (Brooklyn)	15	27			L	
07/31	King Phillip (E. Abington, MA)	26	19		W		
08/09	Olympic (New York)	90	15		W		
08/13	Fairmount (Marlboro, MA)	47	28		W		
08/18	Tri Mountain (Boston)	12	23			L	
08/24	Olympic (Providence, RI)	35	15		W		
08/28	King Phillip (E. Abington, MA)	23	14		W		
09/09	Fairmount (Marlboro, MA)	20	36			L	
09/11	Anderson (Lynn, MA)	102	8		W		
09/25	Harvard (Cambridge, MA)	16	39			L	
10/02	Tri Mountain (Boston)	31	19		W		
10/09	Harvard (Cambridge, MA)	14	32			L	
10/20	Mutual (Springfield, MA)	33	10		W		
10/22	Eckford (Brooklyn)	33	38			L	
10/26	Harvard (Cambridge, MA)	24	36			L	
10/30	Tri Mountain (Boston)	24	12		W		

BATTERS	POS	GP	HL	A	O	R	A	O	H	A	O	TB	A	O
William Joslyn	1B,OF,P	19	53	2	15	53	2	15	45	2	7	64	3	7
James Lovett	2B,P	17	41	2	7	79	4	11	66	3	15	96	5	1
Fred Conant	SS	18	49	2	13	44	2	8	48	2	12	60	3	6
Edward Jewell	3B	7	21	3	0	19	2	5	23	3	2	29	4	1
Mort Rogers	OF,P	23	74	3	5	83	3	14	67	2	21	119	5	4
William Alline	OF	21	63	3	0	61	2	19	67	3	4	98	5	3
A.M. Newton	OF,1B	17	65	3	14	57	3	6	55	3	4	67	3	16
William Bradbury	C	26	71	2	19	94	3	16	87	3	9	129	4	25
Briggs	P,OF	24	55	2	7	91	3	19	88	3	16	138	5	18
George Wilder	2B,SS	16	50	3	2	56	3	8	43	2	11	51	3	3
Dillingham	OF	15	42	2	12	54	3	9	49	3	4	62	4	2
Lowell	OF	9	22	2	4	42	4	6	34	3	7	43	4	7
Henry Dennison	1B	9	26	2	8	28	3	1	29	3	2	47	5	2
Simmons	3B,SS	7	22	3	1	20	2	6						
Mason	2B,1B	5	11	2	1	23	4	3	20	4	0	27	5	2

SOUTHERN   13-7
New Orleans, LA

DATE	OPPONENT	SCORE		W	L	T
02/--	R.E. Lee (New Orleans)	23	33		L	
03/06	Dramatic (Mobile, AL)	82	21	W		
04/11	R.E. Lee (New Orleans)	31	43		L	
04/11	Atlantic (Algiers, LA)	40	46		L	
05/09	Atlantic (Algiers, LA)	77	20	W		
05/10	Fearless (New Orleans)	36	25	W		
05/23	Lone Star (New Orleans)	26	36		L	
05/30	R.E. Lee (New Orleans)	25	19	W		
06/06	R.E. Lee (New Orleans)	25	9	W		
07/04	Lone Star (New Orleans)*	24	26		L	
07/25	Lone Star (New Orleans)	21	22		L	
08/15	Atlantic (St. Louis)	10	4	W		
08/16	Empire (St. Louis)	23	10	W		
08/17	Union (S. Louis)*	35	21	W		
08/--	Bluff City (Memphis)*	25	19	W		
08/20	Kentucky (Louisville)*	43	25	W		
08/21	Eagle (Louisville)	25	22	W		
08/23	Cincinnati (Cincinnati)	3	35		L	
09/12	Picked Nine (New Orleans)	24	14	W		
11/21	Pelican (New Orleans)	27	21	W		

* Box score not available

BATTERS	POS	GP	HL	A	O	R	A	O	H	A	O	TB	A	O
J. Holtzman	1B,OF	*14	31	2	9	59	4	3						
S. Hays	2B,OF	*6	19	3	4	14	2	2						
J. Buddendorf	SS	*14	32	2	10	45	3	3						
O. Bozant	3B	*8	12	2	0	31	3	7						
F. Fay	OF,1B,2B,3B	*14	23	2	1	61	4	5						
L. Kearns	OF	*10	21	3	0	43	4	3						
Chandler	OF,P	*9	9	1	4	38	4	2						
W. Larkin	C	*16	35	2	11	54	3	6						
C. Keefe	P	12	39	3	3	28	2	4						
J. Hennessey	1B	6	18	3	0	14	2	2						
Twomy	3B,OF	6	16	2	4	13	2	1						
Donovan	C	6	21	3	3	8	1	2						

* Hands lost not available for all games

CHAMPION   13-8
Jersey City, NJ

DATE	OPPONENT	SCORE		W	L	T
05/14	Mutual (New York)	14	39		L	
05/17	Atlantic (Brooklyn)	2	52		L	
06/15	Olympic (New York)	26	21	W		
06/29	Eagle (New York)	30	17	W		
07/14	Bergen (Bergen, NJ)	50	4	W		
07/16	Eagle (Flatbush, NY)	8	10		L	
07/20	Alpha (Brooklyn)	16	5	W		
07/27	Gotham (New York)	27	16	W		
07/30	Eagle (New York)	16	14	W		
08/04	Resolute (Elizabeth, NJ)	45	21	W		
08/12	Athlete (Washington Hts., NY)	18	33		L	
09/02	Athletic (Brooklyn)	27	18	W		
09/15	Star (Brooklyn)	13	16		L	
09/21	Gotham (New York)*	27	15	W		
10/09	Star (Brooklyn)	24	9	W		
10/26	Star (Brooklyn)	8	27		L	

CHAMPION (cont.)
Jersey City, NJ

DATE	OPPONENT	SCORE		W	L	T
10/30	Harmonic (Brooklyn)	7	12		L	
11/03	Athletic (Brooklyn)	7	25		L	

(Only scores extant)

* Box score not available

BATTERS	POS	GP	HL	A	O	R	A	O	H	A	O	TB	A	O
Halpin	1B,OF	9	31	3	4	16	1	7						
Willis	2B,P,	14	25	1	11	41	2	13						
H. McMahon	SS,C	10	29	2	9	14	1	4						
Brown	3B,OF	10	29	2	9	27	2	7						
Snowden	OF	12	40	3	4	24	2	0						
Edwards	OF,C	11	29	2	7	24	2	2						
J. McMahon	OF,2B	9	24	2	6	21	2	3						
Boyce	C	5	13	2	3	14	2	4						
Clark	P,1B	12	32	2	8	28	2	4						
Collins	SS,OF,C,3B	7	17	2	3	13	1	6						
Platt	P,3B,OF	7	20	2	6	12	1	5						
Donnelly	2B,SS	6	14	2	2	17	2	3						
Hellmer	OF,3B	6	22	3	4	15	2	3						

GOTHAM 9 - 6
New York, NY

DATE	OPPONENT	SCORE		W	L	T
06/08	Mutual (New York)	15	33		L	
07/01	Empire (New York)	26	38		L	
07/14	Sparta (New York)	54	15	W		
07/19	Orion (New York)	71	18	W		
07/27	Champion (Jersey City, NJ)	16	27		L	
08/03	Eagle (New York)	46	36	W		
08/06	Social (New York)	32	28	W		
08/31	Olympic (New York)*	37	28	W		
09/21	Champion (Jersey City, NJ)*	15	27		L	
10/26	Eagle (New York)	13	21		L	

(Only scores extant)

* Box score not available

BATTERS	POS	GP	HL	A	O	R	A	O	H	A	O	TB	A	O
Marks		8	22	2	6	33	4	1						
Vincent		8	27	3	3	32	4	0						
William Goodspeed		8	22	2	6	25	3	1						
Ed Beadle		7	16	2	2	30	4	2						
Reed		7	20	2	6	29	4	1						
Hall		7	19	2	5	27	3	6						
Murray		7	24	3	3	25	3	4						
Phelan		5	12	2	2	15	3	0						

EMPIRE 9 - 8
New York, NY

DATE	OPPONENT	SCORE		W	L	T
06/17	Social (New York)	42	15	W		
06/24	Alert (S. Orange, NJ)	40	25	W		
07/01	Gotham (New York)	38	26	W		
07/12	Eagle (New York)	41	27	W		
07/19	Athlete (Washington Hts., NY)	23	26		L	

EMPIRE (cont.)
New York, NY

DATE	OPPONENT	SCORE		W	L	T
08/24	Union (Morrisania, NY)	13	45		L	
08/25	Active (New York)	32	21	W		
09/13	Eagle (New York)	29	30		L	
09/19	Eureka (Newark)*	14	6	W		
10/01	Orion (New York)	38	9	W		
10/03	Eureka (Newark)*	9	0	W		
10/07	Athlete (Washington Hts., NY)	23	25		L	
10/12	Orion (New York)*	31	18	W		
10/20	Union (Morrisania, NY)	16	17		L	
11/04	Eagle (New York)	5	26		L	

(Only scores extant)

* Box score not available

BATTERS	POS	GP	HL	A	O	R	A	O	H	A	O	TB	A	O
Josephs	1B	5	18	3	3	15	3	0						
Kelly	2B,3B	9	20	2	2	42	4	6						
Murphy	SS	8	19	2	3	33	4	1						
R. McGown	3B	5	16	3	1	10	2	0						
Vosge	OF,P	12	35	2	11	33	2	9						
Higham	OF,C,SS	12	28	2	4	47	3	11						
Griffin	OF,SS	10	28	2	8	24	2	4						
J. Miller	C,1B	8	18	2	2	32	4	0						
L. Miller	P,OF	5	20	4	0	12	2	2						
Andrew Gedney	OF	3	10	3	1	13	4	1						
Wilson	SS,C	8	24	3	0	23	2	7						

HARMONIC   9-9
Brooklyn, NY

DATE	OPPONENT	SCORE			W	L	T
06/26	Eckford (Brooklyn)	6	58			L	
07/05	Liberty (Norwalk, CT)*	23	22		W		
07/21	Excelsior (Brooklyn)	22	30			L	
07/24	Eagle (Flatbush, NY)	24	22		W		
07/31	Star (Brooklyn)	25	42			L	
08/06	Mutual (New York)	11	46			L	
08/10	Eagle (New York)	35	31	(10)	W		
08/14	Quickstep (Staten Island, NY)	39	23		W		
08/18	Eagle (Flatbush, NY)*	40	20		W		
08/28	Eureka (Brooklyn)*	35	24		W		
09/01	Excelsior (Brooklyn)	17	23			L	
09/16	Atlantic (Brooklyn)	12	38			L	
09/20	Eckford (Brooklyn)	23	30			L	
09/30	Atlantic (Brooklyn)*	9	22			L	
10/08	Powhatan (Brooklyn)*	18	12		W		
10/16	Star (Brooklyn)	11	27			L	
10/30	Champion (Jersey City, NJ)	12	7		W		

(Only scores extant)

* Box score not available

BATTERS	POS	GP	HL	A	O	R	A	O	H	A	O	TB	A	O
Fenniman	1B,3B	7	20	2	6	25	3	4						
L.S. Lewis	2B,P,3B	8	23	2	7	17	2	1						
W.J. Bennett	SS,2B	8	24	3	0	16	2	0						
Brown	3B,2B	10	30	3	0	22	2	2						
Larkin	OF	10	28	2	8	28	2	8						
Crosby	OF	10	27	2	7	27	2	7						
C. Hatch	OF,C,3B	6	21	3	3	11	1	5						
Nat Hicks	C	4	11	2	3	8	2	2						
J. Hatch	P,SS	7	21	3	0	17	2	3						

ATHLETIC   9 - 10 - 1
Brooklyn, NY

DATE	OPPONENT	SCORE			W	L	T
06/24	Eckford (Brooklyn)	5	32			L	
06/27	Powhatan (Brooklyn)	25	55			L	
07/10	Alpha (Brooklyn)	31	33	(10)		L	
07/13	Excelsior (Brooklyn)	17	16		W		
07/16	Atlantic (Brooklyn)	22	30			L	
07/21	Eckford (Brooklyn)	5	43			L	
07/29	Suffolk (Huntington, NY)	15	3		W		
08/12	Atlantic (Brooklyn)	8	29			L	
08/25	Alpha (Brooklyn)	32	23		W		
09/02	Champion (Jersey City, NJ)	18	27			L	
09/04	Star (Brooklyn)	10	57			L	
09/28	Quickstep (Staten Island, NY)	43	23		W		
10/06	Powhatan (Brooklyn)	24	24				T
10/22	Powhatan (Brooklyn)	13	28			L	
11/03	Champion (Jersey City, NJ)	25	7		W		

(Only scores extant)

BATTERS	POS	GP	HL	A	O	R	A	O	H	A	O	TB	A	O
Martin	1B,OF,3B	7	18	2	4	18	2	4						
Noonan	2B,SS,3B	14	32	2	4	46	3	4						
T. Madden	SS,2B	9	19	2	1	22	2	4						
Ireland	3B	12	37	3	1	26	2	2						
Wiggins	OF,2B,P	12	34	2	10	31	2	7						
H. Madden	OF,1B	10	32	3	2	17	1	7						
Edwards	OF,2B,SS	12	40	3	4	29	2	5						
George Price	C	15	42	2	12	39	2	9						
Richardson	P,OF	11	31	2	9	29	2	7						
George Cook	OF	10	30	3	0	16	1	6						
Hendrickson	1B	5	17	3	2	8	1	3						

MANSFIELD   8 - 2
Middletown, CT

DATE	OPPONENT	SCORE		W	L	T
06/18	Wesleyan Freshmen (Middletown)	26	17	W		
07/05	Pequot (New London, CT)	37	16	W		
07/10	Wesleyan (Middletown)	38	31	W		
07/14	Wesleyan (Middletown)	39	33	W		
07/22	Bristol (Bristol, CT)	14	22		L	
07/30	Mineola (Middletown)	58	21	W		
08/06	Bristol (Bristol, CT)	30	28	W		
08/14	Seymour (Middletown)	36	26	W		
08/25	Bristol (Bristol, CT)	11	25		L	
10/02	Quinnipack (Wallingford, CT)	39	9	W		

BATTERS	POS	GP	HL	A	O	R	A	O	H	A	O	TB	A	O
Johnson	1B	6	17	2	5	19	3	1						
Seth Plumb	2B	4	12	3	0	16	4	0						
Shay	SS	10	25	2	5	38	3	8						
Smith	3B	9	26	2	8	37	4	1						
Tipper	OF	10	22	2	2	50	5	0						
Douglass	OF	10	36	3	6	30	3	0						
Edwards	OF	2	4	2	0	9	4	1						
Selden Plumb	C	6	18	3	0	23	3	5						
Bentley	P	9	32	3	5	33	3	6						
Arnold	SS	6	12	2	0	24	4	0						
Young		3	10	3	1	5	1	2						

MUTUAL   8-3
Janesville, WI

DATE	OPPONENT	SCORE		W	L	T
07/05	Titan (Janesville)	56	47	W		
07/17	Make or Brake (Monroe, WI)	*9	0	W		
07/19	Athlete (Whitewater, WI)	29	38		L	
08/06	Athlete (Whitewater, WI)	43	41	W		
08/18	Athlete (Whitewater, WI)	35	30	W		
08/27	Capital City (Madison, WI)	14	8	W		
09/03	Capital City (Madison, WI)	17	19		L	
09/11	Cream City (Milwaukee)	55	46	W		
09/17	Athlete (Whitewater, WI)	50	24	W		
09/20	Aetna (Chicago)	18	37		L	
09/28	Capital City (Madison, WI)	*9	0	W		

* Forfeit

BATTERS	POS	GP	HL	A	O	R	A	O	H	A	O	TB	A	O
Conant	1B	8	22	2	6	32	4	0						
E. Smith	2B	9	33	3	6	30	3	3						
Heller	SS	9	15	1	4	45	5	0						
Ed Smith	3B	5	19	3	4	11	2	1						
Sutherland	OF	9	31	2	4	29	3	2						
St. John	OF	8	19	2	3	36	4	0						
T. Smith	OF,1B	4	14	3	2	15	3	3						
Lonaghen	C,OF	9	18	2	0	30	3	3						
Hitchcock	P	9	24	2	6	36	4	0						
Pullen	C	3	8	2	2	11	3	2						
Bump	OF,3B	3	9	3	0	11	3	2						
Marston	3B	2	2	1	0	14	7	0						
Stoddard	OF	2	3	1	1	6	3	0						
White	OF	1	5	5	0	5	5	0						

EAGLE   8-5
New York, NY

DATE	OPPONENT	SCORE			W	L	T
06/17	Athlete (Washington Hts., NY)	25	19		W		
06/24	Ivanhoe (Sing Sing, NY)	52	28		W		
06/29	Champion (Jersey City, NJ)	17	30			L	
07/09	Ivanhoe (Sing Sing, NY)*	43	12		W		
07/12	Empire (New York)	27	41			L	
07/20	Bergen (Bergen, NJ)	29	25		W		
07/30	Champion (Jersey City, NJ)	14	16			L	
08/03	Gotham (New York)	36	46			L	
08/10	Harmonic (Brooklyn)	31	35	(10)		L	
09/13	Empire (New York)	30	29		W		
10/26	Gotham (New York)	21	13		W		
11/04	Empire (New York)	26	5		W		

(Only scores extant)

* Box score not available

BATTERS	POS	GP	HL	A	O	R	A	O	H	A	O	TB	A	O
Norton	1B	8	19	2	3	26	3	2	29	3	5	36	4	4
T. Gaughan	2B	12	44	3	8	32	2	8	27	2	5	34	3	1
Kane	SS,C	*8	20	2	6	22	3	1	29	3	5	34	4	2
W. Gallagher	3B,OF	*12	29	2	7	38	3	5	45	3	10	51	4	3
Fleet	OF,2B	*11	24	2	6	24	2	6	24	2	2	29	2	7
Bruin	OF,3B	*10	18	2	4	22	3	1	40	4	0	46	4	6
Winicott	OF	9	24	2	6	26	2	8	32	3	5	39	4	3
Nat Hicks	C	*6	13	2	3	15	3	0	19	3	1	23	3	5
Stevens	P,OF	*12	27	2	7	38	3	8	53	4	5	59	4	11

EAGLE (cont.)
New York, NY

BATTERS	POS	GP	HL	A	O	R	A	O	H	A	O	TB	A	O
A. Gaughan	1B,SS,3B	*6	11	2	1	20	4	0	28	4	4	34	5	4

* Hands lost and runs not counted in all games

R.E. LEE 7 - 3
New Orleans, LA

DATE	OPPONENT	SCORE		W	L	T
02/28	Pelican (New Orleans)	48	25	W		
02/--	Southern (New Orleans)	33	23	W		
03/15	Atlantic (Algiers, LA)	33	20	W		
03/21	Atlantic (Algiers, LA)	34	17	W		
04/11	Southern (New Orleans)	43	31	W		
05/30	Southern (New Orleans)	19	25		L	
06/06	Southern (New Orleans)	9	25		L	
07/11	Lone Star (New Orleans)	10	14		L	
08/22	Lone Star (New Orleans)*	25	23	W		
10/10	Surprise (New Orleans)*	--	--	W		

* Box score not available

BATTERS	POS	GP	HL	A	O	R	A	O	H	A	O	TB	A	O
J. Hennessey	1B	*5	7	3	1	18	3	3						
William Hatton	2B,3B,SS	*5	8	2	2	14	2	4						
J. Levy	SS	*5	12	4	0	10	2	2						
A. Johnson	3B,1B,OF	*7	5	2	1	22	3	1						
Rendon	OF,C	*7	5	1	2	21	3	0						
P. Lauer	OF,3B	*7	8	2	2	21	3	0						
P. Donovan	OF	*5	7	3	1	14	2	4						
V.C. Bertel	C,1B	*7	9	3	0	17	2	3						
James Donovan	P	*6	10	3	1	15	2	3						

* Hands lost not available for all games

ATHLETE 7 - 4
Washington Hts., NY

DATE	OPPONENT	SCORE		W	L	T
05/27	Rival (New York)*	19	29		L	
06/11	Alpha (Brooklyn)	27	32		L	
06/17	Eagle (New York)	19	25		L	
07/19	Empire (New York)	26	23	W		
08/05	Bergen (Bergen, NJ)	17	16	W		
08/12	Champion (Jersey City, NJ)	33	18	W		
09/15	Bergen (Bergen, NJ)*	35	18	W		
09/23	Powhatan (Brooklyn)*	13	29		L	
09/30	Union (Morrisania, NY)	30	15	W		
10/07	Empire (New York)	25	23	W		

(Only scores extant)

* Box score not available

BATTERS	POS	GP	HL	A	O	R	A	O	H	A	O	TB	A	O
Truax		*7	16	2	2	22	3	1	13	3	1	23	5	3
McManus		*7	18	2	4	20	2	6	14	3	2	20	5	0
Barry		*6	17	2	5	18	3	0	10	3	1	15	5	0
Valentine		*6	15	2	3	21	3	3	10	3	1	13	4	1
Sloane		*6	18	3	0	15	2	3	13	3	1	17	4	1

* Hits and total bases not available for all games

ATHLETIC
Chicago, IL
7 - 4

DATE	OPPONENT	SCORE		W	L	T
06/02	Amateur (Chicago)	38	53		L	
06/12	Enterprise (Chicago)	55	43	W		
06/28	Enterprise (Chicago)	34	15	W		
07/05	Cream City (Milwaukee)	20	34		L	
07/12	Aetna (Chicago)	34	21	W		
07/19	Amateur (Chicago)	50	36	W		
07/29	Aetna (Chicago)	25	19	W		
08/11	Garden City (Chicago)	26	42		L	
08/28	Amateur (Chicago)	45	33	W		
09/08	Garden City (Chicago)	16	36		L	
10/12	Eureka (Chicago)	41	21	W		

BATTERS	POS	GP	HL	A	O	R	A	O	H	A	O	TB	A	O
Butler		11	35	3	2	43	3	10						
Stambough		11	40	3	7	40	3	7						
Bredberg		11	23	2	1	52	4	8						
Reynolds		10	22	2	2	44	4	4						
Graves		10	33	3	3	35	3	5						
H. Taylor		9	28	3	1	37	4	1						
Boardman		8	21	2	5	34	4	2						
Keane		8	21	2	5	32	4	0						
Dorgan		6	13	2	1	24	4	0						
Mears		3	9	3	0	9	3	0						
Powers		3	10	3	1	6	2	0						

PELICAN
New Orleans, LA
7 - 6

DATE	OPPONENT	SCORE		W	L	T
01/31	Washington (New Orleans)	33	5	W		
02/07	Washington (New Orleans)	30	9	W		
02/28	R.E. Lee (New Orleans)	25	48		L	
03/21	Crusader (New Orleans)	31	28	W		
04/04	Lone Star (New Orleans)	17	35		L	
04/25	Lone Star (New Orleans)	5	18		L	
05/16	Lone Star (New Orleans)	19	41		L	
05/30	Atlantic (Algiers, LA)*	29	27	W		
07/11	Morgan (New Orleans)	12	60		L	
08/15	Hope (New Orleans)	19	12	W		
09/26	Hope (New Orleans)*	56	6	W		
10/10	Washington (New Orleans)*	31	16	W		
11/21	Southern (New Orleans)	21	27		L	

* Box score not available

BATTERS	POS	GP	HL	A	O	R	A	O	H	A	O	TB	A	O
James Murtha		*10	17	2	1	31	3	1						
P. Ford		*9	11	1	3	28	3	1						
J. Blanchard		*8	18	3	0	22	2	6						
Short		*7	11	1	5	24	3	3						
T. Mahan		*7	19	3	1	20	2	6						
Morton		*6	13	2	3	22	3	4						
R. Hutchinson		*6	9	2	1	18	3	0						

NIAGARA   7 - 7
Buffalo, NY

DATE	OPPONENT	SCORE		W	L	T
06/03	Cincinnati (Cincinnati)	6	42		L	
06/08	Columbia (Buffalo)	209	10	W		
07/01	Independent (Dundas, ON)*	49	13	W		
07/27	Union (Buffalo)	25	17	W		
07/29	Central City (Syracuse, NY)	16	11	W		
08/07	Central City (Syracuse, NY)	15	18		L	
08/09	Forest City (Cleveland)	36	40		L	
08/16	Ontario (Oswego, NY)*	36	15	W		
08/19	Eckford (Brooklyn)	18	24		L	
08/27	Independent (Dundas, ON)*	40	20	W		
08/31	Alert (Rochester, NY)	19	15	W		
09/01	Sherman (Utica, NY)*	28	39		L	
09/09	Union (Lansingburgh, NY)*	9	34		L	
09/16	Forest City (Cleveland)	22	32		L	

* Box score not available

BATTERS	POS	GP	HL	A	O	R	A	O	H	A	O	TB	A	O
Hawley		9	25	2	7	47	5	2						
Emerson		9	20	2	2	45	5	0						
Van Velsor		9	28	3	1	34	3	7						
A. Holley		8	20	2	4	38	4	6						
Atwater		8	29	3	5	13	1	5						
M. Holley		6	17	2	5	35	5	5						
Lewis		5	13	2	3	17	3	2						

TRI MOUNTAIN   7 - 9
Boston, MA

DATE	OPPONENT	SCORE		W	L	T
05/24	Mutual (New York)	17	69		L	
06/10	Cincinnati (Cincinnati)	12	40		L	
07/03	King Phillip (E. Abington, MA)	30	19	W		
07/05	Union (Lansingburgh, NY)	24	63		L	
07/06	National (Albany)*	42	43		L	
07/23	Fairmount (Marlboro, MA)	17	40		L	
08/07	Olympic (New York)	80	14	W		
08/18	Lowell (Boston)	23	12	W		
09/03	Clipper (Lowell, MA)	22	15	W		
09/23	Olympic (Providence)*	39	38	W		
09/29	Clipper (Lowell, MA)*	33	15	W		
10/02	Lowell (Boston)	19	31		L	
10/06	Olympic (Providence)	40	41		L	
10/18	Mutual (Springfield, MA)*	46	17	W		
10/21	Eckford (Brooklyn)	17	26		L	
10/30	Lowell (Boston)	12	24		L	

* Box score not available

BATTERS	POS	GP	HL	A	O	R	A	O	H	A	O	TB	A	O
Jones		13	38	2	11	45	3	5						
Sullivan		12	32	2	8	46	3	10						
Record		12	23	1	11	43	3	7						
Kelly		12	34	2	10	39	3	3						
Frank Barrows		12	33	2	9	35	2	11						
French		12	38	3	2	31	2	7						
O'Brien		10	22	2	2	38	3	8						
Putnam		8	31	3	7	21	2	5						

MUTUAL 6-4
Springfield, MA

DATE	OPPONENT	SCORE		W	L	T
06/09	Cincinnati (Cincinnati)	5	80		L	
07/01	Comet (Chicopee, MA)	21	9	W		
07/05	Upton (Boston)	51	16	W		
07/13	Old Elm (Pittsfield, MA)	40	16	W		
09/04	Amherst (Amherst, MA)	21	6	W		
09/23	Hampden (Chicopee, MA)	49	33	W		
10/09	Clipper (Lowell, MA)	17	7	W		
10/18	Tri Mountain (Boston)	17	46		L	
10/19	Harvard (Cambridge, MA)	1	26		L	
10/20	Lowell (Boston)	10	33		L	

BATTERS	POS	GP	HL	A	O	R	A	O	H	A	O	TB	A	O
Field	1B,OF	8	10	1	2	31	3	7						
Shaw	2B,SS	10	18	1	8	30	3	0						
Donovan	SS	6	17	2	5	11	1	5						
Kelley	3B	5	15	3	0	8	1	3						
Gibbons	OF,SS	10	33	3	3	16	1	6						
Emerson	OF,1B	9	22	2	4	21	2	3						
Kennsick	OF	9	32	3	5	25	2	7						
Kellogg	C,OF	9	21	2	3	29	3	2						
Beach	P	10	26	2	6	22	2	2						

DETROIT 6-7
Detroit, MI

DATE	OPPONENT	SCORE		W	L	T
07/01	Mystic (Detroit)*	68	5	W		
07/05	Forest City (Cleveland)*	10	25		L	
07/23	Forest City (Cleveland)	9	54		L	
07/29	Forest City (Rockford, IL)	10	32		L	
07/31	Central City (Syracuse, NY)	30	14	W		
08/06	Empire (Bay City, MI)*	37	17	W		
08/08	Hercules (Flint, MI)*	20	16	W		
08/18	Eckford (Brooklyn)	12	42		L	
08/30	Olympic (Detroit)*	119	12	W		
09/03	Alert (Rochester, NY)	9	30		L	
09/25	Ann Arbor (Ann Arbor, MI)*	#19	21	W		
10/09	Ann Arbor (Ann Arbor, MI)	12	19		L	
10/21	Ann Arbor (Ann Arbor, MI)*	19	21	(10)	L	

* Box score not available
\# Umpire awarded win to Detroit after Ann Arbor refused to play ninth inning in rain.

BATTERS	POS	GP	HL	A	O	R	A	O	H	A	O	TB	A	O
Hull	1B	6	17	2	5	8	1	2						
Brown	2B	4	14	3	2	9	2	1						
Webster	SS,C	6	11	1	5	11	1	5						
Sheehan	3B	3	13	4	1	4	1	1						
M. Ward	OF,2B	6	12	2	0	11	1	5						
Presley	OF	5	10	2	0	7	1	2						
Standish	OF,3B	4	15	3	3	1	0	1						
Collins	C,SS	5	12	2	2	12	2	2						
C. Ward	P	6	20	3	2	7	1	1						

ALERT 6-7
Rochester, NY

DATE	OPPONENT	SCORE		W	L	T
06/04	Cincinnati (Cincinnati)	9	18		L	
08/05	Sherman (Utica, NY)*	25	21	W		

ALERT (cont.)
Rochester, NY

DATE	OPPONENT	SCORE		W	L	T
08/06	National (Albany, NY)*	39	15	W		
08/07	Union (Lansingburgh, NY)*	15	53		L	
08/09	Central City (Syracuse, NY)	34	13	W		
08/11	Eckford (Brooklyn)	27	38		L	
08/---	Ontario (Oswego, NY)*	50	23	W		
08/31	Niagara (Buffalo)	15	19		L	
09/01	Forest City (Cleveland)	29	34		L	
09/02	Cincinnati (Cincinnati)	19	32		L	
09/03	Detroit (Detroit)	30	9	W		
09/14	Livingston (Genesee, NY)*	42	15	W		
09/15	Forest City (Cleveland)	8	18		L	

(Only scores extant)
* Box score not available

BATTERS	POS	GP	HL	A	O	R	A	O	H	A	O	TB	A	O
G. Ward		8	21	2	5	23	2	7						
Glenn		8	19	2	3	22	2	6						
Gene Kimball		8	22	2	6	20	2	4						
Ezra Sutton		8	26	3	2	19	2	3						
Huddleston		8	25	3	1	17	2	1						
W. Jackson		8	27	3	3	16	2	0						
McKelvey		8	28	3	4	15	1	7						
Hoy		7	19	2	5	19	2	5						

BUCKEYE 6 - 8
Cincinnati, OH

DATE	OPPONENT	SCORE		W	L	T
05/08	Great Western (Cincinnati)	36	16	W		
05/26	Covington (Covington, KY)	36	23	W		
07/12	Olympic (Washington)	11	36		L	
07/22	Cincinnati (Cincinnati)*	15	71		L	
07/24	Kentucky (Louisville, KY)	28	9	W		
07/26	Forest City (Rockford, IL)	1	40		L	
07/27	Empire (St. Louis)*	13	27		L	
08/14	Eckford (Brooklyn)	16	37		L	
08/31	Cincinnati (Cincinnati)	8	103		L	
09/04	Blue Stocking (Cleves, OH)*	68	28	W		
09/10	Olympic (Pittsburgh)*	23	24		L	

(Only scores extant)
* Box score not available

BATTERS	POS	GP	HL	A	O	R	A	O	H	A	O	TB	A	O
Doyle		7	21	3	0	20	2	6						
W.H. Boake		6	13	2	1	22	3	4						
J.P. Mack		6	13	2	1	13	2	1						
W.P. Wright		6	23	3	5	10	1	4						
Lowe		6	17	2	5	8	1	2						

PASTIME 6 - 8
Baltimore, MD

DATE	OPPONENT	SCORE		W	L	T
06/17	Olympic (Washington)	15	22		L	
07/16	Maryland (Baltimore)	19	55		L	
08/18	Oriental (New York)	15	16		L	
08/26	Mutual (New York)	13	21		L	
09/02	Athletic (Philadelphia)	29	33		L	

JEFFERSON (cont.)
Washington, DC

DATE	OPPONENT	SCORE		W	L	T
09/10	Union (Washington)	46	24	W		
09/13	National (Washington)	15	46		L	
09/20	Maryland (Baltimore)	19	29		L	
09/30	National (Washington)	15	23		L	
10/09	Union (Culpepper, VA)	23	9	W		
10/13	Union (Washington)	21	20	W		
11/18	Monitor (Annapolis, MD)	19	16	W		

BATTERS	POS	GP	HL	A	O	R	A	O	H	A	O	TB	A	O
McClelland		12	30	2	6	38	3	2	30	2	6			
Anderson		12	28	2	4	32	2	8	28	2	4			
A. Finney		12	37	3	1	23	1	11	22	1	10			
J. Doyle		11	36	3	3	23	2	1	23	2	1			
McCauley		11	35	3	2	18	1	7	17	1	6			
Lake		8	19	2	3	25	3	1	24	3	0			
Church		8	14	1	6	16	2	0	21	2	5			
Morgan		7	17	2	3	16	2	2	14	2	0			

SOCIAL   5 - 9
New York, NY

DATE	OPPONENT	SCORE		W	L	T
06/17	Empire (New York)	15	42		L	
06/24	Union (Hudson City, NJ)*	73	29	W		
07/14	Union (Hudson City, NJ)	25	31		L	
07/30	Mutual (New York)	10	31		L	
08/06	Gotham (New York)	28	32		L	
08/18	Bergen (Bergen, NJ)	26	31		L	
09/01	Sparta (New York)*	33	28	W		
09/18	Union (Morrisania, NY)*	26	17	W		
11/05	Union (Morrisania, NY)	17	26		L	

(Only scores extant)

* Box score not available

BATTERS	POS	GP	HL	A	O	R	A	O	H	A	O	TB	A	O
William Bell		6	12	2	0	19	2	5						
J. Clute		5	8	1	3	20	4	0						
Ryerson		5	12	2	2	11	2	1						
McKewen		5	16	3	1	10	2	0						

OLYMPIC   5 - 10
Philadelphia, PA

DATE	OPPONENT	SCORE		W	L	T
04/28	Athletic (Philadelphia)	23	36		L	
05/14	Keystone (Philadelphia)	19	10	W		
05/13	Expert (Philadelphia)	26	35		L	
05/22	Keystone (Philadelphia)	20	15	W		
05/26	Athletic (Philadelphia)	29	45		L	
06/17	Athletic (Philadelphia)	26	36		L	
06/19	Cincinnati (Cincinnati)	11	22		L	
07/15	Intrepid (Philadelphia)	34	12	W		
09/14	Keystone (Philadelphia)	37	23	W		
09/25	Athletic (Philadelphia)	7	18		L	
09/28	Keystone (Philadelphia)	21	7	W		

OLYMPIC (cont.)
Philadelphia, PA

DATE	OPPONENT	SCORE		W	L	T
10/02	Athletic (Philadelphia)	17	21		L	
10/22	Expert (Philadelphia)	15	20		L	

(Only scores extant)

BATTERS	POS	GP	HL	A	O	R	A	O	H	A	O	TB	A	O
Severn	1B	*8	14	2	2	14	2	2	20	2	4	35	4	3
Kern	2B	*15	35	2	9	41	3	2	32	2	2	37	2	7
Horgesheimer	SS	7	21	3	0	18	2	4	19	2	5	25	3	4
Harry Schafer	3B	*11	19	1	9	37	3	7	39	3	6	52	4	8
Clinton	OF,1B	*15	43	3	4	29	2	3	33	2	3	44	2	14
Oram	OF,1B	*13	26	2	4	25	2	3	28	2	2	35	2	9
Roth	OF	*10	26	3	2	20	2	4	21	2	1	29	2	9
Miller	C	*15	44	3	5	24	1	10	32	2	2	37	2	7
Rorke	P,C,SS	*14	28	2	4	29	2	5	45	3	3	52	3	10
Lovett	P	*6	18	3	3	9	1	4	10	1	4	13	2	1

* Hands lost and runs not available for all games

UNION   5 - 10
Morrisania, NY

DATE	OPPONENT	SCORE		W	L	T
07/30	Ross (Harlem, NY)	25	21	W		
08/05	Atlantic (Brooklyn)	8	34		L	
08/18	Mutual (New York)	8	83		L	
08/24	Empire (New York)	45	13	W		
09/07	Oriental (New York)	16	20		L	
09/13	Mutual (New York)	10	26		L	
09/18	Social (New York)*	17	26		L	
09/21	Eckford (Brooklyn)	11	18		L	
09/30	Athlete (Washington Hts., NY)	15	30		L	
10/06	Atlantic (Brooklyn)*	14	24		L	
10/20	Empire (New York)	17	16	W		
11/05	Social (New York)	26	17	W		

(Only scores extant)

* Box score not available

BATTERS	POS	GP	HL	A	O	R	A	O	H	A	O	TB	A	O
Baker	1B,OF	6	22	3	4	5	0	5						
John Goldie	2B,1B	5	10	2	0	17	3	2						
Tom Haines	SS	8	15	1	7	19	2	3						
Weidberg	3B,OF	8	23	2	7	11	1	3						
Harry Austin	OF,2B,C	10	28	2	8	27	2	7						
Whelan	OF,3B,1B	6	16	2	4	11	1	5						
Ten Eyke	OF,3B	4	10	2	2	5	1	1						
Carsie	C	4	8	2	0	9	2	1						
Lyons	P,OF	8	24	3	0	18	2	2						
Reynolds	2B,SS	4	6	1	2	13	3	1						
George Smith	3B,OF,1B	4	10	2	2	10	2	2						

POWHATAN   5 - 12 - 1
Brooklyn, NY

DATE	OPPONENT	SCORE		W	L	T
05/03	Atlantic (Brooklyn)	1	17		L	
05/25	Eagle (Flatbush, NY)	56	10	W		
06/17	Atlantic (Brooklyn)	8	55		L	

POWHATAN (cont.)
Brooklyn, NY

DATE	OPPONENT	SCORE			W	L	T
06/27	Athletic (Brooklyn)	55	25		W		
07/12	Eckford (Brooklyn)	12	52			L	
07/25	Star (Brooklyn)	11	26			L	
09/02	Mutual (New York)	12	49			L	
09/18	Star (Brooklyn)	19	42			L	
09/23	Athlete (Washington Hts., NY)	29	13		W		
10/06	Athletic (Brooklyn)	24	24	(11)			T
10/08	Harmonic (Brooklyn)	12	18			L	
10/22	Athletic (Brooklyn)	28	13		W		
10/18	Eckford (Brooklyn)	4	45			L	

(Only scores extant)

* Box score not available

BATTERS	POS	GP	HL	A	O	R	A	O	H	A	O	TB	A	O
Stark	1B	9	17	1	8	22	2	4						
E.P. Beavans	2B	10	30	3	0	17	1	7						
Proctor	SS	14	36	2	8	33	2	5						
Hartman	3B,C	13	38	2	11	32	2	6						
Tom York	OF	14	42	3	0	33	2	5						
Berger	OF,2B	7	13	1	6	24	3	3						
Booth	OF	5	17	3	2	6	1	1						
Bass	C	13	39	3	0	37	2	11						
Brower	P	10	24	2	4	24	2	4						

LONE STAR   4 - 1
St. Louis, MO

DATE	OPPONENT	SCORE		W	L	T
05/16	Atlantic (St. Louis)	26	37		L	
05/---	Lone Star (Alma, IL)	38	23	W		
06/19	Atlantic (St. Louis)	28	22	W		
07/25	Rowena (St. Louis)	31	11	W		
07/---	Aetna (St. Louis)	32	10	W		

BATTERS	POS	GP	HL	A	O	R	A	O	H	A	O	TB	A	O
Nagle		5	11	2	1	19	3	4						
Johnson		5	14	2	4	17	3	2						
Roehl		5	16	3	1	16	3	1						
Haltmann		5	15	3	0	14	2	4						

ATLANTIC   4 - 2
St. Louis, MO

DATE	OPPONENT	SCORE		W	L	T
05/16	Lone Star (St. Louis)	37	26	W		
06/19	Lone Star (St. Louis)	22	28		L	
08/15	Southern (New Orleans)	4	10		L	
08/22	Lone Star (Alma, IL)	27	23	W		
08/29	Active (St. Louis)	40	22	W		
11/---	Empire (St. Louis)	11	7	W		

BATTERS	POS	GP	HL	A	O	R	A	O	H	A	O	TB	A	O
W.R. Peterson		5	11	2	1	20	4	0						
Smith		5	11	2	1	19	3	4						
Reuble		5	18	3	3	13	2	3						
Balser		5	14	2	4	13	2	3						
Herring		5	14	2	4	9	2	1						
E. Chenot		5	19	3	4	10	2	0						

MAPLE LEAF 4 - 2
Guelph, ON

DATE	OPPONENT	SCORE		W	L	T
06/30	Young Canadian (Woodstock, ON)	57	38	W		
---/---	Victoria (?)	34	45		L	
---/---	Independent (?)	28	40		L	
---/---	Victoria (?)	76	33	W		
---/---	Young Canadian (Woodstock, ON)	30	16	W		
08/24	Tecumseh (?)	43	20	W		

BATTERS	POS	GP	HL	A	O	R	A	O	H	A	O	TB	A	O
W. Hewer	1B	4	12	3	0	17	4	1						
J. Coulson	2B	6	14	2	2	35	5	5						
T. Smith	SS	6	16	2	4	29	4	5						
C. Maddock	3B	6	14	2	2	33	5	3						
H. Steele	OF	6	17	2	5	31	5	1						
J. Goldie	OF	6	17	2	5	34	5	4						
H. McLean	OF	3	8	2	2	15	5	0						
J. Nichols	C	6	18	3	0	27	4	3						
W. Sunley	P	6	22	3	4	26	4	2						

FEARLESS 4 - 4
New Orleans, LA

DATE	OPPONENT	SCORE		W	L	T
04/11	Washington (New Orleans)	32	34		L	
04/---	Washington (New Orleans)	28	22	W		
05/10	Southern (New Orleans)	25	36		L	
06/27	Washington (New Orleans)	20	8	W		
07/18	Lone Star (New Orleans)*	3	18		L	
07/25	Surprise (New Orleans)	17	10	W		
08/15	Surprise (New Orleans)	22	12	W		
10/02	Lone Star (New Orleans)*	21	26		L	

* Box score not available

BATTERS	POS	GP	HL	A	O	R	A	O	H	A	O	TB	A	O
J.V. Guillots		6	21	3	3	13	2	1						
D. Kletter		5	14	2	4	17	2	5						
M.C. Ullmer		5	17	3	2	11	2	1						
F. Prete		4	8	2	0	13	3	1						
J. Myers		4	10	2	2	12	3	0						
J. Chenville		4	10	2	2	13	2	3						
N. Sartorius		4	8	2	0	11	2	3						
George W. Wright		4	10	2	2	11	2	3						

BERGEN 4 - 5
Bergen, NJ

DATE	OPPONENT	SCORE		W	L	T
07/14	Champion (Jersey City, NJ)	4	50		L	
07/20	Eagle (New York)	25	29		L	
08/05	Athlete (Washington Hts., NY)	16	17		L	
08/09	Hoyt (New York)*	44	41	W		
08/18	Social (New York)	31	26	W		
09/07	Olympic (New York)	32	19	W		
09/15	Athlete (Washington Hts., NY)*	18	35		L	
09/21	Communipaw (New Jersey)	61	9	W		
---/---	Communipaw (New Jersey)*	9	16		L	

* Box score not available

BERGEN (cont.)
Bergen, NJ

BATTERS	POS	GP	HL	A	O	R	A	O	H	A	O	TB	A	O
James Arbuckle, Jr.		6	12	2	0	23	3	5						
Stringham		6	14	2	2	20	3	2						
James Arbuckle		6	20	3	2	18	3	0						
Craven		5	16	3	1	16	3	1						

NATIONAL 4 - 6
Albany, NY

DATE	OPPONENT	SCORE		W	L	T
06/08	Cincinnati (Cincinnati)	8	49		L	
06/18	Ancient City (Schnectady, NY)	40	2	W		
06/25	Champion (W. Troy, NY)	40	22	W		
07/05	Live Oak (Albany)	46	23	W		
07/06	Tri Mountain (Boston)*	43	42	W		
07/13	Harvard (Cambridge, MA)*	17	58		L	
07/22	Union (Lansingburgh, NY)*	14	53		L	
08/06	Alert (Rochester, NY)*	15	39		L	
08/10	Independent (Amsterdam, NY)	27	28		L	
08/12	Ancient City (Schnectady, NY)	31	37		L	

* Box score not available

BATTERS	POS	GP	HL	A	O	R	A	O	H	A	O	TB	A	O
McDonald		6	14	2	2	25	4	1						
Cantwell		6	17	2	5	23	3	5						
Spellman		6	16	2	4	23	2	5						
Woolverton		5	11	2	1	21	4	1						

WASHINGTON 4 - 8
New Orleans, LA

DATE	OPPONENT	SCORE		W	L	T
01/31	Pelican (New Orleans)	5	33		L	
02/07	Pelican (New Orleans)	9	30		L	
04/11	Fearless (New Orleans)	34	32	W		
04/---	Fearless (New Orleans)	22	28		L	
05/02	Lone Star (New Orleans)*	22	45		L	
05/09	Lone Star (New Orleans)	31	44		L	
05/---	Comet (New Orleans)*	23	66		L	
06/27	Fearless (New Orleans)	8	20		L	
08/15	Comet (New Orleans)	37	29	W		
10/10	Pelican (New Orleans)*	16	31		L	
11/18	Magnolia (New Orleans)	18	6	W		
11/28	Magnolia (New Orleans)	35	9	W		

(Only scores extant)

* Box score not available

BATTERS	POS	GP	HL	A	O	R	A	O	H	A	O	TB	A	O
P. Everett		*6	10	2	0	23	3	5						
E. Wilcox		6	16	2	4	16	2	4						
J. Foley		*6	13	2	3	13	2	1						
T. Jones		6	19	3	1	12	2	0						
Lambert		*5	11	2	3	15	3	0						
F. Oberle		5	14	2	4	14	2	4						

* Hands lost not available for all games

CENTRAL CITY   4 - 10
Syracuse, NY

DATE	OPPONENT	SCORE		W	L	T
06/17	Pastime (Little Falls, NY)	26	27		L	
07/29	Niagara (Buffalo)	11	16		L	
07/30	Forest City (Cleveland)	23	29		L	
07/31	Detroit (Detroit)	14	30		L	
08/04	Cincinnati (Cincinnati)	9	37		L	
08/05	Cincinnati (Cincinnati)	22	36		L	
08/07	Niagara (Buffalo)	18	15	W		
08/09	Alert (Rochester, NY)	13	34		L	
08/10	Eckford (Brooklyn)	13	41		L	
08/14	Forest City (Cleveland)	11	39		L	
08/27	Olympic (Canandaigua, NY)	29	17	W		
09/--	Sherman (Utica, NY)	28	15	W		
09/--	Sherman (Utica, NY)	30	6	W		
10/09	Ontario (Oswego, NY)*	27	29		L	

* Box score not available

BATTERS	POS	GP	HL	A	O	R	A	O	H	A	O	TB	A	O
Ferrer	1B,OF	8	26	3	2	16	2	0						
Johnson	2B,OF	10	31	3	1	19	1	9						
White	SS,C,1B	10	31	3	1	22	2	2						
Cruttendon	3B	7	24	3	3	9	1	2						
Stark	OF,2B	10	23	2	3	25	2	5						
Colton	OF	7	20	2	6	18	2	4						
Porter	OF	7	25	3	4	12	1	5						
Grace	C,3B	13	33	2	7	29	2	3						
Dodge	P,OF	10	32	3	2	19	1	9						
Adams	SS	6	16	2	4	10	1	4						
Yale	1B	5	15	3	0	14	2	4						

ALPHA   4 - 11
Brooklyn, NY

DATE	OPPONENT	SCORE			W	L	T
04/16	Atlantic (Brooklyn)	11	42			L	
05/10	Atlantic (Brooklyn)*	14	45			L	
05/16	Atlantic (Brooklyn)	16	32			L	
05/27	Eckford (Brooklyn)	3	30			L	
06/11	Athlete (Washington Hts., NY)	32	27		W		
06/14	Atlantic (Brooklyn)	6	34			L	
06/26	Star (Brooklyn)	15	17			L	
07/10	Athletic (Brooklyn)	33	31	(10)	W		
07/20	Champion (Jersey City, NJ)	5	16			L	
07/24	Star (Brooklyn)	20	31			L	
08/03	Excelsior (Brooklyn)	10	9		W		
08/25	Athletic (Brooklyn)	23	32			L	
09/03	Eckford (Brooklyn)	17	30			L	

(Only scores extant)

* Box score not available

BATTERS	POS	GP	HL	A	O	R	A	O	H	A	O	TB	A	O
Kennedy	1B	*6	17	2	5	17	2	5	10	2	2	12	2	0
James	2B,C	*9	27	3	0	19	2	1	18	2	2	26	3	2
Munn	SS	*7	19	2	5	17	2	4	9	1	4	15	3	0
Moody	3B,C	*7	21	3	0	12	1	5	7	1	2	11	2	1
Valentine	OF	*10	32	3	2	17	1	7	14	1	5	20	2	2
E. Jackson	OF,3B	*9	31	3	4	11	1	2	9	1	3	12	2	0
Remsen	OF	*9	25	2	7	21	2	3	19	2	5	31	4	3
Fredericks	C,3B,OF	*7	21	3	0	12	1	5	14	2	4	12	4	1
Hillyer	P	*10	24	2	4	17	1	7	21	2	5	34	4	2

ALPHA (cont.)
Brooklyn, NY

BATTERS	POS	GP	HL	A	O	R	A	O	H	A	O	TB	A	O
Wood	OF,2B	*6	20	3	2	13	2	1	12	2	2	14	2	4

* Hits and total bases not available for all games

ORIENTAL 4 - 13
New York, NY

DATE	OPPONENT	SCORE	W	L	T
06/04	Mutual (New York)	6 16		L	
06/11	Mutual (New York)	15 20		L	
06/24	Sparta (New York)	59 17	W		
07/05	Lone Star (Middletown, NY)	74 25	W		
07/19	Eckford (Brooklyn)	15 33		L	
07/23	Atlantic (Brooklyn)	3 81		L	
08/02	Eckford (Brooklyn)	12 25		L	
08/16	Athletic (Philadelphia)	24 49		L	
08/17	Keystone (Philadelphia)	17 45		L	
08/18	Pastime (Baltimore)	16 15	W		
08/19	Maryland (Baltimore)	15 28		L	
08/20	National (Washington)	8 48		L	
09/07	Union (Morrisania, NY)	20 16	W		
09/24	National (Washington)	21 36		L	
09/30	Star (Brooklyn)	9 18		L	
10/08	Atlantic (Brooklyn)*	18 32		L	
10/16	Mutual (New York)	11 22		L	

* Box score not available

BATTERS	POS	GP	HL	A	O	R	A	O	H	A	O	TB	A	O
Delmadge	1B	15	46	3	1	36	2	6						
H.C. Galliker	2B,C	15	37	2	7	36	2	6						
Coffee	SS	9	19	2	1	25	2	7						
McGee	3B,P,OF	13	40	3	1	34	2	8						
Heineman	OF	13	42	3	3	26	2	0						
Perrine	OF	8	24	3	0	20	2	4						
C. Smith	OF	8	25	3	1	22	2	6						
George Bunting	C,2B	16	38	2	6	39	2	7						
R.J. Fitzsimmons	P,OF	13	41	3	2	21	1	8						
Delaney	SS	5	14	2	4	10	2	0						
Milt Sears	1B,2B	5	16	3	1	6	1	1						

EXCELSIOR 3 - 2
Farmington, WV

DATE	OPPONENT	SCORE	W	L	T
06/26	Franklin (White Rock, WV)	45 39	W		
07/31	Eureka (Fairmount, WV)	27 54		L	
08/28	Expert (Mannington, WV)	28 26	W		
09/04	Expert (Mannington, WV)	50 16	W		
09/29	Baltic (Wheeling, WV)	33 83		L	

BATTERS	POS	GP	HL	A	O	R	A	O	H	A	O	TB	A	O
F.T. Morgan	1B	4	14	3	2	14	3	2						
J. B. Fletcher	2B	3	7	2	1	14	4	2						
F.H. Morgan	SS	3	8	2	2	12	4	0						
H. Randall	3B,2B	4	14	3	2	17	4	1						
R. Downs	OF,3B,2B	4	9	2	1	20	5	0						
Haught	OF,2B	4	14	3	2	15	3	3						

EXCELSIOR (cont.)
Farmington, WV

BATTERS	POS	GP	HL	A	O	R	A	O	H	A	O	TB	A	O
Carpenter	OF	3	4	1	1	12	4	0						
Downs	C	5	15	3	0	22	4	2						
M.D. Randall	P,OF	4	11	2	3	16	4	0						
J.P. Fletcher	P,OF	4	11	2	3	14	3	2						
Jones	SS	2	7	3	1	8	4	0						
Cooper	3B	1	5	5	0	4	4	0						
J. Davis	OF	1	1	1	0	4	4	0						
Shroyer	P	1	3	3	0	3	3	0						
Davis	1B	1	3	3	0	3	3	0						
Parish	2B	1	5	5	0	2	2	0						

ATLANTIC 3 - 5
Algiers, LA

DATE	OPPONENT	SCORE	W	L	T
01/31	Lone Star (New Orleans)	25 33		L	
02/21	Lone Star (New Orleans)	27 20	W		
02/28	Lone Star (New Orleans)	60 40	W		
03/15	R.E. Lee (New Orleans)	20 33		L	
03/21	R.E. Lee (New Orleans)	17 34		L	
04/11	Southern (New Orleans)	46 40	W		
05/09	Southern (New Orleans)	20 77		L	
05/30	Pelican (New Orleans)*	27 29		L	

* Box score not available

BATTERS	POS	GP	HL	A	O	R	A	O	H	A	O	TB	A	O
James Higgins	1B,2B	*5	2	2	0	18	3	3						
H. Belcher	2B,SS	*6	6	3	0	19	3	1						
J. McKee	SS	*5	3	3	0	6	1	1						
W. Morton	3B	*4	8	4	0	14	3	2						
J. Smith	OF,1B	*7	2	1	0	30	4	2						
G. Cooley	OF,C	*6	10	5	0	14	2	2						
T. Houston	OF	*4	7	3	1	15	3	3						
C. Steele	C,3B	*7	3	1	1	31	4	3						
E. Foley	P	*4	3	1	1	20	5	0						
E. Wright	1B	*5	2	2	0	16	3	1						

* Hands lost not counted in all games

YALE 1 - 4
New Haven, CT

DATE	OPPONENT	SCORE	W	L	T
06/09	Mutual (New York)	16 18		L	
06/23	Mutual (New York)	5 15		L	
06/28	Williams (Williamstown, MA)	26 8	W		
07/05	Harvard (Cambridge, MA)	24 41		L	
10/20	Eckford (Brooklyn)	8 24		L	

BATTERS	POS	GP	HL	A	O	R	A	O	H	A	O	TB	A	O
French	1B,SS	5	19	3	4	5	1	0						
Wheeler	2B	3	11	3	2	5	1	2						
McCutcheon	SS	3	8	2	2	6	2	0						
McClintock	3B	4	14	3	2	7	1	3						
Condict	OF	4	13	3	1	5	1	1						
Denning	OF	4	9	2	1	12	3	0						

YALE (cont.)
New Haven, CT

BATTERS	POS	GP	HL	A	O	R	A	O	H	A	O	TB	A	O
Lewis	OF	4	10	2	2	9	2	1						
G. Richards	C	5	14	2	4	8	1	3						
Hooker	P	4	12	3	0	8	2	0						
Chapman	1B,3B	2	6	3	0	5	2	1						
Thomas	P	1	2	2	0	3	3	0						
Selden	2B	1	4	4	0	2	2	0						
Payson	2B	1	3	3	0	1	1	0						
Day	OF	1	3	3	0	1	1	0						
B. Richards	SS	1	2	2	0	1	1	0						
Buck	OF	1	3	3	0	1	1	0						
Faulkner	OF	1	3	3	0	0	0	0						

OLYMPIC   0 - 18
New York, NY

DATE	OPPONENT	SCORE		W	L	T
05/04	Mutual (New York)	8	38		L	
05/11	Mutual (New York)*	9	57		L	
05/17	Eckford (Brooklyn)	5	60		L	
05/24	Eckford (Brooklyn)*	3	35		L	
05/27	Atlantic (Brooklyn)	7	89		L	
06/15	Champion (Jersey City, NJ)	21	26		L	
08/04	Excelsior (Worcester, MA)	26	29		L	
08/06	Fairmount (Marlboro, MA)	17	48		L	
08/07	Tri Mountain (Boston)	14	80		L	
08/09	Lowell (Boston)	15	90		L	
08/10	Clipper (Lowell, MA)	20	84		L	
08/27	Atlantic (Brooklyn)	10	89		L	
08/31	Gotham (New York)*	28	37		L	
09/07	Bergen (Bergen, NJ)	19	32		L	

(Only scores extant)

* Box score not available

BATTERS	POS	GP	HL	A	O	R	A	O	H	A	O	TB	A	O
Hope Waddell	1B	11	34	3	1	19	1	8						
McCahill	2B,SS,C	7	22	3	1	10	1	3						
Tracy	SS	7	24	3	3	11	1	4						
White	3B,OF,2B	9	26	2	8	19	2	1						
Conover	OF	6	15	2	3	15	2	3						
Jones	OF	6	23	3	5	9	1	3						
Scott	OF	5	15	3	0	12	2	2						
Myers	C,P	7	22	3	1	13	1	6						
Sutton	P	6	9	1	3	12	2	0						
Edwards	C,2B	5	12	2	2	11	2	1						

AMATEUR TEAM TOTALS

TEAM	CITY/STATE	GP	W	L	T	PCT	R	OR
Lone Star	New Orleans, LA	25	22	3	0	.880	806	504
Forest City	Rockford, IL	24	20	4	0	.833	1174	287
Empire	St. Louis, MO	23	19	4	0	.826	834	492
Fairmount	Marlboro, MA	20	17	3	0	.850	747	426
Star	Brooklyn, NY	22	16	6	0	.727	618	338
Clipper	Lowell, MA	19	14	4	1	.763	510	296
Harvard	Cambridge, MA	20	11	5	1	.725	593	353
Lowell	Boston, MA	27	14	13	0	.519	821	602

AMATEUR TEAM TOTALS (cont.)

TEAM	CITY/STATE	GP	W	L	T	PCT	R	OR
Champion	Jersey City, NJ	21	13	8	0	.619	434	388
Southern	New Orleans, LA	20	13	7	0	.650	625	471
Gotham	New York, NY	15	9	6	0	.600	485	386
Empire	New York, NY	17	9	8	0	.529	437	401
Harmonic	Brooklyn, NY	18	9	9	0	.509	509	441
Athletic	Brooklyn, NY	20	9	10	1	.475	406	547
Mansfield	Middletown, CT	10	8	2	0	.800	328	228
Mutual	Janesville, WI	11	8	3	0	.727	335	290
Eagle	New York, NY	13	8	5	0	.615	391	327
Olympic	Pittsburgh, PA	8	7	1	0	.875	266	172
R.E. Lee	New Orleans, LA	10	7	3	0	.700	254	203
Athlete	Washington Hts., NY	11	7	4	0	.636	267	241
Athletic	Chicago, IL	11	7	4	0	.636	384	353
Pelican	New Orleans, LA	13	7	6	0	.538	328	332
Niagara	Buffalo, NY	14	7	7	0	.500	528	330
Tri Mountain	Boston, MA	16	7	9	0	.437	473	507
Mutual	Springfield, MA	10	6	4	0	.600	232	272
Alert	Rochester, NY	13	6	7	0	.462	342	308
Eagle	Flatbush, NY	13	6	7	0	.462	146	360
Detroit	Detroit, MI	13	6	7	0	.438	374	308
Buckeye	Cincinnati, OH	14	6	8	0	.429	317	514
Pastime	Baltimore, MD	14	6	8	0	.429	380	318
Olive	Philadelphia, PA	7	5	2	0	.714	270	195
Clipper	Glassboro, NJ	8	5	3	0	.625	286	
City Item	Philadelphia, PA	9	5	4	0	.556	279	285
Resolute	Elizabeth, NJ	10	5	5	0	.500	292	295
Excelsior	Brooklyn, NY	12	5	7	0	.417	196	261
Jefferson	Washington, DC	14	5	9	0	.357	292	450
Social	New York, NY	14	5	9	0	.357	391	434
Olympic	Philadelphia, PA	15	5	10	0	.333	305	345
Union	Morrisania, NY	15	5	10	0	.333	349	399
Powhatan	Brooklyn, NY	18	5	12	1	.306	390	453
Atalanta	Stoneham, MA	5	4	1	0	.800	437	108
Buckskin	Gloversville, NY	5	4	1	0	.800	197	108
Lone Star	St. Louis, MO	5	4	1	0	.800	155	103
Atlantic	St. Louis, MO	6	4	2	0	.667	141	116
Maple Leaf	Guelph, ON	6	4	2	0	.667	268	192
Fearless	New Orleans, LA	8	4	4	0	.500	168	166
Bergen	Bergen, NJ	9	4	5	0	.444	240	242
Intrepid	Philadelphia, PA	9	4	5	0	.444	203	206
National	Albany, NY	10	4	6	0	.400	281	353
Washington	New Orleans, LA	12	4	8	0	.333	260	373
Central City	Syracuse, NY	14	4	10	0	.286	274	371
Alpha	Brooklyn, NY	15	4	11	0	.267	262	401
Oriental	New York, NY	17	4	13	0	.235	343	526
Wide Awake	Taunton, MA	4	3	1	0	.750	165	102
Excelsior	Farmington, WV	5	3	2	0	.600	183	218
Expert	Philadelphia, PA	8	3	4	1	.437	225	295
Atlantic	Algiers, LA	8	3	5	0	.375	242	306
Dartmouth	Hanover, NH	4	2	2	0	.500	91	100
Salmon	Lowell, MA	4	2	2	0	.500	121	129
Old Point	Ft. Monroe, VA	5	2	2	1	.500	129	116
Sparta	New York, NY	5	2	3	0	.400	143	198
Excelsior	Worcester, MA	7	3	4	0	.429	176	209
Kentucky	Louisville, KY	8	2	6	0	.250	178	287
Sherman	Utica, NY	5	1	3	1	.300	90	120
Anderson	Lynn, MA	5	1	4	0	.200	118	256
Orion	New York, NY	5	1	4	0	.200	132	217
Ancient City	Schnectady, NY	5	1	4	0	.200	102	267
Comet	New Orleans, LA	5	1	4	0	.200	154	171
Yale	New Haven, CT	5	1	4	0	.200	79	106
Union	Washington, DC	10	1	9	0	.100	156	364
King Phillip	E. Abington, MA	4	0	4	0	.000	69	100
Surprise	New Orleans, LA	5	0	5	0	.000	49	96
Active	New York, NY	6	0	6	0	.000	94	201
Independent	Mansfield, OH	6	0	6	0	.000	92	302

AMATEUR TEAM TOTALS (cont.)

TEAM	CITY/STATE	GP	W	L	T	PCT	R	OR
Union	St. Louis, MO	7	0	7	0	.000	153	265
Olympic	New York, NY	18	0	18	0	.000	286	963

OTHER AMATEUR TEAMS

TEAM	CITY/STATE
Active	New Orleans, LA
Active	Wappinger Falls, NY
Aetna	Chicago, IL
Aetna	Jersey City, NJ
Alert	Philadelphia, PA
Amateur	Chicago, IL
Americus	Newark, NJ
Americus	Philadelphia, PA
Amity	Brooklyn, NY
Anderson	Lynn, MA
Androscoggin	Lewiston, ME
Ann Arbor	Ann Arbor, MI
Antioch	Yellow Springs, OH
Arcadia	Doylestown, PA
Arctic	New York, NY
Atlantic	Elizabeth, NJ
Atlantic	Philadelphia, PA
Atlantic	San Francisco, CA
Atlantic	San Francisco, CA
Bachelor	Philadelphia, PA
Baltic	Wheeling, WV
Beloit College	Beloit, WI
Boanerges	Hiram College, OH
Buckskin	Gloversville, NY
Capital City	Montgomery, AL
Chelsea	Long Branch, NJ
Chestnut St. Th,	Philadelphia, PA
Clipper	Monmouth, IL
Commonwealth	Philadelphia, PA
Covington	Covington, KY
Cream City	Milwaukee, WI
Crusader	New Orleans, LA
Delaware	Port Jervis, NY
Dexter	Quincy, IL
Dramatic	Mobile, AL
Eagle	San Francisco, CA
Empire	New Orleans, LA
Eon	Portland, ME
Eureka	E. New York, NY
Eureka	Milford, MA
Eureka	Newark, NJ
Excelsior	New Orleans, LA
Excelsior	Newark, NJ
Excelsior	Worcester, MA
Fulton	New York, NY
Geary	Philadelphia, PA
Gramercy	New York, NY
Granite	Lynn, MA
Great Western	Cincinnati, OH
Greenville	Greenville, AL
Gulf City	Mobile, AL
Hancock	New Orleans, LA
Harlem	New York, NY
Harvard	Harvard, IL
Hero	New Orleans, LA
Hickory	McConnellsville, OH

OTHER AMATEUR TEAMS (cont.)

TEAM	CITY/STATE
Holt	Newport, KY
Hope	New Orleans, LA
Howard	N. Bridgewater, MA
Intrepid	Philadelphia, PA
Invincible	Wetumpka, AL
Iron State	St. Louis, MO
Ivanhoe	Sing Sing, NY
Jasper	New York, NY
Jefferson	New York, NY
Kearsarge	Concord, NH
Kearsarge	Stoneham, MA
Kekionga	Ft. Wayne, IN
Kickenepawling	Johnstown, PA
Knickerbocker	Albany, NY
Lawrence	Bedford, IN
Liberty	New Brunswick, NJ
Liberty	Norwalk, CT
Liberty	Springfield, IL
Lone Star	Alma, IL
Magnolia	Marion, AL
Magnolia	St. Louis, MO
Malvern	Philadelphia, PA
Marion	Jersey City, NJ
Metacomet	Taunton, MA
Mohawk	Brooklyn, NY
Momoweta	Greenport, NY
Montgomery	Montgomery, AL
Morgan	New Orleans, LA
Mountain City	Pottsville, PA
Mountaineer	Ebensburgh, PA
Mutual	Selma, AL
Mystic	Rochester, NY
Naval	Norfolk, VA
Neptune	Easton, PA
Newark	Newark, NJ
Niagara Falls	Niagara Falls, NY
Nichols	Sandwich, MA
Occidental	Quincy, IL
Old Elm	Pittsfield, MA
Olympic	Burlington, VT
Olympic	Providence, RI
Olympic	Rock Point, VT
Omaha	Omaha, NE
Ontario	Oswego, NY
Oriental	Greenpoint, NY
Otoes	Omaha, NE
Pacific	Mobile, AL
Pacific	San Francisco, CA
Pacific	San Francisco, CA
Pastime	Little Falls, NY
Peconic	Brooklyn, NY
Princeton	Princeton, NJ
Quequechan	Fall River, MA
Raritan	S. Amboy, NJ
Relic	Jacksonville, IL
Rescue	Philadelphia, PA
Reserve	Hudson, OH
Resolute	Brooklyn, NY
Resolute	Oberlin, OH
Revere	Boston, MA
Riverside	Cattawissa, PA
Riverside	Holyoke, MA
Riverside	Portsmouth, OH
Rollstone	Fitchburg, MA
Rose Hill	Fordham, NY
Ross	Harlem, NY

OTHER AMATEUR TEAMS (cont.)

TEAM	CITY/STATE
Rowena	St. Louis, MO
Roxborough	Manayunk, PA
Schuylkill	Reading, PA
St. Elmo	Mobile, AL
St. Louis	St. Louis, MO
Stamford	Stamford, CT
Star	New Brunswick, NJ
Star	Painsesville, OH
Stonewall	Wetumpka, AL
Suffolk	Huntington, NY
Turner	St. Louis, MO
Una	Mt. Vernon, NY
Union	Camden, NJ
Union	Cohoes, NY
Union	Hudson City, NJ
Upton	Boston, MA
Wamsutta	New Bedford, MA
Wissahickon	Germantown, PA

1870
END GAME

By 1870, the National Association was faltering. Several forces were rising in the game which diluted its ability to govern the game properly. The most noteworthy of the Association's problems was its sheer size. It is very difficult to effectively govern a group numbering over 500 spread across the country. The solution of letting state associations govern the body of teams did alleviate the minutia of day to day operation but it led to other problems. With state associations voting as a block, a few teams, usually professional nines, could conceivably control large quantities of votes.

The professional teams viewed baseball differently than the bulk of the other teams for one primary reason. By employing the best possible players, the pro teams placed winning above all else. Consequently, a good team would generate much interest thus serving as a source of money. This concept was an anathema to the amateurs, but they felt helpless, swept along with the professional tide.

Two more Association problems were rising to a head by the end of the decade: (1) the quandry of players called "revolvers" who jumped from team to team and (2) the championship question. Revolving had been a problem ever since professionalism had crept into baseball. Players were constantly being lured from team to team with the promise of more lucre, sometimes in the middle of the season. Secondly, the way the championship was one or lost via a best-of-three series didn't always reward the best team. The so-called champions could simply avoid a tough opponent thus retaining their laurels through inactivity. The Athletics of Philadelphia were victims of this on more than one occasion. The Association was generally toothless to stop these practices. They could threaten teams with expulsion, but they rarely did. The truth was becoming apparent. The Association needed its members more than the members needed the Association.

At the December 1869 convention the conflict between professionals and amateurs rose to the surface. This was summarized in a *New York Clipper* editorial:

> At a fair estimate, there are not far from a thousand regularly organized base ball clubs located in our country, from Maine to California, and from the St. Lawrence to the Gulf of Mexico. Of these not fifty can be ranked in any way as professional clubs; indeed a contemporary limits the list to sixteen. And yet it is the ambition of this small minority to rule the whole thousand.

Further on, the *Clipper* suggested a solution:

> The result of all this, it is thought, must necessarily be either the withdrawal of amateur clubs from the association or the dismissal of professional clubs. This is the issue, it seems, which the controlling interest in the recent Convention has forced upon the fraternity.

In the year to come, it would be seen how this prophecy would come to pass.

On the field in 1870, a new entrant entered the fray modeled after baseball's must successful franchise to date. Late in 1869, a series of ads were placed in the *Clipper* seeking players for a team in Chicago called the Chicago club. Much as the Red Stockings had done the year before, the Chicago club was endeavoring to create the best professional nine in the land. The advertisements worked. Soon the Chicago club had signed several seasoned pros including Levi Meyerle and Ned Cuthbert. To further copy the Cincinnati outfit, the Chicago club wore knickers with long stockings—not red but white. Thereafter, the team would be known as the White Stockings.

Joining the White Stockings for the 1870 Association season were 14 other professional teams. Before too long, two of the group would play a game to end all games.

As the season started, the Red Stocking machine marched on. After touring to the east and west the year before, Cincinnati turned its attention to the south in April 1870. Playing a series of games in Louisiana, Tennessee and Kentucky, the team romped at will, winning them all handily.

As May turned to June, the Red Stockings left on another eastern tour. Here they carved a swath of victories through upper-state New York and New England. On June 13th, after arriving in New York City, the Cincinnati club bested the Mutuals 16–3, pushing its winning-streak to 89 games. The opponent the next day would be Brooklyn's Atlantic club.

On the 14th of June, many thousands of baseball fans jammed the Capitoline Grounds, the Atlantics' home ballpark, paying 50 cents a head to see the mighty Cincinnatis. The game remained close throughout as the Red Stockings nursed a 5-4 lead into the seventh. The home team tied up the match in the bottom of the eighth and neither team scored in the ninth. To the surprise of all, the jubilant Atlantics had apparently held the Red Stockings to a 5-5 tie.

Not content with a draw, the captain of the Red Stockings, Harry Wright, demanded a continuation. Association rules stipulated that if one team wanted to play a tie to its conclusion, the other team had to comply. Wright, confident that his team would eventually prevail, convinced the umpire that play should continue.

Neither team scored in the tenth and the Cincinnati nine came to the plate in the top of the eleventh. Here several well-placed hits garnered them two runs. It looked like Wright's insistence had paid off. Not done yet, the Atlantics took their turn in the bottom of the eleventh. To the consternation of the Cincinnatis, the first two Brooklyn batters reached base and scored, helped greatly by a wallop into the overflow crowd. One of the next batters, George Zettlein, hit a ball that the Cincinnati first sacker couldn't handle, allowing Bob Ferguson to score the eighth and winning run. The fabulous streak was over.

As mentioned in the Chadwick scrapbooks, the crestfallen Red Stocking president Aaron Champion sent a telegram back to the faithful fans of Cincinnati. It read: "Atlantics 8, Red Stockings 7. The finest game ever played. Our boys did nobly, but fortune was against us. Eleven innings played. Though beaten, not disgraced."

The lustre gone, the Red Stockings meandered through the rest of their schedule losing five more games while tying one. Still, they finished with the best professional record in the land (27-6-1). The new White Stockings finished with the second best pro record followed by the Athletics. In all games, the Mutual, Cincinnati, Chicago and Athletic clubs each won more than 65 each.

Like before, the championship for 1870 reached a murky ending. The Red Stockings finished with the best record, but lost out again to the eccentricities of the schedule. The Atlantics, by virtue of their second loss to the Mutuals on September 22, turned the crown over to them. Later, the New York nine lost two to the White Stockings (the second in controversial fashion), giving the tainted pennant to them. For the fourth year in a row, the team with the best record had been left pennantless.

The sporting press did their best to alleviate the championship confusion. During the summer a table was published showing how the top five pro teams (Chicago, Athletic, Mutual, Cincinnati and Atlantic) were faring against one another. Although largely ignored, this first set of team standings was a landmark event.

For the first time, in computing averages, the reported statistics for some of the professional teams were compiled in two sections: (1) games against professional teams and (2) games against all teams. In matches with professionals only, the best marks were garnered by the Athletics Wes Fisler with 85 hits, 139 total bases and (using the decimal system) a 2.36 and 3.86 average respectively. In all games, a trio of Red Stockings came away with the honors. Fred Waterman cuffed opposing pitchers for 278 hits, while Charles Gould ran up 419 total bases. The peerless George Wright finished with the highest average in each (4.27) and (7.08)

Among the amateur teams, the Lone Star squad of New Orleans finished with the most wins (32) but once again the Brooklyn Stars (24–9) were considered the amateur champions as they beat the Harvards of Cambridge, Massachusetts (31–12) for the second time in November. The highest amateur averages were posted by two members of the Lone Stars. William Condon swatted the most hits (161) leading to the most total bases (251). His teammate A.B. Johnston obtained the highest average in each category (4.19) and (5.79).

For two teams, the professional White Stockings and the amateur Stars (Brooklyn), a new statistic was unveiled in the season-ending statistics. The two teams kept track of the number of times each player batted. Into this number was divided his hits, thus giving birth to the modern batting average. Quickly seen as the best method of determining a batter's strength, at-bats were added to game reports the next spring to help determine batting averages. With this addition, the box score evolved into a form easily recognizable today.

After the season, delegates gathered for the annual convention of the National Association in November. As reported in the *Clipper*, it was not altogether a satisfactory affair:

> ...before the convention in question closed its proceedings the fact was

> realized that the convention was neither more or less than a gathering of professional club managers...This convention, and the remarkable proceedings which characterized it shows that the last feather had been placed on the camel's back, and under the pressure of the control of a clique of professional managers the National Association gave up the ghost, and after a reputable existence of ten years and a decline in health during the last three, it adjourned *sine die* on the 30th of November, 1870.

Although speaking metaphorically, the words rang true. This November meeting would be the last convention of the National Association.

Through the last 14 years, for better or for worse, the National Association had governed baseball. In the early days, the Association had nurtured the game, overseeing its growth from coast to coast and helping to codify its statistics. But in 1870, with the Association so large, and so plagued with the great gulf between the amateurs and professionals, it was time for a change. It was time to say goodbye to baseball's first era before getting ready to greet its next.

PROFESSIONAL TEAMS

MUTUAL 68 - 17 - 3   (29 - 15 - 3)
New York, NY

DATE	OPPONENT	SCORE		W	L	T
05/03	Oriental (New York)	29	5	W		
05/04	Union (Morrisania, NY)#	11	4	W		
05/06	Union (Morrisania, NY)#	17	14	W		
05/07	Star (Brooklyn)	3	14		L	
05/19	Oriental (New York)	30	1	W		
05/20	Eckford (Brooklyn)#	22	8	W		
05/25	Resolute (Elizabeth, NJ)	54	18	W		
05/26	Rose Hill (Fordham, NY)	21	6	W		
05/30	Forest City (Rockford, IL)#	21	13	W		
06/02	Athletic (Brooklyn)	38	9	W		
06/03	Eckford (Brooklyn)#	13	13			T
06/06	Eckford (Brooklyn)#	18	15	W		
06/07	Social (New York)	40	5	W		
06/08	Union (Morrisania, NY)#	13	19		L	
06/09	Resolute (Elizabeth, NJ)	37	18	W		
06/13	Cincinnati (Cincinnati)#	3	16		L	
06/16	Union (Lansingburgh, NY)#	10	10			T
06/17	Tri Mountain (Boston)#	25	11	W		
06/18	Lowell (Boston)	35	20	W		
06/20	Fairmount (Marlboro, MA)	22	13	W		
06/21	Clipper (Lowell, MA)	34	14	W		
06/22	Harvard (Cambridge, MA)	22	24		L	
06/25	Yale (New Haven, CT)	49	12	W		
06/27	Alpha (Brooklyn)	25	4	W		
06/28	Atlantic (Brooklyn)#	13	15		L	
07/01	Rose Hill (Fordham, NY)	27	18	W		
07/04	Athletic (Philadelphia)#	15	24		L	
07/06	Chicago (Chicago)#	13	4	W		
07/11	Maryland (Baltimore)#	21	10	W		
07/12	Pastime (Baltimore)	34	18	W		
07/13	Olympic (Washington)#	29	8	W		
07/14	National (Washington)#	11	1	W		
07/16	Wheeling (Wheeling, WV)	48	14	W		
07/19	Riverside (Portsmouth, OH)#	31	17	W		
07/20	Harvard (Cambridge, MA)	22	15	W		
07/22	Amateur (Chicago)	65	11	W		
07/23	Chicago (Chicago)#	9	0	W		
07/25	Forest City (Rockford, IL)#	15	4	W		
07/29	Forest City (Cleveland)#	5	7		L	
07/30	Cincinnati (Cincinnati)#	12	15		L	
08/02	Eckford (Brooklyn)#	19	9	W		
08/03	Pastime (Baltimore)	29	7	W		
08/09	Atlantic (Brooklyn)#	9	7	W		
08/11	Athletic (Brooklyn)	17	10	W		
08/16	Forest City (Cleveland)#	10	9	W		
08/18	Athletic (Philadelphia)#	21	8	W		
08/19	Keystone (Philadelphia)	34	8	W		
08/23	Excelsior (Brooklyn)	23	5	W		
08/24	Forest City (Cleveland)#	16	15	W		
08/25	Union (Morrisania, NY)#	18	10	W		
08/26	Union (Lansingburgh, NY)#	24	13	W		
08/29	Athletic (Philadelphia)#	7	11		L	
09/01	Eckford (Brooklyn)#	27	8	W		
09/03	Union (Morrisania, NY)#	12	1	W		
09/04	Yale (New Haven, CT)	29	4	W		
09/10	Star (Brooklyn)	16	7	W		
09/13	Olympic (Washington)#	29	4	W		
09/14	Eckford (Brooklyn)#	35	6	W		
09/15	Athletic (Philadelphia)#	11	10	W		
09/16	Expert (Philadelphia)	29	4	W		
09/19	Union (Lansingburgh, NY)	19	24		L	
09/22	Atlantic (Brooklyn)#	10	4	W		
09/24	Trenton (Trenton, NJ)	19	0	W		

MUTUAL (cont.)
New York, NY

DATE	OPPONENT	SCORE		W	L	T
09/27	Chicago (Chicago)#	11	22		L	
09/29	Mansfield (Middletown, CT)	50	20	W		
10/01	Star (Brooklyn)	13	8	W		
10/05	Union (Lansingburgh, NY)#	12	9	W		
10/10	Atlantic (Brooklyn)#	4	8		L	
10/15	Harvard (Cambridge, MA)	24	13	W		
10/18	Athletic (Philadelphia)#	12	12			T
10/19	Yale (New Haven, CT)	31	9	W		
10/24	Athletic (Philadelphia)#	12	17		L	
10/25	Cincinnati (Cincinnati)#	1	7		L	
10/28	Athletic (Philadelphia)#	6	4	W		
11/01	Chicago (Chicago#	*5	7		L	
11/02	Cincinnati (Cincinnati)#	7	23		L	
11/05	Atlantic (Brooklyn)#	13	9	W		
11/10	Athletic (Philadelphia)#	19	23		L	
11/17	Montgomery (Montgomery, AL)	46	4	W		
11/18	Lone Star (New Orleans, LA)	28	2	W		
11/24	Southern (New Orleans, LA)	37	5	W		
11/24	R.E. Lee (New Orleans, LA)	19	1	W		
11/24	Lone Star (New Orleans, LA)	26	1	W		
11/27	Southern (New Orleans, LA)	36	6	W		
11/27	Lone Star (New Orleans, LA)	13	5	W		
11/30	R.E. Lee (New Orleans, LA)	15	8	W		
12/04	Southern (New Orleans, LA)	26	16	W		
12/04	R.E. Lee (New Orleans, LA)	22	9	W		

\# Professional games
* 13-12 Mutual in ninth when New York club left field in protest; score reverted to eighth inning.

(All Games)

BATTERS	POS	GP	HL	AVG	R	AVG	H	AVG	TB	AVG
Ev Mills	1B	56					135	2.41	186	3.32
Marty Swandell	2B	47					88	1.87	108	2.30
John Hatfield	SS	57					139	2.44	197	3.46
Jack Nelson	3B	57					130	2.28	169	2.96
Dave Eggler	OF	59					147	2.49	190	3.22
Dan Patterson	OF	58					118	2.03	149	2.56
Al Martin	OF,P	52					104	2.00	112	2.15
Charley Mills	C	58					91	1.57	133	2.29
Rynie Wolters	P	51					102	2.00	114	2.23
Dick Higham	2B	9					10	1.11	18	2.00
Billy McMahon	OF	8					15	1.88	17	2.13
George Flanly	2B	7					15	2.14	17	2.43

(Professional Games)

BATTERS	POS	GP	HL	AVG	R	AVG	H	AVG	TB	AVG
Ev Mills	1B	36					79	2.19	116	3.22
Marty Swandell	2B	30					46	1.53	56	1.87
John Hatfield	SS	37					75	2.03	108	2.92
Jack Nelson	3B	38					74	1.95	98	2.58
Dave Eggler	OF	38					77	2.03	101	2.66
Dan Patterson	OF	38					65	1.71	88	2.32
Al Martin										
Charley Mills	C	38					59	1.55	72	1.89
Rynie Wolters	P	35					54	1.54	76	2.17

CINCINNATI 67 - 6 - 1 (27 - 6 - 1)
Cincinnati, OH

DATE	OPPONENT	SCORE			W	L	T
04/21	Eagle (Louisville, KY)	94	7		W		
04/25	Pelican (New Orleans, LA)	51	1		W		
04/26	Southern (New Orleans)	79	6		W		
04/28	Atlantic (Algiers, LA)	39	6		W		
04/29	Lone Star (New Orleans, LA)	26	7		W		
04/30	R.E. Lee (New Orleans, LA)	24	4		W		
05/04	Oriental (Memphis, TN)	100	2		W		
05/12	Forest City (Cleveland)#	12	2		W		
05/13	Forest City (Cleveland)#	24	10		W		
05/20	College Hill (College Hill, OH)	72	10		W		
05/23	Orion (Lexington, KY)	75	0		W		
05/25	Union (Urbana, OH)	108	3		W		
05/26	Dayton (Dayton, OH)	104	9		W		
05/29	Riverside (Portsmouth,OH)#	32	3		W		
05/31	Forest City (Cleveland)#	27	13		W		
06/01	Flour City (Rochester, NY)	56	13		W		
06/02	Ontario (Oswego, NY)	46	4		W		
06/03	Old Elm (Pittsfield, MA)	66	9		W		
06/04	Harvard (Cambridge, MA)	46	15		W		
06/06	Lowell (Boston)	17	4		W		
06/08	Clipper (Lowell, MA)	32	5		W		
06/09	Tri Mountain (Boston, MA)#	30	6		W		
06/10	Fairmount (Marlboro, MA)	77	16		W		
06/13	Mutual (New York)#	16	3		W		
06/14	Atlantic (Brooklyn)#	7	8	(11)		L	
06/15	Union (Morrisania, NY)#	14	0		W		
06/16	Resolute (Elizabeth, NJ)	22	7		W		
06/17	Eckford (Brooklyn)#	24	7		W		
06/18	Star (Brooklyn)	16	11		W		
06/20	Amateur (Newark)	53	2		W		
06/21	Intrepid (Philadelphia)	52	14		W		
06/22	Athletic (Philadelphia)#	27	25		W		
06/23	Keystone (Philadelphia)	37	26		W		
06/24	Pastime (Baltimore)	30	8		W		
06/25	Maryland (Baltimore)#	30	13		W		
06/27	Olympic (Washington)#	35	24		W		
06/28	National (Washington)#	30	10		W		
07/02	Forest City (Rockford, IL)#	14	13		W		
07/04	Forest City (Rockford, IL)#	24	7		W		
07/09	Amateur (Chicago)	56	19		W		
07/11	Forest City (Rockford, IL)#	16	16				T
07/13	Kekionga (Ft. Wayne, IN)	70	1		W		
07/15	Eagle (Louisville, KY)	39	8		W		
07/18	Harvard (Cambridge, MA)	20	17		W		
07/27	Athletic (Philadelphia)#	7	11			L	
07/30	Mutual (New York)#	15	12		W		
08/02	Maryland (Baltimore)#	25	9		W		
08/04	Lightfoot (Lebanon, OH)	66	6		W		
08/05	Indianapolis (Indianapolis)	61	8		W		
08/06	Olympic (Washington)#	38	3		W		
08/09	Union (Lansingburgh, NY)#	34	9		W		
08/12	Lone Star (New Orleans, LA)	49	11		W		
08/22	Live Oak (Cincinnati)	46	2		W		
08/23	Amateur (Wash. Ct. House, OH)	72	6		W		
08/26	Riverside (Portsmouth, OH)#	29	27		W		
08/31	Live Oak (Cincinnati)	35	12		W		
09/02	Atlantic (Brooklyn)#	14	3		W		
09/07	Chicago (Chicago)#	6	10			L	
09/15	Riverside (Portsmouth, OH)#	12	1		W		
09/20	Resolute (Hamilton, OH)	36	4		W		
09/21	Dayton (Dayton, OH)	79	12		W		
09/24	Holt (Newport, KY)	32	7		W		
09/27	Indianapolis (Indianapolis, IN)	43	2		W		
09/28	Union (St. Louis)	28	1		W		
09/29	Empire (St. Louis)	7	5		W		
10/06	Forest City (Cleveland)#	18	15		W		

CINCINNATI (cont.)
Cincinnati, OH

DATE	OPPONENT	SCORE	W	L	T
10/13	Chicago (Chicago)#	13 16		L	
10/15	Forest City (Rockford, IL)#	5 12		L	
10/22	Athletic (Philadelphia)#	15 8	W		
10/24	Union (Lansingburgh, NY)	12 7	W		
10/25	Mutual (New York)#	7 1	W		
10/26	Atlantic (Brooklyn)#	7 11		L	
11/02	Mutual (New York)#	23 7	W		
11/05	Forest City (Cleveland)#	27 16	W		

Professional games

(All Games)

BATTERS	POS	GP	HL	AVG	R	AVG	H	AVG	TB	AVG
Charles Gould	1B	74					266	3.59	419	5.66
Charlie Sweasy	2B	73					232	3.17	396	5.42
George Wright	SS	58					248	4.27	411	7.08
Fred Waterman	3B	72					278	3.86	414	5.75
Andy Leonard	OF,SS	74					269	3.63	424	5.70
Harry Wright	OF,P	74					257	3.47	363	4.94
Cal McVey	OF	72					262	3.63	389	5.40
Doug Allison	C	55					178	3.23	245	4.45
Asa Brainard	P	66					217	3.28	284	4.30
Dean	OF,C	33					112	3.05	178	5.56
Atwater	OF,P	16					72	4.05	100	6.25

PITCHERS	IP	R	BB	AVG
Asa Brainard	440	440	47	1.00
Harry Wright	108	123	1	1.14
Atwater	93	83	11	0.89

CHICAGO 65 - 8 (22 - 7)
Chicago, IL

DATE	OPPONENT	SCORE	W	L	T
04/21	Amateur (Chicago)	75 12	W		
04/23	Garden City (Chicago)	48 2	W		
04/29	Union (St. Louis)	47 1	W		
04/30	Empire (St. Louis)	36 8	W		
05/06	Atlantic (Algiers, LA)	51 0	W		
05/08	Lone Star (New Orleans, LA)	18 10	W		
05/09	R.E. Lee (New Orleans, LA)	24 14	W		
05/11	Southern (New Orleans, LA)	41 9	W		
05/13	Bluff City (Memphis, TN)	157 1	W		
05/16	Grove City (Kankakee, IL)	111 5	W		
05/21	Amateur (Chicago)	49 4	W		
05/24	Garden City (Chicago)	46 12	W		
05/27	Mutual (Janesville, WI)	74 5	W		
05/28	Cream City (Milwaukee)	71 19	W		
05/31	Athletic (Chicago)	39 5	W		
06/03	Forest City (Cleveland)#	15 9	W		
06/07	Garden City (Chicago)	24 11	W		
06/10	Active (Clinton, IA)	96 7	W		
06/11	Amateur (Chicago)	52 13	W		
06/15	Picked Nine (Chicago)	17 13	W		
06/16	Forest City (Rockford, IL)#	28 14	W		
06/20	Forest City (Cleveland)#	24 8	W		
06/21	Niagara (Buffalo)	64 14	W		
06/22	Flour City (Rochester, NY)	46 20	W		
06/24	Ontario (Oswego, NY)	108 12	W		
06/25	Eckford (Syracuse, NY)	30 15	W		
06/27	Union (Lansingburgh, NY)#	25 21	W		

CHICAGO (cont.)
Chicago, IL

DATE	OPPONENT	SCORE		W	L	T
06/28	Lowell (Boston)	43	25	W		
06/29	Tri Mountain (Boston)#	36	16	W		
06/30	Harvard (Cambridge, MA)	33	7	W		
07/02	Yale (New Haven, CT)	35	8	W		
07/04	Atlantic (Brooklyn)#	20	30		L	
07/06	Mutual (New York)#	4	13		L	
07/08	Union (Morrisania, NY)#	28	12	W		
07/09	Star (Brooklyn)	9	6	W		
07/11	Athletic (Philadelphia)#	12	17		L	
07/12	Keystone (Philadelphia)	23	18	W		
07/13	W. Philadelphia (Philadelphia)	18	9	W		
07/14	Maryland (Baltimore)#	46	9	W		
07/15	Pastime (Baltimore)	32	13	W		
07/16	Olympic (Washington)#	27	9	W		
07/18	National (Washington)#	24	6	W		
07/23	Mutual (New York)#	0	9		L	
07/26	Harvard (Cambridge, MA)	6	11		L	
08/01	Athletic (Philadelphia)	11	18		L	
08/03	Lone Star (New Orleans, LA)	42	8	W		
08/04	Union (Lansingburgh, NY)#	11	16		L	
08/05	Maryland (Baltimore)#	28	15	W		
08/10	Olympic (Washington)#	16	15	W		
08/11	Aetna (Chicago)	43	8	W		
08/17	Athletic (Chicago)	28	12	W		
08/24	Active (Chicago)	54	6	W		
08/26	Forest City (Rockford, IL)#	7	14		L	
08/30	Atlantic (Brooklyn)#	12	4	W		
09/02	Forest City (Rockford, IL)	13	6	W		
09/07	Cincinnati (Cincinnati)#	10	6	W		
09/08	Eagle (Louisville)	22	12	W		
09/17	Forest City (Cleveland)#	9	7	W		
09/20	Eckford (Brooklyn)#	22	8	W		
09/24	Atlantic (Brooklyn)#	9	4	W		
09/26	Athletic (Philadelphia)#	12	11	W		
09/27	Mutual (New York)#	22	11	W		
09/30	Kekionga (Ft. Wayne, IN)	@16	13	W		
10/01	Aetna (Chicago)	37	9	W		
10/07	Active (Chicago)	20	2	W		
10/08	Amateur (Chicago)	23	12	W		
10/13	Cincinnati (Cincinnati)#	16	13	W		
10/19	Kekionga (Ft. Wayne, IN)	15	2	W		
10/22	Forest City (Rockford, IL)#	10	6	W		
10/24	Atlantic (St. Louis)	46	8	W		
10/25	Empire (St. Louis)	46	10	W		
10/26	Bloomington (Bloomington, IL)	61	6	W		
11/01	Mutual (New York)#	$7	5	W		

@ 13-12 Kekionga after 5 innings, sixth and final inning played under protest.
$ 13-12 Mutual in ninth when New York club left field in protest; score reverted to eighth inning.
# Professional games

(All Games)

BATTERS	POS	GP	HL	AVG	R	AVG	H	AVG	TB	AVG
Bub McAtee	1B	54					188	3.48	231	4.28
James Wood	2B,P	66					237	3.59	363	5.50
Ed Duffy	SS	20					39	1.95	64	3.20
Levi Meyerle	3B,P	63					213	3.38	327	5.19
Ned Cuthbert	OF	68					238	3.50	372	5.47
Fred Treacey	OF	64					227	3.39	373	5.83
Clipper Flynn	OF	61					215	3.52	284	4.66
Charley Hodes	C	46					172	3.74	239	5.19
Ed Pinkham	P	59					213	3.61	358	6.07
Mart King	OF,SS,3B,C	45					171	3.80	244	5.42
Keerle	OF	9					27	3.00	38	4.22
Burns	P	9					11	1.22	14	1.55

CHICAGO (cont.)
Chicago, IL

PITCHERS	IP	H	AVG
Ed Pinkham	330	367	1.11
Levi Meyerle	217	257	1.18
Burns	24	17	0.71
James Wood	9	7	0.77

(Professional Games)

BATTERS	POS	GP	AB	R	AVG	H	AVG	TB	AVG	BA
Bub McAtee	1B	24	139			54	2.25	78	3.25	.388
Jimmy Wood	2B	25	139			58	2.32	81	3.24	.417
Ed Duffy	SS	11	53			12	1.09	24	2.18	.226
Levi Meyerle	3B	23	116			42	1.83	71	3.09	.362
Ned Cuthbert	OF	25	135			56	2.24	82	3.28	.415
Clipper Flynn	OF	24	129			62	2.58	76	3.17	.481
Fred Treacey	OF	22	115			44	2.00	79	3.59	.383
Mart King	C	15	78			31	2.06	40	2.66	.397
Ed Pinkham	P	20	103			42	2.10	66	3.30	.408
Charley Hodes	C	11	65			23	2.09	29	2.64	.354
Keerle	OF	3	13			5	1.66	9	3.00	.385
Burns	P	5	26			4	0.80	5	1.00	.192

ATHLETIC
Philadelphia, PA

65 - 11 - 1   (26 - 11 - 1)

DATE	OPPONENT	SCORE		W	L	T
04/21	Intrepid (Philadelphia)	41	7	W		
04/25	Maryland (Baltimore)#	34	16	W		
04/28	Maryland (Baltimore)#	23	9	W		
04/30	Pastime (Baltimore)	34	12	W		
05/05	Keystone (Philadelphia)	28	13	W		
05/07	Expert (Philadelphia)	47	6	W		
05/13	Union (Morrisania, NY)#	6	7		L	
05/14	Pastime (Baltimore)	32	10	W		
05/16	Olympic (Washington)#	29	13	W		
05/18	Union (Morrisania, NY)#	31	11	W		
05/19	Olympic (Washington)#	11	14		L	
05/23	Harvard (Cambridge, MA)	20	8	W		
05/24	Lowell (Boston)	22	11	W		
05/25	Tri Mountain (Boston)#	45	4	W		
05/26	Yale (New Haven, CT)	29	12	W		
05/30	Atlantic (Brooklyn)#	18	13	W		
06/01	Forest City (Rockford, IL)#	16	10	W		
06/04	Keystone (Philadelphia)	12	1	W		
06/08	Union (Lansingburgh, NY)#	41	6	W		
06/18	Princeton (Princeton, NJ)	22	4	W		
06/20	Atlantic (Brooklyn)#	19	3	W		
06/22	Cincinnati (Cincinnati)#	25	27		L	
06/24	Trenton (Trenton, NJ)	48	11	W		
06/27	Union (Morrisania, NY)#	51	20	W		
06/28	Princeton (Princeton, NJ)	24	7	W		
07/04	Mutual (New York)#	24	15	W		
07/07	W. Philadelphia (Philadelphia)	50	1	W		
07/09	Expert (Philadelphia)	40	13	W		
07/11	Chicago (Chicago)#	17	12	W		
07/14	Keystone (Philadelphia)	30	19	W		
07/18	Olympic (Washington)#	25	15	W		
07/22	Maryland (Baltimore)#	24	13	W		
07/25	Atlantic (Pittsburgh)	24	2	W		
07/27	Cincinnati (Cincinnati)#	11	7	W		
07/28	Riverside (Portsmouth, OH)	15	2	W		
07/30	Kekionga (Ft. Wayne, IN)	110	5	W		
08/01	Chicago (Chicago)#	18	11	W		

ATHLETIC (cont.)
Philadelphia, PA

DATE	OPPONENT	SCORE			W	L	T
08/03	Forest City (Rockford, IL)#	10	15			L	
08/06	Forest City (Cleveland)#	28	7		W		
08/08	Niagara (Buffalo)	30	4		W		
08/10	Harvard (Cambridge, MA)	27	9		W		
08/13	Tuttle & Bailey (New York)	39	0		W		
08/15	Excelsior (Norristown, PA)	40	2		W		
08/18	Mutual (New York)#	8	21			L	
08/20	Pastime (Germantown, PA)	27	3		W		
08/21	Forest City (Cleveland)#	19	11		W		
08/24	W. Philadelphia (Philadelphia)	24	12		W		
08/27	Excelsior (Norristown, PA)	50	2		W		
08/29	Mutual (New York)#	12	7		W		
08/31	Union (Lansingburgh, NY)#	11	2		W		
09/02	Mansfield (Middletown, CT)	32	5		W		
09/06	Expert (Philadelphia)	21	9		W		
09/12	Excelsior (Philadelphia)	80	4		W		
09/14	Olympic (Washington)#	30	4		W		
09/15	Mutual (New York)#	10	11			L	
09/24	Union (Lansingburgh, NY)#	10	15			L	
09/26	Chicago (Chicago)#	11	12			L	
09/27	Schuylkill (Reading, PA)	45	7		W		
09/29	Active (Renova, PA)	69	20		W		
10/05	Excelsior (Philadelphia, PA)	32	2		W		
10/08	Expert (Philadelphia, PA)	11	5		W		
10/10	W. Philadelphia (Philadelphia)	34	18		W		
10/15	Cohocksink (Philadelphia)	55	0		W		
10/17	Atlantic (Brooklyn)#	11	7		W		
10/18	Mutual (New York)#	12	12	(10)			T
10/19	Atlantic (Brooklyn)#	15	3		W		
10/22	Cincinnati (Cincinnati)#	8	15			L	
10/24	Mutual (New York)#	17	12		W		
10/28	Mutual (New York)#	4	6			L	
10/29	Eddington (Eddington, NJ)	57	11		W		
10/31	Intrepid (Philadelphia)	31	12		W		
11/02	Brandywine (W. Chester, PA)	42	2		W		
11/05	Trenton (Trenton, NJ)	36	7		W		
11/07	Intrepid (Philadelphia)	45	4		W		
11/10	Mutual (New York)#	23	19		W		
11/11	Brandywine (W. Chester, PA)	48	9		W		
11/14	Atlantic (Brooklyn)#	12	14			L	

\# Professional games

(All Games)

BATTERS	POS	GP	HL	AVG	R	AVG	H	AVG	TB	AVG
Wes Fisler	1B	74					234	3.16	370	5.00
Al Reach	2B	76					231	3.03	331	4.36
John Radcliff	SS	73					210	2.87	321	4.39
Tom Pratt	3B	70					201	2.87	282	4.03
John Sensenderfer	OF	73					225	3.08	338	4.63
George Bechtel	OF	69					206	2.98	293	4.25
Tom Berry	OF	55					158	2.87	214	3.89
Fergy Malone	C	74					241	3.25	370	5.00
Dick McBride	P	72					230	3.19	334	4.64
Harry Schafer	OF	35					121	3.45	188	5.37

(Professional Games)

BATTERS	POS	GP	HL	AVG	R	AVG	H	AVG	TB	AVG
Wes Fisler	1B	36					85	2.36	139	3.86
Al Reach	2B	37					75	2.02	113	3.05
John Radcliff	SS	37					71	1.91	116	3.10
Tom Pratt	3B	37					71	1.91	106	2.86
John Sensenderfer	OF	36					83	2.30	121	3.35
George Bechtel	OF	36					63	1.75	84	2.33

ATHLETIC (cont.)
Philadelphia, PA

BATTERS	POS	GP	HL	AVG	R	AVG	H	AVG	TB	AVG
Tom Berry	OF	25					36	1.44	52	2.08
Fergy Malone	C	37					86	2.32	132	3.56
Dick McBride	P	36					83	2.30	132	3.66
Harry Schafer	OF	10					20	2.00	26	2.66

FOREST CITY   42 - 13 - 1   (10 - 13 - 1)
Rockford, IL

DATE	OPPONENT	SCORE			W	L	T
05/11	Kaw Valley (Lawrence, KS)	41	6		W		
05/12	Picked Nine (Topeka, KS)	97	13		W		
05/16	Picked Nine (Rockford)	28	7		W		
05/18	Maple Leaf (Hamilton, ON)	65	3		W		
05/19	Niagara (Buffalo)	44	13		W		
05/20	Eckford (Syracuse, NY)	57	16		W		
05/23	Union (Lansingburgh, NY)#	21	3		W		
05/25	Mutual (Springfield, MA)	36	4		W		
05/30	Mutual (New York)#	13	21			L	
05/31	Atlantic (Brooklyn)#	17	16		W		
06/02	Athletic (Philadelphia)#	10	16			L	
06/04	Pastime (Baltimore)	21	11		W		
06/06	Olympic (Washington)#	10	19			L	
06/07	Olympic (Washington)#	8	7		W		
06/08	National (Washington)#	10	4		W		
06/08	Jefferson (Washington)	15	6		W		
06/13	Forest City (Cleveland)#	9	21			L	
06/14	Forest City (Cleveland)#	24	18		W		
06/16	Chicago (Chicago)#	14	28			L	
06/30	Amateur (Chicago)	53	28		W		
07/02	Cincinnati (Cincinnati)#	13	14			L	
07/04	Cincinnati (Cincinnati)#	7	24			L	
07/06	Riverside (Portsmouth, OH)#	37	7		W		
07/08	Kekionga (Ft. Wayne, IN)	32	3		W		
07/11	Cincinnati (Cincinnati)#	16	16				T
07/18	Potter Palmer (Chicago)	49	0		W		
07/25	Mutual (New York)#	4	15			L	
07/30	Lone Star (New Orleans, LA)	44	8		W		
08/03	Athletic (Philadelphia)#	15	10		W		
08/04	Maryland (Baltimore)#	11	4		W		
08/06	Union (Lansingburgh, NY)#	29	31			L	
08/08	Olympic (Washington)#	13	24			L	
08/20	Plow Boy (Stillman Valley, IL)	21	4		W		
08/26	Chicago (Chicago)#	14	7		W		
08/29	Atlantic (Brooklyn)#	13	14	(12)		L	
09/01	Mutual (Janesville, WI)	69	4		W		
09/02	Cream City (Milwaukee)	52	3		W		
09/03	Valley City (Grand Rapids, MI)	32	7		W		
09/05	Chicago (Chicago)#	6	13			L	
09/13	Elgin (Elgin, IL)	72	3		W		
09/14	Aurora (Aurora, IL)	29	7		W		
09/15	Aetna (Chicago)	35	3		W		
09/16	Marshall (Marshalltown, IA)	17	3		W		
09/17	Marshall (Marshalltown, IA)	34	5		W		
09/19	Star (Waverly, IA)	59	4		W		
09/20	Excelsior (Manchester, IA)	68	7		W		
09/21	Key City (Dubuque, IA)	79	1		W		
09/22	Active (Clinton, IA)	59	13		W		
09/29	Shabonna (Ottawa, IL)	17	2		W		
09/30	Des Moines (Des Moines, IA)	32	9		W		
10/01	Des Moines (Des Moines, IA)	24	2		W		
10/03	Otoe (Nebraska City, NE)	70	6		W		
10/07	Appanoe (Ottumwa, IA)	48	3		W		

FOREST CITY (cont.)
Rockford, IL

DATE	OPPONENT	SCORE		W	L	T
10/08	Crescent (Ottumwa, IA)	41	2	W		
10/15	Cincinnati (Cincinnati)#	12	5	W		
10/22	Chicago (Chicago)#	6	10		L	

Professional games

(All Games)

BATTERS	POS	GP	HL	AVG	R	AVG	H	AVG	TB	AVG
Joe Doyle	1B	50					111	2.22	144	2.88
Bob Addy	2B	56					204	3.64	283	5.05
Ross Barnes	SS	56					177	3.16	243	4.34
Tom Foley	3B	53					163	3.08	205	3.87
Joe Simmons	OF	56					203	3.63	286	5.11
Gat Stires	OF	55					179	3.25	278	4.96
Fred Cone	OF	39					127	3.25	158	4.05
Scott Hastings	C	54					170	3.15	216	4.00
Al Spalding	P	55					164	2.98	202	3.67
Barstow	OF,1B	21					63	3.00	87	4.14
Al Barker	OF	11					37	3.36	42	3.81

(Professional Games)

BATTERS	POS	GP	HL	AVG	R	AVG	H	AVG	TB	AVG
Joe Doyle	1B	22					28	1.27	40	1.82
Bob Addy	2B	22					47	2.14	68	3.09
Tom Foley	3B	22					38	1.73	44	2.00
Ross Barnes	SS	22					50	2.27	64	2.91
Joe Simmons	OF	22					47	2.14	66	3.00
Gat Stires	OF	21					41	1.95	67	3.19
Fred Cone	OF	13					15	1.15	21	1.62
Scott Hastings	C	22					42	1.91	53	2.41
Al Spalding	P	22					36	1.64	49	2.23
Barstow	OF	10					18	1.80	29	2.90

ATLANTIC   41 - 17   (20 - 16)
Brooklyn, NY

DATE	OPPONENT	SCORE			W	L	T
04/17	Union (Morrisania, NY)#	24	10		W		
04/25	Union (Morrisania, NY)#	10	26			L	
04/27	Harmonic (Brooklyn)	25	20		W		
05/02	Union (Morrisania, NY)#	36	23		W		
05/05	Harmonic (Brooklyn)	29	6		W		
05/09	Eagle (New York)	54	5		W		
05/13	Resolute (Elizabeth, NJ)	19	0		W		
05/14	Star (Brooklyn)	8	1		W		
05/16	Union (Lansingburgh, NY)#	23	18		W		
05/18	Eckford (Brooklyn)#	39	6		W		
05/19	Harmonic (Brooklyn)	25	20		W		
05/23	Olympic (Washington)#	39	7		W		
05/24	National (Washington)#	31	9		W		
05/25	Maryland (Baltimore)#	13	12		W		
05/26	Pastime (Baltimore)	22	5		W		
05/28	Keystone (Philadelphia)	35	1		W		
05/30	Athletic (Philadelphia)#	13	18			L	
05/31	Forest City (Rockford, IL)#	16	17			L	
06/06	Union (Lansingburgh, NY)#	31	32			L	
06/09	Athletic (Brooklyn)	52	5		W		
06/14	Cincinnati (Cincinnati)#	8	7	(11)	W		
06/20	Athletic (Philadelphia)#	3	19			L	
06/24	Eckford (Brooklyn)#	22	8		W		

ATLANTIC (cont.)
Brooklyn, NY

DATE	OPPONENT	SCORE			W	L	T
06/28	Mutual (New York)	15	13		W		
06/30	Union (Brooklyn)	38	8		W		
07/01	Union (Morrisania, NY)#	22	11		W		
07/04	Chicago (Chicago)#	30	20		W		
07/11	Alpha (Brooklyn)	21	4		W		
07/14	Resolute (Elizabeth, NJ)	29	3		W		
07/18	Union (Lansingburgh, NY)#	14	31			L	
07/26	Pickott Benefit (Brooklyn)	29	9		W		
07/29	Pastime (Baltimore)	27	7		W		
08/09	Mutual (New York)#	7	9			L	
08/12	Harvard (Cambridge, MA)	13	4		W		
08/16	Forest City (Cleveland)#	15	9		W		
08/19	Alpha (Brooklyn)	34	17		W		
08/22	Union (Morrisania, NY)#	24	21		W		
08/29	Forest City (Rockford, IL)#	14	13	(12)	W		
08/30	Chicago (Chicago)#	4	12			L	
08/31	Amateur (Chicago)	62	14		W		
09/02	Cincinnati (Cincinnati)#	3	14			L	
09/05	Forest City (Cleveland)#	13	15			L	
09/06	Niagara (Buffalo)	24	3		W		
09/07	Flour City (Rochester, NY)	29	15		W		
09/12	Olympic (Washington)#	29	26		W		
09/15	Athletic (Brooklyn)	16	12		W		
09/22	Mutual (New York)#	4	10			L	
09/25	Chicago (Chicago)#	4	9			L	
10/04	Union (Lansingburgh, NY)#	10	12	(11)		L	
10/08	Star (Brooklyn)	24	31			L	
10/10	Mutual (New York)#	8	4		W		
10/11	Union (Lansingburgh, NY)#	12	5		W		
10/17	Athletic (Philadelphia)#	7	11			L	
10/19	Athletic (Philadelphia)#	3	15			L	
10/26	Cincinnati (Cincinnati)#	11	7		W		
11/02	Athletic (Philadelphia)#	14	12		W		
11/05	Mutual (New York)#	9	13			L	
11/24	Oriental (New York)	16	4		W		

Professional games

(All Games)

BATTERS	POS	GP	HL	AVG	R	AVG	H	AVG	TB	AVG
Joe Start	1B	56					161	2.88	269	4.41
Lip Pike	2B	58					144	2.48	266	4.58
Dickey Pearce	SS	55					129	2.35	165	3.00
Charles Smith	3B	56					127	2.27	182	3.25
John Chapman	OF	58					150	2.58	210	3.62
George Hall	OF	58					118	2.03	174	3.00
Dan McDonald	OF	56					102	1.82	158	2.82
Bob Ferguson	C	54					126	2.33	187	3.46
George Zettlein	P	46					86	1.87	107	2.33
Munn	OF,C	6					10	1.67	15	2.50

(Professional Games)*

BATTERS	POS	GP	HL	AVG	R	AVG	H	AVG	TB	AVG
Joe Start	1B	36					99	2.75	149	4.14
Lip Pike	2B	36					84	2.33	153	4.25
Dickey Pearce	SS	34					85	2.50	100	2.94
Charles Smith	3B	36					73	2.03	100	2.78
John Chapman	OF	36					86	2.39	119	3.31
George Hall	OF	36					67	1.86	99	2.75
Dan McDonald	OF	36					61	1.69	83	2.31

ATLANTIC (cont.)
Brooklyn, NY

BATTERS	POS	GP	HL	AVG	R	AVG	H	AVG	TB	AVG
Bob Ferguson	C	36					81	2.25	104	2.88
George Zettlein	P	33					51	1.55	64	1.93

* As originally calculated, averages only included 21 professional games. They have been adjusted to reflect all 36 professional games.

UNION 30 - 15 - 1   (11 - 13 - 1)
Lansingburgh, NY

DATE	OPPONENT	SCORE			W	L	T
05/03	Old Elm (Pittsfield, MA)	28	14		W		
05/16	Atlantic (Brooklyn)#	18	23			L	
05/18	Buckskin (Gloversville, NY)	29	6		W		
05/23	Forest City (Rockford, IL)#	3	21			L	
05/30	Union (Morrisania, NY)#	27	18		W		
06/04	Putnam (Troy, NY)	59	17		W		
06/06	Atlantic (Brooklyn)#	32	31		W		
06/07	Keystone (Philadelphia)	41	20		W		
06/08	Athletic (Philadelphia)#	6	41			L	
06/11	Pastime (Baltimore)	15	9		W		
06/13	Maryland (Baltimore)#	13	15			L	
06/16	Mutual (New York)#	10	10				T
06/27	Chicago (Chicago)#	21	25			L	
07/04	Oriental (New York)	88	9		W		
07/07	Harvard (Cambridge, MA)	13	25			L	
07/13	Buckskin (Gloversville, NY)	29	12		W		
07/18	Atlantic (Brooklyn)#	31	14		W		
07/27	Union (Morrisania, NY)#	10	12			L	
07/29	Utica (Utica, NY)	48	8		W		
08/01	Pastime (Baltimore)	6	23			L	
08/02	Niagara (Buffalo)	27	24		W		
08/03	Forest City (Cleveland)#	6	17			L	
08/04	Chicago (Chicago)#	16	11		W		
08/06	Forest City (Rockford, IL)#	31	29		W		
08/09	Cincinnati (Cincinnati)#	8	34			L	
08/13	Forest City (Cleveland)#	19	11		W		
08/18	Dunderberg (Peekskill, NY)	81	1		W		
08/26	Mutual (NewYork)#	13	24			L	
08/31	Athletic (Philadelphia)#	2	11			L	
09/06	Lone Star (Catskill, NY)	82	6		W		
09/10	Olympic (Washington)#	17	9		W		
09/16	Alert (Schenectady, NY)	42	11		W		
09/19	Mutual (New York)#	24	19		W		
09/21	Pastime (Baltimore)	22	7		W		
09/23	Expert (Philadelphia)	21	16		W		
09/24	Athletic (Philadelphia)#	15	10		W		
09/25	Olympic (Washington)#	19	15		W		
09/26	Pastime (Baltimore)	32	14		W		
09/28	Putnam (Troy, NY)	13	5		W		
09/29	Utica (Utica, NY)	21	11		W		
10/04	Atlantic (Brooklyn)#	12	10	(11)	W		
10/05	Mutual (New York)#	9	12			L	
10/11	Atlantic (Brooklyn)#	5	12			L	
10/13	Picked Nine (Albany, NY)	34	7		W		
10/17	Putnam (Troy, NY)	45	9		W		
10/24	Cincinnati (Cincinnati)#	7	12			L	

Professional games

(All Games)

BATTERS	POS	GP	HL	AVG	R	AVG	H	AVG	TB	AVG
Cherokee Fisher	1B,P	46					141	3.06	213	4.63
Billy Dick	2B	21					58	2.76	66	3.14

UNION (cont.)
Lansingburgh, NY

BATTERS	POS	GP	HL	AVG	R	AVG	H	AVG	TB	AVG
Dick Flowers	SS	46					136	2.95	192	4.17
Steve Bellan	3B	40					91	2.28	119	2.98
Steve King	OF	46					149	3.23	212	4.61
Jim Foran	OF	39					109	2.79	149	3.82
Tom York	OF	38					113	2.97	170	4.47
Mike McGeary	C	37					101	2.72	137	3.70
John McMullin	P	33					78	2.36	119	3.61
Woolverton	SS	19					65	3.42	113	5.94
Cal Penfield	OF	15					46	3.07	63	4.20
Bill Craver	2B	14					28	2.00	40	2.86
Hollister	1B	12					35	2.92	58	4.83

OLYMPIC
Washington, DC

29 - 21 (10 - 18)

DATE	OPPONENT	SCORE		W	L	T
05/02	Maryland (Baltimore)#	14	8	W		
05/13	Maryland (Baltimore)#	21	15	W		
05/16	Athletic (Philadelphia)#	13	29		L	
05/19	Athletic (Philadelphia)#	14	11	W		
05/23	Atlantic (Brooklyn)#	7	39		L	
05/31	National (Washington)#	2	6		L	
06/06	Forest City (Rockford, IL)#	19	10	W		
06/07	Forest City (Rockford, IL)#	7	8		L	
06/10	Star (Brooklyn)	*0	9		L	
06/15	Pastime (Baltimore)	14	16		L	
06/17	National (Washington)#	13	8	W		
06/22	Pastime (Baltimore)	27	20	W		
06/24	National (Washington)#	14	23		L	
06/27	Cincinnati (Cincinnati)#	24	35		L	
07/04	Union (Morrisania, NY)#	14	5	W		
07/08	National (Washington)#	43	15	W		
07/11	Jefferson (Washington)	34	11	W		
07/13	Mutual (New York)#	8	29		L	
07/15	Rosedale (Washington)	45	15	W		
07/16	Chicago (Chicago)#	9	27		L	
07/18	Athletic (Philadelphia)#	15	25		L	
07/20	Jefferson (Washington)	47	6	W		
07/23	Arlington (Washington)	49	14	W		
07/27	W. Philadelphia (Philadelphia)	26	4	W		
07/29	Maryland (Baltimore)#	18	15	W		
08/02	Maryland (Baltimore)#	32	12	W		
08/03	Harvard (Cambridge, MA)	18	7	W		
08/06	Cincinnati (Cincinnati)#	3	38		L	
08/08	Forest City (Rockford, IL)#	24	13	W		
08/10	Chicago (Chicago)#	15	16		L	
08/11	Indianapolis (Indianapolis)	44	11	W		
08/26	Forest City (Cleveland)#	17	18		L	
09/02	Osceola (Pittsburgh)	38	0	W		
09/03	Forest City (Cleveland)#	13	25		L	
09/05	Niagara (Buffalo)	25	9	W		
09/06	Flour City (Rochester, NY)	42	18	W		
09/07	Ontario (Oswego, NY)	31	16	W		
09/08	Alert (Schenectady, NY)	26	9	W		
09/09	Buckskin (Gloversville, NY)	25	3	W		
09/10	Union (Lansingburgh, NY)#	9	17		L	
09/12	Atlantic (Brooklyn)#	26	29		L	
09/13	Mutual (New York)#	4	29		L	
09/14	Athletic (Philadelphia)#	4	30		L	
09/15	W. Philadelphia (Philadelphia)	25	17	W		
09/20	Olympic (Baltimore)	13	20		L	
09/21	Arlington (Washington)	28	26	W		

OLYMPIC (cont.)
Washington, DC

DATE	OPPONENT	SCORE		W	L	T
09/23	Active (Washington)	44	6	W		
09/25	Union (Lansingburgh, NY)#	15	19		L	
10/01	Washington (Washington)	16	7	W		
10/06	Washington (Washington)	16	7	W		

\# Professional games
* Forfeit

(All Games)

BATTERS	POS	GP	HL	AVG	R	AVG	H	AVG	TB	AVG
Nick Young	1B,OF	25					73	2.92	91	3.64
Andrew Gibney	2B,3B	18					44	2.44	55	3.05
Davy Force	SS,C	45					119	2.64	165	3.67
Philip Culp	3B,SS	23					36	1.56	44	1.91
Henry Burroughs	OF	40					91	2.28	138	3.45
Dick Hurley	OF,2B,1B	37					84	2.27	126	3.41
A.V Robinson	OF	21					52	2.48	64	3.05
Ewell	C	42					92	2.19	125	2.98
Ed Leech	P	42					108	2.57	139	3.31
George Fox		27					65	2.41	90	3.33
Harry Berthrong	C,OF	27					65	2.41	80	2.96
John Hollingshead	1B,2B	18					31	1.72	48	2.67
Frank Norton	2B	17					42	2.47	60	3.53
John Glenn	OF	14					29	2.07	41	2.93
Bob Reach	OF,SS	12					34	2.83	44	3.67

(Professional Games)

BATTERS	POS	GP	HL	AVG	R	AVG	H	AVG	TB	AVG
Nick Young	1B	10					26	2.60	38	3.80
Andrew Gibney	2B,3B	15					33	2.20	38	2.53
Davy Force	SS,C	27					65	2.41	96	3.56
Philip Culp	3B,SS	16					25	1.56	28	1.75
Henry Burroughs	OF	26					52	2.00	80	3.08
Dick Hurley	OF,2B,1B	22					42	1.91	57	2.59
A.V. Robinson	OF	14					29	2.09	38	2.70
Ewell	C	26					40	1.53	56	2.16
Ed Leech	P	26					53	2.04	61	2.34
George Fox		19					41	2.16	57	3.00
Harry Berthrong	C	11					22	2.00	24	2.18
John Glenn	OF	9					16	1.77	24	2.64
Frank Norton	2B	7					13	1.86	18	2.57
John Hollingshead	1B,2B	7					13	1.86	18	2.57
Bob Reach	OF,SS	5					14	2.80	17	3.67

FOREST CITY   25 - 16   (9 - 15)
Cleveland, OH

DATE	OPPONENT	SCORE		W	L	T
05/10	Resolute (Oberlin, OH)	31	14	W		
05/12	Cincinnati (Cincinnati)#	2	12		L	
05/13	Cincinnati (Cincinnati)#	10	24		L	
05/16	Atlantic Railway (Cleveland)	132	1	W		
05/25	Seneca (Oil City, PA)	42	9	W		
05/26	Mutual (Meadville, PA)	20	1	W		
05/27	Athletic (Jamestown, NY)	46	2	W		
05/31	Cincinnati (Cincinnati)#	13	27		L	
06/03	Chicago (Chicago)#	9	15		L	
06/13	Forest City (Rockford, IL)#	21	12	W		
06/14	Forest City (Rockford, IL)#	18	21		L	
06/18	Resolute (Oberlin, OH)	54	26	W		

FOREST CITY (cont.)
Cleveland, OH

DATE	OPPONENT	SCORE		W	L	T
06/20	Chicago (Chicago)#	8	24		L	
07/04	Flour City (Rochester, NY)	28	13	W		
07/15	Harvard (Cambridge, MA)	14	9	W		
07/16	Harvard (Cambridge, MA)	7	15		L	
07/23	Mutual (Meadville, PA)	57	5	W		
07/29	Mutual (New York)#	7	5	W		
08/03	Union (Lansingburgh, NY)#	17	6	W		
08/06	Athletic (Philadelphia)#	7	28		L	
08/11	Niagara (Buffalo)	26	5	W		
08/12	Flour City (Rochester, NY)	29	2	W		
08/13	Union (Lansingburgh, NY)#	11	19		L	
08/15	Atlantic (Brooklyn)#	9	15		L	
08/16	Mutual (New York)#	9	10		L	
08/18	Eckford (Brooklyn)#	13	0	W		
08/19	Union (Morrisania, NY)#	19	15	W		
08/20	Star (Brooklyn)	9	7	W		
08/21	Athletic (Philadelphia)#	11	19		L	
08/23	Mutual (New York)#	15	16		L	
08/25	Pastime (Baltimore)	22	18	W		
08/26	Olympic (Washington)#	18	17	W		
08/27	National (Washington)#	67	12	W		
08/30	Allegheny (Pittsburgh)	17	6	W		
08/31	Allegheny (Pittsburgh)	26	3	W		
09/03	Olympic (Washington)#	25	13	W		
09/05	Atlantic (Brooklyn)#	15	13	W		
09/16	Una (Kalamazoo, MI)	47	5	W		
09/17	Chicago (Chicago)#	7	9		L	
10/06	Cincinnati (Cincinnati)#	15	18		L	
11/05	Cincinnati (Cincinnati)#	16	27		L	

Professional games

(All Games)

BATTERS	POS	GP	HL	AVG	R	AVG	H	AVG	TB	AVG
James Carlton	1B	37					85	2.29	116	3.13
Gene Kimball	2B	37					96	2.59	129	3.48
John Ward	SS	35					77	2.20	105	3.00
Ezra Sutton	3B	35					124	3.54	177	5.05
George Heubel	OF	37					100	2.70	131	3.54
Art Allison	OF	36					98	2.72	147	4.08
E. White	OF	19					50	2.63	58	3.05
James White	C,P	36					108	3.00	184	5.11
Al Pratt	P	34					85	2.50	125	3.67
Parker	OF	7					21	3.00	26	3.71
Chick Fulmer	OF,P	8					12	1.50	15	1.87
H. Brown	OF	4					10	2.50	13	3.25
A.R. Smith	OF	8					32	4.00	51	6.37

PITCHERS	IP	R	AVG
Al Pratt	248	359	1.44
James White	74	79	1.06
Chick Fulmer	4	6	1.50

UNION   20 - 19   (7 - 18)
Morrisania, NY

DATE	OPPONENT	SCORE		W	L	T
04/24	Atlantic (Brooklyn)#	10	24		L	
04/25	Atlantic (Brooklyn)#	26	10	W		
05/02	Atlantic (Brooklyn)#	23	36		L	
05/04	Mutual (New York)#	4	11		L	

UNION (cont.)
Morrisania, NY

DATE	OPPONENT	SCORE		W	L	T
05/05	Rose Hill (Fordham, NY)	16	10	W		
05/06	Mutual (New York)#	14	17		L	
05/13	Athletic (Philadelphia)#	7	6	W		
05/18	Athletic (Philadelphia)#	11	31		L	
05/19	Keystone (Philadelphia)	18	13	W		
05/23	Eckford (Brooklyn)#	9	21		L	
05/30	Union (Lansingburgh, NY)#	18	27		L	
06/02	Rose Hill (Fordham, NY)	35	8	W		
06/08	Mutual (New York, NY)#	19	13	W		
06/09	Eckford (Brooklyn)#	28	20	W		
06/15	Cincinnati (Cincinnati)#	0	14		L	
06/22	Eckford (Brooklyn)#	22	9	W		
06/23	Jasper (New York)	30	3	W		
06/27	Athletic (Philadelphia)#	20	51		L	
06/28	Jasper (New York)	26	17	W		
07/01	Atlantic (Brooklyn)#	11	22		L	
07/04	Olympic (Washington)#	5	14		L	
07/05	National (Washington)#	34	13	W		
07/06	Maryland (Baltimore)#	5	21		L	
07/07	Pastime (Baltimore)	26	23	W		
07/08	Chicago (Chicago)#	12	28		L	
07/19	Unknown (New York)	26	13	W		
07/22	Lexington (New York)	24	17	W		
07/23	Lexington (New York)	56	12	W		
07/26	Hope (New York)	73	10	W		
07/27	Union (Lansingburgh, NY)#	12	10	W		
07/29	Social (New York)	34	11	W		
08/01	Resolute (Elizabeth, NJ)	36	13	W		
08/02	Pastime (Baltimore)	12	10	W		
08/03	Warren (New York)	17	18		L	
08/05	Eckford (Brooklyn)#	12	17		L	
08/19	Forest City (Cleveland)#	15	19		L	
08/22	Atlantic (Brooklyn)#	21	24		L	
08/25	Mutual (New York)#	10	18		L	
09/03	Mutual (New York)#	1	12		L	

Professional games

(All Games)

BATTERS	POS	GP	HL	AVG	R	AVG	H	AVG	TB	AVG
Brown	1B	8					12	1.50	21	2.62
Dick Higham	2B	26					61	2.34	88	3.38
John Bass	SS	19					40	2.11	66	3.47
Ed Shelley	3B	24					41	1.71	61	2.54
Al Gedney	OF	26					56	2.15	73	2.81
Henry Austin	OF	24					44	1.83	55	2.29
John Kenney	OF,3B	23					29	1.26	38	1.65
Dave Birdsall	C	18					29	1.61	42	2.33
Charley Pabor	P	27					45	1.66	80	2.96
Reynolds	OF	15					27	1.80	33	2.20
Jim Holdsworth	3B	11					23	2.09	31	2.82
Charley Bearman	1B	7					12	1.71	12	1.71

ECKFORD
Brooklyn, NY

13 - 16 - 1   (2 - 12 - 1)

DATE	OPPONENT	SCORE		W	L	T
04/27	Oriental (New York)	21	15	W		
05/05	Oriental (New York)	19	4	W		
05/18	Atlantic (Brooklyn)#	6	39		L	
05/20	Mutual (New York)#	8	22		L	
05/21	Star (Brooklyn)	9	15		L	

ECKFORD (cont.)
Brooklyn, NY

DATE	OPPONENT	SCORE		W	L	T
05/23	Union (Morrisania, NY)#	21	9	W		
06/01	Resolute (Elizabeth, NJ)	14	17		L	
06/03	Mutual (New York)#	13	13			T
06/04	Star (Brooklyn)	6	24		L	
06/06	Mutual (New York)#	15	18		L	
06/09	Union (Morrisania, NY)#	20	28		L	
06/14	Excelsior (Brooklyn)	24	10	W		
06/16	Osceola (Brooklyn)	29	11	W		
06/17	Cincinnati (Cincinnati)#	7	24		L	
06/22	Union (Morrisania, NY)#	9	22		L	
06/24	Atlantic (Brooklyn)#	8	22		L	
06/28	Resolute (Elizabeth, NJ)	10	31		L	
06/30	Athletic (Brooklyn)	19	7	W		
07/12	Athletic (Brooklyn)	16	13	W		
07/15	Equity (Brooklyn)	69	12	W		
07/16	Grammercy (New York)	37	18	W		
07/23	Harmonic (Brooklyn)	37	13	W		
07/28	Irving (New York)	19	7	W		
07/30	Bergen (Bergen, NJ)	37	8	W		
08/02	Mutual (New York)#	9	19		L	
08/05	Union (Morrisania, NY)#	17	12	W		
08/18	Forest City (Cleveland)#	0	13		L	
09/01	Mutual (New York)#	8	27		L	
09/14	Mutual (New York)#	6	35		L	
09/23	Chicago (Chicago)#	8	22		L	

Professional games

(All Games)

BATTERS	POS	GP	HL	AVG	R	AVG	H	AVG	TB	AVG
Andy Allison	1B	21					44	2.09	53	2.52
Malone	2B	5					7	1.40	8	1.60
Tom Devyr	SS	8					10	1.25	12	1.50
Ed Duffy	3B,SS	21					46	2.19	64	3.04
Josh Snyder	OF	19					25	1.32	31	1.63
Richard Hunt	OF	15					34	2.27	44	2.93
Coniglan	OF	14					23	1.64	27	1.93
James Snyder	C	19					20	1.05	30	1.58
Joe McDermott	P	20					28	1.40	40	2.00
Charles Hunt	OF	9					14	1.55	17	1.88
Lynch	OF	8					12	1.50	12	1.50
Reach	SS	6					6	1.00	8	1.33
George Price	C	5					8	1.60	9	1.80
Nat Jewett	C	5					7	1.40	12	2.40

MARYLAND   9 - 18   (2 - 14)
Baltimore, MD

DATE	OPPONENT	SCORE		W	L	T
04/25	Athletic (Philadelphia)#	16	34		L	
04/28	Athletic (Philadelphia)#	9	23		L	
05/02	Olympic (Washington)#	8	14		L	
05/13	Olympic (Washington)#	15	21		L	
05/18	Pastime (Baltimore)	17	6	W		
05/25	Atlantic (Brooklyn)#	12	13		L	
06/07	Star (Brooklyn)@	7	28		L	
06/13	Union (Lansingburgh, NY)#@	15	13	W		
06/25	Cincinnati (Cincinnati)#	13	30		L	
07/02*	Olympic (Washington)#@	12	32		L	
07/04	Pastime (Baltimore)	32	20	W		
07/04	Keystone (Philadelphia)	38	13	W		
07/06	Union (Morrisania, NY)#	21	5	W		

MARYLAND (cont.)
Baltimore, MD

DATE	OPPONENT	SCORE		W	L	T
07/11	Mutual (New York)#@	10	21		L	
07/14	Chicago (Chicago)#	9	46		L	
07/19	Olympic (Baltimore)@	32	12	W		
07/22	Athletic (Philadelphia)#	13	24		L	
07/23	Expert (Philadelphia)	28	36		L	
07/29	Olympic (Washington)#	15	18		L	
08/01	Indianapolis (Indianapolis)@	24	7	W		
08/02	Cincinnati (Cincinnati)#	9	25		L	
08/04	Forest City (Rockford, IL)#@	4	11		L	
08/05	Chicago (Chicago)#@	15	28		L	
08/22	Olympic (Baltimore)	23	22	W		
08/27	Pastime (Baltimore)	10	7	W		
09/02	Pastime (Baltimore)@	10	25		L	
09/09	Pastime (Baltimore)	5	37		L	

\# Professional games
* Date under dispute
@ Boxscore not available

(All Games)

BATTERS	POS	GP	HL	AVG	R	AVG	H	AVG	TB	AVG
Tom Forker	1B	14	48	3.43	20	1.43				
Charley Bearman	2B	8	21	2.63	16	2.00				
Wally Goldsmith	SS	15	35	2.35	28	1.87				
Tom Carey	3B	12	30	2.50	25	2.08				
Ed Mincher	OF	13	40	3.08	23	1.77				
Tully Worthington	OF	11	25	2.27	26	2.36				
Mike Hooper	OF	10	24	2.40	24	2.40				
Bill Lennon	C	13	41	3.15	23	1.77				
Bobby Mathews	P	14	52	3.71	22	1.57				
Sam Armstrong	OF	5	17	3.40	6	1.20				
Kernan	3B,2B	5	16	3.20	4	0.80				

(Professional Games)

BATTERS	POS	GP	HL	AVG	R	AVG	H	AVG	TB	AVG
Tom Forker	1B	10	35	3.50	10	1.00				
Charley Bearman	2B	6	16	2.67	11	1.83				
Wally Goldsmith	SS	11	27	2.45	15	1.36				
Tom Carey	3B	9	24	2.67	13	1.44				
Tully Worthington	OF	9	22	2.44	17	1.89				
Ed Mincher	OF	9	27	3.00	10	1.11				
Mike Hooper	OF	8	20	2.50	14	1.75				
Bill Lennon	C	9	24	2.67	12	1.33				
Bobby Mathews	P	11	42	3.81	11	1.00				
Kernan	3B,2B	5	16	3.20	4	0.80				
Sam Armstrong	OF	4	13	3.25	4	1.00				

TRI MOUNTAIN   6 - 7   (0 - 4)
Boston, MA

DATE	OPPONENT	SCORE		W	L	T
04/16	Revere (Boston)	22	5	W		
04/23	Revere (Boston)	45	9	W		
04/30	Excelsior (Boston)	31	18	W		
05/07	Una (Boston)	11	7	W		
05/25	Athletic (Philadelphia)#	4	45		L	
06/01	Fairmount (Marlboro, MA)@	11	13		L	
06/09	Cincinnati (Cincinnati)#	6	30		L	
06/17	Mutual (New York)#	11	25		L	
06/25	Harvard (Cambridge, MA)	17	21		L	

TRI MOUNTAIN (cont.)
Boston, MA

DATE	OPPONENT	SCORE		W	L	T
06/29	Chicago (Chicago)#	16	36		L	
08/03	Mansfield (Middletown, CT)	37	7	W		
09/24	Clipper (Lowell, MA)@	21	22		L	
10/27	Kearsarge (Stoneham, MA)@	15	13	W		

\# Professional games
@ Boxscore not available

(All Games)

BATTERS	POS	GP	HL	AVG	R	AVG	H	AVG	TB	AVG
Record	1B	10	34	3.40	19	1.90				
Frank Barrows	2B	10	26	2.60	27	2.70				
Freeman	SS	7	18	2.57	18	2.57				
W. Pratt	3B,OF	5	18	3.60	5	1.00				
Sanderson	OF	10	28	2.80	22	2.20				
Kelly	OF	6	17	2.83	18	3.00				
Putnam	OF	5	12	2.40	11	2.20				
Sullivan	C,3B	7	19	2.71	11	1.57				
Jackson	P	6	15	2.50	8	1.33				
Harris	OF	5	18	3.60	8	1.60				

(Professional Games)

BATTERS	POS	GP	HL	AVG	R	AVG	H	AVG	TB	AVG
Record	1B	4	16	4.00	3	0.75				
Frank Barrows	2B	4	10	2.50	5	1.25				
Freeman	SS	3	8	2.67	4	1.33				
W. Pratt	3B,OF	2	7	3.50	0	0.00				
Sanderson	OF	4	11	2.75	6	1.50				
Kelley	OF	2	6	3.00	4	2.00				
Putnam	OF	2	6	3.00	0	0.00				
Sullivan	C,3B	4	14	3.50	2	0.50				
Jackson	P	4	11	2.75	4	1.00				
Harris	OF	1	4	4.00	0	0.00				

NATIONAL 5 - 12 (2 - 9)
Washington, DC

DATE	OPPONENT	SCORE		W	L	T
05/04	Jefferson (Washington)	20	21		L	
05/16	Jefferson (Washington)	29	3	W		
05/24	Atlantic (Brooklyn)#	9	31		L	
05/31	Olympic (Washington)#	6	2	W		
06/08	Forest City (Rockford, IL)#	4	10		L	
06/11	Star (Brooklyn)	9	5	W		
06/14	Pastime (Baltimore)	18	8	W		
06/17	Olympic (Washington)#	8	13		L	
06/24	Olympic (Washington)#@	23	14	W		
06/28	Cincinnati (Cincinnati)#	10	30		L	
07/05	Union (Morrisania, NY)#	13	34		L	
07/08	Olympic (Washington)#	15	43		L	
07/14	Mutual (New York)#@	1	11		L	
07/18	Chicago (Chicago)#@	6	24		L	
07/25	W. Philadelphia (Philadelphia)	24	27		L	
08/04	Harvard (Cambridge, MA)@	13	39		L	
08/27	Forest City (Cleveland)#@	12	67		L	

\# Professional games
@ Boxscore not available

NATIONAL (cont.)
Washington, DC

(All Games)

BATTERS	POS	GP	HL	AVG	R	AVG	H	AVG	TB	AVG
Hodges	1B	11	28	2.55	19	1.73				
Dennis Coughlin	2B	11	27	2.45	19	1.73				
Pete Shreves	SS,P	8	27	3.38	10	1.25				
Lake	3B	7	18	2.57	14	2.00				
Sy Studley	OF	11	34	3.09	19	1.73				
John Glenn	OF	9	19	2.11	15	1.67				
John Hollingshead	OF,2B	11	31	2.82	18	1.63				
Nat Hicks	C	9	21	2.33	13	1.44				
Hoy	P,OF	9	23	2.56	12	1.33				
Strong	3B,P	7	20	2.86	8	1.14				

(Professional Games)

BATTERS	POS	GP	HL	AVG	R	AVG	H	AVG	TB	AVG
Hodges	1B	6	12	2.00	10	1.67				
Dennis Coughlin	2B	7	19	2.71	7	1.00				
Pete Shreves	SS,P	4	14	3.50	4	1.00				
Strong	3B,P	4	11	2.75	2	0.50				
Sy Studley	OF	7	21	3.00	8	1.14				
John Hollingshead	OF,2B	7	20	2.86	9	1.29				
John Glenn	OF	5	10	2.00	6	1.20				
Nat Hicks	C	6	13	2.17	10	1.67				
Hoy	P,OF	5	15	3.00	2	0.40				
Lake	3B	3	9	3.00	2	0.67				

RIVERSIDE 3 - 6 (0 - 6)
Portsmouth, OH

DATE	OPPONENT	SCORE		W	L	T
05/29	Cincinnati (Cincinnati)#	3	32		L	
06/10	Independent (Ripley, OH)@	46	9	W		
07/06	Forest City (Rockford, IL)#@	7	37		L	
07/19	Mutual (New York)#	17	31		L	
07/27	Athletic (Philadelphia)#	2	15		L	
08/10	Lone Star (New Orleans, LA)@	33	11	W		
08/26	Cincinnati (Cincinnati)#	27	29		L	
09/15	Cincinnati (Cincinnati)#	1	12		L	
09/16	Live Oak (Cincinnati)@	25	9	W		

Professional games
@ Boxscore not available

(Professional Games)

BATTERS	POS	GP	HL	AVG	R	AVG	H	AVG	TB	AVG
Milt Sears	1B	3			1	0.33				
H.C. Galliker	2B,1B	5			10	2.00				
Tom Haines	SS	5			6	1.20				
Davis	3B	4			5	1.25				
Huddleston	OF	5			6	1.20				
Adkins	OF	4			3	0.75				
John Riley	OF,SS	4			6	1.50				
George Bunting	C	5			5	1.00				
R.J. Fitzsimmons	P	5			5	1.00				

TEAM STANDINGS   (Professional Games Only)

CLUB	Cin	Chi	Ath	Mut	Atl	UL	FCR	FCC	Oly	UM	Nat	Eck	Ma	TM	Riv	W	L	T	PCT
Cincinnati	x	0	2	4	1	2	*2	5	2	1	1	1	2	1	3	27	6	1	.809
Chicago	2	x	1	2	2	1	3	3	2	1	1	1	2	1	0	22	7	0	.759
Athletic	1	2	x	*4	4	2	1	2	3	2	0	0	3	1	1	26	11	1	.697
Mutual	0	2	*3	x	3	*2	2	2	4	1	*5	1	1	1	1	29	15	3	.649
Atlantic	2	1	1	2	x	2	1	1	2	4	1	2	1	0	0	20	16	0	.556
Union (L)	0	1	1	*1	3	x	1	1	2	1	0	0	0	0	0	11	13	1	.460
Forest City (R)	*1	1	1	0	1	1	x	1	1	0	1	0	1	0	1	10	13	1	.438
Forest City (C)	0	0	0	1	1	1	1	x	2	1	1	1	0	0	0	9	15	0	.375
Olympic	0	0	1	0	0	0	2	0	x	1	2	0	4	0	0	10	18	0	.357
Union (M)	0	0	1	1	1	1	0	0	0	x	1	2	0	0	0	7	18	0	.280
National	0	0	0	0	0	0	0	0	2	0	x	0	0	0	0	2	9	0	.182
Eckford	0	0	0	*0	0	0	0	0	0	2	0	x	0	0	0	2	12	1	.167
Maryland	0	0	0	0	0	1	0	0 ·	0	1	0	0	x	0	0	2	14	0	.125
Tri Mountain	0	0	0	0	0	0	0	0	0	0	0	0	0	x	0	0	4	0	.000
Riverside	0	0	0	0	0	0	0	0	0	0	0	0	0	0	x	0	6	0	.000

* Mutual and Eckford, Mutual and Union (L), Cincinnati and Forest City (R) and Mutual and Athletic played tie games.

PROFESSIONAL TEAM TOTALS

TEAM	CITY/STATE	GP	W	L	T	PCT	R	OR
Mutual	New York, NY	88	68	17	3	.790	1913	899
Cincinnati	Cincinnati, OH	74	67	6	1	.912	2770	648
Chicago	Chicago, IL	73	65	8	0	.890	2480	749
Athletic	Philadelphia, PA	77	65	11	1	.851	2222	710
Forest City	Rockford, IL	56	42	13	1	.759	1772	553
Atlantic	Brooklyn, NY	58	41	17	0	.707	1211	698
Union	Lansingburgh, NY	46	30	15	1	.663	1150	700
Olympic	Washington, DC	50	29	21	0	.580	1050	805
Forest City	Cleveland, OH	41	25	16	0	.610	969	521
Union	Morrisania, NY	39	20	19	0	.513	778	666
Eckford	Brooklyn, NY	30	13	16	1	.450	521	530
Maryland	Baltimore, MD	27	9	18	0	.333	422	571
Tri Mountain	Boston, MA	13	6	7	0	.462	247	251
National	Washington, DC	17	5	12	0	.294	220	382
Riverside	Portsmouth, OH	9	3	6	0	.333	161	185

AMATEUR TEAMS

LONE STAR   32 - 17
New Orleans, LA

DATE	OPPONENT	SCORE		W	L	T
12/05/69	Hancock (New Orleans)*	47	24	W		
12/12/69	Comet (New Orleans)*	54	14	W		
12/19/69	Pickwick (New Orleans)*	37	7	W		
12/29/69	Mutual (New York)	10	16		L	
01/09	Jackson (New Orleans)	84	2	W		
01/30	Jackson (New Orleans)	34	4	W		
02/13	Magnolia (New Orleans)	66	8	W		
02/20	Stonewall (New Orleans)	71	16	W		
03/06	Pelican (New Orleans)	22	15	W		
03/20	Pelican (New Orleans)	41	27	W		
03/27	Atlantic (Algiers, LA)	52	27	W		
04/02	Fearless (New Orleans)	52	8	W		

LONE STAR (cont.)
New Orleans

DATE	OPPONENT	SCORE		W	L	T
04/21	Southern (New Orleans)	36	21	W		
04/24	Southern (New Orleans)	18	27		L	
04/29	Cincinnati (Cincinnati)	7	26		L	
05/08	Chicago (Chicago)	10	18		L	
05/15	Southern (New Orleans)	20	25		L	
05/29	Southern (New Orleans)	20	30		L	
06/19	Hancock (New Orleans)	57	2	W		
06/25	Creole (New Orleans)	26	3	W		
07/04	R.E. Lee (New Orleans)	14	6	W		
07/10	Picked Nine (New Orleans)	56	13	W		
07/21	Bluff City (Memphis, TN)	54	12	W		
07/24	Empire (St. Louis)	29	16	W		
07/25	Union (St. Louis)	35	34	W		
07/26	Liberty (Springfield, IL)	23	33		L	
07/29	Liberty (Springfield, IL)	21	24		L	
07/30	Forest City (Rockford, IL)	8	44		L	
08/02	Athletic (Chicago)	24	19	W		
08/03	Grove City (Kankakee, IL)	28	7	W		
08/04	Chicago (Chicago)	8	42		L	
08/05	Garden City (Chicago)	24	11	W		
08/08	Indianapolis (Indianapolis)	19	4	W		
08/10	Riverside (Portsmouth, OH)	11	33		L	
08/12	Cincinnati (Cincinnati)	11	47		L	
08/14	Nashville (Nashville, TN)	18	14	W		
08/28	Crescent (New Orleans)	13	4	W		
09/11	Crescent (New Orleans)	16	6	W		
09/25	Southern (New Orleans)	23	4	W		
10/02	R.E. Lee (New Orleans)	15	24		L	
10/16	R.E. Lee (New Orleans)	26	8	W		
10/30	R.E. Lee (New Orleans)	11	14		L	
11/10	Atlantic (St. Louis)	41	8	W		
11/13	Mississippi (New Orleans)	20	0	W		
11/16	Montgomery (Montgomery, AL)	25	11	W		
11/18	Mutual (New York)	2	28		L	
11/24	Mutual (New York)	1	26		L	
11/27	Mutual (New York)	5	13		L	
12/04	Excelsior (New Orleans)	24	12	W		

* Games also counted in 1869 season totals.

BATTERS	POS	GP	HL	AVG	R	AVG	H	AVG	TB	AVG
D. Schwartz	1B	24					61	2.54	96	4.00
C. Waterman	2B	11					20	1.82	31	2.82
A.B. Johnston	3B	38					159	**4.19**	220	**5.79**
J. Waterman	SS	38					95	2.50	126	3.32
William Tracy	OF,P	48					130	2.71	230	4.79
George Scott	OF	45					121	2.69	191	4.24
William Carson	OF	44					139	3.16	222	5.05
R.M. Thebault	C	35					108	3.09	187	5.34
William Condon	P	45					**161**	3.58	**251**	5.58
J.G. Amar	OF,3B	23					84	3.65	135	5.87
F. Waterman	OF	15					40	2.67	45	3.00
M.H. Redon	OF	18					34	1.89	42	2.33
J. Oberlander	2B	9					10	1.11	10	1.11

HARVARD   31 - 11
Cambridge, MA

DATE	OPPONENT	SCORE		W	L	T
05/14	Lowell (Boston)	28	5	W		
05/20	Clipper (Lowell, MA)	47	11	W		
05/21	Fairmount (Marlboro, MA)	60	12	W		

HARVARD (cont.)
Cambridge, MA

DATE	OPPONENT	SCORE		W	L	T
05/23	Athletic (Philadelphia)	8	20		L	
06/04	Cincinnati (Cincinnati)	15	46		L	
06/18	Brown (Providence, RI)	36	21	W		
06/22	Mutual (New York)	24	22	W		
06/25	Tri Mountain (Boston)	21	17	W		
06/27	Lowell (Boston)	36	12	W		
06/30	Chicago (Chicago)	7	33		L	
07/01	Princeton (Princeton, NJ)	26	13	W		
07/04	Yale (New Haven, CT)	24	22	W		
07/05	Rose Hill (Fordham, NY)	17	2	W		
07/07	Union (Lansingburgh, NY)	25	13	W		
07/08	Utica (Utica, NY)	31	23	W		
07/11	Eckford (Syracuse, NY)	30	7	W		
07/12	Ontario (Oswego, NY)	33	6	W		
07/13	Niagara (Buffalo)	28	14	W		
07/14	Niagara (Lockport, NY)	62	4	W		
07/15	Forest City (Cleveland)	9	14		L	
07/16	Forest City (Cleveland)	15	7	W		
07/18	Cincinnati (Cincinnati)	17	20		L	
07/20	Mutual (New York)	15	22		L	
07/21	Eagle (Louisville)	56	14	W		
07/26	Chicago (Chicago)	11	6	W		
07/27	Cream City (Milwaukee)	41	13	W		
07/28	Amateur (Chicago)	45	11	W		
07/30	Indianapolis (Indianapolis)	45	9	W		
08/03	Olympic (Washington)	7	18		L	
08/04	National (Washington)	39	13	W		
08/05	Maryland [amateur] (Baltimore)	44	11	W		
08/06	Pastime (Baltimore)	30	11	W		
08/08	Intrepid (Philadelphia)	33	11	W		
08/10	Athletic (Philadelphia)	9	27		L	
08/12	Atlantic (Brooklyn)	4	13		L	
08/13	Star (Brooklyn)	12	6	W		
08/16	Picked Nine (Boston)	18	16	W		
10/01	Lowell (Boston)	29	6	W		
10/08	Fairmount (Marlboro, MA)	30	1	W		
10/22	Mutual (New York)	13	24		L	
10/29	Brown (Providence, RI)	55	24	W		
11/02	Star (Brooklyn)	7	11		L	

BATTERS	POS	GP	HL	AVG	R	AVG	H	AVG	TB	AVG
Perrin	1B	36					81	2.25	100	2.78
White	2B	40					115	2.87	175	4.37
Percy Austin	SS	28					64	2.28	83	2.96
John Reynolds	3B	36					67	1.89	87	2.42
William Eustis	OF	41					123	3.00	185	4.51
James Wells	OF	40					104	2.60	142	3.55
Thorpe	OF	33					79	2.39	120	3.63
Archie Bush	C	41					134	3.27	201	4.90
Goodwin	P	34					65	1.91	90	2.65
Nathaniel Smith	2B	7					18	2.57	26	3.71
Barnes	OF	11					28	2.54	37	3.36
Gardner Willard	3B	10					25	2.50	37	3.70

STAR 24 - 9
Brooklyn, NY

DATE	OPPONENT	SCORE		W	L	T
05/07	Mutual (New York)	14	3	W		
05/14	Atlantic (Brooklyn)	1	8		L	
05/18	Resolute (Elizabeth, NJ)	22	9	W		
05/21	Eckford (Brooklyn)	15	9	W		

STAR (cont.)
Brooklyn, NY

DATE	OPPONENT	SCORE		W	L	T
06/04	Eckford (Brooklyn)	24	6	W		
06/08	Pastime (Baltimore)	25	18	W		
06/07	Maryland (Baltimore)	28	7	W		
06/10	Olympic (Washington)	*9	0	W		
06/11	National (Washington)	5	9		L	
06/18	Cincinnati (Cincinnati)	11	16		L	
06/25	Eagle (Flatbush, NY)	96	0	W		
06/---	Alpha (Brooklyn)	*9	0	W		
07/04	Mansfield (Middletown, CT)	44	9	W		
07/04	Wesleyan (Middletown, CT)	54	10	W		
07/09	Chicago (Chicago)	6	9		L	
07/12	Osceola (Brooklyn)	39	7	W		
07/23	Resolute (Elizabeth, NJ)	27	5	W		
07/30	Pastime (Baltimore)	7	10		L	
08/09	Champion (Jersey City, NJ)	26	10	W		
08/13	Harvard (Cambridge, MA)	6	12		L	
08/18	Warren (New York)	33	4	W		
08/20	Forest City (Cleveland)	7	9		L	
08/25	Amateur (Newark)	42	13	W		
08/27	Alpha (Brooklyn)	19	1	W		
09/03	Champion (Jersey City, NJ)	25	1	W		
09/10	Mutual (New York)	7	16		L	
09/14	Pastime (Baltimore)	18	13	W		
09/24	Harmonic (Brooklyn)	23	11	W		
09/27	Osceola (Brooklyn)	28	10	W		
10/01	Mutual (New York)	8	13		L	
10/08	Atlantic (Brooklyn)	31	24	W		
10/15	Athletic (Brooklyn)	6	2	W		
11/02	Harvard (Cambridge, MA)	11	7	W		

* Forfeit

BATTERS	POS	GP	AB	R	AVG	H	AVG	TB	AVG	BA
Packer	1B	29	158			72	2.48	85	2.93	.456
E.P. Beavans	2B	30	174			57	1.90	81	2.70	.328
Hy Dollard	SS	29	175			68	2.34	104	3.59	.389
Bob Manly	3B	18	100			36	2.00	45	2.50	.360
John Clyne	OF	31	189			85	2.74	112	3.61	.450
Fraley Rogers	OF	30	192			84	2.80	132	4.40	.438
Herb Worth	OF	30	172			72	2.40	101	3.37	.419
Herbert Jewell	C	20	124			63	3.15	80	4.00	.508
Candy Cummings	P	26	154			49	1.88	73	2.81	.318
Nat Hicks	C	13	80			33	2.54	45	3.46	.413
M.M. Rogers	OF	5	29			15	3.00	19	3.80	.517

MANSFIELD   21 - 13
Middletown, CT

DATE	OPPONENT	SCORE			W	L	T
05/15	Wesleyan (Middletown)	45	35		W		
05/16	Central City (Middletown)	39	14		W		
05/31	Meriden (Meriden, CT)	32	19		W		
06/01	Wesleyan (Middletown)	44	19		W		
06/04	Quinnipack (Wallingford, CT)	50	15		W		
06/10	Hutchings (Hartford, CT)	36	21		W		
06/24	Mutual (Springfield, MA)	12	31			L	
07/02	Aetna (New Britain, CT)	29	15		W		
07/04	Star (Brooklyn)	9	44			L	
07/07	Aetna (New Britain, CT)	29	15		W		
07/24	Wesleyan (Middletown)	37	13		W		
08/02	Lowell (Boston)	30	34	(10)		L	
08/03	Tri Mountain (Boston)	7	37			L	
08/04	Clipper (Lowell, MA)	17	21			L	

MANSFIELD (cont.)
Middletown, CT

DATE	OPPONENT	SCORE		W	L	T
08/05	Fairmount (Marlboro, MA)	11	36		L	
08/06	Mutual (Springfield, MA)	30	34		L	
08/13	Bridgeport (Bridgeport, CT)	24	7	W		
08/19	Osceola (Stratford, CT)	15	11	W		
08/20	Meriden (Meriden, CT)	13	8	W		
09/02	Athletic (Philadelphia)	5	32		L	
09/03	Osceola (Stratford, CT)	*9	0	W		
09/09	Warren (New York)	4	15		L	
09/10	Warren (New York)	28	20	W		
09/10	Meriden (Meriden, CT)	16	28		L	
09/15	Bristol (Bristol, RI)	51	28	W		
09/24	Unca (Portland, CT)	44	19	W		
09/28	Yale (New Haven, CT)	11	29		L	
09/29	Mutual (New York)	20	50		L	
09/30	Union (Brooklyn)	35	25	W		
10/06	Meriden (Meriden, CT)	26	10	W		
10/07	Yale (New Haven, CT)	11	40		L	
10/14	Mutual (New Haven, CT)	39	20	W		
10/29	New Britain (New Britain, CT)	48	17	W		
11/04	Union (Brooklyn)	19	17	W		

BATTERS	POS	GP	HL	AVG	R	AVG	H	AVG	TB	AVG
Noble	1B	19					50	2.63	63	3.32
Furniss	2B	26					61	2.35	83	3.19
Fields	SS	24					55	2.29	78	3.25
Tipper	3B	21					44	2.10	59	2.81
Arnold	OF	27					68	2.52	89	3.30
Smith	OF,P	24					62	2.58	86	3.58
Douglas	OF	12					18	1.50	19	1.58
Selden Plumb	C	20					45	2.25	62	3.10
Bentley	P	26					53	2.04	78	3.00
Seth Plumb	OF	9					21	2.33	32	3.56
Shay	2B	7								
Marks	1B	5					15	3.00	21	4.20
Webster	OF	4					3	0.75	3	0.75
H.A. Plumb	1B	3					6	2.00	6	2.00

INDIANAPOLIS   17 - 10
Indianapolis, IN

DATE	OPPONENT	SCORE		W	L	T
06/17	Franklin (Franklin, IN)	20	40		L	
06/23	Kekionga (Ft. Wayne, IN)	27	40		L	
06/23	Franklin (Franklin, IN)	23	16	W		
07/01	Picked Nine (Indianapolis)	25	8	W		
07/02	Lone Star (Indianapolis)	67	1	W		
07/04	Kekionga (Ft. Wayne, IN)	27	50		L	
07/05	Star (Peru, IN)	51	14	W		
07/06	National (Indianapolis)	34	5	W		
07/12	Union (Stilesville, IN)	44	10	W		
07/13	Clipper (Indianapolis)	69	9	W		
07/22	Lafayette (Lafayette, IN)	50	11	W		
07/25	Athletic (Columbus, OH)	69	16	W		
07/28	Athletic (Logansport, IN)	26	3	W		
07/30	Harvard (Cambridge, MA)	9	45		L	
08/02	Maryland (Baltimore)	7	24		L	
08/05	Cincinnati (Cincinnati)	8	61		L	
08/08	Lone Star (New Orleans, LA)	4	19		L	
08/11	Olympic (Washington)	11	44		L	
08/16	Shelbyville (Shelbyville, IN)	79	25	W		
08/18	Athletic (Columbus, OH)	33	18	W		

INDIANAPOLIS (cont.)
Indianapolis, IN

DATE	OPPONENT	SCORE		W	L	T
08/19	Riverside (Evansville, IN)	47	17	W		
08/24	Excelsior (Jeffersonville, IN)	71	23	W		
08/25	Eagle (Louisville, KY)	8	20		L	
08/26	Eagle (Louisville, KY)	42	32	W		
08/27	Athletic (Logansport, IN)	18	17	W		
09/01	Riverside (Evansville, IN)	18	14	W		
09/27	Cincinnati (Cincinnati)	2	43		L	

BATTERS	POS	GP	HL	AVG	R	AVG	H	AVG	TB	AVG
F. Ketcham	1B	19					41	2.16	65	3.43
Sharpe	2B	23					59	2.56	83	3.61
Morrison	SS	26					65	2.50	93	3.58
E. Ketcham	3B	25					60	2.40	80	3.20
McDonald	OF	23					71	3.07	96	4.17
Parr	OF	22					50	2.27	82	3.73
Williams	OF	18					36	2.00	43	2.39
Bixby	C	18					53	2.94	86	4.78
Hopkinson	P	22					74	3.36	95	4.32
Sheets	OF,C	14					37	2.64	48	3.43

RESOLUTE 14 - 11
Elizabeth, NJ

DATE	OPPONENT	SCORE		W	L	T
05/07	Atlantic (Elizabeth)	38	8	W		
05/13	Atlantic (Brooklyn)	0	19		L	
05/18	Star (Brooklyn)	9	22		L	
05/25	Mutual (New York)	18	54		L	
06/01	Eckford (Brooklyn)	17	14	W		
06/07	Oriental (New York)	22	14	W		
06/09	Mutual (New York)	18	37		L	
06/14	Amateur (Newark)	23	12	W		
06/16	Cincinnati (Cincinnati)	7	22		L	
06/22	Harmonic (Brooklyn)	17	14	W		
06/29	Eckford (Brooklyn)	31	10	W		
07/07	Neptune (Easton, PA)	40	23	W		
07/14	Atlantic (Brooklyn)	3	29		L	
07/23	Star (Brooklyn)	5	27		L	
07/29	Athletic (Brooklyn)*	14	12	W		
08/01	Union (Morrisania, NY)	13	36		L	
08/05	Trenton (Trenton, NJ)*	24	13	W		
08/09	Athletic (Brooklyn)*	26	31		L	
08/26	Active (Newark)*	39	12	W		
09/29	Atlantic (Elizabeth)*	57	6	W		
10/06	Amateur (Newark)	11	21		L	
10/13	Neptune (Easton, PA)*	23	16	W		
11/01	Active (Newark)	9	14		L	
11/07	Active (Newark)*	26	14	W		
11/10	Amateur (Newark)	28	17	W		

* Box score not available

BATTERS	POS	GP	HL	AVG	R	AVG	H	AVG	TB	AVG
Mike Campbell	1B	16			30	1.88				
Ritter	2B	15			35	2.33				
William Greathead	SS	8			8	1.00				
James Forsyth	3B,OF,C	14			26	1.86				
Amory	OF	13			20	1.54				
Beardsley	OF	11			29	2.64				
Laing	OF,SS,2B	8			17	2.13				
John Farrow	C	13			27	2.08				
Hugh Campbell	P	14			22	1.57				

RESOLUTE (cont.)
Elizabeth, NJ

BATTERS	POS	GP	HL	AVG	R	AVG	H	AVG	TB	AVG
Stevens	C	6			14	2.33				

SOUTHERN   13 - 8
New Orleans, LA

DATE	OPPONENT	SCORE		W	L	T
01/09	Pelican (New Orleans)	51	17	W		
02/16	Atlantic (Algiers, LA)	23	22	W		
02/20	Creole (New Orleans)	46	23	W		
02/27	Pelican (New Orleans)	44	29	W		
03/06	Comet (New Orleans)	44	8	W		
03/13	Crescent (New Orleans)	86	20	W		
03/27	Surprise (New Orleans)	51	9	W		
04/04	R.E. Lee (New Orleans)	22	12	W		
04/17	R.E. Lee (New Orleans)	24	21	W		
04/21	Lone Star (New Orleans)	21	36		L	
04/24	Lone Star (New Orleans)	27	18	W		
04/26	Cincinnati (Cincinnati)	6	79		L	
05/11	Chicago (Chicago)	9	41		L	
05/15	Lone Star (New Orleans)	25	20	W		
05/29	Lone Star (New Orleans)*	30	20	W		
06/12	Hancock (New Orleans)*	13	17		L	
09/04	Washington (New Orleans)	29	7	W		
09/25	Lone Star (New Orleans)*	4	23		L	
11/24	Mutual (New York)	5	37		L	
11/27	Mutual (New York)	6	36		L	
12/04	Mutual (New York)*	16	26		L	

* Box score not available

BATTERS	POS	GP	HL	AVG	R	AVG	H	AVG	TB	AVG
J. Hennessey	1B,C,OF	15	41	2.73	60	4.00				
W. Larkin	2B,OF	10	22	2.20	42	4.20				
O'Keefe	SS,OF,P	14	44	3.14	43	3.07				
Holzman	3B,OF	14	43	3.07	62	4.43				
J. Buddendorf	OF,SS	16	43	2.69	51	3.19				
F. Fay	OF,C,P	14	32	2.29	48	3.43				
Chandler	OF	10	33	3.30	39	3.90				
Donovan	C,OF	13	30	2.31	42	3.23				
Winn	P,2B	15	41	2.73	41	2.73				
Bradenburgh	P	5	10	2.00	17	3.20				

AETNA   12 - 4
Chicago, IL

DATE	OPPONENT	SCORE		W	L	T
05/28	Eureka (Chicago)	36	19	W		
06/02	Athletic (Chicago)	19	22		L	
06/23	Eureka (Chicago)	67	12	W		
07/04	Mystic (Detroit)	31	13	W		
08/03	Liberty (Chicago)	49	30	W		
08/11	Chicago (Chicago)	8	43		L	
08/25	Amateur (Chicago	*9	0	W		
08/25	Picked Nine (Chicago)	17	13	W		
08/29	Athletic (Chicago)	24	13	W		
09/08	Transit (Chicago)	36	12	W		
09/13	Athletic (Chicago)	41	24	W		
09/15	Forest City (Rockford, IL)	3	35		L	

AETNA (cont.)
Chicago, IL

DATE	OPPONENT	SCORE		W	L	T
09/28	Amateur (Chicago)	26	21	W		
10/01	Chicago (Chicago)	9	37		L	
10/20	Kekionga (Ft. Wayne, IN)	9	8	W		
10/29	Liberty (Chicago)	41	10	W		

BATTERS	POS	GP	HL	AVG	R	AVG	H	AVG	TB	AVG
Lynch	1B	15					37	2.47	49	3.27
Gillan	2B	13					22	1.69	30	2.30
Hallinan	SS	14					35	2.50	58	4.14
Hanifan	3B	15					39	2.60	54	3.60
Ward	OF	15					38	2.53	51	3.40
O'Laughlin	OF	15					36	2.40	44	2.93
Long	OF	14					27	1.93	30	2.14
Quinn	C	12					27	2.25	39	3.25
Reid	P	15					34	2.27	44	2.93

AMATEUR   12 - 8
Newark, NJ

DATE	OPPONENT	SCORE		W	L	T
05/14	Eckford (Newark)*	41	7	W		
05/19	Liberty (New Brunswick, NJ)*	25	14	W		
05/24	Bergen (Bergen, NJ)*	27	6	W		
05/26	Atlantic (Elizabeth, NJ)*	63	15	W		
06/02	Champion (Jersey City, NJ)	8	16		L	
06/14	Resolute (Elizabeth, NJ)	12	23		L	
06/20	Cincinnati (Cincinnati)	2	53		L	
06/23	Champion (Jersey City, NJ)*	28	20	W		
07/---	Harmonic (Brooklyn)*	24	12	W		
07/26	Bergen (Bergen, NJ)*	15	8	W		
07/28	Champion (Jersey City, NJ)	17	1	W		
07/30	Alpha (Brooklyn)*	19	23		L	
08/18	Bergen (Bergen, NJ)*	21	34		L	
08/25	Star (Brooklyn)*	13	42		L	
09/08	Active (New York)	11	8	W		
09/15	Bergen (Bergen, NJ)*	22	4	W		
09/22	Active (New York)*	39	14	W		
10/06	Resolute (Elizabeth, NJ)	21	11	W		
10/22	Princeton (Princeton, NJ)	13	17		L	
11/10	Resolute (Elizabeth, NJ)	17	28		L	

* Box score not available

BATTERS	POS	GP	HL	AVG	R	AVG	H	AVG	TB	AVG
H. Beam	1B	3	11	3.67	3	1.00				
W. Thorn	2B,P	5	12	2.40	10	2.00				
Welsh	SS	6	19	3.17	7	1.17				
W. Ward	3B	6	16	2.67	6	1.00				
E. Beam	OF	4	12	3.00	1	0.25				
Van Wagenen	OF	5	13	2.60	5	1.00				
McGovern	OF	3	12	4.00	4	1.33				
Sam Wright	C	6	15	2.50	10	1.67				
Grill	P,2B	5	14	2.80	6	1.20				
J. Ward	1B	3	5	1.67	6	2.00				

ATHLETIC 11 - 11
Brooklyn, NY

DATE	OPPONENT	SCORE		W	L	T
---/---	Oriental (New York)	20	10	W		
06/02	Mutual (New York)	9	38		L	
06/09	Atlantic (Brooklyn)	15	52		L	
06/14	Union (Brooklyn)	26	7	W		
06/30	Eckford (Brooklyn)	7	19		L	
07/29	Resolute (Elizabeth, NJ)	12	14		L	
07/12	Eckford (Brooklyn)	13	16		L	
07/20	Alpha (Brooklyn)	9	13		L	
---/---	Champion (Jersey City, NJ)	23	26		L	
---/---	Enterprise (Brooklyn)	27	34		L	
08/09	Resolute (Elizabeth, NJ)	31	26	W		
08/11	Mutual (New York)	10	17		L	
08/15	Enterprise (Brooklyn)	26	4	W		
---/---	Dunderberg (Peekskill, NY)	53	20	W		
09/01	Stamford (Stamford, CT)	40	12	W		
09/06	Champion (Jersey City, NJ)	23	15	W		
09/13	Enterprise (Brooklyn)	45	6	W		
---/---	Union (Brooklyn)	68	26	W		
09/21	Atlantic (Brooklyn)	12	16		L	
09/28	Alpha (Brooklyn)	31	19	W		
10/04	Champion (Jersey City, NJ)	30	20	W		
10/15	Star (Brooklyn)	2	6		L	

BATTERS	POS	GP	HL	AVG	R	AVG	H	AVG	TB	AVG
Bennett	1B,SS	14					39	2.79	56	4.00
Booth	2B	17					56	3.29	83	4.88
Bond	SS	15					40	2.67	52	3.47
Proctor	3B	21					81	3.86	106	5.05
Wiggins	OF,2B	18					55	3.06	95	5.28
Ireland	OF	18					41	2.28	50	2.78
George Cook	OF	10					26	2.60	32	3.20
Noonan	C,SS	22					70	3.18	94	4.27
Richardson	P,1B	22					71	3.22	90	4.09
George Price	OF	9					25	2.78	40	4.44
Naylor	P,1B	4					4	1.00	6	1.50

EAGLE 10 - 1
San Francisco, CA

DATE	OPPONENT	SCORE		W	L	T
04/09	Santa Clara (Santa Clara, CA)	32	22	W		
06/25	Silver Star (Carson City, NV)	34	16	W		
06/28	Silver Star (Carson City, NV)	35	23	W		
07/04	Atlantic (San Francisco)	23	19	W		
07/14	Atlantic (San Francisco)	25	11	W		
09/09	Sacramento (Sacramento)	70	14	W		
10/06	Liberty (San Francisco)	47	28	W		
10/19	Liberty (San Francisco)	33	32	W		
11/12	Vallejo (Vallejo)	30	22	W		
11/24	Vallejo (Vallejo)	36	38		L	
11/30	Vallejo (Vallejo)	39	11	W		

BATTERS	POS	GP	HL	AVG	R	AVG	H	AVG	TB	AVG
Fisher	1B	10					26	2.60	33	3.30
C. Keating	2B	10					27	2.70	49	4.90
Calvert	SS	11					35	3.18	51	4.64
Taylor	3B	9					30	3.33	48	5.33
Strand	OF	11					27	2.45	35	3.18
Beck	OF,1B	9					26	2.88	39	4.33
Hicks	OF	5					8	1.60	11	2.20

EAGLE (cont.)
San Francisco, CA

BATTERS	POS	GP	HL	AVG	R	AVG	H	AVG	TB	AVG
Curran	C	11					34	3.09	57	5.18
Miller	P	9					23	2.56	33	3.67
D. Keating	3B,OF	5					13	2.60	23	4.60

CORNELL 9 - 2
Ithaca, NY

DATE	OPPONENT	SCORE		W	L	T
05/07	Normal (Cortland, NY)	12	24		L	
05/14	Bush (Ithaca)	32	15	W		
05/18	University Press (Ithaca)	56	6	W		
05/21	Friendship (Ithaca)	24	12	W		
05/28	Friendship (Ithaca)	51	18	W		
06/04	Creeper (Groton, NY)	38	14	W		
06/04	Normal (Cortland, NY)	27	31		L	
06/07	Forest City (Ithaca)	31	20	W		
06/10	University Press (Ithaca)	50	17	W		
06/19	Alert (Dundas, ON)	65	20	W		
09/22	Ulysses (Trumansburg, NY)	31	15	W		

BATTERS	POS	GP	HL	AVG	R	AVG	H	AVG	TB	AVG
Jillett		8					44	5.50	53	6.63
C. Smith		7					33	4.71	43	6.14
Rathbone		6					31	5.13	37	6.13
Hurd		6					29	4.83	32	5.33
Bruggeman		6					25	4.17	30	5.00
Gamgie		6					26	4.33	30	5.00
Wright		5					22	4.40	27	5.40
Gavigan		5					21	4.20	25	5.00

OSCEOLA 9 - 3
Pittsburgh, PA

DATE	OPPONENT	SCORE		W	L	T
05/21	Lawrence (Pittsburgh)	29	24	W		
06/11	Rapids (New York State)	19	5	W		
06/25	Shoo Fly (Temperanceville, PA)	68	11	W		
07/09	Good Will (Pittsburgh)	49	14	W		
07/15	Allegheny (Pittsburgh)	21	37		L	
08/06	Laurence (Pittsburgh)	17	27		L	
08/17	Hope (Birmingham, PA)	27	22	W		
09/02	Olympic (Washington)	0	38		L	
09/24	Lawrence (Pittsburgh)	38	23	W		
10/15	Lawrence (Pittsburgh)	14	13	W		
10/22	Shoo Fly (Temperanceville, PA)	27	13	W		
10/28	Atlantic (Pittsburgh)	*9	0	W		

* Forfeit

BATTERS	POS	GP	HL	AVG	R	AVG	H	AVG	TB	AVG
Kober	1B	11					33	3.00	41	3.73
Riley	2B	11					36	3.27	50	4.55
J.A. Fox	SS	11					40	3.64	61	5.55
Johns	3B	9					27	3.00	38	4.22
Metzger	OF	9					26	2.89	36	4.00
Davis	OF	8					16	2.00	20	2.50
Bell	OF	7					16	2.29	21	3.00

OSCEOLA (cont.)
Pittsburgh, PA

BATTERS	POS	GP	HL	AVG	R	AVG	H	AVG	TB	AVG
Stevens	C	11					33	3.00	39	3.55
Shannon	P	9					20	2.22	30	3.33

PASTIME 9 - 22 - 1
Baltimore, MD

DATE	OPPONENT	SCORE		W	L	T
04/30	Athletic (Philadelphia)	21	34		L	
05/14	Athletic (Philadelphia)	10	32		L	
05/18	Maryland (Baltimore)	6	17		L	
05/26	Atlantic (Brooklyn)*	5	22		L	
06/04	Forest City (Rockford)*	11	21		L	
06/08	Star (Brooklyn)*	18	25		L	
06/11	Union (Lansingburgh, NY)*	9	15		L	
06/14	National (Washington)	8	18		L	
06/15	Olympic (Washington)*	16	14	W		
06/22	Olympic (Washington)*	20	27		L	
06/24	Cincinnati (Cincinnati)	8	30		L	
06/30	Unknown (Washington)	40	16	W		
07/04	Maryland (Baltimore)	20	32		L	
07/12	Mutual (New York)*	18	34		L	
07/15	Chicago (Chicago)	13	32		L	
07/29	Atlantic (Brooklyn)	7	27		L	
07/30	Star (Brooklyn)	10	7	W		
08/01	Union (Lansingburgh, NY)	23	6	W		
08/02	Union (Morrisania, NY)	10	12		L	
08/03	Mutual (New York)	7	29		L	
08/06	Harvard (Cambridge, MA)*	12	30		L	
08/19	Olympic (Baltimore)*	46	6	W		
08/25	Forest City (Cleveland)	18	22		L	
08/27	Maryland (Baltimore)	7	10		L	
09/02	Maryland (Baltimore)*	25	10	W		
09/09	Maryland (Baltimore)	37	5	W		
09/19	Flour City (Rochester, NY)	25	16	W		
09/21	Union (Lansingburgh, NY)*	7	22		L	
09/23	Excelsior (Brooklyn)	17	17			T
09/24	Star (Brooklyn)	13	18		L	
09/27	Union (Lansingburgh, NY)	14	32		L	
10/05	Arlington (Washington)*	15	14	W		

* Box score not available

BATTERS	POS	GP	HL	AVG	R	AVG	H	AVG	TB	AVG
Southard	1B,SS	6			13	2.17				
Popplein	2B	14			40	2.86				
Annan	SS	10			19	1.90				
Bailey	3B	13			29	2.23				
Chenowith	OF	15			29	1.93				
Doyle	OF	14			16	1.14				
Lucas	OF,1B	8			14	1.75				
Williams	C,2B	11			17	1.55				
McDonald	P,C,OF	15			19	1.27				
Buck	SS,2B	9			22	2.44				
Reese	1B,C	6			9	1.50				
Barrett	C	5			11	2.20				
Turnbull	P	5			6	1.20				

LONE STAR 8 - 4
Catskill, NY

DATE	OPPONENT	SCORE		W	L	T
08/04	Oneida (Bloomfield, NJ)	33	25	W		
08/13	Niagara (Saugerties, NY)	25	40		L	
08/15	Hudson (Hudson City, NJ)	42	33	W		
08/26	Active (Wappinger Falls, NY)	34	49		L	
08/29	Riverside (Coxsackie, NY)	24	8	W		
09/02	Mutual (Catskill, NY)	46	29	W		
09/06	Union (Lansingburgh, NY)	6	82		L	
09/08	Excelsior (Leeds, NY)	46	6	W		
09/09	Mutual (Catskill, NY)	54	20	W		
09/20	Knickerbocker (Hudson, NY)	36	25	W		
09/22	Excelsior (Leeds, NY)	33	35		L	
09/29	Ulster (Saugerties, NY)	35	26	W		

BATTERS	POS	GP	HL	AVG	R	AVG	H	AVG	TB	AVG
H. Wilcox		12					45	3.75	67	5.58
Cornwall		12					36	3.00	49	4.08
Pease		11					39	3.55	45	4.09
E. Wilcox		10					37	3.70	54	5.40
Tolley		10					37	3.70	42	4.20
Fiero		10					26	2.60	32	3.20
Day		8					32	4.00	51	6.38
McArthur		8					30	3.75	45	5.63
Carlow		5					16	3.20	24	4.80
Beach		5					10	2.00	13	2.60

MUTUAL 8 - 7
Meadville, PA

DATE	OPPONENT	SCORE		W	L	T
05/19	Seneca (Oil City, PA)	7	19		L	
05/26	Forest City (Cleveland)	1	20		L	
06/21	Athletic (Jamestown, NY)	27	36		L	
06/30	Athletic (Jamestown, NY)	36	18	W		
07/19	Forest City (Cleveland)	5	57		L	
08/13	Shoo Fly (Cochranton, PA)	56	6	W		
08/15	Oil Stockings (Franklin, PA)	28	11	W		
08/17	Amateur (Greenville, PA)	76	25	W		
08/22	Union (Mercer, PA)	19	34		L	
08/28	Union (Mercer, PA)	10	39		L	
08/31	Black Stockings (Union, PA)	53	11	W		
09/01	Picked Nine (Meadville)	72	10	W		
09/16	Athletic (Jamestown, NY)	15	9	W		
10/24	Seneca (Oil City, PA)	18	39		L	

(Only scores extant)

BATTERS	POS	GP	HL	AVG	R	AVG	H	AVG	TB	AVG
McCoy		15			64	4.27				
Sargeant		15			54	3.60				
Lane		12			38	3.17				
Carnahan		14			60	4.29				
Blystone		13			39	3.00				
Honeywell		12			44	3.67				
J. McClintock		11			40	3.64				
E. McClintock		9			33	3.67				
S. McClintock		9			8	0.89				
Rose		8			29	3.63				
Branyan		5			21	4.20				

LIVE OAK   6 - 4
Cincinnati, OH

DATE	OPPONENT	SCORE		W	L	T
08/23	Cincinnati (Cincinnati)	2	46		L	
08/24	Resolute (Cincinnati)	15	14	W		
08/25	Mutual (Springfield, OH)	26	12	W		
08/26	Union (Urbana, OH)	32	11	W		
08/31	Cincinnati (Cincinnati)	12	35		L	
09/16	Riverside (Portsmouth, OH)	9	25		L	
09/22	Star (Covington, KY)	25	23	W		
10/---	Resolute (Hamilton, OH)	11	19		L	
10/---	Metropolitan (Cincinnati)	28	16	W		
11/07	Excelsior (Cincinnati)	36	20	W		

(Only scores extant)

BATTERS	POS	GP	HL	AVG	R	AVG	H	AVG	TB	AVG
Lowe	1B	14					26	1.86	42	3.00
W.P. Wright	2B	17					37	2.18	60	3.53
Smith	SS,P,OF	14					36	2.57	60	4.29
Bettens	3B	8					13	1.63	17	2.13
W.H. Boake	OF	15					22	1.47	30	2.00
J.L. Boake	OF	15					19	1.27	22	1.47
Jones	OF,C	8					11	1.38	16	2.00
Griffith	C	15					26	1.73	51	3.40
Colburn	P	10					20	2.00	30	3.00
Kalisch	3B	6					13	2.17	14	2.33
Langdon	SS	6					12	2.00	20	3.33
DeMar	P	5					7	1.40	19	3.80
Russell	C	5					2	0.40	2	0.40

LOWELL   6 - 13
Boston, MA

DATE	OPPONENT	SCORE			W	L	T
05/14	Harvard (Cambridge, MA)	5	28			L	
05/21	Kearsarge (Stoneham, MA)*	33	9		W		
05/24	Athletic (Philadelphia)	11	22			L	
06/01	Clipper (Lowell, MA)	28	14		W		
06/06	Cincinnati (Cincinnati)	4	17			L	
06/17	Yale (New Haven, CT)*	8	14			L	
06/18	Mutual (New York)	20	35			L	
06/21	Fairmount (Marlboro, MA)	15	19			L	
06/23	Nichols (Sandwich, MA)*	60	15		W		
06/27	Harvard (Cambridge, MA)	12	36			L	
06/28	Chicago (Chicago)	25	43			L	
06/---	Brown (Providence, RI)*	20	15		W		
07/04	Princeton (Princeton, NJ)	16	36			L	
07/30	Kearsarge (Stoneham, MA)	17	27			L	
08/02	Mansfield (Middleton, CT)	34	30	(10)	W		
09/20	Fairmount (Marlboro, MA)	12	17			L	
09/23	King Phillip (E. Abington, MA)*	27	19		W		
09/24	Kearsarge (Stoneham, MA)*	5	--			L	
10/01	Harvard (Cambridge, MA)*	6	29			L	

* Box score not available

BATTERS	POS	GP	HL	AVG	R	AVG	H	AVG	TB	AVG
Reed	1B,SS	10	31	3.10	12	1.20				
Edward Jewell	2B	6	16	2.67	9	1.50				
Fred Conant	SS,1B	6	22	3.67	4	0.67				
William Joslyn	3B	5	15	3.00	11	2.20				
Briggs	OF	10	32	3.20	18	1.80				
A.M. Newton	OF,3B	8	23	2.88	11	1.38				
Gorham	OF	7	18	2.57	17	2.43				

LOWELL (cont.)
Boston, MA

BATTERS	POS	GP	HL	AVG	R	AVG	H	AVG	TB	AVG
William Bradbury	C	11	29	2.64	21	1.91				
Mort Rogers	P,OF	11	35	3.18	23	2.09				
William Alline	OF	6	18	3.00	13	2.17				
Bettley	1B	5	11	2.20	15	3.00				

WASHINGTON   5 - 2
Washington, DC

DATE	OPPONENT	SCORE		W	L	T
10/01	Olympic (Washington)	7	16		L	
10/05	Atlantic (Washington)	26	14	W		
10/06	Olympic (Washington)	7	16		L	
10/12	Atlantic (Washington)	49	8	W		
10/18	Active (Washington)	19	8	W		
10/26	Star (?)	32	6	W		
11/12	Active (Washington)	15	7	W		

BATTERS	POS	GP	HL	AVG	R	AVG	H	AVG	TB	AVG
A.V. Robinson		7					17	2.43	32	4.57
J. Doyle		7					15	2.14	26	3.71
Owens		7					16	2.29	22	3.14
Martin		7					13	1.86	15	2.14
Anderson		6					14	2.33	20	3.33
Dennis Coughlin		6					10	1.67	14	2.33
Harry McLean		6					10	1.67	12	2.00
Gould		6					6	1.00	7	1.17

EXCELSIOR   5 - 3 - 1
Brooklyn, NY

DATE	OPPONENT	SCORE		W	L	T
06/14	Eckford (Brooklyn)	10	24		L	
07/01	Alert (S. Orange, NJ)	6	31		L	
07/04	Dunderberg (Peekskill, NY)	18	12	W		
07/13	Alpha (Brooklyn)	23	18	W		
08/11	Leatherstocking (Doylestown, NY)	31	8	W		
08/23	Mutual (New York)	5	23		L	
09/20	Dunderberg (Peekskill, NY)	30	5	W		
09/23	Pastime (Baltimore)	17	17			T
10/12	Athletic (Brooklyn)	16	10	W		

BATTERS	POS	GP	HL	AVG	R	AVG	H	AVG	TB	AVG
Eddy	1B	6					13	2.13	18	3.00
George Chauncey	2B	5					11	2.20	13	2.60
Dohrmann	SS,OF	5					9	1.80	11	2.20
Thompson	3B,SS	5					13	2.60	26	5.20
Dan Chauncey	OF	7					14	2.00	18	2.40
Milton Sweet	OF,P	6					11	1.83	13	2.13
Lockett	OF	5					9	1.80	12	2.40
C. Miller	C	5					8	1.60	13	2.60
Tom Watts	P	7					14	2.00		

PELICAN 5 - 7
New Orleans, LA

DATE	OPPONENT	SCORE		W	L	T
01/09	Surprise (New Orleans)	17	51		L	
02/16	Surprise (New Orleans)	19	14	W		
02/27	Southern (New Orleans)	29	44		L	
03/06	Lone Star (New Orleans)	15	22		L	
03/13	Washington (New Orleans)	40	11	W		
03/20	Lone Star (New Orleans)	27	41		L	
04/03	Washington (New Orleans)*	56	23	W		
04/25	Cincinnati (Cincinnati)	1	51		L	
05/08	Surprise (New Orleans)*	67	14	W		
05/22	Stonewall (New Orleans)	58	12	W		
06/---	Atlantic (Algiers, LA)*	28	29		L	
10/16	Quickstep (New Orleans)*	18	24		L	

* Box score not available

BATTERS	POS	GP	HL	AVG	R	AVG	H	AVG	TB	AVG
Buchanan	1B	8	26	3.25	20	2.50				
Short	2B,SS,3B	8	15	1.88	31	3.88				
Dietrich	SS	5	17	3.40	7	1.40				
Tate	3B	5	16	3.20	13	2.60				
Ford	OF,1B,2B	8	26	3.25	27	3.38				
James Murtha	OF,C,SS	6	14	2.33	18	3.00				
J. Blanchard	OF	5	21	4.20	11	2.20				
Culligan	C	6	25	4.17	15	2.50				
Bell	P,3B	7	28	4.00	16	2.29				
T. Mahan	C,SS	5	15	3.00	18	3.60				

ROSE HILL 3 - 6
Fordham, NY

DATE	OPPONENT	SCORE		W	L	T
05/05	Union (Morrisania, NY)	10	16		L	
05/26	Mutual (New York)	6	21		L	
06/01	Yale (New Haven, CT)	19	13	W		
06/02	Union (Morrisania, NY)*	8	35		L	
07/02	Alpha (Brooklyn)	15	7	W		
07/01	Mutual (New York)	18	27		L	
07/05	Harvard (Cambridge, MA)	2	17		L	
10/18	Princeton (Princeton, NJ)	18	22		L	
11/17	Alert (New York)*	34	22	W		

* Box score not available

BATTERS	POS	GP	HL	AVG	R	AVG	H	AVG	TB	AVG
McManus	1B	5	14	2.80	12	2.40				
McDermott	2B	7	18	2.57	12	1.71				
Tremp	SS	5	16	3.20	12	2.40				
W. Gallagher	3B,OF	6	18	3.00	11	1.83				
Dooley	OF	7	20	2.86	12	1.71				
Gleavy	OF,3B,C	7	23	3.29	11	1.57				
Swayne	OF,1B	6	18	3.00	9	1.50				
Villa	C	6	20	3.33	7	1.17				
Burns	P	6	14	2.33	6	1.00				

HARMONIC 3-9-1
Brooklyn, NY

DATE	OPPONENT	SCORE		W	L	T
04/27	Atlantic (Brooklyn)	20	25		L	
05/03	Alpha (Brooklyn)	15	25		L	
05/05	Atlantic (Brooklyn)	6	29		L	
05/19	Atlantic (Brooklyn)	20	25		L	
06/22	Resolute (Elizabeth, NJ)	14	17		L	
07/04	Waverly (Fishkill, NY)	50	8	W		
07/23	Eckford (Brooklyn)	13	37		L	
07/---	Amateur (Newark)	12	24		L	
08/19	Aetna (New Jersey)	44	27	W		
09/14	Star (Brooklyn)	11	23		L	
09/19	Dunderberg (Peekskill, NY)	27	10	W		
10/01	Eagle (Flatbush, NY)	20	20			T
10/21	Champion (Jersey City, NJ)	14	16		L	

BATTERS	POS	GP	HL	AVG	R	AVG	H	AVG	TB	AVG
Crosby	1B,3B	6					14	2.33	19	3.13
Brown	2B,C	5					7	1.40	9	1.80
Fenniman	SS,OF	5					15	3.00	20	4.00
J. Hatch	3B,SS,P	7					10	1.43	11	1.57
L.S. Lewis	OF,P,2B	7					16	2.29	21	3.00
Murphy	OF	5					12	2.40	15	3.00
Larkin	OF	5					16	3.20	18	3.60
Silleck	C,2B	5					15	3.00	18	3.60
Sullivan	P	5					8	1.60	10	2.00

ALPHA 3-10
Brooklyn, NY

DATE	OPPONENT	SCORE		W	L	T
05/30	Harmonic (Brooklyn)	15	25		L	
06/09	Champion (Jersey City, NJ)	1	12		L	
06/27	Mutual (New York)	4	25		L	
07/02	Rose Hill (Fordham, NY)	14	29		L	
07/04	Buckskin (Gloversville, NY)	12	38		L	
07/11	Atlantic (Brooklyn)	4	21		L	
07/13	Excelsior (Brooklyn)	18	23		L	
07/16	Eagle (Flatbush, NY)	48	18	W		
07/19	Athletic (Brooklyn)	13	9	W		
07/30	Amateur (Newark)	23	10	W		
08/19	Atlantic (Brooklyn)	17	34		L	
08/27	Star (Brooklyn)	1	19		L	
09/28	Athletic (Brooklyn)	19	31		L	

BATTERS	POS	GP	HL	AVG	R	AVG	H	AVG	TB	AVG
Stark	1B	4	8	2.00	11	2.75				
Fred Crane	2B	5					8	1.60	10	2.00
James	SS	6					11	1.83	15	2.50
Hall	3B	6					13	2.17	16	2.67
Valentine	OF	6					6	1.00	9	1.50
E. Jackson	OF	5					13	2.60	18	3.30
Remsen	OF	5					12	2.40	20	4.00
Moody	C	5					10	2.00	13	2.60
Hillyer	P	5					8	1.60	11	2.20

FLOUR CITY   0 - 9
Rochester, NY

DATE	OPPONENT	SCORE		W	L	T
06/01	Cincinnati (Cincinnati)	13	56		L	
06/22	Chicago (Chicago)	20	46		L	
07/04	Forest City (Cleveland)	13	28		L	
08/12	Forest City (Cleveland)	2	29		L	
09/06	Olympic (Washington)*	18	42		L	
09/07	Atlantic (Brooklyn)	15	29		L	
09/13	Maple Leaf (Guelph, ON)	17	45		L	
09/19	Pastime (Baltimore)	16	25		L	
10/07	Maple Leaf (Guelph, ON)*	8	47		L	

* Box score not available

BATTERS	POS	GP	HL	AVG	R	AVG	H	AVG	TB	AVG
Campbell	1B	7	23	3.29	9	1.29				
G. Ward	2B	4	14	3.50	6	1.50				
W. Jackson	SS	7	13	1.86	17	2.43				
Charles McKelvey	3B,OF	7	20	2.86	11	1.57				
J.A. McKelvey, Jr.	OF,2B	7	18	2.57	11	1.57				
Baird	OF,C	6	18	3.00	8	1.33				
Carruthers	OF	5	14	2.80	8	1.60				
Thayer	C,3B	6	17	2.83	5	0.83				
Ball	P	5	18	3.60	7	1.40				
Sabin	2B,3B	4	16	4.00	4	1.00				

AMATEUR TEAM TOTALS

TEAM	CITY/STATE	GP	W	L	T	PCT	R	OR
Lone Star	New Orleans, LA	49	32	17	0	.653	1369	837
Harvard	Cambridge, MA	42	31	11	0	.738	1142	611
Star	Brooklyn, NY	33	24	9	0	.727	726	281
Mansfield	Middletown, CT	34	21	13	0	.616	875	779
Indianapolis	Indianapolis, IN	27	17	10	0	.630	889	625
Resolute	Elizabeth, NJ	25	14	11	0	.560	518	497
Southern	New Orleans, LA	21	13	8	0	.619	582	521
Aetna	Chicago, IL	16	12	4	0	.750	425	312
Amateur	Newark, NJ	20	12	8	0	.600	438	356
Expert	Philadelphia, PA	*28	11	9	0	.550	606	412
Athletic	Brooklyn, NY	22	11	11	0	.500	532	416
Eagle	San Francisco, CA	11	10	1	0	.909	404	236
Kaw Valley	Lawrence, KS	13	10	3	0	.769	448	284
Washington	New Orleans, LA	15	10	5	0	.667	425	415
Cornell	Ithaca, NY	11	9	2	0	.818	417	192
Osceola	Pittsburgh, PA	12	9	3	0	.750	318	227
Trenton	Trenton, NJ	14	9	5	0	.643	450	299
R.E. Lee	New Orleans, LA	17	9	8	0	.529	359	266
Pastime	Baltimore, MD	32	9	22	1	.297	516	652
Lone Star	Catskill, NY	12	8	4	0	.667	414	378
Mutual	Meadville, PA	14	7	7	0	.500	486	356
Social	New York, NY	8	6	2	0	.750	252	191
Live Oak	Cincinnati, OH	10	6	4	0	.600	196	221
Kekionga	Ft. Wayne, IN	12	6	6	0	.500	236	335
Lowell	Boston, MA	19	6	13	0	.316	358	425
Washington	Washington, DC	7	5	2	0	.714	155	75
Excelsior	Brooklyn, NY	9	5	3	1	.611	156	148
Fairmount	Marlboro, MA	10	5	5	0	.500	211	289
W. Philadelphia	Philadelphia, PA	11	5	6	0	.455	186	267
Champion	Jersey City, NJ	12	5	7	0	.417	185	216
Pelican	New Orleans, LA	12	5	7	0	.417	375	336
Maple Leaf	Guelph, ON	4	4	0	0	1.000	190	61
Active	New Orleans, LA	8	4	4	0	.500	277	229
Surprise	New Orleans, LA	10	4	6	0	.400	234	338

AMATEUR TEAM TOTALS (cont.)

TEAM	CITY/STATE	GP	W	L	T	PCT	R	OR
Yale	New Haven, CT	11	4	7	0	.364	194	267
Fearless	New Orleans, LA	5	3	2	0	.600	119	128
Mutual	Springfield, MA	6	3	3	0	.500	126	146
Princeton	Princeton, NJ	6	3	3	0	.500	99	119
Union	Brooklyn, NY	8	3	5	0	.375	195	260
Rose Hill	Fordham, NY	9	3	6	0	.333	130	180
Harmonic	Brooklyn, NY	13	3	9	1	.269	266	286
Alpha	Brooklyn, NY	13	3	10	0	.231	189	294
Allegheny	Pittsburgh, PA	5	2	3	0	.400	76	93
Hancock	New Orleans, LA	5	2	3	0	.400	86	159
Bergen	Bergen, NJ	6	2	4	0	.333	80	109
Buckskin	Gloversville, NY	6	2	4	0	.333	114	108
Ontario	Oswego, NY	6	2	4	0	.333	104	252
Clipper	Lowell, MA	7	2	5	0	.286	153	208
Enterprise	Brooklyn, NY	7	2	5	0	.286	113	200
Jefferson	Washington, DC	9	2	7	0	.222	118	252
Intrepid	Philadelphia, PA	13	2	11	0	.154	186	395
Keystone	Philadelphia, PA	14	2	12	0	.143	226	376
Osceola	Brooklyn, NY	4	1	3	0	.250	76	114
Neptune	Easton, PA	5	1	4	0	.200	101	117
Stonewall	New Orleans, LA	5	1	4	0	.200	110	219
Empire	St. Louis, MO	6	1	5	0	.167	87	185
Pickwick	New Orleans, LA	6	1	5	0	.167	109	213
Atlantic	Algiers, LA	8	1	7	0	.125	151	326
Niagara	Buffalo, NY	10	1	9	0	.100	188	345
Gramercy	New York, NY	4	0	4	0	.000	64	115
Union	St. Louis, MO	5	0	5	0	.000	79	203
Crescent	New Orleans, LA	6	0	6	0	.000	55	196
Oriental	New York, NY	7	0	7	0	.000	53	157
Flour City	Rochester, NY	9	0	9	0	.000	122	347

* Some scores missing

OTHER AMATEUR TEAMS

TEAM	CITY/STATE
Active	Chicago, IL
Active	Clinton, IA
Active	Renova, PA
Active	Washington, DC
Alert	S. Orange, NJ
Alert	Schnectady, NY
Amateur	Chicago, IL
Amateur	Wash. Ct. House, OH
America	Marysville, CA
Ann Arbor	Ann Arbor, MI
Appanoe	Ottumwa, IA
Arlington	Washington, DC
Athletic	Chicago, IL
Athletic	Jamestown, NY
Atlantic	San Francisco, CA
Atlantic	St. Louis, MO
Atlantic Railway	Cleveland, OH
Aurora	Aurora, IL
Awkward	Philadelphia, PA
Bachelor	Philadelphia, PA
Bloomington	Bloomington, IL
Bluff City	Memphis, TN
Brandywine	W. Chester, PA
Brown	Providence, RI
Capital	Sacramento, CA
City Item	Philadelphia, PA

OTHER AMATEUR TEAMS (cont.)

TEAM	CITY/STATE
Cohocksink	Philadelphia, PA
College Hill	College Hill, OH
Comet	New Orleans, LA
Cream City	Milwaukee, WI
Creole	New Orleans, LA
Crescent	Ottumwa, IA
Dayton	Dayton, OH
Des Moines	Des Moines, IA
Detroit	Detroit, MI
Dunderberg	Peekskill, NY
Eagle	Flatbush, NY
Eagle	Louisville, KY
Eagle	New York, NY
Eckford	Syracuse, NY
Eddington	Eddington, NJ
Elgin	Elgin, IL
Empire	Detroit, MI
Equity	Brooklyn, NY
Excelsior	Boston, MA
Excelsior	Manchester, IA
Excelsior	New Orleans, LA
Excelsior	Norristown, PA
Excelsior	Philadelphia, PA
Exercise	Philadelphia, PA
Franklin	Philadelphia, PA
Garden City	Chicago, IL
Gotham	New York, NY
Grove City	Kankakee, IL
Holt	Newport, KY
Hope	New York, NY
Independent	Ripley, OH
Irving	New York, NY
James Page	Philadelphia, PA
Jasper	New York, NY
Kearsarge	Stoneham, MA
Key City	Dubuque, IA
Lexington	New York, NY
Liberty	Springfield, IL
Lightfoot	Lebanon, OH
Magnolia	New Orleans, LA
Maple Leaf	Hamilton, ON
Marshall	Marshalltown, IA
Mississippi	New Orleans, LA
Montgomery	Montgomery, AL
Mount Vernon	Manayunk, PA
Mutual	Janesville, WI
Mystic	Detroit, MI
Nashville	Nashville, TN
National	Philadelphia, PA
Niagara	Lockport, NY
Oakleaf	Stockton, CA
Occidental	Oakland, CA
Ogemas	Flint, MI
Old Elm	Pittsfield, MA
Olive	Philadelphia, PA
Olympic	Baltimore, MD
Olympic	Philadelphia, PA
Olympic	Pittsburgh, PA
Oriental	Memphis, TN
Orion	Lexington, KY
Orion	New York, NY
Otoe	Nebraska City, NE
Ours	Philadelphia, PA
Pastime	Germantown, PA
Pastime	Philadelphia, PA
Pioneer	Philadelphia, PA

OTHER AMATEUR TEAMS (cont.)

TEAM	CITY/STATE
Plow Boy	Stillman Valley, IL
Potomac	Washington, DC
Potter Palmer	Chicago, IL
Resolute	Hamilton, OH
Resolute	Oberlin, OH
Revere	Boston, MA
Rosedale	Washington, DC
Sacramento	Sacramento, CA
Schuylkill	Reading, PA
Seneca	Oil City, PA
Shabonna	Ottawa, IL
Star	Waverly, IA
Tuttle & Bailey	New York, NY
Una	Boston, MA
Una	Kalamazoo, MI
Union	Urbana, OH
Unknown	New York, NY
Utica	Utica, NY
Vallejo	Vallejo, CA
Valley City	Grand Rapids, MI
Village	Philadelphia, PA
Wesleyan	Middletown, CT
Wheeling	Wheeling, WV
Wide Awake	Oakland, CA

POSTLUDE
BREAKING AWAY

In March 1871, ten members of the National Association met in New York for the purpose of forming a new group. This new group, dubbed the National Association of Professional Base Ball Players, contained the following clubs: Mutual (New York), Athletic (Philadelphia), Olympic (Washington, D.C.), White Stocking (Chicago), Red Stocking (Boston), Forest City (Rockford), Forest City (Cleveland), Kekionga (Ft. Wayne, Ind.), National (Washington, D.C.) and Haymakers (Troy, N.Y.). All of the above entries had fielded pro teams in 1870 with the exception of the Kekiongas and the Red Stocking outfit of Boston. (The Haymakers of Troy was a new name for the Unions of Lansingburgh, N.Y.) This act essentially killed the National Association.

Noticeably absent from this august group were two of the strongest nines of 1870—the Atlantics and Red Stockings. The Atlantics chose not to join while the Red Stockings were not able to. Following the end of the 1870 season, the backers of the Cincinnati club withdrew their support, causing the famous nine to disband.

To counter the professionals, several amateur teams also met in March 1871 to form a group of their own. Calling themselves the National Association of Amateur Base Ball Players, the 33 teams formed a contingent, as the *New York Clipper* said, "...which reminded those present of the good old days of amateur playing which prevailed some ten years ago." The roster of teams had a familiar feel as three of the oldest New York clubs, the Knickerbocker, Gotham and Eagle, joined the group.

In the first professional season, the Athletics of Philadelphia with a 22-7 record earned the 1871 pennant based upon their record alone and not upon whom they played and when. Continuing on for another four years, the professional National Association evolved into the National League in 1876, the very same National League of professional baseball today.

During the amateur's first season alone, the Stars of Brooklyn, with a record of 30–13, were considered the best team. After one more convention in March 1872, the amateur National Association withered away due to lack of interest.

To answer the question of why the professional organization flourished, and why both the old National Association and the new amateur group foundered, one can turn to the nature of professional and amateur athletics. Playing baseball for money is a business. To succeed, it needs to be run in a logical and organized manner. Conversely, amateur sports are played ostensibly for fun. Any organization it might need would be only sufficient to keep it going. With the problems inherent in a multi-state entity like both amateur Associations, it was just not worthwhile to keep a national organization up and running.

Just because a national amateur association didn't survive past the mid 1870s, it didn't mean that interest in non-professional baseball waned. On the contrary, interest in the game continued to increase through the decades, serviced adequately by a range of state-wide and local entities. To this very day, these groups keep baseball alive in all corners of the country, carrying interest in the game far beyond the narrow confines of professional teams.

SELECTED BIBLIOGRAPHY

ARTICLES

Alvarez, Mark. "William Henry Wright." *Baseball's First Stars*, 1996. Society for American Baseball Research.
Brock, Darryl. "How Many Games Did the 1869 Red Stockings Win?"*The Baseball Research Journal*, 1987. Society for American Baseball Research.
Ivor-Campbell, Frederick. "Alexander Joy Cartwright." *Baseball's First Stars*, 1996. Society for American Baseball Research.
_____. "Henry Chadwick." *Baseball's First Stars*, 1996. Society for American Baseball Research.
_____. "George Wright." *Baseball's First Stars*, 1996. Society for American Baseball Research.
_____. "Joseph Start." *Nineteenth Century Stars*, 1989. Society for American Baseball Research.
Overfield, Joseph M. "Asa Brainard." *Nineteenth Century Stars*, 1989. Society for American Baseball Research.
_____. "Weston Dickson Fisler." *Nineteenth Century Stars*, 1989. Society for American Baseball Research.
_____. "David W. Force." *Nineteenth Century Stars*, 1989. Society for American Baseball Research.
_____. "Lipman Emmanuel Pike." *Nineteenth Century Stars*, 1989. Society for American Baseball Research.
_____. "Alfred James Reach." *Nineteenth Century Stars*, 1989. Society for American Baseball Research.
Phelps, Frank V. "Robert V. Ferguson." *Nineteenth Century Stars*, 1989. Society for American Baseball Research.

ARTICLES (cont.)

_____. "Richard J. Pearce." *Nineteenth Century Stars*, 1989. Society for American Baseball Research.

Richardson, Bob, and Jim Sumner. "Andrew Jackson Leonard." *Nineteenth Century Stars*, 1989. Society for American Baseball Research.

Rucker, Mark. "Jim Creighton." *Nineteenth Century Stars*, 1989. Society for American Baseball Research.

_____. "M. Mortimer Rogers." *Nineteenth Century Stars*, 1989. Society for American Baseball Research.

Shieber, Tom. "The Evolution of the Baseball Diamond." *The Baseball Research Journal*, 1994. Society for American Baseball Research.

Smith, Duane A. "Dickey Pearce: Baseball's First Great Shortstop." *The National Pastime*, 1990. Society for American Baseball Research.

Smith, James D. "George William Hall." *Nineteenth Century Stars*, 1989. Society for American Baseball Research.

_____. "Levi Samuel Meyerle." *Nineteenth Century Stars*, 1989. Society for American Baseball Research.

Thorn, John. "Daniel Lucius Adams." *Baseball's First Stars*, 1996. Society for American Baseball Research.

Thorn, John, and Mark Rucker, eds. "Special Pictorial Issue: The Nineteenth Century." *The National Pastime*, 1984. Society for American Baseball Research.

Tiemann, Robert L. "James Leon Wood." *Baseball's First Stars*, 1996. Society for American Baseball Research.

BOOKS

Adelman, Melvin L. *A Sporting Time: New York City and the Rise of Modern Athletics, 1820–1970*. Urbana: University of Illinois Press, 1986.

Brock, Darryl. *If I Never Get Back*. New York: Crown, 1989.

Bucek, Jeanine, ed. dir. *The Baseball Encyclopedia*. (Tenth edition). New York: Macmillan, 1996.

Chadwick, Henry, comp. *The Base Ball Player's Book of Reference*. New York: J.C. Harvey, 1870.

BOOKS (cont.)

Church, S.R. *Base Ball: 1845–1871.* 1902. Reprint Princeton: Pyne, 1974.

Dennison, A.L. *The Dennison Family.* Exeter, New Hampshire: The News-Letter Press, 1906.

Dyja, Thomas. *Playing for a Kingdom.* New York: Harcourt Brace, 1997.

Ellard, Harry. *Baseball in Cincinnati—A History.* Cincinnati: Johnson & Hardin, 1907.

Goldstein, Warren Jay. *Playing for Keeps—A History of Early Baseball.* Ithaca, NY: Cornell University Press, 1989.

Guschov, Stephen D. *The Red Stockings of Cincinnati: Baseball's First All-Professional Team and Its Historic 1869 and 1870 Seasons.* Jefferson, North Carolina: McFarland, 1998.

Kirsch, George B. *The Creation of American Team Sports; Baseball and Cricket, 1838-1872.* Urbana: University of Illinois Press, 1989.

Orem, Preston D. *Baseball, from Newspaper Accounts.* Altadena, California: self-published, 1961.

Peverelly, Charles. *American Pastimes.* New York: self-published, 1866.

Richter, Francis C. *A Brief History of Base Ball.* Philadelphia: Sporting Life, 1909.

_____. *Richter's History and Records of Baseball.* Philadelphia: self-published, 1914.

Ryczek, William J. *When Johnny Came Sliding Home: The Post–Civil War Baseball Boom, 1865–1870.* Jefferson, North Carolina: McFar-land, 1998.

Seymour, Harold. *Baseball: The Early Years.* New York: Oxford Uni-versity Press, 1960.

Spalding, Albert Goodwill. *America's National Game.* New York: American Sports, 1911.

Spink, A.H. *The National Game.* St. Louis: National Game, 1910.

Sullivan, Dean A., ed. *Early Innings: A Documentary History of Baseball, 1825-1908.* Lincoln: University of Nebraska Press, 1995.

Thorn, John, and Peter Palmer, eds. *Total Baseball IV.* New York: Viking, 1995.

GUIDES

Beadle's Dime Base Ball Player, 1860–1875.
Chadwick's Base Ball Manual, 1870–1871.
De Witt's Base-ball Guide, 1869–1872.

NEWSPAPERS

American Chronicle of Sports and Pastimes, 1868.
Baseball Players Chronicle, 1867.
National Chronicle, 1869–1870.
New England Base Ballist, 1868.
New York Clipper, 1857–1872.
Porter's Spirit of the Times, 1857–1859.

OTHER

Chadwick Scorebooks, 1860–1870.
Chadwick Scrapbooks, 1858–1870.
Constitution and By-Laws of the Excelsior Base Ball Club, 1860.
Constitution and By-Laws of the National Association of Base Ball Players, 1859–1869.

INDEX

Abbott 136
Abbott 216
Abel 172, 209
Aber 164
Abercrombie 133
Abrams, William 36, 49, 69, 79, 89, 99, 114, 148, 152, 197, 248
Achilles (Morrison, IL) 230
Ackerson, G. 124, 174
Acme (New York, NY) 223; (Waukegan, IL) 230
Active (Baltimore, MD) 230; (Ballston Spa, NY) 182, 230; (Buffalo, NY) 159, 180, 230; (Chicago, IL) 293, 325; (Clinton, IA) 292, 296, 325; (Indianapolis, IN) 150, 182, 191–192, 196, 203, 211, 218, 229; (New Orleans, LA) 281, 324; (New York, NY) 85, 87–90, 93, 98, 99, 100, 102–103, 107–108, 114, 116–117, 119–122, 130, 132, 137, 147, 155, 175, 181, 215, 229, 280; (Newark, NJ) 147, 150–151, 155, 160, 173, 182, 313;

(Quincy, MA) 202, 230; (Renova, PA) 295, 325; (St. Louis, MO) 201, 230, 273; (Wappinger Falls, NY) 198, 243, 281, 319; (Washington, DC) 301, 321, 325
Acushnet (Acushnet, MA) 214
Acushnet, MA (Acushnet) 214
Adams 88, 102
Adams 129
Adams 135
Adams 153, 213, 276
Adams 157
Adams, Daniel 2–3, 11, 26, 37
Addison, NY (Meteor) 165, 168, 177, 184, 234
Addy, Bob 202, 240, 255, 297
Adkins 307
Adriatic (Newark, NJ) 11, 23–24, 46–47, 49, 60, 63, 72; (Philadelphia, PA) 67, 269
Adsit, C. 165
Adsit, J. 165
Aetna (Chicago, IL) 255, 263, 265, 281, 293, 296, 314, 324; (Jersey City, NJ) 281; (New Britain, CT)

311; (St. Louis, MO) 201, 213, 273; (Windsor Locks, CT) 230
Agallian (Middletown, CT) 182
Aiken, Albro 114, 148
Aitken, W. 157, 204
Alaska (Brooklyn, NY) 195, 217, 230
Albany, NY (Champion) 44, 53; (Eckford) 87, 108, 138, 182; (Knickerbocker) 81, 87, 93, 102–103, 108, 128, 137, 151–153, 178, 180, 233, 282; (Live Oak) 198, 275; (National) 103, 108, 114, 116, 128, 137, 147, 152–153, 181, 190–196, 198, 200, 212, 221, 229, 242, 248, 257, 266, 268, 275, 280; (Union College) 87
Albert 62
Albertson 216
Albertson, George 131, 216, 252
Albro 50, 69
Alcott 213
Alden 132, 222
Aldic, VA (Awkward) 171
Alert (Charleston, SC)

-335-

219, 230; (Cumberland, MD) 182, 230; (Danville, PA) 114, 135, 137, 182; (Dundee, ON) 317; (Elmira, NY) 168, 175, 177, 182, 230; (Hartford, CT) 182, 230; (New York, NY) 322; (Norwalk, CT) 169, 181, 227, 230; (Paterson, NJ) 230; (Philadelphia, PA) 114, 125, 138, 182, 230, 281; (Poultney, VT) 182, 231; (Plainville, OH) 202; (Rochester, NY) 159, 205, 242–243, 248, 250, 267, 275–276, 280; (S. Orange, NJ) 217, 260, 270, 321, 325; (Schnectady, NY) 325; (Washington, DC) 249
Alexandria, VA (Mt. Vernon) 171; (Old Dominion) 171; (Pioneer) 156, 164, 171, 181, 215, 235
Alfred, University of (New York) 165
Algiers, LA (Atlantic) 254, 259, 264–265, 278, 280, 291–292, 308, 314, 322, 325
Allegheny (Allegheny, PA) 137, 182, 230; (Pittsburgh, PA) 190, 193, 203, 219, 302, 317, 325
Allegheny City, PA (Enterprise) 183, 232
Allegheny College (Meadville, PA) 166
Allegheny, PA (Allegheny) 137, 182, 230; (Enterprise) 164; (Olympic) 163–164
Allen 150, 154

Allen 253
Allen 256
Allen, L. 161
Allen, T. 80, 92, 178
Allentown, PA (Star) 143
Alline, William 162, 202, 258, 321
Allison 161
Allison, Andy 168, 195, 244, 304
Allison, Art 209, 250, 302
Allison, Doug 193, 209, 239, 243, 292
Alma, IL (Lone Star) 201, 213, 273, 282
Alpha (Brooklyn, NY) 216–217, 223, 227, 229, 243, 245, 256, 262, 264, 270, 276, 280, 289, 298, 311, 315–316, 321–323, 325; (Chicago, IL) 231; (Philadelphia, PA) 231; (Springfield, VT) 182, 231
Alpha, OH (Enterprise) 232
Alpine (New York, NY) 57, 63, 72
Alston 157
Alton, IL (Wide Awake) 229
Altoona, IL (Walnut) 236
Altoona, PA (Mountain) 77, 86, 98, 109, 138, 184; (Mountain Star) 234; (Star) 185
Alvin (Philadelphia) 144–145, 156, 163, 181, 204
Amar, J.G. 309
Amateur (Carlisle, PA) 231; (Chicago, IL) 182, 231, 255, 265, 281, 289, 291–293, 296, 298, 310, 314–315, 325; (Greenville,

PA) 319; (Newark, NJ) 291, 311, 313, 315, 323–324; (Oswego, NY) 153; (Philadelphia, PA) 149, 182, 231; (Princeton, IL) 231; (Wash. Ct. House, OH) 291, 325
America (Marysville, CA) 325
American (Indianapolis, IN) 231
Americus (Newark, NJ) 101, 105, 109, 120, 124, 131, 135, 137, 160, 162, 173, 176, 180, 231, 281; (Philadelphia, PA) 281; (Yorkville, NY) 206, 211, 220, 222, 230
Ames 133, 154, 198
Amherst (Amherst, MA) 267
Amherst, MA (Amherst) 267
Amity (Brooklyn, NY) 39, 281
Amory 313
Amsterdam, NY (Independent) 275
Amulet (Waterbury, VT) 182, 231
Anchor (Pittsburgh, PA) 182, 231
Ancient City (Schnectady, NY) 248, 275, 280
Anderson 26
Anderson 34
Anderson 70
Anderson 126, 156, 215, 271, 321
Anderson 163
Anderson 225
Anderson (Lynn, MA) 255, 257–258, 280–281
Anderson, IN (Lone Star) 183, 234
Anderson, R.H. 48

INDEX

Anderson, W. 18
Andreas 38
Andrews 179, 224
Androscoggin (Lewiston, ME) 216, 255, 281
Ann Arbor (Ann Arbor, MI) 267, 281, 325
Ann Arbor, MI (Ann Arbor) 267, 281, 325; (University) 219
Annan 199, 269, 318
Annapolis, MD (Monitor) 271; (Severn) 156, 161
Anspach 129
Antietam (Hagerstown, MD) 182
Antioch (Yellow Springs, OH) 242, 281
Appanoe (Ottumwa, IA) 296, 325
Appleton, WI (Badger) 231
Arbuckle, James 275
Arbuckle, Jr., James 275
Arcadia (Doylestown, PA) 244, 281
Archer 167
Arctic (Baltimore, MD) 199, 231, 250; (New York, NY) 281; (Philadelphia, PA) 143, 145–146, 149, 156, 160, 162, 181, 231
Arden 150
Arlington (Washington, DC) 300, 318, 325
Armfield 9
Armistead 262
Armour 71
Armstrong 136
Armstrong (Philadelphia, PA) 182, 231
Armstrong, Sam 199, 251, 305
Arnold 262, 312
Asbury College (Greencastle, IN) 211
Ashland (New York, NY) 39, 52
Ashmead 51
Associate (Baltimore, MD) 231
Asten 211
Astoria (Astoria, NY) 39, 52
Astoria, NY (Astoria) 39, 52
Atalanta (Geneva, NY) 182, 231; (Stoneham, MA) 257, 258, 280
Athenian (Philadelphia, PA) 182, 231
Athlete (St. Louis, MO) 209, 231; (Washington Hts., NY) 147, 151, 155, 182, 197, 206, 220, 229, 259–261, 263–264, 272–274, 276, 280; (Wheaton, IL) 231; (Whitewater, WI) 263;
Athletic (Baltimore, MD) 269; (Boston, MA) 198, 202; (Brooklyn, NY) 191, 195, 197, 216–217, 223, 230–231, 243, 246, 256, 259–260, 262, 265, 270, 272–273, 276, 280, 289, 297–298, 304, 311, 313, 316, 324–325; (Chicago, IL) 292–293, 309, 314; (Columbus, OH) 312; (Jamestown, NY) 301, 319, 325; (Logansport, IN) 312–313; (Memphis, TN) 182, 231; (Monmouth, IL) 231; (Philadelphia, PA) 28, 63, 67, 75–78, 81, 85–86, 91, 93, 96, 98–104, 106–108, 112, 114–115, 117, 119, 121, 125–126, 129–131, 135, 137, 143–147, 149, 152, 154, 156, 158, 161–162, 168, 172, 180, 186–188, 190–191, 193–196, 198, 200–201, 203–205, 209–213, 216, 218–219, 221, 224–225, 229, 242, 244, 246–252, 254, 257, 268, 271–272, 276, 289–294, 296–300, 302–305, 307–310, 312, 318, 320, 328; (Portland, ME) 182, 231; (Selma, AL) 231; (Springfield, IL) 231
Atlanta (Tremont, NY) 147, 151, 167, 171, 182, 231
Atlantic (Algiers, LA) 254, 259, 264–265, 278, 280, 291–292, 308, 314, 322, 325; (Brooklyn, NY) 2, 5–7, 9–10, 12–14, 19–20, 24–25, 27, 31–32, 35–39, 43–45, 48–52, 54–55, 57–60, 62, 66–67, 70, 76–78, 81, 83, 85–91, 93–104, 106–108, 111, 115–117, 119–122, 125, 131–132, 134, 137, 140, 143, 145–148, 151–152, 157–158, 163, 167–168, 172, 176, 180, 186–188, 190–196, 198–201, 204–207, 209–213, 215–216, 219, 221, 223–229, 242–245, 247–248, 251–254, 256, 259, 261–262, 272–273, 276–277, 279, 285, 289, 290–297, 299, 300, 302–304, 306, 308, 310, 313, 316, 318,

323–324, 328; (Buffalo, NY) 231; (Chicago, IL) 144, 157, 166, 170, 181, 191–192, 196, 228, 230, 231; (Elizabeth, NJ) 281, 313, 315; (Jamaica, NY) 36, 39, 50, 52, 115, 124–125, 137, 182; (Memphis, TN) 182, 231; (Milwaukee, WI) 231; (Philadelphia, PA) 281; (Pittsburgh, PA) 164, 182, 231, 294, 317; (San Francisco, CA) 242, 281, 316, 325; (Springfield, IL) 231; (St. Louis, MO) 201, 209–210, 220, 229, 259, 273, 280, 293, 309, 325; (Trenton, NJ) 143, 163, 182, 231; (Washington, DC) 321; Atlantic Railway (Cleveland, OH) 301, 325
Atwater 205, 266, 292
Auburn (Auburn, NY) 153, 181, 192, 198, 231
Auburn, NY (Auburn) 153, 181, 192, 198, 231
Augusta, ME (Cushnoc) 216; (Dirigo) 255
Aurora (Aurora, IL) 296, 325; (Chicago, IL) 231; (Plattsburgh, NY) 182, 231
Aurora, IL (Aurora) 296; (Black Hawk) 231
Austin, Henry 99, 114, 148, 192, 272, 303
Austin, Percy 198, 257, 310
Auten 25
Avenue (Cincinnati, OH) 203, 231
Awkard (Aldic, VA) 171; (Philadelphia, PA) 182, 325
Aymer, James G. 254
Ayres 121

Babcock 132
Babcock 166
Babcock, Alec 46, 58
Babcock, Edward 173
Babcock, Elisha 173
Babcock, William 9
Bachelor (Philadelphia, PA) 143–144, 162, 181, 190, 213, 218, 230, 281, 325
Bachman 177
Bacot 131
Baden 226
Badger 165
Badger 179
Badger (Appleton, WI) 231; (Beloit, WI) 231; (Columbus, WI) 231
Bailey 179
Bailey 204
Bailey 207
Bailey 318
Bailey, A. 107, 121, 151, 226, 253
Bailey, George 124
Baird 324
Baker 10
Baker 24
Baker 166
Baker 203
Baker 272
Balcolm 11, 24, 36, 50
Bald Eagle (Carlisle, PA) 231
Baldwin 127
Baldwin 134
Baldwin 221
Baldwin, P. 48
Ball 221, 324
Ballston Spa, NY (Active) 182, 230
Balser 273
Baltic (Belleville, NJ) 47; (Belvidere, NJ) 63; (New York, NY) 5–7, 10, 14, 18, 20, 22, 25, 27, 31, 38–39, 53, 63, 81, 231; (St. Louis, MO) 231; (Wheeling, WV) 193, 280
Baltimore, MD (Active) 230; (Arctic) 199, 231, 250; (Associate) 231; (Athletic) 269; (Dexter) 232; (Enterprise) 143, 183, 193, 199–200, 208, 215, 222, 229; (Eureka) 232; (Excelsior) 52, 63; (Lake) 233; (Maryland) 144, 156, 158, 162, 181, 191, 194, 199–200, 204, 208, 229, 242–252, 254, 268–269, 271, 277, 289, 291, 293–294, 296–297, 299–300, 303–304, 308, 310–312, 318; (Mutual) 234; (Olympic) 269, 300, 305, 318, 326; (Paragon) 235; (Pastime) 144, 146, 151, 181, 199–200, 208, 235, 245, 247–248, 250–252, 268, 270, 277, 280, 289, 291, 293–294, 296–300, 302–306, 310–311, 318, 321, 324; (Patapaco) 199; (Prince George) 235; (Resolute) 235
Banker 157
Barber 131
Barclay 221
Barker 159
Barker, Al 202, 255, 297
Barnes 310
Barnes, Ross 202, 255, 297
Barnett 59
Barnum 159
Barre 36

INDEX

Barrett 223
Barrett 249
Barrett 318
Barron 214
Barrows, Frank 148, 200, 266, 306
Barry 24
Barry 26
Barry 206, 264
Barstow 297
Bartlett 23
Barto 22
Bass 208
Bass 227, 273
Bass, John 303
Bassett 165
Bassett 213
Bassford 69
Batavia, NY (Star) 159
Bateman 154, 224
Bates 203
Baton Rouge, LA (Capital) 231; (Red Stick) 235
Baulch 212
Bay City, MI (Empire) 267; (Valley) 23
Bayard 164
Beach 166
Beach 170, 319
Beach 267
Beach, Waddy 32, 45, 57, 67, 76, 120, 201
Beadle, Ed 91, 103, 127, 177, 260
Beals, Tommy 148
Beam, E. 315
Beam, H. 315
Bean 229
Beans 176
Bear 150
Beard 169
Beard, J. 18, 35, 51, 76
Beardsley 22
Beardsley 270, 313
Bearman, Charley 146, 194, 197, 248, 303, 305
Beavans, E.P. 178, 273, 311

Beaver Dam, WI (Wayland) 236
Bechtel, George 150, 172, 209, 216, 252, 295
Beck 39
Beck 316
Becklar 218
Bedford (Brooklyn, NY) 7, 14
Bedford, IN (Lawrence) 282
Beebe 21
Beebe 228
Beers 36
Beggs 203
Behr 118
Belcher, H. 278
Belden 10
Belknap 33
Bell 169
Bell 270
Bell 317
Bell 322
Bell, William 79, 88, 105, 124, 163, 271
Bell, W. 180
Bellan, Steve 193, 248, 300
Belleville, NJ (Baltic) 47
Belmont (Philadelphia, PA) 160, 231
Beloit College (Beloit, WI) 255, 281
Beloit, WI (Badger) 231; (Beloit College) 255, 281; (Comet) 232; (Eagle) 232
Belvidere, IL (Phoenix) 184, 235
Belvidere, NJ (Baltic) 63
Benedict (Philadelphia, PA) 63
Benedict, E. 48
Benner 270
Bennett 24
Bennett 36, 50
Bennett 50, 71, 125

Bennett 127
Bennett 173
Bennett, C. 135
Bennett, J.J. 227
Bennett, W.J. 227, 261, 316
Bensel 106
Bensell 33, 47
Benson 10, 18, 34, 49, 61, 88
Benson 26, 38
Benson 220
Bentley 262, 312
Bergen 19
Bergen 60
Bergen 62
Bergen 127
Bergen 131
Bergen, A. 179
Bergen, A.V. 125, 178
Bergen, L.M. 9, 19
Bergen, W. 179
Bergen, W.G. 174
Bergen (Bergen, NJ) 155, 173, 182, 205, 214, 230, 247, 259, 263–264, 271, 274, 279–280, 304, 315, 325
Bergen, NJ (Bergen) 155, 173, 182, 205, 214, 230, 247, 259, 263–264, 271, 274, 279–280, 304, 315, 325; (Quickstep) 63
Berger 273
Berkenstock, Nate 77, 86, 98, 115
Berry 14
Berry 128
Berry, J. 201
Berry, Tom 143, 190, 245, 295–296
Bertel, V.C. 264
Berthrong, Harry 106, 117, 144, 208, 301
Bertie, F. 218
Bertie, M. 218
Bertis 25
Bettens 320
Bettinger 141, 159, 205

Bettley 321
Betts 122
Betts 175
Beverly, NJ (Friendship) 149, 183
Biddle 135
Bielaski 164, 222
Biggs 24, 31, 36
Billings, Hosea 168
Binghamton (Binghamton, NY) 153, 168, 182, 231
Binghamton, NY (Binghamton) 153, 168, 182, 231
Birdsall 131
Birdsall, Dave 21, 71, 79, 89, 99, 114, 148, 192, 252, 303
Birmingham, PA (Hope) 317
Bishop, I.W. 174
Bixby 9, 23, 33, 47, 61
Bixby 313
Black 203
Black Hawk (Aurora, IL) 231
Black Stockings (Union, PA) 319
Blackstone (Providence, RI) 212, 214
Blackwell 123
Blair 166
Blair, J. 136
Blair, W. 136
Blakeslee 157
Blakeslee, J.W. 129
Blakeslee, V. 130
Blanchard, J. 265, 322
Blanchester, OH (Olympian) 234
Bliss 80
Bliss 103, 153
Bliss, Frank 151
Bliss, William 45
Bliven 155, 197
Bloomfield, NJ (Oneida) 319
Bloomington (Bloomington, IL) 157, 190–192, 196, 230, 293, 325
Bloomington, IL (Bloomington) 157, 190–192, 196, 230, 293, 325
Bloomsburg, PA (Independent) 245
Bloor, L. 179
Blue Stocking (Cleves, OH) 268
Blue Wing (New Boston, OH) 231
Bluff City (Memphis, TN) 182, 231, 259, 292, 309, 325
Blystone 319
Boake, J.L. 165, 320
Boake, W.H. 165, 268, 320
Boanerges (Hiram College, OH) 249, 281
Boardman 228, 265
Bodell 212
Boerum, Polkert 9, 19, 32, 45, 58
Bogart 35, 51, 57, 68, 90
Bogart, H. 26
Bogart, J.A. 26
Bogart, P. 26
Bogle 36, 50, 69, 89
Bomeisler, Ted 90, 101, 119
Bond 316
Bonney, R.B. 173
Boone 129
Booraem 214
Booth 11, 24, 36
Booth 206, 273, 316
Booth 225
Borden 157, 218
Bordentown, NJ (Columbia) 114–115, 138, 145, 163, 182, 190, 232
Borker, J.H. 197
Borland 50
Boston, MA (Athletic) 198, 202; (Bowdoin) 53, 63, 69; (Brookline) 182, 231; (Excelsior) 255, 326; (Granite) 154; (Lowell) 69, 132, 136–137, 148, 154–155, 161, 181, 198, 202, 210, 229, 242, 244, 247, 255–258, 266, 279, 289, 291, 293–294, 309–311, 320, 324; (Red Stockings) 328; (Revere) 282, 305, 327; (Somerset) 255; (Tri Mountain) 69, 148, 161, 180, 191, 194–196, 198–199, 223, 227, 229, 242, 244, 246, 248, 255, 257–258, 266–267, 275, 279–280, 289, 291, 293–294, 305, 308, 311; (Una) 305, 327; (Upton) 255, 267, 283; (Winthrop) 185, 237
Bostwick, H.P. 44, 69
Boswell 153, 213
Botsford 52
Boughton 58
Bound Brook, NJ (Minerva) 184
Bourquin 213
Bouse 228
Bowditch 198
Bowdoin (Boston, MA) 53, 63, 69
Bower City (Janesville, WI) 231
Bowery (New York, NY) 223
Bowie 92
Bowman 218
Boyce 219
Boyce 260
Boyd 36
Boyd 50, 59
Boyd 52, 59
Boyd 88, 102, 126
Boyd 135
Boyle 37
Boynton 257

Bozant, O. 259
Bradbeer 250
Bradbury 150, 228
Bradbury, William 180, 202, 258, 321
Braden 208
Bradenburgh 314
Bradford 35
Bradish 59
Brady 179
Brainard, Asa 44, 69, 78, 87, 104, 116, 144, 193, 239, 243, 292
Brainard, H. 31, 33, 69, 78, 87
Braisted, P.D. 174
Bramhall, G. 134
Branch 204
Brandon 11
Brandow 24
Brandywine (W. Chester, PA) 154, 172, 180, 190, 218, 224, 230, 245, 295, 325
Brantner, J. 179
Branyan 319
Bratton 125
Braughton 136
Bredberg 228, 265
Brenner 171
Brensriger 169
Bridgeport (Bridgeport, CT) 182, 210, 231, 312
Bridgeport, CT (Bridgeport) 182, 210, 231, 312
Bridgeton (Bridgeton, NJ) 77
Bridgeton, NJ (Bridgeton) 77
Brientnall, H. 48, 90, 101, 119, 176
Briggs 14, 22
Briggs 127
Briggs 258, 320
Brigham, A. 256
Brigham, H. 179, 224, 256
Brigham, W. 224, 256

Brinckerhoff 9, 23, 33, 47, 61
Bristol (Bristol, CT) 262; (Bristol, RI) 312; (Philadelphia, PA) 143;
Bristol, CT (Bristol) 262
Bristol, RI (Bristol) 312
Bristol, VT (Green Mountain) 183, 233
Bronx, NY (Woodlawn) 59
Brookline (Boston, MA) 182, 231
Brooklyn (Brooklyn, NY) 51, 53, 59, 63, 72
Brooklyn, NY (Alaska) 195, 217, 230; (Alpha) 216–217, 223, 227, 229, 243, 245, 256, 259, 262, 264, 270, 276, 280, 289, 298, 311, 315, 316, 321–323, 325; (Amity) 39, 281; (Athletic) 191, 195, 197, 216–217, 223, 230, 243, 246, 256, 259–260, 262, 270, 272–273, 276, 280, 289, 297–298, 304, 311, 313, 316, 321, 323–324; (Atlantic) 2, 5–7, 9–10, 12–14, 19–20, 24–25, 27, 31–32, 35–39, 43–45, 48–52, 54–55, 57–60, 62, 66–67, 70, 76–78, 81, 83, 85–91, 93–104, 106–108, 111, 115–117, 119–122, 125, 131–132, 134, 137, 140, 143, 145–148, 151–152, 157–158, 163, 167–168, 172, 176, 180, 186–188, 190–196, 198–201, 204–207, 209–213, 215, 216, 219, 221,

223–229, 242–245, 247–248, 251–254, 256, 259, 261–262, 272–273, 276–277, 279, 285, 289, 291–297, 299–300, 302–304, 306, 308, 310, 313, 316, 318, 323–324, 328; (Bedford) 7, 14; (Brooklyn) 51, 53, 59, 63, 72; (Capitoline) 223; (Charter Oak) 30–32, 36, 39, 44, 46–48, 51–52, 55, 63, 68–69, 72, 81; (Clinton) 138, 182; (Columbia) 6; (Constellation) 49, 81, 93, 122, 127, 130, 133, 137, 182; (Contest) 116, 121, 128, 136, 137, 182; (Continental) 7, 9, 12, 13–14, 20–22, 25, 27, 32, 39, 44, 53, 63, 72, 81; (Dictator) 182; (Eckford) 5–7, 9–10, 12, 14, 20, 22, 25, 27–28, 31–35, 37, 39, 44–45, 52, 55, 57–62, 66–68, 70–71, 74–77, 79–81, 84–85, 90–93, 98, 100–104, 107–108, 114–116, 118–121, 127, 130, 132, 135, 137, 143, 145–148, 151, 155, 167–168, 172, 175–176, 178, 181, 190–192, 194–195, 198–200, 204, 210, 214–216, 222–223, 226, 229, 242–243, 245–251, 253–254, 257–258, 261–262, 266–268, 270, 272–273, 276–279, 289, 291, 293, 297, 302–303, 308, 310, 311, 313, 316, 321, 323; (Enterprise) 44–45, 47, 50, 52, 57–58, 62–63, 67, 72, 86–87, 91–93, 100–104, 107–108, 114, 116, 118–120, 124, 128–130, 133, 137, 183, 316, 325; (Equity) 304, 326; (Eureka) 261; (Excelsior) 2, 5, 7, 11–14, 19–20, 23–27, 29–39, 42–46, 48–49, 51–52, 54, 63, 65, 68–69, 71, 77–79, 81, 85–86, 89–93, 98–99, 103, 106–108, 114, 116–119, 121–123, 125, 128–129, 133–134, 137, 139, 144, 147, 154–155, 161, 168, 171, 175–177, 180, 204, 217, 220, 223, 229, 243, 249, 251, 261, 262, 270, 276, 280, 289, 304, 318, 321, 324; (Exercise) 39, 50, 53, 57–59, 62, 63, 72; (Favorita) 72, 81; (Greenwood) 118, 123–124, 128–129, 136–137, 183; (Hamilton) 21, 39, 47, 50, 53, 58–59, 61–63, 72, 81, 93; (Harmonic) 217, 225, 227, 230, 243, 246–247, 256, 260–261, 263, 270, 273, 280, 297, 304, 311, 313, 315, 323, 325; (Harmony) 5–7; (Hiawatha) 21, 39, 53; (Independent) 44, 46, 49, 52, 116, 118–119, 123, 125, 137, 145, 155, 167, 171, 176, 178, 181, 206, 214, 225, 227, 230; (Intrepid) 171, 183, 233; (Ivanhoe) 39; (Marion) 234; (Mohawk) 25, 118, 123–125, 132, 134, 136–137, 146, 155, 167–168, 171, 176, 181, 191–192, 194–195, 198, 230, 282; (Morphy) 53; (Nassau) 7, 13–14, 40; (Niagara) 32, 64; (Olympic) 7, 40; (Orchard) 151, 184, 235; (Oriental) 22–23, 27, 35, 39; (Osceola) 21, 27, 40, 256, 304, 311, 325; (Pastime) 19, 22–23, 27, 31, 33–34, 36, 39, 53, 63; (Peconic) 115–116, 118–119, 125, 134, 137, 155, 177, 181, 206, 216–217, 223, 230, 282; (Phoenix) 21; (Powhatan) 59, 63, 69, 71, 118, 123–124, 134–137, 152, 157, 168, 171, 178, 181, 235, 244–245, 247, 256, 261–262, 264, 272, 280; (Putnam) 5–6, 9, 13–14, 19–20, 25–27, 31–33, 35–36, 39, 44–45, 48–49, 52, 63, 72; (Resolute) 69–70, 76, 78, 80, 81, 85–91, 93, 98, 100, 102–104, 108–109, 123, 138, 178, 181, 235, 282; (Star) 31–32, 37, 39, 44–45, 51–52, 59, 62–63, 65, 68–69, 71, 76–81, 85, 87–88, 90, 92–93, 98–99, 104, 107–108, 114–118, 121, 123, 132, 137, 148–149, 151, 158, 167–168, 171, 173, 176, 181, 191–192, 194, 196, 200, 206, 210–211, 215, 225, 229, 246–247, 249, 256, 258–259, 261–262, 273, 276–277, 279, 289–291, 293, 297–298, 300, 302–304, 306, 310–311, 313, 315–316, 318, 323–324, 329; (Union) 80–81, 246, 298, 312, 316, 325; (Vigilant) 53; (Wayne) 138, 185; (Williamsburgh) 122, 138, 185

Brooks 26
Brookshaw, B. 165, 196
Brookville, PA (Wild Cat) 185, 237
Brothers 221
Brower 25, 38
Brower 122, 273
Brown 13
Brown 13, 20, 32, 45, 57,67, 92
Brown 21
Brown 38
Brown 71, 125, 178
Brown 105, 125, 145
Brown 124
Brown 128
Brown 163
Brown 166
Brown 197
Brown 206
Brown 211
Brown 219, 267
Brown 220
Brown 252
Brown 260
Brown 261, 323
Brown 303
Brown, C. 204
Brown, E. 49
Brown, Ed 57,67, 75–76, 86, 100, 120
Brown, H. 203, 250, 302
Brown, H. 225
Brown, Oliver 246
Brown, R. 25
Brown (Providence, RI)

198, 202, 258, 310, 320, 325
Browne 124
Browne 227
Browne, H.B. 171
Brownlee 214
Bruggeman 317
Bruin 263
Brumaghim 153
Brush 50
Buchanan 322
Buck 210, 279
Buck 222
Buck 251, 318
Buckeye (Cincinnati, OH) 144, 150, 165, 181, 190–193, 195, 201–203, 209–211, 213, 218–219, 225, 228–229, 242–243, 255, 268, 280; (Dayton, OH) 165
Buckhorn (Indianapolis, IN) 231
Buckley, T. 91, 107, 121, 151, 226, 253
Buckskin (Gloversville, NY) 248, 280–281, 299–300, 323, 325
Budd 157, 210
Buddendorf, J. 259, 314
Buffalo (Buffalo, NY) 182, 231
Buffalo, NY (Active) 159, 180, 230; (Atlantic) 231; (Buffalo) 182, 231; (Columbia) 266; (Mutual) 159; (Niagara) 39, 44, 53, 147, 153, 159, 181, 190–191, 193, 205, 210, 212, 219, 229, 242–243, 248, 250, 266, 268, 275, 280, 292, 295–296, 298–300, 302, 325; (Union) 266
Bump 263
Bunce, F.L. 123

Bunce, H.L. 123
Bunting 121, 160
Bunting 124
Bunting, George 222, 277, 307
Burbanks 212
Burchard, W. 158
Burd 61
Burleigh 162, 216
Burlington (Burlington, NJ) 115, 138, 182; (Burlington, VT) 182, 231
Burlington, IA (Crescent) 232; (Western) 185
Burlington, NJ (Burlington) 115, 138, 182; (New Jersey) 138, 184
Burlington, VT (Burlington) 182, 231; (Champion) 182, 231; (Home) 183, 233; (Nonpareil) 184, 234; (Olympic) 282; (U.V.M.) 185, 236
Burns, S. 18, 35, 51, 57, 68
Burns 227
Burns 293, 294, 322
Burr 12, 20, 23, 35, 48, 67
Burrillville, RI (Wide Awake) 212
Burroughs 90, 120
Burroughs, Henry 301
Burroughs, Joseph 219
Burt 204, 250
Burt 205
Burtis 34, 46, 68
Burtiss 159
Burton, T. 170
Burwell, William 171
Bush 92
Bush, Archie 103, 128, 198, 199, 258, 310
Bush (Ithaca, NY) 317
Bussell 211
Butler 101, 120

Butler 127
Butler 228, 265
Butler, Percy 134, 152, 207
Buttrick 207
Byerly 135
Bynner 21
Byrd 136
Byrne 227
Byrnes 135, 163, 217
Byxbee 169

Cabanne 159, 209
Cabot, VT (Winooski) 185, 237
Cairo, IL (Eclipse) 232; (Independent) 233
Calder 212
Caledonia (Danville, VT) 231
California, OH (Greenwood) 202, 203, 218, 233
Callahan 60
Callahan 177
Calloway, Fred 89, 101, 119, 176
Calvert 60
Calvert 161
Calvert 316
Cambridge, MA (Eagle) 198–199; (Harvard) 115–117, 119, 122, 133, 137, 143, 154–155, 161, 180, 198, 200, 202, 207, 210, 216, 221, 229, 242–244, 246, 248, 252, 255–258, 267, 275, 278–279, 289–291, 294–295, 298–301, 305–306, 309, 311–312, 318, 322, 324; (Sophomore) 185, 236
Camden (Camden, NJ) 85–86, 91, 115, 125, 129, 131, 137, 143, 144–145, 154, 181, 213, 231

Camden, NJ (Camden) 85–86, 91, 115, 125, 129, 131, 137, 143, 144–145, 154, 181, 213, 231; (Ralston) 146; (Union) 143, 145–147, 181, 190, 204, 209, 213, 218, 229, 244, 283
Camp 170
Campbell 45, 56–57, 67, 76
Campbell 122, 175
Campbell 153
Campbell 324
Campbell, Hugh 107, 121, 151, 226, 253, 313
Campbell, J. 121
Campbell, Mike 121, 151, 226, 253, 313
Canandigua, NY (Olympic) 276
Canacadea (Hornellsville, NY) 165, 181, 231
Canseraga, NY (Star) 165
Cantwell 199, 275
Capital (Baton Rouge, LA) 231; (Columbus, OH) 144, 182, 193, 231; (Madison, WI) 182; (Sacramento, CA) 325
Capital City (Madison, WI) 192, 201, 224, 228, 230, 263; (Montgomery, AL) 231, 281
Capitol (Springfield, IL) 157; (Washington, DC) 164, 181, 231
Capitoline (Brooklyn, NY) 223
Carey, Tom 305
Carhart 92
Carlisle, PA (Amateur) 231; (Bald Eagle) 231
Carlow 319
Carlton 175
Carlton, James 247, 302

Carlton, S. 244
Carnahan 166, 319
Carpenter 164
Carpenter 278
Carr, H.C. 209
Carrigan 170
Carroll 23, 36, 46
Carroll 165
Carroll 220
Carruthers 324
Carsie 272
Carson, William 254, 309
Carson City, NV (Silver Star) 316
Carter 207, 257
Cartwright, Alexander 2
Case 136
Cassiday 132
Castleton, VT (Clipper) 182, 232
Catamount (Ridgeway, PA) 231
Cate 130
Caton 150
Catskill, NY (Lone Star) 170, 181, 234, 299, 319, 324; (Mutual) 319
Cattawissa, PA (Riverside) 244, 282
Catto, Octavius 141
Caulkins 13
Cazenovia (Syracuse, NY) 153
Cedar Grove (Fishkill, NY) 138, 182
Centerville, IN (Central) 231
Central (Centerville, IN) 231
Central City (Jackson, MI) 192; (Middletown, CT) 311; (Selma, AL) 231; (Syracuse, NY) 138, 153, 180, 190–192, 196, 198, 205, 212, 229, 242–243, 250, 266–268, 276, 280

Centralia, IL (Egyptian) 157
Chadwick, Henry 41, 42, 43
Chadwick, P. 13
Challenge (Rogersville, NY) 165
Chamberlin 39
Chambers 220
Champaign, IL (Empire) 232
Champion (Albany, NY) 53; (Burlington, VT) 182, 231; (Jersey City) 146, 154, 158, 175, 177, 180, 194, 197, 205–206, 217, 223, 226, 229, 245–246, 256, 259, 260–264, 269, 274, 276, 279–280, 311, 315–316, 323–324; (New York) 53; (W. Troy, NY) 198, 275
Champion, Aaron 238, 285
Champlain (Vergennes, VT) 182, 232
Chandler 259, 314
Chapin 90, 107
Chapman 49
Chapman 134
Chapman 279
Chapman, Curtis 246
Chapman, J. 174
Chapman, John 50, 59, 70, 77, 84, 85, 98, 115, 145, 188, 191, 298
Chappell 70
Charles 160
Charleston, SC (Alert) 219, 230
Charter Oak(Brooklyn, NY) 30–32, 36, 39, 46, 51–52, 55, 63, 68–69, 72, 81; (Hartford, CT) 114, 122, 129, 132, 137, 143, 155, 176, 181, 202, 232
Chase 135, 217

INDEX

Chatham (Chatham, NY) 152
Chatham, NY (Chatham) 152
Chattanooga, TN (Lightfoot) 183; (Lookout) 138, 184
Chauncey, Dan 155, 218, 270, 321
Chauncey, George 270, 321
Cheeseman 221
Chelsea (Long Branch, NJ) 281; (New York, NY) 39, 53, 63
Chenoa, IL (Lone Star) 234
Chenot, E. 201, 273
Chenowith 208, 262, 318
Chenville, J. 274
Chesapeake (Hampton, VA) 212
Chesney 255
Chester (Norwich, CT) 137, 182
Chester, PA (Columbia) 218
Chesterfield (Queen Anne Cty., MD) 232
Chestnut St. Th. (Philadelphia, PA) 149, 160, 182, 281, 209, 230, 252
Chicago (Chicago, IL) 232, 284, 289–306, 308, 309–311, 314–315, 318, 320, 324
Chicago, IL (Active) 293, 325; (Aetna) 255, 263, 265, 281, 293, 296, 314, 324; (Alpha) 231; (Amateur) 182, 231, 255, 265, 281, 289, 291–293, 296, 298, 310, 314–315, 325; (Athletic) 231, 265, 280, 292–293, 309, 314, 325; (Atlantic) 144, 157, 166, 170, 181, 191–192, 196, 228, 230–231; (Aurora) 231; (Chicago) 232, 284, 289–306, 308–311, 314–315, 318, 320, 324; (Comet) 232; (Enterprise) 210, 232, 265; (Eureka) 166, 170, 181, 191, 210, 232, 265, 314; (Excelsior) 144, 157, 170, 180, 190, 192–193, 196, 201, 203, 205, 209–210, 219, 229; (Garden City) 157, 166, 170, 224, 233, 255, 265, 292, 309, 326; (Liberty) 314–315; (National) 234; (Potter Palmer) 296, 327; (Resolute) 166, 235; (Transit) 314; (Union) 236; (White Stockings) 328
Chicopee, MA (Comet) 267; (Hampden) 267
Chilton, B. 70
Chipcase 33
Chittendon (Milton, VT) 182, 232
Church 207, 257
Church 271
Churchill 106
Churchville (Churchville, NY) 159
Churchville, NY (Churchville) 159
Cincinnati (Cincinnati, OH) 144, 150, 165, 180, 190–196, 198, 200, 202–205, 208, 211, 216, 218, 226, 228–229, 238, 239–245, 247–255, 257–259, 266–268, 271, 275–276, 284–285, 289–291, 293–315, 318, 320, 322, 324, 328
Cincinnati, OH (Avenue) 203, 231; (Buckeye) 144, 150, 165, 181, 190–193, 195, 201–203, 209–211, 213, 218–219, 229, 242–245, 268, 280; (Cincinnati) 144, 150, 165, 180, 190–196, 198, 200, 202–205, 208, 211, 216, 218, 226, 228–229, 238, 239–245, 247–255, 257–259, 266–268, 271, 275–276, 284–285, 289–291, 293–315, 318, 320, 322, 324, 328; (Crescent) 232; (East End) 218, 232; (Excelsior) 320; (Great Western) 193, 195, 196, 202, 211, 218, 226, 229, 242, 268, 281; (Harmony) 233; (Ironsides) 233; (I.X.L.) 233; (Laurel) 233; (Live Oak) 150, 165, 181, 193, 196, 202–203, 211, 218, 229, 291, 307, 320, 324; (Metropolitan) 320; (Pastime) 235; (Red Hook) 235; (Resolute) 320; (Social) 236; (Walnut Hill) 203
City Item (Philadelphia, PA) 252, 269, 325
Clancy, L. 18, 35, 51, 57
Clark 125, 178
Clark 131
Clark 135
Clark 158
Clark 219
Clark 260
Clark, R. 105

Clarke 26
Clarke 26
Clarke 90, 105
Clarke 164
Clarke 180
Clarke 203
Claybourne (St. Michael's, MD) 232
Clear, A.W. 164, 222
Clear, R.L. 164
Cleveland 210
Cleveland, OH (Atlantic Railway) 301, 325; (Forest City) 192–193, 196, 203, 219, 225, 227, 228–229, 242–243, 248–249, 254, 266–268, 275, 289, 291–293, 295–296, 298–301, 303–304, 306, 308, 311, 318–319, 324, 328; (Railway Union) 174, 192, 193, 196, 203, 227, 230
Cleves, OH (Blue Stocking) 268
Clifton (Clifton, NY) 159, 205
Clifton, NY (Clifton) 159, 205; (Enterprise) 138, 183, 232
Cliker 153
Clinton 172, 209, 253, 272
Clinton (Brooklyn, NY) 138, 182
Clinton, IA (Active) 292, 296, 325; (Pacific) 184, 235
Clinton, IL (Eureka) 232
Clinton, WI (Crescent) 232
Clipper (Castleton, VT) 182, 232; (Glassboro, NJ) 280; (Indianapolis, IN) 312; (Lowell, MA) 207, 229, 257, 266–267, 279, 289,
291, 306, 309, 311, 320, 325; (Monmouth, IL) 232, 255, 281; (Nashua, NH) 257
Clute, J. 217, 271
Clyne, John 78, 87, 104, 116, 155, 206, 256, 311
Coatesville, PA (Excelsior) 149, 153, 183, 233
Cobleskill, NY (Excelsior) 153
Cochranton, PA (Shoo Fly) 319
Cocker 123
Coe 62
Coe 169
Coffee 277
Cohen 34, 46, 62, 68, 91, 103
Cohocksink (Philadelphia, PA) 295, 326
Cohoes, NY (Phil. Sheridan) 181, 235; (Union) 153, 198, 221, 236, 283
Colburn 320
Cold Spring (Philadelphia, PA) 232
Cold Spring, NY (Undercliff) 126, 128, 137, 185, 236
Cole, George 13, 19, 31, 60
Coleman 61
Coleman 169
Coles 22
Colgate 71
College Hill (College Hill, OH) 291, 326
College Hill, OH (College Hill) 291, 326
Collins, J. 48
Collins 90, 107
Collins, Sammy 69, 79, 89, 99
Collins 101, 121
Collins 118
Collins 169
Collins 175, 215
Collins 206
Collins 219, 267
Collins 260
Colton 276
Columbia (Bordentown, NJ) 114–115, 138, 145, 163, 182, 190, 232; (Columbia, OH) 196, 203, 232; (New York, NY) 221, 232; (Chester, PA) 154
Columbia, OH (Columbia) 196, 203, 232
Columbia, PA (Mutual) 234
Columbian (New York) 39
Columbus, OH (Athletic) 312; (Capital) 144, 182, 231, 293; (Irvington) 183, 233; (Railroad) 193, 235
Columbus, WI (Badger) 231
Colvin, W.S. 124, 172
Colyer 58
Comet (Beloit, WI) 232; (Chicago, IL) 232; (Chicopee, MA) 267; (New Orleans, LA) 254, 275, 280, 308, 314, 326
Commercial (St. Louis, MO) 213, 232
Commerford 10, 25, 33, 34, 47, 61, 129
Commonwealth (Philadelphia, PA) 143–144, 149, 156, 158, 162, 172, 180, 190, 200, 213, 218, 224, 229, 281
Communipaw (New Jersey) 270, 274
Comstock 166
Comstock 170
Comstock 211
Conant 263
Conant, Fred 202, 258, 320

Concord, NH
(Kearsarge) 282
Condict 210, 278
Condon, William 254,
286, 309
Conduit 59
Cone, Fred 166, 202,
255, 297
Coniglan 304
Conklin 50
Conklin 219
Conlan 223
Connell 46, 127, 177
Conner 60
Conner, Ned 147, 216
Connor 26
Connor, Edwin 19, 32
Connorton 108
Conover 12
Conover 279
Conover, J. 24
Constellation (Brooklyn, NY) 49, 81, 93,
122, 127, 130, 133,
137, 182
Contest (Brooklyn, NY)
116, 121, 128,
136–137, 182;
(Philadelphia, PA)
232
Continental (Brooklyn,
NY) 7, 9, 12–14,
20–22, 25, 27, 32, 44,
39, 53, 63, 72, 81;
(Delavan, WI) 232;
(Jersey City, NJ) 63;
(Washington, DC)
144, 156, 158, 164, 182
Conway, G. 207, 257
Conway, J. 207
Cook, George 69, 78,
108, 119, 155, 207,
262, 316
Cooke 219
Cooley, G. 278
Coolidge 207, 257
Coon 105
Cooney 178
Cooper 278
Cooper, C. 25, 38

Cope, Elias 105, 125,
147, 201, 251
Copec (Covington, KY)
193, 203
Corey 87, 103
Cornell (Ithaca, NY)
317, 324
Cornell, W. 22
Corning, NY (Monitor)
177, 184, 234
Cornish 24
Cornwall 170, 319
Cornwall, NY
(Idlewild) 183
Cornwell, George 119,
217
Cornwell, R. 50, 58, 92,
108, 119
Cornwell, W. 93, 108,
119
Cortelew, H.S. 24, 127
Cortelew, W.H. 24, 127
Cortland, NY (Normal)
317
Coughlin, Dennis 208,
251, 307, 321
Coulson, J. 274
Coulter 130
Coulter, W.E. 173
Courtney 103
Courtney 169, 195, 244
Covington (Covington,
KY) 268, 281
Covington, KY (Copec)
193, 203; (Covington)
268, 281; (Star) 320
Cowing 205
Coxsackie, NY (Riverside) 319
Crafts 180
Craig, James 48
Crane, Fred 58, 70, 77,
85, 96, 98, 115–116,
149, 191, 246, 323
Craven 221
Craven 275
Craver, Bill 152, 197,
239, 248, 300
Crawford 26
Crawford 50

Crawford 100
Crawford 153
Crawford, Harry 121,
151
Creagh 92
Creagh 178
Cream City (Milwaukee, WI) 170, 191–
192, 224, 228, 230,
242, 263, 265, 281,
292, 296, 310, 326
Creamer 220
Creeper (Groton, NY)
317
Crees 161
Cregan 206
Creighton (Norfolk,
VA) 161, 180, 212,
232
Creighton, James 33,
44, 64–66, 69, 238
Creole (New Orleans,
LA) 309, 314, 326
Crescent (Cincinnati,
OH) 232; (Burlington, IA) 232;
(Clinton, WI) 232;
(New Lisbon, OH)
182, 232; (New
Orleans) 309, 314,
325; (Ottumwa, IA)
297, 326; (St. Albans,
VT) 182, 232;
(Sycamore, IL) 232
Croasdale 129
Crombie 228
Crooker 211
Crosby 148, 200
Crosby 261, 323
Crowell 37
Crusader (New
Orleans, LA) 265, 281
Cruttendon 153, 213,
276
Cudlipp 11, 25
Culligan 322
Culp, Phillip 216, 252,
301
Culpepper, VA (Union)
271

Culyer 18, 34, 49, 61
Cumberland, MD (Alert) 182, 230
Cummings, Candy 116, 155, 206, 256, 311
Curran 317
Currier 39
Currier 106
Curry 61
Curry 166
Curtis 13
Curtis 34
Curtis, J. 18
Cushing 218
Cushnoc (Augusta, ME) 216
Cuthbert, Ned 105, 125, 143, 172, 190, 245, 284, 293, 294
Cuthill 132
Cypress (E. New York, NY) 182, 195, 207, 232

Dakin 12, 20, 35, 49, 87
Dallon, W. 179
Dalton 51
Dalton 124
Dalton, H. 79, 163
Dalton, T. 79, 105, 163
Daly 142, 179
Danby, IL (Rustic) 157
Daniels 126, 156, 215
Danville, IL (Vermillion) 185, 236
Danville, IN (Paragon) 235
Danville, PA (Alert) 114, 135, 137, 182
Danville, VT (Caledonia) 231
Darlington 224
Dartmouth (Hanover, NH) 257, 280
Davenport 62
Davenport 77
Davenport 129, 176, 195
Davidson 12
Davidson, J.C. 174

Davies, D. 152
Davis 11, 26, 37, 52, 220
Davis 60
Davis 106
Davis 134
Davis 197
Davis 207, 257
Davis 226, 307
Davis 278
Davis 317
Davis, G.H. 23, 134
Davis, H.L. 174
Davis, J. 278
Davis, William H. 168
Davison, R. 48
Dawson 219
Day 170, 319
Day 279
Dayton, A. 13, 17, 19, 36
Dayton, A.J. 9
Dayton, G. 36
Dayton, J. 36
Dayton 131, 173
Dayton (Dayton, OH) 291, 326
Dayton, OH (Buckeye) 165; (Dayton) 291, 326
De Mott 106
De Witt 212
Deady 211
Deal, W.M. 105, 125
Dean 60
Dean 211, 292
DeBeck, B.O.M. 165
DeBost 12, 26, 37, 52
Decker 21
Delaney 155
Delaney 221
Delaney 277
Delano, G. 179
Delany, C. 174
Delavan, WI (Continental) 232
Delavarge 87
Delaware (Delaware, OH) 182, 232; (Port Jervis, NY) 173, 281

Delaware, OH (Delaware) 182, 232
DeLille 219
Delisser 118
Delmadge 277
DeMar 320
Demarest 60
Demarest 133
Denison 158, 201, 249
Denmead 131, 197
Denning 210, 278
Dennis 136, 216
Dennison, Henry 162, 202, 258
Denton 23
Des Moines (Des Moines, IA) 296, 326
Des Moines, IA (Des Moines) 296, 326
Deshong 145, 269
Detroit (Detroit, MI) 48, 52, 157, 190–192, 196, 203, 205, 210, 219, 230, 243, 249, 255, 267, 268, 275, 280, 326
Detroit, MI (Detroit) 48, 52, 157, 190–192, 196, 203, 205, 210, 219, 230, 243, 249, 255, 267, 268, 275, 280, 326; (Early Riser) 48; (Empire) 326; (Franklin) 48; (Mystic) 267, 314, 32; (O.K.) 219; (Olympic) 234, 267
Devine 160
Devine 175
Devyr, Tom 67, 76, 86, 96, 100, 146, 194, 244, 247, 304
Dewey 38, 49, 61, 67
Dexter (Baltimore, MD) 232; (Massillon, OH) 225; (Quincy, IL) 281
Dexter 180
Diamond (Newton, OH) 232

Diamond State (Wilmington, DE) 182
Dick 58
Dick, Billy 105, 125, 147, 201, 252, 299
Dickens 225
Dickerson 11
Dickinson 24
Dictator (Brooklyn, NY) 182
Diehl 157, 269
Dielman 212
Dietrich 322
Dillingham 258
Dingler 131
Dingrus 159
Dirigo (Philadelphia, PA) 146, 182, 190, 216, 232; (St. Louis, MO) 201, 232
Dixon, IL (Riverside) 235
Doane 170
Dockney, Patsy 91, 103, 115, 194, 196
Dodge 153, 213, 276
Dodson 129
Dohrmann 270, 321
Dolan 179, 224
Dollard, Hy 206, 256, 311
Donahue, John 168
Donaldson, W. 180
Doneldson 62
Donn 161
Donnelly 155, 197, 260
Donohue 145, 209, 213
Donovan 259, 314
Donovan 267
Donovan, James 264
Donovan, P. 264
Dooley 322
Doremus 107, 133
Dorgan 228, 265
Dorsett 221
Dorsey 172, 209
Doubleday 214, 228
Douglas 170, 262, 312
Dover, NJ (Randolph) 184

Downington, PA (Penn) 154
Downs 130, 167
Downs 278
Downs, R. 277
Doyle 161
Doyle 199, 318
Doyle 213
Doyle, J. 156, 215, 271, 321
Doyle, Joe 196, 268, 297
Doylestown, NY (Leatherstocking) 321
Doylestown, PA (Arcadia) 244, 281
Dramatic (Mobile, AL) 230, 254, 259, 281
Drinkhouse 169
Drummond, F. 171
Dubuque, IA (Excelsior) 183, 233; (Key City) 296, 326
Duffy, Ed 47, 76, 86, 96, 100, 293, 294, 304
Dumon, J.J. 48
Duncan 102, 130, 158
Duncan, R. 159, 209
Duncan, W. 159
Dundas, ON (Alert) 317; (Independent) 266
Dunderberg (Peekskill, NY) 299, 316, 321, 323, 326
Dunham 122
Dunkell 160
Dunkirk, NY (Empire) 159, 165
Dunlap 106
Dunn, D.A. 254
Dupignac, Andrew 11, 34, 127, 175
Durell, E. 11, 24, 38, 50, 69, 89, 99
Durell, F. 69
Durkee 14, 22
Durnham, Samuel 152
Dusenberry 61
Dusenberry 130

Duval 106
Dyer 21, 38

E Pluribus Unum (New York, NY) 39, 53
Eagle (Beloit, WI) 232; (Cambridge, MA) 198–199; (Flatbush, NY) 178, 182, 232, 245–246, 256, 259, 261, 272, 280, 311, 323, 326; (Florence, MA) 148, 152; (Louisville, KY) 192, 225, 259, 291, 293, 310, 313, 326; (Natick, MA) 162, 200, 207; (New York, NY) 2, 4–5, 7, 9–12, 14, 18–19, 23, 26–27, 31, 33–36, 38–39, 47, 49, 51–52, 57, 60–63, 67–68, 71, 76–77, 79–81, 85–87, 89, 90–93, 98, 100–103, 107–108, 118, 120, 122–123, 127, 129–132, 137, 177, 181, 197, 205, 217, 220, 226, 229, 259–261, 263–264, 274, 280, 297, 326, 328; (Norristown, PA) 145; (Providence, RI) 214; (San Francisco, CA) 242, 281, 316, 324; (Sparta, WI) 182, 232; (St. Albans, VT) 182, 232; (W. Troy, NY) 182, 232
Earl 59, 71, 77, 125, 178
Early Riser (Detroit, MI) 48
Earnest (Riverhead, NY) 182, 232
Earthquake (New Harmony, IN) 232
East Abington, MA (King Phillip) 148, 258, 266, 280, 320

East Cambridge, MA
  (Eureka) 148, 183,
  198, 223, 232;
  (Shields) 148
East End (Cincinnati,
  OH) 218, 232
East Hampton, MA
  (Williston) 185
East Liberty, PA
  (Mutual) 184, 225,
  230
East Liverpool, OH
  (Etruria) 183, 232
East New York, NY
  (Cypress) 182, 195,
  207, 232; (Eureka) 281
Eastin 141, 159
Easton 209
Easton 219
Easton, PA (Neptune)
  151, 169, 181, 190,
  234, 270, 313, 282, 325
Eaton 91
Eaton 161
Eaton 170
Eaton, George 118, 226,
  253
Eaton (Meriden, CT)
  232
Ebbetts, George 100,
  118, 215
Ebensburgh, PA
  (Mountaineer) 245,
  282
Eberhardt 159
Eby 163, 221
Eckendorf 204
Eckford (Albany, NY)
  87, 108, 138, 182;
  (Brooklyn, NY) 5–7,
  9–10, 12, 14, 20, 22,
  25, 27–28, 31–35, 37,
  39, 44–45, 52, 55,
  57–62, 66–68, 70–71,
  74–77, 79–81, 84–85,
  90–93, 98, 100–104,
  107–108, 114–116,
  118–121, 127, 130,
  132, 135, 137, 143,
  145–148, 151, 155,
167–168, 172,
  175–176, 178, 181,
  190–192, 194–195,
  198–200, 204, 210,
  214–216, 222–223,
  226, 229, 242–243,
  245–251, 253–254,
  257–258, 261–262,
  266–268, 270,
  272–273, 276–279,
  289, 291, 293, 297,
  302–303, 308, 310,
  311, 313, 316, 321,
  323; (Newark, NJ)
  315; (Syracuse, NY)
  292, 296, 326
Eclectic (New York,
  NY) 105–106, 108,
  118–121, 123–124,
  126–127, 130, 135,
  137, 145, 147, 151,
  154–155, 160, 162,
  181, 232
Eclipse (Cairo, IL) 232
Ecliptic (Middletown,
  CT) 170, 181, 232
Eddington (Eddington,
  NJ) 295, 326
Eddington, NJ (Eddington) 295, 326
Eddy 270, 321
Edwards 108, 119
Edwards 131, 155, 197,
  260
Edwards 148
Edwards 262
Edwards 262
Edwards 279
Edwards, C.H. 124, 172
Edwards, H. 225
Edwards, J. 179
Edwards, R. 123, 171
Eel River (Loganport,
  IN) 232
Eels 38
Eggler, Dave 195, 247,
  290
Eggler, John 244
Egyptian (Centralia, IL)
  157
Ehrman 173
Elgin (Elgin, IL) 232,
  296, 326
Elgin, IL (Elgin) 232,
  296, 326
Elizabeth, NJ (Atlantic)
  281, 313, 315; (Resolute) 123, 167, 169,
  184, 197, 230,
  243–244, 253, 259,
  269, 280, 289, 291,
  297–298, 303–304,
  310–311, 313,
  315–316, 323–324;
  (Union) 44, 53, 63, 72;
  (Unknown) 214, 236
Ellard 150
Ellard, Harry 241
Ellicott (Jamestown,
  NY) 165, 166
Elliott 212
Ellis, E.A. 180
Ellis, G.H. 180
Ellis, J. 168
Elmendorf 217
Elmendorf, Anthony
  116, 217
Elmira, NY (Alert) 168,
  175, 177, 182, 230;
  (Excelsior) 168, 177,
  181, 233; (Hector) 168,
  183; (Hope) 183;
  (Social) 236; (Union)
  168, 177, 181, 236
Elsden, R. 48
Elysian Field 2
Emerson 205, 266
Emerson 267
Emmett (Westerly, RI)
  212
Emmons 51
Empire (Champaign,
  IL) 232
Empire (Bay City, MI)
  267; (Detroit, MI)
  326; (Dunkirk, NY)
  159, 165; (New
  Orleans, LA) 281;
  (New York, NY) 4–5,
  7, 9–12, 14, 18, 23,

25–27, 31–33, 35–37, 39, 44, 47, 49, 51–52, 57, 60–61, 63, 71, 76, 78–80, 85, 87–93, 98–105, 107–108, 114, 118–120, 129–130, 132, 137, 148, 151, 155, 157, 167, 174, 178, 180, 205, 211, 217, 226, 230, 260, 263–264, 271–272, 280; (Placedale, RI) 182, 232; (San Francisco, CA) 232; (St. Louis, MO) 138, 144, 159, 183, 190, 191–192, 196, 209, 213, 220, 229, 242, 255, 259, 268, 273, 291–293, 309, 325; (Washington, DC) 144, 156, 158, 181, 232
Endeavor (New York, NY) 160, 183, 192, 194, 197, 215, 232
Englewood (Englewood, NJ) 63
Englewood, NJ (Englewood) 63; (Palisade) 184
English 134
Enterprise (Allegheny City, PA) 164, 183, 232; (Alpha, OH) 232; (Baltimore, MD) 143, 183, 193, 199, 208, 229; (Brooklyn, NY) 44–45, 50, 52, 57–58, 62–63, 67, 72, 86–87, 91–93, 100–104, 107–108, 114, 116, 118–120, 124, 128–130, 133, 137, 183, 316, 325; (Chicago, IL) 210, 232, 265; (Clifton, NY) 138, 183, 207, 214, 227, 232; (Indianapolis, IN) 232; (Philadelphia, PA)

183; (Renovo, PA) 232; (Troy, NY) 87, 88
Eon (Portland, ME) 136–137, 143, 162, 181, 198, 216, 229, 258, 281
Equity (Brooklyn, NY) 304, 326; (Philadelphia, PA) 63, 129, 138, 183, 232
Erie (Erie, PA) 190
Erie, PA (Erie) 190
Ertsberger 128, 199
Esculapian (New York, NY) 39, 53
Essex (New Brunswick, NJ) 232
Estes 38, 71
Ethan Allen (Winooski, VT) 183, 232
Etheridge, C. 13, 19, 31
Etruria (E. Liverpool, OH) 183, 232
Eureka (Baltimore, MD) 232; (Brooklyn, NY) 261; (Chicago, IL) 166, 170, 181, 190–191, 210, 232, 265, 314; (Clinton, IL) 232; (E. Cambridge, MA) 148, 183, 198, 223, 232; (E. New York, NY) 281; (Fairmont, WV) 277; (Lowell, MA) 257; (Memphis, TN) 232; (Milford, MA) 281; (Newark, NJ) 47, 50, 52, 58, 63, 67–68, 72, 76–77, 81, 85, 88–89, 93, 95, 98–101, 106–108, 114–116, 118–120, 130, 132–133, 137, 146–148, 150–152, 155, 160, 173, 176, 181, 191, 197, 207, 230, 261, 281; (Pittsburgh, OH) 232; (Pittsburgh, PA) 183

Eustis, William 198, 258, 310
Evans 62
Evans 136, 216
Evans, C. 131
Evansville, IN (Evansville) 172; (Resolute) 172, 181, 235; (Riverside) 313
Everett (Oshkosh, WI) 179, 183, 232
Everett, P. 275
Everts 166
Ewell 147, 216, 252, 301
Excello (Middleton, OH) 233
Excelsior (Baltimore, MD) 44, 52, 63; (Boston, MA) 255, 326; (Brooklyn, NY) 2, 5, 7, 11–14, 19–20, 23–27, 29–39, 42–46, 48–49, 51–52, 54, 63, 65, 68–69, 71, 77–79, 81, 85–86, 89–93, 98–99, 103, 106–108, 114, 116–119, 121–123, 125, 128–129, 133–134, 137, 139, 144, 147, 154–155, 161, 168, 171, 175–177, 180, 204, 217, 220, 223, 229, 243, 249, 251, 261, 262, 270, 276, 280, 289, 304, 318, 321, 324; (Chicago, IL) 144, 157, 170, 180, 190, 192–193, 196, 201, 203, 205, 209–210, 219, 229; (Cincinnati, OH) 320; (Coatesville, PA) 149, 153, 183, 233; (Cobleskill, NY) 153; (Dubuque, IA) 183, 233; (Elmira, NY) 168, 177, 181, 233; (Farmington, WV) 277, 280; (Jefferson-

ville, IN) 313; (Leeds, NY) 319; (Manchester, IA) 183, 233, 296, 326; (Mt. Joy, PA) 233; (New Orleans, LA) 281, 309, 326; (Newark, NJ) 281; (Norristown, PA) 295, 326; (Paterson, NJ) 151, 154, 183, 233; (Philadelphia, PA) 183, 295, 326; (Ridgewood, NJ) 173; (Rochester, NY) 147–148, 153, 167–168, 181, 190, 193, 196, 205, 230; (St. Louis, MO) 183, 233; (Worcester, MA) 255, 257, 279–281
Exercise (Brooklyn, NY) 39, 50, 53, 57–59, 62, 63, 72; (New York, NY) 158, 183, 220, 233; (Philadelphia, PA) 326;
Expert (Mannington, WV) 277; (Philadelphia, PA) 233, 244, 252, 271, 272, 280, 289, 294–295, 299, 305, 324
Express (Indianapolis, IN) 233

Fackler 213
Fair Haven, CT (Pine Grove) 184, 235
Fairbanks, Henry 33, 44
Fairmount (Fairmount, OH) 233; (Marlboro, MA) 179, 183, 200, 223, 230, 255, 257–258, 266, 279, 289, 291, 305, 309–310, 312, 320, 324
Fairmount, OH (Fairmount) 233

Fairmount, WV (Eureka) 277
Faitoute 101, 119
Falkenbergh 37
Fall River, MA (Quequechan) 282
Fallkill (Poughkeepsie, NY) 138, 183
Fanley 223
Fanwood (New York, NY) 206, 211
Farentum, PA (Ristori) 184, 235
Farley 160
Farmington, WV (Excelsior) 277, 280
Farr 178
Farrar 253
Farrell 101
Farrow, John 313
Fashion Race Course 16
Faulkner 279
Favorita (Brooklyn, NY) 72, 81
Fay, F. 259, 314
Fays 10, 18, 34
Fear Naught (Middlebury, VT) 183, 233
Fearless (New Orleans) 254, 259, 274–275, 280, 308, 325
Febiger 196
Felton 179, 224, 256
Fenniman 225, 261, 323
Ferdon 11, 24, 36, 38
Ferguson, Bob 108, 115, 149, 188, 191, 246, 298–299
Ferrer 276
Fesler 169
Field 70
Field 267
Fields 135
Fields 157
Fields 312
Fiero 170, 319
Finn 26
Finnegan, John 173
Finney 208

Finney, A. 126, 156, 215, 271
First Ward (Philadelphia, PA) 146, 183, 233
Fish 37
Fisher 88, 102
Fisher 229
Fisher 316
Fisher, Cherokee 172, 196, 248, 299
Fisher, Jr., Joseph 173
Fisher, W. 25, 38
Fishkill, NY (Cedar Grove) 138, 182; (Waverly) 323
Fisler, Wes 115, 143, 188, 190, 245, 286, 295
Fitchburg, MA (Rollstone) 202, 235, 282
Fitzgerald 123
Fitzgerald, G. 269
Fitzgerald, Hill 269
Fitzgerald, Rob 269
Fitzgibbons 214
Fitzsimmons, R.J. 208, 277, 307
Flagg, G.A. 133, 154
Flanders, Pete 78, 90, 104, 122, 167
Flanly, George 33, 44, 69, 78, 87, 104, 116, 155, 194, 247, 290
Flatbush, NY (Eagle) 178, 182, 232, 245–246, 256, 259–260, 272, 280, 311, 323, 326
Fleet 263
Fleet, R 13, 31
Fletcher, George 87, 104, 116, 144
Fletcher, J.B. 277
Fletcher, J.P. 278
Flint, MI (Hercules) 267; (Ogemas) 326
Florence, MA (Eagle) 148, 152
Flour City (Rochester, NY) 44, 63, 291–292,

298, 300–301, 318, 324–325
Flowers, Dick 145, 216, 252, 300
Flynn 93
Flynn, Clipper 152, 197, 248, 293, 294
Foley, E. 278
Foley, J. 275
Foley, Tom 157, 210, 255, 297
Folsom 21
Folsom, F. 48
Fond du Lac, WI (Fountain City) 233; (Whitewater) 237
Foote, C.S. 165
Foran, Jim 245, 300
Force, Davy 158, 201, 249, 301
Ford 87, 103
Ford 106, 119
Ford 322
Ford, George 175
Ford, P. 265
Fordham, NY (Rose Hill) 89, 215, 243, 247, 282, 289, 303, 322–324
Forest City (Cleveland, OH) 192–193, 196, 203, 219, 225, 227–229, 242–243, 248–249, 254, 266–268, 275, 289, 291–293, 295–296, 298–301, 303–304, 306, 308, 311, 318–319, 324, 328; (Ithaca, NY) 317; (Middletown, CT) 183, 233; (Rockford, IL) 140, 144, 157, 190–192, 196, 201, 210, 228, 229, 242, 255, 268, 279, 289, 291–293, 295–301, 305–309, 314, 328; (Savannah, GA) 219
Forker 33, 51, 59, 118
Forker, W. 59

Forker, Tom 208, 251, 305
Forrister 135
Forsyth 25, 34, 46, 62, 68, 80
Forsyth, James 270, 313
Fort Clark (Peoria, IL) 183, 233
Fort Dodge, IA (Wahkonsa) 185
Fort Leavenworth, KS (Frontier) 138, 183
Fort Monroe (Ft. Monroe, VA) 251
Fort Monroe, VA (Ft. Monroe) 251; (Old Point) 161, 280; (Ordinance) 161
Fort Scott (Ft. Scott, KS) 183
Fort Scott, KS (Ft. Scott) 183
Fort Wayne, IN (Kekionga) 233, 242, 282, 291, 293–294, 296, 312, 315, 324, 328
Foster 135
Foster 136
Foster 222
Foster, B. 25
Foulks 169
Fountain City (Fond du Lac, WI) 233
Fox 159
Fox, George 101, 117, 144, 208, 251, 301
Fox, J.A. 179, 317
Foxboro, MA (Norfolk) 200
Frankford, PA (Osceola) 184, 235
Frankhouse, C. 175
Franklin 148, 200
Franklin (Detroit, MI) 48; (Franklin, IN) 233, 312; (Philadelphia, PA) 269, 326; (White Rock, WV) 277

Franklin, IN (Franklin) 233, 312
Franklin, PA (Oil Stockings) 319
Fraternity (S. Boston, MA) 148, 161, 181, 233
Frazier, F.A. 105
Fredericks 276
Freeland 51
Freeman 148, 200, 306
Freeman 159, 209
Freeman 218
French 266
French 278
French, L. 227
Friendship (Beverly, NJ) 149, 183; (Ithaca, NY) 317
Frisbee 11, 50
Frontier (Ft. Leavenworth, KS) 138, 183
Fruin, Jerry 37, 214
Fry 218
Fryatt 101
Fuller 33, 52
Fullerton, Daniel 173
Fulmer, Chick 204, 253, 302
Fulton (Fulton, IL) 233; (Fulton, NY) 212; (New York, NY) 151, 155, 168, 175, 181, 233, 281
Fulton Market (New York, NY) 122, 127, 132–133, 137
Fulton, IL (Fulton) 233
Fulton, NY (Fulton) 212
Furey 36
Furey, John 168
Furness 157
Furniss 312

Galbraith, Samuel 127, 152
Gallagher, W. 205, 263, 322

Galliker 208
Galliker, H.C. 277, 307
Galpin 59, 70, 77
Galvin, John 60, 77, 84, 85, 98, 115, 149, 194
Gambrier, OH (Occidental) 184
Gamgie 317
Garden City (Chicago, IL) 157, 166, 170, 224, 233, 255, 265, 292, 309, 326
Gardner 87, 153
Garlick 203
Garrison 126
Garvey 129
Garvin 150
Gaskill, Charles 77, 86, 98, 115
Gaskins 166
Gaughan, A. 264
Gaughan, T. 205, 263
Gaunt 34, 49
Gavagan, P. 18, 35, 51
Gavigan 317
Gaynor 69
Geary (Philadelphia, PA) 144, 149, 156, 162, 180, 190, 200, 204, 209, 213, 216, 229, 281
Gedney, Al 303
Gedney, Andrew 174, 247, 261
Gelston 8–9, 23, 33
Gelwicks 160
Genesee, IL (Pioneer) 235
Genesee, NY (Livingston) 268
Geneva, NY (Atalanta) 182, 231
Gerard, L. 24
Gerhart 135
Germantown (Philadelphia, PA) 183
Germantown, PA (Pastime) 295, 326; (Wissahickon) 245, 283
Gesner 12, 20, 23, 35

Gibbons 267
Gibbs 12
Gibney, Andrew 91, 103, 144, 208, 251, 301
Gibson 49
Gibson 129
Gifford 11, 24, 36, 49
Gignoux 59
Gillan 315
Gillen, A. 179, 217
Gillespie 12, 20, 35, 49
Gilman 9
Glading 160
Glassboro, NJ (Clipper) 280
Glastenbury (Glastenbury, CT) 233
Glastenbury, CT (Glastenbury) 233
Gleavy 322
Glenn 268
Glenn, John 301, 307
Glover 124, 163
Glover, C. 105
Glover, W. 105
Gloversville, NY (Buckskin) 248, 280–281, 299–300, 323, 325
Goff 18
Goldie, J. 274
Goldie, John 60, 68, 76, 86, 100, 114, 117, 147, 192, 272
Goldsmith, Wally 199, 208, 251, 305
Good Intent (New Utrecht, NY) 39, 53, 63, 72
Good Will (Pittsburgh, PA) 317
Gooding, W.C. 214
Goodspeed, William 127, 177, 260
Goodwin 258, 310
Gordon 161
Gordon 171
Gorff 10
Gorham 320
Gorman 208
Gorman, Arthur 106

Goshen (Goshen, NY) 88
Goshen, NY (Goshen) 88; (Monitor) 88, 93, 102, 109, 121, 138, 184
Gosman 214
Gotham (New York, NY) 2, 4–5, 7, 9–10, 14, 18–20, 25, 27, 31–35, 39, 46–47, 50–52, 57–58, 61–63, 67–68, 70–71, 76, 78–81, 85, 87–88, 90–93, 98, 99, 100–103, 107–108, 114, 117, 123–124, 126–127, 132, 137, 160, 174, 176, 181, 197, 204, 226, 230, 247, 259–260, 263, 271, 279–280, 326, 328
Gough 34, 131
Gould 180
Gould 199
Gould 321
Gould, Charles 165, 193, 239, 243, 286, 292
Govans (Govans, MD) 233
Govans, MD (Govans) 233
Grace 153
Grace 220
Grace 276
Grady 34
Graff 71
Graham 105
Gramercy (New York, NY) 192, 200, 207, 211, 215, 227, 230, 247, 304, 281, 325
Grand Rapids, MI (Kent) 233; (Valley City) 296, 327
Granger 60
Granite (Boston, MA) 154; (Lynn, MA) 255, 258, 281; (New York, NY) 183, 233
Grant 150, 193
Gratz 86

Graves 177
Graves 228, 265
Gray 13
Gray 178
Great Western (Cincinnati, OH) 193, 195–196, 202, 211, 218, 226, 229, 242, 268, 281
Greathead, William 160, 253, 313
Green 18, 35
Green Bay, WI (Star) 236
Green Island, NY (Union) 87
Green Mountain (Bristol, VT) 183, 233
Greencastle, IN (Asbury College) 211
Greene 212
Greenfield, MA (Star) 161
Greenleaf 159, 209
Greenman 130
Greenpoint, NY (Oriental) 114, 120, 127, 134–135, 137, 147, 149, 151, 153, 157, 162–163, 175, 180, 191, 207, 221–222, 227, 229, 269, 282
Greenport, NY (Momoweta) 184, 234, 282
Greenville (Greenville, AL) 233, 281
Greenville, AL (Greenville) 233, 281
Greenville, PA (Amateur) 319
Greenwood 167
Greenwood (Brooklyn, NY) 118, 123–124, 128–129, 136–137, 183; (California, OH) 202, 203, 218, 233
Greer 57, 60
Greglietta 33
Gregory 23

Grenelle, William 12, 26
Griffin 261
Griffith 320
Grill 315
Grim 169
Griswold 11–12, 34, 46, 62
Groton, NY (Creeper) 317
Grove City (Kankakee, IL) 292, 309, 326
Grover 207
Grover, E. 168
Grum, George 12, 20, 32, 45, 57, 101, 120, 169, 195
Grum, John 30, 32, 43, 45, 57, 120, 169, 195
Guelph, ON (Maple Leaf) 274, 280, 324
Guernsey 206
Guillots, J.V. 274
Gulf City (Mobile, AL) 233, 281
Gulick, Charles 44
Gulick (New York, NY) 233
Gwynn, Joseph 147, 216, 252
Gymnast (Philadelphia, PA) 183
Gymnastic (Washington, DC) 164, 183

Hackes 136
Hackett 25, 34, 46
Hageman 163
Hagerstown, MD (Antietam) 182
Haines, Tom 105, 118, 175, 215, 272, 307
Haines 166
Halbach 150, 209, 252
Hall 21
Hall 62
Hall 134
Hall 260
Hall 323
Hall, George 119, 155, 206, 256, 298

Hallinan 315
Halpin 197, 260
Halsey 62
Halsey 88, 102, 126
Haltmann 273
Hamberger 150
Hamilton (Brooklyn, NY) 21, 39, 47, 50, 53, 58–59, 61–63, 72, 81, 93; (Jersey City, NJ) 32, 39, 47, 53
Hamilton College (Syracuse, NY) 153
Hamilton, OH (Resolute) 291, 320, 327
Hamilton, ON (Maple Leaf) 296, 326
Hamilton, Tice 9, 19, 31, 45
Hampden (Chicopee, MA) 267; (Springfield, MA) 152–153, 200
Hampton, VA (Chesapeake) 212
Hancock (New Orleans, LA) 254, 282, 308–309, 314, 325
Hanifan 315
Hanna 203, 250
Hannegan, Bernard 36, 50, 69, 79, 89, 99, 114
Hannon, F.J. 165
Hanover, NH (Dartmouth) 257, 280
Harden 166
Hardenbrook 223
Hardenburg 228
Hargesheimer 162
Harlem (New York, NY) 7, 11, 14, 19–20, 25, 27, 31–32, 37, 39, 47, 52, 57, 63, 67–68, 70–71, 81, 116, 124, 132, 146, 171, 183, 192, 194, 206, 211, 215, 220, 226, 227, 229, 281
Harlem, NY (Ross) 247, 272, 283

Harmon 132
Harmon 179
Harmonic (Brooklyn, NY) 217, 225, 227, 230, 243, 246–247, 256, 260–261, 263, 270, 273, 280, 297, 304, 311, 313, 315, 323, 325; (Staten Island, NY) 214
Harmony (Brooklyn, NY) 5–7, 14; (Cincinnati, OH) 233
Harriman 214
Harris 35, 51, 57, 68, 76, 86, 100
Harris 148
Harris 306
Harrisburg, PA (Tyrolean) 143, 185, 236; (Keystone) 183, 233
Harrop 157, 204
Harry Clay (Philadelphia, PA) 143, 145, 149, 169, 181, 200, 204, 216, 218, 229
Harshman, John 175
Hart 158
Hart 212
Hartford, CT (Alert) 182, 230; (Charter Oak) 114, 122, 129, 132, 137, 155, 176, 181, 202, 232; (Howard) 183, 233; (Hutchings) 311; (Oriental) 235
Hartman 134
Hartman 154, 224
Hartman 273
Harvard (Cambridge, MA) 115–117, 119, 122, 133, 137, 143, 154–155, 161, 180, 198, 200, 202, 207, 210, 216, 221, 229, 242–244, 246, 248, 252, 255, 256–258, 267, 275, 278–279, 289–291, 294–295, 298–301, 305–306, 309, 311–312, 318, 322, 324; (Harvard, IL) 255
Harvard, IL (Harvard) 255
Harvey 60
Hastings 166
Hastings, Scott 240, 255, 297
Hasty 212
Hatch, C. 169, 261
Hatch, J. 169, 261, 323
Hatfield, John 100, 103, 117, 118, 146, 188, 193, 247, 290
Hathaway 130, 167
Hatton, William 264
Haug 269
Haught 277
Haviland 177
Havre (Havre de Grace, MD) 233
Havre de Grace, MD (Havre) 233
Hawes 202
Hawkeye (Stillman Valley, IL) 255
Hawkhurst, W. 32, 45, 58
Hawkins, M. 25
Hawley 205, 266
Hayden 169
Haydock 34, 49, 61
Hayes 161
Hayes, M. 221
Hayes, P. 221
Hayhurst, Hicks 86, 98, 112, 115, 143, 190, 245
Haymakers (Troy, NY) 328
Hays, S. 259
Hayward 52
Hazard 177
Hazelton 214
Hazlehurst 199
Hazzard 23, 47
Headford 20
Hector (Elmira, NY) 168, 183
Hedden, E.O. 174
Heffern 160
Heineman 277
Heller 263
Helling 172
Hellmer 260
Helm 174
Helms 160
Helms 211
Hempstead, NY (Washington) 40, 53
Hendrickson 262
Hennessey, J. 259, 264, 314
Henry 11, 22, 59, 70
Henry 253, 269
Henry Eckford (New York, NY) 49, 51, 60–61, 63, 68, 72, 77–81, 93
Hercules (Flint, MI) 267
Hero (New Orleans, LA) 281
Herring 201, 273
Herse 204
Heslin 219
Heubel, George 145, 209, 245, 302
Hewer, W. 274
Hiawatha (Brooklyn, NY) 21, 39, 53; (Kitanning, PA) 163–164, 183
Hibbard 89, 100, 118
Hibernia (Phoenixville, PA) 224
Hickory (McConnelsville, OH) 150, 165, 193, 281, 233; (New Rutland, IL) 233
Hicks 316
Hicks, Nat 133, 205, 261, 263, 307, 311
Higgins, James 278
Higham, Dick 261, 290, 303

Highland Falls, NY (West Point) 185
Hightstown, NJ (Mohican) 184
Hilderbrant, M. 24
Hilliard 136
Hills 123
Hillyer 178, 276, 323
Hinchman 219
Hinsdale 106, 220
Hiram College, OH (Boanerges) 249, 281
Hitchcock 263
Hoagland 106
Hoagland 118
Hobby, William 127, 152, 207
Hoboken (Hoboken, NJ) 18, 32–33, 35, 38–39, 53
Hoboken, NJ (Hoboken) 18, 32–33, 35, 38–39, 53; (Monmouth) 184
Hockanum (N. Manchester, CT) 183, 233
Hodes, Charley 195, 244, 293, 294
Hodges 117, 208, 307
Hogan 127
Holabird 203
Holden, H. 25, 38
Holder, John 9, 19, 31, 44
Holdsworth, Jim 303
Holley, Alfred 205, 266
Holley, M. 205, 266
Hollidaysburg, PA (Juniata) 183
Hollingshead, John 252, 301, 307
Hollister 300
Holloway 159
Holmes 195
Holmes, Ed 134, 152, 207
Holmes, Elijah 134, 152, 207
Holmes, J. 171
Holt 59

Holt (Newport, KY) 150, 165, 282, 291, 326
Holt, E. 23, 36
Holt, G. 24, 36
Holt, S. 52
Holtzman, J. 259
Holyoke, MA (Riverside) 282
Holzman 314
Homans 106
Home (Burlington, VT) 183, 233
Honeywell 166, 319
Hooker 210, 279
Hooper 161
Hooper, Mike 199, 251, 305
Hoosier (Lafayette, IN) 233
Hope 163
Hope (Birmingham, PA) 317; (Elmira, NY) 183; (New Orleans, LA) 265, 282; (New York, NY) 303, 326; (Saratoga Spr., NY) 183, 233; (St. Louis, MO) 159, 201, 233
Hope and Anchor (Pawtucket, RI) 212
Hopkins 46, 62
Hopkins 150, 209
Hopkins 206
Hopkinson 313
Horgesheimer 272
Hornellsville, NY (Canacadea) 165, 181, 231
Horner, L. 213
Horton, C.H. 173
Horton, J.D. 173
Hosford (Lowell, MA) 207
Hosford, Samuel 130, 158
Hough 60, 129
Hough 166
Houseman 9, 23, 33

Houser 169
Houston, T. 278
Howard 217
Howard (Hartford, CT) 183, 233; (New Bedford, MA) 200; (N. Bridgewater, MA) 202, 282
Howe 33, 47, 61
Howe, Con 150, 193
Howe, G.H. 174
Howell 145
Howell 161
Howland, N.E. 214
Hoy 268, 307
Hoyt (New York, NY) 274
Hoyt 10, 12, 18, 34
Hoyt 157
Hubbell 123
Hubbs 122, 175
Huddleson 226
Huddleston 226, 307
Huddleston 268
Hudson 21
Hudson 179, 224, 256
Hudson (Hudson, NY) 152–153, 183; (Hudson City, NJ) 319
Hudson City, NJ (Union) 197, 230, 271, 283
Hudson River (Newburgh, NY) 44, 53, 63, 67, 76, 78, 80–81, 85, 87–88, 90, 92–93, 99–100, 102–103, 105, 107–108, 114, 124, 126, 128, 137, 145, 151–152, 181, 196, 233
Hudson, NY (Hudson) 152–153, 183; (Knickerbocker) 319
Hudson, OH (Reserve) 282
Hudson, W.F. 71, 79, 89, 99, 114, 148
Hughes 21, 38
Hull 267
Hulme 154

Humphrey, G. 105, 124
Humphrey, M. 105, 124
Hunkidori (Wheeling, WV) 183
Hunnewell 133, 154, 198
Hunt 221
Hunt, Charles 57, 68, 76, 86, 100, 117, 146, 194, 246–247, 304
Hunt, Richard 117, 146, 194, 247, 256, 304
Hunter 59
Huntington 171
Huntington, NY (Suffolk) 185, 236, 262, 283
Huntington, PA (Social) 185
Hurd 317
Hurley, Dick 196, 239, 249, 301
Hurn 129
Hussey 47, 61
Hutchings (Hartford, CT) 311
Hutchings, J. 24
Hutchins 161
Hutchins, B. 168
Hutchinson, R. 265
Hyatt 69, 79
Hyde 127
Hylen 177

Ibbottson 59
Ictoria (Kethsburg, IL) 233
Idell, J. 38
Idell, T. 39
Idlewild (Cornwall, NY) 183
Iglehart 173
Illinois (Morris, IL) 255
Independent (Amsterdam, NY) 275; (Bloomsburg, PA) 245; (Brooklyn, NY) 44, 46, 49, 52, 116, 118, 121–123, 125, 136, 137, 145, 155, 167, 171, 176, 178, 181, 206, 214, 225, 227, 230; (Cairo, IL) 233; (Dundas, ON) 266; (Johnstown, PA) 183; (Mansfield, OH) 203, 242–243, 248–249, 255, 280; (New London, CT) 233; (New York, NY) 18, 39, 63, 72, 81; (Petersburg, VA) 161; (Ripley, OH) 307, 326; (Somerville, NJ) 24
Indian Queen (Phoenixville, PA) 154
Indianapolis (Indianapolis, IN) 291, 300, 305, 309–310, 312, 324
Indianapolis, IN (Active) 150, 182, 190–193, 196, 203, 211, 218, 229; (American) 231; (Buckhorn) 231; (Clipper) 312; (Enterprise) 232; (Express) 233; (Indianapolis) 291, 300, 305, 309–310, 312, 324; (Lone Star) 312; (Marion) 242; (Mutual) 211; (National) 312; (Pioneer) 211, 235; (Railroad) ; (Western) 144, 150, 165, 172, 181, 211, 236; (Western Star) 211, 236
Ingals 170
Ingle 173
Interior (Washington, DC) 144, 156, 158, 164, 183, 233
Intrepid (Brooklyn, NY) 171, 183, 233; (La Crosse, WI) 233; (Philadelphia, PA) 244, 266, 271, 281, 291, 294, 295, 310, 325
Invincible (Wetumpka, AL) 233, 282
Ireland 316
Ireland, John 19
Iron State (St. Louis, MO) 282
Ironsides (Cincinnati, OH) 233
Irvine 227
Irving (New York, NY) 304, 326
Irvington (Columbus, OH) 183, 233 (Irvington, NJ) 111–112, 114–115, 118, 120–121, 123–124, 128, 133, 137, 144–145, 147–148, 150, 152, 167–169, 176, 180, 191, 194–195, 221, 226, 230, 242–247, 253–254, 269
Irvington, NJ (Irvington) 111–112, 114–115, 118, 120–121, 123–124, 128, 133, 137, 144–145, 147–148, 150, 152, 167–169, 176, 180, 191, 194–195, 221, 226, 230, 242–247, 253–254, 269
Irwin 71, 125
Irwin 219
Ithaca, NY (Bush) 317; (Cornell) 317, 324; (Forest City) 317; (Friendship) 317; (University Press) 317
Ivanhoe (Brooklyn, NY) 39; (Sing Sing, NY) 197, 207, 230, 263, 282
I.X.L. (Cincinnati, OH) 233; (S. Zanesville, OH) 233

Jackson (New Orleans, LA) 308
Jackson 20, 35
Jackson 21
Jackson 50
Jackson 60
Jackson 227, 306
Jackson, E. 217, 276, 323
Jackson, W. 268, 324
Jackson, MI (Central City) 192
Jacksonville, IL (Relic) 255, 282
Jamaica (Jamaica Plains, MA) 183, 233
Jamaica Plains, MA (Jamaica) 183, 233
Jamaica, NY (Atlantic) 36, 39, 50, 52, 137, 182; (Liberty) 183, 234
James 124, 206, 276, 323
James Page (Philadelphia, PA) 160, 326
Jamestown, NY (Athletic) 301, 319, 325; (Ellicott) 165, 166
Janes 129
Janesville, WI (Bower City) 231; (Mutual) 229, 263, 280, 292, 296, 326; (Titan) 263; (Western Star) 236
Jarvis 167
Jasper (New York, NY) 243, 282, 303, 326
Jefferson (New York, NY) 35, 46, 51–52, 57, 60–61 63, 67–68, 71, 81, 93, 127, 130, 135, 145–146, 158, 173–174, 176, 181, 197, 205, 217, 226, 230, 282; (Washington, DC) 106, 117, 125, 132, 137, 156, 158, 171, 180, 200, 208, 215, 222, 229, 248–251, 270, 280, 296, 300, 306, 325
Jeffersonville, IN (Excelsior) 313
Jennings 166
Jeralemon 121
Jerold 69
Jerome 37, 59, 70
Jersey City, NJ (Aetna) 281; (Champion) 146, 154, 158, 175, 177, 180, 194, 197, 205–206, 217, 223, 226, 229, 245–246, 256, 259–264, 269, 274, 276, 279–280, 311, 315–316, 323–324; (Continental) 63; (Hamilton) 32, 39, 47, 53; (Marion) 282; (National) 120, 121, 131, 132, 135, 137, 184
Jewell, Edward 108, 123, 162, 202, 258, 320
Jewell, Herbert 104, 116, 119, 155, 206, 256, 311
Jewett, Nat 79, 88, 102, 117, 146, 194, 244, 304
Jillett 317
Joesbury 170
Johns 317
Johnson 10
Johnson 62
Johnson 128
Johnson 153, 213, 276
Johnson 155, 197
Johnson 163
Johnson 204
Johnson 213
Johnson 262
Johnson 273
Johnson, A. 264
Johnson, Joseph 167, 206, 256
Johnson, William 150, 193
Johnston, A.B. 309
Johnston, J.B. 286
Johnstown, PA (Independent) 183; (Kickenepawling) 181, 233, 245, 282
Jones 162
Jones 178
Jones 208
Jones 218, 320
Jones 223, 279
Jones 224
Jones 266
Jones 278
Jones, C.E 164
Jones, Charles 165
Jones, T. 275
Josephs 261
Joslyn, William 162, 202, 258, 320
Joyce 121, 160
Joyce, George 126, 156, 215, 251
Juneau (Milwaukee, WI) 233
Juniata (Hollidaysburg, PA) 183

Kahmar 143, 190
Kalamazoo, MI (Una) 302, 327
Kalisch 203, 320
Kane 133, 205, 263
Kankakee, IL (Grove City) 292, 309, 326
Kanski 21
Katydid (New York, NY) 39, 53
Kaw Valley (Lawrence, KS) 209, 213, 296, 324
Keally, C. 180
Keane 265
Kearney (Rahway, NJ) 119, 121–122, 133, 137, 160, 183
Kearns, L. 259
Kearsarge (Concord, NH) 282; (Stoneham, MA) 199, 202, 207, 257, 282, 306, 320, 326
Keating, D. 317

Keating, C. 316
Keating, L. 254
Keefe, C. 259
Keeler 52
Keenan 157
Keerle 199, 251, 269, 293, 294
Kekionga (Ft. Wayne, IN) 233, 242, 282, 291, 293–294, 296, 312, 315, 324, 328
Kelley 105
Kelley 267
Kelley, H.C. 175, 215
Kelley, T.F. 118, 175, 215
Kelley, William 89, 100, 118, 175, 215
Kellogg 267
Kelly 14
Kelly 20, 35, 59, 70, 78, 90, 108
Kelly 88, 102, 126
Kelly 102
Kelly 148, 200, 266, 306
Kelly 160
Kelly 194
Kelly 261
Kelso 35, 51
Kemper 150
Kendall, William 31
Kendall 161
Kendall (Yorkville, IL) 233
Kennedy 157, 210
Kennedy 276
Kenney, John 149, 192, 246, 303
Kennsick 267
Kensington (Philadelphia, PA) 183
Kent (Grand Rapids, MI) 233
Kent Island (Kent Island, MD) 233
Kent Island, MD (Kent Island) 233
Kentucky (Louisville, KY) 242, 248–249, 259, 268, 280

Kern 157, 204, 272
Kernan 305
Kerr 212
Ketcham, E. 313
Ketcham, F. 313
Ketchum, Dan 12, 20, 35, 67, 71, 99, 114, 148
Kethsburg, IL (Ictoria) 233
Kettleman, J. 25, 38, 71
Kettleton 221
Kewanee (Kewanee, IL) 183, 233
Kewanee, IL (Kewanee) 183, 233
Key City (Dubuque, IA) 296, 326
Keystone (Harrisburg, PA) 183, 233; (Philadelphia, PA) 67, 77, 81, 85–86, 91, 93, 98–99, 101–102, 104, 108, 115–117, 125, 131–132, 137, 143, 145–146, 149, 155, 162, 168, 172, 180, 190–195, 200, 204, 209, 216, 229, 242, 244–252, 254, 257, 269, 271, 277, 289, 291, 293–294, 297, 299, 303–304, 325
Kickenepawling (Johnstown, PA) 181, 233, 245, 282
Kiers 134
Kilt 123
Kimball, Gene 268, 302
Kimberly, B. 44
King Phillip (E. Abington, MA) 148, 258, 266, 280, 320
King 165
King, George 202
King, Mart 152, 197, 248, 293, 294
King, Rufus 193
King, Steve 152, 197, 248, 300
Kingon 228

Kingsbury, S. 168
Kingsland 71
Kinloch 50
Kinzie, G. 170
Kipp 62
Kirk 21
Kirkpatrick, J.B. 131, 174
Kissam, Samuel 12, 19, 26, 37, 106, 220
Kitanning, PA (Hiawatha) 163, 164, 183
Kivelin, P. 18, 35
Klein 101, 120, 169
Kleinfelder, Dan 77, 86, 98, 112, 115, 143, 190, 253
Kletter, D. 274
Knapp 13, 22
Knecht 269
Knickerbocker (Albany, NY) 81, 85, 87–88, 90, 92–93, 102–103, 108, 128, 137, 151–153, 178, 180, 233, 282; (Hudson, NY) 319; (New York, NY) 1, 4–5, 7, 9–11, 14, 18–19, 23, 26–27, 31–33, 37, 39, 44, 52, 63, 72, 81, 105–106, 108, 138, 157–158, 183, 205, 217, 220, 230, 328
Kober 317
Korndaffer (Philadelphia, PA) 183, 233
Kuen 129
Kurtz 164
Kurtz, J.B. 175

La Crosse, WI (Intrepid) 233
Labon 24, 36
Lacour 21
Lafayette (Lafayette, IN) 312
Lafayette, IN (Hoosier) 233; (Lafayette) 312
Laing 195, 270, 313

Laing 195, 270, 313
Lake (Baltimore, MD) 233
Lake 128
Lake 271, 307
Lake Shore (Waukegan, IL) 233
Lamb 123
Lambert 275
Lamoure 103, 153
Lamphier 32, 45, 58
Lane 123
Lane 219
Lane 319
Lane, S. 164
Lang 134
Lang 226
Langdon 320
Langley 78, 87
Lansing 128
Lansingburgh, NY (Union) 115, 143–147, 149, 151–152, 176, 180, 190–191, 193–194, 196, 198, 200, 206, 212, 221, 229, 239, 242–243, 245–248, 250–252, 254, 257, 266, 268–269, 275, 289–304, 308, 318–319, 328
Larkin 224
Larkin 227, 261, 323
Larkin, W. 259, 314
Lasak 12
Lathrop 87
Lauer, P. 264
Laurel (Cincinnati, OH) 233
Laurence (New York, NY) 234; (Pittsburgh, PA) 179, 183, 317
Lawrenceburg, IN (Woolen Mill) 183, 237
Law, J.F. 13, 22
Law, Jr. J. 14, 22
Law, N.B. 13, 22
Lawlor 164

Lawrence 130, 167
Lawrence 164
Lawrence (Bedford, IN) 282
Lawrence, KS (Kaw Valley) 209, 213, 296, 324
Layman 135, 217
Leaning 34
Leatherstocking (Doylestown, NY) 321
Leavenworth, Sonny 152
Leavitt, C. 168
Leavy 10, 49
Lebanon, OH (Lightfoot) 291, 326
Leech, Ed 158, 201, 249, 301
Leeds, NY (Excelsior) 319
Leesburg, VA (Tuscarora) 171
Leggett, Joe 13, 19, 30–31 43–44, 69, 78, 116
Leisure (Philadelphia, PA) 183
Leland 50, 58, 93, 108, 119
Lennon 78, 90
Lennon, Bill 155, 251, 305
Leonard 160
Leonard, Andy 88, 102, 126, 112, 121, 151, 196, 239, 243, 292
Leonore (Philadelphia, PA) 145
LeRoy, NY (Oatka) 159
Lethbridge 178
Levy 34
Levy, J. 264
Lewis 91
Lewis 122
Lewis 170
Lewis 210, 279
Lewis 227
Lewis 229

Lewis 266
Lewis, Billy 121, 151, 226, 247
Lewis, C. 25, 38
Lewis, L.S. 171, 225, 261, 323
Lewisburg, PA (McLaughlin) 234
Lewiston, ME (Androscoggin) 216, 255, 281; (Union) 255
Lex, Harry 176, 120, 210
Lexington (New York, NY) 39, 53, 63, 303, 326
Lexington, KY (Orion) 291, 326
Liberty (Chicago, IL) 314–315; (Jamaica, NY) 183, 234; (New Brunswick, NJ) 16, 19, 24, 27, 39, 45, 53, 58, 63, 114, 117, 126, 131, 137, 173, 183, 234, 269, 282, 315; (Norwalk, CT) 169, 183, 210, 234, 282; (San Francisco, CA) 234, 316; (Springfield, IL) 255, 282, 309, 326
Lightfoot (Chattanooga, TN) 183; (Lebanon, OH) 291, 326; (Madisonville, OH) 234; (Salem, MA) 257
Lillie 221
Lilly, G. 199
Lincoln (Pittsburgh, PA) 163, 181, 234
Lindley 102, 126
Linen, J. 48
Lines, George 226, 253
Lippincott, W. 25, 38
Liscomb 21, 38
Little Falls, NY (Pastime) 276, 282
Littlewood, A. 48, 90, 101, 120, 176

Live Oak (Albany, NY) 198, 275; (Cincinnati, OH) 150, 165, 181, 193, 196, 202–203, 211, 218, 229, 291, 307, 320, 324; (Rochester, NY) 44
Lively (Toledo, OH) 234
Lively Turtle (Rockford, IL) 234
Livingston (Genesee, NY) 268
Lloyd 57
Lockett 270, 321
Lock City (Lockport, NY) 159
Lockport, NY (Lock City) 159; (Niagara) 205, 234, 326
Lockwood 178
Lockwood, J.S. 92, 108, 219
Logan 12
Logan (Mt. Morris, IL) 234; (Mt. Union, PA)
Logansport, IN (Athletic) 312, 313; (Eel River) 232
Lonaghen 263
Lone Star (Alma, IL) 201, 213, 273, 282; (Anderson, IN) 183, 234; (Catskill, NY) 170, 181, 234, 299, 319, 324; (Chenoa, IL) 234; (Indianapolis, IN) 312; (Mattewan, NY) 151, 181, 234; (Middletown, NY) 277; (New Orleans) 254, 259, 264, 265, 274–275, 278–279, 290–293, 296, 307–308, 312, 314, 322, 324; (Springfield, OH) 174, 181, 234, 273, 280
Long 315
Long Branch, NJ

(Chelsea) 281; (Sea Side) 185, 236
Lookout (Chattanooga, TN) 138, 184
Loomis 153
Loper 49, 61
Lord 166
Lorillard (Rhinebeck, NY) 128, 138, 184
Loughery 164
Louisville (Louisville, KY) 138, 144, 150, 165, 184, 190–192, 196, 225, 230
Louisville, KY (Eagle) 192, 225, 259, 291, 293, 310, 313, 326; (Kentucky) 242, 248–249, 259, 268, 280; (Louisville) 138, 144, 150, 165, 184, 190–192, 196, 225, 230; (Olympic) 150, 165, 184, 234
Love 60
Lovett 272
Lovett, James 162, 202, 258
Lowe 207
Lowe 218, 268, 320
Lowell 162, 258
Lowell (Boston, MA) 69, 132, 136–137, 148, 154–155, 161, 181, 198, 202, 210, 229, 242, 244, 247, 255–258, 266, 279, 289, 291, 293–294, 309–311, 320, 324
Lowell, MA (Clipper) 207, 229, 257, 266–267, 279, 289, 291, 306, 309, 311, 320, 325; (Eureka) 257; (Hosford) 207; (Salmon) 207, 257, 280; (Sheridan) 207
Lucas 199, 251, 269, 318

Lucas 209
Luengene 86, 98
Lupton 227
Lusk 252
Lylle 225
Lynch 304
Lynch 315
Lynn, MA (Anderson) 255, 257–258, 280, 281; (Granite) 255, 258, 281
Lynnfield Center, MA (Union) 207
Lyon 169
Lyons 71
Lyons 200
Lyons 272

Mack, J.P. 165, 218, 268
Mackie 147
Madden 224, 256
Madden, H. 223
Madden, James 179
Madden, John 179
Madden, T. 262
Maddock, C. 274
Madison, WI (Capital) 182; (Capital City) 192, 201, 224, 228, 230, 263
Madisonville, OH (Lightfoot) 234
Magee 212
Magill 132
Magill 135
Magnolia (Marion, AL) 282; (New Orleans, LA) 278, 308, 326; (St. Louis, MO) 159, 234, 282
Maguire 172
Mahan, T. 265, 322
Make or Brake (Monroe, WI) 263
Mallison, J. 23
Mallory 50
Mallory 164
Malone 169, 195, 304
Malone, Fergy 86, 105,

INDEX 363

145, 201, 249, 295, 296
Malone, NY (St. Lawrence) 200, 236
Maloney 212
Malta (New York, NY) 63
Malvern (Philadelphia, PA) 156, 209, 218, 230, 282
Manayunk, PA (Masonic) 234; (Pestaricus) 160, 235; (Roxborough) 245, 283;
Manchester, IA (Excelsior) 183, 233, 296, 326
Manhattan (New York, NY) 20, 39, 53, 63, 184, 234
Manly, Bob 33, 51, 70, 78, 104, 122, 167, 206, 256, 311
Mann 11
Mann, Steven 9, 19
Mannington, WV (Expert) 277
Manolt, Harry 12, 20, 30, 32, 45, 57, 66–67, 76, 92, 101, 120, 175
Mansfield (Middletown, CT) 262, 280, 290, 295, 306, 311, 320, 324
Mansfield, OH (Independent) 203, 242–243, 248–249, 255, 280
Mansion (New York, NY) 234
Manson 105, 130
Manwaring 50
Mapes 88, 102
Maple Leaf (Guelph, ON) 274, 280, 324; (Hamilton, ON) 296, 326
Marion (Brooklyn, NY) 234; (Indianapolis, IN) 242; (Jersey City, NJ) 282; (Philadelphia, PA) 184, 234
Marion, AL (Magnolia) 282
Markham, A. 13, 19, 31
Marks 177, 260, 312
Marlboro, MA (Fairmount) 179, 183, 200, 223, 230, 255, 257–258, 266, 279, 289, 291, 305, 309, 310, 312, 320, 324
Marsh 21, 38, 71, 211
Marshall (Marshalltown, IA) 296, 326
Marshalltown, IA (Marshall) 296, 326
Marston 263
Martin 38
Martin 134
Martin 223, 262
Martin 225
Martin 321
Martin, Al 88, 102, 114, 117, 146–147, 192, 195, 244, 290
Martin, W. 161
Marvin (Norwichtown, CT) 184, 234
Maryland (Baltimore, MD) 144, 156, 158, 162, 181, 191, 194, 199–200, 204, 208, 229, 242–252, 254, 268–269, 271, 277, 289, 291, 293–294, 296–297, 299–300, 303–304, 308, 310–312, 318
Marysville, CA (America) 325
Mason 258
Masonic (Manayunk, PA) 234
Massey, F.W. 22, 60, 70
Massillon, OH (Dexter) 225
Masten 14, 20, 35, 49, 69
Mathews 177
Mathews 216
Mathews, Bobby 251, 305
Mattewan, NY (Lone Star) 155, 181, 234
Matthews 150
Maxfield 62
Maxon 62
Maxwell 135
Maxwell, D. 180
Mayhew 121, 160
McAllister 136
McAllister 170
McArthur 319
McAtee, Bub 152, 197, 248, 293, 294
McAuslan 67
McBain 37
McBride, Dick 77, 86, 98, 112, 115, 141, 143, 190, 245, 295, 296
McCahill 279
McCarthy 79
McCarty 71, 125, 178
McCarty 130
McCauley 126, 156, 271
McCauley, A. 179
McClarnan 147, 216, 252
McCleary 115
McCleland, W.W. 164
McClelland 126, 156, 215, 271
McClintock 210, 278
McClintock, E. 319
McClintock, J. 319
McClintock, S. 319
McClintock, T. 164
McClure 128
McClymont 220
McConnell 51
McConnelsville, OH (Hickory) 150, 165, 193, 233, 281
McCord, E.O. 175
McCosker 10, 25, 34, 46
McCoskry, R. 124, 172, 225
McCoy 166, 319

McCrea 167
McCullough 70, 86, 104
McCullough 160
McCusker 161
McCutcheon 45
McCutcheon 210, 278
McDermott 322
McDermott, Joe 304
McDiarmid, Tom 90, 104, 122, 167, 206, 256
McDonald 49
McDonald 87
McDonald 134
McDonald 211, 313
McDonald 220
McDonald 275
McDonald 318
McDonald, Dan 115, 149, 191, 246, 298
McEnery 254
McFarland 91
McFarland 224
McFayden 224
McGeary, Mike 300
McGee 124, 277
McGorran, H. 174
McGovern 315
McGown, R. 261
McGrath 68, 160
McGregor 21
McIlvaine 163
McKee, J. 278
McKeever 34, 46, 62, 68
McKellar 38
McKelvey 268
McKelvey, Charles 324
McKelvey, Jr., J.A. 324
McKelvy, J. 225
McKelvy, S. 225
McKelvy, W.F. 225
McKenna 253
McKenzie 23, 36
McKenzie 69, 78
McKeon, James 152
McKever 76
McKewen 271
McKibben 222
McKiernan 123
McKinstry 12, 20, 35, 48

McLaren 166
McLaughlin 12, 26, 37
McLaughlin (Lewisburg, PA) 234
McLean 150
McLean, H. 274
McLean, Harry 117, 144, 158, 201, 249, 321
McMahon 155
McMahon 35
McMahon, Archie 9, 19, 31, 45, 58
McMahon, Billy 51, 57, 68, 76, 86, 117, 146, 194, 247, 290
McMahon, H. 197, 260
McMahon, J. 197, 260
McManus 206, 264
McManus 220
McManus 322
McMullin, John 147, 196, 245, 300
McNally 157, 210
McNamee 24, 36
McNeil 177
McVey, Cal 211, 239, 243, 292
McVoy 13
Meacham 159
Meadville, PA (Allegheny College) 166; (Mutual) 166, 181, 234, 301–302, 319, 324
Meagher, John 165, 196
Mealey 154
Means 136
Mears (Steubenville, OH) 193
Mears 228, 265
Mechanic (Memphis, TN) 184, 234; (Weymouth, MA) 162
Mechanics (Patterson, PA) 234; (St. Johnsbury, VT) 184, 234
Medford, MA (Tufts) 202
Meech 136

Mehl 127
Meigs 50, 59
Mellier 163, 221
Melton 228
Memphis, TN (Athletic) 182, 231; (Atlantic) 182, 231; (Bluff City) 182, 231, 259, 292, 309, 325; (Eureka) 232; (Mechanic) 184, 234; (Oriental) 291, 326
Mercantile (Philadelphia, PA) 86, 154
Mercer 154, 224
Mercer, PA (Union) 319
Meriden (Meriden, CT) 311–312
Meriden, CT (Eaton) 232; (Meriden) 311–312
Merrell 150
Merritt 26
Mesereau 217
Messerole 20
Metacomet (Taunton, MA) 200, 282
Meteor (Addison, NY) 165, 168, 177, 184, 234
Metropolitan (New York, NY) 21–22, 27, 39, 44, 53, 63, 72, 81, 93
Mettler, S.B. 174
Metzger 317
Meyerle, Levi 150, 209, 245, 284, 293, 294
Meyers 173
Meyers 211
Miami (Yellow Springs, OH) 174, 193
Middlebury (Middlebury, VT) 184, 234
Middlebury, VT (Fear Naught) 183, 233; (Middlebury) 184, 234; (Wide Awake) 185, 237
Middleton, OH (Excello) 233

Middletown, CT (Agallian) 182; (Central City) 311; (Ecliptic) 170, 181, 232; (Forest City) 183, 233; (Mansfield) 62, 280, 290, 295, 306, 311, 320, 324; (Mineola) 262; (Seymour) 262; (Wesleyan) 262, 311, 327
Middletown, NY (Lone Star) 277; (Retaliators) 173; (Walkill) 173, 178, 181, 236
Miles 166
Miles 176
Milford, MA (Eureka) 281
Millard, L. 179
Millard, S.V. 9
Miller 10, 18, 34, 49, 61, 80, 88, 102, 130, 226
Miller 133
Miller 166
Miller 177
Miller 204, 272
Miller 221
Miller 317
Miller, C. 270, 321
Miller, G.P. 165
Miller, J. 222, 261
Miller, L. 222, 261
Miller, S.W. 88, 102, 126
Miller, William 249
Milliken 50
Mills, A. 13, 20, 32, 45, 57, 66–67, 92, 101, 120
Mills, Charley 101, 115, 191, 247, 290
Mills, Ev 89, 101, 119, 176, 194, 226, 247, 290
Millspaugh 88, 102, 126, 177
Milton (Milton, WI) 234
Milton College (Milton, WI) 234

Milton, VT (Chittendon) 182, 232
Milton, WI (Milton) 234 (Milton College) 234
Milwaukee, WI (Atlantic) 231; (Cream City) 170, 191–192, 224, 228, 230, 242, 263, 265, 281, 292, 296, 310, 326; (Juneau) 233; (Monitor) 234
Mimnie 46
Minard 167
Mincher, Ed 199, 208, 251, 305
Mineola (Middletown, CT) 262
Minerva (Bound Brook, NJ) 184; (Philadelphia, PA) 129, 138, 156, 184, 234
Minne 34
Minor 223
Minot 198, 258
Minshall 164
Mishawum (Woburn, MA) 207
Mississippi (New Orleans, LA) 309, 326
Mitchell 51, 59, 70, 78, 90, 96, 104
Mitchell 170
Mitchell, James 104, 116, 155, 217
M.M. Van Dyke (New York, NY) 120–122, 123, 127, 132, 134, 137, 184, 234
Mobile (Mobile, AL) 230
Mobile, AL (Dramatic) 230, 254, 259, 281; (Gulf City) 233, 281; (Mobile) 230; (Pacific) 235, 282; (St. Elmo) 236, 283
Mohawk (Brooklyn,

NY) 25, 118, 123–125, 132, 134, 136–137, 146, 155, 167–168, 171, 176, 181, 191–192, 194–195, 198, 230, 282
Mohican (Hightstown, NJ) 184
Moline (Moline, IL) 234
Moline, IL (Moline) 234
Momoweta (Greenport, NY) 184, 234, 282
Monitor (Annapolis, MD) 271; (Corning, NY) 177, 184, 234; (Goshen, NY) 92–93, 102, 109, 121, 138, 184; (Milwaukee, WI) 234; (Waterbury, CT) 157, 184, 234; (Westport, CT) 184, 234
Monmouth (Hoboken, NJ) 184
Monmouth, IL (Athletic) 231; (Clipper) 232, 255, 281
Monroe, WI (Make or Brake) 263
Montgomery (Montgomery, AL) 229, 282, 290, 309, 326
Montgomery, AL (Capital City) 231, 281; (Montgomery) 229, 282, 290, 309, 326
Monticello (Monticello, NY) 184, 234
Monticello, IA (Unkidori) 185, 236
Monticello, NY (Monticello) 184, 234
Monument (New York, NY) 18, 39, 53
Monumental (Washington, DC) 171
Moody 212
Moody 216
Moody 276, 323
Moore 10, 18, 34, 49, 61

INDEX

Moore 87, 218, 270
Moore 124
Moore 128
Moore 133
Moore 171
Moore, Colonel 77, 111
Moore, H. 23
Moran 118
Morgan 173
Morgan 271
Morgan (New Orleans, LA) 265, 282
Morgan, F.H. 277
Morgan, F.T. 277
Morphy (Brooklyn, NY) 53
Morrell 12
Morrell 217
Morris 135
Morris, C. 51, 59, 70, 90
Morris, T. 13, 30, 33, 52, 70
Morris, IL (Illinois) 255
Morrisania, NY (Union) 5–7, 11, 13–14, 19, 24, 27, 31, 34–36, 39, 44–45, 47–49, 52, 61, 63, 67–71, 76, 79, 81, 86–87, 89, 91–93, 98–108, 112, 114–117, 119–120, 122, 126–130, 132, 134, 136–137, 139–140, 146–152, 162–163, 168, 175–176, 180, 186–187, 191–196, 198, 201, 203, 206, 209–213, 215–216, 219, 224–225, 227–229, 243, 246–247, 261, 264, 271–272, 277, 280, 289, 291, 293–294, 297–300, 302, 304, 306, 308, 313, 318, 322
Morrisey, E. 165
Morrisey, T. 165
Morrison 22
Morrison 80
Morrison 313
Morrison, IL (Achilles) 230
Morristown, NJ (National) 184
Morrow 26, 37, 52
Morrow 160
Morse 38
Mortimer 218
Morton 265
Morton, W. 278
Moss 57
Mott 11, 26, 35, 38, 51, 57, 68, 71, 76, 86
Mount Airy (Philadelphia, PA) 138, 184
Mount Joy, PA (Excelsior) 233
Mount Morris, IL (Logan) 234
Mount Union, PA (Logan) 234
Mount Vernon (Alexandria, VA) 171
Mount Vernon (Manayunk, PA) 326
Mount Vernon, NY (Una) 114, 118, 124, 130, 132, 137, 155, 158, 167, 171, 181, 236, 283
Mountain (Altoona, PA) 77, 86, 98, 109, 138, 184
Mountain City (Pottsville, PA) 244, 282
Mountain Star (Altoona, PA) 234
Mountaineer (Ebensburgh, PA) 245, 282
Mudge 70
Mulholland 104, 125
Mullen 123
Mulliner 131
Mumford 22
Mundell, C.U. 62
Mundell, S. 62
Munn 217, 276, 298
Murphy 37, 47
Murphy 170
Murphy 261
Murphy 323
Murphy, P. 174
Murray 171
Murray 211
Murray 214
Murray 221
Murray 227
Murray 260
Murray, P. 174
Murtha 218
Murtha, James 265, 322
Murtha, W.H. 58, 93, 107, 119
Mussey 203
Mutual (Baltimore, MD) 234; (Buffalo, NY) 159; (Catskill, NY) 319; (Columbia, PA) 234; (E. Liberty, PA) 184, 225, 230; (Indianapolis, IN) 211; (Janesville, WI) 229, 263, 280, 292, 296, 326; (Meadville, PA) 166, 181, 234, 301–302, 319, 324; (New Haven, CT) 312; (New York, NY) 18, 25–27, 31, 33–35, 38–39, 45–47, 49, 51–52, 55, 57–58, 60–62, 67–68, 70–71, 76–81, 85–93, 98–104, 107–108, 114–116, 118–120, 122, 137, 143–149, 151–152, 155, 162, 168, 171–172, 174, 176, 180, 190–200, 204, 206–207, 211, 215–217, 222, 226, 229, 242–243, 245–246, 248–250, 252–254, 256–257, 259–261, 266, 268, 271–272, 277–279, 289, 291–296,

INDEX 367

298–301, 303–308,
311, 313–314, 316,
318, 320–323, 328;
(Philadelphia, PA)
234; (Pittsburgh, PA)
203; (Selma, AL) 282;
(Springfield, MA)
242, 257–258,
266–267, 280, 296,
311–312, 325; (Springfield, OH) 195–196,
203, 234 ; (St. Louis,
MO) 209; (Washington, DC) 209;
Muzzey 136
Myers 10
Myers 60
Myers 157, 204
Myers 221
Myers 279
Myers, J. 274
Myers, S. 172
Mystic (Detroit, MI)
267, 314, 326; (New
York, NY) 79, 93, 99,
102, 105–106, 108,
138, 184; (Rochester,
NY) 282;
Mystic Bridge, CT
(Oceanic) 184, 234

Nagle 106
Nagle 273
Nape 175
Napolean (Napolean,
OH) 234
Napolean, OH
(Napolean) 234
Nashua, NH (Clipper)
257; (Resolute) 257
Nashville (Nashville,
TN) 309, 326
Nashville, TN
(Nashville) 309, 326
Nassau (Brooklyn, NY)
7, 13–14, 21, 40;
(Princeton, NJ) 77–78,
80, 85–86, 89–90, 184,
190–191, 198, 207,
210, 221, 230

Natick, MA (Eagle)
162, 200, 207
National (Albany, NY)
103, 108, 114, 116,
128, 137, 147,
152–153, 181,
190–196, 198, 200,
212, 221, 229, 242,
248, 257, 266, 268,
275, 280; (Chicago,
IL) 234; (Indianapolis, IN) 312; (Jersey
City, NJ) 120–121,
131–132, 135, 137,
184; (Morristown,
NJ) ; (Philadelphia,
PA) 184, 234, 244,
326; (St. Louis, MO)
234; (Washington,
DC) 63, 93, 98, 103,
106, 108, 114, 116–117,
125–127, 132, 137,
139–144, 146, 150–152,
155–159, 164–165, 170,
180, 193, 199–200, 208,
215, 222, 229, 242,
244–252, 254, 270–271,
277, 289, 291, 293,
296–297, 300, 302–303,
306, 308, 310–311, 328
Naval (Norfolk, VA) 282
Naylor 316
Nazareth, PA
(Olympic) 184, 234;
(Viola) 185, 236
Nebraska City, NE
(Otoe) 296, 326
Neff 150
Neibuhr, Fraley 11, 26
Nelson 133
Nelson, Clay 174
Nelson, Jack 168, 195,
244
Neosho (New Utrecht,
NY) 31, 36, 40, 53
Nepperham (Yonkers,
NY) 234
Neptune (Easton, PA)
151, 169, 181, 190,
234, 270, 282, 313, 325

Nestler, E. 158, 226
Nestler. M. 158
Neville 223
New Bedford, MA
(Howard) 200;
(Onward) 214, 235;
(Wamsutta) 185, 202,
214, 229, 283
New Boston, OH (Blue
Wing) 231
New Britain (New
Britain, CT) 184, 234,
312
New Britain, CT
(Aetna) 311; (New
Britain) 184, 234,
312;
New Brunswick, NJ
(Essex) 232; (Liberty)
16, 19, 24, 27, 39, 45,
53, 58, 63, 114, 117,
126, 131, 137, 173,
183, 234, 269, 282,
315; (Star) 120, 123,
126, 131, 135, 137,
160, 163, 173–174,
176, 181, 236, 283
New Harmony, IN
(Earthquake) 232
New Haven, CT (Quinnipiack) 53, 184, 235;
(Yale) 122, 129, 138,
185, 191–192, 195,
198, 202, 206, 210,
221, 229, 278, 280,
325
New Jersey (Burlington, NJ) 138, 184
New Lisbon, OH (Crescent) 182, 232
New London, CT
(Independent) 233;
(Pequot) 147, 181,
235, 262
New Orleans, LA
(Active) 281, 324;
(Comet) 254, 275,
280, 308, 314, 326;
(Creole) 309, 314,
326; (Crescent) 309,

314, 325; (Crusader) 265, 281; (Empire) 281; (Excelsior) 281, 309, 326; (Fearless) 254, 259, 274–275, 280, 308, 325; (Hancock) 254, 282, 308–309, 314, 325; (Hero) 281; (Hope) 265, 282; (Jackson) 308; (Lone Star) 254, 259, 264–265, 274, 275, 278, 279, 290–293, 296, 307–308, 312, 314, 322, 324; (Magnolia) 275, 308, 326; (Mississippi) 309, 326; (Morgan) 265, 282; (Pelican) 254, 259, 264–265, 275, 278, 280, 291, 308, 314, 322, 324; (Pickwick) 254, 308, 325; (Quickstep) 322; (R.E. Lee) 254, 259, 264–265, 278, 280, 290, 291–292, 309, 314; (Southern) 242, 254, 259, 264–265, 273–274, 278, 280, 290–292, 309, 314, 322, 324; (Stonewall) 322, 325; (Surprise) 254, 263, 274, 280, 314, 322, 324; (Washington) 254, 265, 274–275, 280, 314, 322, 324; New Rochelle (New Rochelle, NY) 63

New Rochelle, NY (New Rochelle) 63

New Rutland, IL (Hickory) 233

New Utrecht, NY (Good Intent) 39, 53, 63, 72; (Neosho) 31, 36, 40, 53; (Pacific) 128, 137, 184, 235

New York (New York, NY) 1, 4, 63, 72, 81, 93, 106, 109, 138, 184

New York Cricket Club (New York, NY) 77, 88, 90

New York, NY (Acme) 223; (Active) 85, 87–90, 93, 98–100, 102–103, 107–108, 114, 116–117, 119–122, 130, 132, 137, 147, 155, 175, 181, 191–192, 194, 206, 211, 215, 226, 227, 229, 261, 270, 280, 315; (Alert) 322; (Alpine) 281; (Ashland) 39, 52; (Baltic) 5–7, 10, 14, 18, 20, 22, 25, 27, 31, 38–39, 53, 63, 79, 81, 211, 220, 231; (Bowery) 223; (Champion) 53; (Chelsea) 39, 53, 63; (Columbia) 221, 232; (Columbian) 39; (E Pluribus Unum) 39, 53; (Eagle) 2, 4–5, 7, 9–12, 14, 18–19, 23, 26–27, 31, 33–36, 38–39, 47, 49, 51–52, 57, 60–63, 67–68, 71, 76–77, 79–81, 85–87, 89, 90–93, 98, 100–103, 107–108, 118, 120, 122–123, 127, 129–132, 137, 177, 181, 197, 205, 217, 220, 226, 229, 259–261, 263–264, 274, 280, 297, 326, 328; (Eclectic) 105–106, 108, 118, 119–121, 123–124, 126–127, 130, 135, 137, 145, 147, 151, 154, 155, 160, 162, 181, 232, 297; (Empire) 4–5, 7, 9–12, 14, 18, 23, 25–27, 31–33, 35–37, 39, 44, 47, 49, 51–52, 57, 60–61, 63, 71, 76, 78–80, 85, 87–93, 98–105, 107–108, 114, 118–120, 129–130, 132, 137, 148, 151, 155, 157, 167, 174, 178, 180, 205, 211, 217, 226, 230, 260, 263–264, 271–272, 280; (Endeavor) 160, 183, 192, 194, 197, 215, 232; (Esculapian) 39, 53; (Exercise) 158, 183, 220, 233; (Fanwood) 206, 211; (Fulton) 151, 155, 168, 175, 181, 233, 281; (Fulton Market) 122, 127, 132–133, 137; (Gotham) 2, 4–5, 7, 9–10, 14, 18–20, 25, 27, 31–35, 39, 46–47, 50–52, 57–58, 61–63, 67–68, 70–71, 76, 78–81, 85, 87–88, 90–93, 98, 99, 100–103, 107–108, 114, 117, 123–124, 126–127, 132, 137, 160, 174, 176, 181, 197, 204, 226, 230, 247, 259–260, 263, 271, 279–280, 326, 328; (Gramercy) 192, 200, 207, 211, 215, 227, 230, 247, 281, 304, 325; (Granite) 183, 233; (Gulick) 233; (Harlem) 7, 14, 11, 19–20, 25, 27, 31–32, 37, 39, 45, 47, 52, 57, 63, 67–68, 70–71, 81, 116, 124, 132, 146, 171, 183, 192, 194, 206, 211, 215, 220, 226, 227, 229, 281; (Henry Eckford) 49, 51, 60–61, 63, 68, 72,

INDEX

77–81, 93; (Hope) 303, 326; (Hoyt) 274; (Independent) 18, 39, 63, 72, 81; (Irving) 304, 326; (Jasper) 243, 282, 303, 326; (Jefferson) 35, 46, 51–52, 57, 60–61, 63, 67–68, 71, 81, 93, 127, 130, 135, 145–146, 158, 173–174, 176, 181, 197, 205, 217, 226, 230, 282; (Katydid) 39, 5; (Knickerbocker) 1, 4–5, 9–11, 14, 18, 26–27, 31–33, 37, 39, 44, 52, 63, 72, 81, 105–106, 108, 138, 157–158, 183, 205, 217, 220, 230, 328; (Laurence) 234; (Lexington) 39, 53, 63, 226, 303; (M.M. Van Dyke) 120, 122–123, 127, 132, 134, 137, 184, 234; (Malta) 63; (Manhattan) 20, 39, 53, 63, 184, 234; (Mansion) 234; (Metropolitan) 21–22, 27, 39, 44, 53, 63, 72, 81, 93; (Monument) 18, 39, 53; (Mutual) 18, 25–27, 31, 33–35, 38–39, 45–47, 49, 51–52, 55, 57–58, 60–62, 67–68, 70–71, 76–81, 85–93, 98–104, 107–108, 114–116, 118–120, 122, 137, 143–149, 151–152, 155, 162, 168, 171–172, 174, 176, 180, 190–200, 204, 206–207, 211, 215–217, 222, 226, 229, 242–243, 245–246, 248–250, 252–254, 256–257, 259–261, 266, 268, 271–272, 277–279, 289, 291–296, 298–301, 303–308, 311, 313–314, 316, 318, 320–323, 328; (Mystic) 79, 93, 99, 102, 105–106, 108, 138, 184; (New York) 1, 63, 72, 81, 93, 106, 109, 138, 184; (New York Cricket Club) 77, 88, 90; (Olympic) 223, 230, 235, 241, 243, 245–246, 255, 257–260, 266, 279, 281, 326; (Oriental) 195, 207, 220, 222, 230, 243–244, 246–247, 250–252, 256, 268, 272, 274, 277, 280, 289, 298–299, 303, 313, 316, 325; (Orion) 260–261, 280; (Post Office) 223; (Rival) 264; (Social) 120, 124, 131, 134–135, 137, 174, 185, 194, 197, 205, 217, 226, 229, 247, 260, 271–272, 274, 280, 289, 303, 324; (Sparta) 160, 174, 185, 205, 236, 260, 271, 277, 280; (St. George Cricket Club) 44, 86; (St. Nicholas) 18, 20, 23, 26–27, 33, 40, 53, 63; (Stuyvesant) 27, 40, 53; (Tiger) 40; (Tuttle & Bailey) 295, 327; (Unknown) 303, 327; (Warren) 303, 311–312; (Washington) 2, 4; (World) 155, 185; (Young America) 5

Newark (Newark, NJ) 25, 34, 46–47, 53, 57–58, 60, 63, 67–68, 72, 78, 81, 85–86, 89, 91–93, 99–101, 107–108, 119, 121, 137, 138, 184, 234, 282

Newark, NJ (Active) 147, 150–151, 152, 155, 160, 173, 182, 313; (Adriatic) 11, 23–24, 46–47, 49, 60, 63, 72; (Amateur) 291, 311, 313, 315, 323–324; (Americus) 101, 105, 109, 120, 124, 131, 135, 137, 160, 162–163, 173, 176, 180, 231, 281; (Eckford) 315; (Eureka) 47, 50, 52, 58, 63, 67–68, 72, 76–77, 81, 85, 88–89, 93, 95, 98, 101, 106–108, 114, 115–116, 118, 120, 130, 132–133, 146–148, 150–152, 155, 160, 173, 176, 181, 191, 197, 207, 230, 261, 281; (Excelsior) 281; (Newark) 25, 34, 46–47, 53, 57–58, 60, 63, 67–68, 72, 78, 81, 85–86, 89, 91–93, 99–101, 107, 108, 121, 138, 184, 234, 282; (Pioneer) 99, 101, 103, 105–106, 108, 138, 184

Newberry, J. 48
Newberry, S. 48
Newburgh (Newburgh, NY) 32, 44, 57
Newburgh, NY (Hudson River) 44, 53, 63, 67, 76, 78, 80–81, 85, 87–88, 90, 92–93, 99–100, 102–103, 105, 107–108, 114, 124, 126, 128, 137, 145, 151–152, 181, 196, 233; (Newburgh) 32, 44, 57

Newkirk 10, 38
Newport (Newport, KY) 218
Newport, KY (Holt) 150, 165, 282, 291, 326; (Newport) 218
Newton, A.M. 162, 202, 258, 320
Newton, MA (Waban) 148, 180, 185, 236
Newton, OH (Diamond) 232
Newtown (Newtown, OH) 234
Newtown, OH (Newtown) 234
Niagara (Brooklyn, NY) 32, 64; (Buffalo, NY) 39, 44, 53, 147, 153, 159, 181, 190–191, 193, 205, 210, 212, 219, 229, 242–243, 248, 250, 266, 268, 275, 280, 292, 295, 296, 298–300, 302, 325; (Lockport, NY) 205, 234, 326; (Saugerties, NY) 319
Niagara Falls (Niagara Falls, NY) 159, 234, 282
Niagara Falls, NY (Niagara Falls) 159, 234, 282
Nichols (Sandwich, MA) 282, 320
Nichols, J. 274
Nichols, James 229
Nicholson 69, 79, 99
Niefus, J. 179
Niles, G. 48
Noble 312
Nonpareil (Burlington, VT) 184, 234
Noonan 262, 316
Norfolk (Foxboro, MA) 200
Norfolk, VA (Creighton) 161, 180, 212, 232; (Naval) 282; (Old Point) 212, 229
Normal (Cortland, NY) 317
Norris 224
Norristown, PA (Eagle) 145; (Excelsior) 295, 326
Norrisville, VT (Olympic) 184, 235
North Bridgewater, MA (Howard) 202, 282
North Manchester, CT (Hockanum) 183
Northrup, Harry 47, 89, 101
Norton 39
Norton 133, 205, 263
Norton 148
Norton, Frank 78, 90, 104, 116, 144, 208, 301
Norwalk, CT (Alert) 169, 181, 227, 230; (Liberty) 169, 210, 183, 234, 282
Norway, ME (Pennessewassee) 216
Norwich, CT (Chester) 114, 122, 137, 182; (Riverside) 222, 235; (Uncas) 114, 136, 137, 185
Norwichtown, CT (Marvin) 184, 234
Norwood 211
Noyes, G. 124, 225
Oakland, CA (Occidental) 326; (Wide Awake) 327
Oakleaf (Stockton, CA) 326
Oatka (LeRoy, NY) 159
Oberlander 157, 210
Oberlander, J. 309
Oberle, F. 275
Oberlin, OH (Penfield) 235; (Resolute) 250, 282, 301, 327
O'Brien 148, 200, 266
O'Brien 153
O'Brien 157
O'Brien, Mattie 8–9, 19, 32, 45, 58, 70
O'Brien, Peter 8–9, 17, 19, 31, 45, 58, 70, 77, 85, 98
Ocala, FL (Tropical) 236
Occidental (Gambrier, OH) 184; (Oakland, CA) 326; (Quincy, IL) 234, 242, 255, 282
Oceanic (Mystic Bridge, CT) 184, 234
O'Connell 214
O'Connor 118, 176
O'Connor 227
Oddie 50, 59
O'Flynn 149
Ogborne 160
Ogemas (Flint, MI) 326
Oil City, PA (Seneca) 166, 301, 319, 327
Oil Stockings (Franklin, PA) 319
O.K. (Detroit, MI) 219; (Ottawa, IL) 170, 234; (Zanesville, OH) 234
O'Keefe 201
O'Keefe 314
O'Laughlin 315
Old Dominion (Alexandria, VA) 171
Old Elm (Pittsfield, MA) 248, 267, 282, 291, 299, 326
Old Point (Ft. Monroe, VA) 161, 280
Old Point (Norfolk, VA) 212, 229
Oliphant 163
Olive (Philadelphia, PA) 245, 269, 280, 326
Oliver 223
Oliver, Joe 45, 58, 70, 77, 85
Oliver, John 13, 19, 31, 45, 58, 70, 77
Oliver, T. 48
Olmstead 39

INDEX

Olmsted 163
Olympian (Blanchester, OH) 234; (Oxford, OH) 234
Olympic (Allegheny, PA) 163, 164, 225; (Baltimore, MD) 269, 300, 305, 318, 326; (Brooklyn, NY) 7, 14, 40; (Burlington, VT) 282; (Canandaigua, NY) 276; (Detroit, MI) 234, 267; (Louisville, KY) 150, 165, 184, 234; (Nazareth, PA) 184, 234; (New York, NY) 223, 230, 241, 243, 245–246, 255, 257–260, 266, 279, 281, 326; (Norrisville, VT) 184, 235; (Paterson, NJ) 121, 123–124, 127, 131–132, 137, 155, 173–174, 184, 191–192, 197, 235; (Philadelphia, PA) 2, 63, 67, 85, 115–116, 129, 131–132, 137, 156, 184, 190–191, 193–195, 200, 204, 209, 213, 216–217, 229, 244–245, 252, 271, 280, 326; (Pittsburgh, PA) 190, 193, 242, 268, 280, 326; (Providence, RI) 184, 212, 229, 258, 266, 282; (Rock Point, VT) 282; (S. Brooklyn, NY) 40, 53, 59, 69, 72, 81, 93; (Sheffield, IL) 235; (Washington, DC) 143–145, 156, 158, 164, 180, 190–191, 193–196, 198–200, 204, 206, 208, 215–216, 218, 222, 229, 242–245, 247–252, 254, 256,
268, 270, 289, 291, 293–300, 302, 304–306, 308, 310–312, 317, 321, 324, 328
Omaha (Omaha, NE) 235, 242, 282
Omaha, NE (Omaha) 235, 242, 282; (Otoes) 242, 282
Onawa (Williamsburg, OH) 235
Oneida (Bloomfield, NJ) 319
O'Neil 50, 59, 93, 108
O'Neil 173
O'Neil, J. 170
Ontario (Oswego, NY) 184, 212, 243, 266, 275, 282, 291–292, 300, 325; (Rochester, NY) 85
Onward (New Bedford, MA) 214, 235
Opdycke 209
Oppenheimer, A. 134, 152
Oram 157, 204, 272
Oran 209
Orange County (Orange County, NY) 88
Orange County, NY (Orange County) 88
Orchard (Brooklyn, NY) 151, 184, 235
Ordanance (Ft. Monroe, VA) 161
O'Reilly 212
Oriental (Brooklyn, NY) 22, 23, 27, 35, 39; (Greenpoint, NY) 114, 120, 127, 134–135, 137, 147, 149, 151, 153, 157, 162–163, 175, 180, 191, 207, 221–222, 227, 229, 269, 282; (Hartford, CT) 235; (Memphis, TN) 291, 326; (New York, NY)
195, 207, 220, 222, 230, 243–244, 246–247, 250–252, 256, 268, 272, 274, 277, 280, 325
Orion (Lexington, KY) 291, 326; (New York, NY) 235, 260–261, 280, 326; (Philadelphia, PA) 184
Orr 58–59
Orr 164
Osborn 252
Osborne 61, 91, 120, 176
Osborne, Ballard 202, 255
Osceola (Brooklyn, NY) 21, 27, 40, 256, 304, 311, 325; (Frankford, PA) 184, 235; (Pittsburgh, PA) 317, 324
Oshkosh, WI (Everett) 179, 183, 232
Osterheldt, E. 172
Osterheldt, William 172
Ostrander, William 152, 207
Oswego, NY (Amateur) 153; (Ontario) 184, 212, 243, 266, 268, 275, 282, 291–292, 300, 325
Otoe (Nebraska City, NE) 296, 326
Otoes (Omaha, NE) 242, 282
Ottawa, IL (O.K.) 170, 234; (Shabbonna) 236, 296, 327
Ottumwa, IA (Appanoe) 296, 325; (Crescent) 297, 326
Ours (Philadelphia, PA) 269, 326
Overheiser 21
Overton, J.B. 23
Owen 219
Owens 122
Owens 321

Owensboro (Owensboro, KY) 172
Owensboro, KY (Owensboro) 172
Oxford (Oxford, PA) 154
Oxford, OH (Olympian) 234
Oxford, PA (Oxford) 154
Oyster Bay, NY (Queens) 184, 235

Pabor, Charley 99, 114, 148, 192, 303
Pacific (Clinton, IA) 184, 235; (Mobile, AL) 235, 282; (New Utrecht, NY) 119, 126, 128–129, 135–137, 184, 235; (Philadelphia, PA) 235; (Rochester, NY) 184, 235; (San Francisco, CA) 242, 282
Packer 311
Page, Seaver 71, 89, 100, 126, 156, 175
Painesville, OH (Star) 250, 283
Palisade (Englewood, NJ) 184; (Yonkers, NY) 184
Palmer 136
Paragon (Baltimore, MD) 235; (Danville, IN) 235
Parcher 48
Parisen 39
Parish 278
Parker 24, 36, 50, 69
Parker 133
Parker 154
Parker 207, 257
Parker 302
Parker, Ed 106, 117, 144
Parks 37
Parmalee 22, 35
Parr 313
Pastime (Baltimore, MD) 144, 146, 151, 181, 199–200, 208, 235, 245, 247–248, 250–252, 268, 270, 277, 280, 289, 291, 293–294, 296–300, 302–306, 310–311, 318, 321, 324; (Brooklyn, NY) 19, 22, 23, 27, 31, 33–34, 36, 39, 53, 63; (Cincinnati, OH) 235; (Germantown, PA) 326; (Little Falls, NY) 276, 282; (Philadelphia, PA) 235, 295, 326; (Richmond, VA) 144, 269; (Washington, DC) 171
Patapaco (Baltimore, MD) 199
Patapsco (Westminster, MD) 235
Patchen, E. 33
Patchen, J. 33, 47, 87, 104
Patchen, S. 33, 46
Paterson, NJ (Alert) 230; (Excelsior) 151, 154, 183, 233; (Olympic) 121, 123–124, 127, 131–132, 137, 155, 173–174, 184, 191–192, 197, 235
Patrick 177
Patterson, Dan 79, 86, 100, 117, 290
Patterson, Tom 119, 168, 195, 244
Patterson, PA (Mechanics) 234
Patton 161
Paul 77
Paul, C. 174
Pawling 154, 224
Pawtucket, RI (Hope and Anchor) 212
Paxton, IL (Red Jacket) 235
Payne 62
Payson 279
Peabody 198, 258
Pearce, Dickey 8–9, 19, 31, 45, 56, 58, 70, 77, 84–85, 95, 98, 115–116, 149, 188, 191, 246, 298
Pearsall, A. 30–31, 44, 74
Pearson 132
Pearson 161
Pease 319
Peck, H.S. 123, 172
Peconic (Brooklyn, NY) 115–116, 118–119, 125, 134, 137, 155, 177, 181, 206, 216–217, 223, 230, 282
Peekskill, NY (Dunderberg) 299, 316, 321, 323, 326
Peffers 220
Pelican (New Orleans, LA) 254, 259, 264–265, 275, 278, 280, 291, 308, 314, 322, 324
Penfield (Oberlin, OH) 235
Penfield, Cal 152, 197, 300
Penn (Downington, PA) 154
Penn Treaty (Philadelphia, PA) 184, 235
Pennessewassee (Norway, ME) 216
Penney 223
Pennington 222
Pennington, Albert 47, 101, 119
Pennsylvania (Philadelphia, PA) 160
Peoria, IL (Ft. Clark) 183, 233
Pequonic, CT (Squonnenog) 236
Pequot (New London, CT) 147, 181, 235, 262

Perrin 22
Perrin 257, 310
Perrine 222, 277
Perry (Philadelphia, PA) 145
Perry 171
Perry, C.L. 123
Perry, V.D. 123
Peru, IN (Star) 312
Pestaricus (Manayunk, PA) 160, 235
Petersburg, VA (Independent) 161
Peterson, J. 201
Peterson, W.R. 201, 273
Pharo 143
Pharo, E.A. 157
Pharo, R.F. 157
Phelan 228
Phelan 260
Phelps 219
Phelps, George 19, 32
Philadelphia (Philadelphia, PA) 114–115, 138, 143, 149, 184, 235
Philadelphia, PA (Adriatic) 67, 269; (Alert) 114, 125, 138, 182, 230, 281; (Alpha) 231; (Alvin) 144–145, 156, 163, 181, 204; (Amateur) 149, 182, 231; (Americus) 281; (Arctic) 143, 145–146, 149, 156, 160, 162, 181, 231; (Armstrong) 182, 231; (Athenian) 182, 231; (Athletic) 28, 63, 67, 75–78, 81, 85–86, 91, 93, 96, 98–104, 106–108, 112, 114–115, 117, 119, 121, 125–126, 129–131, 135, 137, 143–147, 149, 152, 154, 156, 158, 161–162, 168, 172, 180, 186–188, 190–191, 193–196, 198, 200–201, 203–205, 209–213, 216, 218–219, 221, 224–225, 229, 242, 244, 246–252, 254, 257, 268, 271–272, 276, 289–294, 296–300, 302–305, 307–310, 312, 318, 320, 328; (Atlantic) 281; (Awkard) 182, 325; (Bachelor) 143–144, 147, 162, 181, 190, 213, 218, 230, 281, 325; (Belmont) 160, 231; (Benedict) 63; (Bristol) 143; (Chestnut St. Th.) 149, 160, 182, 209, 230, 252, 281; (City Item) 252, 269, 325; (Cohocksink) 295, 326; (Cold Spring) 232; (Commonwealth) 143–144, 149, 156, 158, 162, 172, 180, 190, 200, 213, 218, 224, 229, 281; (Expert) 280, 324; (Contest) 232; (Dirigo) 146, 182, 190, 216, 232; (Enterprise) 183; (Equity) 63, 129, 138, 183, 232; (Excelsior) 183, 295, 326; (Exercise) 326; (Expert) 233, 244, 252, 271–272, 289, 294–295, 299, 305; (First Ward) 146, 183, 233; (Franklin) 269, 326; (Geary) 144, 149, 156, 162, 180, 190, 200, 204, 209, 213, 216, 229, 281; (Germantown) 183; (Gymnast) 183; (Hamilton) 143, 154; (Harry Clay) 143, 145, 149, 169, 181, 200, 204, 216, 218, 229; (James Page) 160, 326; (Intrepid) 244, 266, 271, 281, 291, 294, 295, 310, 325; (Kensington) 183; (Keystone) 67, 77, 81, 85–86, 91, 93, 98–99, 101–102, 104, 108, 115–117, 125, 131–132, 137, 143, 145–146, 149, 155, 162, 168, 172, 180, 190–195, 200, 204, 209, 216, 229, 242, 244–252, 254, 257, 269, 271, 277, 289, 291, 293–294, 297, 299, 303–304, 325; (Korndaffer) 183, 233; (Leisure) 183; (Leonore) 145; (Malvern) 156, 209, 218, 230, 282; (Marion) 184, 234; (Mercantile) 86, 154; (Minerva) 129, 138, 156, 184, 234; (Mount Airy) 138, 184; (Mutual) 234; (National) 184, 234, 244, 326; (Olive) 245, 269, 280, 326; (Olympic) 2, 63, 67, 85, 115–116, 129, 131, 137, 156, 184, 190–191, 193–195, 199–200, 204, 209, 213, 216–217, 229, 244–245, 252, 271, 280, 326; (Orion) 184; (Ours) 269, 326; (Pacific) 235; (Pastime) 235, 326; (Pennsylvania) 160; (Penn Treaty) 184, 235; (Perry) 145; (Philadelphia) 114–115, 138, 143, 149, 184, 235; (Pioneer) 327; (Pythian) 141, 269; (Quaker

City) 143–144, 146–147, 149, 151–152, 158, 162, 172, 180, 235; (Raleigh) 184; (Ralston) 235; (Reno) 235; (Rescue) 252, 282; (Rittenhouse) 160, 184, 235; (S.J. Randall) 149, 185, 236; (South Penn) 149; (Spartacus) 224, 236; (Swiftfoot) 138; (Trix) 236; (Typographical) 160, 162, 180, 236; (United) 63; (Village) 327; (W. H. Patterson) 185, 218, 236; (W. Philadelphia) 143, 145–146, 149, 153, 156, 168, 172, 181, 236, 293, 294, 295, 300, 306, 324; (Western Market) 185; (Winona) 63; (Young America) 244
Phil. Sheridan (Cohoes, NY) 181, 235
Phillips 21, 37
Phillips 205
Phoenix (Brooklyn, NY) 22; (Belvidere, IL) 184, 235; (Terre Haute, IN) 235
Phoenixville, PA (Hibernia) 224; (Indian Queen) 154
Pickwick (New Orleans, LA) 254, 308, 325; (St. Louis, MO) 159
Pidge 212
Pidgeon, Frank 13, 20, 28, 32, 45, 67
Pierce 20, 35
Pierce 136
Pierce, O.N. 214
Piermont, NY (Sparkhill) 155, 185
Piggott 219

Pike 60
Pike, Lip 112, 115, 146, 151, 194, 246, 298
Pilch 121
Pinckney 11, 24–25, 36, 50, 69
Pine Grove (Fair Haven, CT) 184, 235
Pinkham, Ed 101, 119, 152, 207, 244, 293, 294
Pinneo 135
Pioneer (Alexandria, VA) 156, 164, 171, 181, 215, 235; (Genesee, IL) 235; (Indianapolis, IN) 211, 235; (Newark, NJ) 99, 101, 103, 105–106, 108, 138, 184; (Philadelphia, PA) 326; (Portland, OR) 184, 235; (Springfield, MA) 184, 235; (Westbrook, ME) 216
Piper 37, 47
Pittman, S. 48
Pittsburgh, PA (Allegheny) 190, 193, 203, 219, 302, 317, 325; (Anchor) 182, 231; (Atlantic) 164, 182, 231, 294, 317; (Eureka) 183, 232; (Good Will) 317; (Laurence) 179, 183, 317; (Lincoln) 163, 181, 234; (Mutual) 203; (Olympic) 190, 193, 242, 268, 280, 326; (Osceola) 300, 317, 324
Pittsfield, MA (Old Elm) 248, 267, 282, 291, 299, 326
Place 9, 23, 33
Placedale, RI (Empire) 182, 232
Plainfield, NJ (Union) 236

Plainville, OH (Alert) 202
Platt 260
Plattsburgh, NY (Aurora) 182, 231
Pleasantville, NY (Star) 185, 192, 236
Plow Boy (Stillman Valley, IL) 296, 327; (Syracuse, NY) 153
Pluck 150
Plumb, H.A. 312
Plumb, Selden 262, 312
Plumb, Seth 262, 312
Pohl 157
Polhemus, H. 19, 31, 44, 69
Pomeroy 13
Popplein 269, 318
Port Chester, NY (Sawpitt) 236; (Washington) 185
Port Jervis, NY (Delaware) 173, 281
Port Richmond, PA (Unity) 185
Porter 153, 213, 276
Porter 177
Portland, CT (Unca) 312
Portland, ME (Athletic) 182, 231; (Eon) 136–137, 143, 162, 181, 198, 216, 229, 258, 281
Portland, OR (Pioneer) 184, 235
Portsmouth, OH (Riverside) 193, 203, 226, 230, 242, 249, 282, 289, 291, 294, 296, 307–309, 320
Post 226
Postley 21
Post Office (New York, NY) 223
Potomac (Washington, DC) 52, 117, 126, 132, 138, 156, 171, 184, 215, 235, 327
Potter 145

Potter Palmer (Chicago, IL) 296, 327
Potts 154
Potts, J. 178
Potts, W. 178
Pottstown (Pottstown, PA) 235
Pottstown, PA (Mountain City) 282; (Pottstown) 235
Pottsville, PA (Mountain City) 244
Poughkeepsie (Poughkeepsie, NY) 53, 88
Poughkeepsie, NY (Falkill) 138, 183; (Poughkeepsie) 53, 88
Poultney, VT (Alert) 182, 231
Pournal, VT (Titan) 185, 236
Povee 60, 70
Powell 51
Powell, W. 18, 35, 51, 57
Powelson, A.V.N. 173
Powers 47
Powers 265
Powers, Mike 153, 199, 248
Powhatan (Brooklyn, NY) 59, 63, 69, 71, 118, 123–124, 134–137, 152, 157, 168, 171, 178, 181, 235, 244–245, 247, 256, 261–262, 264, 272, 280
Prairie (Shannon, IL) 235
Prairie City (Ripon, WI) 235
Pratt, Al 226, 250, 302
Pratt, B. 227
Pratt, Tom 77, 85, 98, 116, 145, 188, 192, 200, 246, 295
Pratt, W. 306
Presley 267
Preston 173

Prete, F. 274
Price 71
Price 166
Price, George 262, 304, 316
Price, John 8, 9, 17, 19, 31, 45, 58, 77
Price, T. 48
Prince George (Baltimore, MD) 235
Princeton (Princeton, NJ) 149, 163, 173, 181, 221, 226, 235, 244–245, 282, 294, 315, 322, 325
Princeton, IL (Amateur) 231
Princeton, NJ (Nassau) 77–78, 80, 85–86, 89–90, 163, 184, 190–191, 198, 207, 210, 221, 230; (Princeton) 149, 163, 173, 181, 221, 226, 235, 244–245, 282, 294, 315, 322, 325
Proctor 273, 316
Prouty 106
Prouty 159
Providence, RI (Blackstone) 212, 214; (Brown) 198, 202, 258, 310, 320, 325; (Eagle) 214; (Olympic) 184, 212, 229, 258, 266, 282; (Rival) 185, 235
Pullen 263
Purcell 221
Purdy 169
Purdy 221
Purtell 46
Putnam 148, 200, 266, 306
Putnam 179
Putnam (Brooklyn, NY) 5–6, 9, 13–14, 19–20, 25–27, 31–33, 35–36, 39, 44–45, 48–49, 52, 63, 72; (Troy, NY) 299

Pythian (Philadelphia) 141, 269

Quaker City (Philadelphia, PA) 143–144, 146–147, 149, 151–152, 158, 162, 172, 180, 235
Quantrell 132, 222
Queen Anne Cty., MD (Chesterfield) 232
Queens (Oyster Bay, NY) 184, 235
Quequechan (Fall River, MA) 282
Quevado, J. 179
Quickstep (Bergen, NJ) 63; (New Orleans, LA) 322; (Staten Island, NY) 261–262; (Toledo, OH) 235
Quincy, IL (Dexter) 281; (Occidental) 234, 242, 255, 282
Quincy, MA (Active) 202, 230
Quinn 127, 158
Quinn 214
Quinn 315
Quinnipack (Wallingford, CT) 262, 311
Quinnipiack (New Haven, CT) 53, 184, 235; (W. Meriden, CT) 235

Radcliff, John 131, 143, 188, 190, 245, 253, 295
Radeau 23
Rahway, NJ (Kearney) 119, 121, 122, 133, 137, 160, 183
Railroad (Columbus, OH) 193, 235; (Indianapolis, IN) 235
Railway Union (Cleveland, OH) 174, 191–193, 196, 203, 227, 230
Raleigh (Philadelphia,

INDEX

Raleigh (Philadelphia, PA) 184
Ralston (Camden, NJ) 146; (Philadelphia, PA) 235
Ran 128
Randall 136
Randall, H. 277
Randall, M.D. 278
Randolph 37, 47
Randolph (Dover, NJ) 184
Rankin 163, 221
Rankin 173
Ransom 131
Raritan (S. Amboy, NJ) 213, 222, 282
Rathbone 317
Ravenna, OH (Star) 225
Rawle, Francis 198, 258
Raymond, J. 60, 174
Reach 304
Reach, Al 57, 67, 76, 92, 98, 112, 115, 141, 143, 188, 190, 245, 295
Reach, Bob 216, 249, 301
Reading, PA (Schuylkill) 244–245, 283, 295, 327
Record 266, 306
Red Hook (Cincinnati, OH) 235
Red Jacket (Paxton, IL) 235
Red Stick (Baton Rouge, LA) 235
Red Stockings (Boston, MA) 328; (Cincinnati, OH) 239–241, 284–285, 328
Reddington 224
Redon, R.H. 309
Reed, F. 23
Reed 60
Reed 107, 133
Reed, James 117
Reed 260
Reed 320

Reeder 169
Reese 251, 318
Reeves 88
Regan 149
Reid 315
Relic (Jacksonville, IL) 255, 282
Remsen 276, 323
Rendon 264
Reno (Philadelphia, PA) 235
Renova, PA (Active) 295, 325; (Enterprise) 232
Republic (Springfield, OH) 174, 235
Rescue (Philadelphia, PA) 252, 282
Reserve (Hudson, OH) 282
Resolute (Baltimore, MD) 235; (Brooklyn, NY) 69–70, 76, 78, 80–81, 85–88, 90–91, 93, 98, 100, 102–104, 108–109, 123, 138, 158, 167, 171, 173, 178, 181, 235, 282; (Chicago, IL) 166, 235; (Cincinnati, OH) 320; (Elizabeth, NJ) 123, 167, 169, 184, 197, 230, 243–244, 253, 259, 269, 280, 289, 291, 297–298, 303–304, 310–311, 313, 315–316, 323–324; (Evansville, IN) 172, 181, 235; (Hamilton, OH) 291, 320, 327; (Nashua, NH) 257; (Oberlin, OH) 250, 282, 301, 327; (St. Louis, MO) 159, 201, 210, 213, 220, 230; (Terre Haute, IN) 235
Retaliators (Middletown, NY) 173
Reuble 273

Revere (Boston, MA) 282, 305, 327
Reynolds 36
Reynolds 155
Reynolds 170
Reynolds 192, 272, 303
Reynolds 228, 265
Reynolds, J. 105
Reynolds, John 258, 310
Reynolds, Thomas 19, 31, 44
Rhinebeck, NY (Lorillard) 128, 138, 184
Rice 180
Richards 119
Richards 129
Richards, B. 279
Richards, G. 279
Richardson 223, 262, 316
Richmond, VA (Pastime) 144, 269; (Union) 185, 236
Richter 220
Ridgeway, PA (Catamount) 231
Ridgewood, NJ (Excelsior) 173
Riegel 220
Riemeyer 203
Riley, John 228, 250, 307
Riley 317
Rinkle 169
Ripley, OH (Independent) 307, 326
Ripon, WI (Prairie City) 235
Ristori (Farentum, PA) 164, 184, 235
Rittenhouse (Philadelphia, PA) 160, 184, 235
Ritter 313
Rival (Providence, RI) 185, 235
Riverhead, NY (Earnest) 182, 232

Rivers 145
Riverside (Cattawissa, PA) 244, 282 (Coxsackie, NY) 319; (Dixon, IL) 235; (Evansville, IN) 313; (Holyoke, MA) 282; (Norwich, CT) 222, 235; (Portsmouth, OH) 193, 203, 226, 230, 242, 249, 282, 289, 291, 294, 296, 307–309, 320
Robbins 21, 23
Robbins 158
R.E. Lee (New Orleans) 254, 259, 264–265, 278, 280, 290–292, 309, 314
Roberts 214
Roberts 220
Robertson 21, 38
Robinson 21
Robinson 48
Robinson 147
Robinson 225
Robinson, A.V. 126, 158, 201, 249, 301, 321
Rochester, NY (Alert) 159, 205, 242–243, 248, 250, 267, 275–276, 280; (Excelsior) 147–148, 153, 167–168, 181, 190, 193, 196, 205, 230; (Flour City) 44, 63, 324, 291, 292, 298, 300–301, 318, 325; (Live Oak) 44; (Mystic) 282; (Ontario) 85; (Pacific) 184, 235
Rock Island, IL (Wasello) 236
Rock Point, VT (Olympic) 282
Rockford, IL (Forest City) 140, 144, 157, 190–192, 196, 201, 210, 228–229, 242, 255, 267–268, 279,
289, 291–301, 305–309, 314, 328 (Lively Turtle) 234; Sonnissippi) 236
Rodman 11
Roe 68
Roe, Charles 168
Roehl 273
Rogers 62
Rogers 89, 100, 118, 175, 215
Rogers, G. 48
Rogers, Fraley 108, 122, 167, 206, 256, 311
Rogers, James 13, 24, 31
Rogers, Mort 80, 92, 108, 162, 202, 258, 321
Rogers, M.M. 311
Rogers, W.H. 178
Rogersville, NY (Challenge) 165
Rollstone (Fitchburg, MA) 202, 235, 282
Rooney 71
Rooney, G. 100
Rooney, William 89, 100
Roosa 11
Rorke 157, 162, 199, 204, 272
Rose 165
Rose 319
Rose Hill (Fordham, NY) 89, 215, 243, 247, 282, 289, 303, 322, 323–324
Rosedale (Washington, DC) 300, 327
Ross 58
Ross 128, 199
Ross 136
Ross (Harlem, NY) 247, 272, 283
Roth 272
Rowena (St. Louis, MO) 273, 283
Rowland 60
Roxborough (Manayunk, PA) 245, 283

Rua 197
Ruder 88
Rural (W. Farrion, PA) 236
Russell 18, 34, 49, 61, 80, 88, 102
Russell 179, 224, 256
Russell 227
Russell 320
Russell, Ed 19, 31, 44, 69
Russell, George 134, 152
Rustic (Danby, IL) 157
Ryan 120, 169
Ryan 171
Ryan 221
Ryder, James 80, 102
Ryder 118
Ryder 124
Ryder 128
Ryerson 271
Ryno 13, 22, 23

Sabin 324
Sacramento (Sacramento, CA) 316, 327
Sacramento, CA (Capital) 325; (Sacramento) 316, 327
Sageman, C. 130, 167
Saint Albans, VT (Crescent) 182, 232; (Eagle) 182, 232
Saint Elmo (Mobile, AL) 236, 283
Saint George Cricket Club (New York, NY) 44, 86
Saint John 263
Saint Johnsbury, VT (Mechanics) 184, 234; (Union) 185, 236
Saint Lawrence (Malone, NY) 200, 236
Saint Louis (St. Louis, MO) 201, 283
Saint Louis, MO (Active) 201, 230, 273; (Aetna) 201, 213, 273; (Athlete) 209,

231; (Atlantic) 201, 209–210, 220, 229, 259, 273, 280, 293, 309, 325; (Baltic) 201, 220, 231; (Commercial) 213, 232; (Dirigo) 201, 232; (Empire) 138, 144, 159, 183, 190–192, 196, 209, 213, 220, 229, 242, 255, 259, 268, 273, 291–293, 309, 325; (Excelsior) 183, 233; (Hope) 159, 201, 233; (Iron State) 282; (Lone Star) 273, 280; (Magnolia) 159, 234, 282; (Mutual) 209; (National) 234; (Pickwick) 159; (Resolute) 159, 201, 210, 213, 220, 230; (Rowena) 273, 283; (St. Louis) 201, 283; (Turner) 283; (Twilight) 236; (Union) 144, 159, 180, 190–193, 196, 201, 209–210, 213, 229, 242, 255, 259, 281, 291, 309, 325
Saint Michael's, MD (Claybourne) 232
Saint Nicholas (New York, NY) 18, 20, 23, 26–27, 33, 40, 53, 63
Salem, MA (Lightfoot) 257
Salem, OH (Independent) 225
Salisbury 38, 47, 61, 90
Salisbury, E.C. 161
Salisbury, L. 161
Salmon (Lowell, MA) 207, 257, 280
Salsman 25
Salters 25
Salts 163
San Francisco, CA (Atlantic) 242, 281, 316, 325; (Eagle) 242, 281, 316, 324; (Empire) 232; (Liberty) 234, 316; (Pacific) 242, 282, 282
Sanders 223
Sanderson 306
Sandford 35
Sandwich, MA (Independent) 214; (Nichols) 282, 320
Sanford 153
Sanger 47
Sans Souci (Connecticut) 236
Santa Clara (Santa Clara, CA) 316
Santa Clara, CA (Santa Clara) 316
Saratoga Springs, NY (Hope) 183, 233
Sargeant 166, 319
Sartorius, N. 274
Saugerties, NY (Niagara) 319; (Ulster) 319
Saunders, A. 62, 79
Saunders 105
Savannah, GA (Forest City) 219
Sawin 179, 224
Sawpitt (Port Chester, NY) 236
Sawyer 255
Saxton 24
Scates, E. 170
Schack 220
Schaeffer 26
Schafer, Harry 162, 190, 204, 272, 295, 296
Schaub 47
Scheidemantle, J. 165
Schell 157
Schenck 163
Schnectady, NY (Alert) 299–300, 325; (Ancient City) 248, 275, 280
Schuylkill (Reading, PA) 244–245, 283, 295, 327
Schwab 33
Schwartz 141, 150
Schwartz, D. 309
Scobell 159
Scott 10
Scott 38
Scott 279
Scott, George 254, 309
Scotton 228
Scranton (Scranton, PA) 169, 185
Scranton, PA (Scranton) 169, 185
Scrimgeour, F. 136
Scrimgeour, J. 136
Sea Side (Long Branch, NJ) 185, 236
Seaman 11
Seaman 201
Seaman, J. 48
Sears 25
Sears 123
Sears, Milt 277, 307
Sebley 213
Sebring 61, 80, 88, 130, 158
Seibert 58, 70
Seinsoth, F. 45, 58, 70, 77
Seinsoth, G. 45, 58
Seinsoth, R. 32, 46, 58
Seinsoth, T. 32
Selbert, Lew 175
Selbert, William 175
Selchow 130
Selden 210, 279
Selma, AL (Athletic) 231; (Central City) 231; (Mutual) 282
Selman, Frank 251
Seneca (Oil City, PA) 166, 301, 319, 327
Sensenderfer, John 115, 141, 143, 190, 245, 295
Severn (Annapolis, MD) 156, 161
Severn 272
Sewell, Charles 168
Seymour (Middletown, CT) 262

INDEX 379

Seymour 159
Seymour 201
Shabbonna (Ottawa, IL) 236, 296, 327
Shaffer, N.B. 90, 107, 133, 177, 205
Shaffer, W.B. 133, 177, 205
Shane, W. 125, 145
Shannon 129
Shannon 318
Shannon, IL (Prairie) 235
Sharpe 313
Shattuck 210
Shaw 154, 198
Shaw 267
Shay 262, 312
Sheehan 267
Sheets 313
Sheffield 204, 250
Sheffield, IL (Olympic) 235
Shelbyville (Shelbyville, IN) 312
Shelbyville, IN (Shelbyville) 312
Sheldon 39
Sheldon, R. 171
Shelley, Ed 192, 251, 303
Shelly 220
Shepard 222
Sheppard 141, 154, 224
Sheridan (Lowell, MA) 207
Sheridan 11, 25
Sherman (Utica) 166, 267, 276, 280
Sherwood, J.E. 165, 196
Shields (E. Cambridge, MA) 148
Shields 47
Shields 125, 178
Shields 156, 215
Shockey 214
Shoo Fly (Cochranton, PA) 319; (Temperanceville, PA) 317
Short 265, 322
Showman 37

Shreves, Pete 127, 158, 194, 307
Shroyer 278
Shugard 120
Shurman 37
Silberman 150
Silleck 118, 176, 323
Silver Star (Carson City, NV) 316
Simmons 162, 258
Simmons 214
Simmons, Joe 103, 158, 188, 210, 297
Simms 88
Simonson 21, 60, 70, 89
Simpson 160
Simpson 165
Sines 48
Sing Sing, NY (Ivanhoe) 197, 207, 223, 230, 263, 282
S.J. Randall (Philadelphia, PA) 149, 185, 236
Skaats 59, 70
Skiff, William 165, 218
Slater 128
Slater 215
Slebern 203
Sloane 136
Sloane 206, 264
Sloane, A. 132
Sloat, J. 61
Sloat, R. 47, 61, 90, 107
Slote 220
Smith 9, 23, 33, 61
Smith 12
Smith 13, 20
Smith 25
Smith 49
Smith 60
Smith 62
Smith 164
Smith 169
Smith 170
Smith 171
Smith 211
Smith 220
Smith 224

Smith 256
Smith 262, 312
Smith 270
Smith 273
Smith 320
Smith, A. 58
Smith, A.R. 250, 302
Smith, A.W. 159, 209
Smith, C. 222, 277
Smith, C. 317
Smith, C.C. 92
Smith, Charles 19, 31, 45, 56, 58, 70, 77, 84–85, 95–96, 98, 149, 191, 246, 298
Smith, E. 50, 59, 107
Smith, E. 263
Smith, Eb 117, 140, 204, 250
Smith, Ed 263
Smith, F. 12
Smith, George 99, 114, 148, 192, 272
Smith, George 165
Smith, H. 10, 18, 34
Smith, J. 12
Smith, J. 133
Smith, J. 278
Smith, James 22
Smith, James 77
Smith, John 22
Smith, Mike 77, 86, 98, 125, 147
Smith, Nathaniel 133, 154, 198, 258, 310
Smith, Sid 70, 77, 85, 98, 115
Smith, T. 78, 104, 122
Smith, T. 263
Smith, T. 274
Smith, T.W. 171
Smithers 211
Snediker 71, 125, 178
Snow 79, 88
Snowden 155, 197, 260
Snyder, James 304
Snyder, John 32, 45, 57, 67, 101
Snyder, Josh 45, 57, 76, 92, 120, 169, 304

Social (Cincinnati, OH) 236 (Elmira, NY) 236; (Huntington, PA) 185; (New York, NY) 120, 124, 131, 134–135, 137, 174, 185, 194, 197, 205, 217, 226, 229, 247, 260, 271–272, 274, 280, 289, 303, 324
Solomon 21
Solomon, A. 127
Somerset (Boston, MA) 255
Somerville, NJ (Independent) 24
Sonnissippi (Rockford, IL) 236
Sophomore (Cambridge, MA) 185, 236
Soule 198
Southard 318
South Penn (Philadelphia, PA) 149
South Amboy, NJ (Raritan) 213, 222, 282
South Boston, MA (Fraternity) 148, 161, 181, 233
South Brooklyn, NY (Olympic) 40, 53, 59, 69, 72, 81, 93
South Orange, NJ (Alert) 217, 260, 270, 321, 325
South Zanesville, OH (I.X.L.) 233
Southern (New Orleans, LA) 242, 254, 259, 264–265, 273–274, 278, 280, 290, 309, 314, 322, 324
Spaight 161
Spalding, Al 140, 202, 255, 297
Spann 211
Sparkhill (Piermont, NY) 155, 160, 174, 185, 205, 260, 271, 277

Sparta (New York, NY) 185, 236, 280
Sparta, WI (Eagle) 182, 232
Spartacus (Philadelphia, PA) 224, 236
Spellman 199, 275
Spence 35, 51, 57, 67
Spofford, S.H. 179
Sprague, Joe 60, 67, 75, 76, 77, 85
Sprague 128
Sprague 154, 198
Sprecher, L.M. 175
Springfield, IL (Athletic) 231; (Atlantic) 231; (Capitol) 157; (Liberty) 255, 282, 309, 326
Springfield, MA (Hampden) 152–153, 200; (Mutual) 242, 257–258, 266–267, 280, 296, 311–312, 325; (Pioneer) 184, 235
Springfield, OH (Lone Star) 174, 181, 234; (Mutual) 195–196, 234; (Republic) 174, 235
Springfield, VT (Alpha) 182, 231
Springsteen, H. 60, 174
Squires 68, 80, 91
Squonnenog (Pequonic, CT) 236
Stambough 265
Stamford (Stamford, CT) 283, 316
Stamford, CT (Stamford) 283, 316
Standbaugh 228
Standish 267
Stanmire 161
Stansbury 12
Stanton 80
Staples 214
Staples, M. 214

Star (Allentown, PA) 143; (Altoona, PA) 185; (Batavia, NY) 159; (Brooklyn, NY) 31–32, 37, 39, 44–45, 51–52, 59, 62–63, 65, 68–69, 71, 76–81, 85, 87–88, 90, 92–93, 98–99, 104, 107–108, 114–118, 121, 123, 132, 137, 148–149, 151, 158, 167–168, 171, 173, 176, 181, 191–192, 194, 196, 200, 206, 210–211, 215, 225, 229, 246–247, 249, 256, 258–259, 261–262, 273, 276–277, 279, 289–291, 293, 297–298, 300, 302–304, 306, 310–311, 313, 315–316, 318, 323–324, 329; (Canseraga, NY) 165; (Covington, KY) 320; (Green Bay, WI) 236; (Greenfield, MA) 161; (New Brunswick, NJ) 120, 123, 126, 131, 135, 137, 160, 163, 173, 174, 176, 181, 236, 283; (Painesville, OH) 250, 283; (Peru, IN) 312; (Pleasantville, NY) 185, 192, 236; (Ravenna, OH) 225; (Virden, IL) 236; (Wakefield, RI) 185, 236; (Wallingford, CT) 236; (Waverly, IA) 296, 327
Stark 134, 178, 273, 323
Stark 276
Start, Joe 50, 56, 58, 70, 77, 85, 95–96, 98, 115, 149, 188, 191, 246, 298
Staten Island, NY (Harmonic) 214; (Quickstep) 261–262; (Unique) 185, 195, 214, 220, 225, 227, 229
Stearns 50

Stearns 92
Stearns 157, 166
Stearns, George 210
Stearns, J.W. 210
Steele, C. 278
Steele, H. 274
Steiner, A. 118, 176
Steiner, J. 118, 176
Stephens 11, 26, 37, 57
Stephens 71
Steubenville, OH (Mears) 193
Stevens 103, 127, 130, 205, 263
Stevens 314
Stevens 318
Stevens, G. 167
Stevens, J.O. 167
Stevens, Richard 12, 221
Stevenson 163
Stewart 148
Stewart 169
Stiehl, C. 180
Stiles 203
Stilesville, IN (Union) 312
Stillman Valley, IL (Hawkeye) 255; (Plow Boy) 255, 327
Stilwaggon 124, 207
Stimson 48
Stimson 199
Stinson 131
Stires, Gat 202, 255, 297
Stockman, Mahlon 91, 100, 118, 151, 194, 253
Stockton, CA (Oakleaf) 326
Stoddard 263
Stokem 79, 91
Stone 126, 156
Stoneham, MA (Atalanta) 257–258, 280; (Kearsarge) 199, 202, 207, 257, 282, 306, 320, 326
Stonewall (New Orleans, LA) 322,
325; (Wetumpka, AL) 236, 283
Storer 122, 175
Storer 150
Story 24, 36
Story, G. 24
Stout, R. 61, 91, 131, 174
Stoutenberg 89
Strand 316
Strawn 165
Strickland 154
Strine 171
Stringham 275
Stroman 160
Strong 24
Strong 307
Stubbs 219
Stubbs 221
Studley, Sy 117, 144, 208, 251, 307
Stump 59
Sturges 24
Stuyvesant (New York, NY) 27, 40, 53
Suffolk (Huntington, NY) 185, 236, 262, 283
Sullivan 104, 122, 167, 206
Sullivan 122
Sullivan 170
Sullivan 200, 266, 306
Sullivan 323
Sumner 162, 202
Sunderling 13
Sunley, W. 274
Surprise (New Orleans, LA) 254, 263, 274, 280, 314, 322, 324; (W. Farms, NY) 114, 118, 132, 137, 167, 185, 236
Susquehanna (Wilkesbarre, PA) 114, 138, 185
Sutherland 263
Sutton 223, 279
Sutton, Ezra 268, 302
Swalton, T. 45
Swandell, Marty 76,
92, 101, 120, 169, 194, 247, 290
Swasey 202
Swayne 322
Sweasy, Charlie 112, 121, 151, 196, 239, 243, 292
Sweeney 213
Sweet, Milton 46, 62, 68, 127, 166, 217, 321
Swiftfoot (Philadelphia, PA) 138
Sycamore, IL (Crescent) 232
Syracuse, NY (Cazenovia) 153; (Central City) 138, 153, 180, 190–192, 196, 198, 205, 212, 229, 242–243, 250, 266–268, 276, 280; (Eckford) 292, 296, 326; (Hamilton College) 153; (Plow Boy) 153

Tallman, J.H. 214
Tallon, Thomas 165
Tanner 205
Tappan 35
Tarentum, PA (Ristori) 164
Tate 123
Tate 322
Taunton, MA (Metacomet) 200, 282; (Wide Awake) 280
Taylor 80
Taylor 106, 221
Taylor 124
Taylor 154, 224
Taylor 204
Taylor 210
Taylor 316
Taylor, A.B. 18, 35, 51, 57
Taylor, H. 170, 228, 265
Taylor, H.B. 18, 35, 51, 57, 68

Taylor, S.S. 168
Taylor, W.S. 124, 172
Telford 153, 213
Telford 164
Temperanceville, PA (Shoo Fly) 317
Temple 207, 257
Ten Eyke 272
Terre Haute, IN (Phoenix) 235; (Resolute) 235
Terrell 61, 107, 176
Terry 129
Thayer 324
Thebault, R. M. 254, 309
Thomas 37
Thomas 70
Thomas 106
Thomas 166
Thomas 207
Thomas 279
Thomas, Charles 48, 89, 101, 119, 176
Thomas, E. 48
Thomas, E.T. 175
Thomas, G. 133
Thomas, H. 133
Thompson 38
Thompson 70
Thompson 71
Thompson 78, 90, 104, 122, 167, 206
Thompson 162
Thompson 173
Thompson 203
Thompson 270, 321
Thompson, B. 21
Thompson, C. 24
Thompson, E. 155
Thompson, E.A. 168
Thompson, G. 21, 71, 211
Thomson (Thomson, IL) 236
Thomson, IL (Thomson) 236
Thorn, Dick 10, 18, 34, 49, 61, 68, 79, 91, 100, 194

Thorn, W. 315
Thorne 91, 107
Thornell 33, 47, 61
Thorpe 134, 178
Thorpe 310
Thwaite, T. 58
Tice 10
Ticknor, Gus 32, 45, 77
Tiers 129
Tiger (New York, NY) 40
Tilden, C. 197
Tipper 262, 312
Tipson 60
Tipton (Tipton, IN) 236
Tipton, IN (Tipton) 236
Titan (Janesville, WI) 263; (Pournal, VT) 185, 236
Titusville, PA (Union) 166, 185
Todd 11, 24, 50
Toledo (Toledo, OH) 236
Toledo, OH (Lively) 234; (Quickstep) 235; (Toledo) 236
Toll 136
Tolley 170, 319
Tomer 225
Tomes, A.F. 22, 60
Tomes, C. 60
Tomes, F.H. 22, 60
Tomlin 218
Tompkins 129
Tooker 11, 25, 34
Tostivan 12
Tostivan 20
Totten 60
Towle 127
Towson (Towson, MD) 236
Towson, MD (Towson) 236
Tracy 33, 52
Tracy 225
Tracy 279
Tracy, William 254, 309
Transit (Chicago, IL) 314

Trayo 135
Treacey, Fred 155, 244, 293, 294
Tremaine 159
Tremont, NY (Atlanta) 147, 151, 167, 171, 182, 231
Tremp 322
Tremper 11
Trenton (Trenton, NJ) 185, 289, 294–295, 313, 324
Trenton, NJ (Atlantic) 143, 163, 182, 231; (Trenton) 185, 289, 294–295, 313, 324; (United) 40
Tri Mountain (Boston, MA) 148, 161, 180, 191, 194, 196, 198–199, 223, 227, 229, 242, 244, 246, 248, 255, 257–258, 266–267, 275, 279–280, 289, 291, 293–294, 305, 308, 311
Trix (Philadelphia, PA) 236
Trojan (Troy, NY) 196, 198, 221, 230
Tropical (Ocala, FL) 236
Troy, NY (Enterprise) 87–88; (Haymakers) 328; (Putnam) 299; (Trojan) 196, 198, 221, 230; (Victory) 44, 53, 63, 71, 81, 85, 128, 138, 152–153, 185, 236
Truax 206, 220, 264
Trumansburg, NY (Ulysses) 317
Trumbull 202, 255
Tryon 39
Tucker 11
Tufts (Medford, MA) 202
Tufts 134
Tuomey 123
Turnbull 269, 318

INDEX

Turner 11, 25, 34, 46, 62, 68
Turner 87
Turner 160
Turner 209
Turner (St. Louis, MO) 283
Tuscarora (Leesburg, VA) 171
Tuttle 23
Tuttle & Bailey (New York, NY) 295, 327
Twilight (St. Louis, MO) 236
Twomy 259
Tynan 123
Typographical (Philadelphia, PA) 160, 162, 180, 236
Tyrell, Joe 91, 119
Tyrolean (Harrisburg, PA) 143, 185, 236

U.V.M. (Burlington, VT) 185, 236
Ullmer, M.C. 274
Ulster (Saugerties, NY) 319
Ulysses (Trumansburg, NY) 317
Umpleby 87, 153, 199
Una (Boston, MA) 305, 327; (Kalamazoo, MI) 302, 327; (Mt. Vernon, NY) 114, 118, 124, 130, 132, 137, 155, 158, 167, 171, 181, 236, 283
Unca (Portland, CT) 312
Uncas (Norwich, CT) 114, 136, 137, 185
Undercliff (Cold Spring, NY) 126, 128, 137, 185, 236
Union (Brooklyn, NY) 80–81, 246, 298, 312, 316, 325; (Buffalo, NY) 266; (Camden, NJ) 143, 145–147, 181, 190, 204, 209, 213, 218, 229, 244, 283; (Chicago, IL) 236; (Cohoes, NY) 153, 198, 221, 236, 283; (Culpepper, VA) 271; (Elizabeth, NJ) 44, 53, 63, 72; (Elmira, NY) 168, 177, 181, 236; (Green Island, NY) 87; (Hudson City, NJ) 197, 230, 271, 283; (Lansingburgh, NY) 115, 143–147, 149, 151–152, 176, 180, 190–191, 193–194, 196, 198, 200, 206, 212, 221, 229, 239, 242–243, 245–248, 250–252, 254, 257, 266, 268–269, 275, 289–304, 308, 318–319, 328; (Lewiston, ME) 255; (Lynnfield Center, MA) 207; (Mercer, PA) 319; (Morrisania, NY) 5–7,11, 13–14, 19, 24, 27, 31, 34–36, 39, 44–45, 47–49, 52, 61, 63, 67–71, 76, 79, 81, 86–87, 89, 91–93, 98–108, 112, 114–117, 119–120, 122, 126–130, 132, 134, 136–137, 139–140, 146–152, 162–163, 168, 175–176, 180, 186–187, 191–196, 198, 201, 203, 206, 209–213, 215–216, 219, 224–225, 227–229, 243, 246–247, 261, 264, 271–272, 277, 280, 289, 291, 293–294, 297–300, 302, 304, 306, 308, 313, 318, 322; (Plainfield, NJ) 236; (Richmond, VA) 185, 236; (St. Johnsbury, VT) 185, 236; (St. Louis, MO) 144, 159, 180, 190–193, 196, 201, 209, 210, 213, 229, 242, 255, 259, 281, 291, 309, 325; (Stilesville, IN) 312; (Titusville, PA) 166, 185; (Urbana, OH) 236, 291, 320, 327; (Washington, DC) 116–117, 125–126, 132, 137, 143–144, 147, 156, 158, 164, 185, 199–200, 208, 215, 222, 230, 248–249, 251, 270, 271, 280
Union College (Albany, NY) 87
Union, PA (Black Stockings) 319
Unionville (Unionville, NY) 120–122, 125, 128, 135, 137, 185, 236
Unionville, NY (Unionville) 120–122, 125, 128, 135, 137, 185, 236
Unique (Staten Island, NY) 185, 195, 214, 220, 225, 227, 229
United (Philadelphia, PA) 63; (Trenton, NJ) 40
United States (Washington, DC) 171
Unity (Port Richmond, PA) 185
University (Ann Arbor, MI) 219
University Press (Ithaca, NY) 317
Unkidori (Monticello, IA) 185, 236
Unknown (Elizabeth, NJ) 214, 236; (New York, NY) 303, 327; (Washington, DC) 318
Upton (Boston, MA) 255, 267, 283
Urbana, OH (Union) 236, 291, 320, 327

Urell, M.E. 117, 132, 222, 249
Urell, W. 22
Utica (Utica, NY) 85, 87, 103, 109, 138, 147, 153, 181, 236, 299, 327
Utica, NY (Sherman) 266–267, 276, 280; (Utica) 85, 87, 103, 109, 138, 147, 153, 181, 236, 299, 327

Vail 11, 25
Vail 221
Valentine 50, 132, 206, 264, 276, 323
Vallejo (Vallejo, CA) 316, 327
Vallejo, CA (Vallejo) 316, 327
Valley (Bay City, MI) 236
Valley City (Grand Rapids, MI) 296, 327
Van Buscheten 223
Van Cott, D. 130, 167
Van Cott, T.G. 11, 25, 34, 46
Van Cott, T.S. 46, 62, 68, 130
Van Cott, W.H. 130, 167
Van Horn 25, 38, 69
Van Houghton, W. 173
Van Houton, C. 48
Van Nice 10, 23, 33, 47, 61
Van Nuyse, M. 24, 127
Van Pelt 128
Van Pelt 129
Van Sciver, W.H. 173
Van Valkenberg 35, 49
Van Velsor 205, 266
Van Wagenen 315
Van Wagner 24
Vanderbilt 13, 20
Vanderbilt, W. 22

Vanderhoef 37, 46, 59
Vanderhoef, J. 151
Vanderveer 71
Vanderveer, A.J. 179
Vanderwerken 38, 46, 62, 89, 100, 215
Vergennes, VT (Champlain) 182, 232
Vermillion (Danville, IL) 185, 236
Verner, J.K. 180
Victory (Troy, NY) 44, 53, 63, 71, 81, 85, 128, 138, 152–153, 185, 236
Vigilant (Brooklyn, NY) 53
Villa 322
Village (Philadelphia, PA) 327
Vincelette 60, 68, 80
Vincent 260
Viola (Nazareth, PA) 185, 236
Virden, IL (Star) 236
Vitt 177, 205
Vogel 135
Voorhees 22
Vosge 226, 261
Vredenburgh, Alfred 11, 26
Waban (Newton, MA) 148, 180, 185, 236
Wachtel 208
Waddell 128, 199
Waddell, Hope 59, 70, 78, 104, 122, 167, 206, 279
Wade 127
Wadlington 22
Wadsworth 10, 25, 46, 62
Wahkonsa (Ft. Dodge, IA) 185
Wakefield, RI (Star) 185, 236
Waldie 129
Walker 52
Walker 159
Walker, Charley 89, 100, 118, 175, 215

Walkill (Middletown, NY) 173, 178, 181, 236
Wallace, C.D. 175
Wallace, William 104, 125, 145
Wallingford, CT (Quinnipack) 262, 311; (Star) 236
Walnut (Altoona, IL) 236
Walnut Hill (Cincinnati, OH) 203
Walnut Hills (Walnut Hills, OH) 236
Walnut Hills, OH (Walnut Hills) 236
Walters 106
Walton 14, 22
Walton, A. 174
Wamsutta (New Bedford, MA) 185, 202, 214, 229, 283
Wandell 9, 23
Wandell 10, 49
Wandell 223
Wanser 127
Wansley, Bill 68, 75, 76, 86, 96, 100
Wanzier 49
Wappinger Falls, NY (Active) 198, 243, 281, 319
Ward, Ed 10, 18, 34, 49, 61, 67, 88, 102, 130
Ward 163
Ward 208
Ward 212
Ward 228, 315
Ward, C. 267
Ward, F.W. 221
Ward, G. 221
Ward, G. 268, 324
Ward, H. 121
Ward, J. 315
Ward, John 152, 197, 250, 302
Ward, M. 267
Ward, W. 121, 315
Wardwell 105

INDEX

Wardwell, G. 128
Wardwell, W. 128
Ware, James 212
Ware, Joseph 212
Warnock, W. 80, 92
Warren (New York, NY) 303, 311, 312
Warsaw (Warsaw, NY) 159
Warsaw, NY (Warsaw) 159
Wasello (Rock Island, IL) 236
Washington (Hempstead, NY) 40, 53; (New Orleans, LA) 254, 265, 274–275, 280, 314, 322, 324; (New York, NY) 2; (Port Chester, NY) 185; (Washington, DC) 301, 321, 324
Washington Ct. House, OH (Amateur) 291, 325
Washington Hts., NY (Athlete) 147, 151, 155, 182, 197, 206, 220, 229, 259–261, 263–264, 272–274, 276, 280
Washington, DC (Active) 301, 321, 325; (Alert) 249; (Arlington) 300, 318, 325; (Atlantic) 321; (Capitol) 144, 156, 158, 164, 171, 181, 231; (Continental) 144, 156, 158, 164, 182; (Empire) 144, 156, 158, 181, 232; (Gymnastic) 164, 183; (Interior) 144, 156, 158, 164, 183, 233; (Jefferson) 106, 117, 125, 132, 137, 143–144, 146, 156, 158, 171, 180, 200, 208, 215, 222, 229, 248–251, 270, 280, 296, 300, 306, 325; (Monumental) 171; (Mutual) 249; (National) 63, 93, 98, 103, 106, 108, 114, 116–117, 125–127, 132, 137, 139–144, 146, 150–152, 155–159, 164–165, 170, 180, 193, 199–200, 208, 215, 222, 229, 242, 244–252, 254, 270–271, 277, 289, 291, 293, 296–297, 300, 302–303, 306, 308, 310–311, 328; (Olympic) 143–145, 156, 158, 164, 180, 190–191, 193–196, 198–200, 204, 206, 208–209, 215–216, 218, 222, 229, 242–245, 247–252, 254, 256, 268, 270, 289, 291, 293–300, 302–306, 308, 310–312, 317, 321, 324, 328; (Pastime) 171; (Potomac) 52, 117, 126, 132, 138, 156, 171, 184, 215, 235, 327; (Rosedale) 300, 327; (Union) 116–117, 125–126, 132, 137, 143–144, 147, 156, 158, 164, 185, 199–200, 208, 215, 222, 230, 248–249, 251, 270–271, 280; (United States) 171; (Unknown) 318; (Washington) 301, 321, 324
Waterbury 169
Waterbury (Waterbury, CT) 114, 119, 122, 129–130, 132, 137, 157, 185, 236
Waterbury, CT (Monitor) 157, 184, 234; (Waterbury) 114, 119, 122, 129, 130–132, 137, 157, 185, 236
Waterbury, VT (Amulet) 182, 231
Waterman, C. 309
Waterman, F. 309
Waterman, Fred 102, 117, 146, 193, 243, 286, 292
Waterman, J. 309
Watts, Tom 146, 270, 321
Watt 162
Waukegan, IL (Acme) 230; (Lake Shore) 233
Waverly (Fishkill, NY) 323
Waverly, IA (Star) 296, 327
Wawassett (Wilmington, DE) 145, 236
Waxham 202
Way 158
Wayland (Beaver Dam, WI) 236
Wayne (Brooklyn, NY) 138, 185
Weaver 26
Weaver 162
Weaver, Charley 125, 172, 216, 252
Weaver, J. 172
Webber, E. 32, 45
Webster (Woburn, MA) 207
Webster 13, 20
Webster 267
Webster 312
Weddie 59
Weed 170
Weeden, J. 80, 92, 178
Weeks, P. 25
Weeks 52, 59
Weeks 118, 176
Weidberg 272
Weir 128
Welch 170
Weldon 161
Welling 12, 20

Welling, Norman 9, 12, 26, 37, 39, 46, 52, 80
Wells 13, 19
Wells 224
Wells, A. 180
Wells, James 198, 258, 310
Welsch 219
Welsh 204
Welsh 315
Welsh, J. 174
Wenona (Wenona, IL) 236
Wenona, IL (Wenona) 236
Wentz 173
Wesleyan (Middletown, CT) 262, 311, 327
West 57
West Chester, PA (Brandywine) 154, 172, 180, 190, 218, 224, 230, 245, 295, 325; (Columbia) 154
West Farms, NY (Surprise) 114, 118, 132, 137, 167, 185, 236
West Farrion, PA (Rural) 236
West Greenville, PA (Ydrad) 166
West Meriden, CT (Quinnipiack) 235
West Philadelphia (Philadelphia, PA) 143, 145–146, 149, 153, 156, 168, 172, 181, 236, 293–295, 300, 306, 324
West Point (Highland Falls, NY) 185
West Troy, NY (Champion) 198, 275; (Eagle) 182, 232
Westbrook, ME (Pioneer) 216
Westbury, CT (Monitor) 234
Westerly, RI (Emmett) 212
Western (Burlington, IA) 185; (Indianapolis, IN) 144, 150, 165, 172, 181, 211, 236
Western Market (Philadelphia, PA) 185
Western Star (Indianapolis, IN) 211, 236; (Janesville, WI) 236
Westervelt 80, 88, 102
Westminster, MD (Patapsco) 235
Westport, CT (Monitor) 184
Wetumpka, AL (Invincible) 233, 282; (Stonewall) 236, 283
Weymouth, MA (Mechanic) 162
W.H. Patterson (Philadelphia, PA) 185, 218, 236
Wheaton, IL (Athlete) 231
Wheeler 22
Wheeler 278
Wheeling (Wheeling, WV) 289, 327
Wheeling, WV (Baltic) 193, 248, 277, 281; (Hunkidori) 183; (Wheeling) 289, 327
Whelan 272
Whitaker 136
White 129
White 207, 257
White 223, 279
White 258, 310
White 263
White 276
White 310
White, E. 302
White, Ed 254
White, James 203, 250, 302
White, L. 204
White Rock, WV (Franklin) 277
White Stockings (Chicago) 284, 328
Whitehead 166
Whitehurst 161
Whitesides 166
Whitewater (Fond du Lac, WI) 237
Whitewater, WI (Athlete) 263
Whiting 62, 78
Whiting, Charles 31, 43–44
Whiting, F. 32, 44
Whiting, John 31, 33, 44
Whitney 116
Whitney 188, 207, 257
Whitney 199
Widdecombe, John A. 175
Wide Awake (Alton, IL) 229; (Burrillville, RI) 212; (Middlebury, VT) 185, 237; (Oakland, CA) 327; (Taunton, MA) 280
Wiggins 316
Wikoff 169
Wilcox 134, 177
Wilcox 214
Wilcox, E. 170, 319
Wilcox, E. 275
Wilcox, H. 170, 319
Wilcox, H.K. 173
Wild Cat (Brookville, PA) 185, 237
Wilder, George 258
Wilder, J. 162
Wildey 51
Wiley 131, 173
Wilkesbarre, PA (Susquehanna) 114, 138, 185
Wilkins, Isaac 77, 86, 98, 115, 143, 190, 245
Willard 220
Willard, Gardner 154, 198, 258, 310
Williams (Williamstown, MA) 221, 257, 278

INDEX 387

Williamstown, MA (Williams) 221, 257, 278
Williams 9, 23, 33, 47, 61
Williams 36
Williams 148
Williams 158
Williams 313
Williams 318
Williams, J. 135
Williams, Will 106, 117, 144, 252
Williamsburg, OH (Onawa) 235
Williamsburgh (Brooklyn, NY) 122, 138, 185
Williamson, Amor 130
Williamsport (Williamsport, PA) 185
Williamsport, PA (Williamsport) 185
Willing 204
Willis 131, 155, 197, 260
Williston (E. Hampton, MA) 185
Wilmington, DE (Diamond State) 182; (Wawassett) 145, 236
Wilson 21
Wilson 80
Wilson 88, 102, 130, 158, 226, 261
Wilson 120
Wilson 126
Wilson 199, 251
Wilson 228
Wilson, G. 92
Wilson, J. 92, 108
Winants 22
Windsor Locks, CT (Aetna) 230
Winicott 263
Winn 314
Winne 87
Winona (Philadelphia, PA) 63
Winooski (Cabot, VT)

185, 237; (Ethan Allen) 183, 232
Winslow 9, 23, 33
Winslow 11
Winthrop (Boston, MA) 185, 237
Wirth 214
Wismer 35
Wissahickon (Germantown, PA) 245, 283
Witt 23
Woburn, MA (Mishawaum) 207; (Webster) 207
Wolters, Rynie 112, 121, 151, 194, 247, 290
Wood 26
Wood 37
Wood 132
Wood 212
Wood 224
Wood 277
Wood, James 21, 38
Wood, James 45, 57, 66–67, 75–76, 92, 195, 244, 293, 294
Wood, John 21, 38
Woodlawn (Bronx, NY) 59
Woodman 169
Woods 223
Woods, Eddie 105, 125, 147, 201, 249, 252
Woodstock, ON (Young Canadian) 85, 191, 243, 274
Woolen Mill (Lawrenceburg, IN) 183, 237
Woolman 143
Woolverton 128, 199, 275, 300
Worcester, MA (Excelsior) 255, 257, 279–281
World (New York, NY) 155, 185
Wormley, T. 168
Worth 78

Worth 90
Worth 206
Worth, Herb 104, 122, 167, 256, 311
Worthington 164
Worthington, Tully 199, 251, 305
Wright 79
Wright 134, 177
Wright 317
Wright, A.H. 124
Wright, E. 278
Wright, Frank 133
Wright, George 52, 91, 114, 127, 141, 144, 192, 239–240, 243, 286, 292
Wright, George W. 274
Wright, Harry 26, 37, 79, 91, 103, 141, 150, 193, 238, 239, 285, 243, 292
Wright, S. 22
Wright, Sam 227
Wright, Sam 315
Wright, W.P. 165, 196, 268, 320
Wright, William 103
Wunder 218
Wurtsboro (Wurtsboro, NY) 173
Wurtsboro, NY (Wurtsboro) 173

Xenia (Xenia, OH) 165, 185, 190, 193, 211, 237
Xenia, OH (Xenia) 165, 185, 190, 193, 211, 237

Yale 153, 213, 276
Yale (New Haven, CT) 122, 129, 138, 185, 191–192, 195, 198, 202, 206, 210, 221, 229, 244, 247, 257, 278, 280, 289, 290, 293–294, 312, 325
Yates, Sam 9, 22–23, 33, 47, 61, 90, 107
Ydrad (W. Greenville, PA) 166

Yeatman, Sam 106, 117, 126, 156, 215, 249
Yellow Springs, OH (Antioch) 242, 281; Miami) 174, 193
Yoder 164
Yohn, C. 211
Yonkers, NY (Nepperham) 234; (Palisade) 184
York, Tom 273, 300
Yorkville, NY (Americus) 206, 211, 220, 222, 230
Yorkville, IL (Kendall) 233

Yost 166
Young 50
Young 180
Young 262
Young, Nick 158, 201, 249, 301
Young, William 13, 17, 19, 31, 44, 69
Young America (New York, NY) 5; (Philadelphia, PA) 244
Young Canadian (Woodstock, ON) 85, 191, 243, 274
Youngs 136

Ypsilanti (Ypsilanti, MI) 48
Ypsilanti, MI (Ypsilanti) 48

Zanesville, OH (O.K.) 234
Zeller, John 60, 68, 76, 86, 100, 17, 146, 157
Zettlein, George 101, 116, 149, 191, 246, 285, 298, 299
Zuill, John 13